ESSENTIALS
OF EDUCATIONAL
MEASUREMENT

ROBERT L. EBEL

Michigan State University

ESSENTIALS
OF EDUCATIONAL
MEASUREMENT

PRENTICE-HALL, INC.   *Englewood Cliffs, New Jersey*

PRENTICE-HALL EDUCATION SERIES

ESSENTIALS OF EDUCATIONAL MEASUREMENT is
the second edition of the book formerly titled
MEASURING EDUCATIONAL ACHIEVEMENT

ISBN: 013–285999-8

Printed in the United States of America

Library of Congress Catalog Card No.:
77–163390

10 9 8 7 6 5 4 3 2 1

Prentice-Hall International, Inc., *London*
Prentice-Hall of Australia, Pty. Ltd., *Sydney*
Prentice-Hall of Canada, Ltd., *Toronto*
Prentice-Hall of India Private Limited, *New Delhi*
Prentice-Hall of Japan, Inc., *Tokyo*

To my teachers and friends
E. F. Lindquist
and
Ben D. Wood
whose leadership in measurement
has done so much for education
whose wisdom and encouragement
have done so much for me

CONTENTS

PART II
CLASSROOM TEST DEVELOPMENT

WHAT SHOULD **3**
ACHIEVEMENT TESTS MEASURE?

55

HOW SHOULD **4**
ACHIEVEMENT BE MEASURED?

81

HOW TO **5**
PLAN A CLASSROOM TEST

97

THE CHARACTERISTICS **6**
AND USES OF ESSAY TESTS

123

PART III

GETTING, INTERPRETING, AND USING TEST SCORES

PART IV
TEST ANALYSIS AND EVALUATION

HOW TO JUDGE **13**
359   THE QUALITY OF A CLASSROOM TEST

HOW TO IMPROVE **14**
383   TEST QUALITY THROUGH ITEM ANALYSIS

HOW TO ESTIMATE, **15**
407   INTERPRET AND IMPROVE TEST RELIABILITY

435   THE VALIDITY OF CLASSROOM TESTS **16**

PART V
PUBLISHED TESTS AND TESTING PROGRAMS

APPENDICES

For myself, I know that, as far as my modest abilities have permitted, I have presented plainly and simply, for the instruction of any who wished to learn, such lessons as I have gained from my own experience, and all else that I have been able to find out for the purpose of the present work. And it is enough for a good man to have taught what he knows.

QUINTILIAN
Institutio Orationem
A.D. 100

PREFACE

Essentials of Educational Measurement is a comprehensive textbook for a solid introductory course in the use of tests in schools and colleges. The five parts of the text deal with these five aspects of educational measurement.

Part 1   History and philosophy
Part 2   Classroom test development
Part 3   Test score interpretation
Part 4   Test analysis and evaluation
Part 5   Standardized tests and testing programs

As an *introductory* text this book explains the special concepts, principles, and procedures of educational measurement in plain language and with frequent illustrations to smooth the path to understanding. It does not assume that the students have had any previous courses in measurement or statistics.

As a text intended for use in *solid* introductory courses it aims at accurate presentation of sound ideas and procedures. The author has been less concerned with how easy an idea may be for students to grasp than with how essential it is to the effective use of tests. Thus the book does not shun the difficult problems and controversial issues that have arisen in contemporary uses of tests. The author has not hesitated to counsel students of education rather directively on how they can use tests most effectively in their teaching.

As a text for courses on the *use* of tests in schools and colleges, the book pays more attention to practical problems and procedures than to theoretical formulations and issues. An effort has been made, however, not only to suggest sound principles and practices, but also to provide as much as possible in the way of philosophical, rational, and empirical bases for understanding and accepting the suggestions offered.

Essentials of Educational Measurement is a successor to *Measuring Educational Achievement*. Much of what appeared in the earlier book reappears here in parts II, III, and IV, sometimes with major revisions, sometimes with only minor changes, but always after careful consideration of ways to improve content, organization, and presentation. Parts I and V are almost entirely new, as is the chapter on oral examinations in Part III. The new book is thus more than a revision of the old. Its extended scope seemed to justify, indeed to require, the new title that was given to it.

To acknowledge completely an author's indebtedness is clearly an impossible task. Most of what I know has been borrowed from others: my teachers, my students, my professional colleagues. My best hope is that I have used reasonably good judgment in selecting from the wealth of information they provided, and that I have not bungled the task of integrating this information into a coherent, dependable structure of knowledge.

ROBERT L. EBEL

ESSENTIALS
OF EDUCATIONAL
MEASUREMENT

PART I

HISTORY
AND PHILOSOPHY

We venture to predict that the mode of examination, by printed questions and written answers, will constitute a new era in the history of our schools.

HORACE MANN

1

EDUCATIONAL MEASUREMENT:
Historical Perspectives

One of the best ways to begin a study of a subject like educational measurement is to review the history of its development. Obviously the means we use today were developed in the past. We will understand their functions and limitations better if we know something of how they came into existence. Most of the problems we face today have long histories. We will be able to judge these problems' importance better, and work toward solving them more effectively, if we know how they arose and how others have tried to cope with them. Finally, a brief survey of the history of measurement in education can provide a unified picture of its scope and its functions, its problems, and its potential. It can provide the essential framework for building a coherent structure of knowledge of the field.

Some milestones in the history of educational measurement are presented in Exhibit 1.1. The remainder of this chapter will be devoted to brief comments on each of them.

One who is particularly interested in the history of testing will find

3

EXHIBIT 1.1

Milestones of Educational Measurement

DATE	LEADER	DEVELOPMENT
2357 B.C.	Emperor Shun	Competitive civil service examinations
1599 A.D.	Society of Jesus	Rules for conducting written examinations
1836	Thomas Campbell	A university to examine and grant degrees
1845	Horace Mann	Replacement of oral by written examinations
1864	George Fisher	Scale book standards for evaluation
1865	Regents of New York	State testing program
1890	James McK. Cattell	Measurements of basic mental faculties
1894	Joseph M. Rice	School reform via survey testing
1899	Charles W. Eliot	College Entrance Examination Board
1903	E. L. Thorndike	Textbook in educational measurement
1905	Alfred Binet	First practical mental test
1908	C. W. Stone	Standard tests of arithmetic
1910	E. L. Thorndike	Handwriting quality scale
1912	Daniel Starch	Reliability of essay grades
1914	Charles Spearman	Factors of intelligence
1917	Arthur Otis	Army Alpha intelligence test
1920	William A. McCall	Use of objective classroom tests
1925	E. K. Strong	Measurement of vocational interest
1926	Carl Brigham	Scholastic aptitude test
1927	Charles K. Taylor	Educational Records Bureau
1928	Ben D. Wood	Pennsylvania study of educational achievement
1929	L. L. Thurstone	Scales for attitude measurement
1929	E. F. Lindquist	Every-pupil testing program
1930	Ben D. Wood	Cooperative Test Service
1931	Ralph Tyler	Tests of developed abilities
1932	Robert M. Hutchins	Board of Examiners
1935	Reynold B. Johnson	Test scoring machine
1936	William S. Learned	Graduate Record Examination
1936	State testing leaders	Invitational Conference on Testing Problems
1938	L. L. Thurstone	Tests of primary mental abilities
1938	Oscar K. Buros	Mental Measurements Yearbooks

DATE	LEADER	DEVELOPMENT
1940	Ben D. Wood	National Teacher Examinations
1943	E. F. Lindquist	Tests of educational development
1947	James B. Conant	Educational Testing Service
1953	E. F. Lindquist	Electronic test processing
1955	John M. Stalnaker	Scholarship examinations
1956	Benjamin S. Bloom	Taxonomy of Educational Objectives
1960	John C. Flanagan	Project TALENT
1961	Torsten Husén	International evaluation of achievement
1964	Francis Keppel	National assessment of educational progress

additional information in the books by DuBois[1] and by Linden[2] and in the chapters by Stanley[3] and Noll.[4]

ANCIENT AND MEDIEVAL

2357 B.C.
CHINESE CIVIL SERVICE EXAMINATIONS

An extensive system of written examinations of educational achievement formed the basis for admission and promotion in the civil service of ancient China.[5, 6] The system persisted until this century and was at least partly responsible for maintaining the internal stability of that society, and its relatively high level of culture, for over two millenia. It provided an alternative to the more usual organizations of ancient society, in which power and privilege were hereditary prerogatives. The Chinese civil service examinations were part of a merit system that rewarded effort and achievement, that gave even the humblest subject the opportunity of becoming one of the ruling elite. This ancient use of exami-

[1] Philip H. DuBois, *A History of Psychological Testing* (Boston: Allyn and Bacon, Inc., 1970), 173 pp.
[2] Kathryn W. Linden and James D. Linden, *Modern Mental Measurement: A Historical Perspective* (Boston: Houghton Mifflin Company, 1968), 111 pp.
[3] Julian C. Stanley, *Measurement in Today's Schools*, 4th ed. (Englewood Cliffs, N.J.: Prentice-Hall, Inc., 1954), chap. 2.
[4] Victor H. Noll, *Introduction to Educational Measurement* (Boston: Houghton Mifflin Company, 1965), chap. 2.
[5] Ping Wen Kuo, *The Chinese System of Public Education*. Contribution to Education No. 64 (New York: Columbia University, Teachers College, 1915), p. 8.
[6] Philip H. DuBois, "A Test Dominated Society: China, 1115 B.C.–1905 A.D." *Proceedings of the 1964 Invitational Conference on Testing Problems* (Princeton, N.J.: Educational Testing Service, 1965).

nations remains today one of the most pervasive and essential in governments throughout the world.

1599 A.D.
JESUIT EXAMINATION RULES

When universities were established in Europe in the Renaissance, examinations were largely oral and frequently took the form of public disputations on controversial questions.[7] But it is much easier to give a poor oral examination than a good one. Further, if most examinees are passed, few complaints concerning its quality are likely to be heard. Under these circumstances the quality of the oral examination is likely to deteriorate, as it did in most of the universities of the Middle Ages. In their report of 1852, the Oxford University commissioners, commenting on the oral examinations that had been used during the previous two centuries, wrote this:

> To render a system of examinations effectual it is indispensable that there should be danger of rejection for inferior candidates, honorable distinctions and suitable rewards for the able and diligent, with examiners of high character, acting upon immediate responsibility to public opinion. In the scheme of Laud[8] all these things were wanting.[9]

The society of Jesus, founded in 1540, placed a high value on education and scholarship. Departing from the popular practice of the times, Jesuits insisted on the use of written examination. In 1599 the society issued a comprehensive statement of the theory and practice of instruction. The statement included a detailed set of rules for the conduct of written school examinations, which ". . . apart from the fact that it is in Latin could be used in an examination room today."[10]

NINETEENTH CENTURY

1836
EXTERNAL EXAMINATIONS FOR DEGREES

In 1836, as a result of competition and friction between two previously established universities, the University of London was chartered

---

[7]S. J. Curtis, *History of Education in Great Britain* (London: University Tutorial Press, Ltd., 1967), p. 64.

[8]William Laud, 1573–1645, english prelate and archbishop of Canterbury. He was executed, but not for giving bad examinations.

[9]James A. Petch, "Examinations," *Encyclopedia Brittanica,* vol. 8 (1960) p. 938.

[10]Petch, "Examinations," p. 937.

to serve primarily as an examining and degree-certifying authority.[11] It had no faculty and no students, and offered no courses. But it rendered an essential service that was extended to students in all parts of the British empire. In recent years a somewhat similar system of credit by examinations has been established by the University of the State of New York.[12]

1845

WRITTEN VS. ORAL EXAMINATIONS

Horace Mann, a towering figure of leadership in the development of public education in the United States, took very seriously his responsibilities as Secretary of the Massachusetts Board of Education. He saw many things that needed improvement and he worked hard and effectively to improve them. One of these was the manner in which local school committees evaluated the education the children were receiving. Typically, they made their evaluations by examining the pupils orally. Like many other oral examinations these tended to degenerate into casual, perfunctory ceremonies, or to become occasions for settling some scores with the schoolmaster.

Because he had become involved in a controversy with the Boston schoolmasters over the effectiveness of some of their methods, Mann felt an especial need for more adequate, more objective evidence of pupil achievements than oral examinations. Written examinations would have a number of advantages.

1. More evidence could be obtained of the achievements of each pupil.
2. A written record of those achievements would be produced.
3. Each pupil would be asked the same questions; thus all would be treated alike.
4. There would be less possibility of favoritism for or bias against particular pupils or teachers.

Horace Mann's arguments were persuasive, and his personality was forceful.[13] Oral examinations began to disappear from the educational scene and to be replaced by written examinations.

1864

SCALE BOOKS FOR EVALUATION

In 1864 the Rev. George Fisher showed how to take some of the guesswork out of educational evaluations, that is, how to make them

---

[11]Curtis, *History of Education in Great Britain*, p. 422.

[12]*College Proficiency Examination Program* (Albany, N. Y.: State Education Department, 1969), p. 106.

[13]Horace Mann, "Report of the Annual Examining Committees of the Boston Grammar and Writing Schools," *Common School Journal*, vol. 7 (1845), 326–36.

more objective. He developed and published scale books that gave examples or specifications of a wide range of levels of quality in handwriting, spelling, mathematics, knowledge of Scripture, and other subjects of study.[14]

The Rev. Fisher's work made no great impact at the time, but fifty years later a number of others, among whom were Thorndike, Ayres, Courtis, Starch, and Odell, used his approach to launch the scientific movement in education early in this century.[15]

Measurements based on scales such as the Rev. Fisher's have valuable content meaning that many test scores lack. Recently there has been renewed interest in this content meaning and renewed efforts to get it via "criterion-referenced" or "domain-referenced" tests.[16] But Fisher-type scales are difficult to construct and tend to have rather short useful lives, especially when they sample only a small fraction of all a pupil is expected to learn in a subject. If teachers emphasize the tasks used on the measuring scale in their teaching, the scale loses its value as a measure of total achievement.

1865

NEW YORK REGENTS EXAMINATIONS

The Regents examination program in New York state, initiated in 1865, was the first, and has been probably the most effective of all of the state-wide programs for testing educational achievement. The first examinations were high school admission tests. Their purpose was to determine how many students enrolled in each public academy were bonafide college preparatory students. The amount of state aid to the academy depended on the number of such students enrolled. These uniform, impartial examinations were well received, and in 1878 a similar program of high school graduation and college admission examinations was instituted.[17]

Over the years, as the scope and enrollments of the secondary schools increased, the Regents examinations were gradually transformed from college preparatory tests into broader evaluation instruments. Local

[14]E. Chadwick, "Statistics of Educational Results," *Museum, A Quarterly Magazine of Education, Literature and Science*, vol. 3 (1864), 479–84.

[15]Daniel Starch, *Educational Measurements* (New York: The Macmillan Company, 1916).

[16]Robert Glaser and Richard C. Cox, "Criterion Reference Testing for the Measurement of Educational Outcomes" in R. A. Weisgerber, ed., *Instructional Process and Media Innovation* (Skokie, Ill.: Rand McNally & Company, 1968).

[17]*Regents Examinations 1865–1965: 100 Years of Quality Control in Education* (Albany, N.Y.: State Education Department, 1965).

schools are encouraged to use Regents examinations as part, but only part, of the basis for evaluating the effectiveness of their programs.

Although much criticism has been directed at the Regents examinations for overemphasizing academic achievement, for encouraging tecahers to teach to the tests, and for limiting the freedom of local schools in curricular innovation, the overall effect of the examinations seems to have been good. Graduates of high schools in New York tend to show higher levels of educational development than those of most other states. Surely not all the credit for this can be given to the Regents examinations, but it seems reasonable to believe that they contributed something.

1890

TESTS OF MENTAL FACULTIES

James McKeen Cattell undertook to measure mental ability (that is, ability to learn) by measuring precisely certain sensory, motor, and basic mental faculties such as visual and auditory sensitivity, rate of tapping, reaction time, speed in naming colors, and judgment of time intervals.[18] He thought that there should be a direct relation between a person's ability in these elemental processes and his ability to use higher mental processes such as reasoning, critical thinking, and creative imagination. He hoped that some combination of these measures could be used to predict academic success. But the results of studies by Seashore,[19] Bagley,[20] Wissler,[21] and others were disappointing. Scores on the basic mental tests bore little relation to each other or to general mental ability as reflected in scholastic success.

Still, the notion that mental ability does consist of a relatively small number of interrelated faculties, or factors, or dimensions, or elements, dies hard. The search for primary mental abilities[22] or for a structure of intellect[23] goes on. Success may not always be elusive. On the other hand, the modern day mental alchemists may be searching for something that simply isn't there.

[18]J. McK., Cattell, "Mental Tests and Measurements," *Mind*, vol. 15 (1890), 373–80.

[19]C. E. Seashore, "Some Psychological Statistics," *University of Iowa Studies in Psychology*, vol. 2 (1899), 1–84.

[20]W. C. Bagley, "On the Correlation of Mental and Motor Ability in School Children," *American Journal of Psychology*, vol. 12 (1900), 193–205.

[21]C. Wissler, "The correlation of mental and physical tests," *Psychological Review, Monograph Supplements*, vol. 8, no. 16 (1901), 62 pp.

[22]L. L. Thurstone, "Primary Mental Abilities," *Psychometric Monographs*, no. 1 (1938).

[23]J. P. Guilford, "Three Faces of Intellect," *American Psychologist*, vol. 14 (1959), 469–79.

1894
SURVEY TESTING FOR SCHOOL REFORM

The modern era of standardized tests and wide-scale testing programs was foreshadowed toward the end of the nineteenth century by a retired physician who had become an educational reformer. Joseph M. Rice used several types of spelling tests administered to thousands of school children to reveal wide differences in achievement and to raise questions about the effectiveness of the instructional methods then in vogue.[24] During the next decade he conducted similar studies, using his own tests, in arithmetic and language.

Dr. Rice was a skillful pioneer in test construction. He was also a strong advocate of scientific methods in the study of educational problems, whose belief in them had developed during his years of study in Germany. His influence did much to launch the scientific movement in education in the first decades of the twentieth century.[25]

1899
COLLEGE ENTRANCE EXAMINATION BOARD

The end of the nineteenth century saw the beginning of the College Entrance Examination Board, an association of colleges and secondary schools established to facilitate the transfer of students from secondary school to college. Diverse entrance requirements of the colleges and varying quality of instruction in the secondary schools had complicated the process of transfer unnecessarily. The proposal was to supplement or to replace some of the course completion requirements with measures of course achievement. Charles W. Eliot, president of Harvard, developed the idea. Nicholas Murrary Butler, later president of Columbia, sold it to the school and college administrators of the Northeast.[26] When the colleges began to use test scores as a basis for admission it became apparent that well qualified applicants were being prepared in free public schools as well as in expensive independent schools. Over the years the College Entrance Entrance Examination Board has been a major factor in shifting the basis for college admission from socioeconomic status to academic aptitude.

[24]J. M. Rice, "The Futility of the Spelling Grind: I" *Forum*, vol. 23 (1897), 163–72.

[25]J. M. Rice, *Scientific Management in Education* (New York: Hinds, Noble and Eldredge, 1914).

[26]Claude M. Fuess, *The College Board: Its First Fifty Years.*   (New York: College Entrance Examination Board, 1950).

EARLY TWENTIETH CENTURY

1903
TEXTBOOK IN EDUCATIONAL MEASUREMENT

The first textbook in educational measurement was published in 1903.[27] Its author, Edward L. Thorndike, who had originally intended to study literature, was attracted to psychology by William James.[28] Franz Boas, the anthropologist, taught him statistics, which he confesses was a bit difficult to learn. His dissertation was on animal learning. This was another first: before his time animals were not allowed in psychological laboratories.

When he undertook the study of human learning, he attacked and discredited the prevailing doctrine of formal discipline. Learning, argued Thorndike, does not consist in the cultivation of faculties such as memory, willpower, reasoning, or imagination. It consists in the formation of vast numbers of specific connections, the strength of which is governed by the laws of readiness, exercise, and effect.

Thorndike believed firmly in the value of experiment and measurement. "Whatever exists at all," he said, "exists in some amount. To know it thoroughly involves knowing its quantity as well as its quality."[29] He and his students produced many of the first scales for measuring educational achievements. The first standardized test of arithmetic was published by C. W. Stone in 1908. Thorndike's own handwriting scale appeared in 1910. He has been characterized as the great toolmaker. The volume and quality of his accomplishments supports the testimony of his contemporaries that he was a prodigious, creative, and efficient worker. More than any other he deserves the designation, "father of modern educational measurements."

1905
INDIVIDUAL INTELLIGENCE TEST

Late in the nineteenth century Alfred Binet, a French student of law, medicine, biology, and finally psychology, became interested in

---

[27]Edward L. Thorndike, *An Introduction to the Theory of Mental and Social Measurements*, (New York: The Science Press, 1903).

[28]Robert S. Woodworth, "Edward Lee Thorndike," *Biographical Memoirs*, vol. 27 (National Academy of Sciences, 1952), 209–37.

[29]Edward L. Thorndike, *Seventeenth Yearbook of the National Society for the Study of Education, Part II* (1918), p. 16.

how the mental processes of judgment, attention, and reasoning might differ in bright and dull children. He tried a wide variety of tests, physical and mental, simple and complex. In 1904, in response to a request from the French Ministry of Education, he began to develop a valid, objective, practical measure of educability that would identify among the nonlearners those whose mental abilities were too limited to permit normal progress in learning.[30] He succeeded so well that his scale became the model for many later ones and the criterion against which the quality of most other mental tests was judged. In the course of his work, Binet also developed an effective technique of scale construction. The concept of mental age was introduced to the world in a revision of his test.

1912

ESSAY TEST RELIABILITY

The efforts of Thorndike and others to objectify the measurement of educational attainments aroused strong opposition. Objective tests were characterized as fragmentary and superficial, suitable perhaps for testing memory of factual details but wholly inadequate for measuring the higher mental processes of logical reasoning, critical evaluation, or creative synthesis. Only an essay test, said the opponents, can adequately test a student's development of these more complex and far more important educational outcomes.

Daniel Starch responded to the attackes on objective tests by launching an attack of his own on essay test grades. In a series of studies in which E. C. Elliott collaborated, Starch exposed the appallingly wide variations in the grades that typical teachers assigned to the same student's answers to questions in geometry, literature, and history.[31] Later studies confirmed these findings in other contexts, and although it has also been shown that essay test answers can be graded reliably when the job is done with great care under careful supervision, the fact that essay tests typically yield highly subjective and unreliable measures of achievement was established beyond dispute.

The studies of Starch and Elliott showed that essay tests were poor measuring instruments. However, they did not answer the main charge against objective tests and they did nothing to support the belief of some test specialists that anything an essay test can do an objective test can

---

[30] Alfred Binet and T. Simon, *The Development of Intelligence in Children*, trans. Elizabeth S. Kite (Baltimore: Williams and Wilkins, 1916).

[31] Daniel Starch and E. C. Elliott, "Reliability of Grading High School Work in English," *School Review*, vol. 20 (September 1912), 442–57; ". . . in Mathematics," *School Review*, vol. 21 (April 1913), 254–59; ". . . in History," *School Review*, vol. 21 (December 1913), 676–81.

do better. True, only a naïve, badly informed critic will still contend that objective tests are limited to simple questions of factual memory. But the possibility remains that an essay test might be measuring something that an objective test can never measure.

A crucial experiment to test this possibility is easy to design. Let the essay test proponent specify concretely what he believes an essay test can measure that an objective test cannot. Let him build an essay test that yields highly reliable scores of this characteristic. Then let an expert objective test constructor try to measure the same thing with high reliability. See how well scores on the two tests correlate. If the correlation is high, the two tests must be measuring the same thing. If it is low, the one must measure something different from what the other measures.

Few experiments of this type have been reported. One reason is that the unique contribution of the essay test has seldom been defined; another is the great difficulty of getting essay test scores of high reliability. However, one study along these lines, done almost half a century ago, led to this conclusion: "...There seems to be no escape from the conclusion that the two types of examination are measuring identical things."[32]

1914

FACTOR ANALYSIS OF TEST SCORES

The growing number of mental tests and the developing tools of statistical analysis gave strong support to the students of mental functions. If it were true, as many believed at one time, that a person's general mental ability consisted in his possession of more or less of a limited number of specific mental abilities or faculties, and if various mental tests call for exercise of different proportions of these faculties, then scores on various pairs of the tests would show various degrees of correlation in a population of persons. Working backward from the correlation coefficients, one can use the statistical techniques of factor analysis to locate and identify hypothetical factors (or faculties) that would account for the correlations observed between the test scores. Charles Spearman in England was one of the pioneers in this endeavor. He developed a two-factor theory of intelligence, one of the factors being general intelligence, or *g*, the other being a factor specific to each test.[33] Other investigators, making different assumptions and using different statistical procedures, arrived at different factorial solutions. A great many factors

---

[32]Donald G. Paterson, "Do New and Old Type Examinations Measure Different Mental Functions?" *School and Society*, vol. 24 (August 21, 1926), 246–48.

[33]Charles Spearman, "The Theory of Two Factors," *Psychological Review*, vol. 21 (1914), 101–15.

have been hypothesized. How unitary, how useful, indeed how real they are remain matters of conjecture.

1917
GROUP INTELLIGENCE TEST

Wars, evil things though they are, have a way of stimulating rapid technological advances. When the United States became involved in World War I, a group of psychologists was assembled in Vineland, New Jersey to apply some of the new knowledge of educational and psychological testing to the selection and classification of military personnel.[34] Arthur Otis was not in the group, but the method he had developed was presented to the group by Lewis Terman and became the model for the Army Alpha. Otis is sometimes credited with having invented the multiple-choice test item, though "firsts" of this kind are often difficult to establish with certainty.

When scores on the Army Alpha were revealed, some people found them quite disturbing. It was reported, for example, that Americans were a nation of fourteen-year-olds intellectually. Questions were raised about the nature and measurement of intelligence. Terman and the young journalist Walter Lippman engaged in a fascinating debate on some of these issues in the pages of the New Republic.[35, 36]

BETWEEN THE WARS

1920
OBJECTIVE CLASSROOM TESTS

The decades between the two world wars were years of rapid development in the techniques and uses of educational measurement. William A. McCall took the lead in urging classroom teachers to use objective tests.[37] Edward K. Strong developed a technique measuring the extent

[34]Robert M. Yerkes, "Psychological Examining in the United States Army," *Memoirs of the National Academy of Sciences,* vol. 15 (1921).

[35]Walter Lippman, "Intelligence Tests," *New Republic,* vol. 32 (1922), 213, 246, 275, 297, 328; vol. 33 (1923), 9, 145, 201.

[36]Lewis Terman, "The Great Conspiracy," *New Republic,* vol. 33 (December 27, 1922), 116–20.

[37]William A. McCall, "A New Kind of School Examination," *Journal of Educational Research,* vol. 1 (January 1920), 33–46.

of a student's interest in each of a large number of vocations.[38] Carl Brigham developed for the College Entrance Examinations Board an objective test of general verbal and quantitative skills, called a scholastic aptitude test, to supplement the essay tests of subject matter achievement.[39] Since 1926 millions of college-bound students have demonstrated the degree of scholastic aptitude they possess by their success, or lack of success, with the tasks presented in successive versions of Carl Brigham's invention.

1927
EDUCATIONAL RECORDS BUREAU

In 1927 the Educational Records Bureau was established by a group of progressive administrators of independent and public schools. Charles K. Taylor was its first director. Ben Wood became director in 1933 and held the position until 1965.[40] The continuing effectiveness of the Educational Records Bureau is attributable in large measure to Ben Wood's good judgment in choosing highly capable assistant directors to manage the operations of the bureau: first Eleanor Perry Wood for several years, then Arthur Traxler for several decades.

The bureau provided for cooperation among the member schools in the selection, purchase, distribution, and scoring of tests, and in the provision of relevant norms for the schools. At an annual conference, supported also by the American Council on Education, discussions by experts of the problems of test selection, use, and interpretation did much to advance the general knowledge of educational measurement techniques.

1928
THE PENNSYLVANIA STUDY

In 1928, supported by a grant from the Carnegie Foundation for the Advancement of Teaching, Ben D. Wood and William S. Learned used objective tests in the first statewide study of educational achievement.[41] One of the disturbing findings was the wide variation in achievement from school to school and from student to student. Another was

---

[38]Edward K. Strong, Jr., "Vocational Interest Test," *Educational Record*, vol. 8 (April 1927), 107–21.

[39]Carl C. Brigham, *A Study Error*, (New York: College Entrance Examination Board, 1932).

[40]Ben D. Wood, "Origin and Work of the Educational Records Bureau," *School and Society*, vol. 34 (December 1931), 835–37.

[41]William S. Learned and Ben D. Wood, *The Student and His Knowledge* (New York: Carnegie Foundation for the Advancement of Teaching, 1938).

the low scores on the tests made by some of the teachers. The tests used were criticized for being too highly factual, but critics could take little comfort in showing that even these "simpler" attainments were being very poorly achieved.

1929
SCALES FOR MEASURING ATTITUDES

Specialists in mental measurement have long been concerned that the units they use are poorly defined and probably unequal. Louis L. Thurstone, attacking the problem of measuring attitudes, proposed the principle that differences that are equally often noticed are equal. That is, if the proportion of judges who declare that statement *B* is more conservative than statement *A* is equal to the proportion of judges who declare statement *C* to be more conservative than statement *B*, then the *B–A* difference is the same as the *C–B* difference. Using this principle, and some rather elaborate procedures for collecting statements expressing attitudes and judging the relative strengths of the attitudes expressed, Thurstone developed a number of attitude scales.[42] Nevertheless, attitudes tend to be numerous, complex, and not subject to easy modification by educational processes. Precise measurement of them has not proved to be a rewarding activity.

1929
IOWA EVERY-PUPIL TESTS

At the urging of President Walter A. Jessup and Dean Paul Packer, and under the technical direction of E. F. Lindquist, a statewide testing program was launched at the University of Iowa in 1929.[43] It began as an academic contest, somewhat like the interscholastic athletic, music, and declamatory contests that had developed. School participation was voluntary, but those who chose to participate agreed to test all their high school pupils in the appropriate subjects. High-scoring students went on to district and finally to state contests where the winners were awarded scholarships. Some of the features of this program were reminiscent of the civil service competitions in ancient China. The success of the high

---

[42]L. L. Thurstone and E. J. Chave, *The Measurement of Attitude* (Chicago: University of Chicago Press, 1929).

[43]William J. Feister and Douglas R. Whitney, "An Interview with Dr. E. F. Lindquist," *Epsilon Bulletin*, vol. 42 (1968), 17028. (Iowa City, Ia.: University of Iowa, College of Education).

school program led to the introduction in 1935 of elementary school objective tests in the basic skills.

1930
COOPERATIVE TEST SERVICE

The growing demand for high-quality tests of educational achievement, and the growing body of specialists skilled in constructing such tests, led in 1930 to the establishment of the Cooperative Test Service under the direction of Ben D. Wood and with the support of the American Council on Education.[44] The mission of this nonprofit agency was to develop and distribute high-quality tests of educational achievement for secondary school and college courses. In this mission it succeeded admirably, though the market for its tests was never large enough to make the agency fully independent financially. Many subsequent leaders in the development of educational measuring techniques served apprenticeships at the Cooperative Test Service.

1931
TESTS OF DEVELOPED ABILITIES

Criticism of emphasis on factual knowledge in achievement tests came also from test specialists. Ralph Tyler, working with the Bureau of Educational Research at Ohio State University, developed and published in 1931 a generalized technique for test construction that began with the definition of objectives in behavioral terms.[45] Typically these objectives emphasized the cultivation of abilities rather than the acquisition of knowledge. Tyler's studies showed that there was not a high correlation between scores on his ability tests and scores on his knowledge tests. He also showed that abilities tend to be retained better than knowledge. His work attracted favorable attention and had considerable influence on the kinds of tests used in wide-scale testing programs. Many teachers, however, found it difficult to define in behavioral terms the important things they were trying to teach.

[44]Ben D. Wood, "The Program of the Cooperative Test Service," in William S. Gray, ed., *Tests and Measurements in Higher Education* (Chicago: University of Chicago Press, 1936).

[45]Ralph W. Tyler, "A Generalized Technique for Constructing Achievement Tests," *Educational Research Bulletin*, vol. 10, no. 8 (April 15, 1931). Reprinted in Ralph W. Tyler, *Constructing Achievement Tests* (Columbus, O.: Ohio State University, Bureau of Educational Research, 1934).

1932
CHICAGO BOARD OF EXAMINERS

The program of general education inaugurated at the University of Chicago under the leadership of its president, Robert M. Hutchins, called for externally constructed examinations for each of the four first-year courses and for the four second-year courses. This task was assigned to a board of examiners composed of distinguished professors.[46] The board appointed L. L. Thurstone as chief examiner, and he assembled an outstanding staff of measurement specialists, including John M. Stalnaker and Ralph W. Tyler. Examiners at the University of Chicago not only developed excellent examinations, they also developed a high level of technical competence in coping with the diverse problems of measuring educational achievement. When time, experience, and smoldering opposition brought radical changes in the program of general education, the functions of the examiners diminished and the board ceased to exist. But through the men and women who learned their trade there, and through the ideas they generated, it left its indelible mark on the technology of educational measurement.

1935
TEST SCORING MACHINE

One of the advantages of the objective test is that the scoring can be done quickly and accurately by routine clerical checking. The use of separate answer sheets and stencil keys, developed during the 1920's, facilitated the clerical operation. But the job is clearly one that could be done by the right sort of machine. Ben Wood urged the president of International Business Machines, Thomas J. Watson, to develop a test scoring machine. IBM tried, but was unable to achieve the necessary accuracy because of variations in the intensity of the marks students made on their papers. Then a Michigan schoolteacher, Reynold B. Johnson, found a solution to the problem, which was to put a high resistance in series with each of the mark-sensing contacts. IBM hired him, and in 1935 a practical electric test scoring machine appeared on the market.[47]

[46]"The Board of Examiners at the University of Chicago," *School and Society*, vol. 35 (January 23, 1932), 116–17.
[47]Arthur E. Traxler, "The IBM Scoring Machine: An Evaluation," *Proceedings of the 1953 Invitational Conference on Testing Problems* (Princeton, N.J.: Educational Testing Service, 1953).

1936
GRADUATE RECORD EXAMINATION

Progressive graduate schools in the mid-1930's began to feel the need for better measures of aptitude for graduate study than could be provided by undergraduate grades. In 1936 experimental work to develop such a test, supported by the Carnegie Foundation for the Advancement of Teaching and conducted at Harvard, Yale, Columbia, and Princeton, led to the inauguration of the Graduate Record Examination program.[48] Initially the program included six profile tests in basic fields of knowledge, plus a dozen or so advanced tests in various subject specialties. Later the profile tests were replaced by verbal and quantitative aptitude tests. Four area tests of educational development were also added to the program, primarily to help undergraduate colleges to evaluate their programs.

Because of the diverse meanings, or sometimes lack of meaning, associated with graduate school grades, evidence as to the predictive validity of Graduate Record Examination Scores is limited and contradictory. It seems clear, however, that those who score high on the G.R.E. have the ability to do good graduate work if they choose to do so, and if the graduate school chooses to recognize and reward it.

1936
INVITATIONAL CONFERENCE ON TESTING

In the mid-1930's a small group of directors of state testing programs began meeting each fall in New York City following the annual conference of the Educational Records Bureau and the Cooperative Test Service. These meetings evolved into an annual invitational conference on testing problems.[49] Measurement specialists present papers on topics of current interest, which are then published in a booklet of proceedings. Fewer than fifty persons attended the first of these conferences before World War II. The Educational Testing Service, when it was established in 1947, took over sponsorship of the conference. In 1970, more than one thousand measurement specialists registered for the annual Saturday meeting.

---

[48]"The Graduate Record Examination," *School and Society*, vol. 54 (September 27, 1941), 241–42.

[49]Anne Anastasi, "The Invitational Conference on Testing Problems," in *Testing Problems in Perspective* (Washington, D.C.: American Council on Education, 1966).

1938
MENTAL MEASUREMENTS YEARBOOKS

The rapidly increasing number of published tests inevitably resulted in the appearance of a number of tests of low quality. It occurred to Oscar K. Buros that the annual publication of a volume of critical reviews of currently available tests could serve a useful purpose. It could guide users to the best tests, and it could persuade test publishers to provide tests of higher quality. The first volume appeared in 1938. Since then five others have been published.[50] The seventh is likely to be published in 1971. Though they have not escaped criticism and are not entirely free of flaws, they have served very well the purposes Buros and his co-workers had in mind. They have come to be recognized as indispensable guides to test selection.

1938
PRIMARY MENTAL ABILITIES

The factor analysis of mental ability that was pioneered by Spearman in England was developed and greatly elaborated in the United States by Louis L. Thurstone. Thurstone was not only a creative statistical analyst, he was also a most influential teacher. Many if not most of those who have become leaders in the field were Thurstone's students at the University of Chicago.[51]

MID-TWENTIETH CENTURY

1940
NATIONAL TEACHER EXAMINATIONS

The use of tests to determine teacher competence or to select qualified teachers for supervisory positions was not an innovation of the 1930's. However, the development of an organized program to prepare high-quality tests of the kinds needed, and to make them conveniently available nationwide, was an innovation. Here again Ben D. Wood

[50]Oscar K. Buros, *The Sixth Mental Measurements Yearbook* (Highland Park, N.J.: The Gryphon Press, 1965).
[51]L. L. Thurstone, "Multiple Factor Analysis," *Psychological Review*, vol. 38 (September 1931), 406–27.

provided the initiative and the educational wisdom that were nesessary to make the enterprise succeed.[52]

1943

TESTS OF EDUCATIONAL DEVELOPMENT

In 1943 a major change was made in the Iowa Every-Pupil high school level tests.[53] In part the change was a consequence of difficulties in continuing the old pattern of end-of-course achievement tests in a variety of high school subjects. New forms of each test had to be developed each year. Some school administrators complained that the tests were dominating the curriculum; that some teachers were spending too much time coaching their pupils to do well on the tests; that once the tests were given, students acted as if nothing important remained to be learned.

But a more important influence was the evolution of a new type of test–one designed to measure general educational development rather than mastery of specific subjects–and of a new function for testing–to facilitate learning rather than to assess it. These tests were given in the early fall instead of spring.

These new Iowa Tests of Educational Development achieved rapid acceptance and popularity. Similar tests were offered by the United States Armed Forces Institute to help the servicemen of World War II to resume educations interrupted by the war. High schools used them as part of the basis for awarding diplomas; colleges used them as a basis for waiving some general education requirements.

No one can doubt that the new test of educational development solved some difficult problems for operators of testing program and met some pressing educational needs. But perhaps one can question whether they should completely replace, or instead should supplement, end-of-course subject matter tests. Pupils still study subjects, and what they achieve mainly is command of knowledge in the subjects area. Perhaps schools need both kinds of tests.

1947

EDUCATIONAL TESTING SERVICE

Before and during World War II a variety of testing programs and services were developed. They were uncoordinated, and some were finan-

[52]David G. Ryans, "The Professional Examination of Teaching Candidates: A Report of the First Annual Administration of the National Teacher Examinations," *School and Society*, vol. 52 (October 5, 1940), 276.

[53]Everet F. Lindquist, *The Iowa Tests of Educational Development: Interpretation and Use of the Test Results by the Classroom Teacher.* (Iowa City, Ia.: University of Iowa, College of Education).

cially and professionally weak. Some educational leaders, particularly President James B. Conant of Harvard, felt that there would be great advantages to combining as many as possible of these into a single strong testing agency. After several years of planning and negotiating, the Educational Testing Service was established in 1947.[54]

Both the American Council on Education and the Carnegie Foundation for the Advancement of Teaching turned over their testing programs and services to ETS and got out of the business themselves. The College Entrance Examination Board turned over to ETS the operation of its programs but remained in existence itself as a policy-making association of colleges and secondary schools.

Since its formation ETS has greatly expanded its operations and its resources, both financial and professional. It has developed a large and talented research staff and has undertaken many research studies on problems in measurement and education. There were those in the beginning who questioned whether the existence of a single colossus in the field of educational testing, created and operated largely in the image of the College Board, would be an unqualified blessing on the American educational scene. But the benign and constructive policies it adopted have allayed those fears. Its success testifies to the vision of its creators and the skill of its leadership.

1953

ELECTRONIC TEST PROCESSING

Despite the availability of the IBM test scoring machine, the tests used in Iowa programs continued to be scored by hand until after 1950. The IBM machine was not well adapted for the scoring of multi-test batteries composed of hundreds of test items. E. F. Lindquist developed efficient equipment and routines for hand scoring by specially trained and closely supervised clerks, but by 1950 it was apparent that the volume of scoring would soon become too large to be handled effectively by these means. Further, the rapid development of computers offered the possibility of simultaneously obtaining, transforming, combining, and analyzing scores.

Backed by the financial resources of the Iowa testing programs and assisted by a small group of electronic and mechanical technicians, Lindquist set to work to devise a high-capacity, computerized electronic test scoring machine.

His successes, reported initially at the 1953 Invitational Conference

---

[54]Henry Chauncey, *Annual Report to the Board of Trustees* (Princeton, N.J.: Educational Testing Service, 1949).

on Testing Problems, led to the establishment of the Measurement Research Center at Iowa.[55] One of the main functions of the center was to provide economical scoring of any widely used test battery, including the Iowa Program tests. Its principal research function has been the development of progressively more refined and sophisticated test scoring devices.[56] Since 1953 other high-capacity computer-coupled scoring machines have been developed, at ETS, IBM, and elsewhere. Their availability has greatly facilitated the wide-scale use of tests in education.

1955

NATIONAL MERIT SCHOLARSHIPS

During the years after World War II there was a rapid increase in the number of corporations offering financial assistance to college students, and in the generosity of their support. This increase was due in part to the corporation's sense of responsibility for supporting institutions that had trained and would be training their technicians and administrators. Contributions also contributed substantially to the corporations' public image.

In many cases the scholarship award winners were chosen from eligible applicants on the basis of competitive examinations and personal data. Initially each corporation undertook to establish and operate its own selection program. But as the number of programs increased, secondary schools began to complain about the demands on them and their students and to call attention to the obvious duplication and inefficiency.

John M. Stalnaker's interest in the use of examinations for scholarship awards had begun before World War II.[57] In 1945 he became director of the Pepsi-Cola Scholarship Program,[58] the forerunner of the National Merit Program, which was established in 1955 with financial support of the Ford Foundation.[59] Through the National Merit program of application, examination, and selection a large number of scholarship donors award some 3000 paying scholarships each year. From the annual

[55] E. F. Lindquist, "The Iowa Electronic Test Processing Equipment" *Proceedings, 1953 Invitational Conference on Testing Problems* (Princeton, N.J.: Educational Testing Service, 1954).

[56] E. F. Lindquist, "The Impact of Machines on Educational Measurement," 68th Yearbook, National Society for the Study of Education, *Part II: Educational Evaluation: New Roles, New Means* (Chicago: University of Chicago Press, 1969).

[57] John M. Stalnaker and M. W. Richardson, "Scholarship Examinations," *The Journal of Higher Education*, vol. 5 (1934), 305–13.

[58] John M. Stalnaker, "A National Scholarship Program: Methods, Problems, Results," in L. L. Thurstone, ed., *Applications of Psychology* (New York: Harper and Row, Publishers, 1952.)

[59] John M. Stalnaker, "Evaluation and the Award of Scholarships," *Educational Evaluation: New Roles, New Means*, chap. 6.

applicant population of about 800,000 some 55,000 are identified with the help of the National Merit Scholarship Qualifying Test for commendation or award. Thus the program not only identifies, honors, and supports high academic talent, it also encourages students and schools to value and to develop such talent.

1956
TAXONOMY OF EDUCATIONAL OBJECTIVES

While he was University Examiner at Chicago, Ralph Tyler periodically invited other college and university examiners to meet and discuss their common interests and problems. One outcome of these meetings was the idea that it would be useful for them to collect, classify, and organize the common objectives of higher education in the form of a taxonomy. Benjamin S. Bloom played a major role in initiating, developing, and completing this project.

Three types of objective were identified—cognitive, affective, and psychomotor. Taxonomies for the first two of these have been published.[60,61] The cognitive taxonomy has become especially well known and has had considerable impact in stimulating the development of tests that "measure more than knowledge." However, questions are still raised about the validity and usefulness of these systems for classifying educational objectives, and about the desirability of making the attainment of these objectives the principal goals of education.

1960
PROJECT TALENT

Project TALENT, conceived by John C. Flanagan, directed by him with the help of panels of educational experts, and supported by the United States Office of Education, was intended to provide substantial nationwide data on the aptitudes, achievements, backgrounds, and career plans of secondary school students. In March, 1960 a two-day battery of tests and questionnaires was administered to 440,000 students in a carefully selected sample of 1,353 secondary schools. The design of the study included plans for followup of the students in the sample 1, 5, 10 and 20 years after their graduation from high school. Efforts were made to develop measures of achievement that would indicate what the student could do, not just how much better or worse he was than the typical student.

---

[60]Benjamin S. Bloom and others, *Taxonomy of Educational Objectives: Cognitive Domain.* (New York: David McKay Company, Inc., 1956).

[61]David R. Krathwohl and others. *Taxonomy of Educational Objectives: Affective Domain.* (New York: David McKay Company, Inc., 1964).

Among the voluminous findings of the study two are worthy of mention in even a brief summary: the wide variations in achievement among pupils of the same age and educational level, and the unrealistic nature of their career plans. Obviously the study is still uncompleted, but it has already produced significant and useful results. A problem that remains is to bring the essence of the findings into the store of information on which educational leaders base their plans and decisions.[62]

1961
INTERNATIONAL ACHIEVEMENT TESTING

Educational research workers, meeting once a year in the late 1950's at the UNESCO Institute for Education in Hamburg, became convinced of the need for instruments and procedures that would permit valid comparisons of educational achievements among nations. A pilot study in 12 countries, using a 120-item test covering science, geography, reading, and nonverbal intelligence, showed that the project was administratively feasible.

The first phase of the actual comparison, based on a mathematics test, involved participation of 12 nations. Israel, with 7 percent of the age group enrolled in mathematics in the final year of secondary education, made the highest mean score on the test. The United States, with 18 percent enrolled, made the lowest. Japan had the highest percentage reaching the 90th percentile on the test.

This International Project for the Evaluation of Educational Achievement (IEA) has become an international, nonprofit, scientific association that aims to conduct similar comparisons in science, civics, English as a foreign language, French as a foreign language, reading comprehension, and literature. Other countries have joined the association. Technical problems of test construction and of score interpretation are formidable but not unsolvable. It is the hope and expectation of IEA that each nation may learn how to improve its own educational techniques and results as a consequence of these studies.[63]

1965
NATIONAL ASSESSMENT

The quarter century that has passed since the end of World War II has been in many ways a golden age of education in the United States,

[62]John C. Flanagan, "The Use of Educational Evaluation," *Educational Evaluation: New Roles, New Means*, chap. 10.

[63]Torsten Husén, "International Impact of Evaluation," *Educational Evaluation: New Roles, New Means*, chap. 14.

A rapid rise of college enrollments began with returning veterans whose continuing education was subsidized generously by the federal government. Russia's initial superiority in space exploration startled the United States into renewed efforts to improve the quality of education. Militant minorities demanded not only that the old inequalities in educational quality and opportunity be removed, but that extra efforts be made on their behalf in the future.

These factors, coupled with very rapid growth of the school-age population and continuing inflation, have caused educational costs to skyrocket. State aid and federal aid have had to bear much of the burden of the higher costs. Increasingly school administrators have been called on to justify increased expenditures by providing evidence of increased pupil learning.

Several states inaugurated mandatory educational testing programs.[64] The federal government felt the need for nationwide data on educational progress. Early in the 1960's the U. S. Commissioner of Education, Francis Keppel, interested John W. Gardner, president of the Carnegie Corporation, in the project. Gardner arranged financial support and in August 1964 appointed members to the Exploratory Committee on the Assessment of Progress in Education, with Ralph Tyler as chairman.[65] The committee met with school people and interested laymen to decide how to use the data and identify problems. It undertook construction of the necessary assessment instruments and the design of sampling and other operational procedures.[66] The initial outrage of some school administrators at the very idea of federal review of the success of their efforts was gradually overcome. The tests were designed and built, and in 1969 test administration began.

How successful these efforts at educational assessment will be, and what influence they will have toward the improvement of education remain to be seen. But so long as our interest and investment in education remain high, this and other efforts to determine how well we are doing, and to suggest how we can do better, are likely to continue.

CONCLUDING OBSERVATIONS

This brings our history of measurement in education up to the 1970's. Counting from the earliest beginnings, the history is a long one.

---

[64]Everett T. Calvert, "Supplemental Report on the 1963 Statewide Testing Program," *California Education*, vol. 2 (January 1965), 3–6.

[65]Ralph W. Tyler, "The Objectives and Plans for a National Assessment of Educational Progress," *Journal of Educational Measurement*, vol. 3 (1966), 1–4.

[66]Jack C. Merwin and Frank B. Womer, "Evaluation in Assessing the Progress of Education to Provide Bases of Public Understanding and Public Policy," *Educational Evaluation: New Roles, New Means*, chap. 13.

But counting the developments that matter to educators in the 1970's, the history is relatively short–only about eighty years. Clearly the history is unfinished. Measurement specialists are hard at work on other developments such as criterion-referenced testing or computer-assisted testing. Some are even at work to eliminate testing as a distinct educational operation by amalgamating it into one continuous process of individually prescribed instruction to a specified level of mastery. Efforts along these lines may or may not succeed. Even if they do, it seems likely that education at the end of the decade will still see tests being used for most of the purposes they are serving more or less well today.

What can we learn, apart from the facts, by viewing this perspective on the history of measurement in education? Perhaps that the problems of educational measurement are persistently perennial–that the problems of what to measure and how to measure it, of objectivity, reliability, validity, and efficiency that bothered our predecessors still bother us. Perhaps that those predecessors were remarkably inventive and resourceful in discovering some solutions to these problems. Perhaps that we owe a great debt to the dynamic innovators who saw a need, and who then committed enough time, effort, persistence, and skill to create the tools and establish the agencies that could satisfy the need. Perhaps that our technical skill in developing tools, procedures, and agencies has been greater than our pedagogical skill in getting teachers to make effective use of the available technology. If teachers could only be taught and persuaded to use well the technology of educational measurement that has already been developed, there could be a quiet revolution in the quality of our testing and teaching almost overnight. Most of the remainder of this book represents an effort to help meet this great current need.

If measurement is to continue to play an increasingly important role in education, measurement workers must be much more than technicians. Unless their efforts are directed by a sound educational philosophy, unless they accept and welcome a greater share of responsibility for the selection and clarification of educational objectives, unless they show much more concern with what they measure as well as with how they measure it, much of their work will prove futile or ineffective.

E. F. LINDQUIST

2

MEASUREMENT AND THE PROCESS OF EDUCATION

Educators disagree as to the role of measurement in education.[1] Some regard tests and grades as mainly destructive in their influence on students, teachers, and the learning process.[2] Others view educational measurements as essential, and constructive.[3]

These differing views of the role of measurement in education are clearly related to different perceptions of the central purpose of formal education. That purpose, some say, is the intellectual development of the

[1] Henry S. Dyer, "Is Testing a Menace to Education?" *New York State Education,*" vol. 59 ILIX (1961), 16–19.
[2] Hillel Black, *They Shall Not Pass* (New York: William Morrow & Company, Inc., 1963).
[3] Henry Chauncey and John E. Dobbin, *Testing: Its Place in Education Today* (New York: Harper and Row, Publishers, 1963).

child, the cultivation of his cognitive competence.[4, 5] Others would give priority to his personal and social development, his security and sense of belonging, his feeling of self-worth, his happiness.[6]

Those who emphasize intellectual development as the principal task of the school tend to support conventional school organization and practices and to seek improvement in education through successive improvements in familiar materials and methods. Those who give higher priority to the pupil's feelings and adjustment tend to favor radical innovations in the direction of flexibility and freedom for pupils and teachers, curriculum, and procedures. Many of them favor getting rid of textbooks, lesson plans, tests, grades, classrooms, even teachers—replacing them with resource materials, projects, self-evaluations, independent study, and learning that is self-motivated and self-directed.

To place all educators in one of two categories—intellectual or humanist, conservative or progressive, scholar or reformer—does considerable violence to the diversity of their views. Nevertheless, it may be instructive to display some of the more important contrasts between points of view about the educational process. This has been attempted in Exhibit 2.1.

Now clearly there are good things on both sides of this table. It is also true that the characteristics here set in opposition to each other are not mutually exclusive. But neither are they mutually complementary. If one member of a pair is given more emphasis, the other is likely to receive less. The two columns of the table reflect, however imperfectly, two quite different orientations to the purposes and processes of education. The differences between them are real and have important consequences in choice of materials and methods, and in results.

Strongest support for the humanistic, progressive point of view comes from some professors of education and from some of their students, particularly among those who plan to teach in the early elementary grades. Strongest support for the intellectual, conservative point of view comes from some leaders in government and business, from the public at large, and from a majority of experienced teachers. Beginning teachers frequently report that one of their major problems in the first years of teaching is readjusting their philosophy of education away from the child-centered, adjustment-oriented ideals they were taught in college toward the more subject-centered, achievement-oriented teaching practiced by the school in which they teach and expected by the community.

[4]Educational Policies Commission, *The Central Purpose of American Education* (Washington, D.C.: National Education Association, 1961).

[5]William C. Bagley, "An Essentialist's Platform for the Advancement of American Education," *Educational Administration and Supervision*, vol. 24 (April 1938), 241–56.

[6]Fred T. Wilhelms, ed., *Evaluation as Feedback and Guide*, 1967 yearbook, Association for Supervision and Curriculum Development (Washington, D. C.: The Association, 1967).

EXHIBIT 2.1

Contrasting Views of Education

DESIGNATIONS

The Progressive View	*The Conventional View*
Humanistic	Intellectual
Experimental	Conventional
Progressive	Conservative

CONCERNS

Pupils	Subjects
Individual needs	Social needs
Feelings	Thoughts
Interests	Accomplishments
Processes of learning	Products of learning

EMPHASES

Perceiving	Knowing
Behaving	Understanding
Becoming	Achieving
Creativity	Mastery
Divergent thinking	Convergent thinking

GOALS

Pupil-determined	Teacher-defined
Adjustment	Competence
Individuality	Excellence

TEACHER ROLES

Motivating	Instructing
Facilitating	Directing
Fellowship	Scholarship

STUDENT ROLES

Leading	Following
Living	Learning
Participating	Studying

PURPOSES OF TESTING

Learning	Measurement
Diagnosis	Evaluation
Guidance	Placement

PROMINENT ADVOCATES

Jean Jacques Rousseau	Aristotle
Johann Heinrich Pestalozzi	John Amos Comenius
Friedrich Froebel	Johann Friedrich Herbart
John Dewey	William C. Bagley
Progressive Education Association	Council for Basic Education
Earl C. Kelley	Arthur Bestor
Arthur W. Combs	Hyman Rickover

EXEMPLARY SCHOOLS

Yverdun (Pestalozzi)	Lyceum of Athens
Chicago Laboratory School	Eton College
Fairhope, Alabama	Phillips Exeter
Summerhill (A. S. Neill)	Evanston Township High School
Melbourne, Florida	Bronx High School of Science

Which orientation is the correct one? Many educators have opinions, but they have difficulty proving them correct. Research can give part of the answer, but only part, for the question of purposes and uses asks more than science is equipped to answer, that is, how things really are. It asks also how things ought to be. "Ought" questions lie in the realm of ethical philosophy—and often they are hard questions.

Hard, yes, but not impossible to answer. If one puts his mind to the task, and spends some time on it, he can arrive at a coherent set of beliefs that takes into account much of what experience and research have to teach us about the goals of education and the uses of measurement in the educational process. If many of us are uncertain about the aims of education it is only partly because the question is hard, only partly because philosophers and researchers offer us no simple, authoritative answers. It is also partly because many of us have spent very little time and energy trying to think clearly about these questions ourselves.

The remainder of the chapter is intended to help make amends for this neglect. It is organized around eight questions having to do with the goals of education and the role of educational measurement. Here they are:

1. What is the principal task of the school?
2. Who is mainly responsible for a person's education?
3. How effective is contemporary education?
4. Can educational achievement be measured?
5. What are the functions of achievement tests?
6. What are the functions of intelligence tests in education?
7. Should schools banish failure?
8. How important is measurement of educational achievement?

An answer to each question will be suggested that seems consistent with the known facts and with the ethical ideals of our society. The student is invited to consider these suggested answers with an open mind. He is not expected to accept them as true simply because the author believes them, but only if, on close examination, they seem to him to be reasonable and constructive. One of the principal purposes of this chapter is to stimulate critical thought and discussion about the purposes of education and about the role of measurement in it.

WHAT IS THE PRINCIPAL TASK OF THE SCHOOL?

When one considers the reasons why schools were built, the reasons why children and adults attend them, and the activities that go on inside them, it seems clear that the principal task of the school is to facilitate cognitive learning. Indeed, this answer may seem too obviously true to require any supporting argument. Yet learning has been challenged by some who argue that the schools should be concerned primarily with one of the following:

a. moral character[7]
b. adjustment to life[8]
c. reconstruction of society[9]
d. self-confidence[10]

Now clearly all of these things are good. Since learning can contribute to each of them, they are not so much alternatives to learning as they are reasons for learning. But should they be given primary emphasis in defining the task of the school? Do they not have more to do with the ends of living than with the means the school should use to help pupils toward those ends?

Those who define the task of the school in terms of character, adjustment, self-confidence or the good society tend to be critical of emphasis on learning in conventional schools. Loving does more than learning to make people happy, they say, and faith is better than reason as a guide to the good life. They tend to oppose structured learning situations, the setting of specific goals, the objective assessment of attainments, and the use of marks to report and record those attainments. They say that a teacher's primary concern should be to send her pupils home in the afternoon thinking better of themselves than when they came to school in the morning. A child's happiness, they say, is more important to society than his ability to read. By thus denying the central role of learning in the activity of the school they find it easy to excuse themselves from teaching, or their pupils from learning, anything very specific.

Many teachers, however, do not agree with those who set "higher"

[7]Ernest M. Ligon, "Education for Moral Character," in Philip H. Phenix, ed., *Philosophies of Education* (New York: John Wiley & Sons, Inc., 1961).

[8]*Life Adjustment Education for Every Youth.* (Washington D.C.: U.S. Office of Education, 1951).

[9]George S. Counts, *Dare the School Build a New Social Order?* (New York: The John Day Company, 1932).

[10]Earl C. Kelley, "The Fully Functioning Self," 1962 Yearbook, Association for Supervision and Curriculum Development, *Perceiving, Behaving, Becoming* (Washington, D.C.: The Association, 1962).

goals than learning for education. While they acknowledge the ultimate importance of character, adjustment, self-confidence, and the good society, they cite at least two reasons why none of them should replace learning the school's primary focus of attention.

The first reason is that the school is a special-purpose social institution. It was designed and developed to do a specific task, that is to facilitate learning. Other agencies are responsible for other parts of the complex task of helping people to live good lives together. There are families and churches, legislative assemblies and courts, publishers and libraries, factories and unions, markets and moneylenders, and so on. To believe that the whole responsibility for ethical character, life adjustment, social reconstruction, or happiness must rest on the schools is as presumptuous as it is foolish.

Let us never doubt the power of education for human betterment. But let us not make the mistake, either, of assuming that the schools can and should undertake to solve directly all the world's problems—war, oppression, poverty, exploitation, inflation, unemployment, anxiety, despair, underdevelopment, or overpopulation. If the schools take the burdens of the world on their shoulders, they are likely to neglect the specific tasks of training, instruction, and education that are their special responsibility. The task of facilitating learning is challenging enough, and important enough, to occupy all of a school's time and to consume all of its energy and resources.

The second reason for believing that the schools should continue to emphasize learning is the basic, instrumental importance of learning all human affairs. With his gift of language, man is specially equipped for learning. Cognitive excellence is his unique excellence. The more he knows and understands, the better, more effective, and happier he is likely to be.

How better can a school help a child toward happiness than by increasing his knowledge and understanding of himself and the world in which he lives? By what other means can his adjustment be facilitated, his character developed, or his ability to contribute to society increased? Is not cognitive learning effective in reaching all these goals? And is there any other means?

Yes, there is one. It is the psychological process called conditioning.[11] It makes use of rewards and punishments to establish specific, habitual responses to certain specific conditions. Much of our behavior was molded, especially during our first of years life, by processes of conditioning. Even as adults we are still subject to its influences. If the school were concerned solely with training: if its sole mission was to establish certain specific, unvarying responses or behavior patterns; then it should depend heavily

[11]Ernest R. Hilgard and Donald G. Marquis, *Conditioning and Learning.* (New York: Appleton-Century-Crofts, 1940).

on conditioning. For conditioning could probably get that job done faster and more surely than could cognitive learning. But what conditioning can not do is to give a person flexibility and freedom. Conditioning is better suited to the training of horses or dogs to obey than to the education of human beings to live happy, useful lives as free men.

Those who object to emphasis on learning as the school's primary task may do so because they think of learning as academic specialization, designed mainly to prepare a person for further learning, and remote from the practical concerns of living. No doubt some of what all schools have taught warrants this judgment. But learning need not be, and ought not to be, the learning of useless things. It can and should be the student's main road to effective living. When it is, it merits recognition as the primary task of the school.

WHO IS MAINLY RESPONSIBLE FOR A PERSON'S EDUCATION?

Three parties share most of the responsibility for education; the family, the society through its schools, and the individual. But it is the individual who ultimately can determine, and must therefore accept responsibility for, the success or failure of his education. As a free human being he can choose not to become educated, and if he so chooses there is not much that his family or the schools can do about it.

When a child is very young his activities are easier to influence and his own responsibility is more limited. During that period his family is in control and must be responsible for laying the foundations of his education. Because all learning builds on prior learning, the first years are of utmost importance. If his educational foundation is strong and extensive, he is fortunate. If not, its deficiencies may handicap him the rest of his life.

Later, when a child has achieved more self-sufficiency and more self-control, he is ready for more formal schooling. A society is responsible for providing the best schools and the best teaching it can afford. Although education is more highly valued today throughout the world than it has ever been before, most societies still have not fully recognized and fully accepted their educational responsibilities. Many of them do much, but most of them need to do a great deal more.

With increasing years the young person achieves increasing freedom, and must accept increasing responsibility. If he succeeds in school he can take most of the credit for it. If he fails, he must accept most of the blame. The schools can provide opportunities; they cannot guarantee results. Of course the school should try to help a student who is having difficulty. But it should never even seem to say to him, "Just relax. The job of educating you is our job. We will take care of everything." The school can't do it. Even if it could it probably shouldn't. A free person could hardly learn to live a responsible live under those conditions. The price of individual freedom is individual responsibility.

HOW EFFECTIVE IS CONTEMPORARY EDUCATION?

Contemporary education is about as effective as imperfect human beings striving to facilitate a highly complex and difficult process are likely to make it in the forseeable future. This means that it falls somewhat short of ideal effectiveness. It also means that it stands very much ahead of total ineffectiveness.

Despite the criticisms that are leveled with almost predictable regularity at conventional school practices,[12] which are usually accompanied by grandiose proposals for sweeping reform, there is much wisdom and virtue in the usual classroom procedures. What schools and teachers have learned to do in centuries of efforts to facilitate learning is, on the whole, wise and effective. It reflects the experiences of many talented and dedicated teachers. It is the distillate of countless bright ideas that have proved their effectiveness in the classroom.

Of course it is true that not all teachers are wise and skillful and dedicated. Not all of them are well acquainted with the vast stores of educational wisdom that have been accumulated. Few of them teach quite as well as they might. But their deficiencies are more in technique than in intent or general procedures. On the whole the direction of their efforts is sound.

Learning at best is difficult. It calls on both students and teachers to work hard. Results are sometimes disappointing. Honest efforts do not always succeed. Over the ages these difficulties and disappointments have led to repeated, indeed almost continuous, efforts to find better things to teach and better ways of teaching. Often the cry is raised that the true solution to educational problems, the golden key to all knowledge, has been found. But always, in time, the truth that education is still hard work, sometimes unsuccessful, frequently disappointing, emerges. Some good new techniques are retained; the rest are discarded and disappear, perhaps to be rediscovered later by some new educational reformer.

Those who condemn current educational practices and results and who propose radical changes in those practices may belong to one of two groups. The first is composed of those who offer criticisms and sug-

[12]Charles E. Silberman, *Crisis in the Classroom* (New York: Random House, Inc., 1970).

gestions from the sidelines, never having themselves been directly involved in day-to-day school operations. Some of these critics may be perceptive, and creative; if so, their comments ought to be taken seriously. But the fact that their views have been published is no guarantee of the validity of those views. A second group is composed of teachers who, having been put in difficult teaching situations or being burdened with difficult personalities, have blamed their problems not on situation or self but on the educational "establishment." These critics are unlikely to have much to contribute to the general improvement of education.

It is sometimes said that the slow progress of education is due to the unimaginative conservatism of teachers, to their great reluctance to abandon old ways and to try something new. But is this true? Consider how eagerly and how frequently elementary school teachers have embraced the "new math" with its substitution of set theory for some computational arithmetic. Consider the current popularity of the most recent innovations: performance contracting, individually-prescribed instruction, flexible scheduling, team teaching, the middle school, the ungraded primary, and the open classroom. Consider the innovations of the past that have flared up and then died away: the Lancastrian monitorial system, the Dalton (contract) plan, the project method, the Gary (platoon) plan of school organization, the Morrison (unit + mastery) method, and progressive education. The list could easily be made much longer.

Surely it is true that current educational practices are subject to improvement. Surely we need wiser and more skillful teachers, and a better selection of ideas and skills to teach. The point is simply that one should look more to increasing wisdom and skill of teachers and curriculum builders than to revolutionary innovations in content or method for the improvement of education. We will do well to concentrate our attention on doing more skillfully the sorts of things we are already trying to do, than on search for some radical solution to educational problems.

CAN EDUCATIONAL ACHIEVEMENT BE MEASURED?

Education is an extensive, diverse, complex enterprise, not only in terms of the achievements it seeks to develop but also in terms of the means by which it seeks to develop them. Our understanding of the nature and process of education is far from perfect. Hence it is easy to agree that we do not now know how to measure all important educational outcomes. *But in principle, all important outcomes of education are measurable.* They may not be measurable with the tests currently available. They may not even be measurable in principle, using only paper-and-pencil tests. But if they are known to be important, they must be measurable.

To be important an outcome of education must make an observable difference. That is, at some time, under some circumstances, a person who has more of it must behave differently from a person who has less of it. If different degrees or amounts of an educational achievement never make any observable difference, what evidence can be found to show that it is, in fact, important?

But if such differences can be observed, then the achievement is measurable, for all measurement requires is verifiable observation of a more-less relationship. Can integrity be measured? It can if verifiable differences in integrity can be observed among men. Can mother love be measured? If observers can agree that a hen shows more mother love than a female trout, or that Mrs. *A* shows more love for her children than Mrs. *B*, then mother love can be measured.

The argument, then, is this. To be important an educational outcome must make a difference. If it makes a difference, the basis for measurement exists.

To say that *A* shows more of trait *X* than *B* may not seem like much of a measurement. Where are the numbers? Yet out of a series of such more-less comparisons a scale for measuring the trait or property can be constructed. The Ayres scale for measuring the quality of handwriting is a familiar example of this.[13] If a sequence of numbers is assigned to the sequence of steps or intervals that make up the scale, then the scale can yield quantitative measurements. If used carefully by a skilled judge, it yields measurements that are reasonably objective (that is free from errors associated with specific judges) and reliable (that is, free from errors associated with use of a particular set of test items or tasks).

Are some outcomes of education essentially qualitative rather than quantitative? If so, is it reasonable to expect that these qualitative outcomes can be measured?

It is certainly true that some differences between persons are not usually thought of as more-less differences. This person is a man; that one is a woman. This person has blue eyes; that one has brown. This person speaks only French; that one speaks only German. But we can express these qualitative differences in quantitative terms. This person has more of the characteristics of a man; that one has less. This person has more eye-blueness; that one has less. This person has more ability to speak French; that one has less.

We may think of the weight of a man, his age, or the size of his bank account as quantities, while regarding his health, his friendliness, or his honesty as qualities. But it is also possible to regard all of them—

---

[13]L. P. Ayres, *A Scale for Measuring the Quality of Handwriting of School Children*, Division of Education, Bulletin 113 (New York: Russell Sage Foundation, 1912).

weight, age, savings, health, friendliness and honesty—as qualities. And if they serve to differentiate him from other men, because he exhibits more or less of them than other men, they become quantitative qualities. It is difficult to think of any quality that interests us that cannot also be quantified. "Whatever exists at all exists in some amount," said E. L. Thorndike.[14] And William A. McCall has added, "Anything that exists in amount can be measured."[15]

It is easy to show that mental measurement falls far short of the standards of logical soundness that have been set for physical measurement.[16] The best it ordinarily can do is to provide an approximate rank ordering of individuals in terms of their ability to perform a more or less well-defined set of tasks. The units used in measuring this ability cannot be shown to be equal. The zero point on the ability scale is not clearly defined.

Because of these limitations some of the things we often do with test scores, such as finding means, standard deviations, and correlation coefficients, ought not to be done if strict mathematical logic holds sway. But we often find it practically useful to do them none the less. When strict logic conflicts with practical utility, it is the utility that usually wins, as it probably should.

On the other hand, the logical limitations of test scores mean that they are unlikely to contribute to the formulation of psychological laws that can compare in precision with, say, the laws of motion. But then, development of precise laws of human behavior is unlikely on other, more fundamental grounds. Deficiencies in the scales of measurement are not the only, nor the most serious, problems in this area.

It is well for us to recognize the logical limitations of the units and scales used in educational measurement. But it is also well not to be so much impressed by these limitations that we stop doing the useful things we can do despite them. One of those useful things is to measure educational achievement.

Are some outcomes of education too intangible to be measured? No doubt there are some that we speak of often, like critical thinking or good citizenship, that are so difficult to define satisfactorily that we have given up trying to define them specifically. To this extent they are intangible, hard to measure, and hard to teach purposefully. We may feel intuitively that critical thinking and good citizenship are immensely

[14]E. L. Thorndike, *The Seventeenth Yearbook of the National Society for the Study of Education*, Part II (Bloomington, Ill.: Public School Publishing Company, 1918), p. 16.

[15]William A. McCall, *Measurement* (New York: The Macmillan Company, 1939), p. 15.

[16]B. Othanel Smith, *Logical aspects of educational measurement* (New York: Columbia University Press, 1938).

important. But if we don't know very clearly what we mean by those terms, it is hard to show that the concepts they might stand for are in fact important.

The processes of education that a particular student experiences probably have subtle and wholly unforeseen effects on him, and possibly on no one else. Some of these effects may not become apparent until long after the student has left school. These, too, could be regarded as intangible outcomes. It is unlikely that any current tests, or any that could conceivably be built, would measure these intangibles satisfactorily. In individual instances they might be crucially important. But since they may be largely accidental, subtle, and quite possibly long delayed in their influence, the practical need to measure them may be no greater than the practical possibility of measuring them.

Some of the belief that certain important outcomes of education are difficult to measure may stem from a confusion between measurement and prediction. For example, most people agree that it is quite difficult at present to measure motivation or creativity. But those who want to measure motivation or creativity are interested mainly in future prospects, not in present status or past achievements. They are less interested in the motivation or the creative achievements a person has shown in the past than in how hard he will work and how successfully he will create in the future.

Difficult as the problems of measuring some complex human traits are, they are much simpler than the problems of predicting unusual future success, especially if that success requires a fortunate coincidence of many influences. To help keep our thinking straight we probably should not charge those difficulties to the limitations of educational measurement. We might charge them in part to the somewhat indefinite generality of the concepts (motivation, creativity, and so on), in part to the complexity of human behavior, and in part to our cherished, if partly imaginary, freedom of choice and action.

Finally, it should be recognized that paper-and-pencil tests do have some limitations. They are well adapted to testing verbal knowledge and understanding and ability to solve verbal and numerical problems. These are important educational outcomes, but they are not all. One would not expect to get far using a paper-and-pencil test to measure children's physical development. Perhaps such a test could be made to yield somewhat better measures of the social effectiveness of adults, but even here the paper-and-pencil test is likely to be seriously limited. Both performance tests of physical development and controlled observations of behavior in social situations would be expected to offer more promise than a paper-and-pencil test.

However, it is important to remember that the use of alternative measures of achievement does not in any way lessen the need for objectivity, relevance, reliability, and validity. To achieve these qualities of excellence in measurement may well be even more difficult in performance testing and observational rating than it is in paper-and-pencil testing. But the usefulness of the measurements depends on them.

WHAT ARE THE FUNCTIONS OF ACHIEVEMENT TESTS?

There are good reasons to believe that the measurement of educational achievement is essential to effective formal education. Formal education is a complex process, requiring a great deal of time and money and the cooperative efforts of many people. Efforts must be directed toward the attainment of specific goals. Education is not automatically or uniformly successful. Some methods are more effective than others. Efficient use of learning resources often requires special motivation, guidance, and assistance. All of those concerned with the process of education —students, teachers, parents, and school officials—need to know periodically how successful their efforts have been, so that they can decide which practices to continue and which to change. It is the function of educational measurement to provide them with this knowledge.

To teach without evaluating the results of teaching would be foolish. Those who suggest that schools do not need tests, or might even do a better job of educating students if tests were prohibited, seldom go so far as to argue that evaluation is not needed. They seldom suggest that learning can be promoted effectively by teachers and students who have no particular goals in view, and who pay no attention to the results of their efforts. If tests were abandoned, some other means of assessing educational achievement would have to be used in their place. No other means that is as efficient, as dependable, and as beneficial to the process of education has yet been discovered.

The major function of a classroom test is to measure student achievement and thus to contribute to the evaluation of his educational progress and attainments. This is a matter of considerable importance. To say, as some critics of testing have said, that what a student knows and can do is more important than his score on a test or his grade in a course implies, quite incorrectly in most cases, that knowledge and scores are independent or unrelated. To say that testing solely to measure achievement has no educational value also implies, and again quite incorrectly in most cases, that test scores are unrelated to educational efforts, that they do not reward and reinforce effective study, that they do not penalize unproductive efforts or tend to discourage lack of effort.

Tests can, and often do, help teachers and professors to give more valid, reliable grades. Because these grades are intended to summarize concisely a comprehensive evaluation of the student's achievement, because they are reported to the student and his parents to indicate the effectiveness of his efforts, because they are entered in the school record and may help to determine honors and opportunities for further education or future employment, it is important that teachers and professors take seriously their responsibilities for assigning accurate, meaningful grades. Students are urged, quite properly, not to study *merely* to earn high grades. But, in terms of the student's present self-perceptions and his future opportunities, there is nothing "mere" about the grades he receives.

A second major function of classroom tests is to motivate and direct student learning. The experience of almost all students and teachers supports the view that students do tend to study harder when they expect an examination than when they do not and that they emphasize in studying those things on which they expect to be tested. If the students know in advance they will be tested, if they know what the test will require, and if the test does a good job of measuring the achievement of essential course objectives, then its motivating and guiding influence will be most wholesome.

Anticipated tests are sometimes regarded as extrinsic motivators of learning efforts, less desirable or effective than intrinsic motivators would be. Learning should be its own reward, it is said. Fortunately, no choice need be made between extrinsic and intrinsic motivation. Both contribute to learning. Withdrawal of either would be likely to lessen the learning of most students. For a fortunate few, intrinsic motivation may be strong enough to stimulate all the effort to learn that the student ought to put forth. For the great majority, however, the motivation provided by tests and other influential factors is indispensable.

Classroom tests have other useful educational functions. Constructing them, if the job is approached carefully, should cause an instructor to think carefully about the goals of instruction in a course. It should lead him to define those goals operationally in terms of the kind of tasks a student must be able to handle to demonstrate achivement of the goals. On the student's part the process of taking a classroom test, and of discussing the scoring of it afterward, can be a richly rewarding learning experience. As Stroud has said,

> It is probably not extravagant to say that the contribution made to a student's store of knowledge by the taking of an examination is as great, minute for minute, as any other enterprise he engages in.[17]

Hence, testing and teaching need not be considered as mutually exclusive, as competitors for the valuable classroom hours. They are intimately related parts of the total educational process.

[17]James B. Stroud, *Psychology in Education* (New York: David McKay Company, Inc., 1946), p. 476.

Awareness of the important direct contributions of test taking to student learning can lead to unwarranted disparagement of tests as measuring instruments. It is sometimes said, for example, that tests should be used to promote learning *rather than* to measure achievement, as if these two uses were somehow in conflict and mutually exclusive. Or the suggestion may be made that pupils who have taken a test will learn more if the test is not graded.

Efforts to increase the direct contributions of testing to learning, which lead to such things as giving "tests" that are not graded and using questions that have no right answers, obviously decrease the value of the tests as measuring instruments. Thus the important indirect contributions are weakened or lost altogether. The results of the test no longer really matter and there is no good reason to take them very seriously. In these circumstances even the direct contributions of the test to learning are likely to be small. It is better to concentrate on making tests the best possible measures of achievement, so that their powerful indirect contribution to learning will also be good. If ways can then be found, as they probably can, to maximize direct learning from the tests, without detracting from the measurement they yield, so much the better. But the direct teaching function of a test is always secondary. Its primary function, the one that justifies its place in the educational process, is measurement.

Richardson and Stalnaker, two leaders in the development of modern educational achievement testing, have insisted that

> an achievement examination need not have direct pedagogical value in itself. . . . The purpose of achievement examining is essentially measurement for certifying academic credit. . . . An achievement examination is good or valid if it simply does a good job of measuring what it purports to measure.[18]

An educational test that does not promote learning somehow is of questionable utility. But the promotion of learning is a complex enterprise, requiring a variety of tools. Tests can be, and usually are, highly important tools for the promotion of learning, but if their usefulness were judged solely in terms of what the student learns while taking them, the greater part of their importance would be overlooked. Their indirect influence in promoting learning is far more potent than their direct influence.

It probably goes without saying that the educational value of a test depends on its quality and on the skill of the teacher in using it. Good tests, properly used, can make valuable contributions to a student's education. Poor tests, or tests misused, will contribute less and might even do educational harm.

[18]M. W. Richardson and J. M. Stalnaker, "Comments on Achievement Examinations," *Journal of Educational Research*, vol. 28 (1935), 425–32.

WHAT ARE THE FUNCTIONS OF INTELLIGENCE TESTS IN EDUCATION?

The obvious fact that some young people learn more, and learn it more easily, than others has led some educators to assume that they must have been born brighter. It has led some to believe that if one is not born bright there is not much he can do about it, and to believe that one of the school's major tasks is to identify, as early as possible, those who have been gifted with the potential for educational development. As a result, it has led to the widespread use of intelligence tests to identify the gifted as well as those less favorably endowed.

Between this view and the alternative—that mental ability is a developed ability—there is a long history of controversy. Beyond any reasonable doubt inheritance plays an important role in determining a person's physical characteristics. Yet even with these, how a person lives and what he does have much to do with how he develops. One can gain weight by overeating or lose it by dieting. One can develop muscles by exercise or let them grow flabby with disuse. One can maintain health by wholesome moderation or let it deteriorate through excess.

The biological basis for learning—the sense organs, nervous system, and brain—are physical characteristics too. It is reasonable to believe that heredity has something to do in their development, and that as a result one person develops better equipment for learning than another. These differences could make a difference in how easily or how much a person learns. But except in a few cases of extreme mental deficiency, we have no clear notion of what these differences are. Among normal persons we have no direct evidence that any such differences even exist.

In contrast, there is good evidence that mental ability does develop. There are no mental operations that a person was born knowing how to do, none that were not learned. Some of these learned abilities are crucial to further learning. In the learning of some of them fortunate accidents play an important role. Not all of them are learned equally soon or equally well by all developing persons.

Because each of us has unique opportunities and experiences and makes unique efforts, each of us develops a unique personality made up of a special pattern of abilities, habits, interests, attitudes, and ideals. No two humans, not even identical twins growing up in the same household, have identical experiences. Each develops his own individuality. As psychoanalysis has taught us, the human personality is very sensitive to specific incidents or accidents. Small causes in experience can have great consequences in the developing personality.

These differences in personality greatly affect our educational development. Some of us come to love learning, others to be indifferent, and others to dislike it. Some of us become scholars; others become artists; still others become executives or businessmen. The differences also affect our lives in other ways. Some pursue fame; others money; others pleasure; and still others contentment. The possibilities for variation in our personal characteristics resulting from diverse experiences are so great that we do not need to assume important biological differences to account for our differences in ability to learn, and in our other achievements.

Experimental studies of the relative effects of heredity and environment on mental ability, often based on comparisons of test scores of identical twins with those of other brothers and sisters raised in the same or different households, are inconsistent and inconclusive.[19] Such testing presents many problems. The degree of genetic similarity of different individuals is difficult to establish; complete identity of environments is impossible to maintain; the possibility of experimenter bias in individual testing of intelligence is difficult to avoid; uncertainty about the nature of intelligence and about appropriate means of measuring it cloud the findings. There is little promise that future studies can solve the problems that have rendered previous studies inconclusive.

The hypothesis that mental ability is inherited is not necessary from a scientific point of view. Socially and educationally it is more likely to harm than to help. Therefore it seems most reasonable and useful to regard mental ability as largely a developed ability.

The cumulative nature of learning is illustrated by the gradual progress a child makes in learning to read, to write, to add, and to handle successively more difficult mental tasks. Courses are arranged in sequence and prerequisites are established so that students will not attempt, or be allowed to try, learning something they are not ready to learn. How often, and how correctly, do teachers account for learning difficulties on the grounds of inadequate preparation?

Of course not everything a person has learned contributes to learning everything else he will learn. Some elements are powerful tools to use in future learning; others are of almost no value. But no new knowledge can be added to a person's store unless some knowledge previously gained is on hand to give it meaning and value.

One of the corollaries of this belief is that the foundations of learning, established in the very early years, are of utmost importance. Another is that deficiencies in early learning are likely to constitute continuing handicaps. Yet another is that breadth and depth of understanding are not often easy prizes, quickly won. More often they reward years of patient effort.

[19]George D. Stoddard, *The Meaning of Intelligence* (New York: The Macmillan Company, 1943).

Finally, a most important corollary is that the potential of most human beings for educational development is, in principle, virtually unlimited. That the potential is seldom realized is more the fault of ourselves than of our cells.

Few of us work hard enough to learn all we possibly could. Most of us, probably for good reasons of health, happiness, or social participation, develop only a fraction of the mental capacity we possess. We are somewhat like automobiles moving at various speeds along the highway. What determines each car's speed is not usually the maximum speed it could attain. It is rather the purposes and the habits of the driver. The different levels of educational achievement of different individuals are probably no more determined by their maximum capacity for development than the different speeds of the cars are determined by their maximum possible speeds.

Of course no car can travel at infinite speed, and no human's capacity for learning is infinite. But it is impossible to say for either cars or humans, "Here is a limit that cannot possibly be exceeded." Given time enough, and opportunity enough, and desire enough, almost any ability can be developed by almost anyone.

It is reasonable to believe on the evidence now available that limitations on native ability do not seriously limit any man's potential for developing wisdom or goodness, or for serving society. What is needed is education to develop man's almost unlimited potential. Our function as teachers is to foster that development.

What has all this to say about the functions of intelligence tests in education? It says that they probably do not function as they are widely assumed to function, that is, as measures of native capacity or innate brightness. It says that we are probably mistaken if we think that achievement is limited by capacity. Instead we should think of capacity as something expanded by achievement. It does *not* say that intelligence tests should be dropped from school testing programs. If they are good tests they can provide good indications of the breadth and strength of a child's foundations for further learning, and hence can be used to predict whether the next stages of educational development will come easily or with difficulty. What it does say is that intelligence, as measured by a good intelligence test, is both a consequence of past achievement and a prerequisite for future achievement.

SHOULD SCHOOLS BANISH FAILURE?

Failure is often a traumatic experience. No normal person enjoys failing at something he has undertaken to do. Because of its disturbing, upsetting effects, some educational leaders have sought to banish it completely from the process of education.[20] In this they seem unwise on two grounds.

First, one cannot banish failure without also banishing any meaningful experience of success. If success is inevitable, where is the honor and the joy in it? Is it not possibility of failure that makes success sweet? It is not possible for a team or a player to win without some other team or player losing. Of course one could eliminate failure by eliminating competition, but only at the cost of slowing progress drastically and taking much of the zest out of living. Even if a person competes only with himself, as some educators unrealistically claim that he should, he can not always win or there is no real competition. The pain of failure is part of the price one must pay for the privilege of enjoying success.

Second, developing men and women need to learn to cope with failure, which they will surely encounter in life. An education that forbids the experience of failure does not help one to learn to withstand the heavy blows that life is almost certain to strike.

In a good life the successes outnumber the failures. So should it be in a good educational experience. No child in school should be faced with constant failure. If he is, something is wrong with the school or with the child that ought to be corrected. Perhaps goals or aspirations have been too high. Perhaps opportunities for different kinds of excellence and success have been too restricted. Perhaps the child gains some kind of revenge on his parents or on society by failing. Consistent failure never need be, and never should be, accepted as inevitable.

The world is full of a diversity of occupations in which men and women can develop excellence. Some make heavy demands on intellectual development. Others call for special social, mechanical, athletic, or artistic development. In each of these broad categories there is a wide variety of specific occupations. Finding happiness and fulfillment in life is partly a matter of finding an agreeable occupation in a field that is not already overcrowded, and working at it long enough and hard enough to achieve excellence. In most fields of human endeavor excellence is in constantly short supply.

Why do so many of us fail to achieve excellence? Perhaps because we are not sufficiently content to be excellent in modest occupations. Perhaps because we overestimate our talents and underestimate the effort required to develop them. Perhaps because we think democracy demands equality in benefits from society regardless of inequality in contributions to society.

Schools that define excellency too narrowly as excellence in the traditional academic fields of study, that offer too little diversity in fields where excellence can be developed, recognized, and rewarded, may also

[20]William Glasser, *Schools Without Failure* (New York: Harper and Row, Publishers, 1969).

be partly to blame. So may overcommitment to a uniform program of general or liberal education for all. Different attainments among men and women need to be encouraged, not suppressed. Diverse avenues to excellence need to be kept open by the schools, and students should be encouraged to explore them.

Whenever goals are reasonably challenging and standards reasonably high, failures are bound to occur. Kept to a minimum, they constitute a valuable part of a person's education. Schools may refuse to recognize failure, but a good school cannot and will not try to banish it.

HOW IMPORTANT IS MEASUREMENT OF EDUCATIONAL ACHIEVEMENT?

The view that classroom tests are important and that they could be, and ought to be, much better than they often are is shared by most school teachers and college professors. Occasionally one hears the suggestion that education could go on perfectly well, perhaps much better than it has in the past, if tests and testing were abolished. Others accept tests grudgingly as a "necessary evil" in education. But the view of the great majority of teachers at all levels is that periodic assessment of educational progress is essential to effective education and that good tests afford very useful assistance to teachers in making those assessments.

One would have difficulty in finding among those who are inclined to discount the value of tests a teacher or professor who is not concerned about quality in education—about the achievements of his students, the adequacy of their previous preparation, his own success as a teacher, and the effectiveness of the whole enterprise of education. But quality is a matter of degree. Unless some means exist for measuring it, for distinguishing between higher and lower quality, between better and poorer achievement, concern for quality will not mean very much. If tests are abandoned, it must be on the ground that better means are available for measuring educational achievement.

It is easy to understand why tests are sometimes characterized as a "necessary evil" in education. Almost all students, but especially students of average or inferior ability, approach a test with apprehension. Those who do less well than they had expected can easily find some basis for regarding the examination as unfair. Cheating on examinations is reported often enough to cast some shadows of disrepute over the whole enterprise.

Instructors, too, sometimes dislike to assume the role of examiners. Most of them prefer to be helpful rather than critical. There is something inconsiderate about probing the minds of other human beings and passing judgment on their shortcomings. There is even something presumptuous in assuming the right to set the standards by which others will be judged. And if the instructor has learned that he is not an infallible examiner, if he has experienced the critical retaliation of students who have been unfairly judged, his wishful dreams of education freed from the torments of examining and evaluation are also easy to understand. No doubt he sometimes feels like the Sergeant of Police in *The Pirates of Penzance*, who sings, "Taking one consideration with another, a policeman's lot is not a happy one."

Unfortunately, there is no effective substitute for tests or examinations in most classrooms. Even in a generally critical leaflet on some aspects of contemporary testing in the public schools, the authors say,

> To teach without testing is unthinkable. Appraisal of outcomes is an essential feedback of teaching. The evaluation process enables those involved to get their bearings, to know in which direction they are going.[21]

Anxiety, unfairness, dishonesty, humiliation, and presumptuousness can be and should be minimized, but the process of examining and evaluating cannot be dispensed with if education is to proceed effectively.

Those who would abolish tests, or who regard them as a necessary evil usually do not mean to imply that good education is possible without any assessment of student achievement whatsoever. What they sometimes do suggest is that a good teacher, working with a class of reasonable size, has no need for tests in order to make sufficiently accurate judgments of student achievement. They may also suggest that the tests they have seen or have even used themselves leave so much to be desired that a teacher is better off without the kind of "help" such tests are likely to give. In some cases they may indeed be right in this judgment. No doubt some bad tests have actually been worse than no tests at all.

But again, the majority of teachers and professors are keenly aware of the limited and unsatisfactory bases they ordinarily have for judging the relative achievement of various students and of the fallibility of their subjective judgments when based on the irregular, uncontrolled observations they can make in their classroom or office. They welcome the help that tests can give in providing a more extensive and objective basis for judgment. For testing is not really an alternative to teacher observation of student behavior. It is simply a specialized technique for extending, refining, efficiently recording, and summarizing those observations.

Some people who know little about mental measurement have been led to expect something close to magic to result from it. They are sure to be disappointed. Test scores are powerful educational tools, but they are only tools. They will not give direct, complete answers to the practical

---

[21]Joint Committee of the American Association of School Administrators, *Testing, Testing, Testing* (Washington, D.C.: American Association of School Administrators, 1962), p. 9.

educational questions that bother teachers and students. They will not point unequivocally to a specific course of action in a given set of circumstances. They may indicate that something needs to be done. They may provide data that will help in deciding what to do. But they will not make the decision.

Those who expect tests to do more than they can do may overreact to the disappointment in store for them. They may, in their frustration, assert that all tests are worthless. This is not true. If properly used, tests can be worth a great deal. It is not the fault of the tests that too much is sometimes expected of them.

The tendency of some who use tests but are not thoroughly familiar with them to expect too much is encouraged by a few test specialists who have cloaked the process of testing and the interpretation of test scores in mystery. It is too complex, they imply, to be dealt with by any but the fully initiated. Test scores should never be reported directly, they say, to anyone who has not been specially trained to interpret them.

Now it is quite true that the meaning of some test scores is obscure, but this is due more often to the test constructor's own confusion than to any technical complexity in the scores he obtains. It is also true that test scores have been misinterpreted by those who do not understand fully how they were derived and the limits of their meaning. But openness and explanation would seem to be a better cure for this fault than secrecy and mystery.

There is nothing inherently complex or technical about the processes of measuring educational achievement. First, a field of knowledge is defined, then a class of tasks appropriate for testing command of that knowledge is defined. Test items are written and administered, and answers are scored as correct or incorrect. The number answered correctly is then reported as a proportion of the total number presented, or in comparison with the number correct given by some reference group of students.

In general the best test scores are the most straightforward and the easiest to interpret. One should be skeptical of the meaning of any test score that cannot be explained to a layman in a paragraph or two, or in ten minutes. Few specialists in educational measurement are so much brighter than their fellow men that they need to withhold what they know in order to protect others from error. Education is a public concern that involves the cooperative efforts of many people; secrecy and mystery have no place in it.

A final few words about the tendency of progressively oriented teachers to deplore and to avoid the use of tests and grades. One possible explanation of this tendency is that it reflects an overgeneralization of the ideal of democracy: the misconception that democracy demands more than equality of opportunity and equality of voice in the determination of public policy; that it demands also the pretence that men are equal in all respects. Some progressive educators deplore the pursuit of excellence in the schools on the grounds that it fosters an intellectual elite, which is intolerable in a democracy. John Gardner has argued the opposite point of view persuasively.[22]

A possible objection to the tendency of progressively oriented teachers to deplore testing and grading is that it involves a logical inconsistency. Consider how a progressively oriented teacher might respond to this series of questions:

1. Do you believe in good education?
2. Is it desirable to base judgments of the goodness of an educational program at least partly on the achievements of students?
3. Is it desirable for those judgments to be as accurate as is feasible and to be reported meaningfully to others?
4. Can tests be used to improve the accuracy with which judgments of achievement are made?
5. Can degrees of quality be reported meaningfully by using a scale of numbers or letters?
6. Should a school that hopes to establish or maintain its goodness use tests and grades?

Most teachers answer "yes" to the first three questions without hesitation. Those with progressive inclinations may answer "Yes, but. . ." to questions 4 and 5, mentioning the poor quality of tests or grades, undesirable side effects, or other faults in their qualifying statements. If these faults should be minimized, as most of them can be, the answers become "yes" without qualification. Given "yes" answers to the first five questions, a "yes" to the sixth becomes almost inevitable. The point of the whole demonstration is this: it is logically inconsistent to support good schools and at the same time to oppose testing and grading.

SUMMARY

The main ideas of this chapter can be summarized in the following 30 propositions.

1. Educators who place primary emphasis on cognitive outcomes (knowledge, understanding) tend to favor the use of tests and grades; those who emphasize affective outcomes (feelings, values) tend to resist their use.
2. Philosophically most educators embrace one of two quite different sets of values; humanistic and progressive or intellectual and conservative.
3. Educators ought to spend more time developing a coherent set of beliefs about the purposes and processes of education.

[22]John W. Gardner, *Excellence: Can We Be Equal and Excellent Too?* (New York: Harper and Row, Publishers, 1961).

4. There are good reasons for believing that the principal task of the school is to facilitate cognitive learning.
5. There are two means that schools can use to help children become effective, happy adults; cultivating their cognitive abilities, and molding their behavior by processes of conditioning.
6. Cognitive competence provides a better basis for the good life of a free man than does conditioned behavior.
7. Responsibility for an individual's education is shared by his family and by the society in which he lives, but the major share of it belongs to the individual himself.
8. Improvements in education are less likely to come out of radical innovations than out of gradual perfection of age-old, time-tested educational practices.
9. There are good reasons for questioning the validity of sweeping indictments of conventional school practices.
10. Educators seem to err more often in the direction of gullibility than in the direction of skepticism when faced with proposed innovations in education.
11. Any important outcome of education is necessarily measurable, but not necessarily by means of a paper-and-pencil test.
12. It is a mistake to believe that qualities cannot be measured.
13. The fact that educational measurements fail to meet high standards of mathematical soundness does not destroy their educational value.
14. Educational outcomes that are said to be intangible because they are not clearly defined are as difficult to attain through purposeful teaching as they are to measure through achievement tests.
15. Any measurement of an educational achievement should be relevant, reliable, and objective, regardless of whether it is a paper-and-pencil test or some other technique, such as a performance test or a rating of observed behavior.
16. The measurement of educational achievement is essential to effective formal education.
17. The primary function of a classroom test is to measure student achievement.
18. Classroom tests can help to motivate and to direct student achievement, and can provide learning exercises.
19. The development of a good classroom test requires the instructor to define the course objectives in specific, operational terms.
20. The indirect contributions of testing to the process of learning are more important than the direct contributions.
21. Mental ability is a developed ability.
22. All learning builds on prior learning.
23. There is no ceiling on the potential of most human beings for educational development.
24. Developed intelligence is both a consequence of past achievement and a prerequisite for future achievement.
25. Occasional failure is a normal experience in life, and is a valuable part of a person's educational experience.
26. Many diverse avenues of excellence are open to men and women.
27. Good achievement in education is fostered by the use of good tests of educational achievement.
28. Most teachers recognize the essential role of measurement in education.
29. There is no magic in educational measurement, and there should be no mystery about it.
30. It is logically inconsistent for those who support good schools to oppose measurement of educational achievements.

CLASSROOM
TEST DEVELOPMENT

3

WHAT SHOULD
ACHIEVEMENT TESTS MEASURE?

THE DUAL PROBLEMS OF TEST CONSTRUCTION

The test constructor faces two major problems. The first is to determine what to measure, and the second is to decide how to measure it. In general, books and articles on educational testing offer more help in solving the second problem than the first. But the quality of an educational achievement test depends on how well *both* problems have been solved. How well the first problem is solved largely determines what is sometimes called the *relevance* of the test. By "relevance" we mean the apparent or obvious logical relationship between what the process of testing requires the student to do and what the process of education undertook to teach him to do. How well the second problem is solved has a great deal to do with the *reliability* of the test and its practicality. By "reliability" we mean the consistency of the measurement of a particular achievement from time to time or from test to test. To the degree that a test has this kind of relevance and yields reliable scores, it can claim to be a *valid* test. A valid test of educational achievement is one composed of relevant tasks and yielding reliable scores.[1]

If the test constructor has sound and specific ideas about what constitutes educational achievement in the area of the test, he knows what to measure. But these sound and specific ideas are sometimes hard to get. For one thing, there is far more of knowledge, understanding, ability, skill, and effective behavior available for us to learn in the world than any one person could possibly learn. Teachers and students are constantly faced with the need to make choices between many varied things to be taught and to be learned. We keep asking ourselves and others the question Herbert Spencer asked and tried to answer a century ago. "What knowledge is of most worth?"[2] Benjamin Franklin recognized the same problem. "It would be well if they could be taught everything that is useful and everything that is ornamental: but art is long and their time is short. It is therefore proposed that they learn those things that are likely to be most useful and most ornamental."[3]

The problems of the test constructor thus have much in common with those of the curriculum maker, the textbook writer, and the classroom teacher. The test constructor, however, can borrow ideas from all of the other three. If those whose guidance he accepts are themselves well educated and if they have thought long and carefully about what achievements are of most worth, the test constructor may build a good test with their help. But the problem is not a simple one. In the foreseeable future educators will probably have to get along as best they can with somewhat imperfect, uncertain answers to the question of what to test. This, of course, is no excuse for not trying to find the best available answers, which are doubtless much better than those we often give or accept.

There is another school of thought about how to produce good tests. Instead of trying to build relevance into the tests, with rational decisions about what kinds of tasks will provide valid measures of a particular kind of achievement, the proponents of this school advocate an experimental approach. Try any kind of question or task you can think of that might work, they say, and retain in the test only those that do work, or work best. The difficulty with this approach is that it requires some basis for judging how well an item "works" as an indicator of achievement.

---

[1]The concepts of test reliability and test validity are much more complex than these simple definitions may imply. They will be discussed in greater detail in subsequent chapters.

[2]Herbert Spencer, *Education: Intellectual, Moral and Physical* (New York: A. L. Burt; London: G. Manwaring, 1861).

[3]Thomas Woody, *Educational Views of Benjamin Franklin* (New York: McGraw-Hill Book Company, 1931), p. 158.

Usually this implies some other, and presumably better, measure of the achievement in question. But this is precisely what we were setting out to create. If we already had it, we probably would not need to worry about building the new test. The use of empirical (experimental) approaches to test development does not circumvent the need for rational decisions and value judgments with respect to what should be measured. If they are not applied to the test, they have to be applied in choosing the standards by which the test is to be judged.

Publishers of standardized tests of educational achievement and directors of wide-scale testing programs that use achievement tests face the special problem of how to make a single test suitable for students who have been taught by different teachers using different textbooks and learning materials in courses having different orientations. The usual solution is to base the test on the elements thought to be most commonly taught. If the differences are too great to make this solution feasible, separate tests have to be provided.

The classroom teacher's problems would seem to be much simpler since only one teacher, one or the same set of textbooks, and a single approach to teaching are involved. But the advantage is less than it might seem. If a particular teacher's instruction and testing do not emphasize substantially the same achievements as those of most other teachers of the same subjects, his students may not have achieved what is expected of them. Thus the test constructor must ask not only, "Do *I* consider this achievement worth having?" but also, "Do *most* good teachers of the subject regard this particular knowledge or ability worth having?"

Some differences between teachers, texts, courses, and tests are not only tolerable but probably essential if teaching is to have its maximum vitality and person-to-person effectiveness. But if the differences become too great, particularly in the more elementary courses, the students may suffer later. Thus the classroom teacher needs to be concerned about the general validity and acceptability of his value judgments and approaches to teaching. If a wholesale revision in curriculum and instruction is called for, it had best not be undertaken singlehandedly, in the relative isolation of a single classroom.

THE USES AND LIMITATIONS OF EDUCATIONAL OBJECTIVES IN TEST DEVELOPMENT

An educational achievement test should seek to measure what the process of education has sought to achieve. Hence the test constructor needs to be concerned with educational objectives, both those that relate to the total process of education and those that relate specifically to the course or subject for which the test is being constructed. The tests he builds ought to be as consistent as possible with the educational objectives of the society, the school, and the test constructor himself.

One of the uses of any statement of educational objectives is to remind all concerned that education should be a purposeful activity, not simply a routine ritual. The steady influx of pupils to be educated and the organization of these pupils into a succession of annual class groups, each of which follows much the same program of studies as it advances through the institution, give the process of education a repetitive characteristic that could easily become a fixed routine. Often the educational needs of a society seem to change faster than the programs of the society's educational institutions. Indeed, some educators seem to make a virtue of the traditional in education, regardless of the educational needs of the contemporary society. It is occasionally useful to ask of any subject of study or method of instruction the simple question, "Why?" and to insist on an answer that makes sense. The formulation of educational objectives can be the occasion for asking such questions. Another use of educational objectives, related to the first, is in the redirecting of educational emphases. Often the motivation for this redirection is the observation that instruction in the schools is not adequately meeting the needs of the day. Herbert Spencer's essay on the purposes of education begins by deploring the overemphasis on the *ormanental* in education, to the neglect of the useful.[4] Spencer evaluated knowledge from the standpoint of its contribution to five categories of activity that constitute human life:

1. Self-preservation
2. Securing the necessities of life
3. Rearing and discipline of offspring
4. Maintenance of proper social and political relations
5. Gratification of the tastes and feelings

When the secondary school continued in the traditions of college preparation while rising enrollments were generating needs for terminal, general, and vocational education, the Commission on the Reorganization of Secondary Education sought to redirect its emphases by formulating the now famous seven cardinal principles as the main objectives of education:[5]

1. Health
2. Command of fundamental processes

[4]Spencer, *Education.*
[5]National Education Association Commission on Reorganizing Secondary Education, *Cardinal Principles of Secondary Education*, Bulletin No. 35 (Washington, D.C.: U.S. Office of Education, 1918).

3. Worthy home membership
4. Vocation
5. Citizenship
6. Worthy use of leisure
7. Ethical character

Statements of educational objectives often accompany efforts to reorient instruction in a specific field of study. A group of social studies teachers in the Wisconsin Improvement Program listed these specific goals for teaching in the social studies:[6]

1. Transmit our cultural heritage.
2. Provide intellectual exercise for the discipline of the mind.
3. Promote moral and spiritual values.
4. Develop democratic citizenship.
5. Promote good mental health.
6. Teach important historical facts and generalizations.
7. Promote the attitude that history is interesting and useful.
8. Teach time and space relationships.
9. Promote aesthetic sensitivities.
10. Acquaint students with basic historical references.
11. Provide instruction and practice in the skills of writing notes from lectures, writing essay examinations, locating information, judging the validity of evidence, drawing conclusions from data, skill in working in a group, and facility in oral expression.

Even more narrowly specific statements of objectives can be formulated for specific courses, units of study, or individual lessons.

General statements of educational objectives are useful to the test constructor as guides to the areas to be covered and to the direction of emphasis in his test. Highly specific statements may be useful in suggesting particular questions or types of questions to ask. But statements of objectives have limitations too.

Sometimes instead of aiming to be directive they aim to be inclusive. Instead of suggesting that the schools or the teacher of a particular course do this *instead* of that, they seem to suggest that the schools do both this *and* that, as well as everything that anyone has suggested it might also be good to do. Frequently they include highly attractive terms like "critical thinking," "creative productivity," or "good citizenship," which everyone can endorse but few can define. Such all-inclusive statements of objectives may be of some use as systems of grouping or classification, but they have little directive value.

Another limitation of statements of educational objectives grows out of the very large number of things to be learned and abilities to be acquired. To attempt to list them all would be an enormous task. The

[6]Robert L. Ebel, "The Problem of Evaluation in the Social Studies," *Social Education,* vol. 24 (January, 1960), 6–10.

task of getting agreement on some order of priority would be even greater. And if the job were ever completed, the list would be so long and so subject to criticism that few would ever bother to read it. The alternative of a comprehensive listing in detail of all objectives is to list names or descriptions of only the major categories of objectives. This is the alternative ordinarily chosen. It gives some indication of coverage and emphasis but is usually too general and indefinite to be of much direct help to the test constructor.

It is important to realize, as was pointed out in a recent yearbook of the National Society for the Study of Education, that specific educational goals are not derived by logical deduction from a single basic statement of the meaning and purpose of life.[7] Rather, they seem to arise out of recognitions of specific needs in the complex business of living. As Grieder has said,

> Are not the goals of a society largely unformulated, like the unwritten British Constitution? They develop slowly and through a continuous process of interaction among various segments and levels of a society, and among societies.[8]

Flanagan has proposed an empirical approach to the formulation of educational goals.[9] By collecting and classifying descriptions of actual observations of effective and ineffective behavior in particular fields of activity (the so-called critical incidents), investigators would be able to develop a more general summary listing of the critical requirements for success in that activity. Thus far this suggestion has not made serious inroads into the more conventional armchair procedures for formulating educational objectives.

A serious effort to take some of the vagueness out of statements of educational objectives at the college level has been made by Bloom and his co-workers.[10] They have produced a system for the classification of educational objectives, which they call a "taxonomy." The term "taxonomy" is derived from two Greek words, *taxis*, meaning "arrangement," and *nomos*, meaning "law." Hence a "taxonomy" is a lawful or an orderly arrangement. That part of the study of plants and animals

[7]Warren Findley and others, "The Relation of Testing Programs to Educational Goals," *The Impact and Improvement of School Testing Programs*, part I, chap. 2. Sixty-Second Yearbook of the National Society for the Study of Education (Chicago: The University of Chicago Press, 1963).

[8]Calvin Grieder, "Is It Possible to Word Educational Goals?" *Nation's Schools*, vol. 68 (October 1961), 10ff.

[9]John C. Flanagan, "The Critical Requirements Approach to Educational Objectives," *School and Society*, vol. 71 (May 27, 1950), 321–24.

[10]Benjamin S. Bloom and others, *Taxonomy of Educational Objectives* (New York: David McKay Company Inc., 1956).

that is concerned with classifying them into a succession of ever narrower and more specific groups–phyla, classes, orders, families, and so forth—is biological taxonomy. Bloom's taxonomy is a taxonomy of educational objectives.

The original publication, the book cited, dealt only with cognitive objectives, grouped in six major classes:

1. Knowledge
2. Comprehension
3. Application
4. Analysis
5. Synthesis
6. Evaluation

More recently, the taxonomy has been extended to affective objectives, having to do with attitudes, values, interests, and appreciation. The five major classes of affective objectives in this taxonomy are:

1. Receiving
2. Responding
3. Valuing
4. Organization
5. Characterization

A taxonomy for a third area of educational objectives dealing with the development of psychomotor (muscular) skills is yet to be completed. Since value judgments were specifically outlawed during its development, the taxonomy provides no directive guidance as to objectives of higher or lower priority.

But the taxonomy does attack one of the major limitations of some other formulations of objectives, that is, indefiniteness, for accompanying each description of a subclass of objectives are illustrative items taken from actual tests. Even where the subclasses are not clearly distinct, and the appropriateness of a stated objective or a test item to one rather than another subclass is not clearly apparent, the items do help to reduce the uncertainty regarding what a particular objective or set of objectives means. The taxonomy also provides a collection of illustrative test items that can be most useful to the test constructor.

In summary, the test constructor needs to be informed about and interested in the educational objectives in the field of his test. A good statement of objectives can help him extend and balance the coverage of his test and check on the appropriateness of its emphasis. But even the best such statement is likely to leave him with many item ideas to discover and many value judgments to make. Ordinarily he will need considerable help from course outlines, textbooks, and even other tests in deciding what should go into the test and what should be left out.

BEHAVIORAL GOALS OF EDUCATION

The history of education indicates that most subjects of study were introduced into the educational program in response to real and immediate needs. With changing times these needs sometimes disappeared, but successive generations of scholars who in their turn became teachers tended to continue teaching the same things they had been taught. Partly in response to the persistence of irrelevant knowledge in the curriculum and partly in reaction to the vagueness of many statements of objectives, some educators like Ralph Tyler began to urge that objectives should be defined in terms of desired behavior.[11] The purpose of education, they suggested, is not to accumulate knowledge but to change behavior. Their suggestions have borne fruit in two volumes setting forth the goals of education in behavioral terms.[12] The efforts of a great many carefully selected educators went into the production of these reports the development of which was supervised by Educational Testing Service, with financial support from the Russell Sage Foundation.

The defects in education that led to this development are real and need to be corrected. All knowledge is not of equal worth, as Herbert Spencer argued a century ago. The knowledge that we ask teachers to teach and students to gain command of needs to be reviewed frequently to reassess its power and its relevance to contemporary needs. Educational objectives that are stated so vaguely that it is difficult to learn whether the scholar has attained them or not by observing what he can do are not likely to provide useful guides to either teaching or testing.[13]

But the remedy proposed, that of defining educational objectives in terms of desired behavior, also has shortcomings.[14] It appears to assume that despite the highly complex and rapidly changing world in which we live, a teacher can know years ahead of time how the scholar ought to behave in a given set of circumstances. It also seems to assume that the teacher is entitled to prescribe his behavior for him. Both of these assumptions may be open to serious question. An alternative to defining educational objectives as descriptions of specific acts or general patterns

[11]Ralph W. Tyler, "A Generalized Technique for Constructing Achievement Tests," *Educational Research Bulletin*, vol. 10 (Columbus, O.: Ohio State University, 1931), 199–208.

[12]Nolan C. Kearney, *Elementary School Objectives* (New York: Russell Sage Foundation, 1953); and Will French and others *Behavioral Goals of General Education in High School* (New York: Russell Sage Foundation, 1957).

[13]Robert F. Mager, *Preparing Instructional Objectives* (Palo Alto, Calif.: Fearon Publishers, 1962), 62 pp.

[14]Robert L. Ebel, "Behavioral Objectives: A Close Look," *Phi Delta Kappan*, vol. 52 (1970), 171–73.

of desired behavior is to define them in terms of relevant and powerful knowledge, the command of which seems well calculated to give the scholar the capacity to adapt his behavior effectively in varied, changing situations.

The power of knowledge as a tool for the attainment of human aspirations can hardly be doubted. But knowledge is not all-powerful. It cannot guarantee the results we seek. This leads to the question of what other means might be used to attain our goals. What alternative to reason based on knowledge might the schools cultivate in order to help human beings live better?

One alternative to knowledge and reason as a basis for behavior is simple conditioning. Much of the behavior we exhibit is conditioned behavior. Human beings are almost as adept as other animals at learning to do the things their environment rewards and to avoid the things it punishes. In the case of very young children, conditioning may be the only effective means of education. As our experiences accumulate, as our awareness develops, reflective thought becomes available as a means of problem solving and of education. But the adult remains susceptible to conditioning, however rationally he may seek to behave. Fortunate success or unfortunate failure can encourage or discourage future efforts along the same line. The attitudes and values a person holds, even his beliefs, are attributable to conditioning as well as to reflective thought.

No doubt a case could be made in favor of conditioning as the exclusive means of education in a static society dedicated to the strength and stability of the group. But that is not the kind of a society in which we live nor the ideal to which we are dedicated. We respect the worth and dignity of the individual and seek to facilitate his maximum development as a free man. This means that we must be concerned with the cultivation of his rational powers. Quoting the Educational Policies Commission:

> To be free, a man must be capable of basing his choices and actions on understandings which he himself achieves and on values which he examines for himself. . . . The free man, in short, has a rational grasp of himself, his surroundings, and the relation between them.[15]

Emphasis on desired behavior as an educational outcome has encouraged test builders to write items that describe specific situations and call for the examinee to choose the most appropriate or effective behavior in that situation. Here is example.

Jim has a movie date for Saturday night but is short on cash. His brother Bob has $5.00 that he is willing to loan for a week at 5 percent interest,

[15]National Education Association Educational Policies Commission, *The Central Purpose of American Education* (Washington, D.C.: National Education Association, 1961), p. 4.

provided Jim will give him some security. Jim offers any one of the following items. Which should Bob accept if he is a prudent businessman?

1. Jim's class ring
2. Jim's new sweater
*3. Jim's car keys
4. Jim's football

Items such as this can have the virtue of testing the examinee's ability to behave effectively in a given situation.

But items of this type are subject to two weaknesses. They tend to require lengthy descriptions of the problem setting and thus to become time consuming and inefficient sources of information on achievement. They also tend, because of the difficulty of communicating fully and clearly all the factors that might be relevant to the choice of an answer, to become somewhat ambiguous as problems and somewhat indeterminate as to the correct response. Taken together these weaknesses may account for the rather lower reliability of tests of this type than of more direct measures of knowledge. There is little evidence that the situational tests are more valid measures of command of substantive knowledge than are simpler, more direct tests. The test constructor may wish to experiment with items of this type, but in the absence of empirical evidence of their superiority there are no compelling reasons for insisting on their use.

Those who have urged that educational goals be expressed in terms of desired behavior have wisely sought emphasis on meaningful statements of useful educational outcomes. They have not advocated conditioning as the primary means of human education. They have not tried to promote a static society. The aim they have been pursuing may not be significantly different from that expressed by the phrase "command of substantive knowledge." If so, the foregoing paragraphs may seem more concerned with the use of particular words than about the purposes and means of education.

But it seems important to suggest strongly that the proper starting point of educational planning in a democracy is not the kind of behaviors present adults desire future adults to exhibit, but rather the kind of equipment that will enable them to choose their own behavior intelligently. A major problem of education is to identify the elements of knowledge whose command will be most useful to the student in contributing to a good life for himself, in the best society he can help to develop. From this point of view educational acievement should be judged more in terms of what the student *can* do than in terms of what he typically *does* do. If there is any sizable discrepancy in the long run between the two, something must be wrong either with what education has taught him how to do or with what society rewards him for doing.

THE COGNITIVE OUTCOMES OF EDUCATION

If we look at what actually goes on in our school and college classrooms and laboratories, libraries and lecture halls, it seems reasonable to conclude that the major goal of education is to develop in the scholars a *command of substantive knowledge.* Achievement of this kind of cognitive mastery is clearly not the only concern of teachers and scholars engaged in the process of education. But the command of substantive knowledge is, and ought to be, the central concern of education.

The central role of knowledge acquisition as an educational goal and as a means of attaining other goals and of written tests as a method of assessment is outlined in Exhibit 3.1. Three major goals of education, with a variety of more specific goals under each, are outlined in the column on the left. The center column identifies some of the most effective means for attaining each of the major goals. The column on the right lists in order of general effectiveness the techniques that may be used to assess the degree to which a particular goal has been attained.

EXHIBIT 3.1

Educational Goals, Learning Processes, and Methods of Assessment

EDUCATIONAL GOAL	LEARNING PROCESS	METHOD OF ASSESSMENT
Knowledge		
Concepts	Observing	Written Test
Facts	Reading	Incidental
Reasons	Reflecting	observation
Processes	Expressing	
Skill		
Writing	Observing	Performance
Speaking	Imitation	Test
Typing	Practice	Written test
Drawing	Knowledge	Incidental
Swimming etc.	acquisition	observation
Character		
Personality	Observing	Incidental
Habits	Imitation	observation
Attitudes	Conditioned	Written test
Values	behavior	
Standards	Knowledge	
	acquisition	

Note that knowledge acquisition, in addition to being itself a primary goal, contributes to the attainment of other goals. Note too that written tests provide the most effective means of assessing skills and character. Consider why incidental observation is preferred for character assessment, but listed as the second or third best method for assessing attainment of the other two major goals. If the outline as a whole fails to do justice to the goals and processes of education as you perceive them, consider how such a brief summary of the educational process might be improved. As it now stands, Exhibit 3.1 probably is not the last word that needs to be said on the subject.

A person's knowledge is based on the information he gets, either directly from his own experiences or indirectly from the reports of others. Thus everything that a person has experienced, all the history of his living, *can* become a part of his knowledge. It will become knowledge if he reflects on it, seeking to make sense out of it, until he builds it into a coherent whole. Knowledge is a structure built out of information by processes of thought.

Information by itself is not knowledge. A teacher can give his pupils information. He cannot give them knowledge, for a person's knowledge is a private, personal possession. He must create it himself. He must earn for himself the right to say "I know this," or "I understand that." If his information on important matters is abundant and accurate, and if he thinks about it clearly and persistently, the structure of knowledge he builds will be substantial and useful. But if some of these essentials are lacking, his house of intellect is likely to be only a shanty.

Pursuit of knowledge is clearly the business of scholarship. The power of knowledge has been so generally acknowledged, from ancient to modern times, that it may seem surprising that anyone would challenge cognitive mastery as the central purpose of education. Yet it has been, and is being, challenged. Knowledge alone is not enough, says the businessman. It does not guarantee financial success. Knowledge alone is not enough, says the college president. It does not guarantee scholarly achievement. Knowledge alone is not enough, says the religious leader. It does not guarantee virtue. Knowledge alone is not enough, says the philosopher. It does not guarantee happiness.

They are all right, of course. Knowledge alone is *not* enough. But in this complex world of chance and change no one thing, nor any combination of things, ever will be enough to *guarantee* financial success or scholarly achievement or virtue or happiness. Few would deny that the command of substantive knowledge does contribute mightily to the attainment of these other, more ultimate goals. Further, it is difficult to name any other developed human ability that is likely to contribute more than, or as much as, knowledge to the attainment of these goals.

It is even more difficult to describe what sorts of things the schools ought to be doing to develop the alleged noncognitive ingredients of success, achievement, virtue, or happiness.

But what is *substantive knowledge?* And what is meant by *command* of knowledge? Consider the first question. A whole branch of philosophy, epistemology, is devoted to a study of what substantive knowledge is and how it is acquired. Perhaps a simpler approach will suffice here.

A person's knowledge includes everything that he has experienced as a result of his perceptions of his external environment or as a result of his internal reflections or thought processes. All this history of his living becomes a part of his knowledge. Psychologists suggest that nothing a person has experienced is ever completely and permanently forgotten. It all remains somewhere, however deeply buried and overlaid with other experiences. The problem of learning, in the modern view, is not so much how to get things into the mind as it is how to get them out again when they are needed. The problem is less one of storage than it is of ready access.

As defined in *Webster's New Collegiate Dictionary*, knowledge is:

1. Familiarity gained by actual experience
2. Acquaintance with fact; hence, scope of information
3. The act or state of understanding; cognition
4. That which is gained and preserved by knowing; enlightenment; learning; also, broadly, the sum of information conserved by civilization.

These definitions suggest the scope of the concept of knowledge, and its relationship to or identity with experience, fact, information, understanding, enlightenment, and learning.

The kind of knowledge that schools and colleges are most concerned with is verbal knowledge. To the degree that a person's experiences of external affairs and internal thoughts can be expressed in words, they become a part of his verbal knowledge. Because verbal knowledge can be recorded, thought about, and communicated so conveniently, it is a very powerful form of knowledge. Possession of skill in using verbal knowledge may be the source of, and certainly provides the clearest evidence of, man's superiority over the lower animals.

Schools are sometimes criticized for excessive concern with verbal knowledge, at the expense of nonverbal knowledge growing out of direct, firsthand experiences in the laboratory, the shop, or outside the school room altogether. Such directly obtained knowledge, it is pointed out, provides the foundation on which the truth and usefulness of all verbal knowledge must rest. For some students, and indeed for some scholars as well, that foundation appears to be none too broad and none too firm. To strengthen and extend it is to add important new dimensions to a person's understanding of the words and sentences with which he deals.

All this can be granted without abandoning the proposition that development of a student's command of useful verbal knowledge is the principal function of formal education. Direct experience is essential as a foundation, but it provides little more than the foundation. It is the verbal knowledge through which those experiences are integrated, interpreted, and communicated that makes possible the intelligent behavior of a human being and the culture of a human society.

There is already a great store of recorded human verbal knowledge in the world. Day by day it increases. Indeed it seems to some observers to be increasing so rapidly that they speak frighteningly of the "explosion of knowledge." In some fields, fortunately few, new knowledge appears almost to make an old scholar's learning obsolete in his own lifetime.

Not all of the items in this store of knowledge—the names, dates, events, concepts, ideas, and propositions—are of equal value. Some are are of limited, temporary interest. Some are indefinite and inaccurate. One of the most important and most difficult tasks of the educator is to sort out the more valuable from the less valuable. It is easy to say that those items of knowledge that are most widely useful, or most central to the structure of a body of knowledge, should be regarded as most valuable. But to apply these abstract criteria to specific items in specific areas of knowledge, the educator must make a multitude of difficult decisions usually in the absence of really adequate evidence. The task is not easy, but it is essential. Whether in curriculum construction, test development, or any other activity concerned with the content of education, the educator's first problem is to pass sound judgments on the potential usefulness of various kinds and items of knowledge. He must guide his pupils toward the development of structures of substantive knowledge, that is, knowledge of enduring importance and usefulness.

The second major problem of the educator is to manage the learning process so as to develop the student's *command* of knowledge. To have command of knowledge is to have ready access to it and full comprehension of its scope, limitations, and implications. Hence to develop command of knowledge requires development of relationships between words and things, between instances and generalizations, between concepts and principles. The more of these relationships a person knows, the better his command of the items they relate and the more likely he is to recall them when they might be useful to him. Only when items of information are related to each other do they become parts of a structure of knowledge.

Relating is understanding. Thunder is understood better when it is related to lightning. Fermentation is understood better when it is related to bacteria. Fluid pressure is understood better when it is related to depth and density. In general, the understanding of any separate thing involves seeing its relations to other things. The knowledge a person understands he has command of, and the knowledge he commands he also understands.

Command of knowledge obviously involves thinking, which both requires and produces it. Thus while knowledge and thinking are not identical, they are closely related. To say that the purpose of education is not to acquire knowledge but to develop the ability to think is to establish a false antithesis. Knowledge and thinking are not mutually exclusive or even alternative goals of education. Each demands the other. One cannot be in favor of thinking but opposed to knowledge. Nor can the power to think be increased appreciably except by increasing the store of knowledge at the command of the thinker. Faulty thinking usually reflects limited or erroneous knowledge, or failure to make careful and unbiased use of it.

Substantive knowledge, as the term is used here, encompasses more than knowledge of facts and principles. It includes, for example, both knowledge of words and other symbols and the objects or concepts they stand for. A person who can read general or technical literature in his native language or in a foreign language, or who can read music or a blueprint, demonstrates command of substantive knowledge.

Substantive knowledge encompasses understanding and ability to explain, for understanding consists mainly of knowing the relations between things. To understand the seasons, for example, one must know the relation between the orbital motion of the earth and the declination of the sun and between that declination and the degree of concentration of solar energy on the surface of the earth. The more one *knows* about the relations among these and other relevant factors, the better he *understands* the seasons.

Substantive knowledge also includes mental skills, such as the ability to add fractions, to diagram a sentence, to play chess, or to design a bridge. While it is probably safe to say that the person who exhibits more skill in any of these areas than another person knows more than the other, it is even safer to say that he has better command of the relevant knowledge. Proficiency in mental skills requires ready availability of the relevant knowledge.

Thus a person's knowledge is a very extensive and important aspect of his mental development. But is it all? Surely not. There are also feelings and habits. There are attitudes and values. There are the behavior patterns that constitute a person's character and personality. These other characteristics of a person may be influenced by his knowledge, but they are not part of it. Not quite all of the purposes of a school have to do with command of useful verbal knowledge.

THE PROBLEM OF ISOLATED BITS OF FACTUAL INFORMATION

Objective tests, composed as they are of many separate, independent items, are sometimes supposed to be useful only for measuring isolated bits of factual information. This supposition involves several questionable assumptions:

1. Whatever characterizes a test must also characterize the thing it tests.
2. Information can be, and often is, stored in the form of isolated bits.
3. The questions on objective tests are familiar questions, to which pat answers can be recalled if they ever were learned.

But if the test is a good test consisting largely of novel problems to which answers must be thought through with the help of information previously acquired, and if it is true that the availability of relevant information depends on how well it has been integrated into a consistent, meaningful network of relations, then objective tests are not so severely limited. Discrete items can and usually do test command of knowledge, that is, ability to use it to solve new problems.

Cohen and Nagel have made two comments about knowledge that seem particularly useful in this context.[16] They say (1) that knowledge is of propositions and (2) that a proposition is anything that can be said to be true or false. Propositions are expressed in sentences, but not all sentences are propositions. Those expressing questions or commands cannot be said to be true or false, nor can those that report purely subjective wishes or feelings. Propositions are always declarative sentences about objects or events in the external world. For example:

> The earth is a planet in the solar system.
>
> A body immersed in a fluid is buoyed up by a force equal to the weight of fluid displaced.
>
> As we consume or acquire additional units of any commodity, the satisfaction derived from each additional installment tends to diminish.
>
> William J. Bryan failed in his bid for election to the presidency of the United States in the campaign of 1896.

The relation of propositions such as these to objective test items of the true-false type is direct and simple. Less obvious, but no less true, is the fact that propositions like those above are implicit in most other types of objective test items—multiple-choice, matching, short-answer, or completion. What we test, beyond the student's ability to understand

---

[16]Morris R. Cohen and Ernest Nagel, *An Introduction to Logic and Scientific Method* (New York: Harcourt Brace Jovanovich, 1934), p. 27.

the language used in the test item, is his knowledge of the proposition that makes one answer correct and others incorrect. All of the propositions cited above appear to deserve a place in the "information conserved by civilization." But there are some other sentences expressing propositions that probably do not deserve such preservation. For example:

> Rain fell in New York City on December 6, 1962.
> The cost of living in Canada advanced two-fifths of a point during October 1962.
> Work-limit tests are mentioned on page 366 of *Educational Measurement*, edited by E. F. Lindquist.

Objective test items ought not to be based on propositions such as these but sometimes, unfortunately, they may be.

The closeness of this relation between the propositions that constitute our knowledge and the items needed for our objective tests may suggest a convenient source of good test items. Simply pick out of a good textbook or reference work a number of sentences expressing important propositions and use these as the basis for test items in the desired form. Basically this is an excellent idea, but it does involve some problems.

Relatively few of the sentences encountered in even a good text or reference work are intended to express propositions about the external world. Many are quite indefinite. Many are offered modestly as tentative hypotheses. Many depend heavily on the context for their meaningfulness or accuracy. Many are in the nature of explanatory comments to the reader to help him follow the author's line of thought. Sometimes the basic proposition implicit in a paragraph or section of a text is never stated succinctly and explicitly by the author. Finally, many of the declarative sentences that seem important and necessary in an extended discourse on a topic do not seem important enough in isolation to be selected in the limited sampling of propositions that must constitute a test.

Thus, despite the fact that the major goal of education is to develop in the scholars a command of substantive knowledge and despite the fact that all knowledge is knowledge of propositions, it is not easy to discover ready-made propositions that are suitable as bases for objective test items. To be suitable, propositions need to meet at least four requirements:

1. They must be worded as accurately and unambiguously as the precision of knowledge and language allow in a reasonably concise statement.
2. They must be acceptable as established truth by a preponderance of experts in the field.
3. They must be regarded as the propositions most worthy of knowing and remembering by a preponderance of experts in the field.
4. They must express principles and ideas not generally known by those who have not studied in the field.

The difficulty of finding or creating propositions that meet these standards in some areas of study may raise questions about the value of study in that field. If good examinations are difficult to build in a field, it may be because the supporting structure of substantive knowledge is weak.

THE PROBLEM OF ROTE LEARNING

Concern is sometimes expressed over the emphasis some tests are supposed to place on mere knowledge to the neglect of higher mental processes. Some tests are thought to require nothing more than recognition or simple recall of isolated factual details. Test builders are often urged to shun tests of this type in favor of tests that emphasize comprehension, interpretation, application, analysis, synthesis, or evaluation. They are warned to guard against items that can be answered on the basis of sheer rote memory.

Any test that can be prepared for most effectively by concentration on rote learning and that therefore encourages students to neglect meaning and understanding in their pursuit of knowledge is a bad test. Undoubtedly, too, some students, in some situations, concentrate on memorization of words with little concern for meanings. But the extent of rote learning, and the educational harm it may do, have probably been somewhat exaggerated.

One source of overconcern with rote learning may be failure to distinguish clearly between incomplete understanding, on the one hand, and rote learning on the other. Students, and adults too, sometimes reveal woeful ignorance of important matters. But it may not be quite correct to charge these deficiencies to an excess of rote learning in the schools. Perhaps the trouble is not rote learning, but no learning. Instead of too much learning of the wrong kind, the deficiencies we exhibit may imply too little learning of any kind.

There is another factor that limits somewhat the danger of rote learning. From the point of view of the learner, rote learning is seldom a very attractive occupation. It is dull, hard work, with no promise of any long-term value. A student may engage in it, out of desperation, in the hope of getting by a quiz or examination, but it seldom rewards him with any sense of permanent achievement.

Finally, rote learning is relatively inefficient and ineffective. Even if a student's sole aim is temporary recall of the answers to a set of questions given to him in advance, he will ordinarily find *understanding*, even limited understanding, a better ally than rote learning. For understanding involves perception of simplifying structural unities, in the variety of aspects and details, which aid memory and recall. A student who chooses to rely on rote learning is seldom likely to do as well on a test as one who seeks the aid of understanding, even when the questions in the test call for nothing more than the recall of isolated factual details.

In summary, because rote learning may be far less common than our fears of it imply, because it is generally unattractive and ineffective, the danger that tests that emphasize factual knowledge will reward and encourage rote learning may not be serious.

THE PROBLEM OF MEANINGLESS VERBALIZATION

There is, however, a related danger that may deserve to be taken more seriously. It is the danger of confusing verbal facility and fluency, on the one hand, with command of substantive knowledge on the other. To the degree that test questions demand only acquaintance with verbal stereotypes, with oft-repeated word sequences or associations, to the degree that they may be answered successfully on the basis of word-word associations alone, without clear perceptions of word-thing relationships, to that degree the tests may be measuring superficial verbal facility instead of command of substantive knowledge.

Written tests depend heavily upon words. Words are versatile and essential instruments for thinking and communicating, but they represent the means, not the ends, of learning. Their usefulness to us depends upon our nonverbal knowledge of what they symbolize.

It is possible, indeed it is not uncommon, for speakers or writers to use words with more concern for fluency and grace in expression than for the accuracy of the ideas being expressed. Most students, and most adults as well, recognize and use more words, phrases, even stereotyped sentences than they understand clearly. One of the main responsibilities of the test maker as he works with words in his test questions or with the verbal responses scholars give to some of them is to make sure that mere verbal facility does not pass for substantive knowledge. To do this he must seek original expressions for his ideas, simple and accurate but unconventional. If he uses familiar textbook language, it should be done in such a way that a student who merely recognizes the phrase but does not understand it will be attracted to a wrong answer. He must invent novel questions and novel problem situations so that recognition alone will not provide the answer.

THE PROBLEM OF FORGETTING

The acquisition of knowledge as an educational goal is sometimes discounted on the grounds that (1) most of what is learned is quickly forgotten and (2) it is wasteful of time and effort to "stuff the mind" with facts that are readily available in a set of good reference works. There is some truth in both of these contentions, but they do not argue so strongly as they may seem to against the pursuit of knowledge as the primary goal of education.

Forgetting does occur, of course, but what is forgotten, and how much, depends largely on how much command of the knowledge the student actually achieved, and how well selected (that is, how useful) was the knowledge he sought or was required to pursue. The more command the student achieves, the more he understands or grasps a unifying structure in the knowledge he is studying, the less he is likely to forget, particularly of the central, unifying principles. The more useful the knowledge, the more likely he is to practice and thus maintain his command over it.

Reference works are valuable accessories to the effective use of knowledge, but they are poor substitutes for command of knowledge. How effectively they can be used depends to a considerable degree on how much the user already knows. One whose mind is deliberately kept empty of facts available in reference works is unlikely to have much interest in those facts or to know how to find them if he should be interested. Further, his progress is likely to be very slow. The "ready availability" of facts in good reference works is something of an illusion. Finding the specific fact one needs can be a frustrating, time-consuming enterprise. It is hard to beat a well-stocked mind as a ready source of information.

DEVELOPMENT OF MENTAL ABILITIES AS AN EDUCATIONAL GOAL

The development of mental abilities is sometimes proposed as the primary purpose and goal of education. Stroud, for example, has said, "All education is in large measure a cultivation of the higher mental processes, even instruction in the basic skills or so-called tool subjects."[17] Later, in the same passage he explains, "By the cultivation of the higher mental processes is usually meant instruction in reflective, relational and inferential thinking." C. H. Judd has compiled a book on the subject.[18] But some others are convinced that educators err seriously when they

[17]James B. Stroud, *Psychology in Education* (New York: David McKay Company, Inc., 1946), p. 198.
[18]C. H. Judd, *Education as Cultivation of the Higher Mental Processes* (New York: The Macmillan Company, 1936).

seek to develop general mental abilities rather than to cultivate command of knowledge.[19, 20, 21]

It is not always clear what the term "mental ability" is intended to mean. It could mean no more nor less than "development of ability to think," to use the words of the Educational Policies Commission. Perhaps it is simply intended to emphasize the use of knowledge, as opposed to its possession. If so, development of mental abilities is not so much an alternative to acquisition of knowledge as an extension to include assimilation of knowledge, which is essentially the same extension as that implied by the phrase "command of substantive knowledge." It is hard to see how mental abilities can be developed or can exist apart from knowledge.

The use of the plural term "mental abilities" suggests that several separate abilities are involved. Presumably these are not intended to refer to the so-called mental faculties of attention, memory, imagination, reason, will, temperament, and character that were thought to be independent, general powers of the mind in the nineteenth century. Studies of transfer of training do not support the belief that such abstract mental faculties or abilities exist or that development and strengthening them by study in one area of knowledge will make them available for use in any other area. Presumably a mental ability is something more general than, for example, ability to spell the word *Constantinople*, ability to add 7 and 9, or ability to complete and balance the chemical equation for the preparation of oxygen from potassium chlorate.

Thus it would seem that the concept of mental abilities or processes is quite indefinite. No generally recognized catalog of mental processes with titles and definitions for distinctly different mental processes seems to exist. There is no reliable classification of such processes into higher and lower levels. Even if we agree that the term "mental process" means no more nor less than the term "thinking," we have no very clear notions of what processes may be involved or of how the "higher" processes may differ from the "lower." Daydreaming seems different from problem solving, but at present we can only guess in what way and to what extent different mental processes may be involved.

The indefiniteness of mental abilities is a problem that plagued the authors of the Taxonomy from the beginning of their labors. They solved it as well as may be humanly possible, after years of deliberation. But

---

[19]Edward L. Thorndike, "In Defense of Facts," *Journal of Adult Education*, vol. 7 (1935), 381–88.

[20]Ben D. Wood and F. S. Beers, "Knowledge Versus Thinking?" *Teachers College Record*, vol. 37 (1936) 487–99.

[21]Robert L. Ebel, "Knowledge Versus Ability in Achievement Testing." *Proceedings of the 1969 Invitational Conference on Testing Problems* (Princeton, N.J.: Educational Testing Service, 1970), 117 pp.

they would the last to claim that they succeeded in discovering an underlying simple structure in mental abilities.

To demonstrate the complexity of the problem of identifying and classifying mental abilities the reader is invited to take a little test. In each of the triads below two of the abilities were put in the same major class in the condensed version of the Taxonomy (pp. 201–207).[22] The third was put in a different major class. Your task is to identify this third (dissimilar) ability. Answers appear at the end of the chapter.

1a. Ability to interpret various types of social data
1b. Ability to predict continuation of a trend
1c. Ability to predict the probable effect of a change

2a. Ability to distinguish facts from hypotheses
2b. Ability to indicate logical fallacies in arguments
2c. Ability to recognize unstated assumptions

3a. Ability to comprehend the relationship among the ideas of a passage
3b. Ability to grasp the thought of a work as a whole
3c. Ability to recognize the techniques used in propaganda

It may be apparent after this test that different mental abilities do not fall obviously and neatly into a small number of distinct categories. Like people, mental abilities vary continuously, and probably on many dimensions as well. But it seems unlikely that any small number of distinct, coherent mental processes will ever be discovered to account for any substantial part of the wide range of intellectual achievements men show.

The mind, most educational psychologists now seem to agree, does not consist of separate faculties that can be cultivated independently. It functions as a unit, and all aspects of its functioning—attention, perception, memory, volition, emotion, and so forth—are likely to be involved whenever the mind is active. The objects of thought may be more or less complex and the procession of thoughts may be more or less purposefully directed and controlled, but so far as we now know, the mind probably functions in essentially the same way regardless of its task. It must certainly need different kinds of knowledge to cope effectively with different kinds of problems, knowledge of processes as well as knowledge of content, but there seems to be no good basis for suggesting that different, whether higher or lower, types of mental functions need to be involved.

Examiners frequently classify their test questions in terms of content (knowledge) and process (ability). But even this distinction sometimes gets blurred. Does a problem in simple addition involve knowledge or ability or both? If both, how can the two be distinguished? Why do they

---

[22]Benjamin S. Bloom and others, *Taxonomy of Educational Objectives* (New York: David McKay Company, Inc., 1956).

need to be distinguished? It is conceivable that one student could have mastered the "content" of mathematics, or grammar or literature, better than another and yet be less adept than he is in using the "processes" involved, but the difficulty of clearly distinguishing between content and process makes evidence on this hypothesis hard to get.

Attempts to write test items that will require the highest levels of mental processes involve several hazards. One is that they may be quite difficult and thus call for more than ordinary examinees are capable of delivering. Such items are not likely to contribute much effective measurement. Another is that they may involve fairly complex situations, which require many words to describe and may present the examinee with problems of comprehension and interpretation that may be irrelevant to the main purpose of the examination. Characteristics of this kind are likely to lower the precision and the efficiency of the test question.

In order to describe the items in a test adequately it seems necessary to specify more than the areas or topics of subject matter with which they deal. Categories of mental abilities or processes have sometimes been used to provide a second dimension to the test outline. But in view of the difficulty of distinguishing clearly between different mental abilities and processes, it may be advisable to avoid this mentalistic approach as much as possible. One alternative is to describe different test items in terms of the kind of task they present rather than in terms of the somewhat hypothetical processes that may be involved in their solution. For example, different kinds of questions used in typical classroom tests may:

1. Ask what a particular term means
2. Ask for a particular fact or principle
3. Ask the explanation of something
4. Ask the solution to a problem.

By including a variety of tasks like these the test can probably cover adequately most of the outcomes of instruction in most courses without becoming involved with the intangibilities of mental processes or abilities.

One of the propositions advanced by Richardson and Stalnaker in their "Comments on Achievement Examinations" was this: "Proposition III. The form of a test gives no certain indication of the ability tested." In discussing this proposition they said:

> We wish to digress enough to point out that psychologists do not know what abilities are involved in procedures such as writing examinations. The nature of these mental operations had best be left alone when discussing test form.[23]

This advice was given in 1935, but it would still appear to be sound.

[23]M. W. Richardson and J. M. Stalnaker, "Comments of Achievement Examinations," *Journal of Educational Research*, XXVIII (1935) 425–32.

AFFECTIVE OUTCOMES AS EDUCATIONAL GOALS

Those who teach and those who test are sometimes charged with overemphasis on cognitive learning, with consequent neglect of the effective determiners of behavior. Teachers, it is said, are preoccupied with what their pupils know or do not know, whereas their pupils are more concerned with what they like or dislike, and how they feel; more concerned with being than with knowing. Thus teachers and students may find themselves living in separate worlds. Further, say the critics, the most profound challenges in our society are not cognitive. They are challenges to our social unity and to our individual righteousness, to our ethical standards and to our moral values, to our courage and to our compassion. If the schools focus too much on cognitive learning, they will fail to contribute as they should to meeting those challenges.

These charges and criticisms are not without foundation. Feeling is as real and as important a part of our human nature as is knowing. How a person feels is almost always more important to him than what he knows. How he behaves is almost always more important to others than what he knows. And his behavior is sometimes determined more by how he feels about a situation than by what he knows about it. The way our society copes with the challenges it must face will depend on how society feels about them as well as on what it knows about them.

Well then, should not the school transfer some of its concern from cognitive outcomes and place it on affective outcomes? Probably not, and for two reasons. The first is that some of the affective ends of the school can be reached through cognitive means. Affect and cognition are not independent aspects of the personality. They are closely related. How a person feels about a problem or an event depends in part on what he knows about it. Wisdom doesn't guarantee happiness, but the lack of it often assures great unhappiness. Our affective failures among students—the alienated, the dropouts, even the bright revolutionaries—can almost always be traced to some prior cognitive failure of theirs or ours. Psychologists who try to help people with problems of affect usually employ cognitive means. The psychotherapy they practice is essentially a cognitive process of fostering self-knowledge in the patient.

The second reason why the schools should not emphasize affective outcomes more is that the only noncognitive means a school can use to attain its affective ends is limited in scope and can lead to quite undesirable consequences. That means is the process of conditioning. When a school adopts and enforces (with rewards and punishments) certain rules of behavior it conditions its students to regularly exhibit that kind of behavior. The initial acceptance of the fact that "this is the way things are done around here" is gradually transformed, if the school runs smoothly and satisfactorily on the whole, into the belief that things ought to be done that way.

When a basketball coach insists that his players behave like gentlemen on the court and off, that their speech, dress, and actions be at all times decent and in good taste, he is using conditioning, and most of us applaud both the end and the means. But Hitler used the same process to solidify popular support for his evil purposes. He used it most effectively to gain support from the youth of the nation.

No teacher can afford to ignore the affective side-effects of his efforts to promote cognitive learning. But he should not use his concern for affective outcomes as an excuse for paying less attention to the cognitive outcomes.

Our schools and colleges were established primarily to develop cognitive competence, in the well-founded belief that this was the best the state could do to help boys and girls become effective and happy men and women.

KEY TO ABILITIES CLASSIFICATION TEST (Page 76)

1a. Comprehension	2a. Analysis	3a. Analysis
1b. Comprehension	2b. Evaluation	3b. Comprehension
1c. Application	2c. Analysis	3c. Analysis

SUMMARY

Some of the main ideas developed in this chapter may be summarized in the following 20 statements.

1. Determination of what to measure is a critical, difficult problem in achievement test construction.
2. The need for rational decisions and value judgments with respect to what should be measured cannot be circumvented by using experimental procedures for test validation.
3. Statements of educational objectives are useful in redirecting educational emphases from past to present needs.
4. Guidance in determining what to measure may be obtained from a statement of educational objectives.
5. Some statements of educational objectives are vaguely general instead of being clearly specific, and uncritically inclusive rather than purposefully selective.
6. Objectives defined in terms of desired behavior are concretely meaningful but may emphasize specific end products at the expense of more general means toward those ends.

7. The use of conditioning as a means for improving the effectiveness of human behavior is more appropriate in the early years of life than it is after formal schooling has begun.
8. A major goal of education is to develop in the student a command of substantive knowledge.
9. A person's knowledge consists of everything that he has experienced as a result of his perceptions of external stimuli or internal thought processes.
10. Knowledge is a structure built out of information by processes of thought.
11. Verbal knowledge is a very powerful, uniquely human form of knowledge.
12. The first problem of the educator is to decide what kinds and items of knowledge will be most useful to the student. His second problem is to manage the learning process so that the student develops a command of this body of knowledge.
13. Command of knowledge is demonstrated by its use in problem solving, decision making, explanation, argumentation, and prediction.
14. Separate, independent test items can provide effective tests of a person's command of knowledge in an area.
15. Rote learning cannot lead to command of knowledge and is unlikely to be used extensively by students.
16. Uncritical acceptance of words of vague or uncertain meaning interferes with development of command of knowledge.
17. The greater a student's command of a body of knowledge, the less he is likely to be troubled by forgetting it.
18. General mental abilities are difficult to identify and to define clearly.
19. Items designed to test the higher mental processes tend to be unsatisfactory.
20. The school should seek to attain affective ends by cognitive means.

We have faith that whatever people now measure crudely by mere descriptive words, helped out by comparative and superlative forms, can be measured more precisely and conveniently if ingenuity and labor are set at the task. We have faith also that the objective products produced, rather than the inner condition of the person whence they spring, are the proper point of attack for the measurer, at least in our day and generation.

EDWARD L. THORNDIKE

4

HOW SHOULD ACHIEVEMENT BE MEASURED?

THE PROBLEM OF QUANTIFICATION

Thorndike defended the measurability of human traits by arguing that whatever exists at all exists in some amount. However, characteristics such as intelligence, reading comprehension, or ability to solve story problems in arithmetic do not exist in quite the same sense as children or books or school buildings exist. Although these characteristics are not figments of our imaginations, they are not objects that we can examine and describe as we might a geode, a tornado, or an aardvark. They are conceptions of the human mind—abstractions. They are based on evidence of some kinds of unity and consistency in behavior, but they have no clearly defined, naturally given boundaries. Hence human minds are free to define the scope and limits of these abstract concepts. If they are to speak clearly about them they must define them clearly.

There are good reasons to believe that students are not all alike in intelligence, reading comprehension, or arithmetic ability. But in order to determine vaguely perceived differences more precisely and to express them more conveniently we must develop procedures for quantifying them. That is, we must assign numbers to persons so that differences in the numbers correspond as closely as possible to perceived differences in intelligence, reading comprehension, arithmetic ability, or other specific mental developments. The process of quantifying usually involves two operations: first, the definition of the characteristics to be measured, and second, the construction of some kind of a scale for measuring it.

Actually two definitions are required to identify a characteristic like intelligence or reading comprehension or arithmetic ability reasonably and precisely enough to permit a valid measurement of it. One of these is a descriptive, conceptual definition that indicates in general terms what is to be measured and implies that general procedures may be suitable for measuring it. The other is an operational definition that indicates precisely *what* was measured by specifying precisely *how* it was measured.

Each different test of an educational achievement, and aptitude, or a personality trait thus implies a somewhat different definition, and hence a somewhat different achievement or aptitude or personality trait. There is a persistent illusion among some educators that the "true" definition of intelligence, or creativity, or motivation exists somewhere and only awaits discovery by anyone who is clever enough to find it. That is not the case, however. Human characteristics can be defined by human minds, but their true essence can never be discovered by searching outside the human mind in the real world, for that is not where they exist.

Thus the test of a good definition, conceptual or operational, of some human trait cannot be its correspondence with some external reality. The test must be rather how reasonable, how meaningful, how useful the definition proves to be. When teachers or test constructors make different tests of the same trait that yield different measurements of the same quantity in the same individual, they can and should discuss the differences between them. These differences may be either in the conceptual or in the operational definitions of what they are trying to measure. They should compare the rationales for their conceptual and operational definitions. In some cases they may even gather data related to the precision, the meaningfulness, and the usefulness of the measures they have obtained. None of the tests is likely to be found best beyond question, but explorations of the nature and causes of discrepancies could lead to improvements in some of the tests.

Quantification refers to the process of developing the procedures to be used in measuring some human characteristic. Measurement is the application of those procedures. In education as in science both the quantification and the measurement are usually facilitated by the construction of a special scale. The thermometer is a familiar example of a special scale used to measure temperature. The scales used in educational measurement usually are tests consisting of a number of questions, test items, or tasks. One obtains a measurement from such a scale by adding across all questions the number of correct answer points the examinee has earned on each of them.

From a technical measurement point of view these educational test scales have a number of shortcomings. The scale units, or score points, are probably unequal. Because of this, identity of test score for two persons probably does not indicate identity in amount of achievement. Each measuring instrument yields numbers on a scale that is unique to that instrument. Hence measures obtained from different tests of the same characteristic must usually be connected (often by somewhat questionable procedures) into standard measures before they can be compared meaningfully.

Theoretically oriented measurement specialists have devoted a great deal of attention to these and other limitations of psychometric (mental measurement) scales. They have developed elaborate theories and sophisticated methods for overcoming some of the limitations, and have become specialists in the psychometric science of scaling. But much of what they know how to do is beyond the reach of the typical teacher or test constructor. Even if it were within reach, it probably could not contribute much to the improvement of practical educational measurements. For inadequate as the scales are, the errors they introduce into educational measurements are far less serious than the errors associated with the definition of the trait to be measured and with the selection and presentation of tasks to be included in the test. The basic problems of educational measurement are not problems of scaling, but problems of test planning and item writing. These problems will be considered in the chapters that follow.

CRITERION-REFERENCED AND NORM-REFERENCED MEASUREMENTS

The quantity of a student's achievement can be expressed in either or both of two ways: (1) as the proportion he learned of what he could (or should) have learned, or (2) as the proportion of his class (or peers) who learned less than he did. The first way gives what have been called criterion-referenced, domain-referenced, or universe-defined measurements. The second way gives what are known as norm-referenced measurements.

The essential difference between norm-referenced and criterion-referenced measurements is in the quantitative scales used to express how much the individual can do. In norm-referenced measurement the scale is usually anchored in the middle on some average level of performance for a specific group of individuals. The units on the scale are usually a function of the distribution of performances above and below the average level. In criterion-referenced measurement the scale is usually anchored at the extremities, a score at the top of the scale indicating complete or perfect mastery of some defined abilities, one at the bottom indicating complete absence of those abilities. The scale units consist of subdivisions of this total scale range.

The percent grades that were used almost universally in schools and colleges in this country up to about 1920 represent one type of criterion-referenced measurement. True, the extremities of the scales used for percent grades in most courses were only loosely anchored in poorly defined specifications of what would constitute either perfect comprehension or total lack of mastery. But this measurement deficiency was more a consequence of the great difficulty in developing such definitions than of failure to appreciate their importance. Little has happened to the subject matter of education since 1920 that would make the task of defining complete mastery any easier. If anything, as the scope of our educational content and objectives has broadened, the task has probably become more difficult.

Criterion-referenced measures of educational achievement, when valid ones can be obtained, tell us in meaningful terms what a student knows or can do. They do not tell us how good or how poor his level of knowledge or ability may be. Excellence or deficiency are necessarily relative. The four-minute mile represents excellence in distance running, not in terms of any absolute standards for human speed, but because so few are able to run that fast for that long.

Now in many areas of education we do pursue excellence and are concerned with remedying deficiency. For these purposes we need norm-referenced measures. To say that such measures leave us in the dark about *what* the student is good at doing or poor at doing is seldom reasonable. Usually our knowledge of typical test or course content gives us at least a rough idea of amount of knowledge or degree of ability.

Criterion-referenced measurement may be practical in those few areas of achievement that focus on cultivation of a high degree of skill in the exercise of a limited number of abilities. Where the emphasis is on knowledge and understanding, effective use of criterion-referenced measurements seem much less likely, for knowledge and understanding consist of a complex fabric that owes its strength and beauty to an infinity of tiny fibers of relationship. Knowledge does not come in discrete chunks that can be defined and identified separately.

Another difficulty in the way of establishing meaningful criteria of achievement is that to be generally meaningful they must not represent the interests, values, and standards of just one teacher. Making them generally acceptable calls for committees, meetings, and long struggles to reach at least a verbal consensus, which in some cases serves only to conceal unresolved disagreements over perceptions, values, and standards. These processes involve so much time and trouble that most criterion-referenced type measurements are idiosyncratic. Is this not what was mainly responsible for the great disagreements Starch and Elliott[1] found in their classic studies of the grading of examination papers? To the extent that criteria of achievement are idiosyncratic, they lack validity and useful meaning.

During the 1960's there was a surge of interest in criterion-referenced measurement,[2, 3, 4, 5] which seemed to be better adapted than norm-referenced measurements to programs of individually prescribed instruction,[6] to mastery learning,[7, 8] and to building a science of education.[9] Some articles on these topics suggested that education had been wandering for more than forty years in the wilderness of norm-referenced measurements and that a shift to criterion-referenced measures could lead education to its promised land. However, it is very difficult to obtain good criterion-referenced measures of achievement in many important areas. Further, criterion-referenced measures do not tell us all, or even the most important parts, of what we need to know about the educational achievements of our students. Contrary to the impression that exists in some quarters, criterion-referenced measurements are not a recent development that modern technology has made possible and that effective education requires. The use of criterion-referenced measurements cannot be expected to improve significantly any large proportion of the evaluations of educational achievement we need to make.

[1]Daniel Starch and E. C. Elliott, "Reliability of Grading High School Work in English," *School Review*, vol. 20 (1912), 442–57.

[2]H. G. Osburn, "Item Sampling for Achievement Testing," *Educational and Psychological Measurement*, vol. 28 (1968), 95–104.

[3]Wells Hively, H. L. Patterson, and S. Page, "A 'Universe Defined' System of Arithmetic Achievement Tests," *Journal of Educational Measurement*, vol. 5 (1968), 275–90.

[4]W. James Popham and T. R. Husek, "Implications of Criterion-Referenced Measurement," *Journal of Educational Measurement*, vol. 6 (1969), 1–9.

[5]George B. Simon, "Comments on 'Implications of Criterion Referenced Measurement'," *Journal of Educational Measurement*, vol. 6 (1969), 259–60.

[6]Robert Glaser, "Instructional Technology and the Measurement of Learning Outcomes," *American Psychologist*, vol. 18 (1963), 519–21.

[7]John Carroll, "A Model for School Learning," *Teachers College Record*, vol. 64 (1963), 723–33.

[8]Ben S. Bloom, "Learning for Mastery," Chapter 3 in *Handbook of Formative and Summative Evaluation of Learning*, Benjamin S. Bloom and others (New York: McGraw-Hill Book Company, 1971).

[9]John R. Bormuth, *On the Theory of Achievement Test Items* (Chicago: University of Chicago Press, 1970).

Of course, norm-referenced measurements need to have content meaning as well as relative meaning.[10] We need to understand not just that a student excels or is deficient, but what he does well or poorly. These meanings and understandings are seldom wholly absent when norm-referenced measures are used. They can be made more obviously present and useful if we choose to do so. Good criterion-referenced measures should be obtained and reported whenever possible. However, they seem likely to serve more often as supplements to, than as substitutes for, norm-referenced measurements.

THE VALUE OF CONTROLLED CONDITIONS

Precise measurement requires careful control or standardization of the conditions surrounding it. Obviously this control makes the behavior being measured artificial to some degree, but artificiality is a price that scientists and engineers, as well as psychologists and teachers, have usually found worth paying to achieve precision. For tests intended to measure typical behavior, such as personality, attitude, or interest tests, the price may sometimes be too high. That is, the behavior in the artificial test situation may be so poorly related to typical behavior in a natural situation that precise measurement is wasted effort. But for tests of educational aptitude or achievement, the gain in precision resulting from the controlled conditions that formal testing can afford usually far outweighs the slight loss in relevance of behavior.

Perhaps an illustration from physical ability testing may be helpful here. Judges, watching a group of children at play (the natural situation), could make rough estimates of the relative abilities of the students to run fast, jump high, or throw some object far. But the precision of the estimates obtained in such an uncontrolled, unstandardized situation would probably be quite low. The different judges would not be likely to agree with each other, or even with themselves on different occasions, in the estimates they would report. If precise estimates are desired, the judges, the children, and everyone else concerned would probably prefer to see them made under the standardized and controlled, if somewhat artificial conditions of a regular track meet. No one would worry much about the possibility that the ones who performed best in the track and field events might perform less well on the playground.

Because all pupils in a class usually take the same test of achievement under the same conditions, some critics have concluded that uniform

[10]Robert L. Ebel, "Content Standard Test Scores," *Educational and Psychological Measurement*, vol. 22 (1962), 15–25.

written tests, particularly objective tests, disregard individual differences and even tend to suppress individuality. The fact that some classroom tests are graded by machines has served to strengthen this misconception. Mass testing and machine grading suggest a standardized uniformity in education that seems inconsistent with concern for the individual and his unique needs and potentials.

However, although the tests and the processes of testing are as nearly alike for all the students in a class as we can make them, the scores of the students on the tests are not alike. Those who score high reflect superior ability and achievement. Those who score low reveal deficiencies. Tests tend to reveal differences among students, not to suppress or conceal them. In fact, uniformity in the conditions of testing is a prerequisite to unequivocal indication of individual differences. If the tests are not identical for all students, not all of the differences in their scores can be attributed to differences among them in ability or achievement. The kind of information about individual differences that uniform tests reveal so clearly is essential to identifying and meeting the unique needs of individual students.

The emphasis in this chapter on the value of written tests in extending a teacher's observations of student behavior and making these observations more dependable and precise is not intended to suggest that tests should be the sole means used in judging a student's educational achievement. Some educational objectives may be concerned mainly with the development of physical skills or social behavior. Direct observation is likely to provide a much better basis than a written test for assessing such skills and behavior. Nor should a teacher or professor ignore his own direct observations, in the classroom or elsewhere, of a student's level of understanding or ability to use knowledge, despite the fact that written tests are especially effective in measuring educational outcomes of that kind. The broader the basis of observations on which evaluation rests, the better, provided only that each observation carries no more weight in determining the final result than its appropriateness and accuracy warrant.

THE NEED FOR OBJECTIVITY

A measurement is objective if it can be verified by another independent measurement. If it cannot be, that is, if the measurement reported depends more on the person making the measurement than on the person being measured, it is unlikely to be very dependable or very useful, and there would be little point in reporting it to anyone else.

By this definition of objectivity, it is clear that objective tests do not necessarily yield objective measures and do not provide the only source of such measures. What is "objective" about an objective test is mainly the scoring. Even that is not likely to be perfectly objective if each scorer makes up his own answer key. And if two examiners start from scratch in building, administering, and scoring independent "objective" tests of the same achievement in the same group of students, it is likely that their measures will show definite deficiencies in objectivity as here defined.

It is usually rather difficult to obtain objective measures from an essay test, but it can be done if sufficient care is taken in defining what is to be measured, and in building and using a test that conforms to that definition. The point is that objectivity is a characteristic of the measures obtained, not of the process by which they are obtained.

The objectivity of a set of measure is obviously a matter of degree. None, not even measures of simple physical characteristics like height or weight, is likely to be perfectly objective. Few, however hastily or amateurishly obtained, are likely to be totally lacking in objectivity. But their usefulness and value depend on the degree of objectivity they exhibit. If they are largely the products of chance or whimsy, they will show little objectivity and have little value to anyone other than the person who made them, and probably not much even to him. On the other hand, if the thing being measured has been defined clearly, and if the process of measuring is adequate and competently carried out, it is likely that objective measures, of some value, will be obtained.

WHO SHOULD PREPARE CLASSROOM TESTS?

Most classroom tests must be prepared by the teacher or professor who is teaching the class. While there are many standardized tests of achievement available for broad areas of subject matter, few are specifically appropriate to the content and objectives of a unit of study, which may constitute only a fraction of the whole course of study. Some textbook publishers furnish tests to accompany their texts. These can be helpful, but too often the items included have not been carefully prepared or reviewed critically by other experts in educational measurement or in the subject field itself.

Some public education authorities, like those in New York State, prepare tests for use in statewide programs of achievement testing. Some universities, like Michigan State, maintain evaluation services that are responsible for preparing achievement tests for their basic courses. Since these tests are usually prepared by experts in test construction, working closely with expert teachers of the subjects involved, they usually do an excellent job of measuring educational achievement. But the substanital cost of developing external tests, and the problems of matching the content of the test to the material emphasized in the classroom, make it seem unlikely that they will replace any substantial fraction of teacher-made tests in the forseeable future.

Having to construct tests gives teachers some educational advantages. As has been said, the process of test construction can help the teacher ·clarify and define the educational objectives of a course. Classroom tests prepared by the teacher are likely to fit the content and objectives of a particular course better than would a test prepared by anyone else. Finally, when testing and teaching are in the hands of the same person, they are likely to be more effectively integrated in the total educational process than if the testing were separated from the teaching.

Every test need not be a completely new and original creation of the instructor. There could be, and should be, much more frequent and extensive exchange of test outlines and test items among teachers of similar courses than is usually the case. This idea of cooperation in test construction is not new. It was involved in the establishment of the Cooperative Test Service over thirty years ago. It was advocated by Thurstone in an article in the *AAUP Bulletin* in 1948.[11] To help make the idea effective, a number of organizations have published collections of test items in various fields. Apparently, however the number of teachers who find these collections useful has been too small to encourage expansion or even renewal of these efforts. Few, if any, new or revised collections have been published in the last ten years. Teachers may consider it more trouble to find the items they want to use in these collections than it is to create new items of their own.

Individual teachers of similar courses probably should arrange for cooperative exchange of test items and test plans. Not only will such cooperation tend to reduce the labor of test construction, it will also make the tests less parochial in the educational understanding and values they reflect and, hence, more generally valid measures of educational achievement.

At the very least, a teacher who uses objective tests can establish and maintain a cumulative file of his own items. The best of these can be and should be reused frequently. If the items have been analyzed for discrimination and difficulty (see Chapter 14), and if the analysis data are recorded with the item, the value of such a file as an aid in future test development will be greatly increased.

When the same test item is used repeatedly it may become the subject of special study and thus lose some of its value as an unbiased indicator of the examinees' general level of achievement. Copies of tests or test items, particularly those used in basic required courses enrolling large

[11]Louis L. Thurstone, "The Improvement of Examinations," *American Association of University Professors Bulletin*, vol. 34 (June, 1948), 394–97.

numbers of students, do find their way into student files. Dissemination of information about the questions that might be reused in a crucial examination may be limited by careful supervision of the examination and careful collection of all test copies, but it can hardly be prevented altogether.

How much the reuse of test items needs to be restricted to prevent appreciable loss of test validity depends, obviously, on the circumstances. In some extreme cases it may seem unwise ever to reuse a single item. Such cases are probably rare. In other extreme cases the identical examination has been used term after term in moderately large classes taking required courses with no appreciable loss in validity. But those were good courses and most of the students were motivated to master the content in them, not just to pass a requirement. Hence the pressure on test security and validity was low. Most courses ought to lie closer to that extreme than to the other.

The legendary "fraternity files" of old tests are seldom as complete, as diligently used, or as richly rewarding to their owners as campus folklore might suggest. And for good reasons. The student who, because of low motivation or low ability, has learned dangerously little during the term is unlikely to find much salvation in poring over copies of old tests, even when urged on and helped along by his more scholarly brothers. What do all those words mean? And even if the answers are clearly and accurately shown, how can they all be remembered until time for the examination? When the probabilities (rather than the possibilities) are assessed rationally, the danger of reusing test items tends to diminish. Probably most instructors ought to do more of it rather than less.

SOME REQUIREMENTS FOR EFFECTIVE TESTING

If all teachers and prospective teachers were skilled in the arts of test development and use, there would be little need for professional training in test construction. But on their own testimony, on that of their sometimes suffering students, and on that of visiting experts called in to advise them on their testing problems, teachers do reveal shortcomings in their use of tests.

A good test constructor must know comprehensively and understand throughly the field of knowledge to be covered by the test so that he will be able to ask significant, novel questions, express them properly and plainly, and provide acceptable, correct answers to them. He must be accurately aware of the level and range of understanding and ability in the group to be tested so that he can choose problems of appropriate intrinsic difficultly and present them so that they will have appropriate functional difficulty. He must understand the thought processes of the students and the misconceptions the less capable ones are likely to have so that he can make wrong answers attractive to those of low achievement.

He must be skilled in written expression so that he can communicate clearly and concisely the information and instructions that make up the test and the test items. He must be a master of the techniques of item writing, and well acquainted with the most useful forms of test items, with their unique virtues, limitations, and pitfalls. Finally, he must be willing to spend the time and make the effort necessary to do a competent, workmanlike job.

The traits just enumerated either contribute to good teaching as well as good testing, or contribute uniquely to good testing. More of the shortcomings observed in classroom tests are probably attributable to deficiencies in traits of the first category than in those of the second. But the correction of deficiencies in command of subject matter, and skill in teaching, is beyond the scope of this book. Nothing that can be said about the techniques of test construction and use will enable an incompetent teacher to make a good test. What a book on classroom testing may do is to help good teachers make better tests than they would otherwise.

A point worth mentioning in passing is that some instructors, outstanding in their scholarship and teaching ability, possess rather naïve notions about the requirements for effective measurement of educational achievement. Sometimes it almost seems that there must be a psychological incompatibility between expertness in scholarship of the one hand and willingness to use effective techniques of educational measurement on the other. The nuclear physicist, the economic theorist, the Shakespearean scholar, and many of their expert colleagues may practice and preach primitive and untrustworthy techniques of testing and grading.

The gap between what we know about how educational achievement ought to be measured and what we actually do is sometimes explained away as a failure in communication, which it almost certainly is. The test specialists are blamed for having developed highly abstruse concepts and highly technical jargon that place their special knowledge beyond the reach of the typical teacher. No doubt there is some justification for this charge. But some of the responsibility may belong to the teachers, too. They may have expected that their own native good sense, plus some effortless sleight-of-hand, could qualify them as experts in educational measurement. The matter is not quite that simple, as Henry Dyer has pointed out.

I don't think the business of educational measurement is inherently simple, and I don't think it is something that can be wrapped up in a do-it-yourself kit. Any way you look at it, the measurement of human behavior is bound to be a terribly complex process, since the phenomena of human behavior are themselves as complex as anything in the universe.[12]

COMMON MISTAKES OF TEACHERS IN TESTING

What are some of the mistakes that even expert teachers and eminent professors make in measuring educational achievement? What are some of their unsound practices in classroom testing?

First, they tend to rely too much on their own subjective judgments, on fortuitous observations, and on unverified inferences. The wide difference among different judges in their evaluations of the same evidence of student achievement—that is, the unreliability of those judgments— has been demonstrated over and over again, yet many teachers have never checked on the reliability of any of their tests and may not even have planned those tests purposely to make them as reliable as possible.

Second, some teachers feel obliged to use absolute standards in judging educational achievement, which can almost always be judged more fairly and consistently in relative terms. If most of the students in a class get A's on one test and most of the same students fail another, some teachers prefer to blame the students rather than the test. They believe, contrary to much evidence, that a teacher can set a reasonable passing score on a test simply by looking at the test and without looking at any student answers to it. They believe that "grading on the curve" permits the students to set the (relative and presumably fallible) standards, instead of permitting the teacher (whose standards are presumed to be absolute and infallible) to set them.

Third, both teachers and professors tend to put off test preparation to the last minute and then to do it on a catch-as-catch-can basis. A last-minute test is likely to be a poor test. Further, such a test cannot possibly have the constructive influence in motivating and directing student learning that a good test of educational achievement ought to have and that a test planned and described to students early in the course would have.

Fourth, many teachers use tests that are too inefficient and too short to sample adequately the whole area of understanding and abilities that the course has attempted to develop. Essay tests have many virtues, but efficiency, adequancy of sampling, and reliability of scoring are not among them.

[12]Henry S. Dyer, "What Point of View Should Teachers Have Concerning the Role of Measurement in Education?" *The Fifteenth Yearbook of the National Council on Measurements Used in Education* (East Lansing, Mich.: Michigan State University, 1958).

Fifth, teachers often overemphasize trivial or ephemeral details in their tests, to the neglect of understanding of basic principles and ability to make practical applications. To illustrate, it is probably far more important to understand the forces that brought Henry VIII into conflict with the Pope than to know the name of his second wife. Yet some teachers are more inclined to ask about the specific, incidental details than about the important general principles.

Sixth, the test questions that teachers and professors write, both essay and objective, often suffer from lowered effectiveness due to unintentional ambiguity in the wording of the question or to inclusion of irrelevant clues to the correct response. Too few teachers avoid these hazards by having their tests reviewed by some competent colleague before the tests are used.

Seventh, the inevitable fact that test scores are affected by the questions or tasks included in them tends to be ignored, and the magnitude of the resulting errors (called *sampling errors*) tend to be underestimated by those who make and use classroom tests. Many of them believe that a test score will be perfectly accurate and reliable if no error has been made in scoring the individual items or in adding these to get a total score. Differences as small as one score unit are often taken to indicate significant differences in attainment.

Finally, many teachers and professors do not use the relatively simple techniques of statistical analysis to check on the effectiveness of their tests. A mean score can show whether or not the test was appropriate for the group tested in its general level of difficulty. A standard deviation can show how well or how poorly the test differentiated among students having different levels of attainment. A reliability coefficient can show how much or how little the scores on this test are likely to differ from those the same students would get on an independent, equivalent test.

An analysis of the responses of good and poor students to individual test items can show whether the items discriminate well or poorly and, if poorly, can suggest why and what needs to be done to improve the item. The calculation of these statistics is quite simple. There is no better way for a teacher of professor to continue to improve his skill in testing, and the quality of the tests he uses, than to analyze systematically the results from his tests and to compare the finding of these analyses with ideal standards of test quality, such as those discussed in Chapter. 13.

DEVELOPING SKILL IN CLASSROOM TESTING

Only one who has never faced the problem of constructing an educational test to meet exacting standards of quality is likely to think that the task is simple or that it can be done quickly. Only one who has never tested his own tests by analyzing student performance on them and by listening to student criticism of them is likely to think it easy to write questions that are unambiguous, that are of appropriate difficulty, and that yield scores of high reliability. Articles and books and courses on testing can help instructors to make better classroom tests and to use them more effectively without devoting much more time to the processes. But real improvement is likely to cost them a real increase in time and effort. How far instructors are willing to go along this line will be determined by the value they place on accurate evaluations of achievement and on the satisfaction they get from doing a good job. Some competent, conscientious teachers may be willing to go a considerable distance.

To make a good test one must begin by knowing thoroughly the subject to be tested. Then one must consider carefully which aspects of achievement in the course are important enough to test. One must invent novel tasks to test those achievements. One must word the question carefully so that the intended answer is clearly defensible, but so that those who are not reasonably sure of the right answer will be attracted to a wrong one. One should have a competent colleague review and suggest corrections or improvements. Then one should give the test under properly controlled conditions, and having given it should analyze the items for discrimination and difficulty, and the test scores for reliability. On the basis of the analysis he should revise the items that are weak, and invent substitutes for those that are too weak to save. Only after all this can the test constructor be reasonably sure that he has done a good job. Is it then surprising that many of the tests we use in our classrooms are not very good? Is it surprising that even some published tests leave much to be desired? In view of the difficulty of making really good tests, one might be tempted to give the whole thing up as a bad job, were it not for the crucial role that good tests can play in the improvement of education. Better testing goes hand in hand with better teaching. Perfect tests may be forever beyond our grasp, but there is much we can do to make our tests better. If we want to improve the learning of our students we will do well to make real efforts to improve our tests.

SUMMARY

The main conclusions to be drawn from the discussions presented in this chapter can be summarized in the following 12 propositions.

1. One can quantify a human characteristic by assigning numbers to persons so that the numbers correspond to amounts of the characteristic.

2. The process of quantifying involves two operations, definition of the characteristic and development of a scale for measuring it.
3. Tests provide imperfect but practically useful scales for measuring human characteristics.
4. Achievement tests are given under specially devised and carefully controlled conditions to improve the precision of measurement without impairing seriously its validity.
5. Written tests provide an important basis, but not the only basis, for evaluating student achievement.
6. A measurement must be objective to be useful.
7. Objective test scores are not always objective measurements, and they are not the only source of such measurements.
8. Most classroom tests are and ought to be prepared by the course instructors.
9. Competence in teaching is a necessary, but not a sufficient, condition for expert test construction.
10. Construction of a good objective test requires special knowledge of testing techniques and special skill in the use of language.
11. Some common weaknesses of teacher-made tests are attributable to: (1) reliance on subjective judgments, (2) reliance on absolute standards of judgment, (3) hasty test preparation, (4) use of short, inefficient tests, (5) testing trivia, (6) careless wording of questions, (7) neglect of sampling errors, and (8) failure to analyze the quality of the test.
12. To improve their testing practices substantially, teachers will have to study the techniques of testing more carefully and work longer and harder to solve the problems testing presents.

To make a good examination paper is far more difficult than is commonly supposed. To do so requires much time and thought; but on no part of the educational process can time and thought be better spent.

A. LAWRENCE LOWELL

5

HOW TO
PLAN A CLASSROOM TEST

DECIDE HOW THE TEST IS TO BE USED

Most classroom tests are used only once, at the end of a unit of instruction to measure the relative amounts of achievement of the members of the class. If the instructor can retrieve all copies of the test each time it is used, he may feel secure in reusing the same test with successive classes year after year. This procedure has the great advantage of saving him the trouble of making a new test each time a new class must be tested.

When used in this way, and it is a perfectly sound educational use, the test functions almost exclusively as a measuring instrument. Students have little or no opportunity to learn from the mistakes they made on it. They cannot review the questions critically or question the instructor's judgment concerning the correct answers to any of them. Some instructors whose objective tests are of marginal quality find it easy to live with these limitations.

However, it is also possible to use a test more than once with the same class, and to do so in a way that not only makes the test much more of a learning exercise but also improves the reliability of the scores it yields. The catch is that these procedures require a new test, or at least a substantially new test, for each new class. However, it is possible to create new forms of a test in a way that keeps the task properly manageable.

The dual or triple use of the same test can be arranged in this way. The first use is as a supervised, secure classroom test that differs from usual testing practice in only two small ways. One is that the students are allowed to keep their copy of the test. The second is that they are encouraged to mark the answers they have chosen not only on the separate answer sheet that is to be turned in, but also on the test.

The second use, immediately following the first, is as an unsupervised take-home test. The students are given a second answer sheet that is due to be turned in several days after the in-class test. They are encouraged to meet in small groups with other students to compare answers and, when the answers differ, to discuss justifications for the alternate answers. Of course, they are free to consult textbooks, class notes, and other references. Their aim should be to turn in perfect or near-perfect answer sheets for the take-home test. Each student's score on the take-home answer sheet is added to his score on the in-class answer sheet to give his score for the entire test.

Experience indicates that most students (excepting those few who are overburdened with other duties or who are low in motivation) work hard on the take-home test and learn a considerable amount in the process. Experience indicates also that the sums of scores on in-class and take-home administrations are much more reliable than scores on either administration by itself. Somewhat surprisingly, it often happens that scores on the take-home test are actually more reliable than those on the in-class test. Although the items are identical, the two tests clearly measure somewhat different aspects of achievement. Quickness of intellect probably counts more on the in-class test. Persistence of effort counts more on the take-home. It seems reasonable to claim that the composite provides a more valid measure of achievement than either alone.

The third use of the same test is as a pre-test for the succeeding class. This pre-test serves three functions. It tells the students what kind of test to expect. Since they are allowed to keep copies of the pre-test, it gives them some practice problems against which to test their developing knowledge. Finally, after an item analysis, it tells the instructor which of his questions were too easy to function as proper measures of achievement.

This multiple use of a test, with the attendant requirement of a new test form for each new class, is likely to seem attractive only to instructors who can develop a system for creating new test forms easily. One instructor manages it this way: The first four times he taught the course he built four new test forms with no common test items. After that the test for each succeeding class has been a revision of one of the earlier forms. From one-third to one-half of the items in each revised form are new or are revised (hopefully improved) items from the earlier test. He uses item analysis from in-class, take-home and pre-test administrations to identify the items most in need of revision or replacement.

To use each test form three times and to create a substantially new test for each class undeniably requires both instructor and students to spend more than the usual amount of time on testing. The system may appeal only to measurement specialists, but it does what nonspecialists often urge teachers to do—use measurements to promote learning, not just to assess it. And it results in better tests and better measurements of achievement.

DECIDE WHEN TO TEST

To some extent the frequency and times of classroom testing are determined by institutional regulations on marking and reporting. Most instructors find it necessary or advisable to test at least twice during a semester. Some give hour tests every three or four weeks. Tests given at shorter intervals can sample smaller units of instruction more intensively, but there is no limit to the amount of instruction that can be sampled by a single test and no inherent reason why a test that samples a small unit intensively is better than a test that samples a large unit more diffusely.

Frequent testing has the advantage of providing a more reliable basis for evaluation and of keeping both instructor and students more currently informed of student progress. But preparing and scoring frequent tests could consume a large share of the instructor's time, unless he has a stockpile of good test questions and unless he is equipped to handle test administration and scoring efficiently. It might in extreme cases even encroach undesirably on time for class instruction. Too frequent testing could conceivably lead to overemphasis on test-passing as a goal for study. However, it is probably safe to say that few classes are overexposed to good tests. Educational psychologists have long recognized that taking a classroom test is somewhat like going through a learning program. The educational value of such programs, and of the teaching machines used to present them, have been objects of considerable interest and study in recent years.

If instructors had complete freedom of choice in scheduling their tests, most would probably choose a midmorning hour. Some would prefer a midweek day. This degree of freedom is seldom available and there is little if any evidence or strong logic to support preference for a particular hour or day.

DECIDE WHETHER TO USE AN ESSAY, OBJECTIVE, OR PROBLEM TEST

The most commonly used types of test questions are the essay (or discussion) type, the objective (or short-answer) type, and the mathematical problem type, used widely in mathematics, some sciences, engineering, and a few other subjects. A brief comparison of the characteristics of these types of test questions seems to be in order at this point.

To begin, let us dispose of some common misconceptions. It is not true that one type tests real understanding whereas another tests only superficial knowledge. As Richardson and Stalnaker have said, "The form of a test gives no certain indication of the ability tested."[1] It is not true that luck is a large element in scores on one type and nearly or totally absent in another. On the contrary, all three types can require much the same kind and level of ability, and if carefully handled can yield results of satisfactory reliability and validity, as Stalnaker[2] and Coffman[3] have shown. A good essay test or a good objective test could be constructed so that it would rank a group of students in nearly the same order as that resulting from a good problem test. But this is not to say that all three types can be used interchangeably with equal ease and effectiveness.

Vernon has called attention to evidence that

> while . . . tests of the same objectives employing different forms tend to give discrepant results (e.g., essay and new-type), tests in the same form which are aimed at different school subjects or different intellectual functions inter-correlate very highly. For many purposes the simpler tests show superior validity, and it is doubtful how far the more complex ones do bring in the "higher" intellectual functions at which they are aimed.[4]

Both essay and problem tests are easier to prepare than objective tests. But the objective test can be scored more rapidly and more reliably

[1]M. W. Richardson and J. M. Stalnaker, "Comments on Achievement Examinations," *Journal of Educational Research*, vol. 28 (1935), 425–32.

[2]John M. Stalnaker, "Essay Examinations Reliably Read," *School and Society*, vol. 46 (1937), 671–72.

[3]William E. Coffman, "On the Validity of Essay Tests of Achievement," *Journal of Educational Measurement*, vol. 3 (1966), 151–56.

[4]Philip E. Vernon, *Educational Testing and Test Form Factors*, Research Bulletin 58–3, (Princeton, N.J.: Educational Testing Service, February, 1958).

(unless very special and unusual pains are taken) than either of the other types, particularly the essay type. Where very large groups of students must be tested, the use of objective tests generally permits a gain in efficiency with little if any loss in validity. But where classes are small, the efficiency advantage is in the opposite direction, and essay or problem tests should be preferred.

The problem type has the advantage of greater intrinsic relevance —of greater identity with on-the-job requirements—than either of the other types. Many superficial or purely academic questions have been included in essay and objective tests. But this fault could and should be avoided.

Neither essay nor problem-type tests, because of the length and complexity of the answers they require and because these answers must be written by hand, can sample as widely as is possible in an objective test. Writing is a much slower process than the reading on which objective tests depend. It is sometimes claimed that ability to choose an answer is different from, and less significant than, ability to produce an answer. But most of the evidence indicates that these abilities are highly related.

In considering the relative merits of essay, problem, and objective tests, it is important to remember that the only useful component of any test score is the objectively verifiable component of it, regardless of the type of test from which is was derived. To the degree that a test score reflects the private, subjective, unverifiable impressions and values of one particular scorer, it is deficient in meaning and hence in usefulness to the student who received it or to anyone else who is interested in this ability or achievement.

In objective tests and problem tests there is often a good deal more objectivity than in essay tests. The student usually has a more definite task, and the reasons for giving or withholding credit are more obvious to all concerned. But it is well to remember that even the objective test is based on many subjective decisions as to what to test and how to test it. For the problem test there is an additional element of subjectivity in scoring that is not present in the objective test. How much credit to give for an imperfect answer and which elements to consider in judging degree of perfection are often matters of spur-of-the-moment, subjective decision when scoring problem tests.

In the interest of useful measurement the examiner should seek, whatever test form he uses, to make his measurements as objective as possible. A measurement is objective to the extent that it can be independently verified by other competent measurers. It is entirely conceivable that measurements obtained from a good essay test could be more objective in this sense than measurements obtained from a poor multiple-choice test. On the other hand it is fair to say that those who use essay tests tend to worry less about the objectivity of their measurements and evaluations than those who use multiple-choice tests.

Each of us is a different person, living largely in a unique world created by his own special history of experiences. It is not surprising that we sometimes find it difficult to agree on perceptions, meanings, and values. But since the harmony of our relationships and the effectiveness of our common enterprises depends on agreement, it is important for us to establish as much identity as possible among ourselves in these perceptions, meanings, and values. This is only another way of saying we need to be as objective as possible in all things, including the measurement of achievement.

In most cases teachers have chosen to use the type of question that seems most useful to them, or which they feel most competent to use effectively. However, it is possible that the force of habit and some unwarranted assumptions may have prevented some teachers from using other types that would actually be more advantageous to them. The classroom testing practices of many school and college faculties probably could be improved by periodic review of the types of tests that are being used, in comparison with those that might be used.

IF THE TEST IS TO BE OBJECTIVE, DECIDE WHAT KIND OF OBJECTIVE TEST ITEM TO USE

The most commonly used kinds of objective test items are multiple-choice, true-false, matching, classification, and short-answer. Many other varieties have been described in more comprehensive catalogs of objective test items.[5] However, most of these special varieties have limited merit and applicability. Their unique features do more to change the appearance of the item and often to increase the difficulty of using it, than to improve the item as a measuring instrument.

Two special item types that have achieved some popularity, the true-false with correction and the multiple-response variation of the multiple-choice item, are displayed in Exhibit 5.1. The disadvantages of both appear to outweigh their advantages. Presumably the corrected true-false item is less subject to guessing than the ordinary true-false item and tests recall as well as recognition. However, the added difficulty and uncertainty involved in scoring student responses to it more than offsets whatever slight reduction in guessing or slight increase in recall testing the item might produce. The multiple-response item is essentially a collection of true-false statements. If the statements were presented and scored as

[5]Robert L. Ebel, "Writing the Test Item," in E. F. Lindquist, ed., *Educational Measurement*, (Washington, D.C.: American Council on Education, 1951); and J. Raymond Gerberich, *Specimen Objective Test Items* (New York: David McKay Company, Inc., 1956).

EXHIBIT 5.1

Special Item Types

---

1. True-false with correction

   Directions: If the statement is true as given, write the word "true" on the blank following the item. If it is false, find a substitute for the underlined word or phrase that would make it true. Then, write the substitute on the blank following the item.

Example:	Answer

   0. The use of steam revolutionized transportation in the *17th* century.   0. *19th*

2. Multiple-response

   Directions: Choose the most nearly correct set of responses from among those listed.

Example:	Responses

   0. Our present constitution   1. *a*
      a. Was the outgrowth of a previous failure   2. *a, b*
      b. Was drafted in Philadelphia during the summer (May to September) of 1787   3. *a, b, c*
      c. Was submitted by the Congress to the states for adoption   4. *b, c, d*
      d. Was adopted by the required number of states and put into effect in 1789.   *5. *a, b, c, d*

---

independent true-false statements, they would yield more detailed and reliable information concerning the state of the examinee's knowledge than they can do in multiple-response form. Those critics who urge test makers to abandon the "traditional" multiple-choice and true-false forms and to invent new forms to measure a more varied and more significant array of educational achievement have failed to grasp two important points:

1. *Any* aspect of cognitive educational achievement can be tested by means of either the multiple-choice or the true-false form.
2. What a multiple-choice or true-false item measures is determined much more by its content than by its form.

Multiple-choice and true-false test items are widely applicable. Because of this, because of the many tasks that can be presented in each form, and because of the importance of developing skill in using each form effectively, separate chapters are devoted to true-false and multiple-choice item forms later in this text. Matching, classification, and short-answer items are more limited in applicability, but can be effectively used in special circumstances to test special aspects of achievement.

The multiple-choice form of test item is relatively high in ability to discriminate between better and poorer students. It is somewhat more difficult to write than some other item types, but its advantages seem so apparent that it has become the type most widely used in tests constructed by specialists. Theoretically, and this has been verified in practice, a multiple-choice test with a given number of items can be expected to show as much reliability in its scores as a typical true-false test with almost twice that number of items. Here is an example of the multiple-choice type.

Directions: Write the number of the best answer to the question on the line at the right of the question.

Example: Which is the most appropriate designation for a government in which control is in the hands of a few men?

1. Autonomy   **4**
2. Bureaucracy
3. Feudalism
4. Oligarchy

The true-false item is the simplest to prepare and is also quite widely adaptable. It tends to be less discriminating, item for item, than the multiple-choice type, and somewhat more subject to ambiguity and misinterpretation. Although theoretically a high proportion of true-false items could be answered correctly by blind guessing, in practice the error introduced into true-false test scores by blind guessing tends to be small. This is true because well-motivated examinees taking a reasonable test do very little blind guessing. They almost always find it possible to give a rational answer and much more advantageous to do so than to guess blindly. The problem of guessing on true-false test questions will be discussed in greater detail in Chapter 7. Here is an example of the true-false form.

Directions: If the sentence is essentially true, encircle the letter "T" at the right of the sentence. If it is essentially false, encircle the letter "F".

Example: A substance that serves as a catalyst in a chemical reaction may be recovered unaltered at the end of the reaction.   Ⓣ   F

The matching type is efficient in that the same set of responses can be used with a cluster of several similar stimulus words. But this is also a limitation since it is sometimes difficult to get clusters of questions or stimulus words that are sufficiently similar to make use of the same set of responses. Further, questions whose answers can be no more than a word or a phrase tend to be somewhat superficial and to place a premium on purely verbalistic learning. An example of the matching type is given here.

Directions: On the blank before the title of each literary work place the letter that precedes the name of the person who wrote it.

Literary Works	Authors
b 1. *Paradise Lost*	*a.* Matthew Arnold
	b. John Milton
e 2. *The Innocents Abroad*	*c.* William Shakespeare
	d. Robert Louis Stevenson
d 3. *Treasure Island*	*e.* Mark Twain

The classification type is less familiar than the matching type, but possibly more useful in specific situations. Like the matching type, it uses a single set of responses but applies these to a large number of stimulus situations. An example of the classification type is the following.

Directions: In the following items you are to express the effects of exercise on various body processes and substances. Assume that the organism undergoes no change except those due to exercise. For each item blacken answer space.

    1. If the effect of exercise is to definitely *increase* the quantity described in the item

    2. If the effect of exercise is to definitely *decrease* the quantity described in the item

    3. If exercise should have no *appreciable effect*, or *an unpredictable effect* on quantity described in the item

    27. Rate of heart beat   ■ 2 3

    28. Blood pressure   ■ 2 3

    29. Amount of glucose in the blood   1 ■ 3

    30. Amount of residual air in the lungs   1 ■ 3

    31. Etc.

The short-answer item, in which the student must supply a word, phrase, number, or other symbol is inordinately popular and tends to be used excessively in classroom tests. It is easy to prepare. In the early grades, where emphasis is on the development of vocabulary and the formation of concepts, it can serve a useful function. It has the apparent advantage of requiring the examinee to think of the answer, but this advantage may be more apparent than real. Some studies have shown a very high correlation between scores on tests composed of parallel short-answer and multiple-choice items, when both members of each pair of parallel items are intended to test the same knowledge or ability.[6]

This means that students who are best at producing correct answers tend also to be best at *identifying* them among several alternatives. Accurate measures of how well a student can identify correct answers tend to

    [6]Alvin C. Eurich, "Four Types of Examinations Compared and Evaluated," *Journal of Educational Psychology*, vol. 22 (1931), 268–78; and Desmond L. Cook, "An Investigation of Three Aspects of Free-response and Choice-type Tests at the College Level," *Dissertation Abstracts*, vol. 15 (1955), 1351.

be somewhat easier to get than accurate measures of his ability to produce them. There may be special situations, of course, where the correlation would be much lower.

The disadvantages of the short-answer form are that it is limited to questions that can be answered by a word, phrase, symbol, or number and that its scoring tends to be subjective and tedious. Item writers often find it difficult to phrase good questions on principles, explanations, applications, or predictions that can be answered in a word or phrase and that can be answered satisfactorily by *only* one specific word or phrase. Here are some examples of short answer items.

> *Directions:* On the blank following each of the following questions, partial statements, or words, write the word or number that seems most appropriate.
>
> *Examples:*
> What is the valence of oxygen? **-2**
> The middle section of the body of an insect is called the **thorax**.
> What major river flows through or near each of these cities?

Cairo	**Nile**
Calcutta	**Ganges**
New Orleans	**Mississippi**
Paris	**Seine**
Quebec	**St. Lawrence**

Some authorities suggest that a variety of item types be used in each examination in order to diversify the tasks presented to the examinee. They imply that this will improve the validity of the test or make it more interesting. Others suggest that the test constructor should choose the particular item type that is best suited to the particular questions or problem he wishes to present. There is more merit in the second of these suggestions than in the first, but even the second should not be accepted as an absolute imperative in test construction. Several item forms are quite widely adaptable. A test constructor can safely decide to use primarily a single item type, such as multiple-choice, and to turn to one of the other forms only when it becomes clearly more efficient to do so. The quality of a classroom test depends much more on giving proper weight to various aspects of achievement, and on writing good items of whatever type, than on choice of this or that type of item.

DECIDE HOW LONG THE TEST SHOULD BE IN MINUTES AND ITEMS

The number of questions to include in a test is determined largely by the amount of time available for it. Many tests are limited to 50 minutes, more or less, because that is the scheduled length of the class period. Special examination schedules may provide periods of two hours or longer. In general, the longer the period and the examination, the more reliable the scores obtained from it. However, it is seldom practical or desirable to prepare a classroom test that will require more than three hours.

It is useful to consider the collection of questions, or items, that make up a test as a sample from a hypothetical population of all possible questions that might be used in such a test. A fifth-grade teacher, for example, might obtain 100 words for a final spelling test by taking every fifth word from the total list of 500 words studied during the term. The 500 words constitute the population from which the 100-word sample is drawn. In the case of this example the population of possible questions is real and definite. But for most tests it is not. That is, there is almost no limit to the number of problems that could be invented for use in an algebra test, nor is there any limit to the number of questions that could be stated for use in a history test. Constructors of tests in these subjects, as in most other subjects, have no predetermined, limited list from which to draw the sample of questions to be used in the test. But their tests are samples, nevertheless, because they include only a fraction of the questions that could be asked in each case. A major problem of the test constructor is to make the sample he uses fairly represent the total population of questions that would be appropriate for the test he is building.

The more extensive the area of subject matter or abilities that the test is intended to cover, the larger the population of potential questions. The size of this population places an upper limit on the size of the sample that can be drawn from it. That is, the sample cannot be larger than the population. But population size does not place a *lower* limit on the size of the sample. A population of 1,000 potential items can be sampled by a test of 10, 50, or 100 items. So can a population of 100,000 potential items. The larger the population, the more likely it is to be heterogeneous, that is, to include diverse and semi-independent areas of knowledge or ability. To achieve equally accurate results, a somewhat larger sample is required in a heterogeneous than in a homogeneous field. Apart from this, the size of the population bears only a slight relation to the most advantageous size of sample.

If length of testing time does not determine the length of a test, the accuracy desired in the scores, and the diversity of types of questions in the hypothetical population of questions should determine it. The larger the number of items in the sample, and the more homogeneous the population to be sampled, the more accurate the scores from the test will be as measures of achievement in the field.

For various reasons there is a growing trend to make tests include few enough questions so that most students have time to attempt all of them when working at their own normal rates. One reason for this is that speed of response is not a primary objective of instruction in most high

TABLE 5.1. THE RELATION BETWEEN RATE AND ACCURACY*

Order of Finish	Sum of Scores	Range of Scores
1–10	965	35
11–20	956	32
21–30	940	31
31–40	964	32
41–50	948	52
51–60	955	25
61–70	965	27
71–80	1010	30
81–90	942	24
91–100	968	40

*On a test in educational measurement composed of 125 true-false test items taken by 100 students on November 3, 1969. The mean score on the test was 96.1. The tenth student finished the test after working on it for 50 minutes. The 100th student used 120 minutes.

school and college courses and hence does not contribute valid indications of achievement. In many areas of proficiency, speed and accuracy are not highly correlated. Consider the data of Table 5.1. The sum of the scores for the first 10 students who finished the test was 965. The highest score in that group was 105. The lowest was 71. Thus, the range of scores in that group was 35 score units. Note how little difference there is between the sum of scores for those finishing early, middle, and late. Though the range of scores varies somewhat from group to group, there is no clear tendency for the groups to become more or less variable. One can conclude from these data that on this test there was almost no relation between time spent in taking the test and the number of correct answers given.

A second reason for giving students ample time to work on a test is that examination anxiety, severe enough even in untimed tests, is accentuated when pressure to work rapidly as well as accurately is applied. A third is that efficient use of an instructor's painstakingly produced test requires that most students respond to all of it.[7] In some situations speed tests may be appropriate and valuable, but these situations seem to be the exception, not the rule.

The number of questions that an examinee can answer per minute depends on the kind of questions used, the complexity of the thought processes required to answer it, and the examinee's work habits. The fastest student in a class may finish a test in half the time required by the slowest. For these reasons it is difficult to specify precisely how many items to include in a given test. Experience with similar tests in similar classes is the best guide. Lacking that, the test constructor might assume that

[7]Robert L. Ebel, "Maximizing Test Validity in Fixed Time Limits," *Educational and Psychological Measurement*, vol. 13 (1953), 347–57.

typical multiple-choice items can be answered by even the slower students at the rate of one per minute, and that true-false items can be answered similarly at the rate of two per minute. If the proposed items are longer or more complex than usual, these estimates may need to be revised. The time required by an essay question or a problem depends on the nature of the question or problem. Sometimes it is helpful for the test constructor to specify how much time he wishes the examinee to spend on each question or problem.

DECIDE WHAT EMPHASIS TO GIVE TO VARIOUS ASPECTS OF ACHIEVEMENT

Educational achievement in most courses consists in acquiring command of a fund of usable knowledge and in developing the ability to perform certain tasks. Knowledge can be conveniently divided into knowledge of vocabulary and knowledge about matters of fact. Abilities usually include ability to explain and ability to apply knowledge to the taking of appropriate action in practical situations. Some courses aim to develop other abilities, such as ability to calculate or ability to predict.

A rather detailed analysis of educational objectives for student achievement has been published by Bloom and his associates.[8] Their taxonomy includes test items appropriate for each objective or category of achievement. Dressel and his colleagues have published outlines of test content in terms of subject matter and pupil achievements, and also have presented illustrative items.[9] These are instructive guides for the test constructor to decide what to test and how to test it.

Some of the words used to identify achievements are more impressionistic than objectively meaningful, however. Some categories of educational achievement are based on hypothetical mental functions, such as comprehension, analysis, synthesis, scientific thinking, or recognition, whose functional independence is open to question. Those who currently attempt to describe mental processes and functions may be a little, but not much, better off than sixteenth-century map makers.

So geographers in Afric maps
With savage pictures fill their gaps
And o'er unhabitable downs
Place elephants for want of towns.[10]

---

[8]Benjamin S. Bloom and others, *Taxonomy of Educational Objectives* (New York: David McKay Company, Inc., 1956).

[9]Paul L. Dressel, *Comprehensive Examinations in a Program of General Education* (East Lansing, Mich.: Michigan State College Press, 1949).

[10]Jonathan Swift, "On Poetry, A Rhapsody," *The Portable Swift* (New York: The Viking Press, Inc., 1948), p. 571.

Unless mental processes are directly related to obvious characteristics of different kinds of test questions, it is somewhat difficult to use them confidently in planning a test or analyzing its contents. As Thorndike put it, "We have faith also that the objective products produced, rather than the inner condition of the person whence they spring, are the proper point of attack for the measurer, at least in our day and generation."[11] Occasionally, too, the specified areas of achievement are so closely related to specific units of instruction that it is difficult to regard them as pervasive educational goals.

Most of the questions used in many good classroom tests can be classified with reasonable ease and certainly into one or another of the following seven categories:

1. Understanding of terminology (or vocabulary)
2. Understanding of fact and principle (or generalization)
3. Ability to explain or illustrate (understanding of relationships)
4. Ability to calculate (numerical problems)
5. Ability to predict (what is likely to happen under specified conditions)
6. Ability to recommend appropriate action (in some specific practical problem situation)
7. Ability to make an evaluative judgment

Multiple-choice test items illustrating each of these categories are presented in Exhibit 5.2.

Items belonging to the first category always designate a term to be defined or otherwise identified. Items dealing with facts and principles are based on descriptive statements of the way things are. Items testing explanations usually involve the words "why" or "because." Items belonging to the fourth category require the student to use mathematical processes to get from the given to the required quantities. Items that belong in both categories 5 and 6 are based on descriptions of specific situations. The *prediction* items specify all of the conditions and ask for the future result, whereas the *action* items specify some of the conditions and ask what other conditions (or actions) will lead to a specified result. In judgment items the response options are statements whose appropriateness or quality is to be judged on the basis of criteria specified in the item stem.

The usefulness of these categories in the classification of items testing various aspects of achievement depends on the fact that they are defined mainly in terms of overt item characteristics rather than in terms of presumed mental processes required for successful response. The appropriate proportions of questions in each category will vary from course to course, but the better tests tend to be those with heavier emphasis on application

---

[11]Edward L. Thorndike, Seventeenth Yearbook, of the National Society for the Study of Education, *The Measurement of Educational Products*, part II, "The Nature, Purposes, and General Methods of Measurement of Educational Products," (1918), p. 160.

EXHIBIT 5.2

Multiple-Choice Items Intended to Test Various Aspects of Achievement

I. *Understanding of terminology*
   A. The term "fringe benefits" has been used frequently in recent years in connection with labor contracts. What does the term mean?
      1. Incentive payments for above-average output
      2. Rights of employees to draw overtime pay at higher rates
      3. Rights of employers to share in the profits from inventions of their employees
      *4. Such considerations as paid vacations, retirement plans, and health insurance
   B. What is the technical definition of the term "production"?
      1. Any natural process producing food or other raw materials
      *2. The creation of economic values
      3. The manufacture of finished products
      4. The operation of a profit-making enterprise

II. *Knowledge of fact and principle*
   A. What principle is utilized in radar?
      1. Faint electronic radiations of far-off objects can be detected by supersensitive receivers.
      *2. High-frequency radio waves are reflected by distant objects.
      3. All objects emit infrared rays, even in darkness.
      4. High-frequency radio waves are not transmitted alike by all substances.
   B. The most frequent source of conflict between the western and eastern parts of the United States during the course of the nineteenth century was:
      *1. The issue of currency inflation
      2. The regulation of monopolies
      3. Internal improvements
      4. Isolationism vs. internationalism
      5. Immigration

III. *Ability to explain or illustrate*
   A. If a piece of lead suspended from one arm of a beam balance is balanced with a piece of wood suspended from the other arm, why is the balance lost if the system is placed in a vacuum?
      1. The mass of the wood exceeds the mass of the lead.
      2. The air exerts a greater buoyant force on the lead than on the wood.
      3. The attraction of gravity is greater for the lead than for the wood when both are in a vacuum.
      *4. The wood displaces more air than the lead.
   B. Should merchants and middlemen be classified as producers or nonproducers? Why?
      1. As nonproducers, because they make their living off producers and consumers

2. As producers, because they are regulators and determiners of price

*3. As producers, because they aid in the distribution of goods and bring producer and consumer together

4. As producers, because they assist in the circulation of money

IV. *Ability to calculate*

    A. If the radius of the earth were increased by three feet, its circumference at the equator would be increased by about how much?

        1. 9 feet   *3. 19 feet

        2. 12 feet   4. 28 feet

    B. What is the standard deviation of this set of five measures—1, 2, 3, 4, 5?

        1. 1   4. $\sqrt{10}$

        *2. $\sqrt{2}$ 5. None of these

        3. 9

V. *Ability to predict*

    A. If an electric refrigerator is operated with the door open in a perfectly insulated sealed room, what will happen to the temperature of the room?

     *1. It will rise slowly.

     2. It will remain constant.

     3. It will drop slowly.

     4. It will drop rapidly.

    B. What would happen if the terminals of an ordinary household light bulb were connected to the terminals of an automobile storage battery?

     1. The bulb would light to its natural brilliance.

     *2. The bulb would not glow, though some current would flow through it.

     3. The bulb would explode.

     4. The battery would go dead in a few minutes.

VI. *Ability to recommend appropriate action*

    A. Which of these practices would probably contribute *least* to reliable grades from essay examinations?

     *1. Weighting the items so that the student receives more credit for answering correctly more difficult items.

     2. Advance preparation by the rater of a correct answer to each question.

     3. Correction of one question at a time through all papers.

     4. Concealment of student names from the rater.

    B. "None of these" is an appropriate response for a multiple-choice test item in cases where:

     1. The number of possible responses is limited to two or three.

     *2. The responses provide absolutely correct or incorrect answers.

     3. A large variety of possible responses might be given.

     4. Guessing is apt to be a serious problem.

VII. *Ability to make an evaluative judgment*

    A. Which one of the following sentences is most appropriately worded

for inclusion in an impartial report resulting from an investigation
of a wage policy in a certain locality?

1. The wages of the working people are fixed by the one businessman who is the only large employer in the locality.
2. Since one employer provides a livelihood for the entire population in the locality, he properly determines the wage policy
   for the locality.
3. Since one employer controls the labor market in the locality,
   his policy may not be challenged.
*4. In this locality, where there is only one large employer of labor,
   the wage policy of this employer is really the wage policy of the
   locality.

B. Which of the following quotations has most of the characteristics
   of conventional poetry?
1. "I never saw a purple cow;
   I never hope to see one."
*2. "Announced by all the trumpets of the sky
   Arrives the snow and blasts his ramparts high."
3. "Thou art blind and confined,
   While I am free for I can see."
4. "In purple prose his passion he betrayed
   For verse was difficult.
   Here he never strayed."

of knowledge than on mere ability to reproduce its verbal representations.
But it is more difficult to write good application questions than reproduction questions, and unless the test constructor decides explicitly in
advance what proportion of the questions in his test should relate to each
specified aspect of achievement, and carries out his decision, his test
may suffer.

DECIDE WHETHER THE TEST SHOULD EMPHASIZE COMPLEX TASKS OR EFFICIENT TASKS AS MEASURES OF ACHIEVEMENT

In recent years there has been a trend toward the use of complex
tasks, often based on descriptions of real or imagined situations or requiring the interpretation of data, diagrams, or background information,
in educational achievement tests. A variety of complex test items is illustrated in a publication of the Educational Testing Service[12] as well as in

---

[12]Test Development Division, ETS *Multiple-Choice Questions: A Close Look*
(Princeton, N.J.: Educational Testing Service, 1963).

EXHIBT 5.3

Descriptions of Complex Items

1. The item begins with a description of a dispute among baseball players, team owners, and Social Security officials over off-season unemployment compensation for the players. The examinee is asked whether the players are justified in their demands, not justified, or whether he needs more information before deciding. Then, the examinee is asked whether each one of a series of statements about the case supports his judgment, opposes it, or leaves him unable to say.

(Taxonomy, pp. 196–97)

2. An unusual chemical reaction is described. The examinee is asked to consider which of a series of possible hypotheses about the reaction is tenable and how the tenable hypotheses might be tested.

(Taxonomy, pp. 183–84)

3. The examinee is given a chart on which the expenditures of a state for various purposes over a period of years have been graphed. Then, given a series of statements about the chart, he is asked to judge how much truth there is in each.

(Taxonomy, pp. 118–19)

the Bloom Taxonomy.[13] Some examples of complex items of this type are described in Exhibit 5.3.

There are several reasons for this trend. Since these tasks obviously call for the *use* of knowledge they provide an answer to critics who assert that objective questions test only recognition of isolated factual details. Since the situations and background materials used in the tasks are complex, the items presumably require the examinee to use higher mental processes. Finally, the items are attractive to those who believe that education should be concerned with developing a student's ability to think rather than his command of knowledge (as if knowledge and thinking were independent attainments).

These complex tasks have some undesireable features as test items. Because they tend to be bulky and time-consuming ,they limit the number of responses the examinee can make per hour of testing time. This limitation reduces the size of the sample of observations of his behavior and, hence, reduces the reliability of measurements of his achievement. Tests composed of complex tasks tend to be inefficient in terms of accuracy of measurement per hour of testing.

[13]Benjamin S. Bloom, ed. *Taxonomy of Educational Objectives, Handbook I: Cognitive Domain*, New York: (David McKay Company, Inc., 1956).

Further, the more complex the situation, and the higher the level of mental process required to make some judgment about it, the more difficult it becomes to defend any one answer as the best answer. Complex test items tend to discriminate poorly. They also tend to be inordinately difficult, unless the examiner manages to ask a very easy question about his complex problem situation. Even the strongest advocates of complex situational or interpretive test items do not claim that good items of this type are easy to write.

The inefficiency of these items, the uncertainty of the best answer, and the difficulty of writing good ones could all be tolerated if the complex items did, in fact, measure more important aspects of achievement than can be measured by simpler types. However, there is no good evidence that this is the case. A simple question like, "Will you marry me?" can have the most profound consequences. It can provide a lifetime's crucial test of the wisdom of the man who asks it and of the girl who answers.

It would be a mistake in testing to pursue efficiency wherever it may lead, for it may lead to testing only vocabulary and simple word associations, and these are inadequate for testing all the dimensions of command of knowledge. It is equally a mistake to value the appearance of complexity for its own sake. If the complex item tests a genuinely important achievement that is within the grasp of most students and that cannot be tested in any simpler way, then retain it. If not, seek some other important achievement or seek to test it more simply.

OUTLINE THE CONTENT TO BE COVERED BY THE TEST

An area of information or an ability is appropriate to use as the basis for an objective test item in a classroom test if it has been given specific attention in instruction. Emphasis in an achievement test on things that were not taught or assigned for learning is hard to justify.

One approach to defining the appropriate universe for sampling is to list as topics, in as much detail as seems reasonable, the areas of knowledge and abilities toward which instruction was directed. In the simplest case, where instruction is based on a single text, section headings in the textbook may provide a satisfactory list of such topics. If sections are regarded as about equal in importance, and if there are n times as many of them as of items needed for the test, the instructor might systematically sample every nth topic as the basis for a test item.

If the various sections of the text are not reasonably equal in importance or if no single text provided the basis for teaching, the instructor may wish to create his own list of topics. Perhaps separate lists of vocabulary items, items of information, and topics involving explanation, applications, calculation, or prediction may be required. This last approach may make it easier to maintain the desired balance among the several aspects of achievement. Illustrative portions of lists of topics for various aspects of achievement are shown in Exhibit 5.4

EXHIBIT 5.4

Illustrative Portions of Topic Lists for a Test on Classroom Testing

List A—Vocabulary
1. Aptitude test
2. Bimodal distribution
3. Composite score
4. Expectancy table
5. Factor analysis
6. Etc.

List B—Knowledge
1. Achievement quotients
2. Types of test items
3. Essay tests
4. Kuder-Richardson formulas
5. Educational uses of tests
6. Etc.

List C—Explanation
1. Correction for attenuation
2. Use of standard scores
3. Cross validation
4. Separate answer sheet
5. Guessing correction formula
6. Etc.

List D—Application
1. Reporting scores
2. Test selection
3. Sources of information
4. Judging test quality
5. Item writing
6. Etc.

List E—Calculation
1. Mean
2. Index of item difficulty
3. Index of item discrimination
4. Percentile rank
5. Reliability coefficient
6. Etc.

DECIDE WHAT LEVEL AND DISTRIBUTION OF DIFFICULTIES ARE APPROPRIATE FOR THE QUESTIONS INCLUDED IN THE TEST

There are two ways in which this problem can be approached. One is to include in the test only those problems or questions that any student who has studied successfully should be able to answer. If this is done, most of the students should be expected to answer most of the questions correctly. To put it somewhat differently, so many correct answers are likely to be given that many of the questions will not be very effective in discriminating among various levels of achievement—best, good, average, weak, and poor.

The other approach is to choose the questions likely to contribute most information as to relative levels of achievement among the students tested. This requires preference for somewhat harder questions. The ideal difficulty for these items would be at a point on the difficulty scale midway between zero difficulty (100 percent correct response) and chance level difficulty (50 percent correct for true-false items, 25 percent correct for four-alternative multiple-choice items). This means that the proportion of correct responses to an ideal true-false item would be about 75 percent and to an ideal multiple-choice item about 62.5 percent. This second approach will generally yield more reliable scores for the same amount of testing time, but it may be more worrisome to the students who take it and will not seem to reflect any minimum standards of competence for a passing score.

Some instructors believe that a good test includes some difficult questions to "test" the better students and some easy questions for the poorer students. This belief might be easier to justify if each new unit of study in a course or each new idea required the mastery of all preceding units and ideas presented in the course. In such a course students would differ in how far they had successfully progressed through it rather than in how many separate ideas they had grasped.

Few courses illustrate such perfect sequences of units and ideas. A student who has missed some of the early ideas or done poorly in some of the early units of study will usually be handicapped in later study, but the sequence of development is seldom so rigidly fixed that his early lapses or deficiencies preclude later progress. Foreign language courses and courses in some branches of mathematics and engineering show more sequential dependence than those in other areas, but even in them the dependence is far from absolute.

For most courses of study the difference between good and poor students is less in how far they have gone than in how many things they have learned to know and to do. In such courses, and unless the students are extremely variable and the test extremely reliable, there is no need to vary the difficulty of the questions on purpose. Theoretical analyses and experimental studies demonstrate quite convincingly that in most situations questions that are neither very difficult nor very easy are best. Richardson, for example, found that

> ... a test composed of items of 50 percent difficulty has a general validity which is higher than tests composed of items of any other degree of difficulty.[14]

[14]Marion W. Richardson, "The Relation Between the Difficulty and the Differential Validity of a Test," *Psychometrika*, vol. 1 (1936) 33–49.

And Gulliksen concluded on the basis of a theoretical analysis that

> in order to maximize the reliability and variance of a test the items should have high intercorrelations, all items should be of the same difficulty level, and the level should be as near 50 percent as possible.[15]

DECIDE WHAT MEANS AND WHAT FORMAT TO USE IN PRESENTING THE TEST TO THE STUDENTS

Objective tests are almost always presented to students in printed booklets. Some careful attention to legibility and attractiveness in the arrangement and typing of the copy is usually well worthwhile. The use of separate answer sheets greatly simplifies scoring without adding seriously to the student's problem of response.

EXHIBIT 5.5

A Comparison of Listed and Tandem Responses

LISTED	TANDEM
What does religious tolerance mean?	What does religious tolerance mean? (1) Making all people belong to one church. (2) Believing everything in the Bible. (3) Believing in science instead of the church. (4) Allowing people to believe what they wish.
1. Making all people belong to one church	
2. Believing everything in the Bible	
3. Believing in science instead of the church	
*4. Allowing people to believe what they wish	

As illustrated in Exhibit 5.5 listing responses to multiple-choice items rather than arranging them in tandem makes the student's task easier. Considerable space can be saved if multuple-choice items are printed in double columns rather than across the page. Designation of alternatives by number is simple and convenient, unless many items include

---

[15]Harold Gulliksen, "The Relation of Item Difficulty and Inter-item Correlation to Test Variance and Reliability, "*Psychometrika* vol. 10 (1945) 79–91.

small-digit responses that might be confused with response numbers. In this case letters probably should be used.

If time limits for the test are generous, as they usually should be for achievement tests, the order of presentation of the items has little effect on student scores, as Sax and Cromack have reported.[16] If time is restricted, the items probably should be arranged in order of increasing difficulty. It is reasonable to suppose that to begin a test with one or two easy questions would help to lessen excessive test anxiety. It also seems reasonable to group together items that deal with the same area of subject matter. However, empirical evidence that these practices improve the validity of the test scores is difficult to obtain.

Oral presentation of true-false items can be reasonably satisfactory, but other item forms may be too complex for this means. Some instructors have been well satisfied with the projection of objective test items on a screen in a partly darkened room. The cost of slides or film strips may be less than that of paper and printing, and they may be more convenient to prepare. Further, problems associated with differences among students in rate of work will be largely eliminated. Experiments have shown that most students can be paced to respond to objective test items more quickly than they do when working at their own rates, with no decrease in accuracy of response and no appreciable increase in tension (see Chapter 7).

On the other hand, there are some obvious drawbacks to test administration by visual projection. The student's attention is not fixed so firmly on his own answer sheet. The job of the test administrator is more tedious and limiting. There must be enough light to facilitate marking the answer sheets, but not so much as to make reading the projected test item difficult. Finally, make-up examinations present a serious problem with projected tests. Hence it seems likely that most objective tests will continue to be presented in printed form.

Open-book examinations, in which the examinees are permitted to bring and use textbooks, references, and class notes, have attracted some interest and attention from instructors and educational research workers. Instructors have seen in them a strong incentive for students to study for ability to use knowledge rather than for ability simply to remember it. Such examinations also encourage instructors to eschew recall-type test questions in favor of interpretation and application types. In this light there is much to be said in favor of the open-book examination. On the other hand, students soon learn that the books and notes they bring with them to classes are likely to provide more moral than informational

---

[16]Gilbert Sax and Theodore R. Cromack, "The Effects of Various Forms of Item Arrangements on Test Performance," *Journal of Educational Measurement*, vol. 3 (1966), 309–11.

support. Looking up the facts or formulas needed may take considerable time. The student who tries to make much use of his references is likely to run out of time before completing the test.

Stalnaker reported favorably on experience with open-book examinations in Chicago.[17] Tussing, at El Camino College was also favorable.[18] He reached the following conclusions:

1. Open-book tests can be constructed and used in all the traditional test forms— essay, multiple-choice, true-false, and so forth.
2. Fear and emotional blocking are reduced.
3. There is less emphasis on memory of facts than on practical problems and reasoning.
4. Cheating is eliminated.
5. The approach is adaptable to the measurement of student attitudes.

An experimental comparison of scores on the same multiple-choice examination, administered as an open-book examination in one section and as a closed-book examination in another section of the same course in child psychology, was reported by Kalish.[19] He concluded that although "the group average scores are not affected by the examination approach, the two types of examinations measure significantly different abilities." Kalish also suggested some possible disadvantages of the open-book examination:

1. Study efforts may be reduced.
2. Efforts to overlearn sufficiently to achieve full understanding may be discouraged.
3. Note-passing and copying from other students are less obvious.
4. More superficial knowledge is encouraged.

The take-home test has some of the same characteristics as the open-book test, with an additional advantage and an additional disadvantage. The advantage is removal of the pressure of time, which often limits the effectiveness of a classroom open-book test as a true open-book test. The disadvantage is the loss of assurance that the answers a student submits represent exclusively his own achievements. For this reason the take-home test often functions better as a learning exercise than as an achievement test. Students may be permitted, even encouraged, to collaborate in seeking answers in which they have confidence. The efforts they sometimes put forth and the learning they sometimes achieve under these conditions can be a pleasant surprise to the instructor. But the take-home test must

---

[17]John M. Stalnaker and Ruth C. Stalnaker, "Open Book Examinations: Results," *Journal of Higher Education*, vol. 6 (1935), 214–16.

[18]Lyle Tussing, "A Consideration of the Open-Book Examination," *Educational and Psychological Measurement*, vol. 11 (1951), 597–602.

[19]Richard A. Kalish, "An Experimental Evaluation of the Open-Book Examination," *Journal of Educational Psychology*, vol. 49 (1958), 200–204.

be scored and the scores must count in order to achieve this result. Also, it probably goes without saying, the correct answers should be reported to the students, with opportunity for them to question and discuss. In this, as in most other situations involving the use of tests, it is hazardous to use a test of low or unknown quality. Student cross-examination can be devastating.

DETERMINE TO TEST IMPORTANT OUTCOMES OF INSTRUCTION

It may be important to conclude by reemphasizing the importance, as well as the difficulty, of one crucial area of decisions, the decisions on what to test. Some of the most serious weaknesses of classroom tests are due to uncritical acceptance of conventional answers to this question.

Many teachers admit that their tests do not adequately reflect the really important outcomes of their courses. Some are convinced that no test, and certainly no objective test, could adequately measure student achievement of these objectives. Others are skeptical of this view. They are persuaded that all defensible outcomes of education are inherently objective, and hence testable. The problems of educational measurement, they think, can be solved. So, obviously, do we.

SUMMARY

The principal ideas developed in this chapter may be summarized in 13 statements:

1. By using the same test twice in the same class, first as a supervised tests in class and then as an open-book, freely discussed take-home test, both the reliability of its scores and its value as a learning exercise can be enhanced.
2. More frequent testing tends to provide a more reliable basis for evaluation.
3. The form of a test gives no certain indication of the ability tested.
4. Multiple-choice and true-false items can be used to measure any aspect of cognitive educational achievement.
5. Other item types have more limited usefulness, but may be advantageous in certain circumstances.
6. Whatever form of test or type of item an examiner uses, he should seek to make his measurements as objective as possible.
7. Most classroom tests of achievement should be short enough, in relation to the time available, so that almost all students have time to attempt all of the items.
8. Items intended to test various aspects of achievement can ordinarily be classified more reliably on the basis of overt item characteristics than on the basis of the mental processes they presumably require.

9. Situational or interpretive test items tend to be inefficient, difficult to write, sometimes hard to defend, and unconvincing as measures of the higher mental processes.
10. An outline of topics dealt with in instruction provides a useful basis for developing test items that will sample the desired achievement representatively.
11. In most tests of achievement the items that contribute the greatest amount of useful information are those on which the proportion of correct response is halfway between 100 percent and the expected chance proportion.
12. Objective classroom tests usually are, and should be, presented in printed test booklets.
13. The most crucial decision the test constructor must make is what to test.

The teacher who, without experience or technical training, has endeavored to use objective tests for his own class has often been dissatisfied with the results and rightly so. . . . Nearly every teacher, however, considers himself fully capable of setting a satisfactory essay test in his own course or subject, and of reading the answers at least to his own satisfaction. . . . Norms, correlations, reader or test reliability, and validity do not worry the teacher. If he knows what they are, he ignores them in dealing with his own classroom situation. The popularity of the essay question should not, therefore, be misinterpreted to indicate that it is the most suitable form for many purposes, that it is in a "healthy" condition, or that improvements are not needed.

JOHN M. STALNAKER

6

THE CHARACTERISTICS AND USES OF ESSAY TESTS

SOME DIFFERENCES BETWEEN ESSAY AND OBJECTIVE TESTS

Two major forms of written classroom test are available for general use. These are essay tests (including, for convenience, tests based on numerical problems) and objective tests. One of the first problems of the constructor of a classroom test is to decide which type to use. There are some significant differences between the two that need to be considered in reaching this decision.

1. *An essay test question requires the student to plan his own answer and to express it in his own words. An objective test item requires him to choose among several designated alternatives.*

The task of composing an adequate, original answer to a novel question can be a revealing indication of the level of educational achievement. To recall relevant principles and factual details, the student must have command of an ample store of knowledge. He must be able to relate these facts and principles, to organize them into a coherent and logical progression, and then to do justice to these ideas in his written expression. Recall is involved in the composition of an answer to an essay test question, but it would be a gross oversimplification to characterize an essay test as *simply* a measure of recall.

It is also a gross oversimplification to characterize an objective test as simply a measure of recognition. The task of making a wise choice among superficially plausible alternative answers to a novel question can also be a revealing indication of educational achievement. In this case, also, the student must have command of a wealth of relevant principles and factual details. He must be able to relate these facts and principles and to organize them into a sound basis for decision.

It is sometimes suggested that objective tests are inevitably more superficial and less realistic tests of a student's knowledge than are essay tests, since in suggesting possible answers to him the examiner has done the more important part of his task for him. But most good objective test items require the examinee to develop, by creative, original thought, the *basis* for choice among the alternatives. Good objective test items do not permit correct response on the basis of simple recognition, sheer rote memory, or meaningless verbal association. Consider the nature of the thought processes involved in selecting an answer to this question.

> A child buys jelly beans which the grocer picks up, without regard for color, from a tray containing a mixture of jelly beans of three different colors. What is the smallest number of jelly beans the child can buy and still be certain of getting at least four jelly beans of the same color?

The answers provided are 4, 7, 10, and 12.

Assume that the examinee is seeing this particular problem for the first time, so that he cannot answer it successfully by simple recall of an answer that someone else has told him. Assume, too, that problems of this kind are not of sufficient practical importance to have been made the subjects of special study and direct teaching of techniques for solution. These assumptions call attention to an important general principle of educational measurement. What a test item measures, that is, what a successful response to it indicates, cannot be determined on the basis of the item alone. Consideration must also be given to the examinee's previous experiences. These may differ significantly for different examinees. But in the case of the foregoing problem, the assumptions mentioned above may be quite reasonable.

How much different would the thought processes be, and how much more difficult would the problem be, if no answers were suggested and the task required production of the answer rather than selection? Producing an answer is not necessarily a more complex or difficult task. or one more indicative of achievement, than choosing the best of the available alternatives.

In Cook's study, where the same questions were presented to college students in two forms of a test, one in which the student had to think of and write out an answer, the other in which he simply chose the best of several answers, the correlation between scores for the same students on the two forms was as high as would be expected if both of them were measuring the same achievement.[1] Table IX of Cook's unpublished dissertation shows a correlation of .97 between the scores for 152 college freshmen on two 60-item tests of knowledge of contemporary affairs, one composed of completion (free-response) items and the other of multiple-choice items. When this correlation was corrected for unreliability of the two tests (.87 for the completion test and .86 for the multiple-choice test) it rose to .99. This means that, within the limits of their accuracy of measurement, the two tests appeared to be measuring identical aspects of achievement. Further, as Sax and Collet report, both types seem equally effective in motivating student learning.[2]

Paterson, in a similar study conducted 32 years earlier, came to the same conclusion: ". . . there seems to be no escape from the conclusion that the two types of examinations are measuring identical things."[3]

The game of chess, which few would regard as a simple or superficial exercise in thinking, is essentially a multiple-choice test. At each move the player's problem is to choose the best of a limited number of alternatives. What the alternatives are is always fairly obvious. Even a novice can easily list all the moves permitted by the rules of the game in a particular situation. Ordinarily, a competent player would regard only a few of these as good possibilities. The test of his skill is in the quality of the choices he makes, in his perception of the implications and consequences of the choices he makes. The considerations that make one move better than another in the game of chess is similar in nature, though probably considerably more involved, than the considerations that make one alternative better than another in a good multiple-choice test question.

The making of choices among limited and clearly defined alternatives is a realistic part of the affairs of government, of business, and of ordinary living. Shall we use the atomic bomb or not? Shall we grant employee demands or risk a prolonged strike? Shall we vacation at the

---

[1]Desmond L. Cook, "An Investigation of Three Aspects of Free-response and Choice-type Tests at the College Level," *Dissertation Abstracts*, vol. 15 (1955), 1351.

[2]Gilbert Sax and LeVerne S. Collet, "An Empirical Comparison of the Effects of Recall and Multiple Choice Tests on Student Achievement," *Journal of Educational Measurement*, vol. 5 (1968), 169–73.

[3]Donald G. Paterson, "Do New and Old Type Examinations Measure Different Mental Functions?" *School and Society*, vol. 24. (August 21, 1926), 246–48.

shore or in the mountains? Leaders in government spend much time dealing with the questions that confront them by issuing statements (as if they were essay test questions) and by making choices (as if they were objective test questions). Skill in doing both is valuable to the leader, and leaders are seldom equally good at doing both. But if the populace had a clear choice between a man good at making statements but weak on decisions and another weak on making statements but good at making decisions, is there any doubt which they should choose? The first might find it easier to get elected, but the second would make a better leader.

The contribution of skill in written expression to success in answering essay test questions is both an advantage and a disadvantage. Written expression is an important skill. Essay tests encourage its cultivation and give practice in it (though the practice may sometimes be practice in *bad* writing—hasty, ill-considered, and unpolished). This is the advantage. The disadvantage is that skill in writing, or lack of it, may influence the scorer's judgement regarding the content of the answer. Uniform, legible handwriting and fluent, graceful sentences can compensate for some deficiencies in content. On the other hand, flaws in spelling, grammar, or usage can detract from the scorer's evaluation of the content.

2. *An essay test consists of relatively few, more general questions that call for rather extended answers. An objective test ordinarily consists of many rather specific questions requiring only brief answers.*

Relatively broad essay questions have the advantage of requiring more integration and organization of knowledge than do the more specific objective test questions. But it would not be correct to say that objective test questions deal only with isolated factual details, that they encourage the fragmentation of knowledge. On either an essay or an objective test, the student who has organized and integrated his knowledge, who understands what he knows, will fare better than one who has not. He will remember better what he has learned, and have it more readily available when a test question calls for its use.

The larger number of questions found typically in objective tests gives them a considerable advantage as reliable samples of a field of achievement. In general, the larger the number of independent elements in the sample of tasks used in an achievement test, the more accurately performance on those tasks will reflect achievement in the whole field. The answer to a complex essay test question often does involve many separate elements of achievement, but these are dealt with as a more or less integrated whole by both the student and the grader, not as independent elements.

Few, if any, experimental studies of the sampling reliability of essay tests relative to that of objective tests have been made. The difficulty of obtaining sufficiently reliable grading of essay test answers may be part of the reason. But there have been some theoretical analyses of the problem. Rush has illustrated the direct relation between the extensiveness of the sample of tasks in a test and the precision with which different levels of achievement can be differentiated.[4] Posey has shown that an examinee's luck, or lack of it, in being asked what he happens to know is a much greater factor in the grade he receive in a 10-question test than in one of 100 questions.[5] His charts, reproduced in Figure 6-1, show the distributions of expected scores for three students on three tests. One student is assumed to be able to answer 90 percent of all the questions that might be asked him on the subject of the test. Another is assumed to be able to answer 70 percent of such questions, and the third is assumed capable of answering only 50 percent of them. Of the three tests, one includes 10 questions, the second 20, and the third 100.

Now, suppose each of these three students took not just one 10-item test but 100 of them, with each test made up of 10 questions drawn at random from a supply of 1,000 questions, all different, but all on the same general subject. The 50 percent student is assumed to be able to give acceptable answers to 500 of the 1,000 questions. However, as the dotted line on the top chart shows, he could *not* expect to answer exactly 5 questions out of 10 acceptably on each of the 100 tests, because in the process of sampling some tests would include more, some less, of the questions he could answer.

The number of tests on which each of the three students could expect to make each of the 11 possible scores (zero to 10) is shown in Table 6.1.[6] Note that the 50 percent student could not expect a single score of 10 in all of the 100 tests: he could expect one score of 9, four of 8, and so on. Columns for the other two students can be interpreted similarly.

The variations in scores for these students on equivalent tests, which

---

[4]G. M. Ruch, *The Objective or New-type Examination* (Glenview, Ill.: Scott, Foresman and Company, 1929), p. 56.

[5]Chesley Posey, "Luck and Examination Grades," *Journal of Engineering Education* vol. 23 (1932) 292–96.

[6]Those who are mathematically inclined may know, or may be interested in learning, that the three "Number of tests" columns in Table 6.1 can be obtained

for the 50 percent student by expanding the binomial $(.5R + .5W)^{10}$

for the 70 percent student by expanding the binomial $(.7R + .3W)^{10}$

for the 90 percent student by expanding the binomial $(.9R + .1W)^{10}$

and reducing the coefficient of each term to a percent of the sum of all coefficients for the expanded binomial. The letters R and W refer to right and wrong answers, and their coefficients to the probability of giving a right or wrong answer.

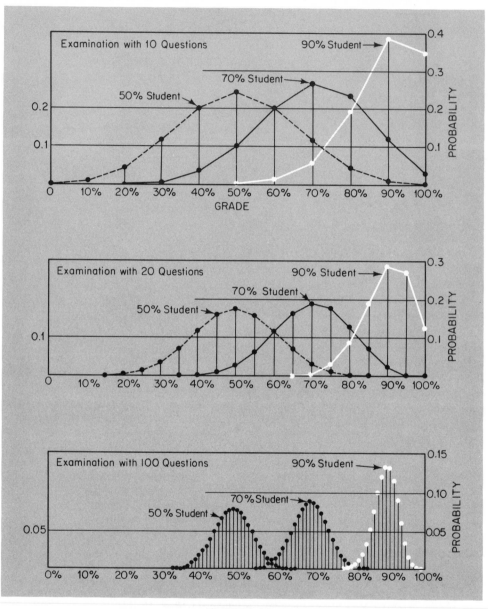

FIGURE 6.1

Relation of the Number of Questions in an Examination to the Sharpness of Discrimination of Different Levels of Ability. (*Source:* Chesley Posey, "Luck and Examination Grades," *Journal of Engineering Education,* vol. 23 (1932) 292–96. Reproduced by permission of Chesley Posey and the *Journal of Engineering Education.*)

TABLE 6.1.   SCORES OF THREE STUDENTS ON 100 10-QUESTION TESTS

| | *Number of Tests Yielding This Score For* | | |
Score	50 Percent Student	70 Percent Student	90 Percent Student
10	0	3	35
9	1	12	38
8	4	23	20
7	12	27	6
6	21	20	1
5	24	10	0
4	21	4	0
3	12	1	0
2	4	0	0
1	1	0	0
0	0	0	0
	100	100	100
Av. Score	5	7	9

differ only in the samples of questions used, are attributed to what are called sampling errors. More precisely, the sampling error is the difference between the score a student gets on a specific sample of questions and the average score he should expect to get in the long run on tests of that kind. Thus, the 50 percent student, whose long-run expectation is for a score of 5 on the 10-item tests, benefits from a sampling error of +4 (9 — 5) on one test and suffers from a sampling error of —4 (1 — 5) on another. There is zero sampling error (5 — 5) in the scores he receives on 24 of the tests. These kinds of sampling errors are present in practically all educational test scores. However, it is important to understand that they are not caused by mistakes in sampling. A perfectly chosen random sample will still be subject to sampling errors simply because it is a random sample.

The point of Posey's charts is that these sampling errors have less serious consequences when the samples are large (100-item tests) than when the samples are small (10-item tests). This is because the spread of scores, expressed as percents, becomes less as the number of questions in the test increases. With less spread there is less overlap in scores for students at different levels of ability. With less overlap, there is a smaller probability that the poorer student will get a higher test score than the better student. In the examination with 100 questions, there is very little chance of a 50 percent student scoring higher than a 70 percent student, and almost no chance of the 70 percent student scoring higher than the 90 percent student. In the examination with only 10 questions, both these chances are much greater.

3. Students spend most of their time in thinking and writing when taking an essay test. They spend most of their time reading and thinking when taking an objective test.

Just as skill in writing may be a somewhat irrelevant factor determining a student's grade on an essay test, so skill in reading may also be a somewhat irrelevant factor determining a student's grade on an objective test. In neither case, ordinarily, can we claim that the test is a pure measure of command of knowledge, uncontaminated by skills of expression or interpretation.

Perhaps a distinction should be made between the kind of routine thinking students do while they are reading an objective test question or writing an essay test answer and the kind of reflective thinking that precedes the writing or follows the reading. Measured in word units, reading is a much faster process than writing. The typical student can probably read at least ten times as many words per minute as he can write. If the objective test questions involve about the same number of words as the essay test answers, a student should be able to spend a greater proportion of his time in reflective thought when taking an objective test than when taking an essay test. Observation of student behavior in taking both kinds of tests indicates that this inference is probably warranted. It would be hard to prove that this fact makes objective tests better than essay tests, but it may help to answer the argument that they are seriously worse.

4. The quality of an objective test is determined largely by the skill of the test constructor. The quality of an essay test is determined largely by the skill of the reader of student answers.

One clear and intentional implication of this statement is that both essay and objective tests vary in quality. If the quality, as measures of educational achievement, were to be determined for all tests, both essay and objective, given at a particular educational institution in a specified year, it is almost a certainty that the difference in quality between the best and poorest of either type would be greater than the difference in quality between the best examples of the two types, or the poorest examples.

It is probably true, on the other hand, that the typical essay test falls farther short of its potential as a measure of educational achievement than does the typical objective test. Fewer systematic efforts are made to improve the quality of essay than of objective types. This may be due in part to the greater difficulty of obtaining data for analysis of essay test quality. It may also be due to the belief of some essay test users that quality is inherent in the form of the test and needs no confirmation or criticism from the statistician.

Writing good objective test items requires a high degree of skill in precise and meaningful verbal expression. Teachers of composition, who specialize in cultivating effective expression and who are themselves highly skilled in this art, should be encouraged to employ that skill more frequently in the writing of objective test items. Perhaps item writing may seem unattractive to some of them because it demands more conventional precision than creative imagination in expression. In item writing, perhaps unlike creative writing, the more nearly a sentence means exactly the same thing to every person who reads it (the less it leaves to the individual's imagination), the more claim it has to respect as an example of literary craftsmanship.

5. *An essay examination is relatively easy to prepare but relatively tedious and difficult to score accurately. A good objective examination is relatively tedious and difficult to prepare but relatively easy to score accurately.*

This difference sometimes is, and usually ought to be, the reason for choosing to use objective tests in some situations and essay tests in others. If a test is to be widely used, with large numbers of students, the instructor is likely to save time in the long run by taking time at the start to prepare a good objective examination. But if the test is destined for limited use, with relatively few students, the instructor is likely to save time by devoting little of it to the preparation of the test (that is, by using an essay test) and by devoting most of his time for the examination to reading the student responses.

Where the line is drawn between a wide-use test and a limited-use test will depend on the preferences of the instructor and on his relative facility as a writer of objective test items or a reader of essay test answers. Some instructors may find objective testing more efficient than essay testing with groups as small as 25. Others may prefer to use essay testing until the groups become larger than 50.

6. *An essay examination affords much freedom for the student to express his individuality in the answer he gives, and much freedom for the scorer to be guided by his individual preferences in scoring the answer. An objective examination affords much freedom for the test constructor to express his knowledge and values but gives the student only the freedom to show, by the proportion of correct answers he gives, how much or how little he knows or can do.*

Beyond any reasonable doubt, and objective test affords less freedom than an essay test. The behavior of both the student and the scorer is more fully controlled. Indeed, the essay test has sometimes to be characterized as a projective test, in which the student's interests and values do more than the examiner's questions to determine what the response will be.[7]

However attractive the word "freedom" and the concept it represents may be, we should remember that its values are specific, not universal. In some situations it is useful, in others harmful. A break in the steering mechanism can increase the freedom of motion of an automobile, perhaps disastrously. A cashier who exercises too much freedom in his use of company funds may get into trouble. Even the freedom that astronauts experience from the pull of gravity can create all kinds of problems.

To a considerable degree, freedom is the enemy of precision in measurement. The more precisely any magnitude is to be measured, the more fully the process of measurement must be described and standardized; the more carefully all the variables that might affect the result must be controlled. Because the objective test item does provide a more uniformly standardized, carefully controlled process of measurement than does the essay test, it is, and should be, regarded as a technical advance in the measurement of educational achievement.

The freedom of the student and the scorer in essay testing, and of the test constructor in objective testing, all contribute to the lack of accuracy, that is, to the unreliability of the scores obtained. To the extent that an essay test question allows a student to choose what he will write about, it permits different students to run different races, and thus increases the difficulty of comparing their performances. The scorer's freedom to express himself in his evaluations also contributes to the unreliability. This freedom also allows him to respond, in his evaluations, to what he already knows or believes about the student. A good answer from a poor student tends to be discounted. A poor answer from a good student tends to be evaluated more highly than its merits deserve.

Essay test scores are subject to irrelevant (or at least questionably relevant) influences such as quality of handwriting and correctness in spelling and grammar.[8] If the scorer reads one student's answers to all the test questions consecutively, instead of reading all students' answers to a single question consecutively, halo effects may distort the scores.[9] That is, if the student does well in answering the first questions, his scores will be higher on the succeeding questions than if he had done poorly on the first questions. Klein and Hart reported the disturbing conclusion that in the grading of essay tests given in law school courses in contracts, individuals who had no law training generally assigned the same grades to

---

[7]Verner M. Sims, "The Essay Examination Is a Projective Technique," *Educational and Psychological Measurement*, vol. 8 (1948), 15–31.

[8]Jon C. Marshall and Jerry M. Powers, "Writing Neatness, Composition Errors, and Essay Grades," *Journal of Educational Measurement*, vol. 6 (1969), 97–101.

[9]Clinton I. Chase, "The Impact of Some Obvious Variables on Essay Test Scores," *Journal of Educational Measurement*, vol. 5 (1968), 315–18.

the papers as did the professors who had taught the courses.[10] This suggests that what the test was measuring essentially was writing skill, not specialized knowledge of law.

Objective test items, particularly multiple-choice items, are sometimes charged with giving students the false idea that there is one and only one right answer to every question. Life really isn't that simple, it is pointed out. An essay test, which permits or encourages diverse answers, and on which the actual conclusion reached is less important than the cogency of the reasons for giving it, is claimed to be truer to life, and hence a better test.

Several aspects of this view warrant comment. It is not at all obvious, in the first place, that students ever do get a generally oversimplified conception of the nature of things by their exposure to the *form* of multiple-choice test items, which is what the critics object to. No evidence to support this contention seems to have been gathered. Nor is its truth obvious on logical grounds. On the contrary, a student who struggles to choose the best of several plausible possibilities, and who sometimes discovers later that his choice was not the best, is likely to be impressed by the complexity of the problem, and by the good case that can sometimes be made, as Banesh Hoffman has shown, for a second- or third-rate answer.[11]

If a test includes questions like these:

1. What is the best form of national government?
2. What is the optimum class size?
3. What is the function of religion?

and if the examinee, to get credit for proper knowledge must answer:

1. The parliamentary system
2. Twenty-five pupils
3. Preparation for eternal life

complaints are certainly in order. These answers *do* imply a simplicity that is seldom found in life to questions of this level of complexity.

The problem here is not in the form, but in the content of the questions. No doubt questions like the last three above have been asked, and answers like these have been expected, in some multiple-choice tests. But objective test items do not need to venture so far into the quicksands of opinion, bias, and dogma as the foregoing questions do. Nor do they need to be limited to such narrowly factual Who? What? When? Where? questions as:

[10]Stephen P. Klein and Frederick M. Hart, "Chance and Systematic Factors Affecting Essay Grades," *Journal of Educational Measurement*, vol. 5 (1968), 197–206.

[11]Banesh Hoffman, *The Tyranny of Testing* (New York: Crowell-Collier and Macmillan, 1962).

Who was the presidential candidate of the Republican party in 1948?
What is the square root of 1936?
In what year was the first artificial Earth satellite launched?
In what state was Abraham Lincoln born?

Between the first extreme of generalization and the second extreme of detail there is ample room for the test constructor to ask significant questions that permit defensible answers. Here are a few examples:

How did the Marshall Plan contribute to European recovery?
What determines the period of revolution of an Earth satellite?
Why does milk sour more quickly in a warm room than in a refrigerator?

When questions like these are used as the basis for multiple-choice test items, the "correct" answers offered are likely to be terse and incomplete. But if the item writer is skilled, such partial correct answers, combined with equally partial incorrect answers, can do all of the job that the test item is intended to do, that is, to discriminate sharply between those who are more capable and those who are less capable of producing an adequate answer to the question.

No brief answer to a complex question is likely to be as adequate as a more extended answer. But this does not mean that a student's command of knowledge related to the question can only be judged on the basis of an extended answer. Nor does it mean that a student of normal intelligence will ever mistake the terse expression of the essence of a correct response for a complete statement of all there is to say on the subject.

Some questions that we encounter in life are indeterminate in the present state of our knowledge. There is no consensus, even among experts, as to the correct answer. Different individuals or groups may believe strongly in quite different answers. It may sometimes be appropriate to refer to such a question in a test so as to determine the student's awareness that it is controversial, or his acquaintance with various points of view respecting it. But a test author should seldom ask such a question and accept only his view as the correct answer, even though he is fairly convinced that in time all other experts will come to agree with him. The scope of verified human knowledge is so wide that neither courses of instruction nor examinations need to hold students responsible for accepting specific beliefs that are being strongly challenged by others.

But for most questions there is sufficient consensus among experts to permit them to differentiate consistently a better answer from a poorer answer. This is all that is required to make the question determinate. If such a question also differentiates clearly between students of high and low achievement, it is likely to be useful in an objective test.

Essay test answers sometimes give the instructor clues to the student's thought processes. But the diverse and random nature of these clues, as well as the uncertainty that the reader will notice them or interpret them correctly, means that they seldom provide reliable indices of the general quality of the student's thought.

The writers of essay test questions sometimes deliberately choose indeterminate issues as the basis for their questions. What the student concludes, they say, is unimportant. The evidence on which he bases his conclusion and the cogency of his arguments in support of it are said to be all-important. These are probably the best justifications that can be afforded for the use of controversial, indeterminate questions in an examination. That they provide an adequate justification is open to question, for more direct, specific, and reliable tests of a student's command of relevant knowledge are available. More direct, specific, and reliable tests of his ability to differentiate sound from unsound arguments are also available. It is difficult to discern any good reason for testing these aspects of achievement by the indirect means and in the poorly controlled setting provided by an indeterminate test question.

The suggestion that the examiner should be more concerned with the student's processes of thinking than with the conclusions he reaches also deserves a close look. There ought to be a reasonably close relation between quality of thought and quality of conclusions. Rarely, by accident, a student might reach the proper conclusion for the wrong reasons. Usually, reaching correct conclusions will require the use of the correct evidence and thought processes. It is impossible in principle for wholly adequate evidence and reasoning to lead to faulty conclusions. In general, a process of thinking can be no better than the conclusion it leads to. Whether the thing produced is an idea or on automobile, the quality of the process of production will always be judged, in the long run, by the quality of the thing it produces.

7. *In objective test items the student's task and the basis on which the examiner will judge the degree to which it has been accomplished are stated more clearly than they are in essay tests.*

Essay test questions can be highly definite, accompanied by detailed, explicit directions to the student. Often they are not. The scoring of answers to essay test questions can also be guided by detailed, explicit directions. Often it is not. The more detailed and explicit the directions to both student and scorer, the more objective and reliable the measurements obtainable from an essay test question.

The fact that objective test items are more definite and explicit than typical essay test questions helps to account for the much more frequent criticisms of the objective test items. Many of these criticisms allege that the best answer is inadequate or that one of the wrong answers is, in fact, as good as, or better than, the answer designated as correct. The source of the trouble is the provision of answers along with the questions, and with the indication that one of these is better than the others.

Essay test questions escape these hazards by leaving the student to create an explicit answer and allowing the scorer to rate its adequacy without producing his own version of an ideal answer or describing the basis of quantifying the difference he perceives between the student's answer and his ideal. The deficiencies of an essay question are seldom so readily available for observation as those of an objective test item.

8. *An objective test permits, and occasionally encourages, guessing. An essay test permits, and occasionally encourages, bluffing.*

A student could guess blindly at the answers to an objective test. If the test were very short and simple, say 10 true-false test items, he might even expect to get a perfect score by blind guessing, once in about every thousand attempts. If he is very poorly prepared, or if the test is inordinately difficult, he might accidentally get a higher score by blind guessing than he would get by considering carefully his response to each question. But seldom if ever would he *expect* to do better by blind guessing. Hence, while blind guessing is possible on an objective test, it is seldom likely to be profitable.

Nor is it likely to be prevalent. Students guess blindly on an examination only when they have no knowledge relevant to the question whatsoever, only when they are running out of time, or when they have run out of the motivation necessary to make the effort to select an answer on rational grounds. The alternative to blind guessing is not certainty of response, but rational consideration of the response. If the student has any knowledge whatever relevant to the questions and if he uses that knowledge to the best of his ability, he is not guessing blindly and his answer to the test question contributes usefully to the measurement of his achievement.

The greater the contribution that blind guessing makes to the determination of student's scores on an examination, the lower the reliability of those scores. If all students were to guess blindly on the answers to all the items in an objective test, the expected value for the reliability of their scores would be zero. Hence, if scores on an objective test show high reliability, it is safe to conclude that the role played by guessing in determining those scores was small. (However, low reliability does not necessarily indicate a large amount of guessing.)Thus, though the possibility and occurrence of guessing on objective tests cannot be denied, the seriousness of its influence on objective test scores is often overestimated.

A corresponding weakness of essay tests is bluffing. A student who is hard put to answer adequately the question asked can transform it subtly into a related question that is easier for him to answer. If he does the task he has substituted for the examiner's task well, the reader may not even notice the substitution. Or the student may concentrate on form rather than on content, on elegant presentation of a few rather simple ideas, in the hope that this may divert the reader's attention to the lack of substantial content.

Not all readers of essay examinations are easy to bluff. Students likely to be most in need of the kind of assistance that bluffing might give them are unlikely to be talented in the art of bluffing. Like guessing on objective tests, the seriousness of the problem of bluffing on essay tests can easily be overestimated.

> 9. *The distribution of numerical scores obtained from an essay test can be controlled to a considerable degree by the grader; that from an objective test is determined almost entirely by the test.*

For most objective tests the maximum possible raw score is determined by the number of questions on the test. Each correct response usually contributes one score unit. Each incorrect response contributes nothing and may, in some cases, result in subtraction of a fraction of a score unit. On a good test the lowest score obtained by any examinee is likely to be not far above the score that might be obtained by blind guessing.

For most essay tests the maximum possible raw score, as well as the minimum passing score, can be determined by the grader. Often the maximum number of points allowed for each of the questions is set so that the maximum possible score on the whole test is 100. Whether the grader allows no points, five points, or even seven points for a seriously inadequate answer is a matter for his own decision. Thus, no matter how inappropriate an essay test may be in difficulty, the grader can adjust his standards so some, but not too many, will receive scores below some preset minimum passing score.

For these reasons the problem of test item difficulty is of much greater concern to those who construct objective tests than it is to those who construct essay tests. Also, the hazards of a predetermined passing score are much greater on an objective than on an essay test.

Some graders of essay test questions will insist that they are not influenced by concern over how many will fail in their grading of essay test answers. They will claim to use *absolute* standards, based on their judgments of how well a student ought to do on a question of the kind being graded. But research studies like those of Starch and Elliott suggest that these so-called absolute standards are, in fact, highly personal and subjective.[12] Reliance on such *absolute* standards, in preference to relative standards (that is, those determined by the performances of other students in the group) almost inevitably lowers the precision of the measurements obtained from essay tests.

SOME SIMILARITIES OF ESSAY AND OBJECTIVE TESTS

The foregoing nine statements call attention to some of the differences between essay and objective tests. There are also some respects in which they are alike.

> *1. Either an essay or an objective test can be used to measure almost any important educational achievement that any written test can measure.*

The "almost" in the foregoing statement is required by the fact that no good objective tests of certain achievements, like the quality of a student's handwriting, exist or are likely to be produced. His spelling ability can be tested objectively. His vocabulary can be tested objectively. His ability to punctuate, capitalize, and apply the principles of grammar and rhetoric can be tested objectively. One substantial study showed that objective tests of ability in written composition correlate more highly with teacher estimates of that ability, based on extensive observation, than do scores on typical essay tests of ability in written composition.[13]

Many of the traits that essay tests have been said to measure, such as critical thinking, originality, and ability to organize and integrate, are not at all clearly defined. The characteristics of answers to essay test questions that serve to indicate which students have more and which have less of these traits are seldom described or illustrated. When the scores awarded to essay test answers are explained or defended, when the reasons why a student did not get the maximum possible on a question are specified, they usually turn out to be some combination of these deficiencies:

1. Incorrect statements were included in the answer.
2. Important ideas necessary to an adequate answer were omitted.
3. Correct statements having little or no relation to the question were included.
4. Unsound conclusions were reached, either because of mistakes in reasoning or because of misapplication of principles.

[12]Daniel Starch and E. C. Elliott, "Reliability of Grading High School Work in English," *School Review*, vol. 20 (1912), 442–57.

[13]Marjorie Olsen, *Summary of Main Findings on the Validity of the 1955 College Board General Composition Tests.* (Princeton, N.J.: Educational Testing Service, 1956).

5. Bad writing obscured the development and exposition of the student's ideas.
6. There were egregious errors in spelling and the mechanics of correct writing.

Mistakes in the first four categories can be attributed either to weaknesses in the student's command of knowledge or to lack of clarity and specificity in the examiner's question. Mistakes in the last two categories indicate weakness in the student's ability in written expression or reflect the difficulties of the hand in keeping up with a mind racing ahead under the pressure of a time-limit test. As essay tests are typically used, the unique functions they have that are beyond the scope of objective tests seem somewhat limited and indefinite. Odell's scales for rating essay test answers suggest strongly that the length of a student's answer may be closely related to the score it receives.[14] Longer answers tend to receive the higher ratings.

2. *Either an essay or an objective test can be used to encourage students to study for understanding of principles, organization and integration of ideas, and application of knowledge to the solution of problems.*

That the nature of the examination expected affects the preparation students make for it is attested by experience, reason, and research.[15] Surveys of student opinion about thirty years ago suggested that students then studied more thoroughly in preparation for essay examinations than for objective examinations. More recent evidence is scanty and inconclusive.

With respect to the influence of examinations on study, the really important question is not how students *say* they study for examinations of different kinds, or even how they *actually* do study, but how these differences affect their achievement. In the absence of adequate evidence on this point, which may be difficult to get, we may turn to some inferences that seem to be reasonable.

1. The kind of study and achievement that a test stimulates is probably more a function of the kind of questions asked on it than of the mode of student response.
2. To the degree that tests in different form measure the same kinds or aspects of achievement, they should stimulate the same kind of study and have the same effect on achievement.

[14]Charles W. Odell, *Scales for Rating Pupils' Answers to Nine Types of Thought Questions in English Literature* (Urbana, Ill.: University of Illinois, Bureau of Educational Research, 1927).
[15]George Meyer, "An Experimental Study of the Old and New Types of Examination: II, Methods of Study," *Journal of Educational Psychology*, vol. 26 (1935), 30–40; and Paul W. Terry, "How Students Review for Objective and Essay Tests," *Elementary School Journal*, vol. 33 (1933), 592–603.

An illustration of the use of essay and objective questions to test essentially the same educational achievement is given in Exhibits 6.1 and 6.2. These tests were devised for use in a dental prosthetics test. The instructor had always used essay questions but was interested in the more reliable scores and greater convenience in scoring that objective tests might afford. He was dubious, however, about the possibility of writing a number of independent objective test items relating to the same complex process without having one question give away the answer to another.

EXHIBIT 6.1

Essay Test Question and Answer

Q. Sometimes a bridge will not go in place properly when being tried in the mouth after being soldered. If the operator should consider it advisable or necessary to unsolder, reassemble, and resolder the bridge, describe how this should be done.

A. The operator should first determine which joint or joints are to be unsoldered. The parts of the bridge should never be separated with a saw or disc, as this leaves a wide space to be filled in with solder. Instead, the bridge should be held in a blow-torch flame in such a way that the flame is directed on the joint to be unsoldered. Only enough heat must be used to melt the solder, and care must be used not to melt or distort an abutment piece.

When the parts of the bridge have been separated, they should be pickled in acid to clean them of oxide. It will be necessary to use a disc or stone to smooth and reduce the amount of solder at the joints before the bridge will go into place in the mouth. This must be done till all parts of the bridge can be reassembled in the mouth.

Place some Parr's flux wax on all contact points of the abutment pieces and pontics (this is done with the pieces outside the mouth), then place all pieces back in the mouth. The Parr's flux wax will hold the parts in place, and the wax is soft enough so the pontics can be moved around to a certain extent to get them in the right position. When positioned properly, the joints should be reinforced with sticky wax, which is hard and brittle and will hold the parts firmly together. Then to further reinforce and strengthen the bridge so the parts will not be disarranged while taking the impression, a short piece of wire about 16 gauge should be bent and placed along the buccal or labial surface of the bridge and the approximating teeth and held firmly in place with sticky wax. All this waxing must be done with the field perfectly dry because any moisture will positively prevent the wax from holding.

Then a small, shallow impression tray is selected, filled with a fast-setting impression plaster and a shallow occlusal impression (if for a posterior bridge) or lingual and incisal impression (if for an anterior bridge) is secured. The impression is removed from the mouth, the bridge also removed and reassembled in the impression, the joints filled with Parr's flux wax, the plaster impression given a coat of separating medium, and the exposed parts of the bridge covered with soldering investment. When the investment is set, the plaster impression is cut away and more soldering investment applied in the proper manner to provide for correct soldering. The case is now ready to be heated and soldered in the regular way.

EXHIBIT 6.2

Corresponding Multiple-choice Items

The following eight items deal with the problem of separating, reassembling, and resoldering a bridge that will not go into place properly after being soldered.

1. Which joint or joints should be separated?
   a. The joint between pontics and smallest abutment piece
   b. Any single joint (the faulty joint must be located by trial and error)
   c. All that were originally soldered
   *d. Only the one or ones which appear responsible for the failure to fit

   Note: Only one of the following two items should be used.

2. Should the joints be separated using a saw or disc rather than heat?
   a. No, because the saw might damage the original castings
   *b. No, because the saw will leave too large a gap to be filled with solder
   c. Yes, because the use of heat might damage the original castings
   d. Yes, because the saw leaves a clean joint ready for resoldering

3. Should the flame be concentrated on the joint to be unsoldered? Why?
   a. No, because the bridge may crack if heated unevenly
   b. No, because the abutments must be thoroughly heated before the solder will melt
   *c. Yes, avoid damage to the other pieces
   d. Yes, to avoid delay in separation

4. After the bridge has been separated what, if anything, needs to be done before reassembling it in the patient's mouth?
   *a. The pieces should be cleaned in acid, and the joints smoothed with a stone
   b. The pieces should be cleaned in acid, but the joints should not be smoothed
   c. The joints should be smoothed, but the pieces need not be cleaned in acid
   d. Reassembling should begin as soon as the bridge has been separated

5. What is used initially to hold the pieces together on reassembly in the patient's mouth?
   a. Sticky wax
   *b. Parr's flux wax
   c. Impression plaster
   d. Soldering investment

6. Which of the following materials—flux wax, sticky wax, metal wire, and soldering investment—are used to hold the pieces of the reassembled bridge in place prior to taking the impression?
   a. All of them
   b. All but metal wire
   *c. All but soldering investment
   d. Only flux wax and sticky wax

7. What precaution is necessary in using sticky wax?
   a. It must not be allowed to touch gum tissues.
   b. It must be applied in separate thin layers to avoid cracking.
   c. The surface to which it is applied must be moist.
   *d. The surface to which it is applied must be dry.

8. What function does the plaster impression have in the process of resoldering the bridge?
   *a. It holds the parts in place while soldering investment is applied.
   b. It holds the parts in place while they are being soldered.
   c. It permits the resoldered bridge to be checked before insertion in the patient's mouth.
   d. It has no function in resoldering the bridge.

To explore this possibility, the professor of dentistry supplied an essay test question and an ideal answer to it. This is displayed in Exhibit 6.1. Then a series of multiple-choice items were written on the basis of this essay-type answer. Eight of these are shown in Exhibit 6.2. Items 2 and 3 are interlocking items. That is, the question asked in item 3 gives some clues as to the best answer to item 2. Hence only one of the two items should be used in any one test.

In view of the many potent factors other than examinations that affect how, and with what success, students study, in view also of the fact that these factors may interact in complex ways to facilitate or to inhibit learning, the chances are small that research will ever demonstrate clearly that either essay or objective tests have the more beneficial influence on study and learning.

3. *The use of both types involves the exercise of subjective judgments.*

In objective testing the subjectivity is concentrated in the process of test construction. In essay testing it affects both the selection and statement of the test questions and the evaluation of student answers. Good objective test construction aims to make the selection of things to test, and the preparation and selection of items to test them, as objective as possible. Good essay testing aims to make the standards for judging the quality of student answers as objective as possible.

The subjectivity of judgments can be reduced by the pooling of expert opinions. This is done in the construction of objective tests for use in wide-scale testing programs by the appointment of committees of examiners to develop the test specifications and to review the individual test items. It is done in the reading of essay answers in a wide-scale testing program by the appointment of committees of readers who develop standards for judging the answers and who compare their scoring of selected answers to achieve as much uniformity as possible. Instructors can seldom manage the extra assistance and effort that these procedures require, but they do represent a standard of excellence to be approached as closely as possible, as often as possible.

4. The value of scores from either type of test is dependent on their objectivity and reliability.

The score on any test is a means of communicating and recording a measurement or an evaluation. It is useful only insofar as it is meaningful. It must mean something to the person who determined it, not only at the moment of determination, but days or weeks later. It must mean as nearly as possible the same thing to the student who receives it as it did to the teacher who assigned it. To the degree that other qualified observers would assign different scores, the measurement lacks objectivity and hence utility. Measurements of school achievement, like other reports, must be trustworthy in order to be useful. To be trustworthy means that they are capable of independent verification. If the same teacher were to assign totally different scores to the same essay test answer on different occasions, or if different teachers were to disagree in the same way, our confidence in the scores would be shaken and their usefulness diminished.

From this point of view, objectivity is an essential characteristic of any measurement, including any test score, whether the score is derived from an objective test or from an essay test. Just as some degree of subjectivity is involved in measuring achievement by means of either essay or objective tests, so some degree of objectivity is essential in the scores that those tests yield.

Some aspects of educational achievement can be measured with high objectivity more easily than other aspects. Some aspects of educational achievement are more important than others. Unfortunately, the most important things are not necessarily the easiest to measure objectively. (We should beware, however, of the fallacy of assuming that if an aspect of education is hard to measure objectively, it is, ipso facto, important—or that if it is easy to measure objectively, it is, ipso facto, trivial.)

We cannot afford to shun the measurement of important aspects of educational achievement simply because it is hard to measure them objectively. But it would be equally bad to settle for alleged measures of these aspects of achievement that are seriously lacking objectivity.

WHEN TO USE ESSAY OR OBJECTIVE TESTS

On the basis of these considerations of the differences and similarities between essay and objective tests, some general recommendations can be summarized.

Use essay tests in the measurement of educational achievement when:

1. The group to be tested is small, and the test should not be reused.
2. The instructor wishes to do all possible to encourage and reward the development of student skill in written expression.
3. The instructor is more interested in exploring the student's attitudes than in measuring his achievements. (Whether an instructor *should* be more interested in attitudes than achievement and whether he should expect an honest expression of attitudes in a test he will evaluate, seem open to question.)
4. The instructor is more confident of his proficiency as a critical reader than as an imaginative writer of good objective test items.
5. Time available for test preparation is shorter than the time available for test grading.

Use objective tests in the measurement of educational achievement when:

1. The group to be tested is large, or the test may be reused.
2. Highly reliable test scores must be obtained as efficiently as possible.
3. Impartiality of evaluation, absolute fairness, and freedom from halo effects are essential.
4. The instructor is more confident of his ability to express objective test items clearly than of his ability to judge essay test answers correctly.
5. There is more pressure for speedy reporting of scores than for speedy test preparation.

Use either essay or objective tests to:

1. Measure almost any important educational achievement a written test can measure.
2. Test understanding and ability to apply principles.
3. Test ability to think critically.
4. Test ability to solve novel problems.
5. Test ability to select relevant facts and principles, to integrate them toward the solution of complex problems.
6. Encourage students to study for command of knowledge.

There may be some teachers who tend to use objective tests when essay tests would serve their purposes better. There certainly are many teachers who tend to use essay tests when objective tests would do a better job of measuring educational achievement. Why are essay tests used so widely? Partly, it may be a matter of tradition. It may be due in part to the belief that objective testing demands more technical skill than they possess. It may be that they know the faults of essay tests are easier to hide than those of objective tests. The main reason, however, is probably their belief, usually unwarranted, that essay tests do a better overall job than objective tests of measuring educational achievement and have a more beneficial effect on student learning.

Essay tests have important uses in educational measurement. They also have serious limitations. It would be well for all teachers to be aware of both. They ought to be on guard against unsubstantiated claims that essay tests can measure undefined and only vaguely perceived "higher-order mental abilities." They ought to question the propriety of using essay tests to determine how well students can do what the instructor has not really tried to teach them to do—to analyze, to synthesize, to organize, to develop original ideas and to express them with clarity, grace, wit, and correctness. Above all, they ought to avoid using an essay test when an objective test could do the job better and more easily.

SUGGESTIONS FOR PREPARING ESSAY TESTS

Both essay and objective tests can make important contributions to the measurement of educational achievement. Although they differ in significant ways and although there are specific situations in which one or the other is especially appropriate, they are to a considerable extent interchangeable. More important than which form is used is how well it is used. Test specialists have paid less attention to the improvement of essay tests than they have to the improvement of objective tests, but this does not mean that essay tests may not be improved.

The most basic and general suggestion for the improvement of essay tests is that the perfomance of essay tests should be evaluated systematicaly against objective standards of test quality set in advance by the test constructor himself. A number of possible standards of quality are suggested in the chapter on judging test quality.

One of the most important standards of quality, and one that has been emphasized in this chapter, is test reliability. In the case of essay tests, score reliability is affected significantly by the reliability with which the answers are read and graded, that is, by the agreement between the grades of different readers. Provision for this kind of check as part of the evaluation of test perfomance would be most desirable.

The quality of the individual questions in an essay test, as reflected in their difficulty and discriminating power, can also be determined by techniques described in Chapter 14. Revision or replacement of items that are too easy or too difficult, that fail to discriminate well for other reasons, or that result in student answers on whose scoring readers tend to disagree will help considerably to improve test reliability. If the items in the test are not to be reused, such an analysis may suggest the kinds of items, or the characteristics of items, most likely to contribute to test reliability. Hence the analysis will contribute indirectly to the improvement of essay tests.

Implicit in what has been said in this chapter about the values and limitations of essay tests are a number of suggestions for improving the questions of which these tests are composed.

1. Ask questions, or set tasks, that will require the student to demonstrate his command of essential knowledge.

Such questions will not simply call for reproduction of materials presented in the textbook or elsewhere. Instead of looking exclusively backward to the past course of instruction, they will also look forward to future applications of the things learned. The questions will be based on novel situations or problems, not on the same ones as were used for instructional purposes.

Many different types of questions may be used as the basis for essay (or objective) test questions. An outline of types of thought questions found in science textbooks has been prepared by Curtis.[16] Similar lists in other subject areas have been prepared by Wesley[17] and by Monroe and Carter.[18]

2. Ask questions that are determinate, in the sense that experts could agree that one answer is better than another.

Indeterminate questions are likely to function in some measure as exercises in exposition, whose relation to effective behavior may be quite remote. Such questions may not be highly relevant to the measurement

[16]Francis D. Curtis, "Types of Thought Questions in Textbooks of Science," *Science Education*, vol. 27 (1943), 60–67.

[17]Edgar B. Wesley and Stanley P. Wronski, *Teaching Social Studies in High Schools*, 4th ed. (Boston: D. C. Heath & Company, 1958), pp. 356–57.

[18]Walter S. Monroe and Ralph E. Carter, *The Use of Different Types of Thought Questions in Secondary Schools and Their Relative Difficulty for Students*, University of Illinois Bulletin, Vol. 20, No. 34 (April 13, 1923).

of a student's useful command of essential knowledge. Further, and most importantly, the absence of a good best answer may make it much more difficult for a reader to judge the student's competence from the answer he gives. On controversial questions, which many indeterminate questions are, the reader's opinions and biases may have considerable influence on his evaluation of the student's answer.

3. *Define the examinee's task as completely and specifically as possible without interfering with measurement of the achievement intended.*

The question should be carefully phrased so that the examinee fully understands what he is expected to do. If it is not clearly evident in the question itself, add an explanation of the basis on which his answer will be evaluated. Do not allow him more freedom than is necessary to measure the desired achievement. If the question permits variation in the extent and detail of the answer given and if you are not testing his judgment on this point, specify about how long his answer is expected to be.

4. *In general, give preference to more specific questions that can be answered more briefly.*

The larger the number of independently scorable questions, the higher the sampling reliability of the test is likely to be. Narrower questions are likely to be less ambiguous to the examinee and easier for scorers to grade reliably. Occasionally the instructor may be required, in order to test some essential aspects of student achievement, to base an essay test on only a few very broad questions. These occasions are not frequent, however, and the instructor should be sure that the need for extended answers is sufficient to warrant the probable loss in score reliability.

5. *Avoid giving the examinee a choice among optional questions unless special circumstances make such options necessary.*

If different examinees answer different questions, the basis for the comparability of their scores is weakened, The scores are likely to be somewhat less variable when students choose the questions they can answer best than when students must answer all the same questions. Hence the reliability of the scores would be expected to be somewhat less. Experimental studies indicate that this expectation is justified.

Meyer found that when college students in psychology were given the choice of omitting one of five essay questions, only 58 percent of them omitted the question on which they would do least well. He "suggested that unless the various questions are weighted in some suitable fashion the choice form of essay examination be discontinued."[19] Stalnaker concluded a survey of the problems involved in the use of optional questions with these words:

> No experimental evidence has been published to show that skills and abilities can be adequately sampled by the use of optional questions; on the other hand, several studies have shown that optional questions complicate measurement and introduce factors of judgment which are extraneous to the ability being measured. For sound sampling, it is recommended that optional questions be avoided and that all examinees be asked to run the same race.[20]

Optional questions are sometimes justified on the ground that giving the student a choice of the questions he is to answer makes the test "fairer" to him. But if all the questions involve, as they ordinarily can, essential aspects of achievement in a course, it is not unfair to any student to ask him to answer all of them. Further, an opportunity to choose among optional questions may not help the well-prepared student at all. It may help the poorly prepared student considerably. This does not make the test fairer to all concerned.

Optional questions may be justifiable when a test of educational achievement must cover a broad area, and when the students who take it have been trained in only part of the whole area. Even in such a situation, however, the advantages of using optional questions may not outweigh the disadvantages. Optional tests, separately scored, might be preferable to a common test, yielding a single score, based on different sets of questions.

6. Test the question by writing an ideal answer to it.

Writing the ideal answer at the time the question is drafted serves an immediate purpose. It gives the test constructor a check on the reasonableness of the questions and the adequacy of his statement of it. He may see how some change in the question could make the question easier, if that seems desirable, or more discriminating, which is always desirable. Also useful, if it can be arranged, is to have someone else who should be able to answer the question try to answer it. Comparison of his answer with that of the test constructor's might shed additional light on its suitability and might suggest additional ways of improving it.

---

[19]George Meyer, "The Choice of Questions on Essay Examinations," *Journal of Educational Psychology*, vol. 30 (1939), 161–71.

[20]John M. Stalnaker, "The Essay Type of Examination," in E. F. Lindquist, ed., *Educational Measurement* (Washington, D.C.: American Council on Education, 1951), p. 506.

The deferred purpose served by drafting an ideal answer to each essay test question is to provide guidance, and a point of reference, for the instructor when he begins to grade the student's answers. If someone other than the instructor is to grade the questions or to help with the grading, the ideal answer is almost indispensable to uniformity in grading.

SUGGESTIONS FOR GRADING ESSAY TESTS

As has been mentioned, the quality of the measurement of educational achievement that results from the use of essay tests is heavily dependent on the quality of the grading process. The competence of the grader is the key to the quality of this process, and no suggestions given here can compensate for deficiencies in that competence. But even competent graders may inadvertently do things that make the results less reliable than they ought to be. Here are some suggestions for the grader of essay test answers to consider if he is anxious to make his work as precise as possible.

1. Use either analytic scoring or global-quality scaling.

In analytic scoring, crucial elements of the ideal answer are identified and scored more or less separately. The higher the proportion of these crucial elements appearing in the student's answer and the less they are contaminated by inaccuracies or irrelevancies, the higher the student's score. Analytic scoring can pay attention not only to the elements of an ideal answer, but also to relations between these elements, that is, to the organization and integration of the answer. But if these relationships are complex and subtle, analytic scoring may prove to be too cumbersome and tedious to be effective.

An illustration of competent and painstaking analytic scoring of essay test answers is provided by the procedures of the Examination Service of the American Institute of Certified Public Accountants.

During the first eight to ten days after the examination, the section chairmen and the reviewers develop the grade sheets, the grading guides, and the notes for the reviewers. The grade sheets for each subject indicate the acceptable items in the answers and their assigned weights. One grade sheet is attached to each candidate's papers; it becomes a permanent record of the points earned. The grading guide describes the concepts, ideas, reasons, entries, amounts, and other items which constitute an acceptable answer; it also provides instructions on how to interpret certain items that may appear on the candidates' papers as well as instructions covering the techniques of grading and scoring. A copy of the grading guide is given to each grader and reviewer.[21]

An alternative is global-quality scaling. In using this method. the grader simply reads the answer for a general impression of its adequacy. He may transform that impression into a numerical grade, record the grade, and go on to the next answer. A better procedure, providing the grader with an opportunity to check the consistency of his grading standards as applied to different papers, involves the sorting of answers into several piles corresponding to different levels of quality. Sorting before marking permits, even encourages, the grader to reconsider his decisions in the light of experience with all the students' answers. It lessens the probability that he would give a higher score to one of two answers which, on rereading, seem to be of equal quality.

Scorers who use the sorting process in connection with global-quality scaling of answers usually try to make the size of each pile approximate some predetermined ideal. That is, they may try to put about the same number in each pile. Or they may try to approximate a normal distribution. With three piles the approximate goals might be:

Low	Middle	High
25%	50%	25%

or with five piles:

Lowest	Lower	Middle	Higher	Highest
5%	25%	40%	25%	5%

Scorers sometimes find it advantageous to use a three-stage process of sorting, dividing the answers after initial reading into three approximately equal piles in the first stage and then subdividing each of these after rereading into three more piles, yielding nine levels of quality in all. The third step in the process is to compare the papers in level 6 (upper third of the original middle group). with those in level 7 (lower third of the original upper group), to make sure that the level-7 papers are actually better than those in level 6. Papers from the upper third of the original lower group (level 3) would also be compared for the same purpose with those from the lower third of the original middle group (level 4).

How many piles to use in the sorting and whether to make the intended distribution equal across piles or roughly normal are matters of preference and convenience. The more piles used, the greater the precision of scoring, provided the answers differ enough, and the scorer is perceptive enough to make confident, reliable decisions as to the classifications of the individual papers.

[21] Association of Certified Public Accountant Examiners, *Report of the CPA Examination Appraisal Commission* (New York: ACPAE, 1961), p. 24.

As part of one dental aptitude test, examinees are required to carve a lump of plaster into some regular shape, such as the block letter "I" shown in Figure 6.2.[22] The lump of plaster supplied to the student has only one smooth flat side to start with. The examinee's task, using a carving

FIGURE 6.2
Block Carving Shape for a Dental Aptitude Test

knife, is to produce an object that resembles the specified shape as closely as possible and on which all angles are right angles, all edges are straight lines, and all surfaces flat.

Initially, the grader scored these objects analytically, measuring and scoring each angle, each edge and each surface. The process seemed more tedious than necessary. The alternative of holistic scoring was tried. The judge would look at each block and then place it on one of several piles graded from "excellent" to "awful." Holistic scoring seemed to yield slightly more consistent ratings for the same student from block to block or from judge to judge than analytic scoring.

As a general rule, global-quality scaling is simpler and faster than analytic scoring. In some situations it may be more reliable. But it does not provide any clear justification of the grade assigned, nor does it give any indication to the student of how his answer fell short of the mark. Analytic scoring can provide such indications It is well suited to questions that are likely to elicit detailed, uniformly structured answers.

An elemental type of analytic scoring, based on frequency of uncommon words, frequency of prepositions, frequency of commas, length of the answer, and other easily quantifiable overt characteristics, has been used by Page in his procedure for grading essays by computer.[23] He has shown that the grades given by the computer agree with those given by human judges about as well as the human judges agree with each other. But since the intercorrelations averaged 0.53 this finding provides no strong support for the reliability of essay test grades obtained by this means. The relevance of grades based on these characteristics is equally open to question.

---

[22]R. V. Smith and H. V. Freeman, "Report on Aptitude Testing in Dentistry at University of Iowa," *Proceedings, 12th Annual Meeting*, American Association of Dental Schools, 1936, pp. 214–28.
[23]Ellis B. Page, "Grading Essays by Computer," *Phi Delta Kappan*, vol. 47 (1966), 238–43.

2. *Grade the answers question by question rather than student by student.*

This means that the grader will read the answers to one question on all students' papers before going on to the next question. Such a procedure is obviously required in the global-quality scaling just described. It is also advantageous in analytic scoring, since concentration of attention on one question at a time helps to develop specialized skill in scoring it.

3. *If possible, conceal from the grader the identity of the student whose answer he is grading.*

The purpose of this procedure is to reduce the possibility that biases or halo effects will influence the scores assigned. Ideally, the answers to different questions would be written on separate sheets of paper, identified only by a code number. These sheets would be arranged into groups by question for the grading process and then recombined by the student for totaling and recording. By this process one can reduce not only the halo effect associated with the student's name and reputation, but also that which might result from high or low scores on preceding answers. The purpose is, of course, to make the essay test scores measure actual achievement, as reflected by perfomance on the test, as accurately as possible.

4. *If possible, arrange for independent grading of the answers, or at least a sample of them.*

Independent grading is the only real check on the objectivity, and hence on the reliability, of the grading. It is troublesome to arrange and time-consuming to carry out, however. Hence it is seldom likely to be undertaken on the initiative of the classroom teacher. But if a school or college were to undertake a serious program for the improvement of essay examinations, such a study of the reliability of essay-test grading would be an excellent way to begin.

To get independent grades, at least two competent readers would have to grade each question, without consulting each other and without knowing what grades the other had assigned. At least 100, preferably 300, answers should be given this double, independent reading. (The answers need not all be to the same question. Reading the answers of 30 students to each of 10 questions would be quite satisfactory.) The correlation between the pairs of grades would indicate the reliability of grading the questions. Then the Spearman-Brown formula could be applied to estimate the reliability of grading for the test as a whole.

SUMMARY

The main conclusions to be drawn from the discussions presented in this chapter can be summarized in the following 22 propositions.

1. An essay demands that a student write well. An objective test demands that he read well.
2. Essay tests ordinarily consist of a few questions that call for extended answers. Objective tests ordinarily consist of many questions that call for brief answers.
3. The difference between a student's score on a particular test and the average of his scores on a large number of similar tests is known as a sampling error.
4. The larger the number of questions in a test the smaller the consequences of sampling errors.
5. The bulk of a student's time is spent in reading and thinking when he takes an objective test. His time is spent mainly in thinking and writing when he takes an essay test.
6. In objective testing the skill of the test constructor is crucial. In essay testing the competence of the scorer is crucial.
7. Essay tests are easier to prepare and harder to score than objective tests.
8. In an essay test the examinee has more freedom to show his individuality, and the scorer more opportunity to depend on his personal opinions, than in an objective test.
9. The examinee's task and the basis for evaluating his performance tend to be specified more clearly on objective than on essay tests.
10. Objective tests sometimes permit guessing. Essay tests sometimes permit bluffing.
11. It is easier for the examiner to control the distribution of essay than of objective test scores.
12. The important aspects of educational achievement that can be measured by objective tests are largely identical with those that can be measured by essay tests.
13. Good objective tests and good essay tests can both test understanding, application problem solving, and the organization of ideas.
14. Subjective judgment is involved in both essay and objective testing.
15. Scores from either essay or objective tests must possess objective meaning to be useful.
16. Essay tests save time when the group to be tested is small. Objective tests save time when the group to be tested is large.
17. Good essay test questions require the student to demonstrate command of essential knowledge.
18. The reliability of essay test scores can be improved by making the questions specific enough so that all good answers must be nearly identical.
19. The reliability of essay test scores can ordinarily be improved by asking more questions that call for short answers than by asking fewer questions that call for long answers.
20. Optional questions should be avoided in essay testing.

21. The quality of an essay question can be tested and reliable scoring facilitated by attempting to write an ideal answer to it.
22. The reliability of reading essay answers can be improved by grading them question by question, by concealing the name of the examinee, and by arranging for several independent gradings.

Taking a true-false test is like having the wind at your back.

LINUS

(CHARLES SCHULZ)

7

TRUE-FALSE TEST ITEMS

From one point of view, as Linus has observed, true-false tests are easier than they ought to be. From another, as many students would testify, they tend to be unecessarily, irrelevantly, and frustratingly difficult. From both points of view there are better ways of measuring achievement than by using true-false questions. This attitude of disapproval is widely shared in educational circles. A few, including, the author of this book, regard true-false test items much more favorably. Therefore the mission of this chapter will be threefold:

1. To consider the indictments against true-false test items
2. To consider arguments in favor of their use
3. To suggest ways of using them effectively.

THE INDICTMENTS

TRIVIALITY

One of the common criticisms of true-false test items is that they are limited to testing for specific, often trivial, factual details. As a result, the critics say, students are encouraged and rewarded for rote learning of bits of factual information, rather than for critical thinking and understanding. In support of this criticism, items like these are cited as typical of true-false tests:

> The author of Don Quixote was Cervantes.   (T)
> The chemical formula for water is H_2O.   (T)
> The Battle of Hastings was fought in 1066.   (T)
> Christopher Columbus was born in Spain.   (F)
> There are six planets in the solar system.   (F)

These are indeed specifically factual questions of the who? what? when? where? or how many? type. If these were the only kinds of questions that could be asked in true-false form, it would surely be of limited value. But it is possible to ask questions that test student's comprehension of broader principles, and his ability to apply them. For example, one can test the student's understanding of an event or of a process:

> King John of England considered the Magna Carta one of his great achievements.   (F)
> In the laboratory preparation of carbon dioxide one of the essential ingredients is limewater.   (F)

One can test the student's knowledge of a functional relationship:

> The more widely the items in a test vary in difficulty, the less widely the scores on the test are likely to vary.   (T)
> If heat is supplied at a constant rate to melt and vaporize a substance, the temperature of the substance will increase at a constant rate also.   (F)

One can test his ability to apply principles:

> It is easier for a poor student to get a good score (80 percent correct) on a true-false test if the test includes only 50 items than if it includes 100 items.   (T)
> If an electric refrigerator is operated in a sealed, insulated room with its door open, the temperature of the room will decrease.   (F)
> The time from moonrise to moonset is usually longer than the time from sunrise to sunset.   (T)

One can test his ability to solve conventional problems:

> The radius of a circle whose area is 75 must be less than 5.   (T)
> The operations required to find the number of kilowatt hours of electricity used by a 60-watt bulb burning three hours a night during the entire month of March are indicated by the formula $(1,000 \times 60) + (3 \times 31)$.   (F).

Clearly true-false items are not necessarily limited to testing the student's recall of trivial factual details. When they do so, the fault is less in the form than in the content of the item.

Looking beyond educational tests, one can find many examples of nontrivial true-false questions in human affairs. When a man accused of murder is on trial for his life, the question before the jury is essentially a true-false question. The medical diagnostician looking at a section of tissue suspected of carcinoma must answer a true-false question. And consider the consequences in human history of efforts to prove or disprove, to sustain or to suppress, propositions like these:

> The earth is the center of the universe.
> Base metals can be transformed into gold.
> Kings derive their authority from God.
> Man has evolved from lower forms.
> White men are naturally superior to colored men.
> Man can initiate and control nuclear reactions.

Surely there is nothing intrinsically trivial about a statement whose truth is open to question.

A test item is significant if it deals with an element of knowledge that is part of a structure of related concepts, ideas or events, and that is likely to be useful on future occasions. Significant items in a test are those that deal with the ends rather than the means of instruction. For every item in a good test it should be possible to give an affirmative answer to the question, "Does this item test an element of knowledge that is really worth knowing?"

It is good for a test constructor to make each item he writes as significant as he can. But if he is writing objective test items he should not expect each of them to appear to have tremendous individual significance. There are, after all, a great many of them in the test. Each one involves directly only one element in a vast and complex structure of knowledge. The substantial significance of a test score rests on the summation of many lesser significances.

There is a second reason why the items of even the best true-false tests may not appear to be highly significant individually. It is that there is typically an inverse relation between an item's apparent significance and the definiteness of its truth or falsity. The requirement that each true-false test item be essentially true or essentially false rules out the use of broad generalizations that might appear to be highly significant, but whose truth has not been and perhaps cannot be definitely established. The generalization may deal with a very important problem, but if its truth is indeterminable it cannot give a significant indication of achievement. Regardless of what form of test item is used, essay or objective, one cannot obtain definite assessments of competence by asking questions that have indefinite answers.

Faced with the difficult problem of finding true propositions of high apparent significance to use as the basis for test items, it is reassuring to recall that, as Howard's study showed, there is a substantial correlation between the indications of achievement given by items of less, and those of more, apparent significance.[1] This means that the degree of apparent significance probably is not a crucial factor in the validity of the measures of achievement obtained. The difference between good and poor command of knowledge in an area of study shows up about as clearly on the less significant items as it does on the more significant ones.

It remains true, however, that the acceptability of a test depends substantially on the apparent significance of the items composing it. The test constructor is well advised to use as many highly significant items in his test as he can succeed in developing.

AMBIGUITY

A second major criticism of true-false test items is that they are frequently ambiguous. Indeed some are, but they need not be if the ideas for the items are carefully chosen and if the items themselves are carefully worded. Further, some of the charges of ambiguity leveled at true-false test items are not well justified. To explain this we must begin by drawing a distinction between intrinsic ambiguity and apparent ambiguity. Students who say, "If I interpret the statement this way, I'd say it is true. But if I interpret it that way, I'd have to say it is false," are complaining about apparent ambiguity. But if experts in the field have the same difficulty in interpreting the same statement, the trouble may be intrinsic ambiguity.

Apparent ambiguity is a result, in part, of inadequacies in the student's knowledge. He has trouble interpreting the statement because the words mean something a little different to him than they do to the expert or because they do not bring to his mind as readily as they do to the expert's the associations necessary to make the intended interpretation clear. Hence apparent ambiguity is not only unavoidable, it may even be useful.

[1] Frederick Thomas Howard, *Complexity of Mental Processes in Science Testing,* Contributions to Education No. 879 New York: Columbia University, Teachers College, 1943).

By making the task of responding correctly harder for the poorly prepared than for the well-prepared student, it can help to discriminate between the two.

Thus a student's report that he does not understand a test question is not necessarily an indictment of the question. It may be, rather, an unintentional confession of his own shortcomings.

Intrinsic ambiguity, on the other hand, the kind of ambiguity that troubles the expert as much as or more than it troubles the novice, is not helpful at all. It probably can never be eliminated, since language is inherently somewhat abstract, general, and imprecise. But in the statements used in true-false test items it should be minimized.

One reason why there is sometimes truth in the charge that true-false test items are ambiguous and lack significance is that teachers sometimes try to use textbook sentences too directly as test items. Even in a well-written text few of the sentences would actually make good true-false test items. Some of the others serve only to keep the reader informed of what the author is trying to do or to remind him of the structure and organization of the discussion. Some are so dependent for their meaning on sentences that precede or follow them that they are almost meaningless out of context. Some are intended only to suggest an idea, not to state it positively and precisely. Some include a whole logical argument, involving two or three propositions, in a single sentence. Some are intended not to describe what is true, but to prescribe what ought to be true. Some are expressed so loosely and so tentatively that there is hardly any possible basis for doubting them. In all the writing we do to preserve the knowledge we have gained and to communicate it to others there seem to be very few naturally occurring nuggets of established knowledge.

For this reason it is seldom possible to find in a text or reference work a sentence that can be copied directly for use as a true statement or transformed by a simple reversal for use as a false statement. The task of writing good true-false test items is more a task of creative writing than of copying. And it may be fortunate that it is so. For it helps the test constructor to avoid the hazard of writing items that would encourage and reward the learning of meaningless verbal sequences.

There is a special source of ambiguity in true-false test items that needs to be guarded against. It is uncertainty on the part of the examinee as to the standards of truth of the examiner. If the statement is not perfect in truth, if it has the slightest flaw, should it be considered false? Probably not; the item writer's task will be easier, and his test will be better, if he directs the examinee to consider as true any statement that has more truth than error in it, or any statement that is more true than its contradiction would be. Then his task is to avoid writing statements that fall in the twilight zone between truth and falsehood.

One way of reducing ambiguity in true-false test items is to use specific rather than general terms wherever possible. Instead of saying "a long test," say "a 100-item test." Instead of saying "a test item of moderate difficulty," say "an item that between 40 percent and 60 percent of the examinees answer correctly."

Another is to write, or at least to think of the items in pairs, one true and one false, such as items 1 to 4 below.

1. An eclipse of the moon can only occur when the moon is full.   (T)
2. An eclipse of the moon can only occur when the moon is new.   (F)
3. The average farm in the united States was larger in 1960 than it was in 1910.   (T)
4. The average farm in the United States was smaller in 1960 than it was in 1910.   (F)

This procedure helps to clarify what the item is testing and to indicate whether or not it is worth testing. It encourages conciseness of expression. It helps avoid items like 5 and 6 below, which have no plausible alternatives and which therefore would make poor true-false test items.

5. Insurance agencies may be either specialized or general.   (T)
6. Camping has a good past, a better present, and an almost unlimited future.   (T)

Of course only one member of any pair is used in the same test. The other is sometimes sufficiently different to be usable in a second test, or in a different form of the test.

A third thing one can do to help solve the problem of definiteness is to write statements that call for comparison between two specified alternatives, as in items 7 and 8 below.

7. The time from moonrise to moonset is generally longer than the time from sunrise to sunset.   (T)
8. The beneficial effect of a guessing correction, if any, is more psychological than statistical.   (T)

Such internal comparison focuses attention clearly on the essential question in the item. Of even greater help is the fact that it avoids the necessity of using arbitrary standards in judging truth or falsity and the resulting possibility that the examiner's standards might differ significantly from those of the examinee.

The fourth thing that helps to avoid indefiniteness in true-false test items is careful review of the items after they have been written. This can be of value even if done by the author of the items himself, after several days have passed, and after the context in which the items were written has been forgotten. It can be of even greater value if done independently by a competent colleague. Independent review is not likely to supply quality to true-false test items that are grossly lacking in it, but it can help to prevent errors and ambiguities in communication that sometimes result from singularity in point of view or mode of expression.

GUESSING

A charge against true-false tests that many take very seriously is that they are subject to gross error introduced by guessing. Several things can be said in response to this charge.

The first is that a distinction needs to be made between blind guessing and informed guessing. Blind guessing adds nothing but error to the test scores. Informed guesses, on the other hand, provide valid indications of achievement. The more a student knows, the more likely that his informed guesses will be correct.

The second is that well-motivated students, taking a test of appropriate difficulty that they have time to finish, are likely to do very little blind guessing on true-false tests. They know that thinking is a surer basis than guessing for determining the correct answer. In a recent study, college students reported an average of only one response in 20 that was equivalent, in their opinion, to a blind guess.[2] Hills and Gladney have shown that scores in the chance range are not significantly different from above-chance scores as predictors of college grades.[3] This suggests that scores in the chance range were not in fact the results of pure chance (blind guessing).

The third is that the influence of blind guessing on the scores of a test diminishes as the test increases in length. On a one-item true-false test a student has a 50 percent chance of getting a perfect score, but on a 2-item test it drops to 25 percent, on a 5-item test to 3 percent, and on a 10-item test to 0.1 percent. On a 100-item test it becomes 0.000,000,000,-000,000,000,000,000,000,08 percent (less than one chance in a million trillion trillion). The chance of getting even a moderately good scores, say 70, on a 100-item true-false test by blind guessing alone is less than one in 1,000.

The fourth and most significant of all is that the reliable scores obtained from true-false tests could not be obtained if they were seriously affected by blind guessing. The effect of blind guessing is to introduce error into the scores and thus to lower their reliability. But true-false classroom tests of 100 items have shown reliability coefficients of 0.75 to 0.85. These values are about as high as can be expected for any classroom test, regardless of the form of test item used. They support the

[2]Robert L. Ebel, "Blind Guessing on Objective Achievement Tests," *Journal of Educational Measurement*, vol. 5 (1968), 321–25.

[3]John R. Hills and Marilyn B. Gladney, "Predicting Grades from Below Chance Test Scores," *Journal of Educational Measurement*, vol. 5 (1968), 45–53.

conclusion that good true-false tests need not be vitiated by guessing.

Some who have a little special knowledge of objective testing believe that the problem of guessing can best be dealt with by "correcting the scores for guessing." This is a misconception. The announcement that a guessing correction will be made when the test is scored may deter some students from guessing, but it only magnifies the differences between the scores of lucky and unlucky guessers. Even its slight effect in deterring guesses has only a negligible effect on the validity of the test scores. If guessing on a true-false test were to be extensive enough to affect the test scores seriously, there is almost nothing that a guessing correction could do to improve the validity of the scores.

A rather elaborate and logically elegant scheme to discourage guessing on true-false and other objective tests has attracted considerable attention in recent years.[4, 5, 6, 7] It is known as confidence weighting. The examinee is required to indicate not only whether he thinks the statement is true or false, but also how certain he is of the correctness of his answer. A correct answer confidently given counts most toward his score. A wrong answer confidently given counts least. One scoring scheme that has been tried uses these weights.

Answer	Score
Confidently correct	10
Diffidently correct	9
No answer (omit)	7
Diffidently wrong	4
Confidently wrong	0

It is possible to show that when these scoring weights are used the examinee is well advised to answer:

Confidently if his chances of being right are 8 in 10 or better.
Diffidently if his chances of being right are 6 in 10 to 8 in 10.
Not at all if his chances of being right are less than 6 in 10.

Confidence weighting can affect both the reliability and the validity of the test scores. It is intended to improve both. But experimental studies of its affect on validity have given conflicting results. Some indications

---

[4]Robert L. Ebel, "Confidence Weighting and Test Reliability," *Journal of Educational Measurement*, vol. 2 (1965), 49–57.

[5]E. H. Shuford, A. Albert, and H. E. Massengill, "Admissible Probability Measurement Procedures," *Psychometrika*, vol. 31 (1966), 125–45.

[6]Robert M. Rippey, "A Comparison of Five Different Scoring Functions for Confidence Tests," *Journal of Educational Measurement*, vol. 7 (1970), 165–70.

[7]Joan J. Michael, "The Reliability of a Multiple Choice Examination under Various Test Taking Instructions," *Journal of Educational Measurement*, vol. 5 (1968), 307–14.

are that it helps substantially, others that it does little good. Significant validity studies are so difficult to design and carry out that few if any have been reported.

If the problem of guessing on true-false tests is not serious, as suggested in this section, it is unlikely that confidence weighting could help very much. An examinee's uncertainty about his certainty may introduce almost as much error into his score as the reduction of guessing can remove. In any case, the present state of our knowledge about confidence weighting does not justify a recommendation that it be used routinely in classroom testing.

HARMFULNESS

Critics of true-false tests sometimes charge that their use has harmful effects on learning; that they encourage students to concentrate on remembering isolated factual details and to rely heavily on rote learning; that they encourage students to accept grossly oversimplified conceptions of truth; that they expose students undesirably to error. Let us consider these charges.

There is no need for true-false test items to emphasize memory for isolated factual details. Good ones emphasize understanding and application. Good ones do not call for specific facts to be recalled; they present novel problems to be solved. Even those that might require recall of factual details do not reward rote learning, for facts are hard to remember in isolation. They are retained and can be recalled better if they are part of a structure of knowledge.

There is reason to believe that rote learning is something of an educational bogey-man, often warned against and used in attempts to influence others, but seldom practiced or observed. Rote learning is not much fun, and it promises few lasting rewards. Most students and teachers properly shun it. Perhaps its supposed prevalence results from an error in inference. It is surely true that rote learning always results in incomplete learning (that is, lack of understanding), but it does not follow that all incomplete learning is the result of too much rote learning. It may simply be the result of too little learning of any sort.

What of the charge that the definiteness of the answers offered, and the categorical way in which they are scored as right or wrong, are likely to give students false notions about the simplicity of truth? Evidence in support of this argument is seldom pressented, and the argument itself is seldom advanced by those who have used true-false tests extensively. They know that students will challenge answers that disagree with their own. They will point out the complexity of the subject with which the item deals and will insist that a case can be made for the alternative answer.

Usually the author concedes that the statement in question is neither perfectly true nor totally false. The discussion of arguments for and against it tends to emphasize, not to conceal, the complexity, the impurity, the relativity of truth. On occasion it leads to the conclusion that the item in question was simply a bad item, poorly conceived or carelessly stated.

Consider finally the charge that true-false test items are educationally harmful on the ground that they expose the student to error. The presentation of false statements as if they might be true may, it has been feared, have a negative suggestion effect, causing the student to believe and remember statements that were never intended to be true. Experimental studies of this effect have found it to be slight, if indeed it exists at all. Ruch tentatively concluded that the negative suggestion effect in true-false tests is probably much smaller than is sometimes assumed and is fully offset by the net positive teaching effects.[8] And as Ross points out,

> Modern psychology recognizes the importance of the total situation or configuration in learning. Whether or not a false statement is dangerous depends largely upon the setting in which it appears. A false statement in the textbook, toward which the characteristic pupil attitude is likely to be one of passive, uncritical acceptance, might easily be serious. But the situation is different with the items in a true-false test. Here the habitual attitude of the modern pupil is one of active, critical challenge.[9]

Considering the limited logical basis for these charges, and the lack of substantial evidence to support them, there seems to be no need to regard any of them as a serious obstacle to the use of true-false items in classroom tests. The contributions of well-conceived and well-developed true-false test items to the educational process can be substantial. The harm some fear they might do is trivial in comparison.

THE DEFENSE

THE CASE FOR TRUE-FALSE TESTS

The basic reason for using true-false test items is that they provide a simple and direct means of measuring the essential outcome of formal education. The argument for the validity of true-false items as measures of educational achievement can be summarized in four statements:

1. The essence of educational achievement is the command of useful verbal knowledge.

[8]G. M. Ruch, *The Objective or New-type Examination* (Chicago: Scott, Foresman and Company, 1929), p. 368.

[9]C. C. Ross, *Measurement in Today's Schools*, 2d ed. (Englewood Cliffs, N.J.: Prentice-Hall, Inc., 1947), p. 349.

2. All verbal knowledge can be expressed in propositions.
3. A proposition is any sentence that can be said to be true or false.
4. The extent of a student's command of a particular area of knowledge is indicated by his success in judging the truth or falsity of propositions related to it.

The first of these statements was considered and defended in Chapter 3. The second is almost self-evident. Is it possible to imagine an element of verbal knowledge that could not be expressed as a proposition? The third is a generally accepted definition. The fourth seems to be a logical consequence of the first three. It might be challenged on the basis of technical weaknesses in true-false items, but if the first three are accepted, it is not likely to be rejected in principle.

To test a person's command of an idea or element of knowledge is to test his understanding of it. A student who can recognize the words in which an idea has been expressed but who cannot recognize the same idea when it is expressed in different words does not have command of it. Or, if he knows the idea only as an isolated fact, without seeing how it is related to other ideas, he has no command of it. Knowledge one has command of is not a miscellaneous collection of separate elements, but an integrated structure. Knowledge one has command of is knowledge one can use to make decisions, draw logical inferences, or solve problems. It is usable knowledge.

Consider how one might test a student's command of Archimedes' Principle. It should not be done by offering him the usual expression of the principle as a true statement, or some slight alteration of it as a false statement, as has been done in items 1 and 2 below.

1. A body immersed in a fluid is buoyed up by a force equal to the weight of the fluid displaced. **(T)**
2. A body immersed in a fluid is buoyed up by a force equal to half of the weight of the fluid displaced. **(F)**

Instead the student might be asked to recognize the principle in some alternative statement of it, as in items 3 and 4 below.

3. If an object having a certain volume is surrounded by a liquid or gas, the upward force on it equals the weight of that volume of the liquid or gas. **(T)**
4. The upward force on an object surrounded by a liquid or gas is equal to the surface area of the object multiplied by the pressure of the liquid or gas surrounding it. **(F)**

Or the student might be required to apply the principle in specific situations such as those described in items 5 and 6 below.

5. The bouyant force on a one-centimeter cube of aluminum is exactly the same as that on a one-centimeter cube of iron when both are immersed in water. **(T)**

6. If an insoluble object is immersed successively in several fluids of different density, the buoyant force upon it in each case will vary inversely with the density of the fluids. (F)

Sometimes the use of an unconventional example can serve to test understanding of a concept.

7. Distilled water is soft water. (T)

It is a popular misconception that true-false test items are limited to testing for simple factual recall. On the contrary, complex and difficult problems can be presented quite effectively in this form.

8. The next term in the series 3, 4, 7, 11, 18 is 29. (T)
9. If the sides of a quadrilateral having two adjacent right angles are consecutive whole numbers, and if the shortest side is one of the two parallel sides, then the area of the trapezoid is 18 square units. (T)

Teachers of courses in history and literature have a special antipathy toward true-false tests, probably because they encounter special problems in using such tests effectively. The basic problem is a lack of dependable generalizations in the subjects they teach—generalizations that would provide the basis for test questions of obvious importance and general significance. The factual details are there, all right, but considered individually they seem too insignificant to provide a respectable basis for judging a student's achievement. These details can be loosely organized into trends and movements and developments, but the generalizations have many exceptions, and the interpretations and explanations are likely to be idiosyncratic and open to serious question. In these fields of scholarship, precise, demonstrably true laws are almost nonexistent.

This is one reason why teachers of history and literature are so favorably disposed toward essay tests, In them. profound and impressive questions can be asked without committing anyone, students or teachers, to any particular answer as the right one. Indeed, some of these teachers take pride in deliberately asking questions that do not have right answers. By doing so they rise above stereotyped ideas and conventional wisdom, stimulating creative thought in their students. This, at least, is the claim.

Yet if they are to use student answers to these questions as bases for measuring achievement in their courses, they must be able to differentiate, however roughly, the better from the poorer. On what basis can this be done, if the question lacks any right answer? Usually it is on the basis of how much the student writes that is true and relevant to the questions, and how well he writes it. Note, however, that what a student writes that is true must consist mainly of factual details in these areas. How well he writes it depends on details of word choice, sentence structure, and organization. Thus the escape from details by way of profound, global questions is only an apparent escape.

The competent teacher of history or literature knows a great deal more about the details of his subject, and about the relations among these details, than any of his students. His subject may lack an elaborate structure of precisely defined concepts and of demonstrable relationships, but it is rich in interesting and illuminating detail. Good teachers of history and literature open doors of vivid, if vicarious, experience to their students. This is what they ought to teach, and the understanding of these experiences is what they ought to test. Details they may be, but they are important details.

There are factual details and limited, qualified generalizations about ancient Greece, and Charlemagne, and the American Revolution, and Mahatma Gandhi that are worth knowing. There are facts about Chaucer and King Lear and Tom Sawyer and Robert Frost that are worth knowing. These facts and their relations constitute the substance of history and literature. Command of the knowledge of these facts is a legitimate, respectable objective for teaching and for testing. Teachers of history and literature can, if they will, make effective use of true-false questions.

Something of subjects and achievements for which true-false items are approprite can be seen in Exhibit 7.1. Included here are items testing factual knowledge, interpretations, computations, and applications. None of the items reproduces a conventional verbalization and hence none is likely to be answered successfully on that basis alone. Item 9, based on a comparison of two things, in this case two quantities, and item 10, based on a conditional if-then proposition, illustrate types that deserve wider use in true-false tests.

Items 8 and 10 illustrate attractive false statements. The student who associates carbon dioxide with limewater on a very superficial basis is likely to mark item 8 true. One who responds to item 10 on the basis of common sense, ignoring the heat absorption and constancy of temperature during melting and vaporization, is likely to mark it as true also.

But none of the items provides a complete pattern, on the basis of which good items can be written by imitation alone. The instructor's thorough mastery of the subject, his skill in verbal communication, and his ingenuity in creating new settings for familiar principles and in devising plausible-looking false statements are the really important qualifications for the writing of effective true-false items.

EQUIVALENCE OF TRUE-FALSE AND MULTIPLE-CHOICE ITEM FORMS

Implicit in most multiple-choice test items are one true statement and several false statements. Like true-false items, multiple-choice items also test knowledge and are based on propositions. Though no experiments of this kind seem to have been reported, it is a reasonable hypothesis

EXHIBIT 7.1

Illustrative True-False Test Items

(T) 1. Hodgkin's disease is characterized by an increase in the size of the lymph nodes.

Subject: Pathology
Level: College
Type: Fact

(F) 2. A receiver in bankruptcy acquires title to the bankrupt's property.

Subject: Business Law
Level: College
Type: Fact

(T) 3. Protective tariffs were consistent with the principles of the mercantilist system.

Subject: Economics
Level: College
Type: Interpretation

(T) 4. An eclipse of the sun can only occur when the moon is new.

Subject: Astronomy
Level: High School
Type: Interpretation

(F) 5. The radius of a circle whose area is 75 would be greater than 5.

Subject: Arithmetic
Level: Upper Grades
Type: Computation

(T) 6. The quantity 11,800 can also be written 11.8×10^3.

Subject: Mathematics
Level: High School
Type: Interpretation

(F) 7. The complete combustion of one molecule of $C_{24}H_{50}$ requires seventy-four molecules of oxygen.

Subject: Chemistry
Level: High School
Type: Computation

(F) 8. Limewater is a convenient source of carbon dioxide.

Subject: Chemistry
Level: High School
Type: Fact

(T) 9. More heat energy is required to warm a gallon of cool water from 50°F. to 80°F. than to heat a pint of the same cool water to boiling point.

Subject: Physics
Level: High School
Type: Computation

(F) 10. If heat is supplied at a constant rate to melt and vaporize a substance, the temperature of the substance will increase at a constant rate also.

Subject: Physics
Level: High School
Type: Application

that most multiple-choice test items could be converted into equivalent true-false test items with no serious change in what is measured or in the precision of measurement. If the conversion were done properly, there might even be an improvement in the reliability of the scores obtained.[10]

Exhibit 7.2 illustrates corresponding items in multiple-choice and

[10]M. A. Burmester and L. A. Olson, "Comparison of Item Statistics for Items in Multiple Choice and Alternate Response Form," *Science Education*, vol. 50 (1966), 467–70.

true-false forms designed to test essentially the same aspects of achievement. None of the items in either version tests recall of isolated, factual

EXHIBIT 7.2

Corresponding Multiple-choice and True-False Test Items

Multiple-choice Version	True-False Version

1. James wants to put a fence around a garden that is 60 feet long and 45 feet wide. How many feet of fencing will he need?
  a. 90 feet   *c.* 120 feet
  b. 105 feet **d.* 210 feet
	1*a.* It will take 105 feet of fencing to put a fence around a garden that is 60 feet long and 45 feet wide. **(F)**

2. The equation $X^2 + Y^2 = 4$ is represented graphically by
*a. a circle
  b. an ellipse
  c. a parabola with its base on the X-axis
	1*b.* It will take 210 feet of fencing to put a fence around a garden that is 60 feet long and 45 feet wide. **(T)**
	2*a.* The graph of $X^2 + Y^2 = 4$ is a circle. **(T)**
	2*b.* The graph of $X^2 + Y^2 = 9$ is an ellipse. **(F)**
	2*c.* The graph of $X^2 + Y^2 = 1$ is a parabola with its base on the Y-axis. **(F)**

3. How can one generate enough electric current to light a flashlight bulb?
  a. By rubbing two good conductors of electricity together
  b. By dipping two strips of zinc in dilute sulphuric acid
  c. By connecting the north pole of a magnet to the south pole, using a coil of wire
*d. By rotating a coil of wire rapidly near a strong magnet
	3*a.* One can generate enough electric current to light a flashlight bulb by dipping two strips of zinc in dilute sulphuric acid. **(F)**
	3*b.* One can generate enough electric current to light a flashlight bulb by rotating a coil of wire rapidly near a strong magnet. **(T)**

4. What does religious tolerance mean?
  a. Admitting everyone to the same church
  b. Accepting religious teachings on faith
  c. Altering religious belief so that it does not conflict with science
*d. Allowing people to believe what they wish
	4*a.* Religous tolerance means admitting everyone to the same church. **(F)**
	4*b.* Religious tolerance means allowing people to believe what they wish. **(T)**
	4*c.* Religious tolerance means altering religious beliefs so that they do not conflict with science. **(F)**

details that are likely to have been taught directly. All of the items require explanation, interpretation, or application. Each of the multiple-choice questions has been used as a basis for several true-false questions, only one of which could be used in any one test, However. the relative brevity of the true-false items means that more such items, yielding more independent item scores, can be answered in a test of the same duration.

The prevailing preference for the multiple-choice form of test item has led some item writers to use this form when the content of the item is really better suited to the true-false form. Two illustrations are presented in Exhibit 7.3 These two multiple-choice items are essentially collections

EXHIBIT 7.3

Items Better Suited to True-False Than to Multiple-choice Form

MULTIPLE-CHOICE VERSION	TRUE-FALSE VERSION	
1. Which of these is not characteristic of a virus?	1*a.* A virus can live only in plant and animal cells.	(T)
a. It can live only in plant and animal cells.	1*b.* A virus can reproduce itself.	(T)
b. It can reproduce itself.	1*c.* A virus is composed of very large living cells.	(F)
c. It is composed of very large living cells.	1*d.* A virus can cause diseases.	(T)
d. It can cause diseases.	2*a.* The median of a triangle is perpendicular to the side it intersects.	(F)
2. Given $\triangle PQR$ with median *RS.* Which of the following must be true?	2*b.* The median of a triangle bisects the angle from which it is drawn.	(F)
a. RS is prependicular to PQ.	2*c.* A triangle with a median is a right triangle.	(F)
b. *RS* bisects $< QRP.$	2*d.* The median of a triangle divides it into two triangles of equal area.	(T)
c. $\triangle$PQR is a right triangle.		
d. None of the above.		

of true-false statements. When the multiple-choice items are separated into true-false items, all of which could be used in the same test in this case, considerably more information (that is, a larger number of independent item scores) about the student's achievement can be obtained from the same test content.

On the other hand, there are occasional multiple-choice items, such as those involving qualitative comparisons between specific examples, which would probably be more awkward to handle in true-false form. Two illustrations of multiple-choice items of this type are provided in Exhibit 7.4. However, despite occasional exceptions such as these, it seems safe to say that most aspects of educational achievement that can be tested using one of the two forms can also be tested satisfactorily using the other.

EXHIBIT 7.4

Items Better Suited to Multiple-Choice Than to True-False Form

1. Which of the following sentences is stated most emphatically?
   a. If my understanding of the question is correct, this principle is one we cannot afford to accept.
   b. One principle we cannot afford to accept is this one, if my understanding of the question is correct.
   *c. This principle, if my understanding of the question is correct, is one we cannot afford to accept.
   d. This principle is one we cannot afford to accept, if my understanding of the question is correct.

2. Which of the following couplets has the characteristics of Robert Frost's poetry most apparently?
   *a. "I opened the door so my last look
      Should be taken outside a house and book."
   b. " 'Tis the human touch in this world that counts,
      The touch of your hand and mine."
   c. "Dear Girl! the grasses on her grave
      Have forty years been growing."
   d. "Think still of lovely things that are not true.
      Let wish and magic work at will in you."

EFFICIENCY AND EASE OF CONSTRUCTION

In addition to providing intrinsically relevant measures of the essence of educational achievement, true-false test items have the advantage of being quite efficient. The number of independently scorable responses per thousand words of test or per hour of testing time tends to be considerably higher than that for multiple-choice test items. Sometimes this advantage in efficiency of true-false items is lost as a result of ambiguity in the test items or as a result of examinee guessing. If these disadvantages are controlled as they can be by proper test planning and item writing, the higher efficiency of true-false items can be expected to result in test scores of higher reliability. Some instructors who make extensive use of true-false items consistently get reliability coefficients in the eighties for their classroom tests. As classroom test reliabilities go, these values are unusually high.

Compared with other item forms, true-false test items are relatively easy to write. They are simple declarative sentences of the kind that make up most oral and written communications. It is true that the ideas they affirm or deny must be judiciously chosen. It is also true that the ideas chosen must be worded carefully, with a view to maximum precision and clarity, since they stand and must be judged in isolation. For this reason they must be self-contained in meaning, depending wholly on internal content, not on external context. But the basic problem of true-false item writing is no different from the problem of writing for any other purpose of communication. Those who have difficulty in writing good true-false test items probably have trouble expressing themselves clearly and accurately in other situations also.

THE USE OF TRUE-FALSE TEST ITEMS

THE DEVELOPMENT OF TRUE-FALSE TEST ITEMS

The development of a true-false test item (or indeed of a multiple-choice test item) for a classroom test begins when the instructor (the item writer) directs his attention to some segment of knowledge that the instructor has sought to develop in the class. The item writer needs to be in firm command of that segment of knowledge. He should regard it as something that any capable student of the subject ought also to possess. This segment of knowledge is, or easily could be, described in a single paragraph such as those found in good textbook for the subject the class is studying.

Then the item writer must identify in this segment of knowledge a proposition on which to base the test item. The proposition should have these three characteristics:

1. It is essential, not incidental, to have command of that segment of knowledge.
2. It can be defended as a true proposition.
3. It is not obviously true to anyone with good common sense or general information.

That is, a correct answer ought to indicate that the person who gives it has a firm grasp of a segment of knowledge that can only be attained by special study of the subject.

A large part of the art of writing good true-false test items is the art of selecting the right propositions on which to base them. The test constructor's knowledge of the subject being tested, and his educational values, will determine to a considerable degree the quality of his selection of propositions to test.

Some examples of paragraphs presenting segments of special knowledge, and of essential propositions derived from them, are presented in Exhibit 7.5.

EXHIBIT 7.5

Paragraphs and Propositions on Which True-False Test Items Might Be Based

I

PARAGRAPHS

1. Mercantilism was an economic philosophy, prevalent in Europe from the sixteenth to the eighteenth centuries, which assumed that the wealth of a country depended on the amount of gold and silver it possessed. To increase this amount the state regulated international trade so as to encourage export of goods in exchange for precious metals, and to discourage imports. Under this theory national rather than individual interests were given primary consideration.

2. An eclipse occurs when the light from one astronomical body is partially or totally cut off by another. In a solar eclipse the moon blocks off the sunlight by coming directly between the earth and the sun. In a lunar eclipse, the earth's shadow falls across the moon, cutting off the sunlight ordinarily reflected from the moon's surface.

II

PROPOSITIONS

1. The economic philosophy of mercantilism involved government regulation of business to serve national interests.

2. An eclipse is caused by the shadow of one body in the solar system falling on another.

Experienced item writers seldom bother to write out the propositions on which they base their test items. They do, however, keep these propositions in mind as the item writing progresses. When an item writer runs into difficulty in formulating or expressing a true-false test item, it is often helpful for him to ask himself, "Just what is this item supposed to test? What is the proposition on which I am basing it?"

The third step in the process of writing true-false test items is to convert the proposition into a test item, either true or false.

Five suggestions are offered for developing true items. The suggestions are illustrated with items derived from the propositions stated in Exhibit 7.5. No special suggestions for writing false items are offered beyond the general suggestions of wording some contradiction of the true statement so that it sounds plausible. But, following the general recommendation that true-false items be written in pairs, a false version of each true statement is illustrated.

Suggestion 1. Restate the Essential Idea in Different Words.

True Versions	False Versions
Under the mercantile system, laws controlling production and trade are enacted for the purpose of strengthening the entire country.	Under the mercantile system, industries regulate their own production and prices.
When some of the light from a star like the sun to a planet like the earth is blocked by some other body like the moon, an eclipse is said to occur.	When light from a star like the sun is reflected from a planet like the earth onto some other body like the moon, an eclipse is said to occur.

Suggestion 2. Restate a Part of the Original Idea.

True Versions	False Versions
The mercantile system requires legislative support.	The mercantile system requires corporate income taxes.
All eclipses involve shadows.	If light rays could not be bent, eclipses could not occur.

Suggestion 3. Relate the Basic Idea to Some Other Idea.

True Versions	False Versions
Mercantilism and free trade are incompatible.	Mercantilism requires free trade.
An eclipse of the moon can only occur when the moon is full.	An eclipse of the moon can only occur when the moon is new.

Suggestion 4. Develop Implications of the Basic Idea.

True Versions	False Versions
Mercantilism requires a strong central government.	Mercantilism requires strong local autonomy in government.
Prediction of eclipses requires information on the orbital motions of the bodies involved.	Prediction of eclipses requires information on the inclination of the earth's axis.

Suggestion 5. Infer the Effect of Different (Even Impossible) Circumstances.

True Versions	False Versions
If there were no trade between nations, mercantilism would be pointless.	If there were no trade between nations, mercantilism would be far more effective.
If there were no luminous astronomical bodies like the sun, eclipses would not be observed.	Eclipses cannot occur in the presence of luminous stars.

The foregoing are not all the possible true-false items that could be developed on the essential ideas underlying mercantilism and eclipses. Probably some much better than those displayed here could be composed. But these illustrations may serve to show the diverse variations that can be developed as means for testing a student's command of an idea. They may suggest that true-false items are not limited to testing simple recall but can present novel problems for the examinee to think through and attempt to solve.

Each true statement that is included in a test should permit the test constructor to say of it: "The truth of this statement is not obvious to everyone, but I can provide evidence to show that it is essentially true." Each false statement that is included in a test should permit the test constructor to say of it: "This statement reads like a plausibly true statement, but I can provide evidence to show that it is essentially false. "If the items pass these tests, they are likely to be good true-false test items.

REQUIREMENTS FOR GOOD TRUE-FALSE TEST ITEMS

There are five general requirements for a good true-false test item.

1. It should test the examinee's knowledge of an important proposition, one that is likely to be significant and useful in coping with a variety of situations and problems. It should say something worth saying.
2. It should require understanding as well as memory. Simple recall of meaningless words, empty phrases, or sentences learned by rote should not be enough to permit a correct answer.
3. The intended correct answer (true or false) should be easy for the item writer to defend to the satisfaction of competent critics. The true statements should be true enough and the false statements false enough so that an expert would have no difficulty distinguishing between them. Any explanation or qualification needed to justify an unconditional answer should be included in the item.
4. On the other hand, the intended correct answer should be obvious only to those who have good command of the knowledge being tested. It should not be a matter of common knowledge. It should not be given away by an unintended clue. The wrong answer should be made attractive to those who lack the desired command.

5. The item should be expressed as simply, as concisely, and above all as clearly as is consistent with the preceding four requirements. It should be based on a single proposition. Common words should be given preference over technical terms. Sentences should be short and simple in structure. Essentially true statements should not be made false by insertion of the word *not*.

Here are some pairs of true-false test items, good and bad, that illustrate these requirements.

1. The item tests an import idea.

(1) *This:* President Kennedy solved the missile crisis by threatening a blockade of Cuba. (T)

(2) *Not this:* President Kennedy was 12 years older than his wife. (T)

The difference in the ages of President Kennedy and his wife might be a subject for comment in a casual conversation, but it has little to do with the important events of the time. The Cuban missile crisis, on the other hand, brought the United States and Russia to the brink of a horrible war. How this crisis was solved is a far more important element in world history than a difference in ages between a President and his wife.

(3) *This:* Words like *some, usually, all* or *never* should be avoided in writing true-false test items. (F)

(4) *Not this:* Two pitfalls should be avoided in writing true-false test items. (F)

Item 4 is the type of textbook sentence that sets the stage for an important pronouncement, but does not make it. Item 3, on the other hand. tests the examinee's understanding of several important principles. Specific determiners like *some* and *usually* provide irrelevant clues only when used in true statements. If used in false statements they tend to attract wrong answers from the ill-prepared student. Conversely, specific determiners like all or never should be avoided in false statements, but are useful in attracting wrong answers from the uninformed.

(5) *This:* More salt can be dissolved in a pint of warm water than in a pint of cold water. (T)

(6) *Not this:* Some things dissolve in other things. (T)

A statement like that in item 6 is too general to say anything useful. Item 5, on the other hand provides a test of the understanding of an important relationship.

2. The item tests understanding. It does not reward recall of a stereotyped phraseology.

(7) *This:* When a hand pushes a door with a certain force the door pushes back on the hand with the same force. (T)

(8) *Not this:* For every action there is an equal and opposite reaction. (T)

(9) *This:* If the hypotenuse of an isosceles right triangle is seven inches long, each of the two equal legs must be more than five inches long. (F)
(10) *Not this:* The square of the hypotenuse equals the sum of the squares of the other two sides. (T)

Both items 8 and 10 are the familiar wordings of important ideas. These wordings could be learned by rote. To test a student's understanding it is desirable to present specific applications that avoid the stereotyped phrases, as has been done in items 7 and 9.

3. A correct answer to the item is defensible.

(11) *This:* Moist air is less dense than dry air. (T)
(12) *Not this:* Rain clouds are light in weight. (T)

Since a rain cloud seems to float in the air, it might reasonably be called light in weight. On the other hand, a single rain cloud may weigh more than 100,000 tons. One cubic foot of the cloud probably weighs about the same as a cubic foot of air. Since the cloud contains droplets of water, it could weigh more per cubic foot than cloudless dry air. But moist air alone (without water droplets) weighs less per cubic foot than does dry air. Should the item also specify that "other things," for example, pressure and temperature, are equal? It might, but in the absence of mention a reasonable person is justified in assuming that temperature and pressure should not be taken to be variable factors in this situation.

(13) *This:* The proposal that salary schedules for teachers ought to include skill in teaching as one of the determining variables is supported more strongly by teachers' organizations than it is by taxpayers. (F)
(14) *Not this:* Merit is an important factor affecting a teacher's salary. (F)

The first version is much more specific, and much more clearly false than the second. Experts could agree on the answer to the first, but would be troubled by the intrinsic ambiguity of the second. Across the country it is no doubt true that the salaries of good teachers are higher than those of poor teachers. However, it is also true that the salary schedules of many school systems do not include merit as one of the determining factors.

(15) *This:* The twinkling of starlight is due to motion in the earth's atmosphere. (T)
(16) *Not this:* Stars send out light that twinkles. (T)

The answer to the second, unacceptable version of this item could be challenged by a reasonable, well-informed person on the following grounds. It is not the light sent out by the star that twinkles. That light is relatively steady. But, owing to disturbances in our atmosphere, the light that reaches our eyes from the star often appears to twinkle. That the second version is unacceptable is due either to the limited knowledge or to the carelessness in expression of the person who wrote it.

4. The answer to a good test item is not obvious to anyone. It tests special knowledge.

A. It is not self-evident.

(17) *This:* Frozen foods are usually cheaper than canned foods.   (F)
(18) *Not this:* Frozen foods of the highest quality may be ruined in the kitchen.
(T)
(19) *This:* Most local insurance agencies are owned and controlled by one of the major national insurance companies.   (F)
(20) *Not this:* Insurance agencies may be either general or specialized.   (T)

Who could doubt the possibility of cooking any kind of food badly? How plausible is the belief that only general or only specialized insurance agencies could be found? The unacceptable versions above are too obviously true to discriminate high achievement from low. Both read like introductory sentences lifted from a textbook, sentences that set the stage for an important idea but do not themselves express important ideas.

B. To one who lacks the knowledge being tested, a wrong answer should appear more reasonable than the correct one.

(21) *This:* By adding more solute a saturated solution can be made supersaturated.   (F)
(22) *Not this:* A supersaturated solution contains more solute per unit than a saturated solution.   (T)

It appears reasonable to believe that adding more solute would turn a saturated solution into a supersatureatd solution. But those who understand solutions know that it won't work that way. The added solute won't dissolve in a saturated solution. Only by evaporating some of the solvent, or cooling it, can a saturated solution be made supersaturated. The student who tries to use common sense as a substitute for special knowledge is likely to give a wrong answer (which is all his knowledge entitles him to) to the first item.

But the same common sense leads the student of low achievement to answer the second item correctly. Thus the second version fails to function properly as a test of the student's command of knowledge.

5. The item is expressed clearly

A. It is based on a single idea

(23) *This:* The salt dissolved in water can be recovered by evaporation of the solvent.   (T)

(24) *Not this:* Salt can be dissolved in water and can be recovered by evaporation of the solvent. (T)
(25) *Or this:* Salt dissolves in hot water; sugar dissolves in cold water. (T)
(26) *This:* At conception the sex ratio is approximately 3 boys to 2 girls. (T)
(27) *Not this:* Scientists have found that male-producing sperm are stronger and live longer than female-producing sperm, which accounts for the sex ratio at conception of approximately 3 boys to 2 girls. (T)

An item based on a single idea is usually easier to understand than one based on two or more. It is also more efficient. One can obtain a more accurate measurement of a student's achievement by testing separate ideas separately than by lumping them together and scoring one composite answer right or wrong.

The strong inclination of some teachers to use their tests as opportunities for teaching, or their misguided attempts to use textbook sentences as test items, may account for the appearance of items like 28, below.

(28) *Not this:* Life is a continuous process of choice-making, sacrificing one human value for another, which goes through the following steps: spontaneous mental selections regarding everything we want, conflicting preferences hold each other in check, hesitation becomes deliberation as we weigh and compare values, finally choice or preference emerges. (T)
(29) *But this:* A person who deliberates before making choices seldom finds himself forced to sacrifice one good thing in order to attain another. (F)

But if one looks for the central idea in item 28, and asks what misapprehension it might serve to correct, an item like 29 above may emerge. Item 29 is simpler, clearer, and better in almost every way than item 28.

B. It is concise.

(30) *This:* The federal government pays practically all the costs of constructing and maintaining highways that are part of the interstate highway system. (F)
(31) *Not this:* When you see a highway with a marker that reads "Interstate 80," you know that the construction and upkeep of that road is built and maintained by the state and federal governments. (T)

The wording of item 31 is careless and redundant. It is the *highway* that is built and maintained, not its construction and upkeep. The personal touch ("when you see") may give the appearance of practicality, but does not affect what the item really measures at all. Finally, making item 31 true by including state as well as federal governments as supporters of the interstate highway system probably makes the item easier for the uninformed. Item 30 hits the intended mark more clearly because it is more straightforward and concise.

C. *It does not include an artificial, tricky negative*

(32) *This:* Columbus made only four voyages of exploration to the Western Hemisphere. (T)

(33) *Not this:* Columbus did not make four voyages of exploration to the Western Hemisphere. (F)

Some item writers try to turn textbook statements, which are usually true, into false statements for test items simply by inserting the word "not" somewhere in the original statement. The result is usually bad. The item usually carries the clear birthmark of its unnatural origin. It reads awkwardly and invites suspicion, which, if the item is indeed false, is bad. Further, these items tend to be tricky. An unobtrusive "not" in an otherwise wholly true statement may be overlooked by even a well-prepared examinee. Such items put him at an unnecessary and undesirable disadvantage.

WRITING ITEMS TO DISCRIMINATE

The job of a test item is to discriminate between those who have and those who lack command of some element of knowledge. Those who have the command should be able to answer the questions correctly without difficulty. Those who lack it should find the wrong answers attractive. To produce items that will discriminate in this way is one of the arts of item writing. Here are some of the ways in which such items can be produced.

1. *Use more false than true statements in the test.*

When in doubt, students seem more inclined to accept than to challenge propositions presented in a true-false test. Several investigators have found that false statements tend to discriminate somewhat more sharply between students of high and low achievement than do true statements. This may be due to what is called an "acquiescent response set." In the absence of firm knowledge a student seems more likely to accept than to question a declarative statement whose truth or falsity he must judge.

Instructions for preparing true-false tests sometimes suggest that about the same number of false statements as true should be included in the test. But if the false statements tend to be higher in discrimination, it would be advantageous to include a higher proportion of them, perhaps as many as 67 percent. Even if students come to expect more false items than true, little value of this technique is lost. In one study students took a test on which two-thirds of the statements were false. After answering the questions and counting how many they had marked true they were told how many they should have marked true, and were given a chance to change any answers they wished. Most of them changed a number of answers, but they improved their scores very little, on the average. They changed about as many of their answers from right to wrong as from wrong to right.

2. *Word the item so that superficial logic suggests a wrong answer.*

A. A rubber ball weighing 100 grams is floating on the surface of a pool of water exactly half submerged. An additional downward force of 50 grams would be required to submerge it completely.　(F)

The ball is half submerged and weighs 100 grams, which gives one-half of 100 considerable plausibility on a superficial basis. The true case is, of course, that if its weight of 100 grams submerges only half of it, another 100 grams would be required to submerge all of it. Superficial logic also would make the incorrect answers to these questions seem plausible.

B. Since students show a wide range of individual differences, the ideal measurement situation would be achieved if each student could take a different test specially designed to test him.　(F)
C. The output voltage of a transformer is determined in part by the number of turns on the input coil.　(T)
D. A transformer that will increase the voltage of an alternating current can also be used to increase the voltage of a direct current.　(F)

3. *Make the wrong answer consistent with a popular misconception or a popular belief irrelevant to the question.*

E. The effectiveness of tests as tools for measuring achievement is lowered by the apprehension students feel for them.　(F)

Many students do experience test anxiety, but for most of them it facilitates rather than impedes maximum performance.

F. An achievement test should include enough items to keep every student busy during the entire test period.　(F)

Keeping students busy at worthy educational tasks is usually commendable, but in this case it would make rate of work count too heavily, in most cases, as a determinant of the test score.

4. *Use specific determiners in reverse to confound testwiseness.*

In true-false test items extreme words like *always* or *never* tend to be used mainly in false statements by unwary item writers, whereas more moderate words like *some, often,* or *generally* tend to be used mainly in true statements. When they are so used they qualify as "specific determiners" that help testwise but uninformed examinees to answer true-false questions correctly. But some *always* or *never* statements are true and some *often* or *generally* statements are false. Thus these specific determiners can be used to attract the student who is merely testwise to a wrong answer.

   5. *Use phrases in false statements that give them the*
      "ring of truth."

G. The use of better achievement tests will, in itself, contribute little or nothing to better achievement.   (F)

The phrases "in itself" and "little or nothing" impart a tone of sincerity and rightness to the statement that conceals its falseness from the uninformed.

H. To insure comprehensive measurement of each aspect of achievement, different kinds of items must be specifically written, in due proportions, to test each different mental process the course is intended to develop.   (F)

   There is superficial logic to this statement like those illustrated under B above. But it also displays the elaborate statement and careful qualifications that testwise individuals associate mainly with true statements.

   Is a teacher playing fair with his students if he sets out deliberately to make it easy for some of them to give wrong answers to his test items? If he wants to measure achievement validly, that is to distinguish correctly between those who have and those who lack command of a particular element of knowledge, it is the only way he can play fair. The only reason a test constructor sets out to make wrong answers attractive to those who lack command of the knowledge is so that correct answers will truly indicate the achievement they are supposed to indicate.

TYPES AND MODELS OF TRUE-FALSE TEST ITEMS

   A variety of sentence forms may be used in writing true-false test items. This section illustrates 43 different forms, identified by numerals, grouped in 12 type classes, identified by letters. These items all deal with aspects of educational measurement; similar sentence forms should be useful in writing true-false items for other subjects of study. Where a key introductory word or phrase in the item clearly identifies and distinguishes a particular sentence form, these words have been italicized. The same words might be used as starting points in writing similar items in other fields.

A. Factual (noun phrase as subject of a declarative sentence)
1. The short-cut method of estimating the standard deviation, suggested by Lathrop, requires that the range of the test scores be restricted. (F)
2. The standard deviation of an ideal set of stanine test scores is 5. (F)

B. Generalization
3. *All* questions that ask Who? What? When? or Where? are properly classified as factual information questions. (T)
4. *Most* good true-false items are tests of ability to apply information. (T)
5. *Many* teachers who like absolute grading find a percentile scale useful for this purpose. (F)

C. Comparative
6. *The difference between* the raw scores corresponding to the 45th and 55th percentiles *is* likely to be smaller than the difference between the raw scores corresponding to the 5th and 15th percentiles. (T)
7. *Both* of the common Kuder-Richardson formulas for estimating test reliability require specific information on the difficulty of each item in the test. (F)

D. Conditional
8. *If* a distribution of scores has a few extremely low scores, and no correspondingly extreme high scores, the median will be numerically larger than the mean. (T)
9. *When* one has a normal distribution the standard deviation and standard error are considered equivalent. (F)

E. Relational
10. *The larger* the number of scores in a set the larger the standard deviation of those scores must be. (F)
11. *The higher* the average level of discriminating power of the items in a test the more variable the scores that the test is likely to yield. (T)
12. *The lower* the reliability of a set of test scores, the more serious the loss of information when they are transformed into stanines. (F)
13. *Making* a test more reliable *is likely to* make it less valid. (F)
14. *Increasing* the number of categories of marks *tends to* increase the reliability of the marks. (T)
15. *How much* weight one particular component of a final mark carries in determining the final mark *depends on* the mean value of scores for that component. (F)

F. Explanatory
16. *The main reason for* changing normally distributed scores to rectangularly distributed scores *is to* make the scores more reliable. (F)
17. *The purpose of* using extreme groups of 27 percent *is to* maximize the dependable difference in ability between the groups. (T)
18. *One of the factors* that *adversely* affect the reliability of an objective test is the amount of guessing the students do in answering it. (T)
19. *Since* judgments of item relevance are inescapably subjective, they cannot be validated by anyone other than the person who made the judgments originally. (F)
20. *Although* computationally simple, the U-L discrimination index is too heavily biased in favor of middle difficulty items to be of much use to professional test constructors. (F)

G. Exemplary
    21. *An example of* a "factual information" question would be one asking how the horsepower of an engine is calculated. (F)
H. Evidential
    22. *Studies of* the marking standards and practices of different faculty members *reveal that* they tend more toward uniformity than toward diversity. (F)
I. Predictive
    23. *One could expect* to increase the reliability coefficient of a test from 0.30 to 0.60 by doubling the number of items in the test. (F)
J. Procedural
    24. *To* find a variance *one must* add, subtract, multiply, and divide. (T)
    25. *In order to* determine the range of a set of scores *one must* know the number of scores in the set. (F)
    26. *One method of* ensuring that scores from a 100-item test and scores from a 25-item test will carry equal weight *is to* multiply the latter scores by 4. (F)
    27. *One essential step* in the best method of calculating the variance of a set of 100 test scores *is to* find the differences between each of the scores and the mean score. (F)
    28. *Use of* 27 percent extreme groups maximizes the difference in average ability between students in upper and lower groups. (F)
    29. *By* lengthening a moderately reliable test, both its reliability and its validity are necessarily increased. (T)
    30. *The first step* toward improved marking in most schools and colleges should be to replace a single mark, reflecting a student's overall achievement in a course, with a series of several marks to indicate his achievement of several different objectives of the course. (F)
K. Computational (item includes numerical data and requires computation or estimation)
    31. The range of the scores 2, 3, 4, and 6 is 5. (T)
    32. In the set of scores 36, 27, 24, 20 and 18, if the percentile rank of 24 is 50, then the percentile rank of 18 is 0. (F)
L. Evaluative
    33. *A good* test of educational achievement will include more items on facts than on generalizations. (F)
    34. *It is better to* select the criterion groups used in item analysis at random *than* on the basis of total test score. (F)
    35. *The best proportion* of the total group to include in the subgroups used in item analysis *is* 12 percent. (F)
    36. *The maximum variability* of the scores on a test will be achieved when the average discrimination of the items is about 0.50. (F)
    37. *The easiest method* of computing a correlation coefficient *is to* begin by converting each raw score into a z-score. (F)
    38. *It is easy to* demonstrate that when percentile ranks are used, resulting in rectangular distributions of scores, this distribution *is not* an accurate reflection of the "true" distribution of abilities. (F)
    39. *It is difficult to* obtain reliable scores from a group in which the range of abilities is very wide. (F)
    40. *It is possible* to correlate the scores of different students on the same test when only a single score is available for each student. (F)
    41. *It is reasonable* to regard most objective test items whose indices of discrimination are above 0.30 as weak and in need of improvement. (F)

42. *It is necessary to* determine the mean and standard deviation of a set of scores *in order to* construct a frequency distribution of those scores.   (F)
43. *The major drawback to* the equivalent forms approach to the estimation of test reliability *is* that students answering the second test tend to remember their answers to the first.   (F)

SUMMARY

Some of the main ideas developed in this chapter are summarized in the following 25 statements.

1. True-false items can test a student's comprehension of important ideas and his ability to use them in solving problems.
2. It is possible to measure significant achievement in an area without insisting that each item deal with a highly significant proposition or problem.
3. Good true-false items may appear ambiguous to novices but should not appear ambiguous to experts.
4. Few textbook sentences are significant enough, and meaningful enough out of context, to be used as the true statements in a true-false test.
5. Statements that are essentially (but not perfectly) true or essentially (but not totally) false can make good true-false test items.
6. The testmaker can reduce ambiguity by writing items that involve an internal comparison of alternatives.
7. Unlike blind guesses, informed guesses provide valid indications of achievement.
8. In practice guessing is not a serious problem on true-false tests because students tend to do very little blind guessing.
9. Correction of true-false test scores for guessing is neither necessary nor beneficial.
10. The use of confidence-weighted scoring schemes cannot be generally recommended on the basis of empirical data.
11. There is no firm empirical data to support the charges that true-false tests encourage rote learning, oversimplified conceptions of true, or the learning of false ideas.
12. True-false test items provide a simple and direct means of measuring the essential outcome of formal education.
13. A student's command of knowledge in history and literature, as well as in science and other subjects, can be tested by means of true-false questions.
14. Many important aspects of achievement can be tested equally well with either true-false or multiple-choice test items.
15. True-false test items are relatively easy to write.
16. True-false test items provide valid information on essential achievements more efficiently than other item forms.
17. True-false test items should be written on the basis of significant true propositions that are part of the special knowledge of the subject.
18. The answer to a good true-false test item is easy for the item writer to defend, but difficult for a student whose knowledge is superficial to discern.
19. Good true-false statements express single, not multiple, ideas.
20. In general, one cannot create good false statements by inserting the word "not" in a true statement.

21. False statements tend to make more discriminating test items than true statements.
22. Avoid giveaway modifiers like *sometimes, usually,* or *often* in true statements, or *always, never,* or *impossible* in false statements.
23. Using words like *always* or *never* in true statements, and *often* or *usually* in false statements tends to mislead the student who relies on testwiseness to give him a good score.
24. Make false items plausible by using familiar words and phrases in seemingly straightforward factual statements.
25. The writing of good true-false test items is facilitated by the adaptation of one of several generally applicable models of sentence structure.

8

HOW TO WRITE
MULTIPLE-CHOICE TEST ITEMS

THE USE OF MULTIPLE-CHOICE ITEMS IN CLASSROOM TESTING

Multiple-choice test items are currently the most highly regarded
and widely used form of objective test item. They are adaptable to the
measurement of most important educational outcomes—knowledge,
understanding, and judgment; ability to solve problems, to recommend
appropriate action, to make predictions. Almost any understanding or
ability that can be tested by means of any other item form—short answer,
completion, true-false, matching, or essay—can also be tested by means
of multiple-choice test items.

The form of the multiple-choice item, with the stem asking or implying a direct question, provides a realistic, naturally appropriate setting
for testing student achievement. There tends to be less indirectness and

artifice in multiple-choice than in some other item forms. Students often find multiple-choice questions less ambiguous than completion or true-false items. Instructors find it easier to defend the correct answers to them.

Finally, multiple-choice items seem to both instructors and students to be less susceptible to chance errors resulting from gressing than true-false items. It is easy to exaggerate the harm done by guessing, and to place too much emphasis on the need to limit the amount of guessing students do. But however little the harm done by guessing, it does less harm in multiple-choice than in true-false tests.

In spite of their virtues, multiple-choice test items have not escaped the attention of critics. Some of the criticisms reflect a general mistrust of all objective testing techniques. These critics allege that objective test questions are inevitably superficial, ambiguous, and conducive to guessing. They say or imply that the only good way to test is the old way they prefer to use—namely, essay testing. Other critics find fault with specific test items, alleging that the questions are ambiguous, the correct answers incorrect, or the distracters as good as or better than the intended correct answer.

One of the best-known and most persistent critics of objective test items in multiple-choice and true-false form has been Professor Banesh Hoffmann.[1] It is instructive to consider some of the items to which he has objected.

1. The sky is blue.   (true or false)

On a bright, sunny day the sky is blue. On a rainy day it may be gray. On a moonless night it may be black. At sunrise or sunset it may be red. Clearly the item as given is not sufficiently qualified to allow a well-informed, critically minded person to answer it either true or false.

2. George Washington was born on February 22, 1732.   (true or false)

George Washington was actually born on February 11, 1732. We now celebrate his birth on February 22. The reason for the discrepancy is the change from the Julian to the Gregorian Calendar, which occurred in the American Colonies in 1752. The British decreed that the day following September 2, 1752 should be called September 14. This involved a loss of 11 days, but served to put the calendar back in phase with the sun as it had been at the beginning of the Christian era. Thus whether item 2 it called true or false depends on whether the original or the corrected date is intended.

---

[1]Banesh Hoffmann, *The Tyranny of Testing* (New York: Crowell-Collier-Macmillan, 1962).

3. Emperor is the name of
   a. a string quartet
   b. a piano concerto
   c. a violin sonata

The best known "Emperor" is Beethoven's Piano Concerto No. 5. But Haydn's string quartet is also known as the Emperor Quartet. Thus whereas the item might cause no trouble for 99 of 100 examinees, the one-hundredth might protest that it provided two correct answers.

4. Which game is least like the other three?
   a. cricket
   b. billiards
   c. football
   d. hockey

One who knows all of these games, and who wants to give the answer that was probably intended, is likely to choose billiards. It alone is not played on a field (or rink). It alone is not a team game. It alone requires more than one ball (or puck). True, some kind of an argument can be made for each of the other alternatives. But a good argument?

5. If we cannot make the wind blow when and where we wish it to blow we can at least make use of its
   a. source
   b. heat
   c. direction
   d. force
   e. atmosphere

In the context of the question—use made of a blowing wind—force seems clearly the best answer. Again, some argument can be found to support each of the other alternatives, but how good are these, how reasonable?

6. The burning of gasoline in an automobile cylinder involves all of the following except
   a. reduction
   b. decomposition
   c. an exothermic reaction
   d. oxidation
   e. conversion of matter to energy

Theoretically the burning of gasoline must be accompanied by loss of mass, to account for the release of energy under Einstein's equation. Whether this is actually conversion of matter to energy, and whether it is significant enough in amount to deserve mention alongside of the other prominent, measurable characteristics of the reaction seems open to question.

None of these items, except possibly the last, is of the kind here recommended for use in measuring educational achievement. But only the first two are so intrinsically ambiguous as to be useless as test items. Well-informed, fair-minded test takers are not likely to be troubled much by the alleged ambiguities of the other four. Professor Hoffmann is on firm ground when he objects to serious ambiguity in multiple-choice test items. But not all of the ambiguities he sees are serious enough to spoil the items. When he implies that his horrible examples are typical of multiple-choice tests generally, he is on very shaky ground.

Few objective tests or test items are so perfect as to be above reproach from a persistent, perceptive critic. But there are at least two weaknesses in the general indictments that have been issued against all multiple-choice tests and items. First, the criticisms are seldom supported by unbiased experimental data, despite the fact that relevant data would be fairly easy to obtain. Most of the flaws pointed out should lower the discriminating power of the items and the reliability of the test scores. Some of the critics, instead of obtaining or even welcoming experimental evidence, tend to discredit statistical methods of testing the quality of items or tests, without suggesting any procedure to replace it other than their own intuitions (and occasionally those of a few friends) and what seems to them to be plain common sense.

In the second place, the critics seldom attempt seriously to make a good case for a better way of measuring educational achievement. Even the most ardent advocate of objective testing does not claim perfection. He acknowledges that multiple-choice test questions can be subject to serious flaws and that, in general, they are not as clearly meaningful and sharply discriminating as they should be. He agrees wholly with the observation that objective test scores are not as reliable as they might be and ought to be for maximum value. But he is likely to reject the suggestion that multiple-choice testing should be abandoned. He is fairly certain that whatever might replace it would have most of the same shortcomings, probably to an even greater degree. In addition, he has reason to believe that the implied alternative, essay testing, would be much less convenient to use in many situations. He would accept and respect dependable evidence that there are much better ways for measuring educational achievement. But he is not likely to consider seriously any recommendations accompanied by expressions of disdain for experimental evidence.

Multiple-choice test items can serve a useful purpose in the measurement of educational achievement. Their widespread use is a tribute to the competence of modern test makers, not evidence of incompetence. This chapter will present nine suggestions for making effective use of this item form. Then some illustrations of desirable characteristics of multiple-choice test items will be presented.

SUGGESTIONS FOR PREPARING GOOD MULTIPLE-CHOICE TEST ITEMS

1. Develop multiple-choice test items on the basis of independently meaningful and demonstrably valid statements of relevant, important, ideas.

Most items of information about word meanings or matters of fact and the basis of most explanations, decisions, calculations, and predictions can be expressed as statements or propositions. In practice, few item writers take the trouble to express the ideas they are testing in written statements, but ideas of this kind are implicit in most of the questions they ask. Novices at item writing and even some experienced professionals find that explicit statements of item ideas are useful in selecting the most promising ideas and in developing sound multiple-choice test items from them. Samples of topics for items in a test on classroom testing, adequate statements of item ideas related to these topics, and the translation of the ideas into multiple-choice test items are illustrated in Exhibit 8.1.

A good practical reason for basing multiple-choice test items on well-selected statements of appropriate ideas is that statements of this kind provide the foundation for good instruction in many courses. Good materials of instruction—texts, references, lecture notes, and so forth—should provide a convenient source from which to select key statements for conversion into test items.

But many of the statements teachers utter or text authors write are not entirely meaningful apart from the context in which they appear. Many are only suggestive, not definitive. Many are not wholly true or objectively verifiable. Many are not entirely relevant to the purposes of instruction in the course. These statements differ widely in importance. Many are quite trivial. Some teachers invent their own terminology and emphasize their own opinions. Items based on such unique visions of truth are not likely to have the general validity essential to good test items. Some ideas are so commonplace and others so abstruse that questions based on them would almost inevitably be too easy or too difficult to differentiate effectively among levels of achievement in the groups to be tested.

Laws, principles, and generalizations tend to be more important than specific incidents or details. However, the statements of such laws, principles, and generalizations may be memorized as relatively meaningless word sequences. This calls attention to one danger in basing multiple-choice test items on statements identical with those that have been used in instruction. The wording of the item may duplicate the statement so

EXHIBIT 8.1

Examples of Item Topics, Item Ideas, and Test Items for a Test on the
Construction of Classroom Tests

Topic: Table of specifications
Idea: The test constructor should draw up an outline or table of specifications, indicating the relative emphasis that will be given to each
of the various areas of content or objectives of instruction.
Item: What is the principal function of the table of specifications for a
test?
1. To enable the scorer to know which response to each item is correct
2. To help students prepare properly for the test
*3. To guide the test constructor toward writing the appropriate
numbers of various kinds of items
4. To provide data for calculating reliability of test scores
Topic: Test difficulty
Idea: An objective classroom test is of appropriate difficulty if the mean
score is about midway between the maximum possible score and the
expected chance score.
Item: A sixty-item objective test composed of four-response multiple-
choice items is given at the end of a course. What data would provide
the best evidence as to whether or not the test is of appropriate
difficulty?
*1. The class mean of the numbers of items answered correctly is 27.5.
2. The distribution of scores is approximately normal.
3. A few items are answered correctly by all students.
4. The reliability coefficient for the test is 0.50.
Topic: Spearman-Brown formula
Idea: The Spearman-Brown formula is used to estimate the reliability of
a test similar to a given test, but of different length.
Item: When is the Spearman-Brown formula useful in estimating test
reliability?
1. When the same test has been given twice to the same group
2. When the only available data are the number of items in the test
and the mean and standard deviation of the scores
3. When one knows the number of items in the test and the difficulty
of each item
*4. When a coefficient of correlation between scores on the odd-
numbered items and on the even-numbered items in test has been
calculated

closely that verbal memory could provide as good a basis for correct response as would clear understanding. Good item writing avoids this danger
by rephrasing the idea or seeking novel illustrations or applications of

it. The aim of good item writing is to yield evidence of understanding, of command of the idea as a tool in thinking, rather than evidence of recall of the conventional verval expression of the idea. Exhibit 8.2 illustrates some good multiple-choice test items that have been written in a variety of subject fields at a variety of educational levels.

EXHIBIT 8.2

Sample Multiple-Choice Test Question

1. *Writing*   *Judgment*   *College Level*
   Which one of the following sentences is most appropriately worded for inclusion in an impartial report resulting from an investigation of a wage policy in a certain locality?
   (A) The wages of the working people are fixed by the one businessman who is the only large employer in the locality.
   (B) Since one employer provides a livelihood for the entire population in the locality, he properly determines the wage policy for the locality.
   (C) Since one employer controls the labor market in a locality, his policy may not be challenged.
   *(D) In this locality, where there is only one large employer of labor, the wage policy of this employer is really the wage policy of the locality.

2. *Mathematics*   *Novel Problem Solving*   *High School Level*
   If jelly beans come in five colors, how many randomly selected beans must a child buy in order to be certain of getting three beans of the same color?
   (A) 3   (B) 7   *(C) 11   (D) 15

3. *Physics*   *Prediction*   *College Level*
   In a beaker almost full of water a cork is nearly submerged by the pull of a spring. If the beaker is allowed to fall free, what will happen to the cork during the period of free fall?
   (A) It will stay nearly submerged.
   *(B) It will submerge completely.
   (C) It will float higher in the water.
   (D) What happens will depend on the size of the cork and the strength of the spring.

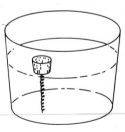

4. *Literature*   *Judgment*   *High School Level*
   Which of the following quotations has most of the characteristics of conventional poetry?

(A) I never saw a purple cow;
   I never hope to see one. . . .
*(B) Announced by all the trumpets of the sky
   Arrives the snow and blasts his ramparts high.
(C) Thou art blind and confined,
   While I am free for I can see.
(D) In purple prose his passion he betrayed
   For verse was difficult. Here he never strayed.

5. *Arithmetic*   *Problem Solving*   *Elementary Level*
What is the product of 5 times 3?
(A) 1 2/3   (B) 8   *(C) 15   (D) 35

6. *United States History*   *Generalization*   *College Level*
The most frequent source of conflict between the western and eastern
parts of the United States during the course of the nineteenth century
was
*(A) the issue of currency inflation.
(B) the regulation of monopolies.
(C) internal improvements.
(D) isolationism vs. internationalism.
(E) immigration.

7. *Economics*   *Decision and Explanation*   *College Level*
Should merchants and middlemen be classified as producers or non-
producers? Why?
(A) As nonproducers, because they make their living off producers and
   consumers.
(B) As producers, because they are regulators and determiners of price.
*(C) As producers, because they aid in the distribution of goods and
   bring producer and consumer together.
(D) As producers, because they assist in the circulation of money.

8. *Physics*   *Prediction*   *High School Level*
If an electric refrigerator is operated with the door open in a perfectly
insulated sealed room, what will happen to the temperature of the
room?
*(A) It will rise slowly.
(B) It will remain constant.
(C) It will drop slowly.
(D) It will drop rapidly.

9. *Economics*   *Definition*   *College Level*
What is the technical definition of the term *production*?
(A) Any natural process producing food or other raw materials.
*(B) The creation of economic values.
(C) The manufacture of finished products.
(D) The operation of a profit-making enterprise.

10. *Literature*   *Factual Knowledge*   *High School Level*
    The poem *Hiawatha* was written by the author of
    (A) *Leaves of Grass.*
    (B) *Thanatopsis.*
    (C) *Israfel.*
    *(D) *The Village Blacksmith.*

11. *Physics*   *Explanation*   *High School Level*
    What cools an electric refrigerator?
    (A) A current of air circulating inside the refrigerator.
    *(B) An expanding gas.
    (C) An insulated metal coil.
    (D) The flow of electricity through a low resistance wire.

To a considerable degree the quality of any educational achievement test depends on the meaningfulness, truthfulness, relevance, and importance of the ideas on which the test items are based. If the test constructor can supplement his own subjective judgments of these qualities with those from competent colleagues, their consensus is likely to yield an even better test.

> 2. *Choose item topics and ideas and write multiple-choice test items with a view to maximizing the discriminating power of the items.*

The uses made of multiple-choice tests of classroom achievement usually require single scores for each student tested. The main purpose of such scores is to summarize and express numerically the student's general level of competence in the area covered by the test. The complex nature of mental abilities, and the limitations of available techniques for assessing them, limit most test scores to relative meaning and limit the precision of even that relative meaning. For a test item to contribute substantially to the precision of relative measures of general competence in a complex, often heterogeneous area of achievement, it must discriminate. That is, students having more of the general competence the test is intended to measure should have greater success than students of less competence in answering each test question correctly.

Methods of measuring the discriminating power of a test item and of improving item discrimination are presented and discussed in Chapter 14. But it is important for the test constructor to keep this requirement in mind during the initial writing of multiple choice or any other type of item for use in an educational test. The job of the item is to discriminate different levels of achievement in the area covered by the course. Most students of high achievement should answer it correctly. Most students of low achievement should miss it. The item writer should choose topics and ideas for testing that are likely to discriminate in this way. He should word the question and the intended correct answer to it and should choose and word the distracters so as to enhance the probable difference between good and poor students in their success on the item.

The basis on which the item discriminates is extremely important. For classroom tests of educational achievement that basis should not be general intelligence, or reading ability, or testwiseness. Each item should require understanding or ability whose development is a special objective of the particular course of study. Even a bright, sophisticated student should have trouble with the item unless he has learned, in that course or elsewhere, the particular understanding or ability the item is testing.

It is sometimes suggested that the final examination for a course should be given as a pretest early in the course so that final course marks can be based on the student's growth during the course, not on what he knew before starting the course as well. Some objections that have been raised to basing marks on apparent growth are discussed in Chapter 12. But there is another, perhaps better, reason for giving the course final as a pretest. Such a procedure will help to identify items that are unlikely to discriminate on the basis of specific course achievement. If most of the students can answer an achievement test question before that achievement has been taught, then either the question is a poor question or that particular achievement need not be taught in the course in question.

3. Arrange to write the initial item drafts so that subsequent revision and assembly into the finished test will be as convenient as possible.

Revision is facilitated if the initial draft is written in pencil and if each item is written, well spaced, on a separate sheet of paper. The sheet should be identified by words or a code indicating what type of question (vocabulary, factual, and so forth) is being asked and what topic it deals with. If based on an explicitly stated item idea, the idea may be written on the page and a specific reference to its source may be indicated. It is best not to number the items until they have been arranged in the order in which they will appear in the test.

Quite naturally the first part of the item to be written is the question or introductory statement. This is usually referred to as the "stem" or "lead" of the item. Not so obviously, the next part to be written in the first draft is the intended answer. The intended answer is the most important alternative and deserves priority in attention while the question it is supposed to answer is fresh in mind. If an adequate answer cannot be written, there is no point in worrying about distracters.

But while the intended answer should be written next after the item, stem, it should not always be written in the space directly below the item stem on the page. Its placement among the responses should be varied randomly even in the first drafts of the items. Unless this is done, an unbiased review of the item is difficult to manage. The best approach to a critical review of the substance of a test item is for the reviewer to act like an examinee—to seek the correct answer to the item. Such an approach obviously requires that the correct answer should not always appear at the same place among the alternatives. One way to manage this operation is to prepare a reasonably random sequence of the digits one to four and use it as a guide to placement of correct responses among the four alternatives. A random sequence can be obtained from a well-shuffled deck of cards if each club is recorded as a one, each diamond as a two, each heart as a three, and each spade as a four.

The otherwise formidable task of item writing can be made more manageable if the total number of items required is divided into a daily quota. An item writer familiar with his material and working from an adequate test plan may be able to turn out the first drafts of 10 promising multiple-choice items in an hour or two. By working this long each day for 10 days, he may produce an entire test.

The order in which test items are arranged in the final form of the test is not critical. If different types of items—multiple choice, matching, and so forth—are included in the same test, there is some advantage in grouping each type together. It is sometimes desirable, for psychological reasons, to begin the test with several rather easy items to help relieve the initial tension examinees sometimes feel. But for most classroom tests the items do not, and should not, vary widely in obvious difficulty. Hence it is not feasible, even if it were considered desirable, to arrange them very precisely in order of difficulty. There is some logic, in arranging the items in topical groups, but little reason to arrange them by type of question (vocabulary, factual, and so forth) unless a separate score on each kind of question is to be obtained.

> 4. *Begin the item with a stem question or incomplete statement to which a reasonably adequate answer or completion can be given concisely and for which plausible wrong answers can be found.*

The function of the item stem is to acquaint the examinee with the problem that is being posed for him. Ideally, it should state or imply a specific question. Although one can sometimes save words without loss of clarity by using an incomplete statement as the item stem, a direct question is often better. Not only does a direct question tend to present the student with a more specific problem, it also may focus the item writer's purposes more clearly and help him to avoid irrelevance or unrelatedness in the distracters. Incidentally, one easy way to start a bad multiple-choice test item is to use the subject of a sentence as the item stem and its predicate as the correct response.

When an incomplete sentence is used as the item stem, the problem it presents to the examinee will usually be clearest if the omitted part comes at the end of the sentence, not the beginning or a middle portion. However, if the part omitted is only a word, short phrase, or number, the location of the missing portion is less crucial.

Novel questions and novel problem situations reward the critical-minded student who has sought to understand what he was taught and penalize the superficial learner. It is usually desirable to avoid using the same questions or problems in a test that were used in instruction. In general, bona fide questions such as would be asked by a person honestly seeking information are likely to be more important than quiz-type questions, which would only be asked by someone who already knew the answer. Here is an example of a bona fide question:

Who were the Huks in the Philippines?
    1. A tribe of primitive head-hunters
  *2. A Communist-supported rebel group
    3. Wealthy Philippine landowners and industrialists
    4. Members of the minority party in the Philippine legislature

This is a question that might occur naturally to a person seeking information. It is not one that has been invented to test a student's recall of particular instructional materials. It is consistent with the idea that the main objectives of instruction are to impart information useful outside the classroom. In contrast, a quiz-type question like the following is less desirable:

J. B. Matthews, one-time employee of Senator McCarthy's subcommittee, charged that a large number of supporters of Communism in the United States would be found in which of these groups?
    1. Wall Street bankers
    2. Newspaper editors
    3. Professional gamblers
  *4. Protestant clergymen

It sometimes seems desirable to phrase the stem question to ask not for the correct answer, but for the incorrect answer. For example, "Which of these is *not* a means of heat transmission?" Such questions should be used sparingly and carefully. They tend to trap the examinee, who easily forgets while pondering his answer that he is looking for a wrong answer, not a correct one. Negatively stated items seem most attractive when used in relation to formal categories or unique lists of causes, factors, and so forth. Frequently such categories and lists are matters of organizational convenience and lack the general validity or importance that make them good bases for test items.

Another common device for adapting multiple-choice items to questions that seem to require several correct answers is to add to the correct answers listed separately the alternative "all of the above" as the correct response. But use of this response is strictly appropriate only if all the preceding alternatives are thoroughly correct answers to the stem question, and even then there is the inherent ambiguity in this device. A correct answer should not be wrong simply because there are other correct answers. "All of the above" should be used sparingly as an alternative to multiple-choice test items.

The response "none of the above" is also sometimes used as the intended answer when no other good answer is provided or as a distracter when a good answer is provided. It is particularly useful in multiple-choice arithmetic or spelling items where the distinction between correctness and error is unequivocal. But this response, like "all of the above," should *not* be used unless the best answer is a thoroughly correct answer.

It is usually desirable to express the stem of the item so that it asks as directly, accurately, and simply as possible for the essential knowledge or ability the item is intended to test. The following item stem seems needlessly complex:

> Considered from an economic viewpoint, which of these proposals to maintain world peace derives the least support from the military potentialities of atomic energy?
> 1. An international police force should be established.
> 2. Permanent programs of universal military training should be adopted.
> *3. Sizes of standing military forces should be increased.
> 4. The remaining democratic nations of the world should enter into a military alliance.

Even after repeated careful readings, the meaning of this item stem is not clear. It involves a negative approach and seems to combine two dissimilar bases for judgment, economics and atomic energy. The wording of this item might seem to reflect lack of clarity in the thinking of the person who wrote it.

Informational preambles that serve only as window dressing and do not help the examinee understand the question he is being asked should ordinarily be avoided. But it is well to specify all conditions and qualifications necessary to make the intended response definitely the best of the available alternatives. If many descriptive or qualifying ideas are required, the clearest expression may be achieved by placing them in separate introductory sentences. In general, the item writer should avoid addressing the examinee personally, as if asking for his opinion rather than for a general truth. Try to avoid implying something in the item stem that is not strictly true, even though the implication does not interfere logically with the choice of a correct response to the item. For example:

> Why is blood plasma often preferred to whole blood for transfusions?
> 1. Whole blood may carry disease germs.

*2. Whole blood must be "typed" to match the blood of the patient.
3. Plasma can be prepared synthetically.
4. Plasma contains more disease-fighting white corpuscles than whole blood.

It is incorrect to state that blood plasma is preferred to whole blood. If whole blood of the proper type is available, it is usually preferred. The stem should ask what advantage blood plasma has over whole blood, for it is true that the plasma need not be typed.

> 5. *Phrase the intended correct response so that it is thoroughly correct or clearly adequate, expressed as clearly and concisely as possible, without providing clues that give it away to the clever but poorly prepared student.*

Ideally, the intended answer to a multiple-choice question should be a thoroughly correct answer, admitting no difference of opinion among adequately informed experts. This kind of absolute correctness, however, is difficult to achieve except in formal logical systems or in statements that simply reproduce other statements. Few, if any, inductive truths or experimentally based generalizations can be regarded as absolutely true. The test constructor must base many of his items on propositions that are not known certainly to be absolutely true but are strongly probable. But he should guard against basing items on statements whose validity would be challenged by competent scholars.

In this connection there are two damaging extremes to avoid. One is failure to quality the question or problem sufficiently to exclude alternative interpretations that lead to different but equally defensible correct answers. The other is qualifying the question in such a way that its truth becomes unequivocal but the question itself becomes inconsequential. For example, it is important to know why the armed forces of the United States were ordered into combat in Korea in 1950, but it is difficult to give a thoroughly correct answer to such a question. On the other hand, it is quite easy to give an unequivocally truthful answer to the question, "What explanation for U.S. military action in Korea was given in an editorial in the *Chicago Tribune* on Friday, June 30, 1950?" But the answer to such a reiterative type of question may not be highly important. The item writer should never settle for a best answer when a correct answer to the same question is available. He should be sure that, in the eyes of competent experts, his best answer is clearly better than any other alternative offered. But he should not avoid important questions, simply because no absolutely and completely correct answer is available for them.

The correct response to a multiple-choice test item sets the pattern for the other responses, the distracters. All responses should be parallel in grammatical structure, semantically similar, and roughly equivalent in length and complexity, since all are intended to be alternative responses to the same question. Obviously the alternatives should be described completely enough to be clearly meaningful, but no words should be wasted in the process and needless structural complexity should be avoided. Parallel structure sometimes requires that all responses should begin with the same word. But if the same group of words is repeated in each response, the possibility of including that phrase only once in the stem should be considered.

Brevity in the responses simplifies the task for the examinee by removing an irrelevant source of difficulty. Brief responses also tend to focus attention on the essential differences among the alternatives offered. Other things being equal, the multiple-choice test item having the shorter responses will be the better. But a test composed largely of items using one-word responses or very short phrases is likely to place more emphasis on vocabulary than on command of knowledge. The item writer should not sacrifice importance and significance in the questions to gain brevity in the responses.

Some irrelevant clues to the correct answer in multiple-choice test items may be due to lack of parallelism in the alternatives offered. There is a tendency for item writers to express the correct answer more carefully and at greater length than the other alternatives. Sometimes revealing key words from the item stem, or their synonyms, are repeated in the correct answer. Sometimes the correct response is more consistent grammatically or semantically with the item stem than are the other responses. Sometimes the correct response is more general and inclusive than any distracter. Sometimes a familiar verbal stereotype is used as the correct answer, so that a student can respond successfully simply by recalling vaguely that he had encountered those same words before. Finally, it sometimes happens that the stem of one item will inadvertently suggest the answer to another item. Here are some examples of items that provide irrelevant clues:

> When used in conjunction with the T-square, the left vertical edge of a triangle is used to draw:
> *1. Vertical lines
> 2. Slant lines
> 3. Horizontal lines
> 4. Inclined lines

The use of the word "vertical" in both the stem and the correct response of this item provides an obvious clue.

> The minor differences among organisms of the same kind are known as:
> 1. Heredity
> *2. Variations
> 3. Adaptation
> 4. Natural selection

The plural term "differences" in the stem calls for a plural response. This points directly to response 2 as the correct response.

> The major weakness of our government under the Articles of Confederation was that
>   1. There were no high officials.
> *2. It lacked power.
>   3. It was very difficult to amend.
>   4. There was only one house in Congress.

There is an obvious relation between lack of power and weakness of government. If one knew nothing about the Articles of Confederation, he would nevertheless tend to choose the correct answer on this common-sense basis alone.

> How did styles in women's clothing in 1950 differ most from those in 1900?
>   1. They showed more beauty.
>   2. They showed more variety.
>   3. They were easier to clean.
> *4. They were easier to live in, to work in, to move in, and were generally less restrictive.

The greater detail used in stating the correct response makes it undesirably obvious.

> History tells us that all nations have enjoyed participation in:
>   1. Gymnastics
>   2. Football
> *3. Physical training of some sort
>   4. Baseball

Response 3 obviously provides a more reasonable completion to the stem statement than any of the other responses. It represents a consistent style of expression. This is one of the dangers inherent in the use of incomplete statement item stems.

All of these irrelevant clues to the correct answer are undesirable, of course, and should be avoided. It is entirely appropriate to plant such clues deliberately in the distracters to mislead the test-wise but poorly prepared student. To give all of the relevant clues—those useful to well-prepared examinees—while avoiding the irrelevant clues is an important part of the art of writing multiple-choice test items.

> 6. *Choose and phrase the incorrect alternatives (distracters) so that they are thoroughly wrong or clearly inadequate, yet plausible enough to appeal to many poorly prepared examinees.*

A troublesome problem for many item writers is that of thinking of three good distracters, after the item stem and the correct answer have been written. Here are some tactics that may be helpful.

1. Define the class of things to which all the alternative answers must belong.

For example, if the question asks what cools an electric refrigerator, the class of possible answers is defined as "things that can cause cooling," such as ice, moving air, expansion of gas, and so forth.

2. Think of things that have some association with terms used in the question.

For the electric refrigerator question above, these might be such things as "flow of electricity through a compressed gas," or "electromagnetic absorption of heat energy."

3. If the item calls for a quantitative answer, make the responses distinctly different points along the same scale.

For example, in response to the question, "How many questions should the average student answer correctly on a good multiple-choice test?" the alternative answers might be 40 percent, 60 percent, 80 percent and 90 percent.

4. Phrase the question so that it calls for a yes or no answer plus an explanation.

For example, as responses to the question, "Did foreign freighters have a competitive advantage over U.S. freighters during the late 1960's? Why?" one could use these responses:

1. yes, because (reason 1)
2. yes, because (reason 2)
3. no, because (reason 3)
4. no, because (reason 4)

5. Use various combinations of two elements as the alternatives.

Thus four responses in some cases might be these.

1. Only A
2. Only B
3. Both A and B
4. Neither A nor B

If the two elements each have two different values, for example rise-fall, rapidly-slowly, they can be combined in this way to give four alternatives.

1. It rises rapidly
2. It rises slowly
3. It falls slowly
4. It falls rapidly

> 6. *Finally, if the desired alternatives are difficult to discover, consider using a different approach in the item stem.*

It is also useful sometimes to back off from the writing job and to ask just what the item is supposed to be testing. If the proposition on which it is based is self-evident, or if a plausible false alternative to it does not exist, the whole idea for the item may have to be discarded, and a new start made with a better idea.

It has occurred to a number of item writers that they might use as distracters the wrong answers students give when they are asked to produce (not choose) short answers to the questions used as multiple-choice item stems.[2] Some useful ideas are quite likely to be obtained in this way, but the gain in quality of items or ease of item writing seldom seems to justify the labor of obtaining the student responses.[3] The unaided ideas of the item writer are likely to be about as good as those he would get from the student responses.

These suggestions, and the illustrative items included in this chapter, should be of some help to the item writer as he seeks to invent plausible distracters for his items. But in the end the quality of those items is likely to be determined largely by his knowledge of the subject matter being tested, the original thinking he does to apply this knowledge to a specific item writing problem, and the time and care he is willing to devote to the task. Despite some recent attempts, it is unlikely that the process of item writing will be successfully mechanized or computerized in the forseeable future.[4,5]

Many multiple-choice test items prove to be too difficult or low in discrimination because the item requires examinees to make very fine distinctions between correct and incorrect responses. Perhaps the item writer's efforts to write plausible distracters led him to incorporate too much truth in them. Or perhaps he used his own keen perceptions of subtle differences in meaning as a standard for estimating the capabilities of

[2]M. R. Loree, *A Study of a Technique for Improving Tests.* Unpublished doctoral dissertation, University of Chicago, 1948.

[3]Richard E. Owens, Gerald S. Hanna and Floyd L. Coppedge, "Comparison of Multiple Choice Tests Using Different Types of Distractor Selection Techniques," *Journal of Educational Measurement,* vol. 7 (1970), 87–90.

[4]John R. Bormuth, *On the Theory of Achievement Test Items* (Chicago: University of Chicago Press, 1970).

[5]John Fremer and Ernest Anastasio, "Computer-assisted Item Writing," I, Spelling Items, *Journal of Educational Measurement,* vol. 6 (1969), 69–74.

his less capable students. To avoid these pitfalls the item writer should seek to maximize the ratio of plausibility to correctness in his distracters. He should ask not only, "Does this distracter look good enough for some students to choose it?" but also, "Could it, by any stretch of the imagination, be defended as a correct answer to the question?" Unless the answer to the first question is "yes" and the second "no," he should try again. The following item illustrates plausible but totally incorrect distracters:

> To what did the title of the Broadway musical *Top Banana* refer?
> 1. The dictator of a Central American country
> 2. The warden of a penitentiary
> *3. The leading comedian in a burlesque theater
> 4. The president of a large fruit company

Bananas are fruits from Central America. The phrase "top banana" sounds like slang which penitentiary inmates might use. Hence these distracters have been well chosen to plant common-sense clues that will attract those who lack the knowledge the item is designed to test.

Common practice in writing multiple-choice test items calls for three or four distracters, so that four or five alternatives are provided in each item. If good distracters are available, the larger the number of alternatives, the more highly discriminating the item is likely to be. However, as one seeks to write more distracters each additional one is likely to be somewhat weaker. There is some merit in setting one's goal at three good distracters to each multiple-choice item and in struggling temporarily to reach this goal. Not all good distracters are immediately apparent. Some will emerge only after considerable brain-racking.

On the other hand, there is no magic in four alternatives and no real reason why all items in a test should have the same number of alternatives. It is quite possible to write a good multiple-choice test item with only two distracters (three responses), and occasionally with only one distracter, as Smith, and Ebel and Williams have shown.[6] After tryout, one can actually improve some items by dropping distracters that don't distract poor students, or that do distract good ones.

A student may sometimes arrive at the correct answer to a multiple-choice test item through a process of elimination. Rejecting responses that seem unsatisfactory, he is finally left with one that he selects as the right answer, not because he has any basis for choosing it directly, but simply because none of the others will do.

---

[6]Kendon Smith, "An Investigation of the Use of 'Double Choice' Items in Testing Achievement," *Journal of Educational Research*, vol. 51 (1958), 387–89; and Robert L. Ebel and Bob J. Williams, "The Effect of Varying the Number of Alternatives per Item on Multiple-choice Vocabulary Test Items," *The 14th Yearbook of the National Council on Measurements Used in Education* (East Lansing, Mich.: Michigan State University, 1957), pp. 63–65.

The availability of this process of elimination is sometimes regarded as a weakness of the multiple-choice item form. A student gets credit for knowing something that he really doesn't know, it is charged. Most specialists in test construction, however, do not disapprove of the process of answering by elimination and do not regard the process as a sign of weakness in multiple-choice items in general, or in an item where the process is particularly useful. (It might be noted in passing that an item that uses the response "none of the above" as a correct answer *requires* the student to answer by a process of elimination.) There are two reasons why this process is not generally deplored by the test specialists.

In the first place, the function of achievement test items is primarily to contribute to a measure of general achievement in an area of study. They are not intended primarily to provide an inventory of which particular bits of knowledge or skills a student has. The achievement of a student who answers items 1, 3, and 5 correctly but misses 2 and 4 is regarded as equal to the achievement of another student who answers items 2, 3, and 4 correctly but misses 1 and 5. Identifying exactly which things a student has achieved or failed to achieve is a matter of secondary importance in an achievement test.

In the second place, the knowledge and ability required to properly eliminate incorrect alternatives can be, and usually is, closely related to the knowledge or ability that would be required to select the correct alternative. If education does not consist in the accumulation of unrelated bits of information, if the development of a meaningful network of related facts and concepts is essential, then the fact that a student responds in a reflective, problem-solving manner, choosing the best answer by rational processes (including the process of elimination), should be applauded rather than deplored.

In practice, few multiple-choice test items are likely to be answered correctly solely by eliminating incorrect choices. Far more often the process of choice will involve comparative judgments of this alternative against that. It is unlikely that an examinee who is totally ignorant of the correct answer would have knowledge enough to eliminate with certainty the incorrect alternatives. This is especially likely to be true if the item is well enough constructed so that all the available alternatives, correct and incorrect, have some obvious basic similarity. For this and the other reasons just given it seems safe to conclude that the problem of answer choice by a process of distracter elimination need not be regarded as a serious one.

7. Word the item as clearly, simply, and correctly as possible.

The purpose of the words and syntax chosen in writing a multiple-choice test item is to communicate explicit meaning as efficiently as possible. Habits of colorful, picturesque, imaginative, creative writing may serve the item writer badly by impairing the precision and definiteness of his communication of thought. Few written words are read with such careful attention to meaning, expressed and implied, as those in objective test items. Item writing makes rigorous demands on the vocabulary and writing skill of the test constructor as well as on his mastery of the subject matter of the test and his familiarity with the characteristics of the students to be tested. Simple carelessness in grammar, usage, punctuation, or spelling may interfere with the effectiveness of an item and will certainly reflect no credit on the item writer. Skill in expository writing and careful exercise of that skill are essential to the production of good objective test items.

8. Modify the item, if necessary, so that it is reasonable to expect about half the examinees to answer the item correctly.

Common sense would suggest that a good test should include some easy and some difficult items along with those of intermediate ease or difficulty. In most classroom tests, however, especially at the high school and college levels, reasonable theoretical models predict and experimental studies confirm that the most reliable and valid scores will be obtained by giving preference to items of medium difficulty.

For free-response items an item of medium difficulty is one that about 50 percent of the examinees answer correctly. For choice-type items, where the possibility of blind guessing exists, an item of medium difficulty can be defined as one on which the proportion of correct responses is midway between the expected chance proportion and 100 percent. Thus a true-false item of medium difficulty would be answered correctly by about 75 percent of the examinees. A multiple-choice item offering five alternative responses would be medium in difficulty when answered correctly by about 60 percent of the examinees (since 60 percent is midway between 20 percent, the chance success proportion for items of this type, and 100 percent).

Items of the same average difficulty for a group have widely different apparent difficulties for specific students. An item that the best student answers incorrectly will be answered correctly by many students of lower ability. In most courses, the best student is distinguished most clearly from the rest not by his superior ability to answer the very hardest questions, but by his ability to answer more questions of all levels of difficulty.

An item so easy that all examinees answer it correctly, or so difficult that none answers it correctly, yields no information about relative levels of achievement. An item of 50 percent difficulty can yield the maximum amount of this kind of information. Fortunately, items in a midrange of difficulty, say from 30 percent to 70 percent success, are almost as productive of differential information as are items of 50 percent difficulty. No item writer can predict precisely how difficult his items are likely to be. If he aims at 50 percent, he is likely to produce items that actually range quite widely in difficulty. The point is that he usually should not deliberately try to write some very easy and other very difficult items.

Some instructors and students disapprove of tests on which the typical student succeeds in answering correctly only about half of the questions. It seems to reflect ineffectiveness of teaching and a low level of mastery of course objectives. It is contrary to the tradition of percentage marking, in which 100 represented perfection and 70 or 75 substantial achievement, but barely enough to justify advancement to the next grade or course.

Objective tests could be built on which the typical student would score 70 percent correct, 75 percent correct, or even higher. But such a test would be relatively inefficient, including many items that nearly all students answer correctly. Items of this kind yield relatively little information useful in differentiating levels of achievement. Further, the notion that traditional percentage standards for marking and passing provide absolute standards of achievement rests on assumptions easily shown to be unreasonable or contrary to fact. In most cases an instructor is well advised to discard this notion and to concentrate on building the most efficient and reliable tests he can. This calls for items of intermediate difficulty, and the closer they cluster about 50 percent, the better the test will ordinarily be.

To some extent the difficulty of a multiple-choice test item is inherent in the idea on which it rests. There are, however, techniques that give the writer of a multiple-choice test item some control over the difficulty of the items he produces on a given topic. He can generally make the stem question easier by making it more general or harder by making it more specific, as the following items illustrate:

> A tariff is a tax on:
> 1. Gifts of money
> *2. Goods brought into a country
> 3. Income of immigrants
> 4. Real estate

Only the most general notions about a tariff are required to successfully respond to this item. It is suitable for use at the lowest level of achievement in this area. A much higher degree of knowledge of tariffs is required to respond successfully to the following item.

> A high protective tariff on Swiss watches in the United States is intended to most directly benefit:
> 1. Swiss watchmakers

    2. United States citizens who buy Swiss watches
    3. United States government officials
  *4. United States watchmakers

This pair of items illustrates how the generality or specificity of a question can be used to help control its difficulty.

    The item writer can make the correct response easier to select by making the alternatives more heterogeneous and harder by making them more homogeneous. In some cases, several items of information or demonstrations of ability can be called for in the same item and the correct response arranged so that a student who knows or can do any one of the several will be able to choose the intended response.

    By using techniques such as these, the test constructor can often salvage an appropriate item idea which seems initially to be much too easy or too difficult. If the techniques seem ineffective, the appropriateness of the idea as a basis for testing achievement may be open to question.

    9. Arrange for competent, independent review and revision of the initial item draft.

    A person reacting to test items written by another can often detect errors, ambiguities, or idiosyncrasies of conception that might interfere with the ability of a test item to discriminate validly among various levels of achievement. If the reviewer also has specific competence in the field covered by the test, his suggestions are likely to be more numerous, more relevant, and more generally helpful. A schoolwide requirement that every objective classroom test be independently reviewed by a staff member other than the author and that the names of both be printed on the final form might do more than any other step to improve the qualtiy of objective classroom tests and the grades based on them. An analogous step, which might also yield great improvement, would be the requirement that each essay test answer be read and graded independently by the instructor and a competent colleague, with the names of each and the grades they each assigned reported to the student.

    If the item writer cannot arrange for independent review of his items, he should put the first drafts aside for a few days and then review them himself. This is not nearly so effective as review by another person, but it is far better than no review at all. In each case the reviewer should ask these questions: Is the item based on an appropriate idea? Does the stem present a clear problem? Is the correct response adequate and better than any other response? Are the distracters likely to attract mainly students of low achievement? Is the wording clear? Is the difficulty appropriate?

    If possible, the reviewer should react to each item as an examinee would, seeking the best answer and then checking his choice against the key. This approach increases his likelihood of detecting serious flaws in the item.

One difficulty is likely to arise when objective test items are reviewed independently, a difficulty that can be minimized if both the item writer and the reviewer are aware of it. It is the tendency for their individual preferences in matters of style to become sources of disagreement on matters irrelevant to the basic quality of the item. Both item writer and reviewer should cultivate the ability to discriminate between essential elements of item quality and incidental item characteristics and focus on the former.

ILLUSTRATIONS OF DESIRABLE AND UNDESIRABLE CHARACTERISTICS OF MULTIPLE-CHOICE TEST ITEMS

The items that follow have been collected from a variety of sources. Some of them were prepared for tests of understanding of contemporary affairs in the early 1950's. Although these may no longer be suitable for use, the principles of item writing they illustrate are still valid. The illustrations have been grouped in nine sets to illustrate characteristics of the item:

A. Topics	*D.* Responses	*G.* Clues
B. Approach	*E.* Distracters	*H.* Difficulty
C. Stem	*F.* Wording	*I.* Arrangement

Brief comments accompany each item to explain its virtues or shortcomings. These items may also serve to suggest the variety of approaches or styles that may be used in formulating multiple-choice test items.

A. Topics
1. *Item permitting a correct answer (desirable, if possible)*
What happened in 1953 to the proposed act of Congress granting statehood to Hawaii?
   a. It was passed by both the House and the Senate.
   b. It was defeated in both the House and the Senate.
   *c. It was passed by the House but not by the Senate.
   d. No act regarding statehood for Hawaii was introduced in either the House or the Senate.

There are some matters of fact that provide a suitable basis for correct answer items. Some judgment is involved in determining whether or not a governor is "successful" (Item 3 below), but no judgment is involved in describing what each house of Congress did with a particular measure.

2. *Item using citation of authority (undesirable)*
   What does Ross say about the Kuder-Richardson method for calculating test reliability?
   *a. It involves assumptions that are likely to be difficult to meet in the ordinary test situation.
   b. It produces coefficients which are higher than those obtained by the split-halves procedure.
   c. It is the simplest and generally most satisfactory method.
   d. It takes account of both pupil errors in response and sampling errors among the items.

What a particular writer has to say on this point is probably less important than what experts generally agree to be true. If there is no consensus among experts on the matter, probably no student should be held responsible for knowing what one writer believes. Incidentally, the current opinion of experts tends to favor the use of the Kuder-Richardson formula.

3. *Item requiring best answer (desirable)*
   Which statement best characterizes the man appointed by President Eisenhower to be Chief Justice of the United States Supreme Court?
   a. An associate justice of the Supreme Court who had once been a professor of law at Harvard.
   *b. A successful governor who had been an unsuccessful candidate for the Republican presidential nomination.
   c. A well-known New York attorney who successfully prosecuted the leaders of the Communist party in the United States.
   d. A Democratic senator from a southern state who had supported Eisenhower's campaign for the presidency.

For many of the most important questions that need to be asked, it is impossible to state an absolutely correct answer within the reasonable limits of a multiple-choice test item. Even if space limitation were not a factor, two experts would probably not agree on the precise wording of the best possible answer. The use of the type of item that has one best answer permits the item writer to ask much more significant questions and frees him from the responsibility of stating a correct answer so precisely that all authorities would agree that the particular wording used was the best possible wording.

4. *Item based on matter of opinion (permissible)*
   Which of these statements is most consistent with Jefferson's concept of democracy?
   a. Democracy is part of the divine plan for mankind.
   b. Democracy requires a strong national government.
   *c. The purpose of government is to promote the welfare of the people.
   d. The purpose of government is to protect the people from radical or subversive minorities.

The responses to this question represent generalizations on the basis of Jefferson's speeches and writings. No authoritative sanction for one particular generalization is likely to be available. Yet scholars familiar with Jefferson's work would probably agree on a best answer to this item. In such cases the use of an item based on expert opinion is entirely justifiable.

   5. *Item admitting no best answer* (*undesirable*)
      Which event in the following list has been of the greatest importance in American history?
      *a. Braddock's defeat
      b. Burr's conspiracy
      c. The Hayes-Tilden contest
      d. The Webster-Hayne debate

It is unlikely that scholars can agree on which of the events listed is of the greatest importance in American history. The importance of an event depends on the point of view of the judge and the context in which he is thinking of it. Unless experts can agree on a best answer, it should not be used as a test item.

   6. *Item dealing with an incidental detail* (*undesirable*)
      This question is based on the advertising campaign of Naumkeag Mills to retain the market leadership of Pequot bed linen. What was the competitive position of Pequot products in 1927?
      a. Ahead of all competitors among all customers
      *b. Strong with institutional buyers but weak with household consumers
      c. Second only to Wamsutta among all customers
      d. Weak with all groups of consumers

This advertising campaign may provide excellent illustrations of the problems involved and the practices to follow in advertising campaigns. But it seems not entirely appropriate to measure a student's ability to handle an advertising campaign by asking him to recall the details of one illustration used in instruction.

   7. *Item based on unique organization of subject matter* (*undesirable*)
      The second principle of education is that the individual:
      a. Gathers knowledge   c. Responds to situations
      b. Makes mistakes   *d. Resents domination

The only person capable of answering this question is one who has studied a particular book or article. Whether a given principle of education is first or second is usually a matter of little importance. Educators have not agreed on any particular list of principles of education or any priority of principles. This item shows an undesirably close tie-up to the organization of subject matter used by a specific instructor or writer.

   8. *Item based on novel question* (*desirable*)
      If the radius of the earth were increased by 3 feet, its circumference at the equator would be increased by about how much?

a. 9 feet	**c.* 19 feet
b. 12 feet	*d.* 28 feet

Requiring a student to predict what would happen under certain unusual, even impossible, circumstances is a good way of measuring his understanding of the principle involved. Mechanical computation of the answer to a problem like the one above is apt to be much more tedious than estimation on the basis of thorough understanding of the relationship.

9. *Item requiring selective recall* (*desirable*)
   Which of the following was an important development in Canada during 1953?
   *a. Rapid business and industrial growth
   b. A severe and widespread economic depression
   c. A marked trend toward Communism in provincial governments
   d. Appearance of a strong movement favoring unification of the United States and Canada

Unless this item had been made the specific object of instruction, it will function as a test of a student's ability to recall a variety of information about Canada, to select that which is relevant, and to base a generalization upon it.

B. *Approach*

10. *Item using descriptive responses* (*desirable*)
    What is monogamy?
    a. Refusal to marry
    b. Marriage of one woman to more than one husband
    c. Marriage of one man to more than one wife
    *d. Marriage of one man to only one wife

Inexperienced item writers tend to seek items having very short responses. This seriously limits the significance and scope of the achievements that can be measured. In an item measuring vocabulary knowledge, it is usually better to place the term to be defined in the item stem and to use definitions or identifications as the responses. The same principle should apply to nonvocabulary items. One-word responses need not be avoided altogether, but they should seldom be prominent in any test.

11. *Item using label responses* (*undesirable*)
    A marriage in which one woman marries one man is called

a. unicameral	*c.* monotheism
b. dualism	**d.* monogamy

This item illustrates how item 10 might be inverted to give one-word responses. But when changed in this way it may be somewhat less realistic. It is true that people frequently search their minds for a word to express a particular concept. But seldom does that concept have the characteristics of a formal definition, such as the stem of item 11. Further, and perhaps more importantly, it is usually somewhat more difficult to get good distracters for a one-word correct response than for a phrase or sentence. When this is true, item discrimination may suffer.

12. *Item showing artificial inversion (undesirable)*
    A man hits a ball into the air to a height of 15 feet or more and it comes down within 2 feet of the net. He is attempting to perfect the
    a. High pass   c. High lob
    b. High volley   *d. High set-up

Item 12 shows artificial inversion of a test item to gain short responses. It is not likely that a coach or a player would often need to be able to to answer a question like the one above. It would seem much more useful for them to know how best to practice a particular maneuver, such as the high set-up. A question asking this directly would look more practical and might even provide better discrimination.

13. *Item using indirect approach (undesirable)*
    Which leaf layer makes it possible for the plants to get the raw materials needed for photosynthesis?
    a. Upper epidermis   c. Spongy layer
    b. Palisade layer   *d. Lower epidermis

It is true that the pores through which the leaf cells of most plants obtain gases needed for photosynthesis occur mainly in the lower epidermis, but it is unnecessarily and undesirably indirect to speak of the lower layer as "making it possible" for the plants to get the raw materials. Further, not all plants have their stomata in the lower epidermis. A notable exception, for example, is the water lily. A direct question on the function of the stomata might be preferable.

14. *Item asking examinee his opinion (undesirable)*
    What do you consider the most important objective of the staff meetings?
    *a. To establish good working relations with your staff
    b. To handle routine matters
    c. To help teachers improve instruction
    d. To practice and exemplify democracy in administration

There is one sense in which any answer to this item must be considered a correct answer. On the other hand, what the item writer obviously wished to determine was the examinee's judgment concerning the most important objective of staff meetings, for the purpose of checking that judgment against authoritative consensus in the matter. It would be better to ask him directly to choose the most important objective of staff meetings. His answer will obviously be what he considers the most important objective, but it will be open to criticism and possible correction if it differs from the judgment of recognized experts.

15. *Item combining two elements to give four responses* (*desirable*)
   What was the general policy of the Eisenhower administration during 1953 with respect to government expenditures and taxes?
   a. Reduction of both expenditures and taxes
   **b.* Reduction of expenditures, no change in taxes
   c. Reduction in taxes, no change in expenditures
   d. No change in either expenditures or taxes

One common difficulty with four-response multiple-choice items is that of securing four good alternatives. An obvious solution to this problem in some cases is to combine two questions with two alternatives each to give the necessary four alternatives.

16. *Item combining a question with an explanation* (*desirable*)
   Has the average size of farms in the United States tended to increase in recent years? Why?
   a. Yes, because as the soil loses its natural fertility more land must be cultivated to maintain the same output
   **b.* Yes, because the use of farm machinery has made large farms more efficient than small farms
   c. No, because the difficulty in securing farm labor has forced many farmers to limit their operations
   d. No, because large family farms tend to be subdivided to provide smaller farms for the children

This is a variation of the preceding type of item in which essentially two questions, having two or more alternatives each, are combined to give four alternatives.

C. Stem

17. *Item using incomplete stem* (*undesirable*)
   Physiology teaches us that
   **a.* The development of vital organs is dependent upon muscular activity.
   b. Strength is independent of muscle size.
   c. The mind and body are not influenced by each other.
   d. Work is not exercise.

Like Item 19, Item 17 poses no specific question. Physiology could teach a variety of things. While there may be somewhat greater danger of this lack of specificity when incomplete sentences are used as item stems, this item would be just as bad if the stem read, "What does physiology teach us?"

18. *Item using negative stem* (*undesirable*)
   In the definition of a mineral, which of the following is incorrect?
   a. It was produced by geologic processes.
   b. It has distinctive physical properties.
   c. It contains one or more elements.
   **d.* Its chemical composition is variable.

Items that are negatively stated, that is, that require an examinee to pick an answer that is not true or characteristic, tend to be somewhat confusing. They appear unusually attractive to examination writers because so much of the instructional material is organized in terms of parallel subheadings under a main topic. This suggests the easy approach, that of asking for something that is *not* one of those subheadings. However, such questions are rarely encountered outside the classroom and thus lack the practical relevance that is usually desirable.

19. *Item asking no specific question* (*undesirable*)
    In comparing the period of heterosexual adjustment of our culture with those of other cultures, it must be concluded that
    *a. There are tremendous differences that can only be explained on a cultural basis.
    b. There are large differences that must be explained by the interaction of biology and the more influential culture.
    c. Although there are some differences, the biological foundation of puberty is fundamental.
    d. In most cultures puberty is the period of heterosexual adjustment.

There is a wide variety of conclusions possible on the basis of a study of a particular period of human development. Until the examinee reads the responses, he has no clear idea of what the question is asking. The item as a whole is not focused on any single specific problem. This opens the way for confusing multiple interpretations.

20. *Item using an introductory sentence* (*permissible*)
    The term "creeping socialism" appeared frequently in political discussions in 1953. Which of these is most often used to illustrate "creeping socialism"?
    *a. Generation and distribution of electric power by the federal government
    b. Communist infiltration of labor unions
    c. Gradual increase in sales and excise taxes
    d. Participation of the United States in international organizations such as the United Nations

The use of a separate sentence frequently adds to the clarity of the item stem if it is necessary to present background information as well as to ask the question itself. Combining these two elements into a single-question sentence probably would make it considerably more complex.

21. *Item including a necessary qualification* (*desirable*)
    What change occurs in the composition of the air in a lighted airtight room in which the only living things are growing green plants?
    a. Carbon dioxide increases and oxygen decreases.
    *b. Carbon dioxide decreases and oxygen increases.
    c. Both carbon dioxide and oxygen increase.
    d. Both carbon dioxide and oxygen decrease.

As originally worded this item simply asked, "What change occurs in the composition of the air in a room in which green plants are growing?" Only if one specifies that the room is lighted, so that photosynthesis can take place, that it is airtight, so that changes in the composition will not be neutralized by ventilation, and that there are no other living things that might consume the oxygen faster than it is produced, is it possible to give a firm answer to this question.

22. *Item involving "window dressing" (undesirable)*
    While ironing her formal, Jane burned her hand accidentally on the hot iron. This was due to a transfer of heat by
    *a. Conduction
    b. Radiation
    c. Convection
    d. Absorption

The introductory sentence suggests that the item involves a practical problem. Actually the question asked calls only for knowledge of technical terminology.

23. *Item involving an "instructional aside" (undesirable)*
    In purifying water for a city water supply, one process is to have the impure water seep through layers of sand and fine and coarse gravel. Here many impurities are left behind. Below are four terms, one of which will describe this process better than the others. Select the correct one.
    a. Sedimentation
    *b. Filtration
    c. Chlorination
    d. Aeration

The primary purpose of a test item is to measure achievement. While much learning may occur during the process of taking a test, deliberate inclusion of instructional materials may reduce its effectiveness as a test more than its instructional value is increased. It might be better to ask the purpose of filtration in purifying city water supplies or the type of filter used.

D. *Responses*
    24. *Item showing inappropriate responses (undesirable)*
        The chief difference between the surface features of Europe and North America is that
        a. The area of Europe is larger.
        b. Europe extends more to the South.
        c. The Volga River is longer than the Missouri-Mississippi.
        *d. The greater highlands and plains of Europe extend in an east-west direction.

Only the correct answer really describes a surface feature of Europe. Either the question should not be limited to "surface features" or the responses given should all conform to that category.

25. *Item showing nonparallel responses* (*undesirable*)
Slavery was first started
*a. At Jamestown settlement
 b. At Plymouth settlement
 c. At the settlement of Rhode Island
 d. A decade before the Civil War

The first three responses are places; the fourth is a time. Use of a direct question stem might help to prevent this type of ambiguity, which could make it possible for more than one answer to be correct.

26. *Item using indistinct responses* (*undesirable*)
Meat can be preserved in brine due to the fact that
 a. Salt is a bacterial poison.
*b. Bacteria cannot withstand the osmotic action of the brine.
 c. Salt alters the chemical composition of the food.
 d. Brine protects the meat from contact with air.

Both responses *a* and *b* could be judged correct. Response *b* simply explains why response *a* is correct. It is undesirable to have only one of two almost equally correct responses be considered the correct response.

27. *Item including complicating elements in the responses* (*undesirable*)
Systematic geography differs from regional geography mainly in that
 a. Systematic geography deals, in the main, with physical geography, whereas regional geography concerns itself essentially with the field of human geography.
 b. Systematic geography studies a region systematically, while regional geography is concerned only with a descriptive account of a region.
*c. Systematic geography studies a single phenomenon in its distribution over the earth in order to supply generalizations for regional geography, which studies the arrangement of phenomena in one given area.
 d. Systematic geography is the modern scientific way of studying differentiation of the earth's surface, while regional geography is the traditional and descriptive way of studying distribution of phenomena in space.

It is a principle of good item writing that the responses should be as simple and clearly distinct as possible. In an item of this type it is very difficult to perceive and keep in mind the essential distinction between the alternative responses. A better question might ask, "What is the characteristic of systematic geography which distinguishes it essentially from regional geography?"

28. *Item using "none of these" appropriately* (*desirable*)
Which word is misspelled?
 a. Contrary   c. Extreme   e. None of these
*b. Tendancy   d. Variable

Whenever each of the responses can be judged unequivocally as correct or incorrect in response to the question posed in the item stem, it is appropriate to use "none of these" as a response. It would also be appropriate to use "all of these" in a similar situation where more than one perfectly correct answer is possible.

29. *Item using "all of these" and "none of these" inappropriately (undesirable)*
    What does the term "growth" mean?
    *a. Maturation   d. All of these
    b. Learning   e. None of these
    c. Development

Since no word means exactly the same as "growth," this item appears more suited to best-answer than to correct-answer form. "All of these" or "none of these" are usually considered inappropriate responses to best-answer items.

30. *Item using quantitative scale of responses (desirable)*
    How did (A) the estimated amount of petroleum discovered in new fields in 1953 compare with (B) the amount extracted from producing fields in the same year?
    a. A was practically zero.
    b. A was about half of B.
    c. A just about equaled B.
    *d. A was greater than B.

In many situations the precise value of a quantitative answer is less important than knowledge of the general level of that value. It is frequently possible to categorize the responses to represent intervals on a scale of quantities. This presents a systematic approach to testing in quantitative situations. The use of code letters for the two quantities to be compared shortens the response options and probably adds to their clarity.

31. *Item using qualitative scale of responses (desirable)*
    Some cases of lung cancer have been attributed to smoking. What was the status of this idea in 1953?
    a. The theory had been clearly established by medical evidence.
    *b. It was a controversial matter and some experts considered the evidence to be inconclusive.
    c. The theory had been clearly disproved by surveys of smokers.
    d. The theory was such a recent development that no tests of it had been completed.

The responses to this item represent a scale of values from complete establishment to complete indefiniteness. The use of a qualitative scale of responses helps to systematize the process of test construction and to suggest desirable responses.

E. *Distracters*

32. *Item using true statements as distracters (desirable)*
    What is the principal advantage of a battery of lead storage cells over a battery of dry cells for automobile starting and lighting?

a. The storage cell furnishes direct current.
b. The voltage of the storage cell is higher.
*c. The current from the storage cell is stronger.
d. The initial cost of the storage cell is less.

It is not necessary that the incorrect responses to a test item be themselves incorrect statements. They simply need to be incorrect answers to the stem question. Lead storage cells do furnish direct current, at a higher voltage than dry cells, but this is not the reason why the storage cell is preferred. Judgments concerning the relevance of knowledge may be as important as judgments concerning its truth. Multiple-choice items should make frequent use of this device for testing an achievement that is sometimes thought to be testable only by using essay examinations.

33. *Item using stereotypes in distracters* (*desirable*)
Which of these has effected the greatest change in domestic plants and animals?
a. Influence of environment on heredity
b. Organic evolution
*c. Selective breeding
d. Survival of the fittest

Phrases like "organic evolution" or "survival of the fittest," which a student may have heard without understanding, provide excellent distracters at the elementary level of discrimination for which this item is intended.

34. *Item using obscure distracters* (*undesirable*)
A chaotic condition

| a. Asymptotic | c. Gauche |
| *b. Confused | d. Permutable |

If the words "chaotic" and "confused" represent an appropriate level of difficulty for this vocabulary test, then the remaining terms used as distracters are obviously too difficult. It is unreasonable to expect the examinee to know for sure that one of them might not be a better synonym for "chaotic" than the intended correct answer. The use of distracters that are less difficult than the correct answer is sometimes criticized because it permits a student to respond successfully by eliminating incorrect responses. However, students who can respond successfully on this basis usually possess more knowledge than those who cannot. Hence the discriminating power of an item is not impaired by this characteristic.

35. *Item using a highly implausible distracter* (*undesirable*)
Which of the following has helped most to increase the average length of human life?
a. Fast driving
b. Avoidance of overeating
c. Wider use of vitamins
*d. Wider use of inoculations

Some teachers may feel that the abilities of some of their students cannot possibly be underestimated, but they should not let this feeling of frustration lead them to employ such an unreasonable distracter as the first response to this item.

36. *Item involving verbal trick (undesirable)*
    Horace Greeley is known for his
    a. Advice to young men not to go west
    b. Discovery of anesthetics
    *c. Editorship of the *New York Tribune*
    d. Humorous anecdotes

Insertion of the "not" in the first response spoils what would otherwise be the best answer to the question. This makes the item test the examinee's alertness more than it tests his knowledge of Horace Greeley.

F. *Wording*
37. *Item using imprecise wording (undesirable)*
    Why do we have the warmest weather in summer?
    a. The sun is nearest the earth in summer.
    *b. The sun's rays strike the earth most directly in summer.
    c. The air is freer of clouds in summer.
    d. The prevailing winds blow from the south in summer.

It is not accurate to say the sun's rays strike the earth any more directly in summer than they do at any other time of the year. What is true is that the sun's rays are more nearly vertical to the surface and hence are concentrated on a smaller area than is true when they strike the earth's surface on a slant.

38. *Item showing needless repetition in responses (undersirable)*
    Which is the best definition for a vein?
    *a. A blood vessel carrying blood going to the heart
    b. A blood vessel carrying blue blood
    c. A blood vessel carrying impure blood
    d. A blood vessel carrying blood away from the heart

This item could probably be improved by using in incomplete statement stem such as, "A vein is a blood vessel carrying——." Occasionally some repetition provides the most convenient way of making the item clear, but in this case the repetition seems excessive.

39. *Item showing ineffective expression (undesirable)*
    Among the factors listed which have contributed to rapid expansion of cut-over land, the most important during recent years has been
    a. Confiscatory taxation of standing timber
    *b. High prices for lumber
    c. Rapid growth of population
    d. Rising standards of living

Item stems should be not only grammatically correct, but should represent the most effective expression of the question idea. Rewording the item to read, "What has been the most important cause for the rapid increase in cut-over lands in recent years?" would seem to improve it.

G. Clues

40. *Item using stereotyped phrases in the correct answer (undesirable)*
    Which best describes what happens when work is done?
    *a. A force operates through a distance.
    b. A force is exerted.
    c. Energy is destroyed.
    d. Potential energy is changed to kinetic.

The statement that work is done whenever a force operates through a distance is a somewhat abstract statement. It could be remembered by one who concentrates on verbal recall almost as well as by one who has grasped the underlying concept of work in concrete situations.

41. *Item using stereotyped answer (undesirable)*
    How did Columbus discover America?
    a. He was blown off his course by a violent storm.
    *b. He was seeking a water route to the Orient.
    c. Queen Isabella sent him to make discoveries.
    d. He was fleeing persecution in Spain.

Stereotyped answers like the one used as the correct response to this item and item 40 could encourage superficial learning. Hence they seldom ought to appear in good test items.

42. *Item whose distracters are too similar (undesirable)*
    The large number of insect species alive today is evidence of
    a. Their relative freedom from attacks of predators
    *b. Perfection of their adaptation to their environment
    c. Their very complex structure
    d. Their great ability to produce many young

In this item the distracters are all much less general than the correct response. This similarity makes the correct response more obvious than it probably ought to be.

43. *Items that interlock (undesirable)*
    What, if anything, developed in 1955 with respect to relations between Egypt and Soviet Russia?
    a. A Russian military force invaded Egypt.
    b. Egypt accused members of the Russian embassy of spying and broke off diplomatic relations.
    c. Soviet Russia supported Egypt's demand for independence from Britain.
    *d. The Egyptian government arranged to buy arms from Soviet Russia.

How did the Western powers react to Egypt's agreement to buy arms from Soviet Russia?
  a. They approved it as a gesture of good will.
  b. They pointed out that it was a private affair between Egypt and Russia.
  *c. They pointed out that it was a threat to peace in the eastern Mediterranean.
  d. They protested that Egypt was aiding a potential enemy.

The second of the two items above provides the answer to the first. Attempts to cover the same small unit of subject matter too intensively, or on diverse levels of comprehension, may lead to interlocking test items. The best preventative is careful review of the items after they have been written.

H. *Difficulty*

44. *Easier item using heterogeneous responses (permissible)*
    An embargo is
  *a. A law or regulation
  b. A kind of boat
  c. An embankment
  d. A foolish adventure

The responses to this item vary widely. Because of their wide differences, only an elementary knowledge of embargoes is required for successful response.

45. *Harder item using homogeneous responses (permissible)*
    An embargo is
  a. A tariff
  b. A customs duty
  *c. The stoppage of goods from entry and departure
  d. An admission of goods free of duty

Although the same question is implied in both items 44 and 45, the homogeneity of the responses in item 45 requires a considerably higher level of knowledge about embargoes and hence makes the item more difficult.

46. *Easier item involving multiple clues (permissible)*
    Which of the following are outstanding contemporary pianists?
  *a. Robert Casadesus and Rudolph Serkin
  b. Patrice Munsel and Marian Anderson
  c. Claude Debussy and Ignace Paderewski
  d. Alan Paton and Alec Guinness

The use of the names of two individuals fitting the specification in the item stem makes it somewhat easier. The examinee need only know one of the contemporary pianists, or know one in each of the three distracters is not a contemporary pianist, to respond successfully.

I. Arrangement

47. *Item with response placed in tandem* (*undesirable*)
The balance sheet report for the Ajax Canning Company would reveal (*a*) The company's profit for the previous fiscal year (**b*) The amount of money owed to its creditors (*c*) The amount of income tax paid (*d*) The amount of sales for the previous fiscal period.

Responses in tandem save some space but are much more difficult to compare in the process of selection than those placed in list form.

48. *Item with unnatural sequence of responses* (*undesirable*)
The population of Denmark is about
   a. 2 million
   b. 15 million
   *c. 4 million
   d. 7 million

Whenever the responses for an item form a quantitative or qualitative scale, they normally should be arranged in order of magnitude from smallest to largest or largest to smallest. This may avoid some confusion on the part of the examinee and eliminate an irrelevant source of error.

SUMMARY

Some of the main ideas developed in this chapter are expressed in the following 24 statements.

1. The most highly regarded and widely used form of objective test item at present is the multiple-choice test.
2. Critics of multiple-choice test items tend to exaggerate the number of faulty items that appear in tests and the seriousness of the consequences of those faults. Evidence in support of their charges and better alternative means of testing are seldom offered by the critics.
3. Multiple-choice test items should be based on sound, significant ideas that can be expressed as independently meaningful propositions.
4. The wording of a multiple-choice item should not follow familiar textbook phraseology so closely that verbal memory without comprehension will provide an adequate basis for response.
5. The main job of most multiple-choice test items is to differentiate between students of higher and lower achievement.
6. Giving the final examination as a pretest will help to identify items that can provide valid measures of specific achievements in the course.
7. Drafting each multiple-choice item in pencil and double spaced on a separate sheet of paper will facilitate revision of the item and its assembly into the test.
8. The stem of a multiple-choice item should state or clearly imply a specific direct question.

9. Item stems including the word "not" and asking in effect for an incorrect answer tend to be superficial in content and confusing to the examinee.
10. The responses "none of the above" and "all of the above" are appropriate only when the answers given to a question are absolutely correct or incorrect (as in spelling or arithmetic problems).
11. The intended answer should be clear, concise, correct, and free of clues.
12. All of the responses to a multiple-choice test item should be parallel in point of view, grammatical structure, and general appearance.
13. The distracters in a multiple-choice item should be definitely incorrect but plausibly attractive to the uninformed.
14. The use of compound responses, including an answer plus an explanation, or some combination of two elements, sometimes solves the problem of providing four good alternative answers to a multiple-choice test question.
15. While most multiple-choice items provide at least four alternative answers, good ones can be written with only two or three alternatives.
16. A student who selects the correct response to a multiple-choice item by eliminating the incorrect responses demonstrates useful achievement.
17. To function properly a multiple-choice item must be expressed in carefully chosen words and critically edited phrases.
18. In general the best multiple-choice test items are those that about half the examinees answer correctly.
19. One can make some multiple-choice items easier by making the question more general and the responses more diverse, or harder by making the question more specific and the responses more similar.
20. Subsequent, and preferably independent, review of the drafts of multiple-choice test items is likely to improve their quality.
21. Some of the most effective multiple-choice test questions call for a best answer rather than an absolutely perfect correct answer.
22. Items testing recall of incidental details of instruction or special organizations of subject matter are ordinarily undesirable.
23. The stem of a multiple-choice item should be expressed as concisely as possible without sacrificing clarity or omitting essential qualifications.
24. The responses to a multiple-choice item should be expressed simply enough to make clear the essential differences among them.
25. True statements that do not provide good answers to the stem question often make good distracters.
26. The responses to a multiple-choice item should be listed rather than written one after another in a compact paragraph.

GETTING, INTERPRETING, AND USING TEST SCORES

In view of their crucial importance in the whole chain of events from the conception of the test to the use of scores in conferences with individuals, it seems highly unfortunate that the giving and scoring of tests are frequently treated very casually by both the authors and the users of tests.

ARTHUR E. TRAXLER

9

HOW TO ADMINISTER AND SCORE AN ACHIEVEMENT TEST

Unless the class is very large, unless the classroom is poorly suited for test administration, or unless other special problems are encountered, test administration usually is the simplest phase of the whole testing process. In the administration of external, standardized tests, the golden rule for the test administrator is: *Follow the directions in the manual precisely.* In classroom testing there usually is no manual and the need for rigidly standardized conditions of test administration is much less. Nevertheless, in test administration, as in most other matters, advanced planning usually pays dividends. Also there are some persistent problems associated with test administration, such as the questions of test time limits, of guessing on objective tests, and of cheating. These topics, together with the problems of efficient scoring of objective tests, will provide the subject matter of this chapter.

TEST PRESENTATION

The questions for essay or problem tests are sometimes written on the chalkboard as the test period begins. This saves duplication costs and helps to maintain the secrecy of the questions, but it gives the teacher the double responsibility of copying the questions and of getting the students started to work on them, at a time when minutes are precious and when everyone is likely to be somewhat tense. And when the blackboard has been erased, no one has a valid record of exactly what the questions were.

Oral dictation of test questions, especially short-answer or true-false questions, has been tried with some success, but most students prefer to be able to look at the question while they are trying to decide on an answer to it. Putting the questions on slides and projecting them in a semidarkened room has also been tried.[1,2] It enables the examiner to pace the students and insures that each examinee will give at least brief consideration to each question. Studies indicate that examinees answer about as many questions correctly when they are forced to hurry as when they choose their own pace. If the rate of question presentation is rapid, more questions can be asked and more reliable scores obtained in a given testing period. But the students are generally unhappy with this kind of time pressure.

Probably the best method of test presentation is to duplicate enough copies so that each student can have one. In printed test copy, legibility of print and of format are prime considerations. Some classroom tests are duplicated unskillfully, on inadequate equipment. Questions may be crowded too closely together. Instead of being listed in a column, the response options to multiple-choice questions may be written in tandem to form a continuous, hard-to-read paragraph. Testers can avoid faults like these by taking pains with the layout and duplication of test copy. Examples of good layouts for true-false and multiple-choice test items are shown in Exhibit 9.1. Some duplication processes permit the use of both sides of the paper. This is economical and, if the papers are

[1]H. A. Curtis and Russell P. Kropp, "A Comparison of Scores Obtained by Administering a Test Normally and Visually," *Journal of Experimental Education*, vol. 24 (1961), 249–60; Curtis and Kropp, *Experimental Analyses of the Effects of Various Modes of Item Presentation on the Scores and Factorial Content of Tests Administered by Visual and Audio-visual Means*, Department of Educational Research and Testing, Florida State University, Tallahassee, Florida, 1962, p. 83.

[2]Robert W. Heckman, Joseph Tiffin, and Richard E. Snow, "Effects of Controlling Item Exposure in Achievement Testing," *Educational and Psychological Measurement*, vol. 27 (1967), 113–25.

EXHIBIT 9.1

Sample Layouts of Objective Test Items

A. True-False Test Items

1. The indirect influence of a test on student learning is greater than its direct influence.
2. Most teachers are quite unaware of the fallibility of their subjective judgments.
3. For assessing a student's typical behavior informal observation is more effective than formal testing.
4. Since pupils differ in ability, the tests used to measure their achievements should, ideally, also differ in difficulty.
5. It is a good thing for students to study with an eye to doing well on the kind of tests they will have to take.

B. Multiple-Choice Test Items

1. In what part of the process of preparing, giving, and scoring an objective test in American history would the help of another history teacher be most valuable?
   (1) In planning the test
   (2) In writing the original item drafts
   (3) In reviewing and revising the original item drafts
   (4) In scoring the answer sheets

2. How important is the assignment of marks as a function of educational achievement tests?
   (1) It has ceased to be important enough to deserve special attention.
   (2) It is definitely less important than the diagnostic values of taking such tests.
   (3) It is important enough to justify special efforts to construct valid and reliable tests.
   (4) It is the only important function of such tests.

3. What is the chief weakness of many achievement tests constructed by classroom teachers?
   (1) They are speed tests rather than power tests.
   (2) They are too difficult.
   (3) They are too long.
   (4) They test memory of details rather than achievement of objectives.

4. Is it desirable for classroom teachers to construct themselves most of the tests they use? Why?
   (1) Yes, because the process of test construction helps the teacher to diagnose student difficulties.
   (2) Yes, because local construction permits the teacher to fit the test to his program of instruction.
   (3) No, because teachers lack the time to do an acceptable job of test construction.
   (4) No, because test construction requires special knowledge and skill that few teachers possess.

stapled only once in the upper lefthand corner, causes the examinees no problems. The use of a separate cover page on which directions to the students are printed helps to emphasize those directions and to keep the students from seeing the questions prematurely. Sample test directions are shown in Exhibit 9.2.

EXHIBIT 9.2

Sample Test Directions

A. FOR A TRUE-FALSE TEST

This test consists of 102 statements. You are to decide whether each statement is true or false, and to record your decision on the answer sheet provided. Your score will be the number of correct decisions you make. It is to your advantage to mark an answer to each item, and to record the answer you give in the test booklet beside the question.

Please use the special pencil provided, and mark each response carefully so that the scoring machine will be able to determine your score accurately.

Identify your answer sheet with your name and the date (July 9, 1970). The name of the test is "465 Midterm." The form is "In Class." No other identifying information is required.

When you finish, turn in your answer sheets and the special pencil. Keep your copy of the test, and be prepared to turn in a revised answer sheet next Monday (July 13, 1970).

B. FOR A MULTIPLE-CHOICE TEST

Please Read These Directions Carefully

REMOVE the answer sheet that is loosely inserted in this booklet and fill in the information called for on the top margin. Then finish reading these directions, but do not open the test booklet until the instructor tells you to do so.

INDICATE your choice of the one best answer to each question by making one solid black pencil mark in the proper space on the answer sheet. If you change your mind, erase the first mark completely. Do not carelessly or intentionally make any other marks on the answer sheet.

IMPROPER marks will reduce your score on this test.

   a. If mismarking (light marks, double marks, stray marks, or improper erasures) causes the test to score differently on two machines, the lower score will be recorded.

   b. If mismarking causes the total number of marks registered by the machine to be greater than the total number of questions in the test, the excess will be subtracted from the score.

DO NOT waste time on difficult questions. You may answer questions even when you are not perfectly sure your answers are correct, but you should avoid wild guessing.

PREPARING THE STUDENTS

In addition to preparing the test for the students, it is important to prepare the students for the test. To begin with, they usually should know that a test is coming. Any important test should be announced well in advance. If a test is to have a desirable effect in motivating and directing efforts to learn, the students not only need to know that a test is coming but they need also to know the kinds of achievement that the test will require them to demonstrate. This means that the instructor should plan his tests *before* the course begins, as part of the overall planning for the course.

Some instructors favor surprise tests in the belief that such tests keep the students studying regularly and discourage cramming. In some situations these tactics may be necessary and effective. Most instructors, however, see some elements of unfairness in surprise tests. Further, cramming is unlikely to be effective with, or to be encouraged by, a test of a student's command of knowledge. Such command cannot be achieved in a few short sessions of intensive cramming. Cramming is most essential and effective if the test requires no more than superficial memory for prominent details. Advance announcement and description of a good test is likely to do more to encourage effective study than the surprise administration of a test, especially if its nature has been kept secret from the students.

DEVELOPING SKILL IN TEST TAKING

In addition to knowing that a test is coming, and to knowing what, in general, to expect in it, the student needs to know how to give a good account of himself on the test. The measurement of a student's achievement requires his active cooperation. If he lacks skill in test taking, his score may fall short of indicating all of his achievement. Test taking is not a highly specialized skill nor is it difficult to master. But almost anyone who has taken more than a few tests can testify from his own experience how easy it is to go astray on an examination, how failure to heed all directions, or carelessness, or unwarranted assumptions, or ignorance of some crucial rule of the game has marred an otherwise creditable test performance.

What are some of the legitimate and essential test-taking skills that an examinee ought to possess?

1. He ought to be aware of the danger of failing to read or listen attentively

when directions for taking the test are presented and of the danger of failing to follow those directions exactly.

2. He should find out the basis on which his responses will be scored. Will points be subtracted for wrong responses or for errors in spelling, grammar, or punctuation? Will any questions carry more weight than others?

3. He should be aware of the premium that most human scorers, and most scoring machines, place on legibility and neatness. Accordingly, he should take pains in writing his answers or marking the answer sheet.

4. He should put himself in the best possible physical and mental shape for taking the test. Fatigue induced by an all-night cram session, even when partially offset by stimulants, is a heavy handicap to the test taker. He should realize that last-minute cramming is a poor substitute for consistent effort throughout the course, particularly if the test he is facing is likely to be a well-constructed measure of his command of knowledge. Some anxiety is useful in keeping the examinee up to doing his best, but jitters are even less helpful than fatigue.

5. He should pace himself so as to have time to consider and respond to all the test questions. This means that he must not puzzle too long over a difficult question or problem, nor extend too long his answer to an essay test question, even when a long answer seems easy to write.

6. He should know that ordinary guessing corrections really do not penalize even blind guessing, but simply seek not to reward it. Hence, he should conclude that his best interests usually will be served by attempting an answer to all questions, even those that he has only a slight basis for answering.

7. In answering an essay question, he should take time to reflect, to plan, and to organize his answer before starting to write. He should decide how much he can afford to write in the time available. And in all cases he should write something, however flimsy it may seem to be, as an answer.

8. If he is making responses on a separate answer sheet, he should check frequently to be sure his mark actually indicates the response he intended and that it is marked in the spaces provided for that question.

9. If possible, he should save time to reread his answers, to detect and correct any careless mistakes.

Since examinations do count, students and their teachers are well advised to spend some time considering how to cope with them most skillfully. Some good books on the subject, giving more detailed help than we have suggested here, are available.[3,4]

THE PROBLEM OF TESTWISENESS

Concern is more often expressed over an excess of test-taking skill than over a deficiency. The suggestion is made that some examinees have developed this skill to such a degree that it enables the examinee to score well on a test for which he is otherwise almost totally unprepared.

[3]Joseph C. Heston, *How to Take a Test* (Chicago: Science Research Associates, 1953); Herschel Manuel, *Taking a Test* (New York: Harcourt Brace Jovanovich, 1956).
[4]Jason Millman and Walter Pauk, *How To Take Tests* (New York: McGraw-Hill Book Company, 1969), p. 176.

There is some real basis for this concern. Certain tests, especially certain kinds of intelligence tests, include novel, unique, highly specialized tasks, such as figure analogies or number series. For test items of this character the main problem of the examinee is to "get the hang of" solving them. They do not reflect previous learning, nor is the skill developed in solving these test problems likely to be practically useful in other settings. Their use in intelligence testing is justified on the grounds that brighter students will get the hang of solving novel problems sooner, and more fully, than duller students.

Items of this type are seldom used in classroom tests. But there are common faults in item writing that may allow an examinee to substitute testwiseness for knowledge. A number of these are mentioned in Part II B of Exhibit 9.3. It is useful for an examinee to be "wise" to all of

EXHIBIT 9.3

Outline of Testwiseness Principles*

I. Elements independent of test constructor or test purpose
   A. Time-using strategy
      1. Begin to work as rapidly as possible with reasonable assurance of accuracy.
      2. Set up a schedule for progress through the test.
      3. Omit or guess at items (see IC and IIB) that resist a quick response.
      4. Mark omitted items, or items that could use further consideration, to assure easy relocation.
      5. Use time remaining after completion of the test to reconsider answers.
   B. Error-avoidance strategy
      1. Pay careful attention to directions, determining clearly the nature of the task and the intended basis for responses.
      2. Pay careful attention to the items, in each case determining clearly the nature of the question.
      3. Ask examiner for clarification when necessary, if doing so is permitted.
      4. Check all answers.
   C. Guessing strategy
      1. Always guess if right answers only are scored.
      2. Always guess if the correction for guessing is less severe than a "correction for guessing" formula that gives an expected score of zero for random responding.
      3. Always guess even if the usual correction or a more severe penalty for guessing is employed, whenever the process of elimination allows a reasonable chance of guessing correctly.
   D. Deductive reasoning strategy
      1. Eliminate options known to be incorrect and choose from among the remaining options.

2. Choose neither or both of two options that imply the correctness of each other.

3. Choose neither or one (but not both) of two statements, one of which, if correct, would imply the incorrectness of the other.

4. Restrict choice to those options that encompass all of two or more given statements known to be correct.

5. Make use of relevant content information in other test items and options.

II. Elements dependent upon the test constructor or purpose

  A. Intent consideration strategy

    1. Interpret and answer questions in view of previous idiosyncratic emphases of the test constructor or in view of the test purpose.

    2. Answer items as the test constructor intended.

    3. Adopt the level of sophistication that is expected.

    4. Consider the relevance of specific detail.

  B. Cue-using strategy

    1. Recognize and make use of any consistent idiosyncracies of the test constructor that distinguish the correct answer from incorrect options. For example:

      a. He makes it longer (shorter) than the incorrect options.

      b. He qualifies it more carefully, or makes it represent a higher degree of generalization.

      c. He includes more false (true) statements.

      d. He places it in certain physical positions among the options (such as in the middle).

      e. He places it in a certain logical position among an ordered set of options (such as the middle of the sequence).

      f. He includes (does not include) it among similar statements, or makes (does not make) it one of a pair of diametrically opposite statements.

      g. He composes (does not compose) it of familiar or stereotyped phraseology.

      h. He does not make it grammatically inconsistent with the stem.

    2. Consider the relevancy of specific detail when answering a given item.

    3. Recognize and make use of specific determiners.

    4. Recognize and make use of resemblances between the options and an aspect of the stem.

    5. Consider the subject matter and difficulty of neighboring items when interpreting and answering a given item.

---

*Jason Millman, Carol H. Bishop, and Robert Ebel, "An Analysis of Testwiseness," *Educational and Psychological Measurement*, vol. 25 (1965), 707–26.

the principles listed in this outline. In a good test, however, the item writer will avoid leaving very many clues of the kind mentioned in II B. Given a test that measures command of knowledge and is free of technical flaws, error in measurement is likely to be due to too little, rather than too much, testwiseness.

THE PROBLEM OF TEST ANXIETY

The problem of test anxiety was mentioned in the preceding section. Anxiety is a frequent side effect of testing, whether that testing occurs in the classroom, on the athletic field, in the art exhibit hall, in the court room, in the conference room where a crucial business decision is being discussed, or in the legislative chamber where a bill is being debated. Test anxiety in the classroom is not something unique. It is a part, though hopefully not too large a part, of life itself.

Because human beings are complex and the situations in which they are tested are diverse, it is unlikely that any simple, universal answers will be found to questions concerning the cause and cure of test anxiety. Some research has been done on test anxiety, particularly among young children. However, the measurement of anxiety is no simple problem. It is not surprising that few generalizations of wide applicability can be defended solidly on the basis of research findings. However, combining what controlled experimentation has reported with common observations of human behavior, it is possible to offer a few generalizations that seem reasonably safe.

1. There is a negative correlation between level of ability and level of test anxiety.[5] Those who are most capable tend to be least anxious when facing a test.
2. There is a positive correlation between level of anxiety and level of aspiration. Those who are most anxious when facing a test tend to be those who have the greatest need or desire to do well on it.
3. Mild degrees of anxiety facilitate and enhance test performance. More extreme degrees are likely to interfere with and depress test performance.
4. The more frequent a student's contact with tests of a specific type given for a specific purpose, the less likely he is to be the victim of extreme anxiety.
5. Test anxiety can be educationally useful if it is distributed, at a relatively low level, throughout the course of instruction, instead of being concentrated, at a relatively high level, just prior to and during an examination. Skillful teaching involves the controlled release of the energy stimulated by test anxiety.

Evidence to support the belief that some students of good or superior achievement characteristically go to pieces and do poorly on every examination is hard to find. Since individuals differ in many respects, it is reasonable to suppose that they may differ also in their tolerance of the kind of

[5]Irwin G. Sarason, "Empirical Findings and Theoretical Problems in the Use of Anxiety Scales," *Psychological Bulletin* (1960), pp. 403–15.

stress that tests generate. On the other hand, it is conceivable that apparent instances of underachievement on tests may actually be instances of overindication of ability in other situations. That is, a student whose achievement is really quite modest may have cultivated the poise, the ready response, the verbal facility, and the pleasing manners that enable him to pass for an accomplished and promising scholar in all save impersonal test situations. All things considered, a teacher is well advised to take with several grains of salt a student's claim that his test performances never do justice to his real achievements.

ADMINISTERING THE TEST

Normally, as suggested earlier, the actual administration of the test involves relatively few and simple problems. Since the time available for the test is usually limited, and seldom as long as some of the students wish, every available minute should be used to good advantage. By giving preliminary instructions before the day of the test, by organizing the test materials for efficient distribution, and by keeping last-minute oral directions and answers to questions as brief as possible, the teacher can start the test promptly to give each student the maximum amount of time to work on it. Corresponding provisions for efficient collection of materials and advance notice to the students that all work must stop when time is called help to conclude the test on time and in an orderly fashion.

To aid the students in pacing themselves, it is helpful for the teacher to write a statement like this on the chalkboard near the beginning of the test.

No more than _____ minutes remain for you to work on this test.
If you have not reached item _____ you are working too slowly.

By changing the numbers entered in these statements every 10 or 15 minutes, the teacher can help the students find time to consider all questions.

During almost any test administration, some students are likely to feel the need of asking some questions. Questions such as those growing out of errors in the test copy or ambiguities in the directions or the test questions require answers if the students are to respond properly. A teacher should help a student to understand the tasks but should stop short of helping him to solve them. Sometimes the dividing line is hard to determine.

Such questions as those stimulated by obvious but noncritical typographical errors should not even be asked. Since the process of asking and answering a question during the course of an examination is always disturbing to others, even if it is done as quietly and discreetly as possible, and since the answer to one student's question might possibly give him an unfair advantage over the others, students should be urged to avoid all but the most necessary questions. Advice to them on this point can well be given prior to the day of the examination.

THE PROBLEM OF CHEATING

In addition to giving directions, answering questions, and helping the students keep track of time, the instructor has at least one other major responsibility during the course of administering a test. That is to prevent cheating, This problem, which students, teachers, and educational administrators tend to agree is serious, seems to receive more attention in the popular press than in technical books and articles on testing. Cheating on examinations is commonly viewed as a sign of declining ethical standards or as an inevitable consequence of increased emphasis on test scores and grades.

Any activity of a student or group of students whose purpose is to give any of them higher grades than they would be likely to receive on the basis of their own achievements is cheating. Thus the term covers a wide variety of activities, such as:

1. The side-long glance at a fellow student's answers
2. The preparation and use of a crib sheet
3. Collusion between two or more students to exchange information on answers during the test
4. Unauthorized copying of questions or stealing of test booklets in anticipation that they may be used again later on
5. Arranging for a substitute to take an examination
6. Stealing or buying copies of an examination before the test is given, or sharing such illicit advance copies with others

Although these various forms of cheating differ in seriousness, none can be viewed with indifference. The typical student has many opportunities to cheat. Some circumstances may even encourage him to, but none justifies him in doing so. A student may conclude, not without some justification, that the ethical standards of many of his fellow students are not very high, at least where cheating on examinations is concerned. He may go on to infer that this fact requires him to lower his own standards or justifies him in doing so. Whatever other conditions may contribute to it, cheating would not occur if all students were to recognize that it is always dishonest and usually unfair.

Some acts of cheating are no doubt motivated by desperation. The more extreme the desperation, the more ambitious and serious the attempt to cheat is likely to be. A cause contributing to cheating is carelessness on the instructor's part in safeguarding the examination copy before it is administered and in supervising the students during the examination.

As already mentioned, emphasis on grades is sometimes blamed as a primary cause of cheating. But since grades are, or should be, symbols of educational achievement, the blame, if any is warranted, should be directed toward emphasis on individual efforts to achieve. No doubt most students would find it easier to resist the temptation to cheat if no advantage of any consequence was likely to result from the cheating. But refusal to recognize and reward achievement may be as effective in reducing achievement as in reducing cheating. Such a price seems too heavy to pay.

Increased use of objective tests has also been blamed as a cause of cheating. The mode of response to objective tests makes some kinds of cheating easier, but the multiplicity of questions makes other kinds of cheating more difficult. No form of test is immune to all forms of cheating. The quality of a test, however, may have a direct bearing on the temptation it offers to students to cheat. Demand for detailed, superficial knowledge encourages the preparation of crib sheets. If the examination seems to the students unlikely to yield valid measures of their real achievements, if it seems unfair to them in terms of the instruction they have received, if their scores seem likely to be determined by irrelevant factors anyway, the "crime" of cheating may seem less serious.

What cures are there for cheating? The basic cure is related to the basic cause. Students and their teachers must recognize that cheating is dishonest and unfair and that it deserves consistent application of appropriate penalties—failure in the course, loss of credit, suspension, or dismissal. Reports on the prevalence of cheating, no doubt sometimes exaggerated, should not be allowed to establish cheating as an acceptable norm for student behavior or to persuade instructors that cheating is inevitable and must be accommodated as gracefully as possible.

It is the responsibility of the instructor to avoid any conditions that make cheating easy—before, during, or after an examination. The security of the examination must be safeguarded while it is being written and duplicated and when it is stored. If the class is large and if the students cannot be seated in alternate seats, alternate forms of the examination should be distributed to students sitting in adjacent seats. One can provide alternate forms satisfactory for this purpose by arranging the same questions in different order. Finally, the instructor should take seriously the task of proctoring his examinations as part of his responsibility to the majority of students who will not cheat and who should not be penalized for their honesty.

A teacher has considerable authority in his own classroom. He should not overuse it under stress or underuse it when the situation requires it. If the teacher is satisfied beyond any reasonable doubt that a student is cheating, the teacher needs no other justification for:

1. Collecting the examination materials and quietly dismissing the student from the room
2. Voiding the results of the examination, requiring an alternative make-up examination, or giving the student a failing grade on the examination
3. Bringing the incident to the attention of the school authorities if further action seems necessary

HONOR SYSTEMS

One frequently mentioned proposal for dealing with problems like cheating involves establishment of an honor system. Honor systems vary, but they have in common a cultivation of the student's sense of responsibility for personal honor and for the honor of the group. They vary in the responsibilities they place on the students for maintaining the system and in the means used for dealing with infractions.

Those honor systems that obligate students to inform designated authorities of the dishonorable acts of other students require a drastic change in one aspect of the code of human behavior—that which forbids talebearing. The honor sought by the honor system thus must be purchased at the price of another kind of honor, that of loyalty to one's close associates. It is not surprising that systems of this kind sometimes break down.

Honor systems seems to work best in educational institutions whose moderate size and rich traditions encourage strong group indentification and loyalties. The spirit of honor on which the system depends seldom arises or maintains itself spontaneously. It must be cultivated carefully and continuously. The things that must be done, or avoided, to maintain personal honor and the honor of the group are usually clearly defined in a code or by well-rehearsed tradition. The degree to which student experience with an honor system in such an environment cultivates a general and lasting spirit of personal honor in a world where no such system is in effect may be open to question. That such systems have worked to limit, or even eliminate, cheating in certain institutions seems beyond doubt. That such systems sometimes break down, disastrously, is also beyond doubt. What is not beyond doubt is the widespread belief that adoption of the honor system is a feasible answer to the problem of cheating on examinations in almost any school or college.

LOSS OF TEST SECURITY

Instructors and administrators, especially at the college level, are occasionally beset by rumors that copies of this or that examination are "out" in advance of the scheduled administration of the examination. Sometimes the rumors are founded on fact. More often they are founded on a misunderstanding and spread in the colloquies of anxious students. Finally the rumor (not so identified, of course) reaches the ears of the instructor, often via one or a number of anonymous telephone calls. What is the instructor to do then?

The first thing to do is to try to determine whether or not the rumor is founded on fact. This is the instructor's responsibility and he should spare no effort in the pursuit of evidence. If he is ready to enlist the aid of his informants and if they are willing to help, even anonymously, the task may be possible. If the informants are unable or unwilling to supply any leads, then they should be told courteously but plainly that their information is worthless and their transmission of it harmful.

If verifiable evidence is obtained that some students have, or have seen, advance copies of the examination, the only reasonable course of action is to prepare a new examination, even if it means changing the form of the examination and possibly losing a night of sleep. But if such evidence cannot be obtained even by searching hard for it, the rumor had probably best be allowed to die as quietly as it will.

Problems of this kind are most likely to arise and to cause most serious difficulties on college campuses. They have occurred in high schools, however. Care in safeguarding the examinations before they are given is the best preventative. But it is also helpful to be ready to respond wisely, and vigorously if the situation warrants, when the rumors that a test is out *do* begin to circulate, as they almost surely will sooner or later.

PROCEDURES FOR TEST SCORING

Student answers to objective test items may be recorded either on the test copy itself or on a separate answer sheet. Tests given in the elementary grades are almost always arranged so that the answers can be recorded in the test booklet. This avoids complicating the task of responding for the beginner. Cashen and Ramseyer found that the test scores of first grade students were lowered substantially when they were required to record their answers on a separate answer sheet.[6] Scores of second grade students were lowered somewhat, but those of third grade students were affected very little. Recording answers in the test booklet lessens the danger of purely clerical errors and makes the corrected test copy easier to use for instructional purposes. The use of a separate answer sheet, on the other hand, makes the scorer's task much easier. It also makes possible the reuse of the test booklet. If a scoring machine is to be used, the answers must be recorded on an answer sheet that the machine is designed to handle. Exhibit 9.4 illustrates an answer sheet designed for hand scoring.

If the answers are to be recorded on the test booklet, space for the answers should be provided near one margin of the test pages. To speed scoring and minimize the chance for errors, the scorer may record correct answers on the columns of a separate answer key card, using one column for each page of answers and positioning the answers in the column so that they will match the answer spaces on the test copy.

In scoring the answers recorded in test booklets, the scorer may find it helpful to mark the answers, using a colored pencil. A short horizontal line through the student's response can be used to indicate a correct response. Sometimes it is advantageous to mark all responses using, in addition to the horizontal line for correct responses, an "X" through the response for an incorrect response and a circle around the answer space to indicate an omitted response.

Responses are indicated on most separate answer sheets by marking one of the several response positions provided opposite the number of each item. Such answer sheets may be scored by hand, using a stencil key with holes punched to correspond to the correct responses. Transparent keys, which can be prepared on the film used to make transparencies for an overhead projector, have some advantages, as Gerlach has noted.[7] When a separate answer sheet and a punched key are used, it is possible to indicate incorrect or omitted items by using a colored pencil to encircle the answer spaces that the student marked wrongly or did not mark at all. This kind of marking is useful when the answer sheets are returned with copies of the test for class discussion.

Most classroom tests of educational achievement are scored by the instructor. If the test is in essay form, the skill and judgment of the instructor or of someone equally competent are essential. The task of scoring an objective test is essentially clerical and can often be handled by some-

[6]Valjean M. Cashen and Gary C. Ramseyer, "The Use of Separate Answer Sheets by Primary Age Children," *Journal of Educational Measurement*, vol. 6 (1969), 155–58.

[7]Vernon S. Gerlach, "Preparing Transparent Keys for Inspecting Answer Sheets," *Journal of Educational Measurement*, vol. 3 (1966), 62.

EXHIBIT 9.4

Standard Answer Sheet

STANDARD ANSWER SHEET

Scores

Test Title: _____

1. _____

Name: _____

2. _____

Last name   first name   initial

3. _____

Section: _____ Date: _____ 195___

4. _____

Directions: Mark a heavy cross (X) in the box corresponding to the answer to each exercise.

a b c d e	a b c d e	a b c d e	a b c d e	a b c d e
1	34	67	100	133
2	35	68	101	134
3	36	69	102	135
4	37	70	103	136
5	38	71	104	137
6	39	72	105	138
7	40	73	106	139
8	41	74	107	140
9	42	75	108	141
10	43	76	109	142
11	44	77	110	143
12	45	78	111	144
13	46	79	112	145
14	47	80	113	146
15	48	81	114	147
16	49	82	115	148
17	50	83	116	149
18	51	84	117	150
19	52	85	118	151
20	53	86	119	152
21	54	87	120	153
22	55	88	121	154
23	56	89	122	155
24	57	90	123	156
25	58	91	124	157
26	59	92	125	158
27	60	93	126	159
28	61	94	127	160
29	62	95	128	161
30	63	96	129	162
31	64	97	130	163
32	65	98	131	164
33	66	99	132	165

one whose time is less expensive than an instructor's time and whose skill and energy are less in demand for other educational tasks.

Some school systems and colleges maintain central scoring services.

Usually these services make use of small scoring machines, several of which are now available. But even if all the scoring is done by hand, a central service has the value of fostering the development of special skills that make for rapid, accurate scoring. Institutional test scoring services often provide statistical and test analysis services as well. Sometimes they offer test duplication services, providing expert assistance in the special problems of test production and in the maintenance of test security.[8]

Instructors sometimes use the class meeting following the test for test scoring, asking each student to check the answers on the paper of one of his classmates. In some situations this may be a reasonable and rewarding use of class time. But often the process tends to be slow and inaccurate. A difficulty encountered by one student on one test paper may interrupt and delay the whole operation. If the student scorers are concentrating on mechanical accuracy of scoring, as they probably should be, the circumstances will not favor much learning as a by-product of the scoring process.

But students can and usually should have the chance to learn from the mistakes they make on a test. Ordinarily the best occasion for this learning is *after* the tests have been scored and the student's answer sheet has been returned to him. The correct answer to each item can be recorded on the blackboard, on a duplicated hand-out, or best of all, on the student's answer sheet itself. With this information each student can satisfy himself of the accuracy with which his answers have been scored. If he also has a copy of the test, he can discover the nature of his mistakes or ask for an explanation, if necessary. The teacher can prevent protracted arguments over the correctness of his choice of correct answers by asking the protesting student to state his case in writing, with a promise of credit if the case seems to merit it. Discussions of this kind contribute to the student's feeling that he is being treated openly and fairly. They can also contribute enough to an increase of the student's command of knowledge to be well worth the time required.

SCORING MACHINES

In recent years various small machines designed for classroom scoring of objective tests have appeared on the educational market. Most of them require the use of specially printed answer sheets or cards. Most of them use an optical system for sensing and an electronic system for counting right and wrong responses. The maximum number of five-alternative

---

[8]Robert L. Ebel, "Improving Evaluation of Educational Outcomes at the College Level," *Proceedings, 1953 Invitational Conference on Testing Problems* (Princeton, N.J.: Educational Testing Service, 1954).

multiple-choice items that can be scored in one pass varies from 25 to about 100. Most of them are equipped to print the score on the student's answer sheet. Some will mark wrong answers and provide data on item difficulty. The smallest is about the size of a portable typewriter; the largest about the size of a mimeograph machine. In cost they range from about $1,000 to about $3,000. In view of the time they can save the teacher, and the accuracy of the scores they yield, they are worthwhile investments for most schools. The manufacturers of several of these machines are identified below. Pictures of the machines are shown in Figure 9.2.

Automata Test Scorer
Automata Corporation
1305 Mansfield Avenue
Richland, Washington 99352

3M Brand Test Scorer
Duplicating Products Division
3M Company Center
St. Paul, Minnesota 55101

Datronics Test Scoring Machine
Rochester Datronics, Inc.
1615 14th Street N.W.
Rochester, Minnesota 55901

Much larger, higher-capacity machines have been developed for use in large school systems, universities, and statewide or nationwide testing agencies.[9] Of course they are much more expensive than the smaller machines. The output of these machines is often coupled to computers, which standardize and summarize the scores, print score distributions and listings, and provide complete analysis of the test data.[10] It is hard to exaggerate the contribution that machines like these can make to the efficient use of objective tests and to their progressive improvement through test analysis. Information on these machines can be obtained by writing to one of the addresses given below.

Measurement Research Center
Box 30
Iowa City, Iowa 52242

Optical Scanning Corporation
Newtown, Pennsylvania 18940

---

[9]J. M. O'Malley and C. Stafford, "Scoring and Analyzing Teacher-made Tests with an IBM 1620," *Educational and Psychological Measurement,* vol. 26 (1966), 715–17.

[10]C. D. Miller and others, "Scoring, Analyzing and Reporting Classroom Tests Using an Optical Reader and 1401 Computer," *Educational and Psychological Measurement,* vol. 27 (1967), 159–64.

(A) Automata 1200

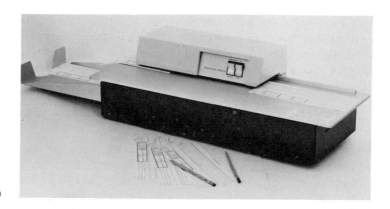

(B) Datronics 500

(C) 3-M Brand
     Test Scorer

FIGURE 9.2
Machines for Scoring Classroom Tests

International Business Machines Corporation
112 East Post Road
White Plains, New York 10601

CORRECTION FOR GUESSING

Scores on objective tests are sometimes corrected for guessing. The purpose of such a correction is to reduce to zero the gain in score expected to result from blind guessing. In other words, a guessing correction is intended to give the student who guesses blindly on certain questions no reasonable expectation of advantage in the long run over the student who omits the same questions.

Suppose a student were to guess blindly on 100 true-false test items. Since there are only two possible answers, one of which is certain to be correct, the student has reason to expect that his blind guesses will be right half of the time. Thus his expected score on the 100-item true-false test would be 50. Another student, knowing no less than the first but reluctant to guess blindly, might attempt no answers. His score would be zero. Without correction for guessing, the score of the first student would be higher than that of the second when, in fact, the two scores should be the same.

To correct the first student's score for guessing, it is necessary to subtract from his score an amount equal to his expected gain from blind guessing. Since on a true-false test he can expect to answer one question wrongly for every question he answers rightly, the number of wrong answers is simply subtracted from the number of right answer. If the questions provided three equally likely answers instead of two, the student would expect to give two wrong answers to every right answer. In this case one would subtract one-half of the number of wrong responses from the number of right responses to correct for guessing. If multiple-choice items list five alternative possible answers to each question, only one of which is correct, the expected ratio of wrong to right answers is 4 to 1 and the guessing correction would call for subtracting one-fourth of the number of wrong answers from the number of right answers.

Logic of this kind leads to a general formula for correction for guessing

$$S = R - \frac{W}{N - 1} \qquad\qquad 9.1$$

in which S stands for the score corrected for guessing, R for the number of questions answered rightly, W for the number of questions answered wrongly, and N for the number of possible alternative answers, equally likely to be chosen in blind guessing. It is easy to see that this formula becomes

$$S = R - W \qquad 9.2$$

in the case of two-alternative (true-false) items, or

$$S = R - \frac{W}{4} \qquad 9.3$$

in the case of five-alternative multiple-choice test items.

Instead of penalizing the student who guesses, one could correct for guessing by rewarding the student who refrains from guessing. That is, instead of subtracting 50 units from the score of the guesser, we could add 50 units to the score of the nonguesser. This too would eliminate the expected advantage from blind guessing. The assumption in this case is that if the nonguesser had guessed, he would have given the right answer to one-half of the true-false items. On three-alternative items he would have been right in his answers to one-third of the items.

Logic of this kind leads to a second general formula for guessing correction

$$S' = R + \frac{O}{N} \qquad 9.4$$

in which S' is the score corrected for guessing on the basis of items omitted, R is the number of items answered correctly, O is the number of items omitted, and N is the number of alternative answers whose choice is equally likely on the basis of blind guessing. Again, it is easy to see that this general formula becomes

$$S' = R + \frac{O}{2} \qquad 9.5$$

in the case of true-false items, or

$$S' = R + \frac{O}{5} \qquad 9.6$$

in the case of five-alternative multiple-choice test items.

If the same set of test scores is corrected for guessing in two different ways, by subtracting a fraction of the wrong answers and by adding a fraction of the omitted answers, two different sets of corrected scores will be obtained. But although the two sets of scores will differ in their average value (with the omit-corrected scores being higher in all cases) and in their variability (with the omit-corrected scores being more variable almost always), the two sets of scores will be perfectly correlated. If student A makes a higher score than student B when the appropriate fractions of their wrong responses are subtracted from the total of their right responses, *A* will also make a higher score than *B* when the appropriate fraction of their items omitted is added to the total of their right responses.

Correction for guessing by subtracting a fraction of the wrong responses is sometimes criticized on the ground that it is based on a false assumption—the assumption that every wrong response is the result of blind guessing. But the falseness of that assumption (and usually it is completely false) does not invalidate the correction formula that rests on it, for no such assumption is made in the formula for guessing correction on the basis of items omitted and yet the two formulas yield scores that agree perfectly in their relative ranking of students. Scores corrected by subtraction may be regarded logically as too low in absolute value, just as those corrected by addition may be regarded logically as too high in absolute value. But they are equally sound in relative value. With scores on tests of educational achievement, the absolute value is usually far less significant than the relative value.

It is also worth noting here that if no items are omitted, scores corrected for guessing by subtracting a fraction of the wrong responses correlate perfectly with the uncorrected scores, that is, with the numbers of right responses. This indicates that the magnitude of the effect of a guessing correction depends on the proportion of items omitted. Only if considerable numbers of items are omitted by at least some of the students will the application of either formula for correction for guessing have an appreciable effect.

Correction for guessing is sometimes misunderstood to mean that the effects of chance on the test scores are eliminated or reduced, that the lucky guesser will, after his score is corrected, fare no better than the unlucky guesser. How far this is from truth is illustrated in Table 9.1. To make the illustration as simple as possible we have assumed that 32 students attempt all 10 items of a true-false test. Each student presumably knew the answers to 5 of the 10 questions. Hence the true score on this test of each of the 32 students should have been 5, as indicated in the second column of Table 9.1.

But they guess, and as usually befalls those who guess, some are luckier than others. The laws of probability indicate that one of the 32 would guess right on all five of the remaining questions, and thus get a total score of 10. Five of the 32 would be lucky on four of the five questions and get scores of 9. One poor soul would be completely unlucky and guess wrong on all five questions. His score would remain at 5, reflecting knowledge but no luck. These facts are shown in the third column of Table 9.1.

Does the application of a guessing-correction formula improve the situation? Look at the fourth column of Table 9.1, which displays the scores obtained by applying Formula 9.2. The differences due to chance

TABLE 9.1. Scores of 32 Students of Equal Ability on a 10-item True-False Test

Scale of Test Scores	True	Frequency Distributions of Scores Uncorrected	Corrected
10		1	1
9		5	
8		10	5
7		10	
6		5	10
5	32	1	
4			10
3			
2			5
1			
0			1

have not been eliminated or even reduced. They have been magnified. Paraphrasing the words of the Bible: To him that hath luck a high score shall be given, even after correction for guessing. From him that hath not luck, even that score which is rightfully his shall be taken away!

Should the scores on objective tests of educational achievement be corrected for guessing? Among the considerations that should influence the instructor's decision are these.

1. Scores corrected for guessing will usually rank students in about the same relative positions as do the uncorrected scores.

Almost all experimental studies of the effect of announced correction for guessing on the reliability and validity of test scores have shown slight, if any, improvement attributable to the correction. Usually the correlation between corrected and uncorrected scores from the same test answers is in the high nineties—nearly perfect in terms of the standards of mental tests. Corrected scores may be slightly more reliable or slightly less reliable than uncorrected scores, depending on whether the correlation between number of items omitted and number answered correctly is positive or negative. Corrected scores may be slightly more valid than uncorrected scores if the correlation between number of items omitted and the criterion scores is positive. If not, they may be slightly less valid.

Some interesting, hitherto unpublished data of the effects of guessing instructions and correction for guessing are presented in Tables 9.2 and 9.3. I am indebted to Professors Paul Blommers and E. F. Lindquist for these data from an unpublished study. They were obtained by first administering the tests under instructions not to guess. Then, before the answer

TABLE 9.2.   EFFECTS OF DIRECTIONS AGAINST GUESSING AND CORRECTION
FOR GUESSING, I

Score[a]	A	B	C
Directions	Don't Guess	Guess	Don't Guess
Correction[b]	No	No	Yes
Mean Score	75.6	80.4	79.6
Standard Deviation	19.76	17.41	17.16
Reliability[c]	0.936	0.898	0.920
Intercorrelation			
With Score A		0.954	0.974
With Score B			0.987

[a]Scores for 360 Army Specialized Training Program trainees on a geography test, taken January 28, 1944, at the State University of Iowa.
[b]The correction was made by adding one-fourth of the number of items omitted to the number answered correctly.
[c]The reliability coefficient was the corrected coefficient of correlation between scores on odd-numbered and even-numbered items.

TABLE 9.3.   EFFECTS OF DIRECTIONS AGAINST GUESSING AND CORRECTION
FOR GUESSING, II

Score[a]	A	B	C	D	E
Directions	Don't Guess	Guess	Guess[b]	Don't Guess	Guess
Correction[c]	No	No	No	Yes	Yes
Mean Score	31.2	33.9	34.2	34.1	34.1
Standard Deviation	13.74	12.67	12.58	12.34	12.57
Reliability[d]	0.933	0.913	0.910	0.916	0.912
Validity[e]			0.809	0.807	
Intercorrelation					
With Score A			0.980	0.981	
With Score C				0.990	

[a]Scores for 362 Army Specialized Training Program trainees on a mathematics test, taken January 28, 1944, at the State University of Iowa.
[b]An artificial guessing procedure was applied to the items omitted despite instructions to mark every item. No artificial guessing procedure was used to obtain score B.
[c]The correction was made by adding one-fifth of the number of items omitted to the number answered correctly.
[d]Based on the correlation between odd- and even-numbered items.
[e]Instructor grades were used as the criterion for validity.

sheets were turned in, the students were given colored pencils and asked to attempt an answer to each item they had omitted. Both sets of responses, the initial incomplete set and the final complete set, were then scored in two ways, with and without correction for guessing.

The tables show that the students in these groups obtained lower mean scores and more variable scores (that is, with larger standard deviations) when they refrained from guessing than when they guessed. When the guessing correction, which in this case involved adding a fraction of the omitted items to the number answered correctly, was applied, the mean of the scores obtained under "do not guess" instructions was raised and the standard deviation lowered, as might be expected. But application of the same correction to scores obtained under "answer every item" instructions, as might be expected also, had little effect on the mean and standard deviation.

On both tests the highest reliability was obtained when students were warned not to guess (that is, when they were told that their scores would be corrected for guessing) but when no guessing correction was actually applied. Obviously such deception could not be practiced in regular test administration and scoring procedures. Of the two feasible alternatives ("do not guess" instructions plus actual correction for guessing, on the one hand, and "answer every item" instructions plus no correction for guessing on the other), there is a slight difference in reliability in favor of the "do not guess" instructions. There is, however, no appreciable difference in validity. In all cases the differences are relatively small and the high intercorrelation between these two alternative scores (*B* and *C* in Table 9.2 and *C* and *D* in Table 9.3) confirms the impression that guessing and correction for guessing made relatively little difference in a pupil's ranking on these tests. These were expertly constructed tests that yielded scores of good reliability. It seems likely that the data reported in Tables 9.2 and 9.3 are reasonably representative of those that would be obtained under similar instructions with other good classroom tests. A recent study by Sabers and Feldt supports this view.[11] Sax and Collet emphasize the important influence of instructions to the examinee on the effectiveness of correction for guessing.[12]

2. The probability of getting a respectable score on a good objective test by blind guessing alone is extremely small.

Suppose the objective test included 100 multiple-choice items, each of which offered five possible answers. A student who took many of such tests and always guessed blindly on every item in such a test would expect to receive an average score of 20. He could expect a score as high as 24 by blind guessing alone on only one test out of six, as high as 28 on only one test out of 44, and as high as 32 on only one test out of 740.

What is the probability of a perfect score on a 100-item true-false test by blind guessing alone? The answer is given by taking the fraction 1/2 (the probability of correct response to one item) and raising it to the one

---

[11]Darrell L. Sabers and Leonard S. Feldt, "An Empirical Study of the Effect of the Correction for Chance Success on the Reliability and Validity of an Aptitude Test," *Journal of Educational Measurement*, vol. 5 (1968), 251–58.

[12]Gilbert Sax and LeVerne Collet, "The Effects of Differing Instructions and Guessing Formulas on Reliability and Validity," *Educational and Psychological Measurement*, vol. 28 (1968), 1127–2236.

hundredth power (the compound probability of all 100 answers being correct in any one test). That fraction, calculated with the help of logarithms, turns out to be

$$\frac{1}{1,268,000,000,000,000,000,000,000,000,000}$$

That is a rather small fraction. It means that in over one and a quarter *nonillion* sets of blindly guessed answers one could expect to find only one perfect paper. If all of the people alive in the world today (say 3,500,000,000) had been doing nothing every day but making blind guesses on 100-item true-false tests (say 10 tests per day) all year long, except Sundays and holidays, (say 3,000 tests per years) and had done so since the beginning of geologic time (say 3 billion years ago) they would produce only 31,500,000,000,000,000,000,000 sets of answers. That number is too small by a factor of 40 million. Thus the kind of nonsense we have described, three and a half billion people taking 3,000 true-false tests per year for three billion years, would have to go on in 40 million other worlds in order to produce one perfect answer sheet to a 100-item true-false test by blind guessing alone.

> 3. *Well-motivated examinees who have time to attempt all items guess blindly on few, if any, items.*

The data presented in Table 9.4 support this generalization. The numbers in line 7 of the table were obtained by asking the students to indicate any items on which they felt their responses were no better than blind guesses. In return for this information the students were promised at least a chance score on those items. That is, if less than half of their guesses were correct, they would be given credit for half of them as correct.

TABLE 9.4.   BLIND GUESSING ON FOUR TRUE-FALSE TESTS*

	Midterm	Final	Midterm	Final
1. Test	Midterm	Final	Midterm	Final
2. Date	7–7–67	7–25–67	10–23–67	12–4–67
3. Number of items	98	89	108	116
4. Number of students	158	158	121	121
5. Responses	15,484	14,062	13,068	14,036
6. Percent correct	76	72	76	71
7. Guesses	486	905	620	1,108
8. Percent of responses	3.1	6.4	4.7	7.9
9. Guesses correct	271	494	336	575
10. Percent correct	56	55	54	52
11. Test reliability	.79	.89	.79	.81

*Robert L. Ebel "Blind Guessing on Objective Achievement Tests," *Journal of Educational Measurement*, vol. 5 (Winter 1968), 321–25.

Under this arrangement the students reported a total of 3,119 guesses out of a total of 56,550 responses, or about 1 in 18. As might be expected, some students reported no guesses at all. A very few students at the other extreme reported that as many as 1 in 4 of their responses were no better than blind guesses.

Some who are concerned about the prevalence of guessing on objective tests would define any response made with less than complete certainty as a guess. Under this definition, naturally, the proportion of guesses would be much higher than that found in the study just reported. But these informed guesses give valuable indications of achievement. If one student's informed guesses turn out to be more frequently correct than another's, it is a good indication that the one has based his guesses on better information than the other.

> 4. *Ordinarily, no moral or educational evil is involved in the encouragement of students to make the best rational guesses they can.*

Guessing is regarded as an evil by those who see in it an attempt by the examinee either to (1) deceive the examiner into thinking he knows something that he really doesn't know or to (2) get by on the basis of slipshod learning. If learning were an all-or-none affair, with perfect mastery or total ignorance the only alternatives, these objections to guessing could carry considerable weight.

But in view of the fact that learning is usually a matter of more-or-less, it seems somewhat unreasonable to ask a student to distinguish clearly what he knows from what he does not know and to answer only those questions that he can answer with complete certainty. Schools and colleges prepare for life, and life is seldom like that. Decisions on life's complex problems are seldom beyond question or doubt. Inevitably most of them require some degree of rational guessing, that is acting on the basis of insufficient evidence. Decision making cannot be avoided when a question or problem arises since the postponement of choice is itself a decision that may turn out well or badly. The most effective persons in life seem to be those whose informed guesses pay off most frequently.

> 5. *A student's rational guesses can provide useful information on his general level of achievement.*

Any test is likely to present tasks that some examinees will not be able to handle with complete assurance. If these examinees do the best they can with such questions, then responses should provide the examiner with more information about their abilities than if they were to omit all such uncertain responses entirely.

Even if it were possible to do so, it would probably be undesirable to measure a student's achievements by counting only the things he thinks he knows beyond the shadow of a doubt, or the abilities he thinks he can exercise flawlessly. The number of such things may be quite small and many of them may be quite unimportant. Further, the more successfully a test probes a student's command of knowledge, the more it requires him to go beyond the recitation of facts and phrases committed to memory, the harder it may be for him to avoid some doubts about the correctness of his choices. If a question is complex and difficult enough to challenge a student's command of knowledge, he is unlikely to arrive at an answer he is completely certain is correct. But uncertain responses can provide good evidence of competence, too. Two students may be uncertain to some degree about all the answers they give on a test, but the student of higher achievement is likely to have more of his uncertain answers turn out to be correct.

6. *If a test is speeded, a guessing correction removes the incentive*
for slower students to guess blindly.

Students who work slowly or who lose track of time when taking a test may be unable to give a considered answer to each question, especially if the test time limits are short. When the test scores are not corrected for guessing, a student who runs out of time can expect a higher score if he guesses blindly than if he does not. Not all students are willing to guess blindly in such circumstances, even when directed to do so. Those who choose not to guess are placed at a disadvantage. Those who do guess blindly make their scores less reliable since the blind guessing adds nothing but random error to their test scores. Correcting test scores for guessing helps solve this problem by removing the incentive to guess blindly on the items the student does not have time to consider.

In some cases a better solution to this problem than correction for guessing may be encouragement of students to work rapidly enough to have time to consider all of the items. Most students could work faster on an examination than they do without serious loss of accuracy in their responses. If they are informed of the passage of time, most will adjust their rates of work so they can finish without guessing. Their scores are then almost certain to be more reliable than if they had guessed blindly on some items, or if a guessing correction had been applied.

7. *Scores corrected for guessing may include irrelevant measures*
of the examinee's testwiseness or willingness to gamble.

Contrary to what students sometimes seem to believe, the typical correction for guessing applies no special penalty to the one who guesses. It simply tends to eliminate the advantage of the student who guesses blindly in preference to omitting items. The testwise student knows he has nothing to lose, and perhaps something to gain, by making use of every hunch and scrap of information in attempting an answer to every item. The test-naïve student or the one who tends to avoid taking chances may be influenced by a guessing correction to omit many items on which his likelihood of correct response is well above the chance level.[13,14] To the degree that scores corrected for guessing give a special advantage to the bold or testwise student, their validity as measures of achievement may suffer.

8. Correction for guessing complicates the scoring task somewhat and tends to lower the accuracy of the scores.

In effect, two scores must be obtained and combined mathematically to yield a single score corrected for guessing. If the tests are scored by hand, as most classroom tests are, both the time required for scoring and the opportunities for error are increased considerably. When machines are used, the speed and accuracy with which formula scores can be obtained depends on the design of the machine and the skill and care with which it is operated. Table 9.5 presents data from a study of scoring accuracy which compared uncorrected with corrected scores when obtained by hand and machine scoring. These data support the general expectation that corrected scores will occasion more errors than uncorrected scores when both are obtained by hand. They indicate that machines can yield corrected scores with the same degree of accuracy as uncorrected scores. The machine used in this study was the Scribe scoring machine of the Educational Testing Service.

TABLE 9.5.   ERRORS IN OBTAINING CORRECTED AND UNCORRECTED TEST SCORES BY HAND AND MACHINE SCORING[a]

Scoring Process	Scoring Formula	Number of Scores Checked	Number of Errors	Percent Without Error
Hand	R	1,599	1	99.94
Hand	R-KW[b]	1,403	15	98.93
Machine	R	6,748	29	99.57
Machine	R-KW[b]	6,558	28	99.57

[a]The data in this table were obtained from an unpublished document, *Addenda to Report of Recommendations to the Testing Operations Board on the Use of Formula and Rights Scores*, Richard W. Watkins, Chairman, Educational Testing Service, Princeton, N.J., June 21, 1962, 8 pp.

[b]In these formulas *K* is a fraction appropriate to the number of alternative answers available in each item, as explained earlier in this chapter. The numerator of the fraction is usually 1. The denominator is usually one less than the number of alternative answers.

[13]Malcolm J. Slakter, "The Penalty for Not Guessing," *Journal of Educational Measurement*, vol. 5 (1968), 141–44.

[14]Malcolm J. Slakter, "The Effect of Guessing Strategy on Objective Test Scores," *Journal of Educational Measurement*, vol. 5 (1968), 217–21.

It is not easy to make a strong case in favor of correcting test scores for guessing on the basis of these considerations. But if correction for guessing does little good, one can also argue that it does little harm. The truth is that ordinarily it makes little difference. If special circumstances seem to require the use of a correction, the instructor can use it with a clear conscience. But his conscience can usually be just as clear, and his life simpler, if he avoids it.

DIFFERENTIAL SCORING WEIGHTS

One obtains all objective test scores by adding weighted response scores. The simplest system of scoring weights and the one most often used is +1 for the correct response to each test item and 0 for any response not correct. Correction for guessing involves a slightly more complex system of scoring weights, such as +1 for each correct response, −1, or −2, or −3, and so on, for each wrong response, and 0 for each omitted response.

Test constructors sometimes suggest that certain items carry more weight than others because they are thought to be more important items, items of better technical quality, more complex or difficult items, or more time-consuming items. For example, in a test composed of 50 true-false items and 25 multiple-choice items, the test constructor may decide that each multiple-choice item should be worth two points and each true-false item only one point.

Reasonable as such differential item weights may seem to be on the surface, they seldom make the test to which they are applied a more reliable or valid measure. Nor do they ordinarily make the test a much worse measure. Like guessing corrections, to which they are closely related, they tend to have relatively small effects. Wilks concluded from a theoretical analysis of the problem that the method of weighting individual items matters little in a long test of intercorrelated items.[15] Aiken reached a similar conclusion.[16] Guilford and his co-workers reported this finding from an empirical study of weighted scoring, concluding that their "logically defensible system of completely weighted scoring did not yield an appreciable gain in either reliability or validity in achievement examina-

[15]S. S. Wilks, "Weighting Systems for Linear Functions of Correlated Variables when There Is No Dependent Variable," *Psychometrika*, vol. 3 (1938), 23–40.
[16]Lewis R. Aiken, Jr., "Another Look at Weighting Test Items," *Journal of Educational Measurement*, vol. 3 (1966), 183–85.

tions of from 20 to 100 items."[17] Phillips,[18] and Sabers and White came to the same conclusion. Sabers and White found

> ... not only that there is little to be gained from weighted scoring, but also that, from the point of view of test construction, weighted scoring is probably not worth the effort. The same advantages can be gained by adding more items or by selecting only the best items from a larger pool. From the administrative point of view, unweighted scoring saves time and offers fewer possibilities for errors in calculating the scores; in addition, the resulting raw scores are probably easier to interpret.[19]

If an achievement test covers two areas, one of which is judged to be twice as important as the other, then twice as many items should be written in relation to the more important area. This will result in more reliable and more valid measures than if an equal number of items is written for each area and those for the more important area are double-weighted.

Complex or time-consuming items should be made, if possible, to yield more than one response that can be independently scored as right or wrong. Very difficult items are likely to contribute less than moderately difficult items to test reliability. Giving the difficult items extra weight lowers the average effectiveness of the items and thus lowers the effectiveness of the test as a whole.

It has occurred to some test constructors that differential weighting of responses to test items might be useful in improving test reliability or validity. For example, in a question like the following:

> A child complains of severe pain and tenderness in the lower abdomen, with nausea. What should the child's mother do?
> 1. Give the child a laxative.
> 2. Put the child to bed.
> 3. Call the doctor.

Choice of the first response might result in a score of -1, of the second in a score of 0, and of the third in a score of $+1$. In this case the scoring weights were determined a priori. It has also been suggested that they might be determined experimentally. so as to maximize test reliability or validity.

---

[17]J. P. Guilford, Constance Lovell, and Ruth M. Williams, "Completely Weighted versus Unweighted Scoring in an Achievement Examination," *Educational and Psychological Measurement*, vol. 2 (1942), 15–21.

[18]Alexander J. Phillips, "Further Evidence Regarding Weighted versus Unweighted Scoring of Examinations," *Educational and Psychological Measurement*, vol. 3 (1943), 151–55.

[19]Darrell L. Sabers and Gordon W. White, "The Effect of Differential Weighting of Individual Item Responses on the Predictive Validity and Reliability of an Aptitude Test," *Journal of Educational Measurement*, vol. 6 (1969), 93–96.

But in this case also the experimental results have been disappointing. Seldom have any appreciable, consistent gains in reliability or validity been found. It seems clear that to gain any real advantage by this means one would need to write items with this purpose specifically in mind. Most item writers, even skilled professionals, have enough difficulty writing items good enough for simple right-or-wrong scoring. To make them good enough for more finely graded differential weighting seems a formidable task. Test improvement via additional, good, simply scored items looks more promising to most item writers.

Exceptions will be found, of course, to the generalization that differential weighting of items, or of item responses, is not worthwhile in the scoring of classroom tests of educational achievement. One such exception is described in the chapter in this book on the use of true-false tests. But it is a good general guide to the constructor of an educational achievement test to settle for simple right-or-wrong scoring of individual items, with each item carrying the same weight as every other item, regardless of its importance, complexity, difficulty, or quality. Increasing the number of scorable units, and making each unit as good as possible, seems better in most situations than differential weighting of items or responses as a means of test imporvement.

SUMMARY

Some of the principal ideas developed in this chapter are summarized in these 20 statements.

1. Students should be told well in advance when an important test is to be given.
2. Students should be taught essential test-taking skills.
3. The test constructor should avoid clues in the test items that enable an examinee to substitute testwiseness for command of knowledge.
4. Test anxiety is seldom a major factor in determining a student's score on a test.
5. The test administrator should help the student to adjust his rate of work on a test to the time available for it.
6. The instructor is responsible for the prevention or punishment of cheating on examinations.
7. The development of honor systems does not afford a generally promising solution to he problem of cheating on examinations.
8. The instructor is responsible for preventing any student from gaining special advance copies of, or advance information about, one of his examinations.
9. The use of separate answer sheets facilitates rapid clerical or machine scoring of objective tests.
10. In recent years a number of good, relatively inexpensive machines have been developed for scoring classroom tests.
11. A guessing correction is sometimes applied to objective test scores to reduce to zero the expected gain from blind guessing.

12. One may correct scores for guessing by subtracting a fraction of the wrong responses or by adding a fraction of the omitted responses.
13. Scores corrected for guessing will usually rank the examinees in about the same order as the uncorrected scores.
14. The probability is small of getting a respectable score on a good objective test by blind guessing alone.
15. Well-motivated examinees who have time to attempt all items do little blind guessing.
16. Students should be encouraged to make rational guesses on the answers to objective test items.
17. A guessing correction removes the incentive for slower students to guess blindly on the final items of a speeded test.
18. Scores corrected for guessing may be influenced by the examinee's readiness, or reluctance, to gamble.
19. A guessing correction may complicate the scoring task and may lower scoring accuracy slightly.
20. Giving different weights to different items in a test, or to different correct or incorrect responses in an item, seldom improves score reliability or validity appreciably.

And the Gileadites took the passages of Jordan before the Ephraimites: and it was so, that when those Ephraimites which were escaped said, Let me go over; that the men of Gilead said unto him, Art thou an Ephraimite? If he say, Nay; then said they unto him, Say now Shibboleth: and he said Sibboleth: for he could not frame to pronounce it right. Then they took him, and slew him at the passages of Jordan: and there fell at that time of the Ephraimites forty and two thousand.

JUDGES, 12: 5–6

10

ORAL EXAMINATIONS

Clearly, the history of oral examinations is a long one. Until about a century ago they were the prevalent form of examination in schools. Now, only occasional voices[1,2,3] are raised to proclaim their virtues as classroom tests. But oral examinations are still popular for some purposes.[4] The final examination of candidates for the degree Doctor of Philosophy is still usually an oral examination. In this situation it serves more of a ceremonial than an evaluative function.[5]

[1]James R. Hartnett, "Oral Examinations," *Improving College and University Teaching*, vol. 13 (Autumn 1965), 208–9.

[2]Grace Graham, "Denmark's Oral Examinations," *Education*, vol. 83 (January 1963), 306–9.

[3]Irving Morrissett, "An Experiment With Oral Examinations," *Journal of Higher Education*, vol. 29 (April 1958), 185–90.

[4]Harold G. Levine and Christine H. McGuire "The Validity and Reliability of Oral Examinations in Assessing Cognitive Skills in Medicine," *Journal of Educational Measurement*, vol. 7 (1970), 63–74.

[5]Otis C. Trimble, *The Final Oral Examination, Purdue University Studies in Higher Education*, no. 25 (November, 1934)

Oral examinations are valued particularly in the certification or selection of professionals whose work involves extensive contacts with people: teachers,[6] medical specialists,[7] police,[8] and other civil servants.[9]

ESSENCE AND VARIATIONS

In essence the oral examination involves two persons, examiner and examinee, face-to-face. The examiner asks questions. The examinee attempts to answer them. The examiner probes with further questions or accepts the answer. Finally he judges the quality of the answers and grades the examinee accordingly. Often the grade is either pass or fail.

Sometimes to improve the objectivity of the examination more than one examiner is used. Sometimes to improve the efficiency of the process, and the fairness of the judgments, several examinees are interviewed simultaneously, giving each a chance to respond to the same questions and to comment on answers given by the other examinees. Sometimes the examinees are directed to question each other, with the examiners acting only as judges, or even with the judging left to the examinees themselves. Hartnett[10] and Brody[11] have described in detail some of these variations on the basic oral examination.

Employment interviews often include a kind of oral examination, and there is some similarity in the principles of good practice for both. The oral examination can be properly regarded as one kind of performance test, but since very special circumstances surround it—the cruciality and stress, the unequal status of the participants—the performance can seldom be regarded as typical behavior.

JUSTIFICATIONS

Obviously the oral examination does involve direct contact and interaction between examiner and examinee. This makes the examination, if not less threatening, at least more personal, and possibly more humane

[6]Richard W. Saxe, "Oral Examinations Evaluate Character, General Fitness," *Chicago Schools Journal*, vol. 44 (December 1962), 123–27.

[7]Harold D. Carter, "How Reliable are Good Oral Examinations?" *California Journal of Educational Research*, vol. 13 (September 1962), 147–53.

[8]C. C. Riggs, *The Oral Interview as a Predictive Device in the Selection of Michigan State Troopers*, Master's Thesis, Michigan State University, 1961.

[9]Samuel H. Ordway, Chairman, *Oral Tests in Public Personnel Selection*, (Chicago: Civil Service Assembly, 1943).

[10]Hartnett, "Oral Examinations."

[11]William Brody and Norman J. Powell, "A New Approach to Oral Testing," *Educational and Psychological Measurement*, vol. 7 (Summer 1947), 289–98.

than written examinations. Some even regard an oral examination as an enjoyable experience.

Personal characteristics that would be impossible to assess on a written test can be evaluated in the face-to-face oral examination: characteristics such as appearance, manner, personality, alertness, forthrightness, stress tolerance, and speech pattern and quality. One can judge the impression the examinee would probably make on others.

When the purpose of the examination is to assess the examinee's knowledge or intellectual abilities, the oral approach permits a flexibility of approach that the written examination usually lacks. The examinee can be asked to expand, to clarify, or to justify his answer. An important point can be probed in depth. Thus a clear picture of the examinee's abilities and limitations may emerge. Those who see cheating as a major problem with written examinations can say that the problem can hardly arise in an oral examination. Even bluffing may be harder to manage effectively in spur-of-the-moment responses to oral questions than on a written exam. Finally, like all good examinations regardless of form, an oral examination can be a learning experience.

However, it is easy for oral examination enthusiasts to claim too much. An oral examination does no better than a written one in assessing intangible, poorly defined traits such as character, creativity, or "general fitness." Those who claim it tests the examinee's ability to think on his feet, or perhaps more accurately to think effectively while under stress, ignore the fact that most people do most of their best thinking while not under stress. Resistance to "choking up" under stress is probably not a very good indicator of overall effectiveness. Above all, advocates of oral examinations should avoid claiming that they measure abilities such as loyalty to the organization, honesty, industry, integrity, or even ability to get along with others, for these are characteristics that examinees have little opportunity to show, or examiners to observe, in the oral examination situation.

LIMITATIONS

Oral examinations are subject to serious limitations, which account for their virtual disappearance as tools for educational evaluation. Because the oral examination is essentially an individual process, it is very time-consuming; particularly if each examination is as long as it needs to be (30 minutes or more) to yield a fair sample of the examinee's abilities; particularly if more than one examiner is used to obtain an objective assessment. These qualities also make oral examinations costly and complex to administer.

The personal contact and interaction between examiner and examinee that is one of the assets of the oral examination is also a liability. It opens the door to prejudice, partiality, and discrimination on grounds other than the relevant traits and abilities. Other influences lower the validity of the examination. For some, as has been suggested above, the stress of the confrontation may upset normally effective mental processes. For others, glibness and pleasantness may help to conceal genuine deficiencies.

But the major limitation of the oral examination is the difficulty of obtaining reasonably reliable scores in reasonable amounts of time. Studies by Hartog,[12] Barnes and Pressey,[13] Riggs,[14] Trimble,[15] and others support this conclusion. On the other hand, as Carter[16] has shown, and as Trimble[17] showed in another study, it is possible to obtain reliable evaluations under certain conditions. If several raters are used, if they are all looking for the same things, and if the examination is long enough and structured so that the examinee will be likely to present a fair picture of his traits and abilities, the oral examination scores can be both reliable and valid. To achieve this result, unfortunately, usually calls for more care and skill and time than most examiners can dedicate to the task.

SUGGESTIONS FOR EFFECTIVE USE

1. Avoid using oral examinations if a written examination can be devised to do the job with reasonable effectiveness.

Seldom should an oral examination be used to assess an examinee's command of knowledge. Written examinations are not nearly so limited in scope or depth as some critics seem to assume. In general, oral examinations should probably be reserved mainly to ceremonial occasions, or to situations in which assessment of personal characteristics is the primary concern. They should not be used to assess intangible, poorly defined traits.

[12]Sir Philip Hartog and E. C. Rhodes, "A Viva Voce (Interview) Examination," *The Marks of Examiners*, chap. 11, pp. 168–78 (London: Macmillan and Company, 1936).
[13]Elinor J. Barnes and S. L. Pressey, "The Reliability and Validity of Oral Examinations," *School and Society*, vol. 30 (November 23, 1929), 719–22.
[14]Riggs, *The Oral Interview*.
[15]Trimble, *The Final Oral Examination*.
[16]Carter, "How Reliable Are Good Oral Examinations?"
[17]Otis C. Trimble, "The Oral Examination: Its Validity and Reliability," *School and Society*, vol. 39 (April 28, 1934), 550–52.

2. Define clearly the purpose of the examination and the basis on which the examinee performances are to be judged.

The traits or abilities to be rated should be defined unambiguously. The scale on which ratings are expressed and the passing score should also be defined. Different kinds of rating scales are described by Saxe, Hartnett, Carter, Graham, Hartog, and Trimble, in the works referred to earlier in this chapter. Proper and improper types of questions and lines of questioning should be specified.

3. Use two or more competent, conscientious, well-trained examiners.

Competence in this context usually means excellence with reference to the traits and abilities on which the examinees are being evaluated. Conscientiousness comes from commitment to the selection or evaluation process, from placing a high value on doing this job well. Examiners who are drafted, and who accept the responsibility with reluctance, may not be conscientious enough.

The training process, at a minimum, should involve prior discussion of the purpose of the examination, the traits to be rated, proper and improper lines of questioning, and the meaning of various scale scores. At a desirable level, the training process would include practice runs to establish common procedures and common bases for judgment. Training can continue as the examination proceeds if continuous checks are made of amount of agreement, and if explanations are sought for instances of extreme disagreement.

4. If possible, arrange for the examinee to be heard in two independent examination sessions, with different panels of examiners.

As Hartog has shown, performance of the same examinee on different occasions may be widely different. The line of questioning may develop quite differently on the two occasions, touching items the examinee knows well in one case, exposing his ignorance in the other. The examinee's assurance may be supported on one occasion and demolished on another. A single examination may be quite an unstable basis for evaluation.

5. Prepare the examinees to give an accurate account of themselves on the examination.

The examinees should know the purpose of the examination, the bases for judging competence, the general nature of the questions to be asked, and the procedures to be followed. If the examiners feel that it is legitimate to ask irrelevant questions or questions impossible to answer (to see whether the examinee can recognize such questions), the examinee ought to be aware of this possibility.

> *6. Arrange to collect data so that the reliability of the scores from each examination can be checked.*

Usually it is impossible to validate the scores on an oral examination statistically. Validity must be built in on the basis of judgments the examiners make. But if examiners disagree, or if the performances of the examinee in different examining sessions are grossly inconsistent, the evaluations are bound to be unreliable and hence cannot possibly be vaild.

CONCLUDING REMARKS

Although the oral approach may appear to afford a superior or easy solution to an examining problem, this rarely proves to be the case. It is not easy to do a good job at oral examining. On closer inspection, the apparent superiority of the oral approach tends to disappear in the wastelands of difficulty and the fogs of unreliability. Sooner or later most examining authorities turn to more precise, more easily manageable methods. It is *possible* to use oral examinations effectively, but it is almost always unattractively difficult to do so.

SUMMARY

Ten main ideas have been developed in this brief chapter on oral examinations:

1. The popularity of oral examinations has waned, but they are still used ceremonially, or for selecting employees who must deal with people directly.
2. Some variations on the simple examiner-examinee interview, involving multiple examiners, multiple examinees, and multiple examining sessions, have been tried and found effective.
3. The oral examination allows for personal contact between examiner and examinee and also allows considerable flexibility in the examining process, but it does not allow for accurate assessment of intangible traits or on-the-job performance characteristics.
4. Oral examinations tend to be time-consuming, to be subject to personal bias, and to yield unreliable measurements.
5. Oral examinations should seldom be used primarily to assess the examinee's command of knowledge.

6. The traits to be rated in an oral examination and the rating scale to be used should be carefully defined in advance.
7. Two or more competent, conscientious examiners should be involved in every important oral examination. Multiple examining sessions are also advisable.
8. Examinees should usually be well informed in advance about the purposes of the examination, and about the bases that will be used in judging their competence.
9. The reliability of the scores from each oral examination should be calculated, to encourage the examiners to do their jobs well and to provide for continuing improvements in the process.
10. It is difficult to give a good oral examination.

I am studying the newer statistical methods under Professor
Boaz, and having a difficult time of it.

EDWARD L. THORNDIKE

11

TEST SCORE STATISTICS

THE STATISTICAL INTERPRETATION OF TEST SCORES

A test score is usually a number. Like any other number a test score,
by itself, has only the meaning given to it by the number system on which
it is based. Consider a test score of 78, for example. From the number
system one can infer that:

a. The 7 refers to 7 tens, and the 8 to 8 units.
b. 78 is more than 77, but less than 79.
c. 78 could be the sum of 52 and 26, or the difference between 93 and 15.

and so on.

But these inferences tell us very little of what we really would like
to know about that test score of 78, which would be answers to questions

like these:

d. Is 78 a high score or a low score?
e. How accurate and dependable is that score?

In order to answer those questions we need to know things like these:

f. What is the highest possible score?
g. What is the highest score and the lowest score any student actually got on this test?
h. What was the average score on this test in the whole class?
i. What percent of the students in the class got higher scores? What percent got lower scores?
j. How were the scores of the class distributed? Were they bunched or spread, and if spread, symmetrically and smoothly or skewed and unevenly?
k. If the student were retested with a different test, how much different would his score be likely to be?

To get answers to questions like these, particularly the last four, we need the help of statistical methods. Statistics is the branch of mathematics dealing with the collection, analysis, interpretation, and presentation of masses of numerical data. It is difficult if not impossible to do an adequate job of interpreting a test score without the help of such concepts as frequency distribution, central tendency (average), variability, percentile ranks, standard scores, and correlation, which statistics provides.

Perhaps a concrete example will help to make clear the useful role that statistics can play in the interpretation of test scores. Exhibit 11.1 presents a sample test report of the sort that one instructor distributes to his students when he returns their answer sheets to them. It shows that the mean score on this test was close to the ideal mean, defined here as a point midway between the maximum possible score (102) and the expected chance score (51). It shows that the scores were much more variable (standard deviation = 10.6) than the specified minimum (8.5), defined here as one-sixth of the range between maximum possible and expected chance scores. It shows that the reliability of the scores was fairly high (0.86) and the probable score error fairly low (2.66). Both of these concepts will be developed in Chapter 15.

The stanine equivalents and grade equivalents tables give the students an indication of how good or poor their individual scores were in relation to the scores of their classmates. On the stanine scale the score intervals are varied so that the distribution of stanine scores is approximately normal. On the grade scale the intervals are all equal, and a 4.0 is equivalent to an A, a 3.0 to a B, and so on. For a graduate level class the average grade is expected to be slightly above 3.0. On this test the average grade was 3.13.

In the test key the number 1 indicates a true statement, the number 2 a false one. The answers are given in rows of eight because that is how

EXHIBIT 11.1

Sample Test Report

Number of students	116	Number of items	102 (TF)
Mean Score	76.6	Ideal mean	76.5
Standard Deviation	10.6	Minimum std. dev.	8.5
Reliability	0.86	Probable error	2.66

	STANINE EQUIVALENTS				GRADE EQUIVALENTS	
9	92–93	3		4.5	93–99	1
8	89–91	9		4.0	86–92	24
7	86–88	13		3.5	79–85	33
6	81–85	25		3.0	72–78	26
5	75–80	22		2.5	65–71	18
4	69–74	17		2.0	58–64	8
3	65–68	13		1.5	51–57	3
2	56–64	9		1.0	44–50	3
1	43–55	5				116
		116				

Average grade = 3.13

Difficult Items (Over 40 percent)

ITEM	DIFFI-CULTY	KEY	DISCRIMI-NATION	PAGE		KEY	
1	51	T	.29	8	1.	1212	1121
2	53	F	.16	3	9.	2212	2111
3	45	T	.07	4	17.	1222	1222
21	50	T	−.07	35	25.	2221	1222
25	45	F	.26	41	33.	2212	2222
30	81	F	−.10	58	41.	2222	1211
47	60	T	.25	91	49.	1222	1121
48	49	T	.33	91	57.	2121	1112
59	57	F	.33	116	65.	2221	2211
61	54	T	−.06	124	73.	1222	1212
62	48	T	.51	127	81.	2121	2212
68	41	T	.45	147	89.	2222	2122
76	46	F	.58	164	97.	2212	11
87	42	T	.26	206			
97	41	F	.61	Lect			
100	55	F	.39	Notes			
101	45	T	.19	Notes			

they appear on the student's answer sheet. Each row of answers is identified by the number of the first item of the row.

The list of difficult items is useful in directing the attention of the class and of the instructor, to the items that a substantial proportion of students answered incorrectly. Indices of difficulty and discrimination and the answer keys and page references are provided for each of the items listed. The meaning and the calculation of indices of difficulty and discrimination are described in Chapter 14.

The student should not hold himself responsible at this point for understanding all of the words and numbers used in Exhibit 11.1 or in the preceding brief discussion of it. Understanding will grow as this and later chapters are studied. Our intent in presenting Exhibit 11.1 here is to suggest that the statistical methods to be studied in this and subsequent chapters *do* have practical usefulness in classroom testing. Statistical methods, like other tools of thinking, are not likely to seem very useful to one who has not yet acquired the ability to use them. One must experience the help they give in order to appreciate their value.

The statistics of test scores to be described in this chapter will be the simplest kinds of descriptive statistics. Even so, some students may find the prospect unnerving if they feel unprepared in mathematics. For them, even the relatively simple mathematics of this chapter may present problems. But, if they are wise, they will not let fear of numbers defeat them before the battle is even joined. Anyone who finds the simple arithmetic of test scores beyond his comprehension probably should consider spending his time doing something other than going to college.

FREQUENCY DISTRIBUTIONS

The first step in the process of describing test scores statistically is to construct a frequency distribution. If the range of scores is greater than 25 score units, a grouped frequency distribution is advantageous. Let us consider a specific example.

Suppose two spelling tests of 100 words each have been given to a class of 25 students. The first test, List A, was dictated on Monday, and the second, List B, composed of entirely different words, on Wednesday. The students' test papers were scored by giving one unit of credit for each word correctly spelled. The scores obtained are shown in Table 11.1. How can these two sets of scores be described statistically? Consider first only the Monday test scores on List A.

Notice that the scores range from a high of 96 for Nathaniel to a low of 61 for Wendell. In order to include all the scores a *range* of 36 score units ($96 - 60 = 36$, or $97 - 61 = 36$) is required. This range is used as one measure of the variability of the scores. To get a more complete picture of the students' scores on this test, a frequency distribution can be constructed.

Grouping the scores into classes simplifies the frequency distribution with no appreciable loss in accuracy. The following suggestions may be helpful in deciding on the size and number of groups.

TABLE 11.1. SCORES OF TWENTY-FIVE PUPILS ON TWO SPELLING TESTS

	List A Monday	List B Wednesday
Aaron	65	67
Barbara	75	72
Ben	66	72
Bud	88	92
Clyde	71	76
Donald	72	72
Dorothy	91	90
Eugene	82	80
Fay	84	80
Frank	76	81
Gary	69	64
Gladys	67	70
Jack	74	78
Jeff	80	77
Jerry	87	90
Joan	91	85
Melville	65	68
Nadine	77	78
Nathaniel	96	94
Patricia	93	87
Peggy	79	78
Perry	84	89
Richard	76	75
Shirley	73	78
Wendell	61	69

1. Find the range of scores (high minus low plus 1).
2. Divide the range by 12, and round to the nearest whole number. That is the number of units to include in each group.
3. Use the lowest score in the distribution as the lowest score in the bottom group.
4. Make all the groups include the same number of score units.

In the case of the List A spelling test scores the range, as we have said, is 36. Thirty-six divided by 12 is 3. The lowest score is 61. Hence the bottom group is 61–63. The next is 64–66, and so on. On this basis the class intervals shown in the left column of Table 11.2 were set up.

Opposite each class interval the scores that fall in it are recorded. Tally marks could be used instead of scores, but when the number of scores is not large, the use of actual score values is convenient and preserves some information that might otherwise be lost. The number of scores falling in each class interval is recorded in the third column headed "Frequency." One can detect in this frequency distribution some signs of

TABLE 11.2. FREQUENCY DISTRIBUTION OF TWENTY-FIVE SCORES ON LIST A

Class Interval	Scores	Frequency
94–96	96	1
91–93	91, 91, 93	3
88–90	88	1
85–87	87	1
82–84	82, 84, 84	3
79–81	80, 79	2
76–78	76, 77, 76	3
73–75	75, 74, 73	3
70–72	71, 72	2
67–69	69, 67	2
64–66	65, 66, 65	3
61–63	61	1
		$n = 25$

the usual tendency for scores to be more concentrated toward the middle of the range. The distribution of scores here is fairly uniform, with some tendency for low scores to be more common than high scores.

The main purpose of the frequency distribution is to give the test constructor an integrated, meaningful picture of the entire distribution scores. It is also useful in showing how any particular score relates to all the other scores in the groups.

THE MEDIAN AND THE MEAN

One useful statistical summary of a set of test scores is some measure of their typical or average value, usually either the *mean* or the *median*. The "median" is either the middle measure of the group (if the group includes an odd number of measures) or the point halfway between the two middle measures (if the number of measures is even). In the case of this set of scores the median is 76. Because the measures are concentrated more in the bottom half than in the top half of the distribution, the median would be expected to fall somewhat below the mean.

The "mean," or more precisely the "arithmetic mean," of a set of measures is obtained by adding all measures and dividing the sum by the number of measures. Expressed as a formula

$$M = \frac{\Sigma X}{N} \qquad\qquad 11.1$$

In which M stands for the mean, Σ means "the sum of," X represents each score in the group, and N stands for the number of scores in the group. For the group of scores from the Monday spelling test, the sum is 1,942, which makes the mean score 77.68.

If the number of scores is large, if the scores themselves are large, and if a calculating machine is not available, one can sometimes save time at the cost of only a slight loss in accuracy by calculating the mean from the frequency distribution.[1] To do this requires a new scale, a deviation scale, whose zero point is located near where we expect the mean to be. The class interval that is expected to contain the mean is designated as zero. If the mean actually does not fall in this interval the calculations will involve larger numbers, but the result will be equally accurate. Successive class intervals above the zero interval are numbered 1, 2, 3, and so forth. Successive class intervals below the zero interval are numbered −1, −2, −3, and so forth. These numbers create a new, simpler deviation scale. They are shown in the third column of Table 11.3.

TABLE 11.3. CALCULATIONS WITH DEVIATION UNITS

Group	Frequency (f)	Deviation (d)	fd	fd²
94–96	1	6	6	36
91–93	3	5	15	75
88–90	1	4	4	16
85–87	1	3	3	9
82–85	3	2	6	12
79–81	2	1	2	2
76–78	3	0	0	0
73–75	3	−1	−3	3
70–72	2	−2	−4	8
67–69	2	−3	−6	18
64–66	3	−4	−12	48
61–63	1	−5	−5	25
Sum	25		6	252

Mean

Deviation units $\quad \frac{6}{25} = .24$

Score units $\quad 3 \times .24 + 77 = 77.72$

Variance

Deviation units $\quad \frac{252}{25} - .24^2 = 10.0224$

Score units $\quad 9 \times 10.0224 = 90.2016$

Standard deviation $\quad \sqrt{90.2016} = 9.50$

[1]Simple hand-operated or more versatile electrically operated desk calculators are available at prices ranging from less than $200 to more than $1,000. The use of such machines can greatly speed up and simplify the statistical calculations described in this chapter. Most schools and colleges have, or should have, one available for faculty use.

On this new, shorter, simpler scale there is one score of 6 (instead of 96), three of 5, one of 4, and so on. There is also one score of −5 (instead of 61), three of −4, two of −3, and so no. The sum of the positive scores is 36. That of the negative scores is 30. Hence the net sum of these new deviation scores is 6. Dividing 6 by 25 gives 0.24 for the mean of the deviation scores.

To translate this deviation score mean to the original score scale one must multiply it by 3, since one deviation score unit is equal to 3 of the original score units, and add 77, since the zero point on the deviation scale corresponds to 77 on the original score scale. These operations yield 77.72 for the estimate of the mean, very close to the value obtained by direct calculation. If the same number of test scores had fallen above as below the midpoints of the class intervals, the two means would have been exactly the same.

A numerical simplification of this kind may not seem worth the mathematical complications it causes and the very slight inaccuracy it introduces in the calculation of the mean. But it can save a great deal of work in the calculation of the standard deviation, as will be illustrated in the next section. Since exactly the same initial steps must be taken in calculating either the mean or the standard deviation by this method, it is advantageous to calculate both of them using the same approach.

Ordinarily the median is easier to determine than the mean. If the set of test scores includes a few extremely high or extremely low scores, the median may give a more reasonable indication of the typical score than does the mean.

> Consider, for example, the set of scores: 8, 9, 10, 11, 22. What is the mean of this set? What is the median? Which best indicates the value of *most* of the scores in the set? Which best indicates the value of *all* the scores in the set?

Because the value of each score in the set affects the value of the mean, the mean tends to be a more stable measure of the average score level than does the median. That is, the mean is likely to vary less from set to set of scores of the same kind than the median. Further, the mean is involved, directly or indirectly, in the calculation of many other statistics. Hence the mean is generally regarded by statisticians as a more precise and useful measure than the median of the central tendency of a set of scores.

If an instructor needs no more than an easily obtained estimate of the typical value of a set of scores, the median is probably the measure to be obtained. But if a fully representative estimate is desired and if other statistics are to be calculated, the mean will usually be preferred.

THE VARIANCE AND THE STANDARD DEVIATION

To provide a concise statistical description of a set of test scores one must take account of variability as well as central tendency. One measure of variability, the range, has already been mentioned. However, since it is determined by only two scores, the highest and the lowest, it is not a particularly stable measure. The standard deviation is a much more reliable and more generally useful measure.

The standard deviation is defined as the square root of the variance. The variance is the mean of the squared deviations of the measures from their mean. Expressed in formulas,

$$\sigma = \sqrt{\frac{\Sigma d^2}{N}} \qquad\qquad 11.2$$

and

$$\sigma^2 = \frac{\Sigma d^2}{N} \qquad\qquad 11.3$$

where σ (sigma) represents the standard deviation, σ^2 (sigma squared) the variance, Σ (upper case or capital sigma) means "the sum of," d is the difference between any score in the group and the mean of all scores in that group, and N represents the number of scores in the group.

For the Monday spelling test scores, the deviation of Aaron's score (65) from the mean of all scores in the group (77.68) is -12.68. The square of -12.68 (-12.68 times -12.68) equals 160.7824. Finding the deviations of all other scores in the group, squaring them, adding the squares, and dividing by the number of scores (25) would give the variance of this set of scores, which is 91.0176. The standard deviation is the square root of the variance, 9.54 in this case.

Some teachers who need to find the standard deviation of a set of test scores may either have forgotten or never have been taught how to find the square root of a number. Various methods are available. The one easiest to explain and to learn how to use is the *guess-and-divide* method. This can be illustrated in finding the square root of 160.7824.

The first problem is to find a number whose square is reasonably close to 160. A table of squares is helpful in this connection. Such a table, or an estimate based on experience, suggests that the square of 12 is 144. This is reasonably close to the number whose square root is needed.

The second step is to divide 160.8 by 12. The quotient is 13.4. The average (mean) of the quotient and the divisor is 12.7. This becomes the divisor. The process of dividing and averaging divisor and quotient is repeated. With each repetition, the divisor and quotient get to be more nearly alike. If the quotient and the divisor are in good agreement after two divisions, their average is accepted as the needed square root. If not, the process is continued. In this example, the average obtained after two divisions, 12.68, appears to be exactly accurate.

To calculate a standard deviation by converting each score into a deviation from the mean of all scores would be to do the job the hard way. Since the deviation of a score is defined as its difference from the mean, so that

$$d = X - M \hspace{4cm} 11.4$$

it is easy to show algebraically that

$$\Sigma d^2 = \Sigma X^2 - \frac{(\Sigma X)^2}{N} \hspace{3cm} 11.5$$

so that

$$\sigma^2 = \frac{\Sigma X^2}{N} - \frac{(\Sigma X)^2}{N^2} \hspace{3cm} 11.6$$

Expressed in words, this formula indicates that the variance of a set of test scores is equal to the difference between two fractions. The larger is the sum of all the squared scores divided by the number of scores. The smaller is the square of the sum of the scores divided by the square of the number of scores. This is the formula actually used to get the variance of the Monday spelling test scores reported above.

This formula is reasonably convenient if the scores are small and few or if a calculating machine is available. When these conditions do not exist, and often they do not in a classroom testing, the same simplification used earlier in estimating the mean can be applied in calculating the standard deviation. That is, the scores can be grouped in intervals, with the intervals given positive and negative score values from some point near the mean. This amounts to using the deviations in the third column of Table 11.3 as if they were actual scores.

The value of fd^2 for each group is obtained by multiplying the fd value by the d value for that group. This process gives the list of numbers shown in the last column of Table 11.3. The sum of these values is 252. This is the sum of all the deviation scores squared. It corresponds to ΣX^2 in formula 11.6.

The sum of the deviation values themselves (ΣX) is 6. The value of N is 25, and of N^2, 625. These values inserted in Formula 11.6 give

$$[\sigma^2] = \tfrac{252}{25} - \tfrac{36}{625} = 10.0800 - .0576 = 10.0224$$

This $[\sigma^2]$ is not the variance desired, since it is expressed in terms of the deviation score scale. One unit on that scale is equal to three units on the original scale. Since scores must be squared to find their variance, the ratio between the units on the two scales must also be squared to make a proper correction. That is, in this case, $\sigma^2 = 9 \, [\sigma^2]$. Hence the variance of these scores, expressed in terms of the original scale, is 90.2016. The square root of this, 9.50, is the value of the standard deviation of these scores.

Lathrop has suggested a short-cut estimate of the standard deviation, assuming a reasonably normal distribution of scores.[2] It is the difference between the sums of the upper and lower one-sixths of the scores, divided by one-half the number of scores. For the List A spelling test scores of Table 11.1, one-sixth of the scores would be 4, to the nearest whole number. The highest four scores are 96, 93, 91, and 91. The lowest four are 61, 65, 65, and 66. Hence the difference between their sums is $371 - 257 = 114$. Dividing 114 by 12.5 gives 9.12, a value in fairly good agreement with those obtained from formulas 11.2 and 11.6. Jenkins has proposed a similar estimate that is slightly less convenient but probably slightly more accurate.[3]

Sometimes at this point students voice a mild complaint. You've taught us *how* to calculate a standard deviation, they say, but we still don't see *why* we should bother. Faced with this reaction most teachers council patience. All in good time, they say. Before you get through the sections in this chapter that deal with normal distribution, with stanines and with correlation coefficients, you will encounter standard deviation again and again and again. You will encounter it also in many of the remaining chapters of the book. Exhibit 11.2 presents some of the questions that can be given much better answers by one who knows what a standard deviation is, and how it can be calculated, than by one who doesn't know and doesn't care. Take it from those who have scrambled up the road to understanding of educational measurement ahead of you. The standard deviation is a useful tool to have along in your mental knapsack.

[2]Robert L. Lathrop, "A Quick but Accurate Approximation to the Standard Deviation of a Distribution," *Journal of Experimental Educational Education*, vol. 29 (March, 1961), 319–21.
[3]W. L. Jenkins, "A Short-cut Method for σ and r," *Educational and Psychological Measurement*, vol. 6 (1946), 533–36.

EXHIBIT 11.2

Uses of the Standard Deviation

A. Expressing precision
    1. How precise is the method of measurement?
    2. How accurately can grade point averages be predicted from this set of aptitude tests?
B. Consideration of chance
    3. What are the chances that a person could get a score of 60 purely by chance on a 100 item true-false test?
    4. What is the influence of blind guessing on test scores?
C. Score interpretation
    5. How good is my score on this test compared with the scores of other students?
    6. How good is a score of 700 on the College Board's Scholastic Aptitude Test?
D. Grading
    7. How were the recommended proportions of A's, B's, and so forth determined in the system of relative grading (grading on the curve)?
    8. What is a stanine?
E. Test planning and evaluating
    9. What is the effect on test scores of using items of uniform, moderate difficulty?
    10. How well does this test discriminate?
F. Reliability estimation
    11. How reliable is this test?
    12. Why are growth measures unreliable?
    13. How did Kuder and Richardson arrive at their formula for test reliability?
G. Equating and weighting
    14. What score on Test A is equivalent to score X on Test B?
    15. How much does this assignment count toward our final mark?
H. Statistical derivation and testing hypotheses
    16. What is meant by the standard error of measurement?
    17. What is a product moment correlation coefficient?
    18. What is covariance?
    19. What are the chances that the apparent superiority of Method A can be attributed entirely to experimental error?

THE NORMAL DISTRIBUTION

Distributions of test scores frequently approximate the normal distribution. For this reason, and because it is convenient to have a standard, idealized model as a point of reference when estimating the charac-

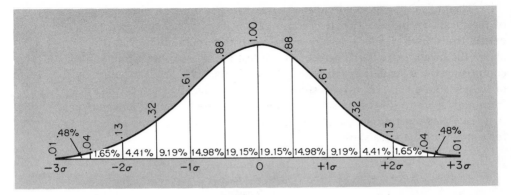

FIGURE 11.1
The Normal Curve

teristics of actual score distributions, we need to pay attention to the normal distribution here. Some systems of standard scores, such as the stanine scores discussed in this chapter, are based on the properties of the normal distribution of scores.

Some of the essential characteristics of the normal distribution are illustrated in Figure 11.1. It is a symmetrical curve, with the mean and median located in the same central position bisecting the area under the curve. The base line of the curve is marked in standard deviation units.

On Figure 11.1 ordinates (vertical lines from the curve to the base line) have been drawn at intervals of one-half of the standard deviation. Taking a convenient arbitrary length for the central ordinate and calling it 1.00, the other ordinates can be expressed as decimal values of the central ordinate. It is helpful to refer to the relative lengths of these ordinates when drawing replicas of the normal curve.

Percentages of the total area under the curve are also indicated for the area between each successive pair of ordinates. It is useful to remember that 68.26 percent of the total area lies between the ordinates located at $+1\sigma$ and -1σ; that 95.46 percent lies between the ordinates at $+2\sigma$ and -2σ, and 99.72 percent between the ordinates at $+3\sigma$ and -3σ. Detailed tables of ordinates and areas under the normal curve are available in good statistical references, such as Blommers and Lindquist and Ferguson.[4] Moonan has published frequency distributions that approximate the normal distribution for various numbers of class intervals and for various numbers of measures.[5]

---

[4]Paul Blommers and E. F. Lindquist, *Elementary Statistical Methods* (Boston: Houghton Mifflin Company, 1960); and George A. Ferguson, *Statistical Analysis in Psychology and Education* (New York: McGraw-Hill Book Company, 1959).

[5]William J. Moonan, "A Table of Normal Distribution Frequencies for Selected Numbers of Class Intervals and Sample Sizes," *Journal of Experimental Education*, vol. 27 (March, 1959), 231–35.

Theoretically, a normal curve extends without limit on either side of the mean. In practice, and for convenience, it is often considered to extend from three standard deviations below to three standard deviations above the mean, since 99.72 percent of the test scores or other measures comprising the distribution fall within those limits. But the distribution of scores from a class of, say, 30 students will not typically show a range from high score to low of six standard deviations. Hoel's figures indicate that the following ratio of range to standard deviation can be expected for samples of the sizes shown.[6]

Sample Size	Typical Range in Standard Deviation Units
10	3.0
50	4.5
100	5.0
1000	6.5

The typical values shown are averages. In some samples of the specified size the observed value of the ratio of range to standard deviation will be considerably more, and in other samples considerably less, than the value indicated. But it may be useful for the instructor to know that in a set of 25 test scores the highest score is more likely to be two than three standard deviations above the mean.

Another point worth nothing is that the points of inflection of the curve occur at $+1\sigma$ and -1σ. As one follows the curve outward from the mean it is at these points that the slope of the curve stops increasing and starts to decrease. Exactly half of the area under the curve is located between ordinates at $+.6745\sigma$ and $-.6745\sigma$. When the normal curve is used to represent chance fluctuations in test scores due to errors of measurement, the value $.6745\sigma$ is referred to as the probable error of measurement. Half the errors are likely to be larger and half smaller than this value. The standard deviation of the normal curve is referred to as the standard error of measurement when the curve itself is used to indicate the expected distribution of errors of measurement. About 32 percent of the errors are likely to be larger and 68 percent smaller than the standard error of measurement.

While it is true, as pointed out at the beginning of this section, that many distributions of test scores do approximate the normal distribution, there is no compelling reason why they ought to. Indeed, to achieve highest

---

[6]Paul G. Hoel, *Introduction to Mathematical Statistics* (New York: John Wiley & Sons, Inc., 1947).

reliability with a given number of test items, a flatter score distribution than the normal distribution is advantageous, one that has more scores at the extremes and fewer in the center. Rummel, working with a college-level mathematics test used to exempt some entering freshmen (about 50 percent) from a course in basic mathematical skills, found that item revisions that flattened the distribution of scores also reduced the errors made in exempting some freshmen and not exempting others.[7]

The test constructor who points with pride to the beautifully normal distribution of scores that his test yields may be using a false standard of quality for his tests. If the scores of his students were determined by their success in matching pennies with him, the distribution of their scores would be approximately normal. Indeed, it is hard to beat pure chance as a generator of normally distributed scores. This does not mean that the normal distributions are always generated by chance errors of measurement. It does mean that such a distribution is not necessarily an indication of quality in a test.

Sometimes tests yield asymmetric or skewed distributions of scores, in which the median score is much nearer the highest score than it is to the lowest, or vice versa. Lord and Cook have reported studies of this characteristic in actual distributions of test scores.[8] If this skewing is not attributable to a few outstandingly capable or incapable students in the group tested, it may be due to excessive ease or excessive difficulty in the test itself. When the test is too easy, students of average achievement may receive scores almost as high as students of outstanding achievement. When it is too hard, students of average achievement may do little better than those of lowest achievement. In either case the distribution of scores is likely to be skewed, or asymmetric. Thus, lack of symmetry in the score distribution may indicate inappropriateness of the test in difficulty. But symmetry is not the same as normality.

PERCENTILE RANKS

Since the scores on different tests, when taken by different groups, can have widely different means, standard deviations, and distributions, it is useful to have some standard scale to which they all can be referred.

[7]Josiah Francis Rummel, "The Modification of a Test to Reduce Errors in the Classification of Examinees," Unpublished dissertation, College of Education, The State University of Iowa, Iowa City, Iowa, 1950.

[8]Frederic M. Lord, "A Summary of Observed Test-score Distributions with Respect to Skewness and Kurtosis," *Educational and Psychological Measurement*, vol. 15 (1955), 383–89; and Desmond L. Cook, "A Replication of Lord's Study of Skewness and Kurtosis of Observed Test-score Distributions," *Educational and Psychological Measurement*, vol. 14 (1959), 81–87.

One such scale is a scale of percentile ranks. Another is a scale of stanine scores. Since both these scales are useful in interpreting and working with the scores from classroom tests, they will be discussed in some detail.

The percentile rank of a given test score can be defined in three similar but significantly different ways. It is the percentage of the scores in a particular distribution of scores that:

1. fall below the given score, or
2. fall at or below the given score, or
3. fall below the midpoint of the given score interval.

Table 11.4 shows the effects of these different definitions on the percentile ranks of five hypothetical test scores. The highest score gets a percentile rank of only 80 under definition 1. The lowest score gets a percentile rank of 20 under definition 2. The average score gets a percentile rank of 40 under definition 1 and of 60 under definition 2. But under definition 3 the average score gets a percentile rank of 50, as it should in a symmetrical distribution of scores, and the highest and lowest scores are both the same distance from the extremes of the percentile scale, as they also should in this situation. For these reasons, definition 3 is usually preferred.

TABLE 11.4.   EFFECT OF DIFFERENT DEFINITIONS OF PERCENTILE RANKS

| Score | Percentile Rank Under Definition | | |
	1	2	3
5	80	100	90
4	60	80	70
3	40	60	50
2	20	40	30
1	0	20	10

There are three steps in the process of calculating the percentile rank equivalents of the scores in a particular set of scores.

1. Prepare a frequency distribution of the scores.
2. Add successive frequencies, starting with the lowest score, to obtain a column of cumulative frequencies.
3. Convert the cumulative frequencies into percentages of the last (highest) cumulative frequency.

These steps are illustrated in Table 11.5.

The first two columns are those of a usual frequency distribution. The next two, only one of which needs to be used, are the cumulative frequency columns, and require a word of explanation.

TABLE 11.5.   COMPUTATION OF PERCENTILE RANKS
Given Scores: 41, 42, 38, 42, 40, 43, 42, 40

Scores	Tally	Cumulative Single	Frequency Doubled	Percent of Frequency	Percentile Rank
44		8.0	16	100.00	100
43	1	7.5	15	93.75	94
42	111	5.5	11	68.75	69
41	1	3.5	7	43.75	44
40	11	2.0	4	25.00	25
39		1.0	2	12.50	13
38	1	0.5	1	6.25	6
37		0	0	0.00	0

According to the third definition of percentiles, which we are using, the cumulative frequencies we need are frequencies below the midpoint of each score interval. We assume that half the scores in each score interval fall below and half above the midpoint of the interval. Thus, we could define the cumulative frequency for each score as the frequency below plus half the frequency in the interval. The score interval for a score of, let us say, 38 is assumed to extend from 37.5 to 38.4999.

Now, if the frequency of occurrence of a given score is an odd number, as it easily can be, our cumulative frequency column will include decimal values, as is evident in the single cumulative frequency column. To avoid this we can use a different definition for our cumulative frequencies: twice the frequency below plus the frequency in the interval whose cumulative frequency we want. This definition leads to the doubled cumulative frequencies of the fourth column of Table 11.5. Many who compute percentile ranks prefer the doubling procedure.

To convert the cumulative frequencies of either kind to percentile ranks we divide each by the highest cumulative frequency and multiply by 100. Usually the percents so obtained are rounded to the nearest whole number. These rounded values, constituting the percentile ranks, are shown in the sixth column of Table 11.5.

In routine calculations of percentiles it is convenient to use a special 10″ × 10″ chart like that shown in Figure 11.2. This chart was used in the University Examinations Service at the State University of Iowa. Holzinger calls a similar chart a *classifier* and notes that Leonard P. Ayres mentioned it in 1920.[9] Each cell in the chart corresponds to one score. The 100 cells cover scores ranging from 0 to 99. The top row accommo-

[9]Karl J. Holzinger, *Statistical Methods for Students in Education* (Boston: Ginn and Company, 1928), pp. 25–26.

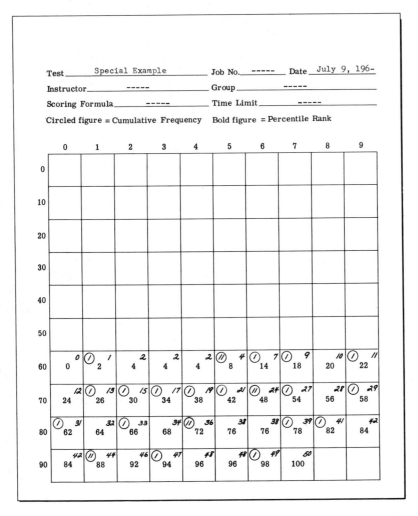

FIGURE 11.2
Frequency Distribution and Percentile Ranks

dates scores from 0 to 9, the second row from 10 to 19, and so on. Blanks are provided at the top of the chart for identifying the data recorded on it.

The scores for Spelling Test List *A* (Table 11.1) have been entered on the chart of Figure 11.2 Note that on this chart the scores have been tallied only once, in the upper left-hand corner of the appropriate square. The cumulative frequencies are written in the upper right-hand corner of the appropriate square. A special rule is followed for adding the tally marks to get the cumulative frequency.

> *To find the cumulative frequency for any score, add to the*
> *cumulative frequency shown in the cell for the next lower score*
> *the number of tally marks in that cell and also the number of tally*
> *marks in the cell of the score for which the cumulative frequency*
> *is desired.*

By this rule each tally mark is added twice, once to contribute to the cumulative frequency for the corresponding score and again to contribute to the cumulative frequency for the next higher score. Thus this rule for addition accomplishes the same result as the double tallying of Table 11.3.

If the percentile rank of a score were defined as the percentage of scores falling below a given score, instead of below the midpoint of the score interval, the computation of the percentile ranks would be somewhat simpler. No double tallying or double addition of tallies would be required. But the percentile scale would all be depressed. It would always give some student's score a percentile rank of 0, but never give any student's score a percentile rank of 100. The mean of all the percentile rank equivalents in a given group would not be 50, as it ought to be logically, but something less than 50. If there are gaps in the distribution of scores, more adjacent test scores will be assigned the same percentile rank equivalent. In sum, the advantages of the more precise definition of a percentile rank seem to justify the slight difficulty it adds to the computation.

INTERPRETATION OF PERCENTILE RANKS

Test scores expressed as percentile ranks are sometimes confused with test scores expressed as percent correct. They are, of course, quite different. A percent correct score is determined by an examinee's performance relative to the content of the test. It expresses the relation between the number of points awarded to a specific examinee's paper and the maximum possible number of points for any paper. Usually the expectation is that few examinees in a group will receive percent correct scores less than some value near 70 percent, which is often set arbitrarily as the passing score. If the group as a whole does well on an examination, the percent correct scores will run higher than if the group as a whole does poorly.

A percentile rank, on the other hand, is determined solely by the relation between a specific examinee's score and the scores of other examinees in the group tested. Percentile ranks must necessarily range from near 0 to near 100, regardless of whether the group as a whole does well or poorly on the examination.

The insensitivity of percentile ranks to general level of group performance might seem to be a disadvantage, and would be if the apparent level of group performance were not so largely determined by unintentional, and to a considerable degree uncontrollable, variations in the difficulty of the test. It is unfortunately true that dependable standards of measurement are seldom provided by the examiner's a priori judgments of how difficult a question is likely to be, and, if it requires the exercise of subjective judgement in scoring, his judgments of how well the student has answered it. The typical unreliability of measures obtained by these means has been demonstrated quite convincingly.

Percentile ranks differ from the original or raw test scores, and many other types of scores derived from them, in another respect. They are rectangularly distributed. Raw score distributions, and those of many other types of scores, generally approximate a normal distribution, more or less. In a normal distribution the scores are concentrated near the middle, with decreasing score frequencies as one moves out to the high and low extremes. In a rectangular distribution the score frequencies are uniform all along the scale. The relation between a normal distribution and a rectangular distribution is illustrated in Figure 11.3.

It is clear from this figure that percentile ranks magnify raw score differences near the middle of the distribution but reduce the raw score differences toward the extremes. Stated in other words, a difference of 10 percentile rank units near the extremes corresponds to a much larger raw score difference than does the same difference in percentile ranks near the mean. Intuition suggests that the raw score distribution, approximately normal, is a more accurate reflection of the "true" distribution of abilities than is the rectangular distribution. But however plausible such an intuition may seem to be, it is difficult to verify by experiment or logical demonstration.

Because the units on the two scales, raw score and percentile rank, are not equal, averages of the two sets of scores may not give consistent results. This is shown in Table 11.6. To simplify the illustration it is assumed that raw scores on each of the three tests are normally distributed with a mean of 50 and a standard deviation of 10. A portion of the table of equivalent raw scores and percentile ranks is reproduced on the right side of Table 11.6. Student A is assumed to have received raw scores of 75, 65, and 70 on the three tests. Student B assumed to have received raw scores of 68, 70, and 69. Note that while Student A has the higher mean raw score, Student B has the higher mean percentile rank.

This example has been chosen purposely to illustrate discrepancies which might arise. Even so, the differences are not very large. In practice, averages based on percentile ranks agree closely with averages based on raw scores. The correlation usually is in the very high nineties.

Can percentile ranks be averaged? Obviously they can, just like any other numbers. We have just done so. But should they be averaged?

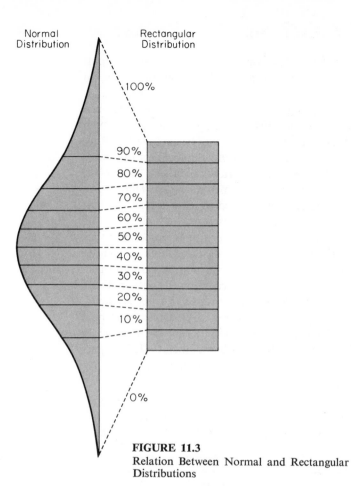

FIGURE 11.3
Relation Between Normal and Rectangular
Distributions

TABLE 11.6. COMPARISON OF SELECTED RAW SCORE AND PERCENTILE
RANK AVERAGES

Student A	Raw Scores	Percentile Ranks	Partial Table of Equivalence Raw Scores	Percentile Ranks
Test 1	75	99.4	75	99.4
Test 2	65	93.3	74	99.2
Test 3	70	97.7	73	98.9
			72	98.6
Mean	70	96.8	71	98.2
			70	97.7
Student B			69	97.1
Test 1	68	96.4	68	96.4
Test 2	70	97.7	67	95.5
Test 3	69	97.1	66	94.5
			65	93.3
Mean	69	97.1		

On this question opinions differ. Those who oppose the practice point out when percentiles are averaged, units that are almost certainly unequal are treated as equal. This, they point out, is mathematically unsound. Others take the position that this logical flaw makes very little difference in practice. Lord, for example, has published a delightful allegory which suggests that even the numbers on football jerseys can be averaged usefully under certain circumstances.[10] One can also note that while raw scores may be less obviously unequal than percentile ranks, neither of them can be shown to be precisely equal in any fundamental sense. Hence any argument on logical grounds against averaging percentiles applies equally, as a matter of principle, to the averaging of raw scores.

If percentile ranks are averaged, it is important to remember that the average of several percentile ranks is not itself a meaningful percentile rank. It is simply a kind of composite score, for which appropriate percentile ranks can be computed. This fact is illustrated by the data in Table 11.7. In the upper section of the table, percentile ranks of three students, good, average, and poor, on four tests are reported. These tests were part of an entrance test battery given to all students entering the College of Liberal Arts at the State University of Iowa in September 1951. The percentiles of all students were averaged and these averages reconverted into percentile ranks.

TABLE 11.7. AN ILLUSTRATION OF THE RELATION BETWEEN AVERAGES
OF PERCENTILE RANKS AND PERCENTILE RANKS OF AVERAGES

	Student		
	A	B	C
Test 1	82	54	3
Test 2	97	68	5
Test 3	98	39	2
Test 4	94	79	11
Average of percentiles	93	60	4
Percentile of averages	99	60	1

Note the difference between the average of the percentiles and the percentile ranks of the averages. These data illustrate a general principle. The percentile rank of the average of several high scores will be higher than the average of the percentile ranks of those scores. The percentile rank of the average of several low scores will be lower than the average of the percentile ranks of those scores. Only with scores whose percentile ranks

[10]Frederic M. Lord, "On the Statistical Treatment of Football Numbers," *American Psychologist*, vol. 8 (1953), 750–51.

fall in the midrange is the percentile rank of their average approximately equal to the average of their percentile ranks.

The results observed here are analogous to those observed often in tests of athletic versatility, such as the decathlon. A competitor need not average a first place finish in the ten component contests in order to finish first in the composite. (Obviously he could not *average* a first place finish without actually finishing first in every event.) It could happen, in fact, that a competitor might win the decathlon without finishing first in any of the ten component events. Overall primacy requires excellence in many of the individual tests but does not require actual primacy in all, or indeed in any, of them.

Once the basic meaning of a percentile rank has been explained, and it is quite easy to explain, scores of this type become extremely useful bases for interpreting a test performance. The scale of percentile ranks is a standard numerical scale, to which the scores from different tests that yield different raw score distributions can all be related. To interpret a raw score on a test one must be familiar with the difficulty level of the tasks composing it. To interpret a percentile rank one must be familiar with the ability level of the group from which the percentile ranks were derived. No test score is wholly self-interpreting, but a simply defined standard scale like that provided by percentile ranks can contribute substantially to test score interpretation.

STANINE STANDARD SCORES

Another convenient and useful basis for score interpretation is provided by the stanine score scale. The term "stanine" was derived from two words, "standard nine," which express its basic meaning. Stanine scores are normally distributed standard scores that range from 1 to 9. They have the convenience of being single-digit scores, which makes them easy to record and to interpret. Although they alter the distribution of raw scores somewhat, forcing it to approximate a normal distribution, the alteration is usually not so radical as that involved in changing raw scores to percentile ranks.

A perfectly normal distribution of stanine scores has a mean of exactly 5 and a standard deviation of approximately 2 stanine score units. Each unit on the stanine scale, except the highest and the lowest unit, is one-half a standard deviation in extent. The middle stanine score unit, 5, extends from one-fourth of a standard deviation below the mean to one-fourth of a standard deviation above it. The limits of other stanine score intervals are shown in Table 11.8. This table also shows what percent of a group should, theoretically, be assigned each stanine score. These

TABLE 11.8. PERCENTAGE OF GROUP THAT SHOULD BE ASSIGNED EACH
STANINE SCORE VALUE

Stanine Score	Verbal Translation	Percent of Group	Interval Limits
9	Highest	4.01	$+1.75\sigma$ to $+\infty$
8	Higher	6.55	$+1.25\sigma$ to $+1.75\sigma$
7	High	12.10	$+ .75\sigma$ to $+1.25\sigma$
6	High average	17.47	$+ .25\sigma$ to $+ .75\sigma$
5	Average	19.74	$- .25\sigma$ to $+ .25\sigma$
4	Low average	17.47	$- .75\sigma$ to $- .25\sigma$
3	Low	12.10	-1.25σ to $- .75\sigma$
2	Lower	6.55	-1.75σ to -1.25σ
1	Lowest	4.01	$-\infty$ to -1.75σ

ideal percentages are obtained from a table of areas under the normal curve, using the interval limits shown in Table 11.8.

The best way of converting a set of raw scores to stanines is to first convert them to percentiles, using the second definition of percentiles mentioned earlier. Then using a similar definition of the cumulative percentages of stanines, assign the stanines as accurately as possible to the raw scores. The process is illustrated in Table 11.9.

The percentile ranks obtained under the second definition of percentiles are shown in the fourth column of Table 11.9. The last column of the table gives the cumulative precentages for the stanine scale. Matching these cumulative stanine percentages as closely as possible with the score percentiles leads to the stanine assignments shown in the fifth column of Table 11.9. For example, since 4.01 of the stanines should be ones, and 4 percent of the scores are scores of 61, the 61 gets a stanine equivalent of 1. Proceeding up the table, using the same reasoning, a score of 65 (12 percent at or below 65) gets a stanine equivalent of 2 (10.56 percent at or below 2), scores of 69, 67, and 66 (24 percent of the scores at or below 69) get stanine equivalents of 3 (22.66 percent of the stanines at or below 3), and so on.

The procedure for determining stanine equivalents just described yields a distribution of stanines that is roughly normal, as near normality as the data will allow. But it is also possible to determine stanine equivalents without attempting to approximate normality. In this procedure the stanine intervals are determined with reference to the mean (M) and standard deviation of the scores, as shown in Table 11.10.

The lower limits for each of the stanine scores (except 1, which has no lower limit) are as defined in the second column of Table 11.10. Applying these definitions to the List A spelling test scores gives the lower limits shown in the third column, and leads to the assignment of stanines to

TABLE 11.9. DETERMINING NORMALIZED STANINE EQUIVALENTS FOR LIST A
SPELLING TEST SCORES

	Score Table				Stanine Table	
Score	Frequency	Cumulative	Percent	Stanine	Stanine	Cumulative Percent
96	1	25	100	9	9	100.00
93	1	24	96	8	8	95.99
91	2	23	92	7	7	89.44
88	1	21	84	7	6	77.34
87	1	20	80	7	5	59.87
84	2	19	76	6	4	40.13
82	1	17	68	6	3	22.66
80	1	16	64	6	2	10.56
79	1	15	60	5	1	4.01
77	1	14	56	5		
76	2	13	52	5		
75	1	11	44	5		
74	1	10	40	4		
73	1	9	36	4		
72	1	8	32	4		
71	1	7	28	4		
69	1	6	24	3		
67	1	5	20	3		
66	1	4	16	3		
65	2	3	12	2		
61	1	1	4	1		

TABLE 11.10. DETERMINING LINEAR STANINE EQUIVALENTS OF TEST SCORES

	I Defining Intervals	*II Spelling Test Data* (Mean = 78.72, σ = 9.50)	
Stanine	Lower Limit	Lower Limit	Scores
9	$M + 1.75\sigma$	94.34	95–96
8	$M + 1.25\sigma$	89.59	90–94
7	$M + 0.75\sigma$	84.84	85–89
6	$M + 0.25\sigma$	80.09	81–84
5	$M - 0.25\sigma$	75.34	76–80
4	$M - 0.75\sigma$	70.59	71–75
3	$M - 1.25\sigma$	65.84	66–70
2	$M - 1.75\sigma$	61.09	62–65
1	—	—	61

scores as shown in the fourth column. Once the lower limit of the ninth
stanine has been determined, the lower limit of each successively lower
stanine can be determined by successively subtracting one-half a standard

deviation (4.75 for this data) from the preceding lower limit. This is simpler than doing all the decimal multiplications and additions or subtractions indicated in the second column of Table 11.10, but leads to the same values for the lower limits.

Note that this linear procedure leads in the cases of only three scores, 75, 80, and 91, to the assignment of stanines different from those assigned by the normalizing procedure. Unless there is good reason for normalizing the stanines (perhaps to correct for extreme skewness in the distribution of raw scores) the simple linear procedure will generally be preferred. It will be used in the procedure for assigning stanine course marks described in Chapter 12.

Transformation of raw scores into stanine scores usually involves some loss of information. That is, some individuals having different raw scores will ordinarily be assigned the same stanine score. Whenever a test yields more than nine different raw scores, and most tests do this, such a loss of differential information will occur. This is the price one must pay for the convenience of using a simple, single-digit, nine-unit score scale. How serious this loss of infromation may be depends in part on the reliability of the test and in part on the use to be made of the scores. The more reliable the test, the more serious the loss of information. In reporting test results to students or parents, when one purpose is to discourage overemphasis on small score differences and another to provide easily interpretable scores, stanines have much to recommend them. The second column of Table 11.8 (p. 294) presents some convenient verbal translations of the various stanine scores.

When test scores and other measures of student achievement in a course are being recorded for subsequent combination into a total as a basis for determination of course grades, stanines have two advantages and one disadvantage. The disadvantage is the loss of information just mentioned. One advantage is the single-digit feature which makes them convenient to record. The other is the fact that they provide a uniform scale for all measures. Scores from whatever source carry equal weight in determining a composite if they are converted to stanines before being combined. If some a priori system of differential weighting is desired, stanines provide the uniform basis needed for applying them. In many situations these advantage will seem slight enough, in comparison with the disadvantage, to make the teacher think twice about recording test scores as stanines.

COEFFICIENTS OF CORRELATION

In dealing with test scores one frequently has need for an index of their relation to other measures. For example, the relation between scores on a reading readiness test given to pupils in the first grade and scores on a test of reading achievement given a year or two later may need to be determined. If the relation is high and if all pupils received the same kind of instruction regardless of their readiness test scores, the readiness test probably would be judged to be a good test because it accurately forecast later achievement.

Another illustration of the need for an index of the relation between sets of test scores is provided by the determination of some kinds of test reliability. If the same test is given twice to the same group, if two different but equivalent forms are given to the same group, or if a single test is split into two equivalent halves that are separately scored, we use an index of the degree of agreement between the pairs of scores for each person as the basis for estimating the test reliability.

The soundest and most widely used measure of the relation between pairs of measures for individuals in a group is the coefficient of correlation, identified more explicitly as the Pearson product-moment coefficient. This coefficient can be simply, though perhaps not clearly, defined as the "mean z-score product." Expressed as a formula,

$$r = \frac{\Sigma z_x z_y}{N} \qquad\qquad 11.7$$

where r is the coefficient of correlation, Σ means "the sum of," z_x is any individual's score on one of the two measures, expressed in standard (z-score) form, z_y is the same individual's score on the related measure, also expressed in standard form, and N is the number of individuals for whom the relation between the paired scores is to be determined. To convert a raw test score or any other measure to standard score form, divide the difference between that score and the mean of all scores by the standard deviation of all the scores.

Converting each score to standard score form before finding the sum of their products would be a very tedious, time-consuming operation. Applying a little algebra to the formula above can convert it to raw score form. The formula then looks more complicated, but it is actually much easier to compute.

$$r = \frac{N\Sigma XY - \Sigma X \Sigma Y}{\sqrt{[N\Sigma X^2 - (\Sigma X)^2][N\Sigma Y^2 - (\Sigma Y)^2]}} \qquad\qquad 11.8$$

The use of capital letters in this formula indicates that we are dealing here with raw scores rather than standard scores.

What this formula means may be easier to understand if we work through a simple numerical example. Suppose we have the scores of five students on each of two 10-item tests, Test X and Test Y, as shown in the first two columns of Table 11.11. The number of pairs of scores to be calculated (N) is 5. The sum of the scores on Test X (ΣX), as well as on Test Y (ΣY) is 40. The sum of the X scores squared (ΣX^2), as well as of the

Y scores squared (ΣY^2), is 330. The sum obtained by multiplying each X by the corresponding Y and adding the five products (ΣXY) is 328.

If we now put these quantities in formula 11.8 we get the expression shown just below the middle of Table 11.11. The numerator boils down easily to 40; the denominator, with somewhat more difficulty, to 50. Since the two bracketed expressions in the denominator are the same, the square root of their product is simply one of them. Finally, 40 divided by 50 gives a correlation coefficient of 0.80.

A point that sometimes causes confusion needs to be mentioned here. The sum of several scores squared (ΣX^2) is *not* the same as the square of their sum ($\Sigma X)^2$. Note in our data that $\Sigma X^2 = 330$ whereas ($\Sigma X)^2 = 1600$. Whether the exponent 2 is inside or outside the parenthesis, that is, whether you square first or add first, makes a great deal of difference.

TABLE 11.11.   COMPUTATION OF A PRODUCT-MOMENT COEFFICIENT OF CORRELATION

	Scores			Products	
X	Y		X^2	XY	Y^2
10	9		100	90	81
9	10		81	90	100
8	8		64	64	64
7	6		49	42	36
6	7		36	42	49
Sums 40	40		330	328	330

$$r = \frac{5 \times 328 - 40 \times 40}{\sqrt{\{5 \times 330 - 40 \times 40\}\{5 \times 330 - 40 \times 40\}}}$$

$$= \frac{1640 - 1600}{1650 - 1600} = \frac{40}{50} = 0.80$$

The example used here is extremely simple, intended only to show what a coefficient of correlation is and how it can be calculated. One would seldom want to calculate a "real" correlation coefficient, which might be based on 30 to 300 pairs of scores whose numerical values might range from a low of 50 to a high of 150, using this kind of paper and pencil computation. A desk calculator is almost the minimum equipment that would be required. A properly programmed computer is even better. When the inter correlations among several variables must be calculated using a desk calculator, the procedures described by Rummel are convenient.[11]

---

[11]J. Francis Rummel, "Procedures for Computation of Zero-order Coefficients Among Several Variables," *Journal of Experimental Education*, vol. 20 (March 1952), 313–18.

OTHER ESTIMATES OF CORRELATION

Another formula for estimating a correlation coefficient is based on differences in rank between the two scores of each pair when the scores from each test have been ranked separately. A different symbol, the Greek letter "rho," is used to indicate that this coefficient of correlation is somewhat different from the Pearson coefficient

$$\rho = 1 - \frac{6\Sigma d^2}{N(N^2 - 1)} \qquad 11.9$$

in which d^2 is the square of the difference between ranks for the scores of any pair and N is the number of pairs of scores.

A simple example to illustrate the application of this formula is shown in Table 11.12. It uses the same scores on Test X and Test Y as were used in Table 11.11 to illustrate the product-moment coefficient, and it gives the same correlation coefficient, 0.80. The scores given in the first two columns are converted to ranks in columns 3 and 4. Column 5 shows the differences squared. Note that only when the difference is one or zero is the squared difference also one or zero. Entering the sum of the squared differences Σd^2, 4 in this case, and the value of N, 5 in this case, in formula 11.9 gives the expression that simplifies to $\rho = 0.80$, as shown in the lower half of Table 11.12.

One slight but common complication in the use of formula 11.10 arises when two or more scores of the same size or value appear in the score distributions. The solution for this complication is to give the repeated scores the average of the ranks they would occupy if each were slightly

TABLE 11.12. CALCULATION OF RANK DIFFERENCE CORRELATION COEFFICIENT

| Scores | | Ranks | | Differences | |
X	Y	X	Y	Simple	Squared
10	9	1	2	1	1
9	10	2	1	1	1
8	8	3	3	0	0
7	6	4	5	1	1
6	7	5	4	1	1

Sum of squared differences = 4

$$\rho = 1 - \frac{6\Sigma d^2}{N(N^2 - 1)}$$

$$= 1 - \frac{24}{120} = 1.00 - 0.20 = 0.80$$

different from the others. If for example, one distribution included the scores in the first line below at the high end of the distribution, the appropriate ranks would be as shown in the second line.

Scores	96	93	91	91	88	87	84	84	82
Ranks	1	2	3.5	3.5	5	6	7.5	7.5	9

Corrlations obtained from the rank difference formula usually will not agree perfectly with product moment correlations from the same pairs of scores, but they are ordinarily quite close. Because they are much easier to compute than the product-moment corrlations, classroom teachers are likely to give preference to them, as they should, when they need to estimate correlation coefficients.

INTERPRETING COEFFICIENTS OF CORRELATION

Coefficients of correlation are widely used in the study of test scores. If calculated accurately they provide precise estimates of the degree of relation in the data on which they are based. But when an obtained coefficient of correlation is used as an estimate of the relationship to be expected in other sets of data obtained under similar conditions, note must be made of the large variations that are often found in coefficients of correlation based on small samples, even when the samples are all drawn from the same population.

This is illustrated in Table 11.13 which shows the range in coeffi-

TABLE 11.13. SAMPLING ERRORS IN CORRELATION COEFFICIENTS*

True Correlation	Sample Size	Limits of Confidence Intervals 50 Percent	95 Percent
.30	10	.05 to .51	−.41 to .78
	30	.18 to .41	−.07 to .60
	100	.24 to .36	.11 to .47
	300	.26 to .34	.19 to .40
.60	10	.41 to .74	−.05 to .89
	30	.51 to .68	.31 to .79
	100	.55 to .64	.46 to .71
	300	.57 to .62	.52 to .67
.90	10	.84 to .94	.62 to .98
	30	.87 to .92	.80 to .95
	100	.886 to .914	.85 to .93
	300	.893 to .907	.88 to .92

*The confidence limits shown in this table were calculated on the basis of the Fisher z statistic, using the method described in Section 15.13 of Paul Blommers and E. F. Lindquist, *Elementary Statistical Methods*, Houghton Mifflin Company (Boston: Houghton Mifflin Company, 1960).

cients that can be expected for samples of various size when the true correlation is 0.30 or 0.60 or 0.90. Table 11.13 should be read in this way:

> If 100 samples of 10 pairs of scores each are drawn from a large population of such pairs in which the true correlation is 0.30 and if the coefficient of correlation is calculated for each pair, 50 of those coefficients would be expected to be more than 0.05 and less than 0.51. Ninety-five would be expected to be above −0.41 and below 0.78. The other five would be expected to be even farther removed from the true value of 0.30.

As the sample size increases and as the value of the true correlation increases, the range of variation of the sample coefficients decreases. Table 11.13 justifies the conclusion that correlation coefficients based on small samples are not very dependable, expecially when the true correlation is moderate or low. A much larger sample is required to yield a precise estimate of the coefficient of correlation than is required for an equally precise estimate of the mean or standard deviations.

How much relationship is implied by correlation coefficients of various values is illustrated in Figure 11.4. The five columns in each diagram represent scores on one variable (X) of 1, 2, 3, 4, and 5 (reading from left to right). These columns could, of course, represent any other set of five equally spaced scores that increase from left to right. The five rows represent similar scores on the other variable, increasing from bottom to top. The distribution of each set of scores is the same in all of the diagrams. That is, there are six scores of middle value, five each of higher and lower scores, and two each of highest and lowest.

The top diagram in the left-hand series illustrates perfect correlation. All the tally marks are in the cells on the diagonal, because the highest scores on one variable are always paired with the highest scores on the other, the second high with the second high, the middle with the middle, and so on. The other diagrams show that as the tally marks depart increasingly from the diagonal, the correlation decreases correspondingly. When the diagram shows a perfectly balanced or symmetrical distribution of tally marks in each of the columns and rows, as the lower left-hand diagram does, the correlation is zero. When the high scores on one variable tend to be associated with low scores on the other, as in the lower right hand diagram, the correlation is negative.

Another way of interpreting a correlation coefficient is to relate it to the coefficients obtained in other more or less familiar situations. Scores on equivalent forms of a well-constructed educational achievement test, administered separately within a few days of each other, should show coefficients of correlation of 0.90 or higher. Scores on good tests intended to predict educational achievement correlate with subsequent good measures of achievement to the extent reflected in coefficients that average about 0.50 and range from about 0.30 to about 0.70, depending on the nature of the achievement, the quality of the measures of promise and of

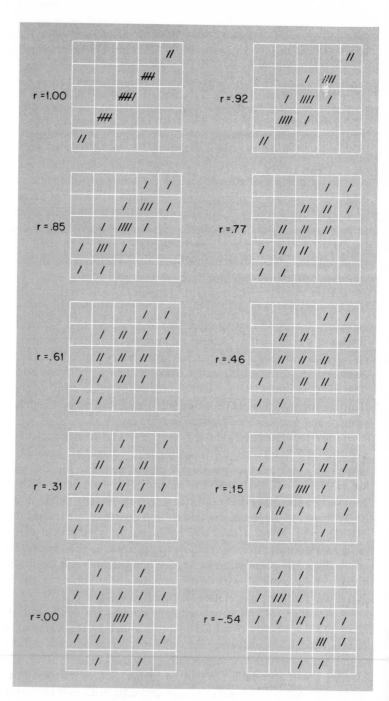

FIGURE 11.4
Simple Scatter Diagrams Illustrating Various Degrees of Correlation

attainment, the interval between the measures, and many other factors. Coefficients of correlation between the scores on individual items of an objective test average about 0.10 but often range from about —0.30 to about 0.50.

Research workers sometimes refer wryly to the "Irish Coefficients" they often obtain when trying out new tests of elusive mental traits. They mean values like 0.02 (O'Two), 0.05, etc. Such coefficients near zero usually mean that the measures bear little or no consistent relation to each other.

Another basis for interpreting a correlation coefficient is to note that it expresses the proportion of independent, equally potent causes influencing performance on the two related tests (or other measures) that are common to both. This principle can be demonstrated using a pair of dice. Both dice are rolled and the total points showing are counted. This gives the first score X of the first pair. Then only one of the dice is picked up and rolled again, leaving the first as it was. Again the total points showing are counted. This gives the second score Y of the first pair. In this case one of two independent, equally potent factors is common to the two scores. The other factor can vary.

In the process above is repeated to yield 50 or 100 pairs of scores and if the coefficient of correlation between the X and Y scores is calculated, a value near 0.50 will be obtained. Instead of two dice, four might be used. If only one of the dice was rerolled to obtain the second score of each pair, a correlation of 0.75 would be expected. If three were rerolled, a correlation of 0.25 would be expected. Using 10 dice and rerolling only one of them should result in an expected coefficient of correlation of 0.90.

Thus when one encounters a correlation coefficient of, say, 0.83, it is reasonable to make this kind of interpretation. If the related measures were determined by the combined effects of 100 independent, equally powerful factors, 83 of the 100 would have to be constant factors. That is, they would have to contribute the same value to each member of the pair of related measures, to yield a coefficient of 0.83. The other 17 factors could vary.

This interpretation is suggestive, but it should not be taken too literally as a description of what actually happens. There is usually no evidence to suggest that the performance of students on any test is the result of the combined influence of a number of independent, equally powerful factors.

OTHER REFERENCES

This chapter has dealt in an introductory fashion with some of the statistics that are useful in dealing with test scores. Many other topics might have been included. Those that were included might have been discussed in more detail. Since they were not, it seems advisable to conclude the chapter with mention of a few other statistical references that the interested student may find useful.

Excellent introductory texts on statistics by Blommers and Lindquist, and by Ferguson, were mentioned earlier in this chapter. A classic in the field, famous for its authoritative and lucid treatment of many problems of test score statistics, is Kelley's *Statistical Method.*[12] Peters and Van Voorhis provide clear explanations and mathematical derivations for a great number of useful statistical procedures.[13]

Considerable attention was given to short-cut statistical procedures in the chapter. Diederich has described some of these and other convenient devices in an interesting, well-written leaflet.[14]

There is no lack of other good references on the statistical treatment of test scores, but perhaps these will suffice to get the interested student started along what could become an absorbing and rewarding line of inquiry.

SUMMARY

Some of the principal ideas developed in this chapter are summarized in these 25 statements.

1. In order to do an adequate job of interpreting a set of test scores it is necessary to understand and use a variety of statistical tools: frequency distributions, standard scores, and measures of central tendency, variability, and correlation.
2. A frequency distribution of scores shows how many scores fall in each group, or at each level, along the score scale.
3. A frequency distribution is useful in showing how any particular score relates to all the other scores in the group.
4. The median is either the middle measure (if the number of measures is odd) or a point midway between the two middle measures (if the number of measures is even).
5. One finds the mean of a set of scores by adding all of the scores and dividing the total by the number of scores.
6. One finds the variance of a set of scores by adding the squared deviations of the scores (from the mean of all scores) and then dividing the total by the number of scores.
7. The standard deviation is the square root of the variance.

[12]Truman L. Kelley, *Statistical Method* (New York: The Macmillan Company, 1924).
    [13]Charles C. Peters and Walter R. Van Voorhis, *Statistical Procedures and Their Mathematical Bases* (New York: McGraw-Hill Book Company, 1940).
    [14]Paul Diederich, *Short-cut Statistics for Tests*, Evaluation and Advisory Service Series No. 5 (Princeton, N.J.: Educational Testing Service, 1960), p. 44.

8. One can sometimes simplify calculation of the mean and of the standard deviation by starting with the frequency distribution and by making use of a deviation scale whose unit is the class interval and whose zero is the midpoint of an interval near the middle of the distribution.

9. Lathrop's short-cut estimate of the standard deviation is obtained by dividing one-half the number of scores into the difference between the sums of upper and lower one-sixths of the scores.

10. The normal curve is a theoretical, symmetric, bell-shaped curve that provides an idealized representation of the frequency distributions of some kinds of experimental data.

11. The larger the number of scores in a group, the greater the expected range of scores in standard deviation units.

12. One can give scores in any set a standard relative meaning by converting them into percentile ranks.

13. The percentile rank of a score is most appropriately defined as the percent of scores in a group that fall below the midpoint of the given score interval.

14. A complete set of percentile ranks yields a frequency distribution that is rectangular in shape.

15. Conversion of normally distributed scores to percentile ranks increases apparent score differences near the center of the distribution and decreases them near the extremes of the distribution.

16. Percentile ranks may be averaged, but the average is not itself a percentile rank.

17. Stanine standard scores are either normally distributed or linearly transformed single-digit scores having a mean of approximately 5 and a standard deviation of approximately 2.

18. Stanines have standard relative meaning and single-digit convenience, but their use involves some loss of precision.

19. The correlation coefficient is a measure of the degree of correspondence between two variables, based on paired values of the variables obtained for each of a number of persons or things.

20. Possible values of the correlation coefficient range from 1.00, expressing perfect positive (direct) relationship, through 0, expressing absence of relationship, to -1.00, expressing perfect negative (inverse) relationship.

21. When scores on two correlated variables are expressed as z-scores (deviations from the mean in standard deviation units), the correlation coefficient is the mean of the z-score products.

22. Correlation coefficients can be estimated simply and quite accurately from differences in the ranks of paired scores.

23. Correlation coefficients obtained from small or medium-sized samples are subject to large sampling errors.

24. The more closely the tally marks in a two-dimensional scatter diagram are clustered along a diagonal, the higher the correlation between the variables represented on the two dimensions.

25. If values of the two variables being correlated can be thought of as the result of influences of a number of independent, equally potent factors, then the correlation coefficient expresses the proportion of those factors making the same (rather than different) contribution to the values in each pair of variables.

The findings of the study strongly support the conclusion that scholastic achievement is a substantial predictor of progress in management in the Bell System. There can be no question but that college recruiting efforts will succeed more in their objective of bringing capable future managers into the business the more they emphasize rank in college graduating class as a criterion of employment.

DONALD S. BRIDGMAN

12

MARKS AND MARKING SYSTEMS

THE PROBLEM OF MARKING

The problem of marking student achievement has been persistently troublesome at all levels of education. Hardly a month goes by without the appearance in some popular magazine or professional journal of an article criticizing current practices or suggesting some new approach. Progressive schools and colleges are constantly experimenting with new systems of marking, or sometimes of not marking. And still the problem seems to remain.

One of the reasons why it remains is that marking is a complex and difficult problem. From some points of view it is even more complex and difficult than the problem of building a good test and using it properly. In an early classic of educational measurement, Thorndike explained some of the reasons why educational achievement often is difficult to measure.

> Measurements which involve human capacities and acts are subject to special difficulties due chiefly to:
> 1. The absence or imperfection of units in which to measure.
> 2. The lack of constancy in the facts to be measured, and
> 3. The extreme complexity of the measurements to be made.[1]

Marks are, of course, measurements of educational achievement.

A second reason why problems of marking are difficult to solve permanently is because marking systems tend to become issues in educational controversies. Odell noted that research on marking systems did not become really significant until after the beginning of the present century.[2] At about the same time, the development of objective tests was ushering in the somewhat controversial "scientific movement" in education. The rise of progressive education in the third and fourth decades of this century, with its emphasis on the uniqueness of the individual, the wholeness of his mental life, freedom and democracy in the classroom, and the child's need for loving reassurance, led to criticisms of the academic narrowness, the competitive pressures, and the common standards of achievement for all pupils implicit in many marking systems. In the sixth and seventh decades renewed emphasis on what is called "basic education" and on the pursuit of academic excellence has been accompanied by pleas for more formal evaluations of achievement and more rigorous standards of attainment.[3]

> Standards! That is a word for every American to write on his bulletin board. We must face the fact that there are a good many things in our national life which are inimical to standards—laziness, complacency, the desire for a fast buck, the American fondness for short cuts, reluctance to criticize slackness, to name only a few. Every thinking American knows in his heart that we must sooner or later come to terms with these failings.[4]

The shifting winds of educational doctrine blow unsteadily even at the same time. Some educational leaders espouse one philosophy, some another. Some teachers find it easy to accept one point of view,

---

[1]E. L. Thorndike, *Mental and Social Measurements*, 2d ed (New York: Teachers College, Columbia University, 1912), chap. 2.

[2]C. W. Odell, "Marks and Marking Systems," in *Encyclopedia of Educational Research*, ed. Walter S. Monroe (New York: The Macmillan Company, 1950), pp. 711–17.

[3]Nelson A. Rockfeller and others, *The Pursuit of Excellence* (Garden City, N.Y.: Doubleday & Company, Inc., 1958), p. 49.

[4]John W. Gardner, *Excellence* (New York: Harper and Row, Publishers, 1961), pp. 158–59.

some another, even when they teach in the same educational institution. Since somewhat different marking systems are implied by each of these different philosophical positions, it is not surprising that differences of opinion, dissatisfaction, and proposals for change tend to characterize instructor reactions to marking systems.

A third reason why marking systems present perennial problems is that they require teachers, whose natural instincts incline them to be helpful guides and counsellors, to stand in judgment over some of their fellow men. This is not the role of friendship and may carry somewhat antisocial overtones.

"Forbear to judge, for we are sinners all," said Shakespeare, echoing the sentiments of the Sermon on the Mount: "Judge not, that ye be not judged." It is never difficult to give a student a good mark, particularly if it is higher than he really expected. But since the reach of many students exceeds their grasp, there are likely to be more occasions for disappointment than pleasure in marks.

For all these reasons, no system of marking is likely to be found that will make the process of marking easy and painless and generally satisfactory. This is not to say that present marking practices are beyond improvement. It is to say that no new marking system, however cleverly devised and conscientiously followed, is likely to solve the basic problems of marking. The real need is not for some new system. Good systems already exist. Odell observed in 1950 that, "Most of the writings since 1938 are so similar to earlier published material that little has been added to either research or opinion in this area."[5] Reviewing articles on marking problems and practices that were written a half century ago, one is struck by their pertinence to the present day. The same problems that were troublesome then are still troublesome. Some of the same remedies that were being proposed then are still being proposed.

Marking procedures, Hadley has pointed out, are about as good or as weak as the teachers who apply them.[6] Few teachers mark as well as they could, or should. Palmer has discussed candidly, but kindly, some of the failures of English teachers in marking the achievements of their students.[7] The more confident a teacher is that he is doing a good job of marking, the less likely he is to be aware of the difficulties of marking, the fallibility of his judgments, and the personal biases he may be reflecting in his marks. Most teachers' marks, says Hadley, are partly fact and partly fancy. The beginning of wisdom in marking is to recognize these

---

[5] Odell, "Marks and Marking Systems."

[6] S. Trevor Hadley, "A School Mark—Fact or Fancy?" *Educational Administration and Supervision*, vol. 40 (1954), 305–12.

[7] Orville Palmer, "Seven Classic Ways of Grading Dishonestly," *The English Journal* (October 1962), pp. 464–67.

shortcomings. The cultivation of wisdom is to work to improve them. For measurements and reports of achievement are essential in education, and no better alternative to marks seems likely to appear.

SOME QUESTIONS AND ANSWERS ABOUT MARKS

The questions in this section relate to some of the issues that have been raised in discussions of school and college marking practices. Brief answers are presented and defended. If any of these answers seem unwarranted, they may serve as springboards to further discussion of the issues involved.

1. Q. Is systematic assessment and reporting of educational progress essential to the long-run effectiveness of schooling?
   A. Education is a complex, difficult process that requires the cooperative efforts of many people: students, teachers, school officials, parents, and others. The assessment and reporting of achievements tend to stimulate and reward the efforts required, and to facilitate effective management of the process.
2. Q. Have marks outlived their usefulness in education?
   A. Marking systems were developed to provide a convenient means for reporting educational achievements. The need for such reporting still exists, and despite numerous efforts, no generally superior (that is, more effective and convenient) system has been developed. Most schools still use marks.
3. Q. Is the use of marks compatible with child-centered education?
   A. There is no useful employment for a teacher who proposes to teach children but not subjects; nor for one who proposes to teach subjects but no children. What education needs, and what it mainly gets, are those who propose to teach subjects *to* children. Such teachers usually find marks useful.
4. Q. Are problems in marking caused mainly by faults in current marking systems and practices?
   A. Because marking is a difficult, emotion-arousing task, it is likely to present problems under the best of all possible systems. That current problems are as frequent and severe as they are, however should be blamed less on the grading systems in use than on the careless incompetence of some who do the grading.
5. Q. Does improvement in educational evaluation call for development of some alternative to marks?
   A. The best hope for improvement in educational evaluation is to persuade teachers that marks are useful tools, and to help them acquire skill in the use of these tools.
6. Q. Are the achievements that marks reflect limited and relatively unimportant among the diverse outcomes of education?
   A. What most teachers try to teach, and what most students try to learn, is useful verbal knowledge. In so doing they develop the cognitive skills that are the power and the glory of humanity. These are the most perva-

sive and important outcomes of education. These are what marks should, can, and often do reflect.

7. Q. Is knowledge now accumulating so rapidly that it is no longer possible to make the acquisition of knowledge the central purpose of education?

   A. The growth of ideas that *could* be known is far greater than the growth of ideas that are important to know. Nevertheless the total of what *someone* ought to know is much too great for any single one to know. Hence the growth of essential knowledge simply indicates that specialization in knowing must also increase. No good alternative to knowing exists. Ability to think, or to learn, is no substitute for knowing what is so. Acquisition of knowledge remains the central purpose of education.

8. Q. Can any single symbol adequately represent the diversity of attainments that make up the outcomes of a good course?

   A. The job of a mark is to indicate, in relative terms, a general level of achievement. This it can do with reasonable adequacy and considerable efficiency. To report achievement of all students in much greater detail usually requires more time and effort than its probable usefulness seems to justify.

9. Q. Do marks set uniform standards of achievement for all, regardless of differences in ability, interest, and so forth?

   A. Marks provide measures of relative achievement. Properly used they report how much was achieved, using the same scale of measurements for all students. But a measuring scale does not indicate how much ought to have been achieved. Standards of achievement may be set by the pupil himself, his parents, or his teacher. These need not be, and ought not to be, the same for all students.

10. Q. Is it true that the marks most students get in their courses have little real meaning?

    A. If it were true in general that marks have little meaning, students, parents, admissions officers, and prospective employers would soon cease using them, and teachers would cease bothering to determine them. But it is not true in general. The cases in which it is substantially true indicate incompetence or indifference on the part of the teacher. A teacher can issue meaningful marks if he knows what he is trying to achieve, and can tell the difference between a student who has achieved more and one who has achieved less of it.

11. Q. Is self-evaluation more important and useful than evaluation by others?

    A. Ultimately the only really effective evaluation is a person's self-evaluation. But a person's assessment of his own achievements is likely to be based on highly subjective perceptions and on idiosyncratic values, and hence to be at least somewhat biased. In business and politics, in science and art, the judgments of others help us to improve our self-evaluations. If we will make the effort, they help us to become better also.

12. Q. Do marks foster competition among students at a level of intensity that is socially and educationally harmful?

    A. Competition stimulates effort and fosters achievement. In sports, in the market place, in all areas of human activity it adds zest to the game of life. But it needs to be balanced by compassionate concern for the welfare and happiness of others. Single-minded, ruthless pursuit of high marks can be as evil as single-minded, ruthless pursuit of money, power, or pleasure. But in each case the evil is the nature of the pursuit, not in the goal. Competition for marks among decent people can be decent and educationally useful.

13. Q. Is emphasis on marks responsible for development of anxiety neuroses, dislike of education, and school dropouts?

A. The source of anxiety, dislike of schooling, and the decision to drop out of school is low achievement, which the marks do not cause but simply report. In the essential processes of adjusting education to individual pupils and individual pupils to education, marks are far more helpful than harmful.

14. Q. Does marking induce students to study just to pass tests, to cram, and to cheat?

A. Studying to pass a good test is good study and leads to good learning. High marks cannot be obtained from a good teacher by last-minute cramming. Cheating on tests, at cards, or in business deals is done for the same purpose—to gain an unfair advantage. The cure is not to stop business deals, or card games, or tests, but to stop the cheating.

15. Q. Do marks discourage creativity by rewarding conforming behavior?

A. If creativity can be taught, marks can be used to report how well a particular student has learned to be creative. If useful creativity must be based on competence, the student who gets high marks is a better bet to be usefully creative than the one who gets low marks. Although some creative persons lead strange lives, there is little in human experience to support the notion that encouraging nonconformity is a good way to develop creativity.

16. Q. If all students in a course attain all the objectives of the course, do they all deserve A's?

A. A mark of A is supposed to mean superior achievement. An achievement that all attain cannot be a superior achievement for any. Students always differ in achievement when challenged by a good, well-taught course to do their best. To teach only as much as the least able student can master is to seriously limit the achievement of the more able.

17. Q. Should marks report achievement alone, or achievement in relation to ability?

A. A mark reports the achievement of a student in a course relative to the achievements of his peers in the same course. If the students differ so widely in ability that they cannot be considered to be peers, they should not be enrolled in the same course. For this reason, because of the problems of assessing ability, and also because of the confusion created when the same mark indicates different degrees of achievement, marks usually should not attempt to report achievement in relation to ability.

18. Q. Is the use of more than five levels of marks justifiable, in view of the unreliability of the bases teachers use in marking?

A. Unless the composite measures of achievement on which marks are based have zero reliability, or only five different values, their conversion into five-valued letter marks will always lower their reliability. The more different levels that a marking system provides, the more reliably that system will report achievement.

19. Q. Is it possible, by adopting a two-level pass-fail system, to avoid the evils of overemphasis on marks while retaining the essential quality control functions of marks?

A. Pass-fail marking reduces emphasis on marks at the cost of reduced emphasis on achievement and reduced interest in precise measurement of achievement. With imprecise measurement more students who should pass are likely to fail, and more who should fail are likely to pass.

In the next and succeeding sections some of the issues raised by these questions will be considered in more detail.

THE NEED FOR MARKS

Most instructors, at all levels of education, seem to agree that marks are necessary. Occasionally a voice is raised to cry that marks are educationally vicious, that they are relics of the dark ages of education.[8] However, as Madsen has pointed out, the claim that abolition of marks would lead to better achievement is, by its very nature, impossible to demonstrate.[9] If we forego measurements of relative achievement, what basis remains for demonstrating that one set of circumstances produces better educational results than another? Comparison of achievements between persons or between methods of teaching is inevitable, Madsen suggests. He concludes that it is the misuse of marks, not their use, that is in need of censure.

The uses made of marks are numerous and crucial. They are used to report a student's educational status to him, to his parents, to his future teachers, and to his prospective employers. They provide a basis for important decisions concerning his educational plans and his occupational career. Education is expensive. To make the best possible use of educational facilities and student talent, it is essential that each student's educational progress be watched carefully and reported as accurately as possible. Reports of course marks serve somewhat the same function in education that financial statements serve in business. In either case, if the reports are inaccurate or unavailable, the venture may become inefficient.

Marks also provide an important means for stimulating, directing, and rewarding the educational efforts of students. This use of marks has been attacked on the ground that it provides extrinsic, artificial, and hence undesirable stimuli and rewards. Indeed, marks are extrinsic, but so are

[8]Dorothy De Zouche, "'The Wound Is Mortal': Marks, Honors, Unsound Activities," *Clearing House*, vol. 19 (1945), 339–44; and H. B. Brooks, "What Can Be Done About Comparative Marks and Formal Report Cards?" *California Journal of Secondary Education*, 10 (1935), 101–6.

[9]I. N. Madsen, "To Mark or Not to Mark," *Elementary School Journal*, vol. 31 (June 1931), 747–55.

most other tangible rewards of effort and achievement. Most workers, including professional workers, are grateful for the intrinsic rewards that sometimes accompany their efforts. But most of them are even more grateful that these are not the only rewards. Few organized, efficient human enterprises can be conducted successfully on the basis of intrinsic rewards alone.

To serve effectively the purpose of stimulating, directing, and rewarding student efforts to learn, marks must be valid. The highest marks must go to those students who have achieved to the highest degree the objectives of instruction in a course. Marks must be based on sufficient evidence. They must report the degree of achievement as precisely as possible under the circumstances. If marks are assigned on the basis of trivial, incidental, or irrelevant achievements or if they are assigned carelessly, their long-run effects on the educational efforts of students cannot be good.

Some students and instructors minimize the importance of marks, suggesting that *what* a person learns is more important than the *mark* he gets. This conception rests on the assumption that there generally is not a high relationship between the amount of useful learning a student achieves and the mark he receives. Others have made the same point by noting that marks should not be regarded as ends in themselves, and by questioning the use of examinations "merely" for the purpose of assigning marks.

It is true that the mark a student receives is not in itself an important educational outcome—by the same token, neither is the degree toward which the student is working, nor the academic rank or scholarly reputation of the professors who teach him. But all of these symbols can be and should be valid indications of important educational attainments. It is desirable, and not impossibly difficult, to make the goal of maximum educational achievement compatible with the goal of highest possible marks. If these two goals are not closely related, the fault would seem to rest with those who teach the courses and who assign the marks. From the point of view of students, parents, teachers, and employers there is nothing "mere" about the marking process and the marks it yields. Stroud has underscored this point.

> If the marks earned in a course of study are made to represent progress toward getting an education, working for marks is *ipso facto* a furtherance of the purposes of education. If the marks are so bad that the student who works for and attains them misses an education, then working for marks is a practice to be eschewed. When marks are given, we are not likely to dissuade pupils from working for them: and there is no sensible reason why we should. It simply does not make sense to grade pupils, to maintain institutional machinery for assembling and recording the gradings, while at the same time telling pupils marks do not amount to much. As a matter of fact they do amount to something and the pupil knows this. If we are

dissatisfied with the results of working for marks we might try to improve the marks.[10]

Marks are necessary. If they are inaccurate, invalid, or meaningless, the remedy lies less in deemphasizing marks than in assigning them more carefully so that they more truly report the extent of important achievements. Instead of seeking to minimize their importance or seeking to find some less painful substitute, perhaps instructors should devote more attention to improving the validity and precision of the marks they assign and to minimizing misinterpretations of marks by students, faculty, and others who use them.

SHORTCOMINGS OF MARKS

The major shortcomings of marks, as they are assigned by many institutions, are twofold: (1) the lack of clearly defined, generally accepted, scrupulously observed definitions of what the various marks should mean and (2) the lack of sufficient relevant, objective evidence to use a basis for assigning marks. One consequence of the first shortcoming is that marking standards and the meanings of marks tend to vary from instructor to instructor, from course to course, from department to department, and from school to school.[11] Another consequence is that instructor biases and idiosyncrasies tend to reduce the validity of the marks. A consequence of the second shortcoming is that the marks tend to be unreliable.

Variability in marking standards and practices has been reported by many investigators. Travers and Gronlund, for example, found wide differences of opinion among the members of a graduate faculty on what various marks should mean and the standards that should be followed in assigning them.[12] Odell reported,

> Where a typical five-letter system is used, the percents of the highest letter are likely to vary from 0 or near 0 to 40 or more; of the next to the highest from about 10 to 50 or more; and of the failure mark from 0 up to 25 or more.[13]

[10]James B. Stroud, *Psychology in Education* (New York: David McKay Co., Inc., 1946), p. 632.

[11]James S. Terwilliger, "Individual Differences in Marking Practices of Secondary School Teachers," *Journal of Educational Measurement*, vol. 5 (1968), 9–15.

[12]Robert M. W. Travers and Norman E. Gronlund, "Meaning of Marks," *Journal of Higher Education*, vol. 21 (1950), 369–74.

[13]Odell, "Marks and Marking Systems."

Some schools and colleges publish, for internal guidance and therapy, periodic summaries of the marks assigned in various courses and departments. In one such unpublished study, instructors in one department were found to be awarding 63 percent A's or B's whereas those in another awarded only 26 percent A's or B's. Course X in one department granted 66 percent A's and B's, whereas Course Y in the same department granted only 28 percent. Each of these two courses, incidentally, enrolled more than 50 students.

Lack of stability in the assignment of grades from year to year is also apparent. Specifically, there appear to be long-run tendencies in many institutions to increase the proportion of high grades issued and to decrease the proportion of low grades. For example, during the years 1936 to 1939 one large institution issued 33 percent A and B grades. From 1951 to 1954 the corresponding proportion of A's and B's had increased to 44 percent. In the same two periods the proportion of D's and F's dropped from 30 to 18 percent.

On the other hand, as Hills and Gladney[14] have reported, the level of marks issued in a college tends to remain about the same even when, as a result of changes in admission policies, the level of ability of the student body has increased substantially. This is an inherent limitation of the kind of relative marking that letter marks were designed to provide. An A among highly able students does not reflect the same level of achievement as an A among less able students. This limitation needs to be recognized. It also needs to be tolerated since there is no good way to overcome it without losing the values of relative marking, which will be discussed later on in this chapter.

The lack of clearly defined, uniform bases for marking and standards for the meanings of various marks tends to allow biases to lower the validity of marks. Often a student's mark has been influenced by the pleasantness of his manner, his willingness to participate in class discussions, his skill in expressing ideas orally or in writing, or his success in building an image of himself as an eager, capable student. Some of these things should not ordinarily be allowed to influence the mark he receives.

Carter found that girls are somewhat more likely to get higher marks than boys of equal ability and achievement.[15] Hadley reported that pupils well liked by teachers tended to get higher marks than pupils of equal ability and achievement who were less well liked.[16] These findings tend to support the accusations of students, and the guilt feelings of instructors, that accomplishment is not the pure and simple basis on which marks

[14]John R. Hills and Marilyn B. Gladney, "Factors Influencing College Grading Standards," *Journal of Educational Measurement*, vol. 5 (1968), 31–39.

[15]Robert S. Carter, "How Invalid Are Marks Assigned by Teachers?" *Journal of Educational Psychology*, vol. 43 (1952), 218–28.

[16]Hadley, "A School Mark—Fact or Fancy?"

are assigned. Indeed, as Palmer has noted, some instructors deliberately use high marks as rewards and low marks as punishments for behavior quite unrelated to the attainment of the objectives of instruction in a course.[17]

The studies of Starch and Elliott on the unreliability of teachers' marks on examination papers are classic demonstrations of the instability of judgments based on presumably absolute standards.[18] Identical copies of an English examination paper were given to 142 English teachers, with instructions to score it on the basis of 100 percent for perfection. Since each teacher looked at only one paper, no relative basis for judgment was available. The scores assigned by the teachers to the same paper ranged all the way from 98 to 50 percent. Similar results were obtained with examination papers in geometry and in history.

Evidently marks such as Starch and Elliott collected for single examination papers are not highly reliable. How is it for composite semester marks? After surveying the evidence, Odell concluded that "the usual reliability of semester marks is indicated by a coefficient of from 0.70 to 0.80, perhaps even of from 0.80 to 0.90." With respect to the validity of marks, and on the basis of admittedly indirect and inadequate evidence, he suggested that "the degree of validity as a measure of mastery of subject matter is fairly high, probably on the average at least not below that represented by a coefficient of correlation of 0.70 and in many cases much higher."[19]

In assessing these estimates of reliability and validity it may be helpful to keep two things in mind. One is that semester marks are based on much more extensive and comprehensive observations of pupil attainments, perhaps as much as or more than 80 hours of observation. One hour of intensive "observation" under the controlled conditions of a well-standardized test of achievement can yield measurements whose reliability may exceed 0.90.

The other thing to keep in mind is that a coefficient of correlation even as high as 0.70 does not reflect very pure and precise measurements of the thing to be measured. In fact, if only half the observations summarized in the mark are completely relevant to the attainment being marked and if the other half are competely irrelevant, the validity of the mark would be about 0.70 (assuming that each observation carries equal weight and that all observations are perfectly reliable). Hence if the summary values for the reliability and validity of semester marks reported

---

[17]Palmer, "Seven Classic Ways of Grading Dishonestly."

[18]Daniel Starch and E. C. Elliott, "Reliability of Grading Work in History," *School Review*, vol. 21 (1913), 676–81; "Reliability of Grading Work in Mathematics," *School Review*, vol. 21 (1913), 254–59; "Reliability of the Grading of High School Work in English," *School Review*, vol. 20 (1912), 442–57.

[19]Odell, "Marks and Marking Systems."

by Odell do not suggest utter chaos, they do suggest that considerable room for improvement remains.

INSTITUTIONAL MARKING SYSTEMS

An obvious method for dealing with one of the major shortcomings of marks—the lack of a clearly defined, scrupulously observed definition of what the various marks should mean—is for a school faculty to develop, adopt, and enforce an institutional marking ststem. Ruch has stressed the point that the marking schemes are essentially matters of definition.[20] Any marking system, he suggests, is somewhat arbitrary. "The adopted marking scheme must be defined. Its sole meaning and value rest upon its definition to pupils, teachers and parents alike."

Travers and Gronlund also emphasize the importance to an institution of clear definition of its marking system.[21] And Odell observes,

> ... when serious attention has been given to the matter and the general principles that should govern marking are agreed upon by a group of teachers, the marks the members of the group assign tend to form distributions much more similar than if this had not been done and their reliability is somewhat improved.[22]

If an institution lacks a clearly defined marking system or if instructors do not assign marks in conformity with the policies that define the system, then the marks will tend to lose their meaning and the marking system will fail to perform its essential functions adequately. A marking system is basically a system of communication. It involves the use of a set of specialized symbols whose meanings ought to be clearly defined and uniformly understood by all concerned. Only to the degree that the marks do have the same meaning for all who use them is it possible for them to serve the purposes of communication meaningfully and precisely.

The meaning of a mark should depend as little as possible on the teacher who issued it or the course to which it pertains. This means that the marking practices of an instructor, of a department, or indeed of an entire educational institution are matters of legitimate concern to other instructors, other departments, and other institutions. It means that a general system of marking ought to be adopted by the faculty and the administration of a school or college. It requires that the meaning of

---

[20]G. M. Ruch, *The Objective or New-type Examination* (Chicago: Scott, Foresman & Company, 1929), pp. 369–402.

[21]Travers and Gronlund, "Meaning of Marks."

[22]Odell, "Marks and Marking Systems."

each mark must be clearly defined. General adherence to this system and to these meanings ought to be expected of all staff members. Such a requirement would in no way infringe the right of each instructor to determine which mark to give to a particular student. But it would limit the right (which some instructors have claimed) to set his own standards or to invent his own meanings for each of the marks issued.

An educational institution that sets out to improve its educational effectiveness by improving its marking practices and to improve its marking practices by developing an institutional marking system is likely to encounter a number of questions such as these on which opinions will differ.

1. Should marks report absolute achievement, in terms of content mastery, or achievements relative to those of other comparable students?
2. Should marks be regarded as measurements or as evaluations?
3. Should marks simply indicate achievement in learning or should they be affected by the student's attitude, effort, character, and similar traits?
4. Should marks report status achieved or amount of growth in achievement?
5. Should a student receive a single composite mark or multiple marks on separate aspects of achievement?
6. Should the marking system report few or many different degrees of achievement?
7. Should letters or numbers be used as the marking symbols?

Each of these questions will be discussed in turn in the sections that follow.

ABSOLUTE VERSUS RELATIVE MARKING

Two major types of marking systems have been in use in the United States since 1900. In the early years of the century almost all marking was in percents. A student who learned all that anyone could learn in a course, whose achievement could therefore be regarded as flawless, could expect a mark of 100 (percent). A student who learned nothing at all would, theoretically, be given a mark of zero. A definite percent of "perfection" usually between 60 and 75 percent was ordinarily regarded as the minimum passing score. Because a student's percent mark is presumably independent of any other student's mark, percent marking is sometimes characterized as "absolute marking."

The second major type of marking system is based on the use of a small number of letter marks, often five, to express various levels of achievement. In the five-letter A-B-C-D-F system, truly outstanding achievement is rewarded with a mark of A. A mark of B indicates above average achievement; C is the average mark; D indicates below average achievement; and F is used to report failure (that is, achievement insufficient to warrant credit for completing a course of study). Because a letter mark is intended to indicate a student's achievement relative to that of his peers, letter marking is sometimes characterized as "relative marking."

A popular term for one variety of relative marking is "grading on the curve." The "curve" referred to is the curve of normal distribution. One method for grading or marking on the curve, using five letter marks, is to determine from the ideal normal curve what proportion of the marks should fall at each of five levels and to follow these proportions as closely as possible in assigning marks. For example, the best 7 percent might get A's, the next best 23 percent get B's, and so on. Another process is to define the limits of the score intervals corresponding to various marks in terms of the mean and standard deviation of the distribution of achievement scores. Those whose scores are more than 1.5 standard deviations above the mean might get A's, those between .5 and 1.5 standard deviations above the mean get B's, and so on. This second process does not guarantee in advance that 7 percent of the students must get A's and 7 percent must fail. If the distribution of achievement is skewed, as it may be, or irregular, as it often is, these characteristics will be reflected in variations in the proportions of each mark assigned.

In the early decades of this century letter marking began to supersede percent marking. A clear majority of educational institutions now uses letter marks. But percent marking is by no means dead. Some schools still use percents instead of letters in their marking systems. Others indicate percent equivalents of the various letter marks they issue. Official examining bodies still prefer to define passing scores in terms of percent, though they often transform test scores, or control the scoring process, to avoid any significant change in the ratio of failures to passes. The controversy that began when percent marking was first seriously attacked, and when the movement to substitute letter marks gained support, continues today. The issue of absolute versus relative marking is still a live one, particularly when relative marking is identified as "grading on the curve."

PERCENT MARKING PROBLEMS

Ruch has criticized percent marking on the ground that it implies a precision that is seldom actually attainable.[23]

[23]Ruch, *The Objective or New-type Examination.*

...a large body of experimental evidence points to the fact that from but five to seven levels of ability are ordinarily recognizable by teachers in marking pupils.... The difference between an "85" and an "86" is a difference at least five times as fine as the human judgment can ordinarily distinguish.

There is substantial basis for this criticism, but it should not be taken too literally. How many levels of ability can be recognized depends on how much good information the teacher has available. No doubt an attempt to decide whether to give a pupil an 85 or an 86 has seemed ridiculous to many teachers. Seldom is a teacher in a position to say, "I am 100 percent certain that this pupil's true mark is 85, not 86 or 84." But given more information as a basis for judgment, the teacher's task might seem less ridiculous. And if a teacher recognizes that he will always have to settle for less than 100 percent confidence in the accuracy of his marks, he may be willing to trade a little of that confidence for a little more precise indication of his best guess at a student's level of achievement. As pointed out elsewhere in this chapter, the use of broad categories in marking tends to reduce the number of wrong marks, but it always sacrifices so much precision in the process that the overall reliability of the marks declines.

The widespread initial use of percent marking and its persistence in modern times suggest that there must be things to be said in its favor. Two advantages are mentioned most often. The first is that percent marking clearly relates achievement to degree of mastery of what was set out to be learned. It does not give high marks to incompetent students simply because they happen to be the best of a bad lot. It does not require that some students receive low marks when they and all their classmates have done well in learning what they were supposed to learn. To know what proportion a student has mastered of a defined set of learning objectives is to know something more, and something less, than to know that he was outstanding, or average, or poor, compared with some other students, in mastering the same set of learning objectives. Achievement cannot be reported fully without reference to what (that is, command of knowledge and utilizable skill) has been achieved.

A second reputed advantage of percent marking is that it provides fixed, standard measures of achievement. This is in contrast to relative grading, where the achievements of the group set standards for what is excellent, average, or very poor in individual achievement. A student whose achievements result in his designation as valedictorian in one school might be regarded as only average in another school. Relative standards are likely to be variable standards.

Unfortunately, percent marking often fails to live up to its promise of providing truly meaningful and stable measures of achievement. To calculate a meaningful percent, two quantities must be measured in common units with reasonable accuracy: (1) the amount available to be learned in a course, and (2) the part of that amount that a particular student did, in fact, learn. These things are so difficult to measure that they are almost never measured. In what units can the material available to be learned be measured? On what basis can an instructor estimate how much might be learned in a particular course?

It is sometimes asserted that standards for marking are inherent in the subject matter itself. But no one ever learns all there is to know about a subject, nor is it possible to ascertain reliably by any known operations what proportion of the theoretical sum total of knowledge in a field any student possesses. It is equally difficult to set any rational minimum standard for passing, in terms of subject matter alone. Educational achievement does not come in separate and equal units that are easy to count and are learned on an all-or-none basis.

A mark of 90 used to be thought to mean that the student who received it had learned 90 percent of what he was expected to learn in a given course. But it takes very little analysis to discover how little meaning there is in such a statement. In what units does one measure amount of knowledge? On what basis can an instructor say how much *should* be learned in a given course? By what operations can one measure the total to be learned and the part the student did learn?

Sometimes those who defend so-called absolute standards argue that the experienced teacher knows what these standards are and that the inexperienced teacher can quickly learn them if he will only try. But this is obviously just a roundabout way of saying that the standards are derived from the observed performances of the students themselves, which means that they are relative and are not absolute measures of subject matter achievement at all. In spite of the arguments in favor of absolute, teacher-determined marking standards, no one has ever described in concrete, operational terms exactly how such standards could be defined and applied.

Few percent marks are ever calculated by division of a measurement of the part learned by a measurement of the total available to be learned. Instead, percent marks almost always reflect a highly subjective judgment, against a somewhat vague and individualistic standard, of the *relative* quality of a student's performance. If he is very good, relative to other students the instructor has, has had, or can imagine having, his percent mark is likely to be high. If not, it is likely to be lower.

The studies by Starch and Elliott, mentioned earlier in this chapter, clearly demonstrated how variable from teacher to teacher these presumably absolute standards of achievement might be. Ruch has illustrated how much this variablility can be reduced when relative marks, based on rankings, are substituted for absolute marks, based on percent.[24]

[24]Ruch, *The Objective or New-type Examination.*

Evidence of these kinds was largely responsible for the shift away from percentage marking and toward letter marking early in this century. Relative standards, based on the average performances of groups of typical students, turn out to be more stable than presumably absolute standards, based on the idiosyncratic judgments of individual instructors.

RELATIVE MARKING PROBLEMS

One of the major problems of relative marking arises from the fact that not all class groups to which marks must be assigned are typical. Some are above and others are below average in general ability and achievement simply because of sampling fluctuations. There may be almost as much chance variation in potential learning ability from one class of 26 students to another class of 26 students as there is in trick-taking potential from one hand of 13 bridge cards to another. Some differences may be the result of self-selection, as when students with special talent or interest elect courses in music, advanced mathematics, or creative writing. Further, able students may tend to elect academically oriented college preparatory courses, whereas less able students may try to get into vocational training courses. Finally, some class differences may be planned deliberately by school officials in the interests of more effective instruction, as when students studying the same subject are grouped on the basis of ability in different classes. Does "grading on the curve" make sense in such atypical classes (which probably constitute a large majority of all classes)?

From one point of view it is absurd to give an A for the best achievement in a low-ability group if identical achievement would have received a mark of C in a group of higher ability. But from another point of view it is equally absurd to deny the possibility of recognizing outstanding achievement among low-ability students with a mark of A, or of recognizing, with marks of C, D, or even F, that students of high ability can do what is for them mediocre, poor, or even failing work.

In many colleges students enrolling to study a foreign language such as German are placed in different classes on the basis of how much German they already know. A student in beginning German has almost the same chance at an A mark as a student in intermediate or advanced German. In some of these same colleges students enrolling in freshman English are also placed in different classes on the basis of how much English they already know. But the student enrolled in the "remedial" course usually has much less likelihood of receiving an A than the student placed in the advanced course. This kind of differential marking, as between beginning German and remedial English, makes sense to those who believe that it is more appropriate to study the one than the other at the college level. But it does not make sense to those who feel that a college can and should teach any college student what he most needs to know, provided only that he is willing to study hard to learn it.

Granting the generalizations that most classes in schools and colleges are atypical and that seriously atypical classes can put serious strains on systems of relative marking, one can still make a case for the advantages in reliability and meaningfulness of a marking system that places more emphasis on relative than on absolute achievement. Absolute standards seem much too difficult to define clearly and with general acceptability to provide in themselves an adequate basis for reliable, meaningful marks.

Variations from class to class in ability and achievement do not preclude reasonable marking on a relative basis. Allowances can be made for the sampling fluctuations in small classes by not insisting on rigorous adherence to a designated ideal distribution in each small, atypical class, but only in the composite distribution of marks for many such classes. One can make provision for a somewhat different "curve" in classes of high ability than in classes of lower ability. But such differences should be public knowledge and should be sanctioned by the whole faculty. Ordinarily they should not be extreme differences. It is unrealistic and psychologically unwise to foster the belief that capable students are entitled to higher marks simply because they are capable. It is equally unrealistic and unwise to create conditions that predestine some students to do below average work and to receive below-average marks in every course they undertake to study. Human beings, fortunately, exhibit a diversity of talents. A good school or college makes provision for developing diverse special talents and for recognizing and rewarding them.

Teachers of subjects like art, music, or physical education sometimes report difficulty in distinguishing reliably as many as five levels of achievement among their students. In such cases the tendency is to use only the top marks of the scale, giving few if any D's or F's. In a few cases where the classes are small and highly selected this practice may be justified. But in others, especially where the problem is lack of reliable measures of achievement rather than sectioning by ability, the practice is not justified. If only three levels of achievement can be distinguished in a large, unselected group, the marks assigned to these levels probably should be B's, C's, and D's rather than A's, B's, and C's.

A basic principle of relative marking is that one should mark a student's achievement by comparing it with the achievement of the student's peers. But who, for example, are the peers of a talented girl studying vocal music? Are they all the girls of her own age in the country, in school and out? Or are they only those girls specializing in vocal music at the same stage in their training as she is? One way, perhaps the best way, to give marks clearly defined operational meaning is to mark a student's performance relative to the performance of other students who are interested in and capable of taking the same course. It is not wholly feasible or reasonable to compare the vocal performance of a girl who is trying to learn to sing exceptionally well with the vocal performance of other girls who are not trying to learn to sing at all. Hence it seems somewhat unreasonable to insist that students with special talents should never be given average marks.

CRITICISMS OF RELATIVE MARKING

One common criticism of relative marking is that it permits the students rather than the teachers to set the standards. This is true. There is the further implication that student-set standards are likely to be low—lower, at least, than those most teachers would set. But this appears not to be true. For when the teachers depart from the proportions of marks recommended in a system of relative marking, they usually seem to do it by giving too many high marks rather than too many low marks.

Another way of stating essentially the same criticism is to claim that relative marking encourages a general slow-down of student effort. The argument is that under a relative system the members of a class can earn just as good marks on the average by taking it easy as by putting forth maximum effort. There is nothing wrong with the abstract logic of this argument, but there is something wrong with its practical psychology. How can any student who agrees to this slow-down be sure that some other student may not work just a bit harder and wind up receiving a higher mark?

Yet another criticism of relative marking is that it requires an instructor to give some low marks and some average marks, even if most of the students in the class learn practically all that he was trying to teach them. Do they not all deserve high marks in such a case? How frequently this hypothetical situation of nearly universal, nearly maximum achievement can be expected to occur is not specified. Some good instructors claim they have never encountered such a case. But even if purely hypothetical, the issue it raises is important and deserves an answer. Actually, two answers can be offered.

The first is that if a high mark implies outstanding, and hence unusual, achievement and if an average mark implies normal, and hence typical, achievement, it is logically inconsistent to give most of the class members a high mark. They should all get average marks since their achievements are about average for the group. None of them have shown outstanding achievement.

The second is that if the students in a class differ appreciably in abilities, preparation, and interests, as they almost always do, the only way that nearly all of them can achieve all that is asked of them is to ask much less than the best could achieve. To equalize achievement by minimizing it deprives some students of the education they could get and may deprive society of the benefits of their fully developed talents. Most good teachers prefer to challenge and to help each pupil to learn as much as he can.

Some instructors have expressed fear that relative marking would lead to such a slow-down. A few students have claimed to know of classes where it happened. But there seems to be little evidence that it ever actually did happen. If it did, the blame might lie more with uninspiring course content or with poor student motivation than with relative marking. Ordinarily the personal competition implicit in relative marking will stimulate as much or more effort to achieve than the impersonal stimulus of an absolute standard of achievement.

In most areas of human activity awards go to individuals who are outstanding in relative, not absolute, terms. There are no absolute standards for speed in running the mile or for distance in throwing the javelin. The winner in any race is determined on a relative basis. Runners on a starting line seldom agree to loaf along simply because there is no absolute standard of speed they have to meet. From the point of view of the individual runner in the 100-yard dash, as well as from that of the individual student majoring in history or chemistry, the best way to achieve outstanding success is to put forth outstanding effort.

A marking system cannot be all things to all men. A single symbol cannot represent low achievement from one point of view (that is, actual degree of content mastery) and high achievement from another (that is, progress in relation to reasonable expectation). What it can and should have is one clearly defined and jealously guarded kind of meaning. School and college faculties have the opportunity and the obligation to establish and maintain clearly defined meanings for the symbols used in their marking systems.

MEASUREMENT OR EVALUATION

As the term is used here, a measurement in education is a quantitative description of how much a student has achieved. A measurement is objective and impersonal, and it can be quite precisely defined in operational terms. An evaluation, on the other hand, is a qualitative judgment of *how good or how satisfactory* the student's performance has been. Evaluations are often based in part on measurments of achievement, but they are also based on many other kinds of evidence. Measurement can describe how much of this ability or that characteristic an individual possesses. But to tell how well educated he is or how well prepared for a particular job, an evaluation is required.

There are several advantages in treating a marking system as a means of reporting measurements of achievement rather than as a means of reporting evaluations. In the first place, evaluations are complex, involving many variables and many considerations that are unique to a particular student. This makes it difficult to report evaluations adequately in a standardized marking system. Judgments of how good a student's educational achievement has been depend not only on how much he has achieved, but also on his opportunity for achievement, the effort he has put forth, and the need that this achievement is likely to serve in his educational and vocational future. It is not easy to make marks valid as *measures* of achievement, but it is next to impossible to make them valid as *evaluations*.

In the second place, because of the many poorly defined and highly individual factors which must be considered in making an evaluation, few teachers have a sufficient basis for making fair evaluations. Some teachers may be well informed about the home background and the personal problems of many of their students and hence can judge quite accurately each student's opportunity to learn and the real effort he has made to learn. But many teachers lack some of this background essential to sound evaluation. Such teachers can help a student to make an honest evaluation of his own achievements, but the teacher can seldom do the whole job alone. And perhaps the teacher should not, even if he could. Imposed evaluations may be not only less accurate than self-evaluations, but less effective also. If students and teachers regard marks as objective measurements of achievement rather than as subjective evaluations, there is greater likelihood that the teachers will assign fair and accurate marks, and there is less likelihood that students will react emotionally so that the relations between student and teacher are damaged.

Consider this analogy. If the scale shows that a man weighs 210 pounds, it is reporting a measurement. The fact may be unpleasant, but there is nothing personal about it and no good cause for anger at the scale. But if a tactless acquaintance suggests that he is getting too fat, the acquaintance is making an evaluation. It can be taken as a personal affront, and a natural reaction is to resent it. The fact that the heavy man may have been thinking the same thing himself does not soothe his feelings very much. In somewhat the same way, the interpretation of marks as evaluations rather than as measurements may have been responsible for some of the tension and unpleasantness associated with their use.

Finally, there may be less need or justification for making a formal report and a permanent record of an evaluation than there is for recording a measurement. Usually it is less important for a future teacher or employer to know that Henry did as well as could be expected of him or that he failed to live up to expectations than to know that he was outstanding in his ability to handle language or mediocre in his mathematical ability. Evaluations are instrumental to specific decisions. Once the decision has been made, there is little to be gained by basking in a favorable evaluation or in agonizing over an unfavorable one. To be successful and to maintain emotional stability, a person must not cherish too long the evaluations, favorable or unfavorable, that others have made of him or that he has made of himself. Measured achievement, on the other hand, often represents a more permanent foundation on which future education and success depend. The more accurately it is reported and the more completely it is recorded, the more soundly a student and his advisors can judge which choices he should make.

A teacher may thus be well advised to regard the marks he assigns in a course as objective, impersonal measures of achievement rather than as subjective, personal evaluations. He may even be able, happily, to persuade his students to accept them on this basis.

ACHIEVEMENT OR ATTITUDE AND EFFORT

Studies such as those by Carter, Hadley, Travers and Gronlund, and others indicate that teachers often base the marks they issue on factors other than degree of achievement of the objectives of instruction. No doubt they will continue to do so, since marks can be useful instruments of social control in the classroom and since some degree of such control is essential to effective teaching. But the use of marks for these purposes must be limited, for it can easily be abused and tends to distort the intended meaning of the mark.

One of the important requirements of a good marking system is that the marks indicate as accurately as possible the extent to which the student has achieved the objectives of instruction in the particular course of study. If improving the student's attitude toward something or improving his willingness to put forth effort for educational achievement is one of the specific objectives of the course and if the instructor has planned specific educational procedures in the course to attain this goal, then it is quite appropriate to consider these things in assigning marks. But often this is not the case. When it is not, attitude and effort probably should be excluded from consideration in determining the mark to be assigned.

Involving judgments of character and citizenship in marking is even more hazardous. Such judgments tend to be impressionistic evaluations rather than objective descriptions. If we like the behavior we call it straightforward, or perhaps thoughtful. If not, we are more likely to call it tactless, or perhaps indecisive. The countercharges of political leaders suggest that what looks like intelligent and courageous statesmanship to those in one party looks like incompetent bungling or spineless expedience to those in the other. Seldom are the traits of good character or good citizenship defined objectively, without the use of value-loaded and question-begging modifiers like "good," "desirable," "effective," or "appropriate."

The result of these difficulties is that valid assessments of character and citizenship are not easy to secure and not often secured. As Odell remarked, in reference to marks reflecting character or citizenship, "In general, the conclusion seems justified that when a mark of this sort is given, it is not highly valid."[25]

STATUS OR GROWTH

Some instructors, seeking to improve the fairness of the marks they issue, attempt to base them on the amount of improvement the student has made rather than on the level of achievement he has reached. Scores on a pretest, and other preliminary observations, are used to provide a basis for estimates of initial status. The difference between these and subsequent test scores and other indications of achievement permits estimates of the amount of change or growth.

Unfortunately these growth measures usually are quite unreliable. Each test score or observation includes its own error of measurement. When these are subtracted from other measurements, the errors tend to accumulate instead of to cancel out. Consequently the difference scores sometimes consist mainly of errors of measurement. Lord, Diederich, and others have pointed out some of the difficulties in using this approach.[26] If his tests are appropriate and reliable, an instructor may safely use the difference between mean pretest and posttest scores as one measure of the effectiveness of his instruction. But few educational tests are good enough to reliably measure short-run gains in educational achievement for individual students.

From some points of view it may seem fairer to use growth rather than final status as a measure of achievement. But, apart from the characteristic unreliability of growth scores just mentioned, there are other

---

[25]Odell, "Marks and Marking Systems."
[26]Frederic M. Lord, "The Measurement of Growth," *Educational and Psychological Measurement*, vol. 16 (1956), 421–37; and Paul B. Diederich, "Pitfalls in the Measurement of Gains in Achievement," *School Review*, vol. 64 (1956), 59–63.

problems. One is that for many educational purposes, knowledge that a student is good, average, or poor when compared with his peers is more important than knowledge that he changed more or less rapidly than they did in a certain period of time. Another is that students who get low scores on the pretest have a considerably greater likelihood of showing subsequent large gains in achievement than their classmates who earned higher initial scores. Students are not slow to grasp this fact when their achievement is judged on the basis of gains. The course of wisdom is for them to make sure that their pretest performance is not so good as to constitute a handicap later on.

One rather strong incentive for marking students on the basis of growth rather than status is to give all students a more nearly equal chance to earn good marks. A student who makes good marks on the basis of status in one course is likely to make good marks in other courses.[27] A student whose marks are high one semsster is likely to get high marks the next semester.[28] The other, darker side of this picture is that status marking condemns some students to low marks in most subjects, semester after semester. Low marks discourage effort. Lack of effort increases the probability of more low marks. So the vicious cycle continues, bringing dislike of learning and early withdrawal from school.

The debilitating effect of low marks on educational interest and effort is probably sufficient to constitute a major educational problem. But whether marking on the basis of growth rather than status provides an effective solution to the problem may be open to question. For one thing, growth measures are usually of rather low reliability, as already indicated. Few students, even poor students, would really favor the substitution of more or less randomly distributed (and hence rather meaningless) praise or blame for consistently dependable measures of status, however discouraging that status might seem to be.

Another limitation of growth measures as an antidote to the discouragement sometimes brought by low-status measures is that they don't really conceal or offset differences in status very effectively. The poor reader knows he is a poor reader, and so do his classmates, even if he gets a good mark for growth in reading. A student who has a hard time with arithmetic is not encouraged very much by the report that, for him, a mediocre score on an arithmetic test represents rather commendable achievement. Students are not likely to forget, nor should they, that in the long run it is competence achieved that will count and that rate of growth is important only as it contributes to status.

What, then, is the answer? Success is important to all of us. None

[27]David Ohlson, "School Marks versus Intelligence Rating," *Educational Administration and Supervision*, vol. 13 (1927), 90–102.

[28]L. W. Ferguson and W. R. Crooks, "Some Characteristics of the Quality Point Ratio," *Journal of General Psychology*, vol. 27 (1942), 111–18.

of us should expect it all of the time, but we should not expect it to be denied all of the time either. Fortunately we do differ in what we can do well. This student is a whiz at mathematics. That one has a talent for languages. This girl is a fine artist. That one can act. This boy is a fine artist. That one is a supersalesman. One trick to successful, happy living, as Robert Frost pointed out, is to "Get up something to say for yourself." What this means, he made clear, is that each person needs to find something he can do better than most other people, if only because he works harder than they to learn how to do that particular thing. And, as John Gardner has pointed out, there are many varieties of excellence.

If students are taught to dislike school by constant reminders of their low achievement, the remedy probably is not to try to persuade them that rate of growth toward achievement is more important than status achieved, for that is a transparent falsehood. The remedy probably is to provide varied opportunities to excel in various kinds of worthwhile achievement. Certainly this can be done within a comprehensive school. It may even be done within a single classroom by an alert, versatile, dedicated teacher. When it is done, marking on the basis of status achieved will no longer mean that some students always win and others always lose. Each can enjoy, as he should, some of the rewards of excellence in his own specialty.

Finally, when reasonable care is taken to enroll students in courses appropriate for their levels of ability and preparatory training, differences in initial status can be limited. In such cases the need to measure achievement in terms of cange is also greatly reduced.

SINGLE OR MULTIPLE MARKS

Achievement in most subjects of study in schools and colleges is complex. There is knowledge to be imparted, understanding to be cultivated, abilities and skills to be developed, attitudes to be fostered, interests to be encouraged, and ideals to be exemplified. Correspondingly, the bases used for determining marks include many aspects or indications of achievement: homework, class participation, test scores, apparent attitude, interest and effort, and even regularity of attendance and helpfulness to the teacher. How can a single symbol do justice to these various aspects of achievement?

The answer of some observers is that it cannot. A mark, they say, is a hodgepodge of uncertain and variable composition. They suggest that the essential step in improving marks is to make them more analytical and descriptive. Multiple marks or written reports have been proposed as improvements over the traditional single letter or number. Bolmeier recommends that marks be analytical enough to be meaningful.[29] Two trends in marking noted by Smith and Dobbin are (1) increased comprehensiveness in the areas of student development being marked and (2) greater specificity in what is marked.[30]

There is considerable merit in these suggestions, and under favorable conditions they can improve marking considerably. But they do involve problems. For one thing, they multiply considerably the already irksome chores of marking. For another, they create additional problems of defining precisely what is to be marked and of distinguishing clearly among the different aspects of achievement. An even more serious problem is that of obtaining sufficient evidence, specific to each aspect of achievement, on which to base a reliable mark. Finally, and largely as a result of the preceding difficulties, the multiple marks exhibit considerable "halo effect." That is, they seem to be determined more by the instructor's overall impression of the student than by his successful analysis and independent measurement of various components of achievement.

Multiple marking is no panacea for the ills of marking. It may well call for more information than the instructor can readily obtain and more effort than the improvement it yields seems to warrant. It may try to tell the student and his parents more than can be told clearly, perhaps even more than they really care to know. Multiple marking is not the only road to improvement in marking and probably not the best road currently available. Much can be done to make single marks more meaningful and more reliable. Perhaps those possibilities should be exploited before the more complex problems of multiple marking are tackled.

HOW MANY STEPS ON THE GRADE SCALE?

A major difference between two systems of marking is that letter marks are usually few in number (five, most commonly) whereas percent marks provide up to 100 different values, of which about 30 are commonly used. Those who advocated letter marks when they were first introduced suggested that the bases on which marks are usually determined are not reliable enough to justify the apparent precision of percent marking. They claimed that the best that most instructors can do is to distinguish about five different levels of achievement. Many instructors seemed to agree with this view.

[29] Edward C. Bolmeier, "Principles Pertaining to Marking and Reporting Pupil Progress," *School Review*, vol. 59 (1951), 15–24.
[30] Ann Z. Smith and John E. Dobbin, "Marks and Marking Systems," in *Encyclopedia of Educational Research*, 3rd ed., ed. Chester W. Harris (New York: The Macmillan Company, 1960), pp. 783–91.

Some proposals for improving marks have gone even farther than the five-letter system in reducing marking categories. The use of only two marks such as "S" for "satisfactory" and "U" for "unsatisfactory," "P" for "pass" and "F" for "fail," or "credit"—"no credit" has been suggested and adopted by some institutions.[31,32] Pass-fail grading enjoyed considerable popularity during the late 1960's, particularly on the more liberally inclined campuses. At the same time there was increased interest in refining the grade scale by adding plus and minus signs to the basic letters, or decimal fractions to the basic numbers.

The notion that marking problems can be simplified and marking errors reduced by using fewer marking categories is an attractive one. Its weakness is exposed by carrying it to the limit. If only one category is used, if everyone is given the same mark, all marking problems vanish, but so does the value of marking. A major shortcoming of two-category marking, and to some degree of five-category marking as well, is this same kind of loss of information. To trade more precisely meaningful marks for marks easier to assign may be a bad bargain for education.

The use of fewer, broader categories in marking does indeed reduce the frequency of errors in marking. That is, with a few broad categories more of the students receive the marks they deserve because fewer wrong marks are available to give them. But each error becomes more crucial. The apparent difference between satisfactory and unsatisfactory, or between a B and a C, is greater than the difference between 87 percent and 88 percent. If a fallible instructor (and all of them, being human, are fallible) gives a student a mark of 86 percent when omniscient wisdom would have assigned a mark of 89 percent, the error has less consequence than if the instructor assigns a C when a B should have been given, or an "unsatisfactory" mark when the mark should have been "satisfactory." Hence the use of fewer categories is no royal road to more reliable marking. And, as noted previously, reducing the number of categories reduces the information conveyed by the mark.

The more reliable the information on which marks are based, the greater the value of a large number of marking categories. But no matter how unreliable that information may be, it is *never* true that few categories report the information more accurately than many categories. This is illustrated in Table 12.1, which may be read as follows: "If marks are based on information having a reliability of 0.95, the use of 2 categories in marking would reduce the reliability to 0.63, of 5 categories to 0.85, and of 10 categories to 0.92. In the case of 15 categories the reduction is very slight, only from 0.95 to 0.94." Other rows in the table may be read similarly. The data in Table 12.1 were prepared from formulas

[31]W. M. Stallings and others, "Pass-Fail Grading Option," *School and Society*, vol. 96 (1968), 179–80.

[32]M. R. Sgan, "First Year of Pass-Fail at Brandeis University: A Report," *Journal of Higher Education*, vol. 40 (1969), 135–44.

TABLE 12.1. LOSS OF RELIABILITY FROM USE OF BROAD CATEGORIES IN MARKING

Reliability of Marking Basis	Reliability of Marks Number of Categories			
	2	5	10	15
0.95	0.63	0.85	0.92	0.94
0.90	0.60	0.80	0.87	0.89
0.80	0.53	0.71	0.78	0.79
0.70	0.47	0.62	0.68	0.69
0.50	0.33	0.45	0.48	0.49

derived and explained by Peters and Van Voorhis.[33] Values in the table assume equally spaced categories and normal distributions of scores and marks.

Table 12.1 illustrates a general proposition of considerable importance.

Regardless of the inaccuracy of the basis for grading, the finer the scale used for reporting the grades, that is the more different grade levels it provides, the more accurate the grade reports will be.

Whenever scores are grouped for purposes of grading, errors are introduced. In some cases the grouping errors will offset, or correct for, measurement errors in the data on which grades are based. But on the whole, the grouping adds more errors than it cancels.[34] The use of very few categories in grading aggravates the problem of unreliability. If maximum reliability of information is the goal, a 5-letter system is better than a 2-letter system, and 10 categories in marking is better than 5. The main arguments for fewer categories in marking must be on grounds of convenience and simplicity, not on grounds of the unreliability of the basis for marking. A system using nine single digits, the stanine system described later in this chapter, seems to offer a reasonable compromise between precision and convenience.

PASS-FAIL GRADING

During the late 1960's successful efforts were made on a number of college campuses and in some public school systems to supplement

[33]Charles C. Peters and Walter R. Van Voorhis, *Statistical Procedures and Their Mathematical Bases* (New York: McGraw-Hill Book Company, 1940), pp. 393–99.
[34]Robert L. Ebel, "The Relation of Scale Fineness to Grade Accuracy," *Journal of Educational Measurement*, vol. 6 (1969), 217–21.

or supplant conventional letter grades with a pass-fail grading system. Several pressures initiated and sustained these efforts: the pressure from faculty members to get rid of grading problems, the pressure from students to get rid of the threat of low grades, and the pressure in the academic community to try something new.

A number of arguments in favor of pass-fail grading were advanced.

1. By the time a student gets to graduate school, or into college, or even into high school, he has proved his ability. He should not be called upon to prove it again and again in every course he takes.
2. Grades are unimportant outside of school. The typical employer doesn't care what kind of grades a person got in school. Grades are poor predictors of later achievement.
3. Many instructors do such a poor job of grading that the grades they issue are almost without meaning.
4. The need to protect his grade point average deters a student from taking courses he wants to take and ought to take outside his major field.
5. The pressure to make high grades forces students into bad study practices such as rote learning and all-night cramming, and drives some to cheat on examinations.
6. The threat of low grades destroys the love of learning that schools ought to foster.

There is some merit in these arguments, but there are also a number of flaws.

1. No man, however successful, ever becomes immune to failure. Those who live good lives never stop trying to do their best, never limit themselves to enterprises whose success is assured in advance. Past success promises future success, but never can guarantee it.
2. Many personal qualities other than academic success contribute to success on the job. We should not expect the first to predict the second infallibly. Nor should we expect success or failure in appreciation of poetry to have much to do with success or failure in managing a grocery. But if there is no relation at all between the competence a student shows in learning how to be a good teacher and his subsequent competence in the classroom, something is seriously wrong with the teacher training program.
3. The better remedy for incompetent grading is to get rid of the incompetence, not to get rid of the grades.
4. The student who is deterred from taking courses outside his major may be acting wisely, if the course he wishes to take is in fact likely to be quite difficult for him to master. The fear of a low grade may be well justified by the student's lack of adequate preparation. Pass-fail grading may encourage him to take the course, but it will not help him at all to master it. On the other hand, if the course is one he really needs and feels able to handle satisfactorily, and if his grade point average is not already dangerously low for other reasons, he is acting quite unwisely if he lets the possibility of a B or C deter him from taking it.
5. If grades are properly given they will not reward rote learning or cramming. Even if badly given they do not justify cheating.
6. Low achievement does more to destroy the love of learning than do the low grades that report that low achievement. Most people come to love doing the things they know they can do well. The grades they get help them to know this.

The arguments against pass-fail grading are less numerous, but may be more substantial.

1. Pass-fail grading removes much of the immediate motivation and reward for efforts to excel.
2. Pass-fail grading leaves the student with an incomplete or an inaccurate record of his achievements.

The practical force of the first of these arguments is such that most systems of exclusive pass-fail grading tend to be short-lived. The force of the second is such that when a pass-fail option is offered to students, few of them decide to make use of it. They know that a transcript loaded with A's and B's will look better to a graduate school admission committee or to a prospective employer than one loaded with pass marks.

Almost every school or college offers some courses in which the aim is to provide certain experiences rather than to develop certain competencies. For such courses neither grades nor pass-fail decisions seem appropriate. Instead, the student who attends enough to get a large proportion of the desired experience should simply be given credit for his attendance. Courses in the appreciation of art, music, or literature, in recreational pursuits, in social problems, or in great issues may belong in this category of ungraded courses. But most other courses do not. Most courses do aim to develop competencies. Such courses call for assessments of achievement, and for them pass-fail grading is a poor substitute for more detailed and precise reporting of achievements.

Most of us want to be valued as persons. Most of us don't particularly want to be evaluated. But we can't enjoy the first without enduring the second. The weakness of pass-fail grading is that by doing a poor job of evaluating it keeps us from doing a good one of valuing.

LETTERS OR NUMBERS

The successful revolt against percent marking was aided by the substitution of letter marks for numbers. Letters helped to emphasize the contrast between clearly relative marking and supposedly absolute percent marking. But the use of letters creates at least two problems. One is that the letters must always be transformed to numbers before they can be added or averaged. The other is that letters imply evaluations of achievement, rather than measurements.

For both these reasons the return to numerical symbols in marking would be advantageous. This advantage must be weighed against the confusion likely to result from introduction of a new set of symbols, with new and unfamiliar meanings. If an educational institution sets out with vigor to improve its marking system, a change in the set of symbols used may help to dramatize and reinforce other, more subtle changes. Since the stanine system of marking seems to afford substantial advantages over the five-letter system, it should receive serious consideration if a change is contemplated.

QUALITY CONTROL IN A MARKING SYSTEM

What a mark means is determined not only by how it was defined when the marking system was adopted, but also, and perhaps more importantly, by the way it is actually used. If an instructor assigns some A's, many B's, some C's, and very few lower marks, then B has become his average mark, not C, as the marking system may have specified. Thus institutional control of marking requires surveillance of the results of the marking process and may require corrective action.

The temptations for instructors to depart from institutional policy in marking are many, and the rationalizations for doing so are not hard to find. Some instructors regard marking as the personal prerogative of the instructor. They may not distinguish between their very considerable freedom to determine which mark a particular student shall receive and their very considerable responsibility to make the meaning of their marks consistent with those of other instructors. To rationalize deviations from overall institutional policy in distribution of marks, they may claim unusual ability or disability in their students, special interest or aptitude in the subject of study, or (usually only by implication) exceptionally fine teaching.

Some instructors yield to the subtle pressures to give more high and fewer low marks. Perhaps they feel inclined to temper justice with mercy. Perhaps they wish to avoid controversy. An instructor seldom has to explain or justify a high mark or to calm the anger of the student who received it. Some instructors may feel that the favorable reputations of their courses among students depend on their generosity with high marks. Many good instructors like their students so much as persons that they find it difficult to disappoint any of them with a low mark, particularly if the student seems to have been trying to learn. These temptations to depart from standard marking practices are understandable as temptations, but most of them do not carry much weight as reasonable justfications. There are indeed some situations that do warrant departure from general institutional policies in marking. But the determination of which situations those are probably cannot be left to the individual instructor concerned if uniformly meaningful marks are desired.

There are several things an educational institution can do to maintain the meaningfulness of the marks issued by its instructors. One is to publish each semester summary distributions of the marks issued in each course by each instructor. This is done systematically by some colleges and has been found quite effective. Another is to record alongside each mark reported to a student or his parents a set of numbers showing the distribution of marks to the student's classmates. The purpose of this is to make the relative meaning of the mark immediately apparent to all concerned.

A somewhat simpler variant of the procedure just described is to accompany each marking symbol by a fraction, the numerator of which shows what percent of the class received higher marks, while the denominator shows what percent received lower marks.

These fractional interpretations may be required only when the instructor has exceeded or fallen short of specified limits for the proportion of marks above or below each category. Such a requirement tends to encourage observance of institutional regulations without preventing necessary exceptions.

Finally, an institution can return to the instructor a set of marks whose distribution among the marking categories is unsatisfactory and ask him to resubmit a revised set of marks.

SYSTEMATIC MARKING PROCEDURES

This and the next two sections are concerned with a particular set of systematic procedures for converting test scores, or composite numerical measures of achievement, into marks. The method is built around the five-unit scale of letter marks that most schools and colleges use currently, though as will be shown it can be adapted to the nine-unit stanine system quite easily.[35]

One of the purposes of any systematic method of assigning marks is to establish greater uniformity among instructors in their marking practices, and hence in the meaning of the marks they issue. A school or college faculty that adopts such a system and requires all faculty members to conform to it in issuing marks will almost certainly improve the uniformity of marking practices and hence make the marks issued much more consistently meaningful. Another purpose is to make the systematic conversion of numerical measures into course marks simple enough to compete successfully with the unsystematic, hit-or-miss procedures that

[35]This method was developed in cooperation with Dean Dewey B. Stuit at the State University of Iowa. It was described in *Technical Bulletin No. 8* of the University Examinations Service, distributed to staff members of the College of Liberal Arts with the approval of the Educational Policy Committee in November, 1954.

some instructors actually do use. To this end the procedures make use of statistics that are easy to determine or can be estimated with sufficient accuracy by short-cut methods.

One basic assumption of the method is that the five-letter marks should represent equal intervals on the score scale. This is an alternative to strict *grading on the curve*, which disregards numerical score values, considers only the rank order of the scores, and gives the top 7 percent A's, the next 23 percent B's, and so on. It is also an alternative to the use of unequal numerical intervals, which usually result when the end points of these intervals are located at gaps or natural breaks in the distribution of scores. Most such gaps are chance affairs, attributable largely to chance errors of measurement. Hence they seldom reflect natural points of division between discrete levels of ability.

Acceptance of this assumption means that there can be no a priori certainty that expected percentages of A's, B's, or any other mark will be assigned. Indeed, in a particular class group there might be no A's or no F's at all. However, in large class groups (and, in the long run, in small class groups) the distribution of letter marks will ordinarily approximate a normal distribution.

The method makes use of the median score as the basic reference point or origin of the letter mark scale. Since there is seldom a meaningful *absolute zero* on any scale of academic achievement, it is almost always necessary to use some other reference point in setting the scale. The median or middle score provides a reference point that is reasonably easy to determine and reasonably stable from one sample to another. If the distribution of scores is skewed, the median is a more typical or representative measure than the mean.

When a five-unit scale is used for measuring achievement, the standard deviation of the test scores provides a unit of convenient size. The usual range of scores in a distribution of 20 to 40 scores equals about four or five standard deviation units. Although the standard deviation is tedious to calculate without machine assistance, it can be estimated quite simply, with reasonable accuracy, for purposes of assigning marks.

Finally, the method of mark assignment here described makes provision for different distributions of marks in classes having different levels of average academic ability. The method does not require such differences, but it does allow for them if the faculty decides in favor of them. Mention was made earlier in the chapter of the differences of opinion that exist in school and college faculties on this question. Probably most faculties would favor giving more high marks in classes of high ability. But when they vote for this policy they also vote, whether explicitly or not, for giving lower than average marks in some other classes. There are both advantages and disadvantages in differentiating levels of marking to correspond with ability levels in various classes.

The means by which marks are adjusted to reflect class ability levels is illustrated in Figure 12.1. Essentially it involves moving the scale of measures on which the marks are to be based up or down in relation to the marking scale. The marking base measures are usually obtained by adding test scores and the numerical equivalents of marks on papers, projects, recitations, and so on. Figure 12.1 shows how marks might be adjusted for classes of two different ability levels, average and exceptional. The marking scale is shown in the center. Distributions of marking base measures are shown as normal distributions. For the class of exceptional ability the distribution of marking base measures is higher on the marking

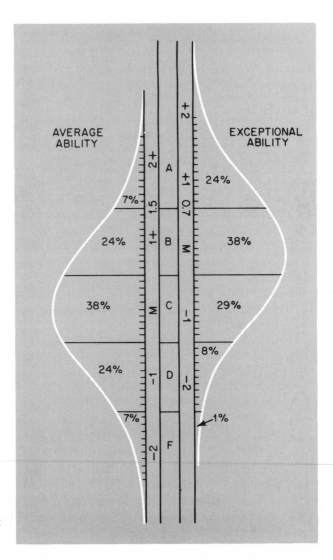

FIGURE 12.1
Adjusting Grades for Different
Ability Levels

scale than it is for the class of average ability. Some details of Figure 12.1 are worth noting.

For a class of average ability the lower limit of the A's is located 1.5 standard deviations above the mean of the measures on which the marks are to be based. With mark intervals of one standard deviation the lower limit of the B's would be 0.5 standard deviations above the mean. The lower limit of the C's would be 0.5 standard deviations *below* the mean, and the lower limit of the D's 1.5 standard deviations below the mean. From a table of areas under the normal curve one can determine that with these limits, 7 percent of the marks would be A's, 24 percent B's, 38 percent C's, 24 percent D's, and 7 percent F's. Using numerical values of 4 for A, 3 for B, 2 for C, 1 for D, and 0 for F, the grade point average for this average level grade distribution is 2.00. Since that grade point average falls exactly in the middle of the distribution of numerical values, its percentile equivalent is 50. The foregoing explains what each of the figures in the fifth row (average ability level) of Table 12.2 means, and how all were derived from the first (lower limit of the A's). But perhaps a second illustration would still be helpful.

For a class of exceptional ability the lower limit of the A's is located only 0.7 standard deviations above the mean of the measures on which the marks are to be based. With mark intervals of one standard deviation, the lower limit of the B's would be 0.3 standard deviations *below* the mean. The lower limit of the C's would be 1.3 standard deviations below the mean, and the lower limit of the D's 2.3 standard deviations below it. From a table of areas under the normal curve one can determine that with these limits 24 percent of the marks would be A's, 38 percent B's, 29 percent C's, 8 percent D's, and 1 percent F's. Using the same numerical values as before (A = 4, B = 3, C = 2, D = 1, F = 0) the grade point average for this exceptional distribution of grades is 2.80. This average is 0.8 standard deviations above the mean (2.00) of a distribution of average (not exceptional) grades. Thus it corresponds to a percentile of 79, for in a normal distribution 79 percent of the measures lie below a point which is 0.8 standard deviations above the mean. Again these statements explain the source and meaning of the figures in the first row (exceptional ability) of Table 12.2.

Mark adjustment data for classes at these two and at five other levels of ability, ranging from somewhat below to well above average, are presented in Table 12.2. The difference between successive levels in the lower limit of the A's is 0.2 standard deviation units. As a necessary but not easily demonstrable consequence of these lower limit differences there are corresponding differences of 0.2 between successive levels in the grade point averages. These differences seem sufficiently small, and the range of levels sufficiently wide, to accommodate most situations in which mark adjustments are needed. Of course the differences could be made smaller

TABLE 12.2.   LETTER MARK DISTRIBUTION STATISTICS FOR CLASSES AT
SEVEN LEVELS OF ABILITY

Ability Level	Lower Limit of A's	Percent of Marks					Ability Measures	
		A	B	C	D	F	GPA	Percentile
Exceptional	0.7	24	38	29	8	1	2.80	79
Superior	0.9	18	36	32	12	2	2.60	73
Good	1.1	14	32	36	15	3	2.40	66
Fair	1.3	10	29	37	20	4	2.20	58
Average	1.5	7	24	38	24	7	2.00	50
Weak	1.7	4	20	37	29	10	1.80	42
Poor	1.9	3	15	36	32	14	1.60	34

or larger, or the range of levels extended if either should seem necessary. The determining value in each row of the table is the first, which tells where the lower limit of the A's is located in standard deviation units above the mean. Given that value and tables of areas under the normal curve, all other figures in the row can be calculated.

Differentiating levels of marking requires uniform ability measures for the pupils in various classes. This could be provided either by scores on some test of academic aptitude or by grade-point averages in previous courses. Of course the mark a particular student receives should not be directly affected by his aptitude test score or his previous grade-point average. Few instructors would argue that one student should get a higher mark than another simply because he is thought to have more ability. His achievement should determine the mark he gets. But since there is a substantial correlation between prior measures of ability and subsequent measures of achievement, it seems reasonable that the average mark in a class of more able students should be higher than the average mark in a class of less able students.

ASSIGNING LETTER MARKS

Four steps are involved in this process of assigning marks.

1. Select from Table 12.2 a distribution of marks appropriate to the level of ability of the class being graded.
2. Calculate the median and the standard deviation of the scores on which the marks are to be based.
3. Determine the lower score limits of the A, B, C, and D mark intervals, using the median, the standard deviation, and the appropriate lower limit factor from Table 12.2.

4. Assign the designated marks to the students whose scores fall in intervals determined for each mark.

Table 12.2 presents mark distribution statistics for classes at seven different levels of academic ability. The first column lists descriptive labels of the ability levels. The last two columns, headed "ability measures," provide means for deciding which level is appropriate for a particular class. If the grade-point averages (GPA) of the class members in their previous course work is known, the mean of these GPA's indicates which ability level is appropriate for the class. If, for example, the class mean of those GPA's was found to be 2.24, the teacher could conclude that this class is slightly above average in ability, so that the level designated "fair" would be appropriate.

If grade point averages are unavailable, inconvenient to use, or undesirable for some other reason, average aptitude test scores can be used in place of the grade point averages. For this purpose, all students in the school or college must have taken the same test or battery of tests, which yields a measure of the academic ability of each student. If the scores of those students are available in the form of local school percentile ranks, then the average of those percentile ranks could also be used to select the appropriate ability level. If, for the hypothetical class we have in mind, that average turned out to be 45, the instructor could conclude that it is below average in ability and that the mark distribution for a *weak* class would be appropriate.

The five columns in the center of Table 12.2 indicate, for each ability level, what percent of the marks would be A's, B's, and so on if the distribution of numerical measures being converted to grades were perfectly normal. Since few distributions are likely to be perfectly normal, the percentage of each mark assigned in any actual case will usually differ somewhat from the percentage indicated in Table 12.2. One could, of course, arrange the numerical measures in rank order and convert them to letter marks on the basis of the "ideal" percentages for a class of the specified level of ability. But, as suggested earlier, this process is open to more of the criticisms of grading on the curve than is the process being described here.

The second step in the process requires calculation of the median and the standard deviation. To calculate the median, follow the steps outlined below.

1. Arrange the scores in order from high to low.
2. If the number of scores is odd, the middle score is the median. The middle score in an odd number of scores is the score whose rank order is represented by the whole number just larger than half the number of scores. For example, in a set of 25 scores the median is the thirteenth score (13 is just larger than 12.5).
3. If the number of scores is even, the median is the average of the two scores

closest to the middle of the distribution. For example, in a set of 26 scores the median is the average of the thirteenth and fourteenth scores.

To estimate the standard deviation this short-cut approximation is recommended.

Divide the difference between the sums of scores in the upper and lower one-sixths of the distribution of scores by one-half of the number of scores in the distribution.

Suppose we have twenty-six scores. The sum of the top four scores (upper one-sixth of the distribution) might be 137. The sum of the bottom four scores (lower one-sixth) might be 69. Then the estimated standard deviation would be

$$\frac{137 - 69}{13} = \frac{68}{13} = 5.23$$

The third step in the process, determining the lower score limits, makes use of the second column of Table 12.2 headed "Lower Limit of A's." The values in this column show how far the lower limit of the score interval for A marks lies above the median, in standard deviation units. In the case of a class of "fair" ability, the A mark interval begins 1.3 standard deviations above the median of the score distribution. In the case of a class of weak ability, the A mark interval begins 1.7 standard deviations above the median. Since the score interval that corresponds to each mark is one standard deviation in extent, once the lower limit of the A interval is determined, the lower limits of the B, C, and D intervals can be found by successive subtractions of the standard deviation from the lower limit of the A's.

As an example of this process consider a set of scores having a median value of 66.2 and a standard deviation of 6.5 for a class whose ability level is regarded by the teacher as "good." Table 12.2 indicates that the lower limit of the A mark interval should be 1.1 standard deviations (6.5) above the median (66.2). Hence this lower limit is 73.35. The lower limit of the B mark interval is one standard deviation less, or 66.85. Similarly, the lower limit of the C marks is found to be 60.35, and of the D marks, 53.85.

The fourth step, assigning the marks, is facilitated by the recording of the score intervals for each letter grade in whole score units. In the example above, A marks would be assigned to all scores of 74 or higher, B marks to scores from 67 to 73, C marks to scores from 61 to 66, D marks to scores from 54 to 60, and F marks to scores of 53 or lower.

Table 12.3 illustrates the application of this method of mark assignment to a sample problem. The previous grade point averages of the students in this class, as well as their aptitude test percentiles, indicate

TABLE 12.3. SAMPLE PROBLEM IN LETTER MARK ASSIGNMENT

A. Data for the problem
  1. Class ability level measures
    a. Mean GPA on previous years' courses 2.17
    b. Mean percentile on aptitude test 56.3
    c. Appropriate grade distribution (Table 12.2) *Fair*
  2. Achievement scores (number of students = 38)

112	100	93	84	78	72	66	51
109	97	91	83	75	71	62	47
106	97	90	82	75	70	59	44
105	95	89	81	75	69	59	
104	95	84	80	74	68	58	

B. Calculations from the data

  1. Median $\dfrac{81 + 80}{2} = 80.5$

  2. Standard deviation $\dfrac{636 - 318}{19} = 16.7$

Marks	Lower Limits	Intervals	Number	Percent
A	$80.5 + 1.3 \times 16.7 = 102.2$	103–112	5	13
B	$102.2 - 16.7 = 85.5$	86–102	9	24
C	$85.5 - 16.7 = 68.8$	69–85	15	39
D	$68.8 - 16.7 = 52.1$	53–68	6	16
F		44–52	3	8
			38	100

that the grade distribution for a class slightly better than average, designated in Table 12.2 as "fair," would be appropriate. Since there are 38 students in the class, the median is the average of the nineteenth and twentieth scores. The top and bottom sixths in a class of 38 include six scores each. Hence the six highest scores, from 100 to 112, are added to obtain the sum of 636. The sum of the six lowest scores, from 44 to 59, is 318. The difference between 636 and 318, divided by half the number of scores, gives the estimated standard deviation.

    Using the lower limit factor of 1.3 (obtained from Table 12.2 for a "fair" class) in conjunction with a standard deviation of 16.7 and a median of 80.5, it is determined that the lower limit of the A mark interval is 102.2. Successive subtractions of the standard deviation give the lower limits of the other mark intervals. From these lower limits the whole number score intervals are easily determined and the appropriate letter mark can be assigned to each numerical score. Note that the actual percentage of scores to which each mark was assigned differs somewhat from the ideal values of Table 12.2 reflecting the fact that the distribution of scores given in Table 12.3 was not perfectly normal.

ASSIGNING STANINES

A system of mark assignment similar to the one just described has also been developed for use with stanine marks. As mentioned earlier in the chapter, a stanine system of marking has some advantages over the five-letter system. Like the method for assigning letter marks, the method for assigning stanines uses the median as a reference (or starting) point. But since the stanine scale has nine intervals instead of five, it is necessary to use half the standard deviation, instead of the standard deviation, as the scale unit. The usual range of a distribution of 20 to 40 scores extends for approximately nine of these semistandard deviation units.

Table 12.4 presents stanine distribution statistics for classes at seven different levels of ability. The first and last columns of Table 12.4 are identical with those of Table 12.2. The lower-limit factors differ because they are expressed in semistandard deviation units rather than full standard deviation units and because they define the lower limit of the top one-ninth rather than the top one-fifth of the score scale. The remaining nine columns indicate expected percentages of each stanine score (if the distribution of scores to be converted is normal) in classes at each level of ability.

TABLE 12.4. STANINE DISTRIBUTION STATISTICS FOR CLASSES AT SEVEN LEVELS OF ABILITY

Ability Level	Lower Limit of 9's	Distribution of Stanines									Ability Measures	
		9	8	7	6	5	4	3	2	1	Mean Stanine	Percentile
Exceptional	1.90	18	16	19	21	13	8	4	1	0	6.60	79
Superior	2.30	13	14	18	20	16	11	6	1	1	6.20	73
Good	2.70	9	11	17	21	17	13	7	3	2	5.80	66
Fair	3.10	6	9	14	20	19	15	10	4	3	5.40	58
Average	3.50	4	7	12	17	20	17	12	7	4	5.00	50
Weak	3.90	3	4	10	15	19	20	14	9	6	4.60	42
Poor	4.30	2	3	7	13	17	21	17	11	9	4.20	34

The use of the term "stanine" to describe these scores is open to criticism on two grounds.

1. True stanines are determined from a rank order of scores, not from the median and half standard deviation of the distribution of scores.
2. True stanines always show the same distribution of scores, not differing distributions depending on the ability level of the class, as indicated in Table 12.4.

But since the scale used is basically a "standard nine" scale, it seems better to use the familiar term "stanine" somewhat imprecisely than to invent some new term. One can, of course, assign stanines on the basis of the percentage distibutions shown in Table 12.4. This process is somewhat simpler than to determine stanine intervals from the median and semi-standard deviation. The only drawback is that use of the percentage distributions involves the questionable assumption that the distribution of achievements in a small class is perfectly normal, or at least that the departures from normality are of no consequence. If one prefers to assume that the irregularities observed in the distribution of raw scores are not due to chance errors of measurement or to peculiarities of the test, but do, in fact, reflect with reasonable accuracy the differences among the students in true achievement, then the linear conversion of raw scores to stanines will be preferred. In most cases either approach will give substantially the same results.

The process of transforming scores to stanines is very much like that of transforming scores to letter marks, as illustrated in Table 12.5.

TABLE 12.5. SAMPLE PROBLEM IN STANINE ASSIGNMENT

A. Data for the problem
  1. Class ability level measures
    a. Mean stanine on previous year's courses 5.34
    b. Mean percentile on aptitude test 56.3
    c. Appropriate grade distribution (Table 12.4) *Fair*
  2. Achievement scores (number of students = 38)

112	100	93	84	78	72	66	51
109	97	91	83	75	71	62	47
106	97	90	82	75	70	59	44
105	95	89	81	75	69	59	
104	95	84	80	74	68	58	

B. Calculations from the data

  1. Median $\dfrac{81 + 80}{2} = 80.5$

  2. Semistandard Deviation $\dfrac{636 - 318}{38} = 8.37$

Stanines	Lower Limits	Intervals	Number	Percent
9	$80.5 + 3.1 \times 8.37 = 106.45$	107–112	2	5
8	$106.45 - 8.37 = 98.08$	99–106	4	11
7	$98.08 - 8.37 = 89.71$	90–98	7	18
6	$89.71 - 8.37 = 81.34$	82–89	5	13
5	$81.34 - 8.37 = 72.97$	73–81	7	18
4	$72.97 - 8.37 = 64.60$	65–72	6	16
3	$64.60 - 8.37 = 56.23$	57–64	4	11
2	$56.23 - 8.37 = 47.86$	48–56	1	3
1		44–47	2	5
			38	100

A distribution that is appropriate to the level of ability of the class is selected from Table 12.4. The median score is calculated. Instead of estimating the standard deviation, however, one estimates half of the standard deviation when stanines are involved. The rule for this estimation is:

> Divide the difference between the sums of scores in the upper and lower one-sixths of the distribution of scores by the number of scores in the distribution.

From the median, the semistandard deviation, and the appropriate lower-limit factor from Table 12.4, calculate the exact values of the lower limits of each stanine score interval. This process is illustrated in the lower section of Table 12.5. Rounding these exact values upward to integral values, the raw score limits of each stanine interval can be determined and the stanine marks assigned. Note that since these stanine marks were assigned on the basis of equal score intervals, the percentages of each stanine mark do not correspond exactly to those anticipated in a normal distribution of scores or marks.

THE BASIS FOR MARKS

When the instructor determines a course mark, as he usually does, by combining marks on daily recitations, homework, term papers, and scores on quizzes and tests, each of the components carries more or less weight in determining the final mark. To obtain marks of maximum validity, the instructor must give each component the proper weight, neither too much nor too little. How can he determine what those weights ought to be? How can he determine what they actually are? If what they are does not correspond to what they should be, what can he do?

It is not easy to give a firm, precise answer to the question of how much influence each component ought to have in determining the final mark. But several guiding principles can be suggested.

In general, the use of several different kinds of indicators of competence is better than use of only one, provided that each of the indicators is relevant to the objectives of the course and provided also that it can be observed or measured with reasonable reliability.

Exclusive reliance on tests, for example, may give an unfair advantage to students who have special test-taking skills and may unfairly handicap students who give the best account of their achievements in discussions, on projects, or in other situations. But irrelevant accomplishments, such as mere glibness, personal charm, or self-assurance, should not be mistaken for solid command of knowledge. Nor should much weight be placed on vague intangibles or subjective impressions that cannot be quantified reliably.

If measures of each component aspect of achievement are highly correlated, the problem of weighting them properly is far less critical than if they are quite unrelated. For most courses the various measurable aspects of achievement are related closely enough so that proper weighting is not a critical problem. The natural "unweighted" weighting will give marks almost as valid as those resulting from more sophisticated statistical procedures.

The actual weight that a component of the final mark does carry depends on the variablility of its measures and the correlations of those measures with measures of the other components. This makes the precise influence of a component quite difficult to determine. As a first approximation to the weight of a component, the standard deviation of the measures of that component serves quite well. If one set of scores is twice as variable as another, the first set is likely to carry about twice the weight of the second.

Table 12.6 shows that the influence (weight) of one component (for example, scores on one test) on a composite (the sum of scores on three tests, in this example) depends on the variability of the test scores. The top section of the table displays the scores of three students, Tom, Dick, and Harry, on three tests, X, Y, and Z, along with their total scores

TABLE 12.6. WEIGHTED TEST SCORES

Tests	X	Y	Z	Total
Student scores				
Tom	53	65	18	136
Dick	50	59	42	151
Harry	47	71	30	148
Student ranks				
Tom	1	2	3	3
Dick	2	3	1	1
Harry	3	1	2	2
Test characteristics				
Total points	100.0	75	50	225.0
Mean score	50.0	65	30	145.0
Standard Deviation	2.5	5	10	6.5
Weighted scores				
Tom	$\frac{\times 4}{212}$	$\frac{\times 2}{130}$	$\frac{\times 1}{18}$	360
Dick	200	118	42	360
Harry	188	142	30	360

on the three tests. Dick has the highest total and Tom the lowest. The next section shows how the students ranked on the three tests. Each of them made the highest score on one test, middle score on a second, and lowest score on the third. Thus the totals of their ranks, and their average ranks, are exactly the same. But note, for future reference, that the ranks of their total scores on the three tests are the same as their ranks on Test Z.

The third section of the table gives the maximum possible scores (total points), the mean scores, and the standard deviations of the scores on the three tests. Test X has the highest number of total points. Test Y has the highest mean score. Test Z has scores with the greatest variability.

On which test was it most important to do well? On which was the payoff for ranking first the highest, and the penalty for ranking last the heaviest? Clearly on Test Z, the test with the greatest variability of scores. Which test ranked the students in the same order as their final ranking, based on total scores? Again the answer is Test Z. Thus the influence of one component on a composite depends not on total points or mean score but on score variability.

Now if the three tests should have carried equal weight, they can be made to do so by weighting their scores to make the standard deviations equal. This is illustrated in the last section of the table. Scores on Test X are multiplied by 4, to change their standard deviation from 2.5 to 10, the same as on Test Z. Scores on Test Y are multiplied by 2, to change their standard deviation to 10 also. With equal standard deviations the tests carry equal weight, and give students having the same average rank on the tests the same total scores.

When the whole possible range of scores is used, score variability is closely related to the extent of the available score scale. This means that scores on a 40-item objective test are likely to carry about four times the weight of scores on a 10-point essay test question, provided that scores extend across the whole range in both cases. But if only a small part of the possible scale of scores is actually used, the length of that scale can be a very misleading guide to the variability of the scores.

In view of the difficulty of determining precisely how much weight each component ought to carry, the difficulty of determining precisely how much weight each component does, in fact, carry seems less serious as an obstacle to valid marks. Further, as we have noted, if the components are quite highly related, the difference between optimum and accidental weighting may be hard to detect, as it affects the validity of the marks. But if the instructor finds a serious discrepancy between what he thinks the component weights ought to be and what they in fact are, two courses are open to him.

One is to multiply the underweighted components by some weighting factor to increase their variability and hence increase the weight they carry. The other is to increase the number of observations of the underweighted component, or the precision with which it is measured, and hence also to increase the weight it carries. Of the two methods, the first is likely to be more convenient. The second is likely to yield the more reliable, and in this case the more valid, marks.

If an instructor has promised his class, for example, that the final mark will be based on five components, weighted as follows:

Contributions in class	15%
Daily assignments	20%
Term paper or project	15%
Midterm test	20%
Final test	30%

then he should plan to obtain enough independent scores on "contributions in class" so that the variability of the total of those scores is about half the variability of the scores on the final test. By the same token, the final test should be half again as long (or include half again as many items) as the midterm test.

A wise instructor will warn his students that the actual weight of each component may differ somewhat from the intended weight. But he can assure them, and rest assured himself, that if he has planned carefully to make the weights what he intended, the inevitable deviations of the actual from the ideal weights will not affect the validity of his marks appreciably.

One final admonition. It is a mistake to convert test scores to letter marks, record these in the grade book, and then reconvert the letter marks to numbers for purposes of calculating the final average. A better procedure is to record the test scores and other numerical measures directly. These can be added, with whatever weighting seems appropriate, to obtain a composite score which can then be converted into the final mark.

Not only does the recording of scores rather than letters usually save time in the long run, it also contributes to accuracy. Whenever a range of scores, some higher, others lower, is converted to the same letter mark, information is lost. Usually this information is not retrieved when the letter marks are changed back to numbers so they can be added or averaged. Each B, whether a high B or a low B in terms of the score on which it was based, is given the same value in the reconversion. Hence to avoid the loss of score information it is usually desirable to record the raw scores, not the scores after conversion to letter marks.

ILLUSTRATION OF MARK DETERMINATION

The process of combining quantitative estimates of achievement on the basis of written work, class observations, quizzes, and tests is illustrated in Table 12.7. This table is intended to represent excerpts from a teacher's class record book showing all the measurements combined to determine the final course mark. In this case all test scores and measures of quality of work on special assignments and projects were recorded numerically. These numerical scores, added together without special weighting, yield the sums, which were then converted into letter marks (and in this case, for purposes of illustration, to stanines as well). The median value of these sums is 432.

The distributions appropriate for a class of exceptional ability were selected, for both marks and stanines, because these were graduate students for whom, according to college rules, any mark below C carries no credit. The names, of course, are fictitious. Values in the bottom row of the table are estimates of the standard deviation of each set of scores. These figures indicate that the final test carried greatest weight, about one-fourth of the total, while the "article reports" assignment carried least weight, about one-fiftieth. The figures in parentheses near the titles for each set of scores indicate the maximum possible value of those scores. Thus the maximum possible total score would have been 710.

It is interesting to note that application of Kuder-Richardson Formula 21 to these scores yields an estimate of about 0.98 for the reliability of the composite scores. Hence whatever other failings these marks may have, they cannot be regarded as seriously unreliable. On the other hand, it is probably unusual for marks in a class to be based on 11 different measures as highly sensitive to student differences and as highly related from measure to measure as these are.

ONE SOLUTION TO TWO PRACTICAL PROBLEMS

Instructors sometimes feel inclined to include marks on daily work in the final course work, not so much to improve the validity of the final mark as to influence students to do the daily work. The daily assignments, after all, are intended to serve primarily as learning exercises, not as measures of achievement. Including these daily work marks also adds considerable labor, often without improving final mark validity appreciably. There is a way of maintaining the incentive to do the daily work while avoiding the labor of adding a multitude of numbers for each student.

TABLE 12.7. CLASS RECORD DATA AND MARK ASSIGNMENT

Subject: Test Construction   Date: First Semester, 1963-64

Sources of Scores	Multiple-Choice Items (20)	True-False Items (20)	Discrimination Item (15)	Article Reports (10)	Midterm Test (150)	Mean and Sigma (35)	Percentile Ranks (30)	Discrimination Indices (30)	Test Project (75)	Take-Home Test (150)	Final Test (175)	Sum (710)	Stanine	Mark
Dates	10-2	10-14	10-25	11-6	11-13	11-28	12-10	12-16	1-15	1-20	1-23			
Names														
Beck, Charles	9	7	7	5	80	21	17	16	53	91	83	389	6	C
Beebe, Paul	16	8	12	9	100	18	19	29	66	133	125	535	9	A
Bell, Marion	3	1	2	1	69	12	20	16	47	88	73	332	4	C
Blinn, Lula	13	18	7	6	102	31	15	16	61	111	125	505	8	A
Bruno, Alice	7	13	10	6	62	14	12	18	43	85	75	345	5	C
Colgan, Mary	10	5	2	7	115	25	25	17	67	86	113	472	8	B
Hooper, Martha	12	5	6	4	70	8	8	14	29	87	23	266	3	D
Horton, Elizabeth	16	16	11	7	124	18	28	22	68	134	135	579	9	A
Kopp, Martha	9	12	6	5	99	15	19	21	55	92	94	427	6	B
Kruse, Theodore	17	16	14	4	108	30	14	20	63	90	120	496	8	A
Merlin, Dawn	14	9	10	6	144	30	18	22	70	125	137	585	9	A
Murphy, Edward	10	5	8	2	75	20	20	11	60	79	97	396	6	C
Peterson, Sandra	5	5	1	2	83	17	13	25	41	69	64	311	4	D
Potter, Marilyn	6	2	3	2	78	22	15	26	62	94	103	412	6	B
Randall, Peggy	4	6	2	7	134	21	24	24	70	145	157	596	9	A
Roman, Mary	8	8	4	2	118	18	18	30	60	136	123	519	9	A
Sautos, Betty	4	2	6	1	83	20	17	18	66	98	86	413	6	B
Shelby, Marilyn	5	7	3	3	104	19	10	24	47	90	70	376	5	C
Silver, Enid	4	4	6	5	98	24	15	17	62	100	104	446	7	B
Snell, Daniel	6	10	3	2	117	18	16	30	50	81	117	437	7	B
Spooner, Janet	9	8	3	4	121	16	14	22	60	93	105	463	7	B
Sweeney, Nancy	5	10	7	1	104	18	19	12	59	107	110	462	7	B
White, Shirley	7	3	4	3	91	20	14	16	46	87	94	381	5	C
Williams, Roberta	3	5	5	5	85	15	10	16	41	109	97	391	6	C
(Standard Deviations)	4.08	4.58	3.33	2.08	20.58	5.58	4.75	5.17	10.08	19.5	27.0	86.75		

This way helps to solve another problem too: the problem of the anguished student who just missed a higher mark by a point or two. Here is the way.

Announce to students that their final marks will be determined primarily by their scores on major tests (midterm and final perhaps) and one or two major papers or projects. After points on these few major measures of achievement have been added, lower limits for each of the marks will be determined. Then for any students whose total puts him within three (or perhaps five) points of the next higher mark, the record of daily work will be reviewed. If the record shows that the student has done the assignments conscientiously and reasonably well, he will be given the next higher mark.

Under this system most students will feel sufficiently motivated to do the daily assignments. They are less likely to feel that only an inconsequential deficiency in achievement kept them from getting a higher mark. Respect for the fairness of the instructor's marking procedures is likely to be enhanced.

SUMMARY

Some of the principal ideas developed in this chapter are summarized in these 35 statements.

1. Marking systems are frequent subjects of educational controversy because the process is difficult, because different educational philosophies call for different marking systems, and because the task is sometimes disagreeable.
2. The belief that "child-centered" education has no need for marks is fallacious.
3. Marks can measure the degree of attainment of the central purpose of education, gaining command of useful verbal knowledge.
4. Marks contribute to valid self-evaluations by the pupil.
5. It is low achievement rather than low marks that is the cause of pupil anxieties and dislike of school.
6. There is no good reason to believe that marking systems tend to suppress creativity.
7. It is unwise to attempt to base marks on achievement in relation to ability.
8. Measurements and reports of achievement are essential in education, and no better means than marks seems likely to appear.
9. To serve effectively their purposes of stimulating, directing, and rewarding student efforts to learn, marks must be valid and reliable.
10. There is nothing wrong with encouraging students to work for high marks if the marks are valid measures of achievement.
11. The major shortcomings of marks are attributable to frequent lack of clearly defined and scrupulously observed meanings for the marks and to frequent lack of sufficient good evidence to use as a basis for assigning marks.
12. Marking standards often vary from instructor to instructor and from institution to institution.
13. Girls usually get higher marks than boys of equal ability and achievement.

14. Marks will tend to lose their meaning if the institution lacks a clearly defined marking system or does not require instructors to mark in conformity with the system.
15. In a majority of the educational institutions in this country, relative marking systems, which make use of letter marks such as A, B, C, D, and F, have replaced presumably absolute marks, which make use of percentages.
16. It is extremely difficult to determine percentage marks so that they do, in fact, express absolute levels of achievement.
17. Evidence of the unreliability of percentage marks, obtained by Starch and Elliott early in this century, was largely responsible for the shift toward letter marking.
18. Variations from class to class in ability and achievement complicate but do not preclude reasonable marking on a relative basis.
19. Relative marking is as likely as absolute marking to stimulate student efforts to achieve.
20. Instructors can simplify some marking problems by regarding a mark as a measurement rather than as an evaluation.
21. Marks should ordinarily be based exclusively on achievement and should not attempt to indicate attitude, effort, or deportment.
22. Marks measuring status tend to be more reliable, more meaningful, and educationally more constructive than marks measuring growth.
23. The discouraging effects of consistently low marks can be counteracted better by providing students with diverse opportunities to excel than by basing marks on growth.
24. The use of multiple marks on various aspects of achievement can improve marking but may cost more in extra effort than the improvement is worth.
25. The more marks available in the system to indicate different levels of achievement, the more reliable the marks will be, but the less convenient the system may be to use.
26. Pass-fail marks cannot do the job that marks are supposed to do as well as more finely graded marks.
27. A return to numerical marks would emphasize their use as measurements and would simplify the calculation of grade point averages.
28. Publication of distributions of marks, course by course, is essential to quality control of the marking system.
29. Relative marking that divides the score scale into equal intervals is an alternative to strict marking on the curve.
30. A system of relative marking that makes provision for different distributions of marks in classes having different levels of average academic ability is possible.
31. An equal-interval relative marking system may require calculation of some average measure like the median and some measure of variability like the standard deviation.
32. In general, the numerical basis for assigning marks should include diverse components, such as contributions in class, homework, projects, and test scores.
33. The weight carried by each component toward determination of the composite depends on the variability of the component scores.
34. Precise weighting of the components of a numerical basis for assigning marks is not crucial to the quality of the marks assigned.
35. Some instructors simplify the process of mark determination, and forestall student discontent, by considering the completeness and quality of class work only for those students whose composite achievement score is near the upper limit of a mark interval.

PART IV

TEST ANALYSIS AND EVALUATION

> I do not believe . . . that inefficient examining can in the long run
> contribute to good training, and I infer from this the belief that
> the only course an examining body can properly take is to strive
> continually to improve its examinations so that they give the
> maximum support to good training.
>
> R. A. C. OLIVER

13

HOW TO
JUDGE THE QUALITY OF
A CLASSROOM TEST

What makes a classroom test a good test? This question concerns both students and instructors whenever a test is given. It is one of the most basic questions confronting those who make and use classroom tests. Too often it goes unanswered or is badly answered for lack of sound standards of quality and convenient techniques of applying them.

Some of the important factors that need to be considered in judging the quality of a test are suggested by the 10 topics and questions that follow:

1. *Relevance.* Have the types of questions included in the test been selected judiciously to test the desired achievements?
2. *Balance.* Does the proportion of items dealing with each aspect of achievement conform with the test constructor's intent, as expressed in the specifications for the test?
3. *Efficiency.* Does the test make efficient use of the instructor's limited time for test preparation and grading and of the student's limited time in the examination period?

4. *Objectivity.* Are the questions clear enough and the answers definite enough so that any expert in the field covered by the test would get a perfect or near-perfect score?

5. *Specificity.* Do the questions require achievements specific to the field covered by the test so that even intelligent, testwise novices who have not studied the field would expect scores near the chance level?

6. *Difficulty.* Are the test questions and the test as a whole appropriate in difficulty, neither too hard nor too easy to function effectively with the examinees for which the test is intended?

7. *Discrimination.* Do the individual questions discriminate sharply between examinees of higher and lower achievement and does the test as a whole yield a wide distribution of scores for students who differ in achievement?

8. *Reliability.* Does the test yield scores that agree with those obtained from equally good independent measurements of the same achievement?

9. *Fairness.* Is the test constructed and administered so that each student has a good, and an equal, chance to demonstrate his real achievement in the area covered by the test?

10. *Speededness.* Is the test appropriate in length for the time available, so that good use is made of the examination period without allowing the examinee's rate of work to have an undue influence on the score he receives?

The answers to some of these questions can be obtained by studying the test itself and the written specifications used in developing it, if any are available. The answers to other questions can be obtained from an analysis of test and item scores.

A sample test analysis report is shown as Exhibit 13.1 on the following page. It consists of an outline of qualities or characteristics, paralleled by three columns of data. The first column suggests certain standards. The second reports data for the test under analysis. The third evaluates these data in relation to the standards. (An earlier version of this approach to the analysis of classroom tests was published in 1954.[1])

Subsequent sections of this chapter, where the test characteristics are discussed in some detail, will present justifications for the ideal standards suggested in the sample test analysis report. Although these standards are reasonable for most classroom tests, they may not all be appropriate to certain special tests. If an instructor feels that some of the standards are not suitable, he may disregard ratings based on them. Better still, he may work out more appropriate standards and reevaluate the test in terms of these new standards.

This analysis is applied most easily to objective tests. It is, however, applicable at least in part to essay-type tests, such as those used in history and literature, and to problem tests, such as those used in physics, mathe-

[1]Robert L. Ebel, "Procedures for the Analysis of Classroom Tests," *Educational and Psychological Measurement,* vol. 14 (1954), 352–64.

EXHIBIT 13.1

Test Analysis Report

Test title: *Educational Measurement* Group Tested: *Graduate Students* N = *40*
Instructor: *Jones* ____ Date of Test: *5/19/-* Score = *Number right*
Number of Items: *50* Choices per Item: *5* Time Limit: *45 minutes*

	Characteristic	Ideal	Actual	Rating
I.	**Relevance and Balance**			
A.	Terminology	less than *20%*	*20%*	*High*
B.	Factual Information	less than *20%*	*18%*	*OK*
C.	Generalization	less than *20%*	*10%*	*OK*
D.	Explanation	more than *10%*	*14%*	*OK*
E.	Calculation	more than *5%*	*12%*	*Good*
F.	Prediction	more than *10%*	*10%*	*OK*
G.	Recommended Action	more than *5%*	*16%*	*Good*
II.	**Discrimination**			
A.	Item			
1.	High (.40 and up)	more than *25%*	*18%*	*Low*
2.	Moderate (.20 to .39)	less than *25%*	*26%*	*O.K.*
3.	Low (.01 to .19)	less than *15%*	*34%*	*High*
4.	Zero or Negative	less than *5%*	*22%*	*High*
B.	Score			
1.	Mean	about *30.0*	*32.5*	*Good*
2.	Standard Deviation	more than *6.67*	*5.84*	*Low*
3.	Reliability	more than *.80*	*.86*	*Good*
4.	Probable Error	more than ____	*1.47*	
III.	**Speededness**			
	Completed Tests	more than *90%*	*97%*	*Good*

matics, and other areas. The only restriction is that individual questions
must be separately scored. The analysis is most significant when applied
to tests given in large classes, but it can provide useful information in
classes as small as 10 or 15 students. Further reference to and explanations of the test analysis report of Exhibit 13.1 will be made in the discussion of the aspects of test quality to which they are related.

RELEVANCE

What "relevance" means, as the term is used here, may be suggested by the example of a set of criteria of relevance for a particular test, such as those presented in Exhibit 13.2. Note that the criteria of relevance are preceded by a brief statement of the purpose of the test. Whether the purpose is a proper purpose or whether these criteria are good criteria, in the sense of specifying the right kind of items for the purpose of this particular test, is not at issue here. For example, the specification that all the items should be in multiple-choice form is somewhat arbitrary and may not be at all crucial to the overall quality of the test. At this point in the discussion we are not concerned primarily with the correctness of specified criteria of relevance. The question that should concern us is whether these criteria are clear and definite enough to limit the test to items of the desired type and comprehensive enough not to exclude any such items. Test specifications should be definite and clear enough to provide unambiguous information to the test constructor or the test reviewer.

In the practical construction of classroom tests, criteria of relevance often are not written. They may exist mainly in the mind of the person who is constructing the test. He may not even be conscious of all of them

EXHIBIT 13.2

Criteria of Relevance for a Test in Educational Measurement

The purpose of this test is to reveal differences among teachers or prospective teachers in their command of knowledge related to the effective use of educational tests in the classroom.

1. All of the items in the test should be in multiple-choice form.
2. Each of the items should require the examinee to demonstrate that he can answer practical questions or solve practical problems related to effective use of educational tests in the classroom.
3. The idea on which the items is based (i.e., the knowledge or ability it tests) should be discussed in some good textbook on classroom testing.
4. The correctness of the keyed correct answer should be verifiable by reference to an authoritative source other than the textbook which suggested the item.
5. No item should use as its stem and correct response any statements consisting of essentially the same word sequence as found in some sentence in the textbook.

all the time. Hence it would be surprising if he were to apply them consistently in writing all the items he puts in the test.

When tests are constructed by committees for wide-scale testing programs, there is usually somewhat greater effort to be explicit about the characteristics desired in the test items. But even in these cases the criteria often are not stated explicitly. To find the work of such committees guided by a collection of explicit statements of the criteria of relevance, similar to those presented in Exhibit 13.2, is probably the exception rather than the rule.

Where several instructors are concerned with teaching the same course, it is quite common for all to share the responsibility for test construction. This practice ought to be extended to single-section courses. Instructors in the same area ought to exchange examinations for review and constructive criticism. It is true that the best instructors give courses that are unique products of their own special abilities, but the important achievements they teach and call for in their tests ought to be things that most of their colleagues would also accept as true and important. No instructor should feel obliged to make all the changes in his test suggested by his colleagues. The ultimate responsibility for its goodness or badness is his. But independent reviews of a test by competent colleagues cost little additional time and often yield large returns in improved quality.

Some specialists in educational testing regard the question of item relevance as inescapably a matter for subjective judgment. The ability to make these judgments soundly, they believe, is what distinguishes the competent from the incompetent test constructor. But relevance is not a purely private affair. It cannot be trusted to wholly subjective (private) decisions. Someone besides the man who makes a test has to believe that it is good. The judgments of the test constructor must eventually pass the test of independent verification. To the extent that they do pass such a test, they cease to be subjective and become objective. For most, if not all, tests of educational achievement it is possible and useful to prepare in advance an explicit statement, comprehensive and concrete, of the qualities desired in the items of the test.

One reason why this task of specifying criteria for desirable test items may not have been more widely attempted is that it can be made to seem hopelessly complex and difficult if one undertakes to specify all the qualities that contribute to the goodness of an item. The degree to which an item lacks some of these qualities will be revealed quite clearly in an item analysis. As an item writer gains skill and experience he gradually learns what to do and what to avoid doing to the end that an increasing proportion of his items will be properly difficult and discriminating. To verbalize all this item-writing wisdom and to obtain agreement on the various, sometimes contradictory, principles suggested is indeed a formidable task.

The goal of the criteria of relevance suggested here is much simpler. Their task is only to provide an answer to the question, "Does an item like this belong in a test intended to serve this particular purpose in this particular set of circumstances?" They are not concerned with such things as item difficulty, possible ambiguity, grammatical flaws, semantic weaknesses, or any other characteristics that may affect the discriminating power of the item but do not affect its intent. Criteria of relevance are not intended to guarantee high-quality items, only to increase the probability that the items included in the test will provide tasks appropriate to the purpose of the test.

Perhaps one point will bear repetition. Making the criteria of relevance explicit does not make them valid. What it does accomplish is to make possible more objective consideration of their validity.

Relevance is one of the aspects of quality in a test. In judging relevance it is most helpful to have a clear statement of the characteristics that make certain items, and only those items, relevant to the purposes of the test. Then the relevance of a test is determined by the extent to which the items in it possess the desired characteristics. Relevance is not easy to objectify, but it does need to be judged as objectively as possible.

BALANCE

Balance is a second aspect of quality in a test. The balance of a test is indicated by the extent to which the proportions of items testing each aspect of achievement correspond to those sepcified for an ideal test of this kind. Balance, like relevance, is not easy to objectify. In order to produce a balanced test, or judge its balance, one must specify distinctly and unambiguously the kind of item that is appropriate to each aspect of achievement. There must be a clear association of each of the aspects of achievement to be tested with each of the types of test items specified.

Most test constructors seek balance in their tests. That is, they hope to make their tests sample representatively all the important aspects of achievement that can be tested effectively. But balance is not always defined clearly or verified specifically. Sometimes, particularly in classroom test construction, it may be left largely to chance.

One of the standard devices of the experienced test constructor who seeks balance in his test is the two-way grid, sometimes called a "test blueprint." The several major areas of content to be covered by the test are assigned to the several rows (or columns) of the grid. The several major kinds of abilities to be developed are assigned to the columns (or rows). Each item may then be classified in one of the cells of the grid. Various numbers of items are assigned to each of the rows and the columns. Knowing the proportions of items specified for a particular row and for a particular column, one can ideally determine the proportion of items appropriate for the cell formed by that row and that column. Travers and Dressel provided an illustration of a test blueprint.[2]

The two-way grid is a good first step toward balance in a test. But it has limitations. For some tests a one-dimensional classification of items may be entirely adequate. Others may require three or four. There is some tendency for content to be related to goals or abilities. Hence the assumption that every cell should be represented by at least one item can be unwarranted. Since the number of cells in the chart equals the number of content areas multiplied by the number of educational goals, there is often a fairly large number of such cells. This leads to a more refined classification of items and a more difficult task of classifying them than may actually be necessary to produce a balanced test.

Another problem in using this device arises from difficulty in providing clear definitions of the categories involved, particularly the goal or ability categories. Content categories, on the other hand, are usually simpler to deal with. In a test for a course in consumer mathematics, for example, it is quite easy to tell whether a given item deals mainly with insurance or with taxation. It is much more difficult to tell whether it deals more with the ability to weigh values than it does with the ability to spend money wisely. Experience suggests that the reliability of a classification of test items in the usual two-way grid may be quite low, especially along the goal or ability dimension.

One way of reducing this difficulty is to classify test items in terms of their overt characteristics as verbal objects instead of on the basis of educational goals to which they seem to relate or mental abilities they presumably require. Another step toward making the measurement of balance more workable is to forego the fine detail in classification demanded by the two-way grid. Instead, one could settle for separate specifications of the desired weighting on each basis for classifying the items, such as item type or content area. Taking these steps might lead to replacement of the two-way grid with separate outlines of categories such as those shown in Exihibit 13.3.

Section I of Exhibit 13.1 summarizes some partial evidence on the relevance and balance of a test in educational measurement. A sheet showing the classification of each item in the test with reference to these categories is shown in Exhibit 13.4. The handwritten numbers identify the test items classified in each category. The basis on which the items were classi-

---

[2]Robert M. W. Travers, *How to Make Achievement Tests* (New York: The Odyssey Press, Inc., 1950), p. 25; and Paul L. Dressel and others, *Comprehensive Examinations in a Program of General Education* (East Lansing, Mich.: Michigan State College Press, 1949), pp. 22, 48, 67, 81, 91.

EXHIBIT 13.3

Distribution of Items Among Content Areas and Question Types
for a Test in Educational Measurement

Content Areas	Items
Nature of educational measurement	2
History of educational measurement	2
Statistical techniques	7
Finding and selecting tests	3
Tests and objectives	3
Teacher-made tests	4
Test tryout and analysis	2
Elementary school testing	5
Secondary school testing	4
Educational aptitude	5
Personality and adjustment	2
Observational techniques	2
School testing programs	5
Using the results of measurement	4
	50

Types of Questions	Items
Terminology	5
Factual information	10
Generalization	15
Explanation	5
Calculation	5
Prediction	5
Recommended action	5
	50

fied is suggested by the Guide to Relevance Categories of Exhibit 13.5. Illustrative examples of items representing each relevance category are provided in Exhibit 13.6.

In general, any course is expected to make some permanent changes in the students who take it—to leave them with new knowledge and understanding, improved and extended abilities, new attitudes, ideals, and interests. But often these long-range goals are neglected when tests are constructed. Instead of being evaluated on the basis of ultimate objectives, the student is sometimes judged on the basis of his memory of what went on from day to day in the class or what he read in preparation for the class sessions.

EXHIBIT 13.4

Relevance Report

Test Title: *Educational Measurement* Group Tested: *Graduate Students* N = *40*

Instructor: *Jones* Date of Test: *5/1/16−* Score:= *Number right*

Number of Items: *50* Choices per Item: *5* Time Limit: *45 minutes*

    A. Terminology

$k = 10$ *5, 6, 11, 16, 17, 29, 37, 38, 41, 48*

20%

    B. Factual Information

$k = 9$ *7, 8, 18, 22, 23, 35, 36, 42, 43*

18%

    C. Generalizations

$k = 5$ *9, 21, 24, 44, 45,*

10%

    D. Explanations

$k = 7$ *1, 10, 19, 20, 28, 34, 49,*

14%

    E. Calculations

$k = 6$ *12, 13, 14, 39, 46, 47*

12%

    F. Predictions

$k = 5$ *2, 3, 27, 40, 50*

10%

    G. Recommended Actions

$k = 8$ *4, 15, 25, 26, 30, 31, 32, 33*

16%

If a test consists mainly of questions requiring recall of some detail in the process of instruction (for example, "How did the lecturer illustrate Hooke's Law?") or requiring reproduction of some unique organization of subject matter (for example, "What were the *three* chief reasons for the failure of the League of Nations?"), it probably does not measure important achievements. If, on the other hand, a majority of the questions deal with applications, explanations, and generalizations, if knowledge of terms and isolated facts is not the sole aim of a large proportion of the questions,

EXHIBIT 13.5

Guide to Relevance Categories

1. *Terminology.* A terminology or vocabulary item tests knowledge of one meaning of a particular word or technical term. It may require choice of:
   a. The statement that best defines a given statement
   b. The term that is best defined by a given statement
   c. The best illustration or example of what the term means
   d. The phrases or sentence in which the term is used most appropriately

2. *Factual Information.* A factual information item requires knowledge of a specific fact or a descriptive detail. Often it is answered primarily on the basis of simple recall. It may ask:
   a. Who? and be answered by the name of a person
   b. What? and be answered by a name or a description
   c. When? and be answered by a date or a time
   d. Where? and be answered by the name of a place
   e. How much? and be answered by a numerical quantity

3. *Generalization.* A generalization item requires knowledge of a descriptive statement having general validity. Such a statement may express:
   a. A law or principle
   b. A general description or characterization
   c. A trend or development
   d. A comparison of types or classes, stating their similarities or differences

   Often such statements include words like "generally," "usually," "normally," or "often."

4. *Explanation.* An explanation item tests understanding. Except in the cases of stereotyped problems or situations it must be answered on the basis of reasoning rather than on the basis of recall. Explanation items
   a. Deal with causes, effects, reasons, purposes, functions, or factors
   b. Involve application of knowledge of relationships
   c. May call for evidence for or against a statement or procedure
   d. Often include words like "why" or "because"

5. *Calculation.* A calculation item states a mathematical problem whose solution always requires the application of principles of mathematics and may require the application of other laws and principles as well. Often the answer is some numerical quantity. Usually a calculation item must be answered by reasoning rather than by recall.

6. *Prediction.* A prediction item describes a specific situation and asks what will result after a period of time or when certain other factors in the situation are changed. It may specify a novel situation, even an impossible situation, and require reasonable inferences.

7. *Recommended Action.* An item of this type tests knowledge of, or ability to determine by rational processes, the most appropriate action in certain specified circumstances.

EXHIBIT 13.6

Illustrative Examples of Question Types
(*The content area represented by each question is indicated in the parenthesis*)

1. *Terminology* (statistical techniques)
   What is meant by the term "error of measurement" as it is used by technically trained specialists?
   a. Any error in test construction, administration, scoring, or interpretation that causes a person to receive different scores on two tests of the same trait.
   b. A test score that is unreliable or invalid as a result of (1) sampling errors in test construction, (2) performance errors on the part of the examinee, or (3) evaluation errors on the part of the scorer.
   *c. The difference between a given measurement and an estimate of the theoretical true value of the quantity measured.
   d. The difference between the obtained score and the predicted score on a trait for a person.

2. *Factual information* (educational aptitude)
   How does one determine a child's mental age on the Stanford-Binet Scale?
   a. By dividing the number of tests passed by the child's age in years.
   *b. By giving a specified number of months of credit for each test passed.
   c. By noting the highest level at which the child answers all tests correctly.
   d. By noting the highest level at which the child answers *any* test correctly.

3. *Generalization* (educational aptitude)
   Expert opinion today assigns how much weight to heredity as a determiner of intelligence?
   *a. Less weight than in 1900
   b. More weight than in 1900
   c. All of the weight
   d. None of the weight

4. *Explanation* (personality and adjustment)
   Why is the Rorschach Test regarded as a projective test?
   a. Because scores on the test provide accurate projections of future performance.
   *b. Because the examinee unintentionally reveals aspects of his own personality in the responses he makes.
   c. Because the simulus material is oridinarily carried on slides that must be projected for viewing.
   d. Because the test is still in an experimental, developmental phase.

5. *Calculation* (educational aptitude)
   What is the I.Q. of an eight-year-old child whose mental age is 10 years?
   a. 80
   b. 90
   *c. 125
   d. The answer cannot be determined from the data given.

6. *Prediction* (test tryout and analysis)

If two forms of a 50-item, 30-minute test are combined to produce a single 100-item, 60-minute test, how variable and reliable will scores from the combined test be (in comparison with those from a single short form)?

*a. More variable and more reliable
 b. More variable but less reliable
 c. Less variable but more reliable
 d. Less variable and less reliable

7. *Recommended Action* (observational techniques)

What should a person who constructs a personality rating scale do about defining the traits to be rated?

*a. He should define them accurately.
 b. He should encourage those who use the scale to develop their own definitions.
 c. He should leave them undefined and encourage those who use the scale to do likewise.
 d. He should limit the scale to traits whose definitions are common knowledge.

---

and if few questions deal with matters of no consequence outside the classroom, the test probably does measure important achievements.

Considerations such as these are reflected in the so-called ideal standards of relevance and balance in the sample test analysis report shown in Exhibit 13.1 earlier in this chapter. Maximum limits of 20 percent each are specified for the informational item categories (terms, facts, generalizations). Minimum limits are specified for the item categories that involve application of information. Lower limits (5 percent) are set for the calculation and action item categories than for the explanation and prediction categories (10 percent), because the former are often more difficult to devise than the latter.

These limits are all somewhat arbitrary. That is, it would be difficult to demonstrate that any of the percentage values indicated is exactly the right value. On the other hand the overlap in function among items in each of the categories is so great than an optimum value for each probably does not exist. Good items in each of the categories can be highly useful in measuring a student's command of knowledge. A good item on terminology is preferable to a bad item on recommended action. The only purpose of the limits suggested in Exhibit 13.1 is to warn item writers to guard against overemphasis on information-type items, and to encourage them to make more use of application-type items.

Unfortunately, the invention and expression of items that demand application of knowledge seems to be a more difficult and exacting task than the construction of informational test items. Cook studied the discrimination and difficulty of objective test items written by 10 college instructors.[3] He found their information items to be slightly more discriminating, and slightly easier, than their application items. Perhaps the information items are shorter, simpler, and less subject to ambiguity. However, the differences Cook found were small and might be eliminated by the use of more care and more skill in the item writing.

EFFICIENCY

A test that yields a large number of independent scorable responses per unit of time is an efficient test, Sacrificing relevance to gain efficiency would obviously be poor strategy in test construction. But if the difference in relevance is slight or uncertain, there are important advantages in the use of efficient item types. An hour-long test composed of efficient item types is likely to be much more reliable than an hour-long test composed of inefficient item types.

If a large group is to be tested or if the same test can be given repeatedly to successive groups, the most efficient use of an instructor's time may call for him to use objective, machine-scorable questions. Such questions are time-consuming to prepare and many more are required than in the case of problem- or essay-type questions. Once prepared, however, they can be scored efficiently and can be used repeatedly. But if a unique test must be prepared for each separate small group, the advantage in efficiency is on the side of the problem- or essay-type test.

The essay test tends to be less efficient than the objective test, partly because it requires the student to spend most of his time in writing rather than in reading. The typical examinee can probably read about 10 times as fast as he can write. Objective questions based on the interpretation of explanatory materials tend to be less efficient than those testing the student's possession of knowledge. Questions involving situational problems tend to be less efficient than those involving factual information. With problem tests the student spends more time thinking than writing. If provision is made for analytic and partial-credit scoring, not just all-or-none scoring, the problem test can be just as efficient as the objective test in its use of the student's time.

Obviously these different item types are ordinarily used to measure somewhat different aspects of achievement. They are not completely interchangeable. On the other hand, the test constructor who wishes

[3]Desmond L. Cook, "A Note on Relevance Categories and Item Statistics," *Educational and Psychological Measurement*, vol. 20, no. 2 (Summer 1960), 321–31.

to measure some specific aspect of achievement ordinarily does have some freedom to choose among several types of items that seem suitable. Some studies, such as that by Cook, have shown that quite different types of test item give essentially equivalent measurements of achievement.[4] It seems reasonable to believe that some improvements could be made in tests of educational achievement by paying attention to the efficiency of the item types used. In judging the quality of a classroom test, the matter of efficiency should always be considered.

OBJECTIVITY

A test question is objective if experts in the field covered by the test all choose the same alternative among the suggested possible answers or if all give essentially the same free-response answer. Casting a question in objective form (multiple-choice, true-false, and so forth) does not automatically produce this kind of objectivity in response since experts sometimes disagree in their choice of the best answer among the possible alternatives. Essay questions, which usually make no claim to objectivity, are nevertheless weakened as devices for measuring educational achievement to the extent that they lack the kind of objectivity (expert agreement in response) just described. Hence, the objectivity of the items included in a classroom test becomes a fourth basis for judging the quality of the test.

When experts disagree in the answers they give to a test question, the fault usually rests in the question. The supposed truth on which the test constructor based the item may be open to question. Or the item writer may have assumed, but failed to state explicitly, all the conditions necessary to make other experts give the same answer he would give to the question. Most fields of study include, in addition to a body of verified knowledge, some opinions that are not shared by all experts and some hypotheses that have not been fully substantiated. Such opinions and hypotheses often are thought-provoking and provide the stimuli for interesting classroom discussions. But they are less suitable than verified knowledge as bases for judging student achievement.

The current trend away from the use of factual or informational types of test questions and toward questions based on generalizations, interpretations, evaluations, and recommended actions seems to increase the room for differences of opinion, even among experts. Though these higher levels

---

[4]Desmond L. Cook, "An Investigation of Three Aspects of Free Response and Choice Type Tests at the College Level," Unpublished dissertation, State University of Iowa, Iowa City, Iowa, 1955.

of understanding and application may appear to provide more significant bases for judging achievement, they may give less reliable measurements of achievement.

In some cases the question in the item writer's mind may have been quite satisfactory but his expression of it in writing somewhat faulty. Perhaps he used words with too little regard for precise meanings. Perhaps the structure of his sentences obscured or distorted the idea he had in mind. Or perhaps he failed to state all the conditions and qualifications necessary to make one, and only one, answer correct. Some of the criticism that has been directed at multiple-choice test items has been stimulated by deficiencies like these in the choice of ideas for test items or in item writing.

To use objectivity as a basis for judging test quality it is necessary to get two or more experts (preferably 5 to 10 of them and preferably experts who took no part in the test development) to answer the questions in the test. The higher the mean score of these experts, the better. If it is less than 90 percent of a perfect score, the test may be judged seriously deficient in objectivity. Even if the mean score is much closer to perfection, the test constructor may wish to identify those items on which the experts expressed the greatest disagreement.

SPECIFICITY

A test shows specificity if a testwise novice in the field covered by the test receives a near-chance score. Specificity is approximately the complement of objectivity.

In the preceding section one consequence of the current preference for questions that emphasize abilities rather than information was mentioned. This was a tendency to reduced objectivity in the test questions. Another consequence is that an examinee's score on such tests may depend to a considerable degree on his general problem-solving or test-taking ability rather than on his specific ability or knowledge. This impairs the test's specificity. Items designed to test interpretations, evaluative judgments, and recommended actions may be more relevant to intelligence or general ability than they are to achievement in a specific area of study. To the degree that any test is a test of reading ability or writing ability or general intelligence, it suffers in specificity.

Emphasis on specificity is intended to focus the test constructor's attention on the desirability of limiting his test to items that require special competence in the specific field of study covered by the test. It assumes that an examinee who has not made a special study of the field covered by a test should make a relatively low score on a test of achievement in that field, regardless of how generally able or intelligent he may be.

To use specificity as a basis for judging test quality it is necessary to get several intelligent and testwise novices to take the test. The lower the mean score of these novices, the better. While it will almost always be well above the expected chance score, it should almost always be less than 20 percent of the difference between chance and perfect scores above the chance score.

Measures of objectivity and specificity were obtained for individual test items in the course of preparing a collection of 245 multiple-choice

EXHIBIT 13.7

Scatter Diagram Showing the Number of Correct Responses by 9 Experts and 10 Novices to Each of 245 Measurement Test Items

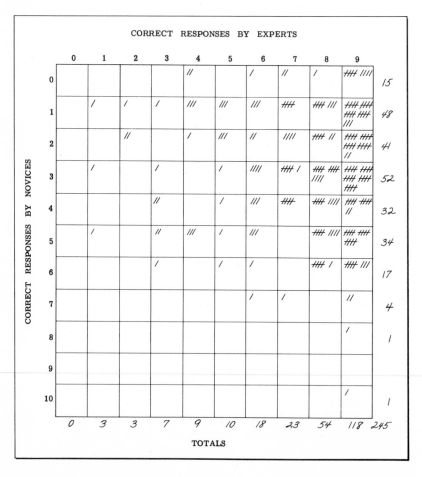

items for a test of teacher competence in educational measurement.[5] Nine experts (specialists in educational measurement) and 10 novices (bright high school seniors) chose what they considered to be the best answers to each of the questions. The results are shown in Exhibit 13.7.

On this chart each tally represents a test item. The top row of squares includes 15 tally marks, indicating the 15 items that none of the novices answered correctly. The 9 tally marks in the upper right-hand square indicate 9 items that all 9 of the experts, but none of the novices, answered correctly. The tally marks in the column of squares on the right indicate the 118 items that were answered correctly by all 9 of the experts.

The best items are represented by marks in the upper right-hand corner of the chart. The poorest would fall in the lower left-hand corner. Items hardest for the combined group of experts and novices would be found in the upper left-hand corner; those easiest for the combined group in the lower right-hand corner.

The mean score of the 9 experts on these 245 items is 208.67, or about 85 percent of a perfect score. The average score of the 10 novices was 73.2. Since 123 of the items were five-choice items, 121 were four-choice items, and one was a three-choice item, the expected chance on the 245 items is 55.2. Hence the mean score of the novices was 9.5 percent of the distance between chance and perfect scores. In terms of the standards suggested above, this test is more satisfactory in specificity than in objectivity.

These data suggest that the test could be improved. More novices than experts answered 13 of the items correctly, and the novices ran dead heats against the experts on 7 more items. Twenty-three of the 245 items were answered correctly by more than half the novices. Twenty-two of the items were missed by more than half of the experts. The test would be considerably improved in objectivity and specificity if about 50 of the items in it were revised or replaced.

DIFFICULTY

In most classroom situations a test in which the average score is somewhat more than half the maximum possible score will be appropriate in difficulty. In the test analysis reported in Exihibit 13.1, a point midway between the maximum possible score and the expected chance score is regarded as the ideal mean. The expected chance score equals the number

---

[5]National Council on Measurement in Education, *Multiple-choice Items for a Test of Teacher Competence in Educational Measurement* (East Lansing, Mich.: Michigan State University, 1962), p. 35.

of items in the test divided by the number of choices per item. Since with 50 five-choice items the expected chance score is 10, the ideal mean in this case is 30 (Section II B.1 of the analysis). If the average score is very much higher or very much lower than the midpoint of the range between highest possible and expected chance scores, the test may be inefficient. That is, it may waste the student's time trying to answer questions that almost no one can answer correctly, or reading and answering questions that almost everyone answers correctly.

The mean score on a test is, of course, determined completely by the mean difficulty of the items composing it. If, for example, in a 60-item test the proportions of correct response to the items have a mean value of 75 percent, the mean score on the test must be 45. Were the items more difficult, on the average, the mean test score would be lower.

In essay or problem tests the average score is determined largely by the choice of the scorer. He may choose to allow 10 points per question but seldom gives less than 5, thus giving some basis for satisfaction to even the poorest student. Or he may choose a more limited range of scores and actually use all of it. If the score for a question is determined by analysis of the student's answer, giving one point for each essential element in the answer, then a question appropriate in difficulty might also show an average score of approximately half of the maximum possible score.

DISCRIMINATION

The discriminating power of an item is indicated by the difference between good and poor students in proportions of correct response. For sound statistical reasons, which are explained in Chapter 14, those students in the top 27 percent on total test score are taken to be "good" students and those in the bottom 27 percent on total test score are taken to be "poor" students. If the difference in proportions of correct response is 0.41 or higher, the item is usually said to be highly discriminating. Other categories of discrimination are similarly identified on the report form (Exhibit 13.1, Section II A). The more items classified as highly or moderately discriminating, the better the test. The sample test left something to be desired in this respect. Too many of the items were low in discriminating power.

In addition to the summary of item discrimination provided on the test report, a separate sheet may be prepared to identify by number the items falling at each level of discriminating power. Such a sheet is shown in Exhibit 13.8. Here again, the handwritten numbers identify items in the test. For tests composed of multiple-choice or true-false items, a copy of the test can be prepared showing the frequency with which good

EXHIBIT 13.8

Discrimination Report

Test Title: *Educational Measurement* Group Tested: *Graduate Students* N = *40*

Instructor: *Jones* Date of Test: *5/19/–* Score = *Number right*

Number of Items: *50* Choices per Item: *5* Time Limit: *45 minutes*

	.95 _____	.90 _____	.85 _____
High	.80 _____	.75 _____	.70 _____
k = 9	.65 _____	.60 *47, 50*	.55 _____
18%	.50 *35, 37, 44*	.48 _____	.46 _____
	.44 *13, 18, 26, 38*	.42 _____	.40 _____
	.38 _____	.36 *12, 19, 23, 40, 48, 49*	.34 _____
Fair	.32 _____	.30 _____	.29 _____
k = 13	.28 _____	.27 *3, 4, 6, 7, 39, 43, 46*	.26 _____
26%	.25 _____	.24 _____	.23 _____
	.22 _____	.21 _____	.20 _____
	.19 _____	.18 *1, 9, 10, 11, 22, 24, 29, 36, 41*	.17 _____
Low	.16 _____	.15 _____	.14 _____
k = 17	.13 _____	.12 _____	.11 _____
34%	.10 _____	.09 *2, 5, 8, 15, 16, 31, 42, 45*	.07 _____
	.05 _____	.03 _____	.01 _____
	.00 _____	.00 *14, 17, 20, 25, 27*	.00 *32, 33*
Zero or Neg.	-.01 _____	-.03 _____	-.05 _____
	-.07 _____	-.09 *21, 34*	-.11 _____
k = 11	-.15 *28*	-.20 _____	-.25 *30*
22%	-.30 _____	-.40 _____	-.50 _____

and poor students chose each alternative. This information is particularly useful in item revision.

If the items in a test tend to discriminate clearly between good and poor students, the test scores will tend to vary widely. This variation permits the total test scores to discriminate clearly, as they are ordinarily intended to do, between students at different levels of ability.

Score variability is measured by the standard deviation (Exhibit 13.1, Section II B). The larger it is, under ordinary conditions, the better the test. A standard deviation of one-sixth the range between highest possible score and the expected chance score is quite satisfactory. For some good tests the standard deviation is more than one-fourth the available range. For poorer tests it may be less than one-tenth the available range. If a test is too hard, too easy, or composed of too many poorly discriminating items, it will yield scores having a small standard deviation. The size of the standard deviation of a set of test scores is an important factor in their reliability. Other things equal, the larger the standard deviation, the higher the reliability of the scores.

RELIABILITY

The index of reliability reported in Section II B of the test analysis of Exhibit 13.1 represents the estimated correlation between the scores on the test and scores on another equivalent test composed of different items but designed to measure the same kind of achievement. A high reliability coefficient indicates that a student's score was not influenced much by the chance selection of certain items rather than other items for inclusion in the test or by the student's luck or lack of luck in guessing correct answers. Some good objective tests have reliability coefficients of 0.90 or more. This level is difficult to achieve consistently with homogeneous class groups and with items that had not previously been tried out, analyzed, and revised. The standard for reliability on this analysis is set somewhat lower at 0.80. The sample test exceeds this minimum standard, with a coefficient of 0.86.

The probable error, shown as 1.47 for the sample test of Exhibit 13.1, is calculated from the reliability coefficient (r) and the standard deviation of the test scores (σ) using the formula:

$$\text{Probable error} = .67\sigma\sqrt{1 - r} = 1.47$$

The probable error indicates the degree of accuracy that can be expected in the test scores. In the case of the sample test, half the scores will be in error (that is, will differ from the theoretical true score values) by less than 1.47 score units. This concept of errors of measurement is discussed more completely in Chapter 15.

No ideal value is specified in Exhibit 13.1 for the probable error, and no evaluative rating is given. This is because the probable error of scores from a good test is not necessarily smaller than that of scores from a poor test, since a good test may yield scores that are more variable (that is, having a larger standard deviation) than the scores from a poor test. Hence good tests may have larger probable errors of measurement than poor tests.

Reliability is often the most significant *statistical* measure of the quality of a classroom test. While validity is generally considered to be more important than reliability, the statistical validity of a classroom test cannot ordinarily be determined. To determine it one needs an external criterion of achievement that is a better measure of true achievement than the test scores themselves. Such a criterion is seldom available. If the items are highly relevant and well balanced and if the scores are highly reliable, the test will necessarily be highly valid as a measure of achievement.

The reliability of a test depends on how sharply the items discriminate between good and poor students, how many items there are, how similar the items are with respect to the ability measured, and how much the students differ from one another in the ability being measured. Thus, it is easier to get a higher reliability of scores in one subject than in another, and with one group of students than with another. The other two factors of reliability, quality and number of items, are under the instructor's control. If the coefficient is too low it can almost always be raised by improving the items used or adding more items, or both. The subject of test reliability is discussed much more fully in Chapter 15.

While the type of reliability just described can also be calculated for essay tests, there is another type which is also important on such tests. It is the degree of agreement between independent scorers or even between independent scorings by the same scorer. Essay tests can be reliably scored, but they often are not. Those who use such tests extensively owe it to their students to demonstrate that the scores assigned were not largely the result of chance judgments of the moment or of the unique opinions of the person scoring them. If an instructor can arrange for competent independent scoring of his essay test papers, scoring reliability can be estimated by the calculation of a correlation coefficient by one of the methods described in Chapter 11.

FAIRNESS

A test is fair to students if it emphasizes the knowledge, understanding, and abilities that were emphasized in the actual teaching of the course. Occasionally a test includes questions that ought to have been covered in the course but were somehow omitted in the instruction of the group being tested. Again, an instructor may evaluate student achievement in a course on the basis of skills, such as ability to spell correctly, which the instructor regards as important but made no attempt to teach in the course. Such tests are not entirely fair to students. Dizney has reported some of the characteristics of test items that students consider unfair.[6]

[6]Henry Dizney, "Characteristics of Classroom Test Items Identified by Students as 'Unfair'," *Journal of Educational Measurement*, vol. 2 (1965), 119–21.

Instructors are in the best position to judge the fairness of a test to their students. A student's opinion on this matter is often biased by his success or lack of success with the test. Probably no effective test has ever been given that was regarded as perfectly fair by all persons taking it. On the other hand, student comments on a test's fairness are often worth securing and considering. If it does nothing more, the request for comments will show the instructor's concern for fairness. And often it can do much more. A student may call attention to ambiguity in a question, to the presence of questions dealing with matters not covered in class, or to omission of questions on matters that were stressed. There are few classroom tests so good that they cannot be improved on the basis of student comments and suggestions.

The administration of a test also affects its fairness. It should be handled efficiently and quietly, with no confusion or disturbance that might interfere with effective performance or give some examinees special advantages. All examinees should be on an equal footing so far as prior knowledge of the examination is concerned. They should have enough advance information about it to be able to prepare properly. The physical environment of heat, light, and space should be comfortable and convenient.

The judgment of the instructor who gave the test provides the best basis for evaluating this aspect of its quality. But here again student comments can be revealing and helpful.

SPEEDEDNESS

A test is unspeeded to the degree that the scores of examinees on it are unaffected by increases in the time allowed for work on it. There is by no means unanimous agreement on the issue of speededness, but the current preference is to remove the pressure of time limitations, at least insofar as one can without seriously lowering overall efficiency in examining. That is, the student's score is made to depend more on what he can do than on how fast he can do it.

Speed obviously is quite important in repetitive, clerical-type operations. Ordinarily, however, it is much less important in critical or creative thinking or in decision making. The fact that good students tend to be quicker than poor students is not in itself a sufficient reason for penalizing the occasional good but slow student. Hence, it is sometimes recommended that test time limits be generous enough for at least 90 percent of the students to attempt an answer to the last question in the test. In the sample test of Exhibit 13.1, 97 percent of the examinees attempted the last item.

If the time limits are made too liberal in an attempt to free all examinees from pressure to hurry, significant parts of the examination period will be wasted by a large proportion of the examinees who work more quickly. Something less than 100 percent completion will ordinarily be considered ideal for most achievement tests. For tests in some courses in which speed of production is one of the goals of instruction and in which speed practice is provided, it may be desirable to minimize rather than to maximize the number of students who complete the test. In such cases there is little waste of examination *time* but there may be much waste of examination *questions* that some of the examinees never reach.

CONCLUDING STATEMENT

Ten aspects of test quality have been identified and discussed in this chapter. For most of them evaluations of the test can be based on evidence gained by studying the test itself or by analyzing the data that it provides. This study and analysis do not themselves improve the test. What they do is to provide some stimulus and some more adequate basis for test improvement. The relevance and balance of the test can be improved. Weak questions identified in the analysis can be revised or discarded. Systematic test analysis provides one of the best available means for the progressive improvement of classroom tests.

SUMMARY

Some of the principal ideas developed in this chapter are summarized in these 12 statements.

1. A good classroom test is relevant, balanced, efficient, objective, specific, difficult, discriminating, reliable, fair, and unspeeded.
2. Test analysis can reveal the extent to which a test possesses the qualities it ought to have.
3. Specific criteria of relevance ought to be written as a basis for determining what kinds of items are appropriate for inclusion in a test.
4. To balance the proportions of items used to test each aspect of achievement, it is helpful to outline categories of content, item type, and so forth, and to specify the number or proportion of items desired in each category.
5. An efficient test includes as many independently scorable responses per unit of testing time as is possible without sacrifice of relevance.
6. The extent to which experts agree on the correct answer to a test question is a measure of its objectivity.
7. If a test question is properly specific, it will not be answered correctly by a significant number of novices who lack special competence in the field covered by the test.

8. A test is appropriate in difficulty if the mean score on it is about midway between the maximum possible score and the expected chance score.
9. The greater the difference between proportions of correct response among students of high and low achievement, the higher the discrimination (discriminating power) of the item.
10. The most significant statistical measure of the quality of a classroom test is its reliability coefficient.
11. A classroom test is fair (or valid) to the extent that it actually demands of students the command of knowledge that the course was intended to develop.
12. Most classroom tests should be essentially unspeeded, so that nearly all examinees have time to attempt all items.

The construction of solid and reliable tests requires consideration of quantitative information regarding the difficulty and discriminating power of each test exercise, or item, that is proposed for use. Such information is provided by item-analysis data.

FREDERICK B. DAVIS

14

HOW TO IMPROVE TEST QUALITY THROUGH ITEM ANALYSIS

THE VALUE OF ITEM ANALYSIS DATA

The analysis of student response to objective test items is a powerful tool for test improvement. Item analysis indicates which items may be too easy or too difficult and which may fail for other reasons to discriminate clearly between the better and the poorer examinees. Item analysis sometimes suggests why an item has not functioned effectively and how it might be improved. A test composed of items revised and selected on the basis of item analysis data is almost certain to be a much more reliable test than one composed of an equal number of untested items. Finally, the teacher who tests his tests through item analysis is likely to improve his skills in test construction much more rapidly than one who does not.

THE PROCESS OF ITEM ANALYSIS

Item analysis begins after the test has been administered and scored. Many different processes of item analysis and many different indices of item quality have been developed.[1] A procedure simple enough to be used regularly by classroom teachers but complete and precise enough to contribute substantially to test improvement has been chosen for detailed discussion in this chapter. It requires the six steps outlined below.

1. Arrange the scored tests or answer sheets in order of score, from high to low.
2. Separate two subgroups of test papers, an upper group, consisting of approximately 27 percent of the total group, who received highest scores on the test, and a lower group consisting of an equal number of papers from those who received lowest scores.
3. Count the number of times each possible response to each item was chosen on the papers of the upper group. Do the same separately for the papers of the lower group.
4. Record these response counts opposite the responses they refer to on a copy of the test.
5. Add the counts from the upper and lower groups to the keyed correct response. Subtract this sum from the maximum possible sum, that is, the sum of the number of papers in upper and lower groups, and divide the difference by that maximum possible sum. Express the quotient as a percentage; that is, multiply the decimal fraction by 100. The result is an index of item difficulty.
6. Subtract the lower group count of correct responses from the upper group count of correct responses. Divide this difference by the maximum possible difference, that is, the number of papers in the upper (or lower) group. This quotient, expressed as a decimal fraction, is the index of discrimination.

AN EXAMPLE OF ITEM ANALYSIS

An illustration of the data obtained by this process for one item is presented in Exhibit 14.1. This item was constructed for a test of understanding of contemporary affairs in 1946. Answer sheets were available for 178 students, so the upper and lower groups consisted of the 48 papers having highest and the 48 having lowest scores. The best answer is marked with an asterisk. The figures in the parentheses following each response

---

[1]Frederick B. Davis, "Item Analysis in Relation to Educational and Psychological Testing," *Psychological Bulletin*, 49 (1952), 97–121; and William W. Turnbull, "A Normalized Graphic Method of Item Analysis," *Journals of Educational Psychology*, vol. 37 (1956), 129–41.

EXHIBIT 14.1

Illustration of Item Analysis Data

26%   What change in life expectancy (number of years a person is likely to
.48   live) has been occurring?
    *(1) It has been increasing (47–24)
    (2) It has been declining due to rising rates of cancer and heart disease
       (0–10)
    (3) It has increased for young people but decreased for older people
       (0–5)
    (4) It has remained about the same (1–7)
       (Omits 0–2)

---

indicate how many of the upper group students (first figure) and how
many of the lower group students (second figure) chose each response.
Of the 48 upper group students, 47 chose the first (correct) response and
one chose the fourth response. Of the 48 lower group students, 24 chose
the first response, 10 the second, 5 the third, and 7 the fourth. Evidently
two of the lower group students failed to respond to the item.

The moderate degree of difficulty of the item is indicated by the
26 percent of incorrect response in the two groups combined, calculated
as follows:

$$47 + 24 = 71 \qquad\qquad 96 - 71 = 25$$
$$25 \div 96 = 0.26 \qquad\qquad 0.26 \times 100 = 26\%$$

The reasonably good level of discrimination is indicated by the difference
of 0.48 in proportions of correct response between upper and lower groups
$[(47 - 24) \div 48 = 0.48]$. Each of the distracters functioned well since
each attracted some responses, largely from students in the lower group.

SELECTION OF THE CRITERION GROUPS

Step 3 in the process of item analysis called for the counting of responses in upper and lower 27 percent groups. Why 27 percent? Why
not upper and lower fourths (25 percent) or thirds (33 percent) or even
halves (50 percent)? The answer is that 27 percent provides the best compromise between two desirable but inconsistent aims: (1) to make the
extreme groups as large as possible and (2) to make the extreme groups
as different as possible. Truman Kelley demonstrated that when extreme
groups, each consisting of approximately 27 percent of the total group

are used, the ratio of the difference in average abilities of the groups to the standard error of their difference, that is, the degree of uncertainty about the size of the real difference, is maximum.[2] By the term "real difference" in the preceding sentence is meant the difference that would be observed in a very large population of students like those in the limited sample whose responses we actually can study.

What Kelley showed was that by taking upper and lower groups of 27 percent of the total group, one can say with the greatest confidence that those in the upper group are superior in the ability measured by the test to those in the lower group. If we were to take upper and lower 10 percent groups the difference in average levels of ability should be greater than with the 27 percent groups, but the 10 percent groups are also much smaller. This means that we can be less sure what their average levels of ability in the two groups really are, and, indeed, less certain that the upper group is really superior to the lower. If we were to take upper and lower 50 percent groups we would have groups of maximum size, but because our basis for classifying them is not perfectly accurate, some students in the upper group probably belong in the lower, and vice versa. This also would reduce our certainty that the upper group is really superior to the lower.

Although upper and lower groups of 27 percent are best, they are not really much better than groups of 25 or 33 percent would be. If one likes to work with simple fractions like one-fourth or one-third, instead of an odd percentage like 27 percent, he should feel free to use upper and lower fourths or thirds. However, he should guard against the intuitive feeling that 33 percent is better than 27 percent because it involves groups of larger size or that 25 percent is better than 27 percent because the difference between the groups is greater. In each case the supposed advantage is slightly more than offset by the opposing disadvantage. The optimum value is 27 percent.

SPECIAL CRITERION GROUPS

The larger the number of papers included in the upper and lower 27 percent groups, the more reliable the analysis data will be. In the analysis of classroom tests it is desirable, where possible, to base the analysis on the answers of several class groups that have taken the same test. Seldom will one who analyzes a classroom test have more data at his disposal than he can use conveniently. But in wide-scale testing programs it some-

[2]Truman L. Kelley, "The Selection of Upper and Lower Groups for the Validation of Test Items," *Journal of Educational Psychology*, vol. 30 (1939), 17–24.

times happens that 27 percent of the total group tested will include several hundred students. The work involved in counting responses varies directly with the number of students in the high and low groups, but the reliability of the indices of discrimination and the item analysis data obtained does not. Increasing the size of the upper and lower groups beyond 100 students each is usually considered to be unprofitable, because the improvement in the precision of the item statistics is small in relation to the effort required to obtain it.

If taking 27 percent of the total group gives more answer sheets than can be handled conveniently, a smaller percentage may be taken. However, it is better to take all of the highest and lowest x percent of the total group than to choose x percent at random from each of the extreme 27 percent groups. In terms of our original purpose, the greater the difference between the groups in average level of ability, the better, so long as groups of reasonable size are obtained.[3] A study by Aschenbrenner demonstrated that the reliability of discrimination indices obtained from extreme 10 percent upper and lower groups tended to be greater than that obtained from extreme 27 percent upper and lower groups when the extreme groups included 100 students each.

It is true, of course, that discrimination indices of this type computed from different upper and lower group proportions are not exactly comparable. That is, if indices of discrimination were calculated for items in the same test first from upper and lower 27 percent groups and then from upper and lower 10 percent groups, one would not expect exactly the same indices for a particular item from the two different proportions. Those from the 10 percent groups would tend to be larger than those from the 27 percent groups. But since the test constructor is seldom faced with the problem of comparing indices of discrimination based on different proportions, the influence of the proportion used on the size of the index obtained seldom induces any errors in item selection. Further, in almost all situations, the use of 27 percent for the upper and lower groups will be convenient as well as logically most defensible.

In ordinary item analyses, no distinction is made between upper-group students having different criterion (total test) scores. The student with the highest criterion score is treated just like the student whose score falls just below the top quarter. Nor is any distinction made among students whose scores place them in the lower group, even though the best of those students may be considerably better than the poorest.

Flanagan has suggested that item response counts, and the discrimination indices obtained from them, could be made more reliable if added weight were given to the responses of students whose criterion scores were

---

[3] Robert L. Ebel, "The Reliability of an Index of Item Discrimination," *Educational and Psychological Measurement*, vol. 11 (1951), pp. 403–9.

extremely high or extremely low.[4] One of several suggestions he offered is that responses on the top 9 percent and bottom 9 percent of the papers be counted twice, with responses on the next 20 percent down from the top and up from the bottom be counted only once. This has the effect of (1) increasing the size of the upper and lower criterion groups and (2) increasing the difference between them in average levels of ability, both of which are desirable. This procedure is likely to be especially helpful in the analysis of classroom tests where the criterion groups usually are quite small at best. Flanagan has demonstrated the effectiveness of this procedure.[5] He has also prepared tables to assist in the determination of correlation coefficients by this weighting procedure.

COUNTING THE RESPONSES

The counting of responses to the items is likely to be the most tedious and time-consuming part of the analysis. However, for many classroom tests the number of papers in each group will be less than 10, which makes the task seem less formidable. If paid clerical help is not available, student volunteers may do the work. It is quite possible to obtain the response counts by a show of hands in class, as Diederich has suggested, or to circulate tally sheets within upper, middle, and lower thirds of the class and have the students record their own responses.[6] Some machines designed for the scoring of classroom tests produce edge-markings of correct or incorrect responses that can be used to get the most essential item analysis data. More complex machines can be programmed to calculate and print the desired indices.

THE INDEX OF DISCRIMINATION

The index of discrimination that results from step 6 was first described by Johnson.[7] Since then it has attracted considerable attention and approval.[8] It is usually designated by the capital letter D. It is simpler

[4]John C. Flanagan, "The Effectiveness of Short Methods for Calculating Correlation Coefficients," *Psychological Bulletin*, vol. 49 (July, 1952), 342–48.

[5]John C. Flanagan, *Calculating Correlation Coefficients* (Pittsburgh, Pa.: American Institute for Research, 1962).

[6]Paul Diederich, "Short-cut Statistics for Teacher-made Tests," *Evaluation and Advisory Service Series No. 5* (Princeton, N.J.: Educational Testing Service, 1960), p. 44.

[7]A. Pemberton Johnson, "Notes on a Suggested Index of Item Validity: The U-L Index," *Journal of Educational Psychology*, vol. 62 (1951), 499–504.

[8]Max D. Engelhart, "A Comparison of Several Item Discrimination Indices," *Journal of Educational Measurement*, vol. 2 (1965), 69–76.

to determine and to explain than such other indices of discrimination as the biserial coefficient of correlation, the tetrachoric coefficient of correlation, Flanagan's coefficient, and Davis' coefficient.[9] It has the very useful property, which most of the correlation indices lack, of being biased in favor of items of middle difficulty. This bias is illustrated in the second column of Table 14.1. If 100 percent of the examinees respond to an item

TABLE 14.1. RELATION OF ITEM DIFFICULTY LEVEL TO MAXIMUM VALUE OF *D* AND TO BITS OF DIFFERENTIAL INFORMATION PROVIDED

Percentage of Correct Response	Maximum Value of D	Bits of Differential Information*
100	0.00	0
90	0.20	36
80	0.40	64
70	0.60	84
60	0.80	96
50	1.00	100
40	0.80	96
30	0.60	84
20	0.40	64
10	0.20	36
0	0.00	0

*In a group of examinees.

correctly, there can be no difference between the upper and lower groups in proportions of correct response. But if only 50 percent of the examinees respond correctly, it is possible that all of those in the upper group and none of those in the lower group responded correctly. In this case the difference in proportion of correct responses would be 1.00 minus 0.00, so that *D* would be 1.00.

Note that the values in the second column of the table are maximum values. They would not be expected to occur often in pracitce. But the expected value of *D* for items of 50 percent difficulty is usually greater than that for items of 40 or 60 percent difficulty, and much greater than that for items of 0 to 100 percent difficulty. Exactly what the expected value of *D* would be for any level of item difficulty depends on other characteristics of the item and the test.

The third column of Table 14.1 reports the number of bits of differential information that an item of a given level of difficulty can supply.

[9]John C. Flanagan, "General Considerations in the Selection of Test Items and a Short Method of Estimating the Product-Moment Coefficient from the Data at the Tails of the Distributions," *Journal of Educational Psychology*, vol. 30 (1939), 674–80; and Frederick B. Davis, "Item Analysis Data," *Harvard Education Papers No. 2*, Graduate School of Education, Harvard University, 1946.

An item that one examinee answers correctly and one examinee misses supplies one bit of differential information for that group of two examinees. If both answered it correctly or missed it, the item would supply no differential information. An item that A, B, C, and D answer correctly but that E and F miss supplies eight bits of differential information. So far as that item is concerned, A shows more ability than E and more than F (two bits of differential information). B shows more than E and more than F (two more bits). Similar statements, four in all, can be made about the relative abilities of C, D, E, and F. Clearly the number of bits of differential information an item can yield is the product of the number who pass and the number who fail it. The figures in the third column were derived by applying this rule, assuming a class of 20 examinees.

If the primary goal of item selection is to maximize test reliability, as it probably should be for most classroom tests, the items having highest discrimination in terms of this index should be chosen. Item difficulty need not be considered directly in item selection, since no item which is much too difficult, or much too easy, can possibly show good discrimination when the Upper-Lower-Difference Index is used.

The second column of Table 14.1 indicates the bias of D in favor of items of middle difficulty. The third column suggests why such a bias may be desirable. Items of middle difficulty have the *potential* of supplying more differential information than do those of extreme ease or difficulty. Note that items in the middle range of difficulty, from 25 to 75 percent, all have at least three-fourths of the maximum potential discrimination.

Of course, not all the discriminations an item affords are likely to be correct discriminations. An item answered correctly by 50 percent of the good students and 50 percent of the poor students provides exactly as many "incorrect" and "correct" discriminations. In the context of item discrimination analysis, the discriminations between good students who answer an item correctly and poor students who miss it are regarded as "correct" discriminations. But discriminations between good students who miss an item and poor students who answer it correctly are regarded as "incorrect" discriminations.

Findley has demonstrated that the index of discrimination D is exctly proportional to the difference between the numbers of correct and incorrect discriminations an item makes.[10] This relationship is illustrated in Table 14.2. The table is based on an examinee group of 37, so that 10 students make up the high-scoring 27 percent and 10 students the low-scoring 27 percent.

The second row of figures in Table 14.2 may be interpreted in this way. If nine good students answer an item correctly and four poor students

[10]Warren G. Findley, "Rationale for the Evaluation of Item Discrimination Statistics," *Educational and Psychological Measurement*, vol. 16 (1956), 175–80.

TABLE 14.2.   ILLUSTRATION OF THE RELATION OF *D* TO THE NET NUMBER
OF CORRECT DISCRIMINATIONS

Correct Responses		Number of Discriminations			Net	Index of
High	Low	Correct	Neutral	Incorrect	Correct	Discrimination
10	7	30	70	0	30	0.30
9	6	36	58	6	30	0.30
8	5	40	50	10	30	0.30
8	4	48	44	8	40	0.40
7	3	49	42	9	40	0.40
6	2	48	44	8	40	0.40
4	2	32	56	12	20	0.20
3	1	27	66	7	20	0.20
2	0	20	80	0	20	0.20

$(10 - 6 = 4)$ miss it, the number of correct discriminations is $9 \times 4 = 36$. But one good student missed the item and six poor students answered it correctly. Hence there were six incorrect discriminations. The net number of correct discriminations is $36 - 6 = 30$. The item, however, fails to discriminate between the nine good and six poor students who gave correct answers, and between the one good and four poor students who gave incorrect answers. Thus the item missed 58 (9×6 plus 1×4) opportunities to discriminate. These are designated as "neutral" discriminations in Table 14.2.

Note that the proportion of net correct discriminations ($30 \div 100 = 0.30$) is exactly equal to the value of the index of discrimination D for an item that 9 of 10 good students and 6 of 10 poor students answer correctly. The two columns to the right of Table 14.2 illustrate this exact proportionality between D and the net number of correct discriminations, or the exact identity of D and the proportion of correct discriminations. Findley proved that this relationship is direct and completely general. The index of discrimination D thus provides an excellent measure of how much useful information about differences in achievement a test item can contribute.

Item discrimination indices of all types are subject to considerable sampling error. The smaller the sample of answer sheets used in the analysis, the larger the sampling errors. An item that appears highly discriminating in one small sample may appear weak or even negative in discrimination in another sample. The values obtained for achievement test items are also sensitive to the kind of instruction the students received relative to the item. Hence the use of refined statistics to measure item discrimination seldom seems to be warranted.

But even though one cannot determine the discrimination indices of individual items reliably using without large samples of student responses, item analysis based on small samples is still worthwhile as a means of overall test improvement. How much better the test composed of most discriminating items can be expected to be will depend on how large the samples and how small the sampling errors are.

THE CRITERION FOR ITEM ANALYSIS

The item analysis described in this chapter, like most item analyses, makes use of an internal criterion for the selection of groups of high and low achievement. That is, the total score on the test whose items are to be analyzed is used as the criterion rather than some other independent (external) measure of achievement. In order to conclude that an item showing high discrimination is a good item, one must assume that the entire test, of which that item is a part, is a good test.

Such an assumption is ordinarily quite reasonable. That is, the test constructor comes close enough to the mark on his first attempt to make the total score on his test a fairly dependable basis for distinguishing between students of high and low achievement. However, it must be conceded that item analysis using an internal criterion can only make a test a better measure of whatever it does measure. To make the test a better measure of what it *ought* to measure (if that should be different from what it *does* measure) one would need to use some better criterion than the total score on the test itself. Obviously this would be an external criterion. However, one should guard against the error of thinking that being external *makes* it better. An external criterion has no real advantage over the internal criterion unless it is a better measure than the test of whatever the test is supposed to measure. Ryans found the available external criteria to be of limited value in validating the items of a professional information test.[11]

The use of total test score as a basis for selecting upper and lower groups for item analysis has two important advantages. The first is relevance. Within limits set by the wisdom and skill of the test constructor, the score on his test does come closer than any other measure is likely to come to measuring what he wished to measure .The second is convenience. The total score on the test whose items are being analyzed is always readily available.

The selection of highly discriminating items, using total test score as the criterion, results in a test whose items are valid measures of what

[11]David G. Ryans, "The Results of Internal Consistency and External Validation Procedures Applied in the Analysis of Test Items Measuring Professional Information," *Educational and Psychological Measurement*, vol. 11 (1951), 549–60.

the whole test measures. In this sense, item analysis is a technique of item validation. But the kind of analysis and selection we have been considering does not demonstrate, and might not even improve, the validity of the test as a whole. What it can do to the test as a whole, and this is no small thing, is to make the test more reliable, and thus probably more valid too.

The fact that the score on an item being analyzed contributes to the total score on the test, the criterion against which the item is being tested, makes the index of discrimination somewhat greater than it would be if the item score did not contribute to the test score.

The total score on a comprehensive test does not always appear to provide the ideal criterion for judging the discriminating power of a particular item in the test. Consider a complex test of English composition, for example, in which various subsets of items test grammar, diction, spelling, punctuation, and organization. Should the students be placed in upper or lower criterion groups on the basis of total score on the entire complex test or would it be better to use as a criterion the score on the spelling test items alone?

When the items in a test can be grouped in fairly distinct subsets or types, as in the English test just mentioned, a subset score provides a more clearly relevant criterion for the items in that subset than does the total test score. Unfortunately, the subset score, based on fewer items, provides a less reliable criterion. Also, on the practical side, the use of different criterion groups complicates the process of analyzing the items in a test.

Finally, if the test is considered to be homogeneous enough so that a single score is adequate for reporting student achievement, then a single score should also be adequate for selecting the upper and lower groups for item analysis.

All things considered, the best procedure for general use seems to be that of using the total test score as the basis for selecting the criterion groups. Only in special circumstances, as when separate scores are to be reported on subsets of items, should consideration be given to the use of criterion scores from more clearly relevant subsets of items.

MUST ALL ITEMS DISCRIMINATE?

In an educational achievement test whose principal function is to distinguish different levels of achievement as clearly as possible, it is desirable for each item to have as high an index of discrimination as possible. Since an item answered correctly by all examinees, or incorrectly by all, cannot discriminate at all, such an item has no place in the kind of achievement test we have been considering.

But items of this sort may be appropriate in another kind of achievement test whose function is to report how many tasks the examinee can perform of some meaningful, clearly defined collection of tasks. For example, such a test might be given to determine how many words on a certain list the individual can spell correctly or how many words on a list of technical terms he can define correctly. Let us refer to this kind of test as a test of "content mastery" to distinguish it from the test of "relative achievement" referred to in the preceding paragraph.

Most tests of educational achievement are and probably should be tests of relative achievement rather than tests of content mastery. It is often difficult to make the score on a test of content mastery clearly meaningful. To achieve this goal, the tasks relevant to an area of content must be defined and described clearly and the process of item writing must be standardized so that irrelevant variations in item difficulty are minimized. Further, scores on tests of content mastery tend to be considerably less reliable than tests of relative achievement for equivalent numbers of items. This lower reliability is a result of including items in the content mastery test regardless of their discriminating power and hence regardless of their contribution to reliability. For these reasons the prevailing emphasis on tests of relative achievement rather than on tests of content mastery seems reasonably well justified.

The preference for items that show a high index of discrimination should not be pushed to the point of excluding from the test those items that are clearly relevant to some aspect of the achievement to be measured by the test, but cannot be made to yield a high index of discrimination. Suppose, for example, that the test specification call for an item covering some information or skill but that all the items written to test this aspect of achievement turn out to have indices of discrimination under 0.20. Suppose, further, that careful examination of the items reveals no serious technical flaws, such as ambiguous or misleading wording, unintended clues, or absence of one clearly defensible best answer. What should the test constructor do?

If the low discrimination is due to the extreme ease or extreme difficulty of the items, they should, if possible, be revised to make them more appropriate in difficulty. If such attempts at revision prove unsuccessful or seem certain to fail, the items should be dropped. However defensible their inclusion may be in principle, they will make in practice little difference in the relative scores of the students.

If the low discrimination is not due to technical weakness in the item or to inappropriate difficulty, the test constructor should review the reasons for including items of this kind in the test. If he remains convinced that they do belong, he should include them regardless of their low discrimination. In fact, he may wish to include more items of this kind than originally planned, so that the relative weakness of each item's contribution to the total score can be offset by the weight of a greater number of such items.

THE INDEX OF ITEM DIFFICULTY

Historically, two measures of item difficulty have been used. One, which is slightly easier than the other to calculate but slightly more confusing to interpret, defines the index of difficulty of a test item as the proportion of a defined group of examinees who answer it correctly. Under this definition the larger the numerical value of the index of discrimination, the *easier* the item. This definition is somewhat illogical and has led some English test specialists to refer to the index as an index of facility (ease) rather than as an index of difficulty. Another way of avoiding the confusion is to define the index of difficulty as the proportion of the group who do not answer the item correctly. This is the definition that will be used in this book.

The index of difficulty of a test item is not solely the property of that item. It reflects also the ability of the group responding to the item. Hence, instead of saying, "The index of difficulty for this item is 56 percent," it would be better to say, "When this item was administered to that particular group, its index of difficulty was 56 percent."

The estimation of item difficulty from the responses of only the upper and lower groups, disregarding the middle group, involves some bias. Omitting the information provided by the middle group also has the effect of reducing the size of sample on which the difficulty index is based. This, in turn, tends to increase sampling errors somewhat. However, the use made of difficulty indices in classroom testing is seldom crucial enough to justify high precision in their determination.

It is sometimes suggested that item-difficulty indices should be corrected for chance success (or guessing) so that the percent reported would indicate what proportion of the group *knew* the answer, instead of including also those who just luckily happened to get it right. Even if such a correction were logically defensible, which is by no means clear, the refinement might be hard to justify in consideration of the use typically made of item-difficulty indices in classroom test construction.

This use will ordinarily involve mainly items of low discrimination and will suggest whether the low discrimination can be attributed to extreme ease or difficulty of the item. Of course, if the results of the test are used for diagnosis of pupil difficulty or of inadequate teaching, the indices of item difficulty will have added significant uses.

DISTRIBUTION OF ITEM DIFFICULTY VALUES

It is quite natual to assume, and many test constructors do assume, that a good test intended to discriminate well over a fairly wide range of levels of achievement must include some easy items to test the poorer students and some difficult items to test the better students. But the facts of educational achievement testing seldom warrant such an assumption. The items in most achievement tests are not like a set of hurdles of different heights, all of which present essentially the same task and differ only in level of difficulty. Achievement test items do differ in difficulty, but they differ also in the kind of task they present.

Suppose a class of 20 students takes a test on which 12 of the students answer item 6 correctly but only 8 answer item 7 correctly. A reasonable assumption is that any student who answered the harder question (item 7) correctly should also answer correctly the easier question (item 6). Anyone who missed the easier question would also be expected to miss the harder. But such assumptions and expectations are often mistaken when applied to educational achievement tests.

Table 14.3 presents data on the responses of 11 student to six test

TABLE 14.3. RESPONSES OF 11 STUDENTS TO SIX TEST ITEMS

Student	A	B	C	D	E	F	G	H	I	J	K
Item 1	+	+	+	+	+	+	+	+	+	0	0
Item 2	+	+	+	+	+	+	0	+	0	0	+
Item 3	+	0	+	0	0	+	+	+	+	0	0
Item 4	+	+	0	+	0	0	+	0	0	+	0
Item 5	+	+	+	+	+	0	0	0	0	0	0
Item 6	+	+	0	0	+	0	0	0	0	+	0

items. A plus (+) in the table represents a correct response, a zero (0) an incorrect response. In this exhibit the students have been arranged in order of ability, and the items in order of difficulty. Note that the item missed by good student *B* was not one of the most difficult items. Poor student *J* missed all of the easier items but managed correct answers to two of the more difficult items.

It is possible to imagine a test which would give highly consistent results across items and across students when administered to a particular group. Results would be called consistent if success by a particular student on a particular item practically guaranteed success on all other items in the test that were easier for the group than that item. Correspondingly, failure on a particular item would almost guarantee failure on all harder items if the student responses were highly consistent. But a test showing such a degree of consistency among the responses would also be characterized by much higher reliability than ordinarily obtained with the same number of items. Such tests can be imagined but are seldom met with in practice. This is another reason why specifications requiring that the test include items ranging widely in difficulty are seldom warranted.

Most item writers produce some items that are ineffective (non-discriminating) because they are too difficult or too easy. Efforts to improve the accuracy with which a test measures, that is, to improve its reliability, usually have the effect of reducing the range of item difficulty rather than increasing it. The differences in difficulty that remain among items highest in discrimination are usually more than adequate to make the test effective in discriminating different levels of achievement over the whole range of abilities for which the test is expected to be used.

Some data from a simple experimental study of the relation between spread of item difficulty values, on the one hand, and spread of test scores and level of reliability coefficients, on the other, are presented in Figure 14.1.

Three synthetic tests of 16 items each were "constructed" by the selection of items from a 61 item trial form of a Contemporary Affairs test. This trial form had been administered to over 300 college freshmen and an item analysis performed to yield indices of difficulty and discrimination for each item. The items constituting the three 16-item tests were selected so as to yield tests differing widely in difficulty distributions.

> In Test C, the items selected were *concentrated* in difficulty values as near the middle of the entire distribution of difficulty values as possible.

> In Test D, the items selected were *distributed* in difficulty values as uniformly as possible over the entire range of available difficulty values.

> In Test E, the items were selected for *extreme* difficulty values, including the eight easiest and the eight most difficult items.

When these three 16-item "tests" were scored on a set of 253 answer sheets for the 61-item tryout form, the distributions of scores displayed in the histograms of Figure 14.1 were obtained. The distributions of item difficulties are indicated by the tally marks along the vertical scales to the left of each histogram.

Note the inverse relation between the spread of item difficulties and the spread of test scores. The wider the dispersion of difficulty values, the more concentrated the distribution of test scores. Note, too, the very low reliability of scores on the test composed only of very easy or very difficult items and the somewhat higher reliability of the scores when items are concentrated near the midpoint in difficulty than when they are distributed in difficulty. In short, the findings of this study support the

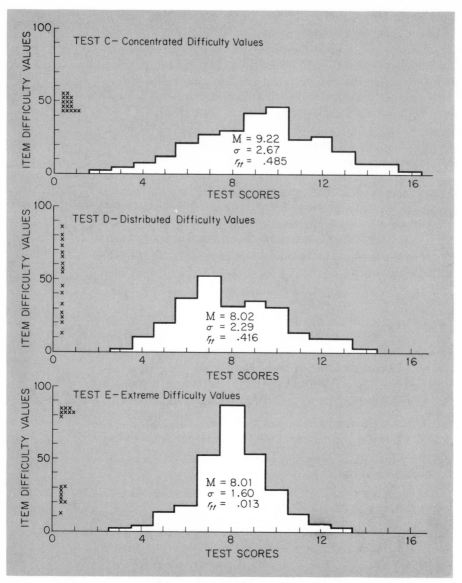

FIGURE 14.1

Relation of Distribution of Test Scores to Distribution of Item Difficulty values

recommendation that items of middle difficulty be favored in the construction of achievement test.

The relation between the spread of item difficulty values and the reliability and validity of a test has been studied analytically and experimentally by a number of other investigators including Cronbach and

Warrington, Lord, and Richardson.[12] Their articles will shed additional light on the nature of the problem and on its optimum solution.

ITEM SELECTION

One of the two direct uses that can be made of indices of discrimination is in the selection of the best (that is, most highly discriminating) items for inclusion in an improved version of the test. How high should the index of discrimination be?

Experience with a wide variety of classroom tests suggests that the indices of item discrimination for most of them can be evaluated on these terms:

Index of Discrimination	*Item Evaluation*
0.40 and up	Very good items
0.30 to 0.39	Reasonably good but possibly subject to improvement
0.20 to 0.29	Marginal items, usually needing and being subject to improvement
Below 0.19	Poor items, to be rejected or improved by revision

It probably goes without saying that no special effort should be made to secure a spread of item discrimination indices. The higher the better. Of two tests otherwise alike, the one in which the average index of item discrimination is the highest will always be the better, that is, the more reliable.

A simple relation can be shown to exist between the sum of the indices of discrimination for the items of a test and the variance of the scores on the test.[13] It is expressed in the formula:

$$\sigma^2 = \frac{(\Sigma D)^2}{6}$$

This formula indicates that score variance is directly proportional to the

[12]Lee J. Cronbach and Willard G. Warrington, "Efficiency of Multiple-choice Tests as a Function of Spread of Item Difficulties," *Psychometrika*, vol. 17 (1952), 127–47; Frederic M. Lord, "The Relation of the Reliability of Multiple-choice Tests to the Distribution of Item Difficulties," *Psychometrika*, vol. 17 (1952), 181–94; and Marion W. Richardson, "The Relation Between the Difficulty and the Differential Validity of a Test," *Psychometrika*, vol. 1 (1936), 33–49.

[13]Robert L. Ebel, "The Relation of Item Discrimination to Test Reliability," *Journal of Educational Measurement*, vol. 4 (Fall 1967), 125–28.

square of the sum of the discrimination indices. Since it is true in general that the larger the score variance for a given number items the higher the reliability of the scores, the formula also indicates that the greater the average value of the discrimination indices, the higher the test reliability is likely to be.

Table 14.4 shows the reliability that can be expected from 100-item

TABLE 14.4.   RELATION OF ITEM DISCRIMINATION TO TEST RELIABILITY FOR A ONE HUNDRED-ITEM TEST

Mean Index of Discrimination	Standard Devition of Scores	Reliability of Scores
0.1225	5.0	0.00
0.16	6.53	0.42
0.20	8.16	0.63
0.30	12.25	0.84
0.40	16.32	0.915
0.50	20.40	0.949

tests whose items have the mean indices of discrimination shown in the first column. These predicted reliability values are based on the assumption that all the items are of 50 percent difficulty. The table indicates that a mean index of discrimination of near 0.40 is needed in order to achieve a reliability of more than 0.90 in a 100-item test. It shows, also, that even in a test of zero reliability the items would show a mean index of discrimination D, of about 0.12. This is due to the fact that the item whose discrimination is being measured contributes itself to the total test scores used as a basis for measuring discrimination.

The fewer the items in the test, the larger this spurious element in the index of discrimination is likely to be. Table 14.5 shows, for tests of various lengths, how large the mean index of discrimination might be for tests of zero reliability. These are essentially minimum values of D for tests of the length indicated. An index of discrimination determined for an item in a short test has a larger spurious element than one for an item in a longer test. These minimum values need to be kept in mind in the interpretation of indices of discrimination of this type.

It is easier to write items that show high discrimination in some fields, like mathematics and foreign languages, than in others, like reading or social studies. Part of the explanation may be that the difference between truth and error, between right and wrong is wider and more distinct in the former. Part of the explanation may also be that the subject matter of mathematics and foreign languages is more tightly organized and dependent on step-by-step mastery. Deficiencies in learning some of the

TABLE 14.5.   VALUES OF *D* INDICATING ZERO RELIABILITY FOR TESTS
OF VARIOUS LENGTH

Number of Items* in the Test	Mean Index of Discrimination D
6	0.50
9	0.40
17	0.30
37	0.20
67	0.15
150	0.10
600	0.05

*Used to determine upper and lower groups, including the item whose discrimination is to be measured.

preliminaries are hard to compensate for by extra efforts subsequently. This has the effect of widening the spread of levels of achievement and making the difference between upper and lower groups much greater in the case of mathematics and foreign languages than it is in the case of reading and social studies. Whatever the explanation, the fact of generally higher levels of item discrimination in some tests than in others seems quite clear and probably should be recognized in evaluating item-discrimination indices in different fields of testing.

ITEM REVISION

The second, and perhaps the more constructive, of the two direct uses that can be made of indices of item discrimination, in conjunction with other analysis data, is in the revision of the test items. Lange, Lehmann, and Mehrens[14] have argued for this use persuasively. Five items illustrating the process of revision on the basis of analysis data are presented and discussed here. These items were written for a test of background knowledge in natural science and were intended for use by high school students. They were administered to a representative group of students in a preliminary tryout. The responses of good and poor students to these items were analyzed, and those items whose analysis data were most satisfactory were selected for the final form of the test. Among the items that were rejected there appeared to be some that might be salvaged by revision. When revisions had been made, the items were tried out with

[14]Allan Lange, Irwin J. Lehmann, and William A. Mehrens, "Using Item Analysis to Improve Tests," *Journal of Educational Measurement*, vol. 4 (1967), 125–28.

another representative group of students and reanalyzed. Results of the tryouts before and after revision for five selected items are indicated in the following paragraphs.

The first item deals with the distinction between the terms "climate" and "weather."

> 63% What, if any, is the distinction between climate and weather?
> 0.13
>   1. There is no important distinction. (1–6)
>   2. Climate is primarily a matter of temperature and rainfall, while weather includes many other natural phenomena. (33–51)
> *3. Climate pertains to longer periods of time than weather. (43–30)
>   4. Weather pertains to natural phenomena on a *local* rather than a *national* scale. (23–13)

This item is somewhat too difficult for the group tested (only 73 correct responses among 200 students) and does not discriminate well (only 13 more good than poor students answered it correctly). Examination of the response counts indicates that the second response was attractive to a considerable number of good students and that the fourth response was more attractive to good students than to poor. Since the stem of the question seemed basically clear and since the intended correct response seemed reasonable, efforts in revision were concentrated on changing distracters 2 and 4. It appeared that response 2 could be made less attractive by making it simpler and somewhat more specific. Since response 4 seemed much too plausible to the better students in the group being tested, it was "spoiled" by substituting a more obviously incorrect response. The revised item (revisions in upper-case letters) reads:

> 38% What, if any, is the distinction between climate and weather?
> 0.58
>   1. There is no important distinction .(2–22)
>   2. CLIMATE IS PRIMARILY A MATTER OF RAINFALL, WHILE WEATHER IS PRIMARILY A MATTER OF TEMPERATURE. (3–25)
> *3. Climate pertains to longer periods of time than weather. (91–33)
>   4. WEATHER IS DETERMINED BY CLOUDS, WHILE CLIMATE IS DETERMINED BY WINDS. (4–20)

Analysis data of the revised item reveal that the revisions were effective. The changed item is much easier and much more highly discriminating than the original. Only nine of the good students chose distracters. Equally important is the fact that these revisions did not appreciably increase the number of poor students choosing the correct response. It is interesting to note that on the second tryout the number of poor students who chose response number I increased markedly, even though this response had not been altered.

The next item deals with the common misconception that meteors are "falling stars."

64% Do stars ever fall to the earth?
0.35 1. Yes. They may be seen often, particularly during certain months. (12–28)
    2. Yes. There are craters caused by falling stars in certain regions of the earth. (30–43)
    3. No. The earth moves too rapidly for its gravitational force to act on the stars. (5–11)
  *4. No. The falling of a single average star would destroy the earth. (53–18)

This item again is somewhat too difficult, though its discriminating power is fairly good. The item might be made somewhat easier by revising the second response. This response can be legitimately criticized as "tricky" because there are *meteor* craters. Hence in the revision, this response alone was changed.

58% Do stars ever fall to the earth?
0.56 1. Yes. They may be seen often, particularly during certain months. (20–68)
    2. NO. PLANETS LIKE THE EARTH HAVE NO ATTRACTION FOR STARS. (1–4)
    3. No. The earth moves too rapidly for its gravitational force to act on the stars. (9–14)
  *4. No. The falling of a single average star would destroy the earth. (70–14)

The change obviously spoiled the attractiveness of the second response. Again it is interesting to note that this change did not increase the proportion of poor students choosing the correct answer but apparently shifted most of their choices to the first response, which had not been changed in the revision.

The next item attempted to get at the notion, important in "dry farming," that cultivation of the soil surface helps to conserve soil moisture.

77% Under which of the following conditions is subsoil moisture most
0.09 likely to come to the surface and evaporate during dry weather?
    1. When the temperature of the soil is high (12–26)
    2. When the soil is cultivated regularly (56–40)
    3. When the air pressure is high (5–16)
  *4. When the soil is closely packed (27–18)

This item is much too difficult and is low in discrimination. The chief offender is response 2. Not only was it attractive to a great many students, but it was even more attractive to the good students than to those of low ability. Since this response to the stem of the items reveals acceptance of an idea exactly opposite to the idea for which we were testing, the data should probably have been interpreted to mean that the item could not be salvaged. However, an attempt was made by writing a new second response.

87% Under which of the following conditions is subsoil moisture most
0.02 likely to come to the surface and evaporate during dry weather?
    1. When the temperature of the soil is high (59–25)
    2. WHEN THE AIR ABOVE THE SOIL IS MOTIONLESS (15–33)
    3. When the air pressure is high (12–30)
  *4. When the soil is closely packed (14–12)

This revision improved the performance of the second response but resulted in no improvement in the item as a whole. In fact, the item is even more difficult and less discriminating than it was before. The notion that closely packed soil facilitates capillary action and thus hastens the loss of soil moisture apparently is not widely enough held to make possible the construction of a discriminating item on this point for this population of students.

The next item deals with cause of shortage in the ground water supply.

52% Water shortages in many localities have been caused by which, if
0.17 any, of these factors?
    1. Removal of natural plant cover allowing faster run-off into streams (17–13)
    2. Increased demands for water in homes, businesses, and industry (15–26)
    3. Neither 1 or 2 (12–22)
  *4. Both 1 and 2 (56–39)

This item is of appropriate difficulty but is not highly discriminating. In this case it appeared that the fault might lie with the design of the item itself. The question was framed in such a way that there were two important correct answers, and hence it was necessary to include each of these as a single, supposedly incorrect response and to make "both" the correct response. This approach is apparently somewhat confusing. Furthermore, no opportunities are provided for the use of bona fide distracters. In the revision one of the correct responses was placed in the stem of the item and three bona fide distracters were provided as follows:

47% WHAT FACTOR, OTHER THAN INCREASED WATER USE,
0.62 HAS BEEN RESPONSIBLE FOR WATER SHORTAGES IN MANY LOCALITIES?
    1. RESTRICTION OF STREAM FLOW BY HYDROELECTRIC DAMS (3–22)
    2. DISTURBANCE OF NORMAL RAINFALL BY ARTIFICIAL RAINMAKING (3–18)
    3. INTENSIVE FARM CULTIVATION, WHICH PERMITS MOST RAINFALL TO SOAK INTO THE GROUND (10–38)

*4. REMOVAL OF NATURAL PLANT COVER ALLOWING
FASTER RUN-OFF INTO STREAMS (84–22)

The item was made somewhat easier and much more discriminating. In this case, the revision process worked in a way that gladdened the heart of the item writer.

The final item in this illustrative series deals with mechanical advantage of a single fixed pulley.

> 88% What is the maximum mechanical advantage obtainable with a
> 0.21 single fixed pulley and a rope that will break under a load of 500
> pounds?
> *1. 1 (22–1)   3. 500 (38–40)
> 2. 2 (20–30)   4. 1,000 (20–29)

This item appeared to discriminate marginally, but it was far too difficult. The item writer assumed that the principal difficulty lay in the abstract nature of the concept of the mechanical advantage. Hence he attempted to rephrase the item using a concrete situation.

> 61%   A WORKMAN LIFTS PLANKS TO THE TOP OF A SCAFFOLD
> −0.07 BY PULLING DOWN ON A ROPE PASSED OVER A SINGLE
> FIXED PULLEY ATTACHED TO THE TOP OF THE SCAF-
> FOLD. THE ROPE WILL BREAK UNDER A LOAD OF 500
> POUNDS, AND THE WORKMAN WEIGHS 200 POUNDS.
> WHAT IS THE HEAVIEST LOAD THE WORKMAN CAN
> LIFT WITH THE PULLEY?
> 1. 100 pounds (1–6)   3. 400 pounds (32–23)
> *2. 200 pounds (35–42)   4. 500 pounds (32–29)

The item in this form was considerably easier, but it turned out to have negative discriminating power. The correct response to the revised item was much more obvious to the poor students than was the correct response in the original item and only somewhat more obvious to the good students. It appears that the problem situation, though completely defensible scientifically, is just complex enough to mislead the good students, while being fairly simple on a superficial basis to the poor students.

The foregoing items do not illustrate all the possible ways in which item analysis data may be interpreted to aid in item revision. What they do is to illustrate the general nature of the process and to indicate that it *may* be highly successful.

SUMMARY

Some of the principal ideas developed in this chapter are summarized in these 16 statements.

1. Item analysis is a useful tool in the progressive improvement of a teacher's classroom tests.
2. Item analysis begins with the counting of responses made by good and poor students to each of the items in the test.
3. It is convenient and statistically defensible to consider as "good" students those whose scores place them in the upper 27 per cent of the total group and to consider as "poor" students those whose scores place them in the lower 27 percent of the total group.
4. Using extreme groups smaller than 27 percent of the total or giving extra weight to the responses on very high-score and very low-score papers may improve the precision of item analysis data.
5. Responses may be counted by hand tally, by show of hands in class, or by machine.
6. A convenient and satisfactory index of discrimination D is simply the difference between upper and lower 27 percent groups in the proportion of correct responses.
7. The value of D can be as great as 1.00 only if the item is of 50 percent difficulty. For extremely easy or extremely difficult items its maximum value will be much lower.
8. The value of D is exactly proportional to the net number of correct discriminations an item makes.
9. While logical objections can be made to the use of the total score on a test as a criterion for analyzing the items in the test, the practical effect of these shortcomings is usually small, and the practical convenience of disregarding them is great.
10. In exceptional circumstances, as when content mastery alone is to be tested or when some essential aspect of achievement is difficult to measure, the inclusion of items of low discrimination in a test may be justified.
11. The proportion of incorrect response to an item in upper and lower 27 percent groups combined provides a satisfactory measure of item difficulty.
12. For most classroom tests it is desirable that all of the items be of middle difficulty, with none of them extremely easy or extremely difficult.
13. In general, the wider the distribution of item difficulty values in a test, the more restricted the distribution of test scores and the lower the reliability of those scores.
14. Good classroom test items should have indices of discrimination of 0.30 or more.
15. The reliability coefficient of a test can be predicted from the number of items in the test and the mean index of discrimination.
16. Data on the response choices of good and poor students can be used as a basis for item revision and improvement.

A very convenient conception is that of the "reliability coefficient" of any system of measurements for any character. By this is meant the coefficient between one half and the other half of several measurements of the same thing.

C. SPEARMAN

15

HOW TO ESTIMATE, INTERPRET, AND IMPROVE TEST RELIABILITY

THE IMPORTANCE OF RELIABILITY

For most tests of educational achievement, the reliability coefficient provides the most revealing statistical index of quality that is ordinarily available.If the scores yielded by any educational achievement test were all perfectly accurate, true scores with no errors attributable to the particular sample of questions used, to alertness, anxiety, fatigue, or other factors that might affect examinee performances, to lucky guesses or unlucky slips, and with no errors caused by the mistakes or biases of the person scoring the test, then the test would have perfect reliability, reflected by a reliability coefficient of 1.00. No educational achievement test, no other type of mental test, and indeed no physical measurement has ever achieved this degree of perfection. Error is unavoidably involved in any measurement, but the goal of measurement specialists in all fields is to reduce these inevitable errors of measurement to a reasonable minimum.

Expertly constructed educational achievement tests often yield reliability coefficients of 0.90 or higher, In contrast. the achievement tests used in many elementary, secondary, and college classrooms often show reliability coefficients of 0.50 or lower. One of the ways of making test scores more reliable is to lengthen the test on which they are based, that is, to include more questions or items in it and to allow more time for it. But a test having a reliability coefficient of 0.50 would need to be increased to nine times its original length to bring its reliability up to 0.90. (The basis for this statement is provided by formula 15.1 on page 413.) Hence, from this point of view, a test having a reliability coefficient of 0.90 is nine times as good as a test having a reliability coefficient of 0.50.

Reliability is a necessary but not sufficient condition for quality in an educational achievement test. The author of a test that yields highly reliable scores may only have succeeded in measuring something irrelevant or trivial with very great precision. On the other hand, the author of a test that yields only unreliable scores has clearly not succeeded in measuring anything very precisely. If a test does not yield reliable scores, whatever other potential merits it may have are blurred and may be largely lost. Only to the degree that test scores are reliable can they be useful for any purpose whatsoever.[1]

Reliability is important to students whose grades are often heavily dependent on the scores they make on educational achievement tests. If they were clearly aware of the importance of test reliability to them, it is likely that they would ask for evidence that the tests used to measure their achievement are not only fair in terms of the purposes of the course, but also are of sufficient technical quality to yield reliable scores.

Reliability is important also to the teacher who is aware that his examinations have shortcomings and who seeks to improve them. Estimates of the reliabilities of his tests would provide the essential information for judging their technical quality and for motivating efforts to improve them. Lengthening an unreliable test is not the only way, and may not be the best way, to improve its reliability. If modern knowledge and techniques of test construction are applied, most educational achievement tests can be made to yield scores having reliability coefficients that at least approach 0.90.

[1] Robert L. Ebel, "The Value of Internal Consistency in Classroom Examinations," *Journal of Educational Measurement*, vol. 5 (1968), 71–73.

THE CONCEPT OF TEST RELIABILITY

One way of clarifying the concept of reliability is to contrast it with validity. These two definitions point up the contrast.

1. The term "reliability" means the consistency with which a set of test scores measure whatever they do measure.
2. The term "validity" means the accuracy with which a set of test scores measure what they ought to measure.

If the perforations on a target made by successive shots from a rifle are all clustered closely, the rifle is performing reliably. If those perforations are all clustered in the bull's-eye, the rifle is also performing validly.

The number of words in a poem can be measured with high reliability. Such a measure would be readily accepted as a valid measure of the length of the poem. It would not, however, be accepted by most poets or literary critics as a valid measure of the literary merit of the poem.

For most tests of educational ahievement no good statistical measure of validity is ordinarily obtainable. To estimate its validity, we must look at the test itself, and, if they are available, at the principles used by the test constructor in deciding what kind of tasks to include in the test. On the other hand, a good estimate of the reliability of the test can be obtained quite simply. Since a test must be reliable if it is to be valid, the statistical analysis of the quality of educational achievement test scores ordinarily places primary emphasis on the reliability of those scores. A test yielding reliable scores is not necessarily valid. But an educational achievement test composed of questions that seem pertinent and significant to expert teachers or professors is very likely to be as valid as it is reliable. This is especially likely if those instructors also have some expertness in educational measurement.

At least three factors contribute to the reliability or unreliability of a set of test scores. One is the appropriateness and definiteness of the task. Tasks that are too easy or too difficult or permit students to make widely divergent interpretation of what is expected of them are not likely to yield highly reliable scores. Another is the constancy or stability of a student's ability to perform the tasks presented in the test. Human beings vary from hour to hour and from day to day in their alertness, energy, emotional balance, and other characteristics. If these personal variables affect a student's test performance appreciably, they will reduce the reliability of the scores. A third is the consistency and objectivity of the person who scores the test. To the extent that the scores he assigns depend upon his notions of the moment rather than on consistent standards, uniformly applied to all the papers he reads, the scores he records will lack reliability.

AN OPERATIONAL DEFINITION OF TEST RELIABILITY

The reliability coefficient for a set of scores from a group of examinees is the coefficient of correlation between that set of scores and another set of scores on an equivalent test obtained independently from the members of the same group.

Three aspects of this definition deserve comment. First, it implies that reliability is not a property of a test by itself but rather of a test when applied to a particular group of examinees. The more appropriate a test is to the level of abilities in the group, the higher the reliability of the scores it will yield. The wider the range of talent in a group, the higher the reliability of the scores yielded by a test of that talent.

Second, the operational definition specifies the use of a correlation coefficient as a measure of reliability. One of the properties of the correlation coefficient is that it provides a relative, rather than an absolute, measure of agreement between the pairs of scores for the same persons. If the differences between scores for the same person are small relative to the differences between scores for different persons, then the test will tend to show a high reliability. But if the differences between scores for the same person are large relative to the differences between persons, then the scores will show low reliability.

Third, the operational definition calls for two or more independent measures, obtained from equivalent tests of the same trait for each member of the group. This is the heart of the definition. The different means by which sets of independent measurements of the same achievement are obtained provide the differences between the various methods for estimating test reliability.

METHODS OF OBTAINING INDEPENDENT SCORES ON EQUIVALENT TESTS

At least five methods have been used for obtaining the independent measurements necessary for estimating test reliability. These methods yield reader reliability, test-retest, equivalent forms, split halves, Kuder-Richardson, or analysis of variance coefficients.

READER RELIABILITY

Tests like essay tests whose scores depend appreciably on the expert judgment of a reader are sometimes scored independently by two or more readers. The correlation between, or among, the multiple sets of ratings for a single set of student examination papers provides a measure of the reliability with which the papers were read.[2] Scorer reliability coefficients are seldom calculated for objective tests, not because scoring errors are never made, but because it is simpler and more meaningful to report the number and sizes of the errors than to report a scoring reliability coefficient. An objective test would have to be scored very carelessly indeed to show anything but a very high coefficient of scoring reliability. Even if over half the answer sheets in a set of 35 were scored wrongly, with errors like those shown below, the coefficient of scoring reliability would still be closer to 0.99 than to 0.98.

Size of Scoring Error	Number of Errors
4	2
3	2
2	5
1	11
0	15
	35

Coefficients of *reader* reliability should not be confused with coefficients of *examinee* reliability or coefficients of *test* reliability. A coefficient of reader reliability indicates how closely two or more readers agree in rating the same set of examination papers. A coefficient of examinee reliability indicates how consistently the examinees perform on the same set of tasks. A coefficient of test reliability indicates how similarly the examinees perform on different, but supposedly equivalent, tasks. Sometimes the reliability of reading an essay test can be quite high, though its test reliability might be quite low. The test-retest reliability coefficient, next to be described, is essentially a measure of examinee reliability. All of the others are essentially measures of test reliability.

TEST-RETEST

Perhaps the simplest obvious method of obtaining repeated measures for the same individuals of the same ability is to give the same test twice.

[2]Robert L. Ebel, "Estimation of the Reliability of Ratings," *Psychometrika*, vol. 16 (December 1951), 407–24.

This would provide two scores for each individual tested. The correlation between the set of scores obtained on the first administration of the test and that obtained on the second administration yields a test-retest reliability coefficient.

A number of objectiions have been raised to the test-retest method. One is that the same set of items is used in both sets. Since this set of items represents only one sample from what is ordinarily a very large population of possible test items, the scores on the retest provide no evidence on how much the scores might change if a different sample of questions was used. Another is that the student's answers to the second test are not independent of their answers to the first. Their responses to the test items on their second presentation may be influenced by memory of the responses they gave the first time. Their responses may also be influenced by discussions of the questions among students between the first and second testings or by other kinds of efforts to learn how to answer the questions that proved troublesome when the test was first administered. A third is that if the interval between the test and the retest is long, errors of measurement may get confused with real changes in student ability as a result of learning. Finally, readministration of the same test simply to determine how reliable it is does not appeal to most students or teachers as a very useful way of spending educational time. Lack of interest on the student's part may sometimes make the second test a much poorer measure than the first, even though the actual test is the same in both cases.

EQUIVALENT FORMS

If two or more parallel forms of a test have been produced in such a way that it seems likely that the scores on these alternate forms will be equivalent and if each student in the group is given both forms of the test, then the correlation between scores on the two forms provides an estimate of their reliability. The major drawback to this approach is that educational achievement tests, particularly those prepared for use in classrooms, are usually produced singly. Parallel alternate forms are not ordinarily available. Even when they are there would be some valid objections from students to duplicate testing simply to obtain an estimate of the reliability of the first test.

SPLIT-HALVES

The difficulties associated with determination of test-retest and equivalent-forms reliability coefficients encouraged the search for more practical alternatives. In one of these, a single test was split into two reasonably equivalent halves. These independent subtests were then used as a source of the two independent scores needed for reliability estimation. One common method of splitting a test has been to score the odd-numbered items and the even-numbered items separately. Then the correlation between scores on the odd- and even-numbered items is calculated. Of course, splitting a test in this way means that the scores whose reliability is determined have been obtained from half-length tests. To obtain an estimate of the reliability of the total test it is necessary to correct or step up the half-test correlation to the expected full-length value. This is done with the help of the Spearman-Brown formula.

The general Spearman-Brown formula, which may be used to predict the increase in reliability resulting from lengthening a test by the addition of items like those in the original test, is:

$$r_n = \frac{nr_s}{(n-1)r_s + 1} \qquad 15.1$$

This formula should be read as follows: "The reliability, r_n, of a test n times as long as a shorter test of known reliability, r_s, is equal to n times the reliability of the shorter test, divided by $(n-1)$ times the reliability of the shorter test, plus 1." If, for example, a given test has a reliability of 0.50 and if its length is increased to nine times the original length by the addition of equivalent items, then the formula indicates that the reliability of the lengthened test may be found by dividing 4.50 by 5.00, which gives 0.90 as the reliability of the lengthened test.

When we need only to predict the realibility of a test twice as long as a given test, as in the case of reliability estimation by the split-half method, the formula is somewhat simpler.

$$r_2 = \frac{2r_s}{r_s + 1} \qquad 15.2$$

If, for example, the correlation between the odd-numbered items and the even-numbered items in a particular test should be 0.82, then the formula indicates that the reliability of the total test should be given by 1.64 divided by 1.82, which is approximately 0.90.

A short-cut method for estimating test reliability from scores on split halves of a test has been proposed by Rulon. The formula[3] he gives is equivalent to this:

$$r = 1 - \frac{\sigma_d^2}{\sigma_s^2} \qquad 15.3$$

---

[3] P. J. Rulon, "A Simplified Procedure for Determining the Reliability of a Test by Split-halves," *Harvard Educational Review*, vol. 9 (January 1939), 99–103.

where σ_d^2 is the variance of the differences between the half test scores and σ_s^2 is the variance of the sum of the half test scores.

There are many ways in which a test may be split into two approximately equal parts. Some of these ways are likely to yield more nearly equivalent tests than others. Hence, the estimate of test reliability obtained may be to some degree a function of the split that is chosen. Lord has shown how wide the variations may be under certain conditions.[4] But if reasonable care is taken in splitting the test into equivalent halves and if the test is reasonably long and homogeneous, these errors are not likely to be serious.

When test scores are corrected for guessing or when special response weighting is used, the split-halves technique probably affords a better combination of accuracy and convenience than any other method of estimating test reliability. Although other formulas, such as those described in the next section, may be advantageous when simple unit-weight rights-only scoring is employed, they become more difficult to handle when applied to tests using multiple scoring weights.

KUDER-RICHARDSON

In the September 1937 issue of *Psychometrika*, Kuder and Richardson published an article, "The Theory of the Estimation of Test Reliability."[5] Included in this paper were a series of formulas, two of which have become widely accepted as a basis for estimating test reliability. Their formula 20 is:

$$r = \frac{k}{k-1}\left[1 - \frac{\Sigma pq}{\sigma^2}\right] \qquad 15.4$$

In this formula k represents the number of items in the test, Σ means "the sum of," p stands for proportion of the responses to one item which is correct, and q the proportion of the responses which are not correct (so that p plus q always equals 1), and σ^2 represents the variance of the scores on the test. This formula requires that the proportion of correct responses to each item be determined and in each case multiplied by the proportion of responses which are not correct .These p times q values for each item are then added for all items. That sum, divided by the variance (square of the standard deviation of the test scores) and subtracted from 1, is then multiplied by the fraction k over k minus 1 (the number of items

[4]Frederic M. Lord, "Sampling Error Due to Choice of Split in Split-half Reliability Coefficients," *Journal of Experimental Education*, vol. 24 (March 1956), 245–49.

[5]G. F. Kuder and M. W. Richardson, "The Theory of the Estimation of Test Reliability," *Psychometrika*, vol. 2 (September 1937), 151–60.

in the test divided by 1 less than the number of items) to obtain an estimate of the reliability of the test scores. Kuder-Richardson formula 20 is applicable only to tests in which one scores the items by giving one point if answered correctly and nothing if not answered correctly. If the scores of the tests are corrected for guessing or if other forms of weighted scoring are used, more complex variations of the formula must be employed.

Use of Kuder-Richardson formula 20 requires information on the difficulty (proportion of correct response) of each item in the test. If the items do not vary widely in difficulty, a reasonably good approximation of the quantity Σpq can be obtained from information on the mean test score, M, and the number of items in the test, k. For example, if the mean score on a test (on which each correct response counts one score unit and no other response or lack of response counts anything) is half the number of items in the test, the average proportion of correct response per item must be .50. In general, the average value of p (which we will designate $\bar{p}$) is

$$\bar{p} = \frac{M}{k}$$

Since $q = 1 - p$, the average value of q (designated $\bar{q}$) must be:

$$\bar{q} = 1 - \frac{M}{k}$$

Substituting these values in formula 15.4 and simplifying gives:

$$r = \frac{k}{k-1}\left[1 - \frac{M(k-M)}{k\sigma^2}\right] \qquad 15.5$$

This is the Kuder-Richardson formula 21.

One limitation of this formula is that it always gives an underestimate of the reliability coefficient when the items vary in difficulty, as they almost always do. If a test includes many items or questions on which the average score is near perfect or near zero, this underestimate could be quite large. If most of the items have average scores of more than 30 percent but less than 70 percent of the maximum possible score, the underestimate is much smaller.

These relations are illustrated in Table 15.1 using hypothetical data for a test of one hundred items. In Test A, all items are at the same 50 percent level of difficulty. In Test B the items vary moderately, and in Test C they vary widely in difficulty. The mean scores of all tests are the same, but the standard deviations differ. It is generally true that tests whose items vary widely in difficulty yield less variable scores than tests whose items are more uniform in difficulty. The reliability estimates at

TABLE 15.1. INFLUENCE OF VARIATIONS IN ITEM DIFFICULTY ON THE ACCURACY OF KUDER-RICHARDSON 21 RELIABILITY ESTIMATES

Proportion of Correct Response	Number of Items		
	Test A	Test B	Test C
1.00			5
0.90			10
0.80			10
0.70		10	10
0.60		25	10
0.50	100	30	10
0.40		25	10
0.30		10	10
0.20			10
0.10			10
0.00			5
Mean Test Score	50	50	50
Standard Deviation	15	12	8
Reliability Coefficient			
K. R. 20	0.898	0.844	0.749
K. R. 21	0.898	0.835	0.615

the bottom of the table were obtained by applying formulas 15.4 and 15.5 to these data.

If the Kuder-Richardson 20 estimates are taken as the more accurate values, it is apparent that Kuder-Richardson 21 gives a perfectly accurate estimate when all items are of the same level of difficulty, as they are in Test A. When the items vary somewhat in difficulty, as in Test B, the Kuder-Richardson 21 coefficient is only slightly under the Kuder-Richardson 20 coefficient. But when the items vary widely, as in Test C, the underestimate is much greater. Hence, before accepting a Kuder-Richardson 21 coefficient as a good estimate of reliability, one would need to be satisfied that few of the items in the test are extremely easy or extremely difficult.

CALCULATION OF RELIABILITY COEFFICIENTS

Exhibit 15.1 displays data that will be used to calculate several commonly used reliability coefficients. Responses of 10 students, identified by letters A through J, to six four-alternative multiple-choice test items, identified by numbers in the column headed "Item Number," are shown

EXHIBIT 15.1

Responses of 10 Students (n = 10) to Six Four-Alternative
Multiple-Choice Test Items (k = 6)

ITEM NUMBER	ANSWER KEY	A	B	C	D	E	F	G	H	I	J	$p(R)$	$q(W)$	$p \cdot q$
1	2	*2*	3	3	4	*2*	1	1	*2*	4	*2*	0.4	0.6	0.24
2	3	*3*	2	4	2	*3*	*3*	*3*	*3*	*3*	*3*	0.7	0.3	0.21
3	2	*2*	*2*	3	*2*	*2*	*2*	1	*2*	*2*	*2*	0.8	0.2	0.16
4	1	*1*	4	*1*	*1*	*1*	3	3	*1*	4	2	0.5	0.5	0.25
5	4	3	*4*	2	*4*	3	*4*	1	*4*	*4*	2	0.5	0.5	0.25
6	4	*4*	1	*4*	1	1	3	2	*4*	2	*4*	0.4	0.6	0.24

Column headers spanning: STUDENT RESPONSES over A–J; PROPORTIONS over $p(R)$ $q(W)$ $p \cdot q$.

$\Sigma pq = 1.35$

Scores — Sums

	A	B	C	D	E	F	G	H	I	J	
Odd (X)	2	2	0	2	2	2	0	3	2	2	$\Sigma X = 17$
Even (Y)	3	0	2	1	2	1	1	3	1	2	$\Sigma Y = 16$
Total ($X + Y$)	5	2	2	3	4	4	1	6	3	4	$\Sigma(X + Y) = 33$

Squares

	A	B	C	D	E	F	G	H	I	J	
Odd (X^2)	4	4	0	4	4	4	0	9	4	4	$\Sigma X^2 = 37$
Even (Y^2)	9	0	4	1	4	1	1	9	1	4	$\Sigma Y^2 = 34$
Total ($X + Y)^2$	25	4	4	9	16	9	1	36	9	16	$\Sigma(X + Y)^2 = 129$

	A	B	C	D	E	F	G	H	I	J	
Products ($X \times Y$)	6	0	0	2	4	2	0	9	2	4	$\Sigma XY = 29$

in the top section of the exhibit. The numbers in each student's column report which alternative he chose as the best answer to each item. The correct answers, those corresponding to the answer key in the second column at the left, have been printed in italics.

To the right of the students-by-items response matrix are three columns of proportions. The first of these, headed p (R) indicates the proportion of correct responses to each item made by these 10 students. The second, headed q (W) gives the proportion that were wrong. Note that $p + q$ always equals one. The third gives the products of each p multiplied by the corresponding q. If an item is scored 1 if correct and zero if wrong or omitted, the pq product gives the variance of the scores on that item. The sum of those products, 1.35 in this case, is one of the quantities needed in calculating K. R. 20.

Moving down Exhibit 15.1, the next three rows of figures show the number of correct answers given by each student to the odd-numbered items (1, 3, and 5); to the even-numbered items (2, 4, and 6); and to all six of the items. The next three rows show the squares of each of the numbers given in the preceeding three. The final row gives the products of scores on odd and on even items for each student. To the right of these seven rows of figures there is a column of sums. Each figure in this column is the sum of the 10 figures preceeding it in the row. These sums will be used in calculating the mean test score, the variance of the test scores, and the correlation of odd-even scores. Preceeding each sum is the algebraic symbol that indicates it in the formulas given in Exhibit 15.2.

EXHIBIT 15.2
Calculation of Reliability Coefficients from Data of Exhibit 15.1

1. MEAN $M = \dfrac{\Sigma(X + Y)}{n} = \dfrac{33}{10} = 3.30$

2. VARIANCE $\sigma^2 = \dfrac{\Sigma(X + Y)^2}{n} - \dfrac{[\Sigma(X + Y)]^2}{n^2} = \dfrac{129}{10} + \dfrac{33^2}{10^2}$

$\sigma^2 = 12.9 - 10.89 = 2.01$

3. ODD-EVEN $r_{oe} = \dfrac{N\Sigma XY - \Sigma X \Sigma Y}{\sqrt{[n\Sigma X^2 - (\Sigma X)^2]}} [n\Sigma Y^2 - (\Sigma Y)^2]$

$= \dfrac{10 \times 29 - 17 \times 16}{\sqrt{[10 \times 37 - 17 \times 17][10 \times 34 - 16 \times 16}}$

$r_{oe} = \dfrac{290 - 272}{\sqrt{[370 - 289][340 - 256]}} = \dfrac{18}{\sqrt{81 \times 84}} = \dfrac{18}{82.5} = 0.218$

4. SPLIT-HALVES (SPEARMAN-BROWN CORRECTION OF ODD-EVEN)

$r_{tt} = \dfrac{2r_{oe}}{1 + r_{oe}} + \dfrac{2 \times .218}{1 + .218} = \dfrac{0.436}{1.218} = 0.36$

5. KUDER-RICHARDSON FORMULA 20

$K. R._{20} = \dfrac{k}{k - 1}\left[1 - \dfrac{\Sigma pq}{\sigma^2}\right]$

$K. R._{20} = \dfrac{6}{5}\left[1 - \dfrac{1.35}{2.01}\right] = 1.2(1 - .67) = \boxed{.36}$

6. KUDER-RICHARDSON FORMULA 21

$K. R._{21} = \dfrac{k}{k - 1}\left[1 - \dfrac{M(k - M)}{k\sigma^2}\right]$

$K. R._{21} = \dfrac{6}{5}\left[1 - \dfrac{3.3(6 - 3.3)}{6 \times 2.01}\right] = 1.2\left(1 - \dfrac{8.91}{12.06}\right) = 1.2 \times 0.26 = \boxed{0.31}$

The six calculations shown in Exhibit 15.2 begin with the six algebraic formulas given in the exhibit. The necessary sums and other values (remember that $n = 10$ and $k = 6$) from Exhibit 15.1 are simply "plugged in" to the formulas, and the indicated multiplications, divisions, additions, and subtractions are carried out. Once the mystery of the symbols is solved, nothing but simple arithmetic remains. But the student probably should not assume that he understands fully and can do the job correctly without testing himself. Copy the six formulas from Exhibit 15.2 and the 10 quantities they require from Exhibit 15.1. Then close the book, do the calculations, and check the results against those given in the book.

It is worth noting that in this example the split-halves and the K. R. 20 coefficients agree perfectly, to the second decimal. K. R. 21 gives a lower value, as it is expected to do when the items vary in difficulty (*p* values) as they do here.

RELIABILITY OF ESSAY TEST SCORES OR RATINGS

A Kuder-Richardson formula that is useful in estimating the reliability of essay test scores or of multiple ratings of the same performance is

$$r = \frac{k}{k-1}\left[1 - \frac{\Sigma\sigma_i^2}{\rho_t^2}\right] \qquad 15.6$$

in which k represents the number of separately scored essay test questions or independent ratings of a performance, ρ_i^2 is the variance of student scores on a particular question or from a particular rater, $\Sigma\rho_i^2$ is the sum of these question or rater variances for all questions or all raters, and σ_t^2 is the variance of the total essay test scores, or the sums of the ratings from all raters.

The application of this formula to scores of five students on the four questions of an essay test is shown in Exhibit 15.3. These scores might also be regarded as the ratings of four judges to the performances of five students. In either case the calculation of a reliability estimate would proceed in the same way.

The five students are identified by letters A through E in the row across the top; the four questions (or raters) by numbers 1 through 4 in the column at the left. Figures in the body of this section of the exhibit are the question scores or ratings. Totals for each question, and those totals squared, are shown in the two columns at the right in the top section of the table. The fifth row of figures gives the sum of scores for each student, the sum of the question sums (and student sums), and the sum of the squared question sums.

The middle section of the exhibit shows the squared scores or ratings, the squared student sums (in the fifth row of figures in this section) and the sums of the squared question scores (in the column to the right of this section). How these values plus those in the top section are used to calculate the total score variance and the sum of item variances is shown in the third section of the table. Finally, substituting these values in formula 15.6 gives the reliability estimate that was sought. Because, in this example, the variation in scores between students is relatively great when

EXHIBIT 15.3

Reliability of Essay Test Scores

1. SCORES AND TOTALS

			Student			
Question	A	B	C	D	E	Total
1	2	6	3	6	6	23
2	1	4	2	3	4	14
3	1	5	1	3	4	14
4	3	6	1	3	3	16
Total	7	21	7	15	17	67

2. SQUARES OF SCORES AND TOTALS

			Student			
Question	A	B	C	D	E	Total
1	4	36	9	36	36	529
2	1	16	4	9	16	196
3	1	25	1	9	16	196
4	9	36	1	9	9	256
Total	49	441	49	225	289	

3. SUMS OF SQUARED SCORES AND TOTALS
   20 question scores squared   283
   5 student totals squared   1053
   4 question totals squared   1177

4. VARIANCES

   Total score $\sigma_t^2 = \dfrac{1053}{5} - \dfrac{67^2}{5^2} = 210.6 - 179.6 = 31.0$

   Sum of item $\Sigma\sigma_i^2 = \dfrac{283}{5} - \dfrac{1177}{5^2} = 56.6 - 47.1 = 9.5$

5. RELIABILITY

   $r = \dfrac{k}{k-1}\left[1 - \dfrac{\Sigma\sigma i^2}{\sigma t^2}\right] = \dfrac{4}{3}\left[1 - \dfrac{9.5}{31.0}\right] = 1.33 \times 0.69 = \boxed{0.92}$

compared to the variation within students, the reliability coefficient is unusually high. Essay test scores and performance ratings are not normally as reliable as this example might suggest.

RELIABILITY AND ERRORS OF MEASUREMENT

A reliability coefficient, as has been said, is an estimate of the coefficient of correlation between one set of scores on a particular test for a particular group of examinees and an independent set of scores on an equivalent test for the same examinees. The higher this coefficient, the more consistently the test is measuring whatever it does measure. Perfect reliability, never actually obtained in practice, would be represented by a coefficient of 1.00. Although reliability coefficients of 0.96 or higher are sometimes reported, most test constructors are reasonably well satisfied if their tests yield reliability coefficients in the vicinity of 0.90. The reliability coefficients ordinarily obtained for teacher-made tests tend to fall considerably short of this goal.

Another way of interpreting a reliability coefficient is to say that it is an expression of the ratio of the variance of true scores to the variance of obtained scores. One obtains the variance of a set of scores by finding how much each score differs from the mean of the set of scores, squaring those differences, adding them, and dividing by the number of scores. By the "hypothetical true score" of an individual on a test is meant the average of a very large number of scores that might be obtained on similar tests, under similar conditions, for the same individual. The difference between the true score and an obtained score is called an "error of measurement." It is assumed that in a very large number of obtained scores for the same person, the errors of measurement will tend to cancel each other, so that the average of a very large number of obtained scores closely approximates the true score for that person.

Table 15.3 shows, in a hypothetical example, how the true score for a specific student on a specific test might be estimated and how that estimate might be used to calculate the error of measurement in each obtained score, and the overall error variance. If student John Doe takes ten 100-word spelling tests, he might get the scores shown in the second column of the table. The mean of these scores is 65. This is our estimate of his true score. It leads to the determination of the errors of measurement shown in the third column. The mean error is zero. The variance of the errors, which one obtains by squaring each error, adding all ten of them and dividing by ten, is 12.4. This 12.4 is the error variance for John Doe on 100-word dictation spelling tests of this type. If we should similarly determine true scores for each of the other students on 100-word spelling tests, we could calculate the variance of their true scores. From this, and the variance of their obtained scores whose calculation was described earlier, we could obtain an estimate of the reliability of the spelling test scores, using the formula

$$r = \frac{\sigma_t^2}{\sigma_o^2} \qquad\qquad 15.7$$

in which r stands for the coefficient of reliability, σ_t^2 represents the variance of the true scores, and σ_o^2 the variance of the obtained scores. But this approach, which requires the giving of a number of tests to each student

TABLE 15.2. HYPOTHETICAL SCORES OF JOHN DOE ON TEN
100-WORD SPELLING TESTS

Test	Score	Error
1	67	+2
2	67	+2
3	59	−6
4	64	−1
5	64	−1
6	70	+5
7	59	−6
8	69	+4
9	65	0
10	66	+1
	650	0

$$\text{MEAN} = \frac{650}{10} = 65 \quad \text{(True Score)}$$

$$\text{ERROR VARIANCE} = \frac{124}{10} = 12.4$$

in order to estimate his true score, is obviously not a very popular one. The main reason for discussing it as a hypothetical possibility here is because of the light it can shed on the interpretation of reliability coefficients.

The relation between obtained scores, true scores, and errors of measurement that we have just discussed can be expressed in the formula:

$$X = \bar{X} + e \qquad\qquad 15.8$$

in which x stands for any test score, $\bar{x}$ for the average of a very large number of similar scores, and e for an error of measurement.

It is ordinarily assumed that errors of measurement are uncorrelated with true scores. In other words, the size of the error of measurement is assumed to be unrelated to the size of the true score. If this is true, the variance of the obtained scores equals the variance of the true scores plus the variance of the errors of measurement. This can be expressed in a formula as follows:

$$\sigma_o^2 = \sigma_t^2 + \sigma_e^2 \qquad\qquad 15.9$$

in which σ_o^2 stands for the variance of the obtained scores, σ_t^2 for the variance of the true scores, and σ_e^2 for the variance of the errors of measurement.

Some of these relations are illustrated numerically in Table 15.3 where the true scores, the errors of measurement, and the obtained scores

TABLE 15.3.   RELIABILITY AND ERRORS OF MEASUREMENT

Students		*True Scores*	*Errors of Measurement*	*Obtained Scores*
Arline		18	−2	16
Dan		9	+1	10
Jean		15	+2	17
John		21	+1	22
Victor		12	−2	10
	Mean	15	0	15
	Variance	18	2.8	20.8

$$\text{Reliability} = \frac{18}{20.8} = 0.865$$

$$\sigma_e = \sqrt{2.8} = 1.67 \quad \text{(direct calculation)}$$
$$\sigma_e = \sqrt{20.8/(1 - 0.865)}$$
$$= 4.56 \times 0.367$$
$$= 1.67 \quad \text{(from formula)}$$

for five students are displayed. Note that for each student, the obtained score equals the true score plus the error of measurement. The mean of the true score is 15, of the errors of measurement 0, which makes the mean of the obtained scores also 15. The variances of true scores, errors of measurement, and obtained scores, calculated as described previously, are given in the next line of the table. The ratio of the variance of the true scores to that of the obtained scores, in this case 0.865, is the reliability of this set of obtained scores.

In almost all practical measurement situations, the only information available is the obtained scores of the persons measured. Their true scores are unknown and the error of measurement associated with each obtained score is also unknown. However, given the standard deviation of the distribution of obtained scores and the reliability coefficient of those scores, one can estimate the standard deviation of the errors of measurement. This quantity is called the "standard error of measurement." By combining equations 15.7 and 15.9 above to eliminate the expression for the variance of the two true scores and then by solving the resulting combined equation for the variance of errors of measurement and taking the square root of both sides, this expression is obtained for the standard error of measurement.

$$\sigma_e = \sigma_o \sqrt{1 - r} \qquad\qquad 15.10$$

When the values for σ_o and r shown in Table 15.3 are substituted in this formula, the value $\sigma_e = 1.67$ is obtained. Note that this is identical with the value obtained when the standard deviation of the errors of measurement is calculated directly. This shows that an estimate of the standard deviation of the errors of measurement can be obtained from the standard deviation and reliability of the obtained scores, without any information about the individual errors of measurement.

The standard error of measurement provides an indication of the absolute accuracy of the test scores. If, for example, the standard error of measurement for a set of scores is 3, then for slightly more than two thirds of the obtained scores (about 68 percent of them) the errors of measurement will be three points or less. For the remainder of scores, of course, the errors of measurement will be greater than three score units.

Another way of expressing the absolute accuracy of test scores is to use the probable error of measurement. For half the scores in any set of scores, the errors of measurement will be no greater than the probable error of measurement for that set. The other half, of course, will have errors greater than the probable error of measurement. The probable error of measurement is somewhat smaller than the standard error of measurement. It is, in fact, 0.6745 times the standard error of measurement.

One of the shortcomings of the reliability coefficient is that its magnitude is not solely dependent upon the quality of the test. It depends also on the variability of the group to which the test is applied. Since the standard error of measurement is affected very little by the variability of the group tested, it is sometimes proposed as a measure of reliability that would be superior to the ordinary reliability coefficient. Unfortunately, the standard error of measurement has shortcoming of its own. For tests using a given type of item, the standard error of measurement is almost entirely dependent upon the number of items in the test and hardly at all upon their quality. This point has been demonstrated by Lord and supported by Swineford.[6]

RELIABILITY, AGREEMENT, AND ACCURACY

Since a reliability coefficient looks like a proportion, some users are tempted to interpret it as the proportion of scores that agree, (are identical). This is not correct. However, it is possible to derive from a

[6]Frederic M. Lord, "Do Tests of the Same Length Have the Same Standard Error of Measurement?" *Educational and Psychological Measurement*, vol. 17 (1957), 501–21; Frederic M. Lord, "Tests of the Same Length Do Have the Same Standard Error of Measurement," *Educational and Psychological Measurement*, vol. 19 (1959), 233–39; and Frances Swineford, "Note on 'Tests of the Same Length Do Have the Same Standard Error of Measurement,'" *Educational and Psychological Measurement*, vol. 19 (1959), 241–42.

correlation coefficient an expression for a proportion or percent of agreement under certain specified conditions. Suppose, for example, a group of individuals is divided into two equal parts on the basis of their scores on some test. Those in the half making the higher scores are placed in one group, and the others in the half making the lower scores are placed in the other group. What percent of the individuals in this group would remain in the same half if their true scores were known? The answer is suggested by Table 15.4. If the reliability coefficient were 0.96, then 95 percent of

TABLE 15.4. INTERPRETING RELIABILITY COEFFICIENTS IN TERMS OF PERCENT OF AGREEMENT

Correlation Coefficient	Percent of Agreement	
	By Halves*	By Thirds**
1.00	100	100
0.96	95	79
0.90	90	73
0.85	87	69
0.81	85	65
0.76	83	62
0.64	80	55
0.49	74	49
0.25	66	40
0.00	50	33

*Robert L. Ebel, "The Frequency of Errors in the Classification of Individuals on the Basis of Fallible Test Scores," *Educational and Psychological Measurement* (Winter 1947), pp. 725–34.
**Joshua A. Fishman, *1957 Supplement to College Board Scores No. 2*, The College Entrance Examination Board, New York, 1957, p. 206.

the individuals in the group would stay in the same half on the basis of their scores as that to which they were originally assigned on the basis of their fallible scores. Only 5 percent would be transferred from the lower half to the upper or from the upper half to the lower. On the other hand, dividing a group into two equal parts on the basis of totally unreliable test scores would be expected to result in 50 percent wrong assignments.

The third column in Table 15.4 illustrates somewhat similar data where the group is divided into thirds. In this case, however, the percent of agreement estimated is between obtained scores on two equivalent forms of a test, each of which yields scores that are somewhat unreliable. It is not, as was true of the percentages in the second column, estimated agreement between obtained scores for one test and estimated true scores for the same test.

The relation between the reliability of the test scores or other bases used in assigning course marks and frequency of error in marking is a topic of special interest. An "error in marking" is any course mark awarded

TABLE 15.5.   ACCURACY IN ASSIGNING 1,000 MARKS ON THE BASIS
OF MEASURES WHOSE RELIABILITY COEFFICIENT IS 0.90*

Assigned Marks	True Marks				
	A	B	C	D	F
A	38	12	0	0	0
B	12	193	45	0	0
C	0	45	310	45	0
D	0	0	45	193	12
F	0	0	0	12	38

*Underlined figures are frequencies of accurately assigned marks.

that differs from the mark that would have been awarded on the basis of a perfectly reliable measure of course achievement. Table 15.5 illustrates these errors for a five-letter marking system when the reliability of the basis for marking is 0.90. This table assumes that 5 percent of the marks assigned are A's, 25 percent are B's, 40 percent are C's, 25 percent are D's, and 5 percent are F's. The table includes 1,000 marks. The first column of this table should be read as follows: "Of the 50 students who should have received marks of A, 38 actually did receive A's and 12 received B's." Since 228 of the marks assigned differ from the true mark that should have been assigned, the percent of incorrect marking is approximately 23 percent. Table 15.6 shows the percent of incorrect marking under a similar marking system when the reliability of the marking basis varies from 1.00 to 0.00.

TABLE 15.6.   ESTIMATED PERCENTAGES OF INCORRECT MARKING
ON THE BASIS OF MEASURES OF DIFFERING DEGREES
OF RELIABILITY, ASSUMING A FIVE-CATEGORY
(5–25–40–25–5) DISTRIBUTION

Reliability of Measures	Percent Incorrect
1.00	0
0.99	5
0.98	9
0.95	15
0.90	23
0.80	33
0.70	40
0.50	50
0.00	70

IMPROVING TEST RELIABILITY

The coefficient of reliability of a set of test scores is related to a number of other characteristics of the test and of the group tested. Typically the reliability coefficient will be greater for scores:

1. from a longer test than from a shorter test
2. from a test composed of more homogeneous items than from a more heterogeneous test
3. from a test composed of more discriminating items than from a test composed of less discriminating items
4. from a test whose items are of middle difficulty than from a test composed mainly of quite difficult or quite easy items
5. from a group having a wide range of ability than from a group more homogeneous in ability
6. from a speeded test than from one all examinees can complete in the time available

The Spearman-Brown formula, discussed earlier in this chapter formula 15.1), indicates the theoretical relation between test reliability and test length. The effect of successive doublings of the length of an original five-item test, the reliability of which was assumed to be 0.20, is shown in Table 15.7. The same data are shown graphically in Figure 15.1.

TABLE 15.7.   RELATION OF TEST LENGTH TO TEST RELIABILITY

Items	Reliability
5	0.20
10	0.33
20	0.50
40	0.67
80	0.80
160	0.89
320	0.94
640	0.97
∞	1.00

As the table and the figure indicate, the higher the reliability of the test, the smaller the increase in reliability with added test length. Adding 60 items to a 20-item test could increase its reliability from 0.50 to 0.80. But adding 80 more items to the 80-item test would raise its reliability

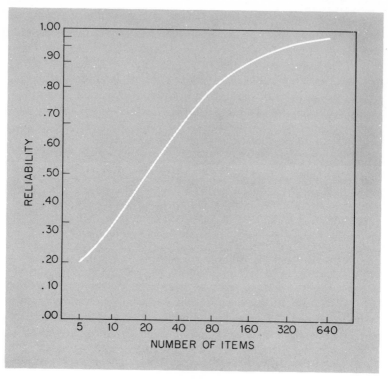

FIGURE 15.1

Relation of Test Length to Test Reliability

only from 0.80 to 0.89. To achieve perfect reliability, an infinite number of items would have to be used, which of course means that perfect reliability cannot be attained by lengthening any unreliable test.

Two assumptions, one statistical, the other psychological, are involved in the use of the Spearman-Brown formula. The statistical assumption is that the material added to the original test to increase its length has the same statistical properties as the original test. That is, the added items should have the same average difficulty as the original items and their addition to the test should not change the average intercorrelation among the test items. The psychological assumption involved is that lengthening the test should not change the way in which the examinees respond to it. If practice on items like those in the test facilitates correct response, if fatigue or boredom inhibits it, or if any other factors make the examinees respond quite differently to the lengthened test, reliability predictions based on the Spearman-Brown formula could be erroneous.

Homogeneity of test content also tends to enhance test reliability. A 100-item test in American history is likely to be more reliable than a

100-item test covering all aspects of achievement in high school. Also the subject matter in some courses, such as mathematics and foreign languages, is more tightly organized, with greater interdependence of facts, principles, abilities, and achievements, than is the subject matter of literature or history. This is another aspect of test content homogeneity that makes high reliability easier to achieve in tests of mathematics and foreign languages than in some other tests of educational achievement.

The items in homogeneous tests tend to have higher indices of discrimination than items in tests covering more diverse content and abilities. But item discrimination is also heavily dependent on the technical quality of the item—on the soundness of the idea underlying the item, the clarity of its expression, and in the case of multiple-choice items, the adequacy of the correct response and the attractiveness of the distracters to examinees of lower ability. The nature and determination of indices of discrimination and their relation to test reliability was discussed in greater detail in the previous chapter. For the present it will be sufficient to say that the relation is close and important. Working to improve the discrimination of the individual items in most classroom tests is probably the most effective means of improving test reliability and, hence, test quality.

The difficulty of a test item affects its contribution to test reliability. An item that all examinees answer correctly, or all miss, contributes nothing to test reliability. An item that just half of the examinees answer correctly is potentially capable of contributing more to test reliability than any item that is more difficult or less difficult. But such an item could also be totally nondiscriminating, in which case it would contribute nothing to the reliability of the test. Item of middle difficulty, that is, from 25 to 75 percent correct response, are all capable of contributing much to test reliability. Items that more than 90 percent or fewer than 10 percent of the examinees answer correctly cannot possibly contribute as much. Contrary to popular belief, a good test seldom needs to include items that vary widely in difficulty.

The reliability coefficient for a set of test scores depends also on the range of talent in the group tested. If an achievement test suitable for use in the middle grades of an elementary school is given to pupils in the fourth, fifth, and sixth grades, the reliability of the complete set of scores will almost certainly be higher than the reliability of the scores for pupils of any one grade.

The reliability coefficient, as we have said, reflects the ratio of true score variance to observed score variance. The wider the range of talent, the greater the true score variance .If the variance of the errors of measurement is unaffected by the range of talent, as should be expected, then the observed score variance will not increase as fast, that is, in the same proportion, as the true score variance. Thus increasing the range of talent, and hence the true score variance, tends to increase the reliability coefficient.

The relation of reliability to score variability can be illustrated further by a research study that failed. The study was intended to find out how the reliability of a test might differ for students at different levels of ability. The investigator divided 1,000 answer sheets from the test into 10 groups of 100 each, putting the 100 answer sheets having highest scores into one group, the 100 next high in a second, and so on. Then he calculated an odd-even reliability coefficient for each of the 10 sets. Much to his surprise, the coefficients he obtained were all negative. He had expected them to be low, but not negative.

The explanation was not hard to find. All the papers in any one group had total scores of nearly the same value. Hence a student who got *more* than half his total score on the odd-numbered items necessarily got *less* than half of his total score on the even-numbered items. A student whose score on the odd-numbered items was lower than that of other students in his group had to get a score on the even-numbered items that was higher—hence the negative odd-even correlation and the resulting negative reliability coefficients. The same results would have been obtained if the Kuder-Richardson formulas had been used, although the explanation is a bit more complicated.

What the investigator should have done was to use as a basis for selecting the different ability groups some measure other than (and independent of) the score on the test he was analyzing. He probably should have included 500 or more answer sheets in each group, too, since the reliabilities he got would probably be quite low and hence subject to large errors unless based on very sizable samples.

Classroom tests are sometimes constructed and scored so that the range of scores obtained is much less than that which is theoretically available. For example, an essay test with a 100-point maximum score may be graded with a view to making 75 a reasonable passing score. This usually limits the effective range of scores to about 30 points. A true-false test, scored only for the number of items answered correctly, has a useful score range of only about half the number of items. A multiple-choice test, on the other hand, may have a useful score range of three-fourths or more of the number of items in the test. Hence a 100-item multiple-choice test is usually more reliable than a 100-item true-false test.

The dependence of test reliability on score variability is illustrated with hypothetical data for three kinds of tests in Figure 15.2. The essay test was assumed to consist of 10 questions, each worth a maximum of 10 points, with a score of 75 on the entire test set in advance as the minimum passing score. The other two tests consist of one hundred items each and are scored by giving one point of credit for each correct answer. There

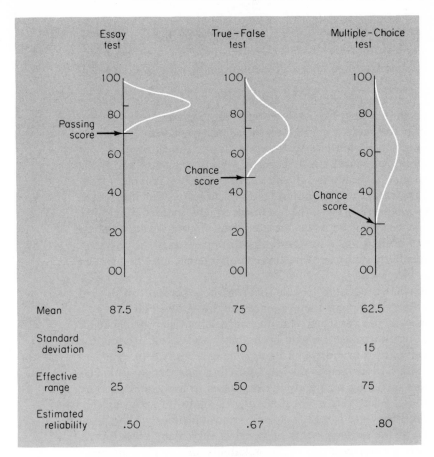

FIGURE 15.2

Hypothetical Score Distributions for Three Tests

is no "correction for guessing" by a subtraction of a fraction of the wrong answers. Each multiple-choice answer is assumed to offer four alternative answers, so that the expected chance score on it is 25. The expected chance score on the true-false test is, of course, 50.

The data at the bottom of Figure 15.2 show the expected difference among the tests in average score (mean), in variability (standard deviation), in effective range, and in reliability. While these are hypothetical data, based on deductions from certain assumptions, they are reasonably representative of the results teachers typically achieve in using tests of these types.

It is possible to construct a 100-item multiple-choice test whose reliability coefficient will be above 0.90, but it is not easy to do and relatively few instructors succeed in doing it. Again, 100-point essay tests can be handled so that their reliability will be as satisfactory as that of a 100-item multiple-choice test. But this also is not easy to do, and few of those who prepare and score classroom tests succeed in doing it without taking special pains.

Scores from a test given to a group under highly speeded conditions will ordinarily show a higher reliability coefficient than would be obtained for scores from the same test given to the same group with time limits generous enough to permit all examinees to finish. But most of the increased reliability of speeded test scores is spurious, an artifact of the method of estimating reliability. If, instead of estimating reliability from a single administration of the speeded test, we were to administer separately timed equivalent forms of the test under equally speeded conditions, the correlation between scores on these equivalent forms would be less than that estimated from a single administration. Hence the apparent increase in reliability that results from speeding a test is usually regarded as a spurious increase.

Here is what causes the trouble. Scores on a speeded test depend not only on how many items the examinee can answer, but also on how fast he can work to answer them. Thus to estimate the reliability of scores on a speeded test one must estimate both ability and speed. By splitting a test into halves or into individual items, one can get two independent estimates of ability. But there is no way of getting independent estimates of speed, short of timing separately the responses to individual items or parts of the test. When this is not done, the estimates of speed are not only dependent, they are forced to appear almost identical. The apparent reliability of the measurements of speed is very high. When this is combined with a valid estimate of the reliability of the measurements of ability, the composite is spuriously inflated. The implication of this is that dependable estimates of test score reliability can be obtained from a single administration of a test only if the speed at which an examinee works is not an important factor in determining his score.

The importance of test reliability as a factor in test quality has been stressed in this chapter. How can the test constructor make more reliable tests? By taking advantage of the factors affecting reliability that are under his control. This means writing, revising, and selecting test items so that they will discriminate as clearly as possible between much and little of the achievement the test is intended to measure. Choosing items of high discrimination will result automatically in choosing items of middle difficulty if the index of discrimination recommended in the next chapter is used. This means also including as many items as possible in the test, so as to make the test as long as possible. When the time available for testing is limited, as it usually is, the test constructor will tend to favor items that are least time-consuming individually.

SUMMARY

Some of the principal ideas developed in this chapter are summarized in these 17 statements.

1. Educational tests always are less than perfectly reliable because of item sampling errors, examinee performance errors, and scoring errors.
2. A test must be reliable to be valid, but reliability does not guarantee validity.
3. "Test reliability" may be defined operationally as the "coefficient of correlation between scores on two equivalent forms of a test for a specified group of examinees."
4. Separate coefficients of test reliability, examinee reliability, and scoring reliability may be obtained.
5. The coefficient of correlation between scores on two reasonably equivalent halves of a test can be corrected by using the Spearman-Brown formula to obtain a good estimate of test reliability.
6. Short-cut estimates of test reliability can be obtained from the sums and the differences of the half-test scores.
7. The Kuder-Richardson formulas yield estimates of test reliability from data on the variability of test scores and item scores and the number of items in the test.
8. The more widely the items in a test vary in difficulty, the more seriously the Kuder-Richardson formulas, particularly formula 21, may underestimate reliability.
9. A reliability coefficient may be interpreted as a ratio of the variance of true (error-free) scores to the variance of obtained (error-affected) scores.
10. The standard error of measurement is an estimate of the general magnitude of errors expressed in test score units.
11. The standard error of measurement is found by multiplying the standard deviation of the scores by the square root of the difference between the reliability coefficient and 1.
12. From the reliability coefficient it is possible to estimate the percentage of agreement between independent measurements when used to classify persons into groups of high, medium, and low achievement.
13. Longer tests composed of more discriminating items are likely to be more reliable than shorter tests composed of less discriminating items.
14. Homogeneous tests are likely to be more reliable than heterogeneous tests.
15. Scores obtained from heterogeneous groups are likely to be more reliable than scores obtained from homogeneous groups.
16. The more variable the scores obtained from a test, the higher its reliability is likely to be.
17. Reliability coefficients obtained from speeded tests tend to be spuriously high.

Examinations comprise a crucial aspect of the whole educational process, since they represent willy-nilly what all the fine words have been about. Moreover examinations furnish practically the only objective evidence of the value of a course of instruction. A published examination (and examinations are always published, whether officially or unofficially) presents a fair statement of the course objectives. All else that is said about the course may be summarily classified in the category of "pious hopes."

M. W. RICHARDSON

16

THE VALIDITY OF CLASSROOM TESTS

THE CONCEPT OF VALIDITY

In the preceeding chapter the concept of validity was distinguished from that of reliability in these two parallel but different definitions.

1. The term "validity" means the accuracy with which a set of test scores measures what it ought to measure.
2. The term "reliability" means the consistency with which a set of test scores measures whatever it does measure.

Having defined reliability in Chapter 15, we proceeded to show how reliability coefficients could be calculated and interpreted. It would be nice if we could treat validity in the same way. Unfortunately, for most tests that are of interest to classroom teachers, quantitative measures of test validity cannot be obtained. Only when tests are used to predict subsequent performance, or used as simpler substitutes for some exact but difficult measurement process, can coefficients of validity ordinarily be obtained. The validity of most classroom tests is a matter of carefully defining what is to be measured, and of relying on expert judgment to determine how well the tests measure it.

Solid evidence supporting the validity of most educational tests is very difficult to obtain. Possibly because of this, test specialists have worried a great deal about the validity problem and have written many articles about it. In contrast, the physical scientists, who probably do a better job of measuring than do psychologists and educators, seem to be relatively indifferent to, even unaware of, the validity problem. They tend to worry more about how accurate and how useful their measurements are than about essentially unanswerable questions which ask whether they are measuring what they *intend* to measure or what their procedures *purport* to measure.

Consider this question, "Which is the more valid measure of central tendency, the mean or the median?" Surely this question has much in common with the question, "Which is the more valid measure of intelligence, the Stanford-Binet or the Wechsler scale for children?" Why is it that the first question is almost never asked, whereas the second is asked frequently? Neither question, it may be pointed out, has ever been answered conclusively. In neither case do we have any independent external criterion to which we can appeal for a decision.

With respect to the first question, our behavior is more like that of the typical scientist; that is, we define the measurements, develop their properties, and use whichever is more appropriate or convenient in a specific situation. With respect to the second, we withhold full confidence in either test in the hope that someone will find an answer to the essentially unanswerable question we have asked. Neither central tendency nor intelligence is a meaningful quantitative concept apart from some specific operations for calculation or some specific testing procedures.

TWO TYPES OF VALIDITY

A great many varieties of validity have been discussed in the rather extensive literature on this subject. Here are brief characterizations of several of these varieties.

"*Concurrent validity* is concerned with the relation of test scores to an accepted contemporary criterion of performance on the variable that the test is intended to measure."[1]

[1]American Educational Research Association, *Technical Recommendations for Achievement Tests* (Washington, D.C.: AERA, 1955), p. 16.

Construct validity is concerned with "what psychological qualities a test measures," and one evaluates it "by demonstrating that certain explanatory constructs account to some degree for performance on the test."[2]

"*Content validity* is concerned with the adequacy of sampling of a specified universe of content."[3]

"*Curricular validity* is determined by examining the content of the test itself and judging the degree to which it is a true measure of the important objectives of the course, or a truly representative sampling of the essential materials of instruction."[4]

Empirical validity "refers to the relation between test scores and a criterion, the latter being an independent and direct measure of that which the test is designed to predict."[5]

"*Face validity* refers, not to what a test necessarily measures, but to what it appears to measure."[6]

"The *factorial validity* of a test is the correlation between that test and the factor common to a group of tests or other measures of behavior . . . . such validity is based on factor analysis."[7]

Intrinsic validity involves the use of experimental techniques other than correlation with a criterion to provide objective, quantitative evidence that the test is measuring what it ought to measure.[8]

"*Predictive validity* is concerned with the relation of test scores to measures on a criterion based on performance at some later time."[9]

"*Validity by definition:* For some tests the objective is defined solely in terms of the population of questions from which the sample comprising the test was drawn, for example, when the ability to handle the 100 number facts of addition is tested by sampling of those number facts."[10]

These varieties of validity are not all distinctly different from each other. In fact, one or two of them are practically identical with one or two others. But enough major differences appear to justify grouping

---

[2]American Psychological Association, Inc., *Technical Recommendations for Psychological Tests and Diagnostic Techniques* (Weshington, D.C.: APA, 1954), p. 14.

[3]*Technical Recommendations*, p. 16.

[4]C. C. Ross and Julian C. Stanley, *Measurement in Today's Schools* (Englewood Cliffs, N.J.: Prentice-Hall, Inc., 1954), p. 101.

[5]Anne Anastasi, *Psychological Testing* (New York: The Macmillan Company, 1954), p. 127.

[6]*Ibid.*, p. 121.

[7]*Ibid.*, p. 123.

[8]Harold Gulliksen, "Intrinsic Validity," *The American Psychologist*, vol. 5 (October 1950), 511.

[9]*Technical Recommendation*, p. 16.

[10]Charles I. Mosier, "A Critical Examination of the Concepts of Face Validity," *Educational and Psychological Measurement*, vol. 7 (Summer 1947), 192.

them into two major categories: those concerned with primary or direct validity and those concerned with secondary or derived validity. A test has direct, primary validity to the extent that the tasks included in it represent faithfully and in due proportion the kinds of tasks that provide an operational definition of the achievement or the trait in question. A test has derived, secondary validity to the extent that the scores it yields correlate with criterion scores that possess direct, primary validity. Thorndike and Hagen suggest a similar dichotomy of types of validity: those which depend primarily on rational analysis and professional judgment (here identified as *direct* validity) and those which depend on empirical and statistical evidence (which are designated here as *derived* validity).[11]

Some types of validity that seem appropriate for each category are listed below:

Direct	*Derived*
Validity by definition	Empirical validity
Content validity	Concurrent validity
Curricular validity	Predictive validity
Intrinsic validity	Factorial validity
Face validity	Construct validity

The distinction between the two categories is not sharp in all cases. For example, it can be argued that factorial validity and construct validity, despite their involvement of multiple measurements and coefficients of correlation, do represent a basic (primary) kind of validity. Still, a distinction seems warranted between primary validity, which must be built into a test and which can be evaluated only by examining critically the decisions of the test constructor, and derived validity, which always involves correlation with some real or hypothetical criterion.

DERIVED VALIDITY

There are two kinds of derived validity that are of principal interest to constructors and users of educational tests: concurrent and predictive. Correlations between scores on a test and criterion measures available at the time the test is given indicate concurrent validity. Correlations between prior test scores and subsequent measures of achievement indicate predictive validity.

[11]Robert L. Thorndike and Elizabeth Hagen, *Measurement and Evaluation in Psychology and Education* (New York: John Wiley & Sons, Inc., 1955), pp. 109–10.

Efforts are sometimes made to determine the concurrent validity of educational achievement tests by correlating the test scores of pupils with the grades teachers assign to the same pupils. If the test scores *were* used to determine grades the correlation would have to be high, whether the test were any good or not. Part of the trouble is that teachers' grades often are not highly reliable. Another part is that the grades usually do, and usually ought to, reflect pupil achievements that the test could not or was not intended to measure. One could reasonably expect students who get grades of A in a biology course to make a higher average score on a biology achievement test than the students who get grades of B. But it would be unreasonable to expect every A student to make a higher score on the test than any B student. Further, one could probably show that the average score of A students in biology on an intelligence test was higher than the average score of the B students. Would this then validate the intelligence test as a biology test?

Predictive validity applies more to aptitude tests than to classroom tests of educational achievement. A case can be made for the contention that all measurement is for purpose of prediction, but this does not alter the fact that there is a great difference between the way aptitude test scores and achievement test scores are typically used. The validities of classroom tests of educational achievement are seldom judged on the basis of how well they predict subsequent achievement.

OPERATIONAL DEFINITIONS

For many achievement tests the most important type of validation, sometimes the only possible type, is direct validation. Rulon has stressed the primary role of direct intrinsic validity for classroom tests in these words.

> What we need is to be able to choose between available test techniques on the basis of what operations we are trying to teach the learner to perform, and what materials we are trying to teach him to perform these operations upon. Both these materials and these operations should be represented in the test situation if the test is to be "obviously valid."
>
> Such a test must always be the criterion by which any not obviously valid test is validated.
>
> The "obviously valid" test is its own criterion.[12]

All types of direct validation require explicitly or by implication a definition of the achievement or trait to be measured. An essential

[12]P. J. Rulon, "On the Validity of Educational Tests," *Harvard Educational Review*, vol. 16 (1946), 290–96.

characteristic of a measurable property, as Cook has pointed out, is that it must be clearly defined and unambiguous.[13] "So long as we stick to operational definitions in discussing and thinking about the abstract concepts used in educational measurements," says Cureton, "we will be on safe ground."[14] To be operationally defined, an achievement must be defined in terms of tasks that will defferentiate between those having more and those having less of that achievement.

There is no better way of making clear what one means by achievement in algebra or chemistry or psychology than by describing how one would measure the amounts of those achievements that other persons possess. Much thinking and writing about educational goals and outcomes is vaguer than it ought to be because words like "intelligence," "motivation," and "creativity" are used freely without definite specification, and probably without any definite conception, of their operational definitions. Good tests of human traits can provide useful operational definitions of those traits.

But many classroom tests do not provide very clear or authoritative definitions of the qualities they measure. They reflect the understandings and values and limitations of a single test author. Even though this test constructor has carefully thought out the basic rationale for the test (and many constructors of classroom tests fail to do this, unfortunately), this rationale may not be clearly evident to one who looks at the test. Thus while one can say that every test does define the trait it measures in some fashion, most classroom tests do not define what they measure very authoritatively or clearly. Usually they would be better tests if their authors would try to make them better operational definitions of what they ought to measure.

Many of the problems of validation that perplex test constructors are really problems of defining operationally the achievement or the trait to be tested. If anxiety, for example, were defined authoritatively, comprehensively, and unequivocally, in terms of the responses to standard test situations that differentiate more anxious from less anxious persons, there would be far less concern about the validity of an anxiety test. The same statement can be made about practically all other traits or achievements that instructors would like to test. The persistent difficulties that plague our efforts to measure some outcomes of education are less attributable to limitations of measurement than to uncertainty about what is to be measured.

Well, then, why not get busy defining in operational terms these

---

[13]Walter W. Cook, "Tests: Achievement," in *Encyclopedia of Educational Research*, ed. Walter S. Monroe, rev. ed. (New York: The Macmillan Company, 1950), p. 1464.

[14]E. E. Cureton, "Validity," in *Educational Measurement*, ed. E. F. Lindquist (Washington, D.C.: American Council on Education, 1951), p. 625.

traits and achievements in which we are interested? We should, but we should not look for quick, easy success. Two obstacles, at least, may be expected. One is the persistent belief that what a word (or a concept) like "anxiety" or "intelligence" or "creativity" means can somehow be discovered by research or by the analysis of data. But language is always invented, and what a term means is always determined by some consensus among past and present users of the term. Research can discover what people *do* mean by the term "anxiety." It cannot reveal what anxiety *ought* to mean. Tests cannot reveal what intelligence *really* is; they can only illustrate what certain test constructors believe that the term "intelligence" ought to mean.

But different tests thus imply different definitions of intelligence or of almost any other trait or achievement for which tests have ever been made. This suggests the second obstacle—the difficulty of reaching substantial agreement on the operational definition of a trait or an achievement. If agreement is not reached, if each test constructor projects his own unique perceptions and values and theories in each test he constructs, without regard for the perceptions and values and theories of others who build similar tests, nothing of general value has been defined and no test of general validity is likely to be produced.

Fortunately, our inability to discover in nature what a term should mean or the absence of any revelation of ultimate criteria for our tests does not condemn us to an endless Babel of competing operational definitions. Not all possible operational definitions of an achievement are likely to be equally reasonable. They are not likely to yield tests that prove equally useful. They are not likely to be publicized with equal vigor and skill. If the concept to be defined is necessary and useful, a consensus on its meaning will emerge in time. The process can be hastened if enough of those concerned with using the concept will dedicate enough of their time and energies to developing a rational consensus. Substantial progress has already been made in defining some traits and achievements in these terms. A great deal more would be useful.

THE ROLE OF JUDGMENT

The dependence of direct intrinsic validity on human judgment makes some test specialists quite uneasy. Human judgment is fallible. Competent judges, as has been implied, may disagree. What these specialists would like to find is a way of determining test validity that does not involve fallible human judgments. Empirical test validation might provide this way if it were not for the problem of finding a valid criterion. But the difficulties and uncertainties involved in getting directly valid criterion measures are exactly as serious and troublesome as those of obtaining directly valid test scores. In fact, the two problems are almost identical, as Anastasi has indicated.[15] There is no means of test validation that is completely empirical, is completely impersonal and objective, and avoids the vagueness and uncertainty of human judgments altogether.

To say that the exercise of judgment is unavoidable in constructing valid tests or determining their validity is not to say that one man's judgment is as good as the next or that any man's judgment is above rational and corrective criticism. The decisions of the test constructor reflect his knowledge and those values. The knowledge may be incomplete. The reasoning may be faulty. Even the values may reflect faulty knowledge or reasoning. Assumptions that have not been, but could be, tested may be involved in the test constructor's decisions.

There is no simple, uniform, wholly objective procedure for determining the validity of a test or of a test item. The judgment of the test constructor is inevitably involved in the process of test construction. But his judgment is not beyond criticism and improvement. It can be refined and given a sounder basis, as Gulliksen has argued persuasively.[16] Not all the differences of opinion among test constructors with respect to questions of relevance are likely to be resolved quickly and surely by rational consideration and further experimental evidence. It is unlikely that a majority of the teachers of any subject will ever agree on one particular test as the ideal test of achievement in that subject. What can be expected is increasing awareness of, and agreement on, the essentials for validity in items purporting to test achievement in that subject. Capable, conscientious teachers are likely to make progressively better tests as they think and discuss what their tests ought to measure and as they invent and try out new tasks for their tests.[17]

TASKS AND TRAITS

This chapter has suggested that the validity of a test can be judged, in part at least, by studying the test itself. But does a test really measure what it appears to measure? Is this a test of scientific understanding,

---

[15] Anne Anastasi, "The Concept of Validity in the Interpretation of Test Scores," *Educational and Psychological Measurement*, vol. 10 (Spring 1950), 67–78.

[16] Gulliksen, "Intrinsic Validity,"

[17] Robert L. Ebel, "Obtaining and Reporting Evidence on Content Validity," *Educational and Psychological Measurement*, vol. 16 (1956), 269–82.

as its title claims, or is it really an intelligence test? Is that a test of intelligence, or is it really only a reading test?

If one is willing to accept as a definition of what a test is measuring a simple description of the tasks that the test requires a student to perform, then what a test appears to measure and what it really does measure will be practically identical. For example, the question, "What is the sum of $\frac{1}{5}$ and $\frac{1}{6}$?" appears to measure, and really does measure (beyond his ability to read), the student's ability to add two particular common fractions. The tasks in most classroom tests of educational achievement can be described as obviously and sensibly as this if one is willing to settle for an obvious, common-sense description.

But some are not. Some prefer to name their tests and describe what their tests are measuring, not in terms of the tasks they present, but in terms of the traits they presumably measure. So we have tests of intelligence, persistence, empathy, rigidity, creativity, anxiety, tolerance, perceptiveness, reasoning, and many other traits. For tests like these, the question of whether the test really measures what it claims to measure does arise, as indeed it should. Does the task of completing a figure analogy measure intelligence? Does ability to suggest unconventional uses for a brick measure creativity? Does ability to repeat a series of digits in reverse order measure memory?

Unfortunately, when such questions do arise, it is usually impossible to find satisfactory answers to them. For the traits these tests are supposed to measure are so highly generalized and so variable from one situation to another that a primary, intrinsically valid trait-defining test is seldom available for them. In the absence of such direct measures of the traits in question it is well nigh impossible to establish the validity of tests that claim to measure the traits indirectly.

Whenever measures of magnitude A, obtained by operations that define magnitude A, correlate with measures of magnitude B, obtained by operations that define magnitude B, then A measures B to some degree, and B measures A. But if we have no measures that define magnitude A, it is impossible to answer the question, "Do the operations we used to obtain measures B really measure A?" For reasons like these we can not always tell for sure whether test B does in fact measure trait A.

The generality of meaning of many trait names and the variability of the behavior attributed to such traits, depending on the specific circumstances, have caused much trouble for those who try to construct tests of these traits. It is not uncommon to find that the scores on three different tests, all purporting to measure the same trait, show intercorrelations of near zero. Further, there is a dangerous tendency to overgeneralize behavior predictions on the basis of trait names. Here is an example.

Applicants for positions on the police force in one city were shown this sign

Throw trash
in the
the trash cans.

and asked to comment on it. If they noticed the repetition of the word "the," they were given credit for perceptiveness and their chances of acceptance were improved.

All would agree that policemen need to be perceptive, to notice and remember important details like the license numbers of certain cars and descriptions of certain people. But there is little evidence, and really not much reason to expect, that people who are good at noticing printing errors in signs will also be good at noticing essential details at the scene of a crime.

Test items like the misprinted sign, which have only a verbal claim to direct relationship to the trait to be measured, do call for empirical validation. But perhaps they should be validated not as measures of perceptiveness, but as predictors of effectiveness on the police force. The trouble is that to do a good job of that kind of empirical validation is extremely difficult. The primary, directly valid measures of effectiveness are hard to design and harder still to use effectively. Fortunately, classroom tests can usually avoid most of these quicksands of trait measurement. If they are built carefully and skillfully enough they can have direct, primary validity.

VALIDITY AND RELIABILITY

The term "validity," as noted earlier in this chapter, is sometimes defined as the "accuracy with which the test measures what it is intended to measure." This is in contrast with "reliability," which can be defined as the "accuracy with which the test measures whatever it does measure." Clearly, a test that measures accurately what it is intended to measure also measures with equal or greater accuracy whatever it does measure. Hence to the degree that a test is valid it must also be reliable. Further, a test cannot measure what it is intended to measure more accurately than it measures whatever it *does* measure.[18] Hence in order to be valid a test must be reliable.

---

[18]This statement is not contradicted by the fact that it is theoretically possible for a test to yield a validity coefficient that is numerically larger than its reliability coefficient for the same examinees. For the validity coefficient can reach its theoretical maximum only if the criterion for validity is a perfectly accurate measure of whatever the test does in fact measure. In that case the difference between what a test is intended to measure and what it does measure has disappeared. If error-free criterion measures are assumed for both reliability and validity, the index of validity can never be larger than the index of reliability.

The converse of the relation just stated between reliability and validity is not necessarily true, however. That is, a reliable test—one that measures accurately whatever it does measure—is not necessarily a valid test—one that measures accurately what it is intended to measure. Reliability is a necessary condition for validity, but it is not a sufficient condition.

Indeed, there is at least the possibility that a test constructor, working to improve the reliability of his test, might actually lower its validity. Some types of ability, like knowledge of word meanings or ability to solve numerical problems, are easier to measure reliably than other things, such as understanding of principles or ability to suggest appropriate action in a practical problem situation. If the test constructor concentrates on the types of ability that can be measured easily, to the neglect of others that also ought to be measured, his test could become more reliable but less valid.

Again, a homogeneous test is likely to be more reliable than a heterogeneous test. But if a course of instruction aims to develop a variety of different abilities or relatively unrelated understandings, an appropriate test of achievement for that course must show corresponding variety, or heterogeneity, in the items it includes. Making the test valid in this case may interfere somewhat with making it reliable.

The selection of items for high indices of discrimination, as pointed out in Chapter 14 on item analysis, tends to make the test more reliable. If the rejected items are low in discrimination because of low technical quality, the reliability is gained at no sacrifice in validity. But if they show low indices of discrimination because they are measuring something different from the majority of items in the test and if that something is an essential part of what the whole test ought to measure, then the elimination of those items from the test would increase reliability at the expense of validity.

None of these possibilities of opposition or interference between reliability and validity justifies any devaluation of high reliability as a goal in test construction. Reliability is essential to validity. The test constructor is not justified in taking shortcuts to reliability by measuring only those things that can be easily measured with high reliability or by making his test more homogeneous than is warranted by the complexity of what he is testing; neither is he justified in settling for an unreliable test. He must try to measure what needs to be measured as reliably as possible. If he does not, the validity of his test will suffer.

VALIDITY AND RELEVANCE

Reliability is clearly an important component of validity. Another component is relevance. A test that measures with a high degree of accuracy what it is intended to measure is highly valid because it is both highly relevant and highly reliable. But a test could be highly reliable, in theory at least, without being highly valid if it lacked a high degree of relevance.

For almost all classroom tests of educational achievement, relevance is a matter of logical analysis and expert judgment. Unlike reliability, it ordinarily cannot be measured statistically, on the basis of experimental data, after the test has been given. Relevance must be built into the test.[19] What a test actually does measure is determined by the test constructor as he works, step by step, to build the test. The cumulative effect of the decisions he makes at each step in the process determines the relevance of the test. If the individual items in the test are relevant, that is, if they require demonstration of mastery of some essential aspect of the course and if they sample proportionally all those essential aspects, then the test as a whole will be relevant.[20]

Much of what this book has had to say about test construction has related to the problem of building relevance into the tests. This is especially true of the chapters on what can be measured, on test planning, and on the writing of true-false and multiple-choice items. But it may be useful to restate here some of the factors that are most likely to affect the relevance of classroom tests of educational achievement.

Chapter 3 suggested that the principal objective of all classroom instruction is to develop in the students a command of useful knowledge. To measure a student's achievement of this objective, a classroom test should present tasks that require a student to demonstrate his command of the knowledge, that is, his ability to use it. It should not reward sheer verbal memory. It should include novel, practical problems that require the application of knowledge. It should not present problems that can be solved by logical reasoning alone. The tasks in the test should require demonstration of achievement of the unique goals of instruction in the particular course. They should not be answerable successfully on the basis of general intelligence alone. The items in the test should be free of irrelevant clues that play into the hands of the sophisticated test taker. Above all, the tasks selected should relate to the most fundamental, the most central, and hence the most useful concepts and principles developed by the course.

The kind of validity we have been discussing, based on relevance and reliability, is the kind most classroom tests of educational achievement ought to have, and indeed the only kind they ordinarily can have. It is primary, direct, intrinsic validity. Sometimes it is referred to as "con-

[19]Edith M. Huddleson, "Test Development on the Basis of Content Validity," *Educational and Psychological Measurement*, vol. 16 (Autumn 1956), 283–93.

[20]Roger T. Lennon, "Assumptions Underlying the Use of Content Validity," *Educational and Psychological Measurement*, vol. 16 (Autumn 1956), 294–304.

tent validity" or "curricular validity." How much of this kind of validity a test possesses cannot be determined by looking at the scores the test yields. Instead one must look at the test itself, at the rationale and specifications for the test, if they are available, and at directions for administering and scoring it.

CHARACTERISTICS OF VALIDITY

The validity of any test is clearly a matter of degree, not an all-or-none quality. Tests are not valid or invalid. They are more or less valid. Further, the validity of a test is not completely determined by the test itself. It depends on the purpose for which the test is used, the group with which it is used, and the way it is administered and scored. Instead of asking, "How valid is this *test*?" it would be more precise to ask, "How valid are the *scores* from this test when it is used in a specified way for a specified purpose with a specified group?" Most classroom tests are constructed with a very specific group and purpose in mind. Flaws in test administration might adversely affect the reliability of the scores but are not likely to affect relevance appreciably.

How long does the validity of a classroom test last? If copies of the test are returned to the students for discussion and remedial instruction after the test was given and if the students who take the same course in successive years have frequent contacts with each other, the validity of a test may be abraded rapidly. Or if the teacher begins to use test content for teaching purposes, that is, to teach for the test directly, then its validity will also suffer. The tasks in any test are only a sample. At best they are a sample of a population of tasks any one of which the student would meet for the first time were it to be included in the test. Direct teaching for any of the tasks in a test tends to spoil the test as a representative sample from a population of novel tasks.

On the other hand, where no extensive use is made of the test for teaching and where contacts between members of successive classes are likely to be few and casual, the same test may retain its validity for a long time. Good tests are hard enough to build to make a teacher or professor consider carefully the pros and cons of using test items for teaching purposes.

SUMMARY

The main conclusion to be drawn from the discussions presented in this chapter can be summarized in the following 18 propositions.

1. Solid evidence supporting the validity of most educational tests is very difficult to obtain.
2. Physical scientists show less concern than psychologists for the validity of their measurements.
3. It is often difficult and seldom essential to secure a conclusive answer to questions asking which of two procedures provides the more valid measure of a particular characteristic.
4. The numerous varieties of validity that have been named and discussed can be grouped into two main types: direct validity and derived validity.
5. Course grades usually do not provide satisfactory criteria for the empirical validation of classroom tests of educational achievement.
6. The best procedures for establishing the validities of tests of educational achievement are usually those involving direct validation.
7. Many of the problems of test validation arise from lack of clear and generally accepted definitions of the thing to be measured.
8. The clearest definitions of quantitative concepts are those that specify the operations involved in measuring the concept.
9. Not all operational definitions of a trait or an achievement will prove to be equally rational or equally useful.
10. One can determine what a trait name, an educational achievement, or any other concept means better by looking for a consensus in the way competent people use the term than by analyzing the correlations among test scores.
11. The exercise of judgment is inescapable in the construction of valid tests. No wholly empirical processes of test validation are available.
12. Test validity can be defined more meaningfully in terms of the tasks the test samples than in terms of the traits it is presumed to measure.
13. To be valid a test must be both relevant and reliable.
14. A test can often, though not always, be made more valid by making it more reliable.
15. Validity can be built into a test of educational achievement by giving careful attention to the relevance of the tasks included in it.
16. Validity is a matter of degree. Tests are not valid or invalid. They are more or less valid.
17. Validity depends on the purposes for which a test is used, the group with which it is used, and the skill with which it is used.
18. Test validity may deteriorate as the test is used repeatedly.

PART V

PUBLISHED TESTS
AND TESTING PROGRAMS

The educational historian who comes to write the story of American education during the 1950's and 1960's can hardly fail to note, as one of its distinctive features, the pervasive use of the standardized test, at every level and for a variety of purposes.

ROGER T. LENNON

THE SCOPE
AND USE
OF PUBLISHED TESTS

THE SCOPE OF PUBLISHED TESTS

Previous chapters in this book have been concerned with tests of educational achievement prepared and used by classroom teachers. Some published tests are also intended to measure what students have learned in specific courses or units of instruction. But many more of them are designed to measure such things as:

Intelligence
Special aptitudes
Special skills or handicaps
Scholastic aptitude
General educational development
Personality traits
Attitudes and interests

451

Occupational proficiency
Professional competence

A more detailed, but still far from exhaustive, outline of human characteristics for which tests have been published is shown in Exhibit 17.1.

EXHIBIT 17.1

Categories of Published Tests*

ACHIEVEMENT BATTERIES	FOREIGN LANGUAGES	VOCATIONS, GENERAL
READING	English	Clerical
General	French	Interests
Oral	German	Manual dexterity
Readiness	Greek	Mechanical ability
Special fields	Hebrew	VOCATIONS, SPECIFIC
Speed	Italian	Accounting
Study skills	Latin	Dentistry
MATHEMATICS	Russian	Engineering
Arithmetic	Spanish	Law
Algebra	FINE ARTS	Medicine
Geometry	Art	Nursing
Trigonometry	Music	Research
SCIENCE	BUSINESS EDUCATION	Selling
General	General	Skilled trades
Biology	Bookkeeping	Supervision
Chemistry	Stenography	Transportation
Physics	Typewriting	MULTI-APTITUDE BATTERIES
SOCIAL STUDIES	MISCELLANEOUS	INTELLIGENCE
Contemporary affairs	Agriculture	Group
Economics	Driving and safety education	Individual
Geography	Education	Specific
History	Etiquette	CHARACTER AND PERSONALITY
ENGLISH	Handwriting	Nonprojective
Composition	Health and physical education	Projective
Literature	Home education	SENSORY-MOTOR
Speech	Industrial arts	Hearing
Spelling	Listening comprehension	Motor
Vocabulary	Marriage and courtship	Vision
	Philosophy	TEST PROGRAMS AND SERIES
	Psychology	COMPUTATION AND SCORING
	Religious education	RECORD AND REPORT FORMS
	Socioeconomic status	SELECTION AND RATING FORMS

*Adapted from Oscar K. Buros, *Tests in Print* (Highland Park, N.J.: The Gryphon Press, 1961), pp. vii–viii.

Names and publishers of tests for each of these traits can be found in *Tests in Print*. A total of 2,104 published tests are listed in this reference. The American Educational Publisher's Institute estimates that during 1969, over 81 million copies of these tests and answer sheets were sold, at a total cost of approximately $22 million.

Clearly, published tests are available for a large number of human traits, educational achievements, and occupational proficienties. Unfortunately, however, the number of characteristics that might be measured, and the distinctly different populations requiring different tests of these characteristics, are many times as large as the number of tests available to measure them. Despite the great variety of published tests, the odds are that a teacher, researcher, or employer who has an infrequently encountered measurement problem will be unable to find a published test to do the job he wants done. Usually it is not possible to say honestly that the desired test ought to be developed, or to suggest that the one who needs it could achieve fame and fortune by developing it. In view of the limited market and the limited life of most tests, the costs of developing an adequate test are too great to make the venture rewarding.

TWO LIMITATIONS OF PUBLISHED TESTS

Even the list of avaliable published tests should be regarded with at least two grains of salt: justifiable skepticism about what some of the tests actually measure, and about the quality of published tests. As to what the tests measure, for example, a test of practical judgment may appear on close inspection to be essentially a test of general information. A test of concept mastery may look remarkably like a vocabulary test. Even an intelligence test may be composed mainly of items that would be quite at home in a battery of achievement tests.

The trouble is that many of the characteristics we say we test are easier to name than to define. It is even more difficult to get a definition that will be generally accepted. The task of building a good test of some trait that has no standard definition and no generally recognized, precise meaning is quite naturally a very difficult one.

This problem is most acute when one is dealing with personality traits and other characteristics of interest to psychologists. But it also afflicts educational achievement tests. Mathematics does not mean the same thing to the teacher of conventional arithmetic as it does to the advocate of "modern" mathematics. Biology teaching that emphasizes function calls for somewhat different achievement than teaching that is organized around a taxonomy of forms. Tests having the same or closely similar titles may actually test quite different kinds of achievement. As is true of psychological traits, it is easier to give the same name to several courses than to get agreement on common content or objectives for them.

As for the quality of published tests, these tests should be, and usually are, prepared more expertly and with greater care than the usual classroom test. But seldom is the job done well enough to draw unqualified praise from the critics. The hard fact is that construction of a good standardized test is such a long, difficult, demanding, and costly job that the test constructor often feels obliged to settle for something less than his ideal of excellence. Teachers need to recognize that while most published tests result from honest effort, the fact that they are called "standardized" is no guarantee of their excellence. Some are very good indeed. Others are mediocre. Still others are so poor that they fully deserve the condemnation they sometimes receive from knowledgeable critics.

DESIRABLE CHARACTERISTICS OF PUBLISHED TESTS

All of the characteristics of a good classroom test mentioned in Chapter 13 apply also to published tests. That is, the items in the test ought to be:

relevant to the purpose of the test,
balanced across all aspects to be tested,
efficient in producing numerous scorable responses,
objective, so experts will all give the same answer,
specific, so they test more than intelligence or general knowledge,
difficult enough, but not too difficult, and
discriminating between those of high and those of low achievement.

All of these qualities contribute to the test's

reliability (consistent measurement of something), and
validity (measurement of what was intended).

Obviously, too, the test should be

fair in what it demands and how it is given,
long enough to give reliable scores, and
speeded enough to make good use of the time available but not so much as to distort measurement of achievement or generate needless anxiety.

In addition to these there are some special characteristics that contribute to the quality of a published test.

1. It should be convenient to administer under standardized conditions.

The scores of a published standardized test are intended to be compared with scores on the same test obtained in other administrations. This means that the directions for administration should be sufficiently detailed and clear, and that the process of administration be uncomplicated enough to make it easy to conduct a standard administration of the test. A test consisting of many short, separately timed subtests is hard to administer uniformly. A very long test is hard to fit into the school schedule and into the interest span of the pupils being tested.

2. It should be convenient to score accurately.

Separate answer sheets, stencil keys, and machine scoring (if one- to three-day service is available) contribute to ease of scoring. If the answer sheets have to be mailed to a central scoring service that can promise no less than two or three week service, the delay may cancel much of the interest and some of the value of the test results. Single-score tests are easier to score than those that provide many part scores on short subtests. Often, in the latter case, the subtest scores based on relatively few test items are highly unreliable.

3. It should yield scores that are easy to interpret correctly.

No test score, even the easiest to interpret, can be properly called self-interpreting. All scores depend on the interpreter's knowledge and good sense to some degree. But the statistical refinements[1] or even the deliberate obscurity[2] built into some test scores makes them particularly difficult to interpret. On the other hand some kinds of test scores, like grade level scores for elementary school tests, are easy to interpret incorrectly. These problems are discussed more fully in Chapter 19.

4. It should be provided with appropriate, dependable norms

One of the main reasons for using a published test is that it provides a basis for comparing the scores of a local group with an external standard of achievement. This is usually provided by the scores of a representative

---

[1] Eric F. Gardner, "Normative Standard Scores," *Educational and Psychological Measurement*, vol. 22 (Spring 1962), 7–14.

[2] William H. Angoff, "Scales with Non-meaningful Origins and Units of Measurement," *Educational and Psychological Measurement*, vol. 22 (Spring 1962), 27–34.

sample from some large population of comparable students. These scores are summarized in tables of norms. But the problems of providing appropriate, dependable norms are not easy for test publishers to solve. These problems, too, are discussed more fully in Chapter 19.

> 5. *If the test is to be used repeatedly, equivalent forms should be provided.*

Forms of a test that can be used interchangeably, with differences in scores on the different forms attributable to differences in the persons tested, not to differences in the tests, are equivalent. Making tests equivalent in this sense calls for painstaking effort. Most publishers of standardized tests, however, seem willing and able to provide reasonably equivalent forms.

> 6. *The cost of the test booklets, answer sheets, and accessory materials should not be high in relation to the value received.*

Competition between test publishers tends to keep test costs as low as sound business management will allow. Like the costs of other educational materials and services, the costs of published tests have increased sharply in recent years. The information provided by a good test is valuable enough, however, to justify the small portion of the educational budget that is ordinarily expended on tests.

One interesting problem has arisen in the pricing of published tests. Separate answer sheets make possible the reuse of test booklets. Reuse limits the sale of the booklets and increases the sale of answer sheets. Publishers are thus driven to recover more of the costs of test development through the sale of answer sheets. But usable answer sheets can sometimes be printed locally (albeit in violation of copyright), and different scoring machines require different answer sheets. These three developments —reusable booklets, home-made answer sheets, and the need to supply different answer sheets for different scoring machines—pose difficult problems, which test publishers have been unable to solve to their complete satisfaction.

THE VALIDITY OF PUBLISHED TESTS

Reviewers of published tests tend to be particularly critical of the lack of evidence of test validity. In this they may sometimes be unreasonable. It is true that validity is such an essential element in the goodness of a test that for a test to to lack it is a fatal flaw. For some tests of special functions, for which unquestionably valid criteria exist, it is reasonable to ask the producer to present evidence of his test's validity. For many other tests, however, no such criteria exist. The test itself may be the most careful attempt yet made to measure what it is trying to test. In those cases, to ask the developer to offer *evidence* that his test is valid is to ask the impossible.

The problem of providing evidence of test validity is similar to the problem of providing evidence that a person has lived a good life. In both cases the evidence of validity, or goodness, is often found in the test, or the life, itself, not in something separate or additional. Whether the life or the test is judged to be valid, or good, depends somewhat on the values and standards of the judge. Usually a test's validity depends to a considerable degree on the circumstances in which it is used. Further, there are some tests to which the very concept of validity, as usually understood, does not apply.[3]

For these reasons, evidence for the validity of published tests is sometimes scanty or lacking altogether. The test user may not find, in advance of his own use of the test, clear evidence that it will be valid for the purposes he has in mind.

CRITICAL TEST REVIEWS AND TEST STANDARDS

One way of working toward higher quality in published tests is to subject them to critical reviews. Several journals, including the *Journal of Consulting Psychology*, the *Journal of Counseling Psychology*, and the *Personnel and Guidance Journal*, publish such reviews regularly. But it is the *Mental Measurements Yearbooks*, edited by Oscar Buros, that provide the most comprehensive and generally useful collections of test descriptions and critical reviews. The *Sixth Mental Measurements Yearbook*, published in 1965, includes entries for 1,219 tests.[4]

Educators who contribute critical test reviews to the *Mental Measurements Yearbook* are carefully selected. Their critical standards are high. Few tests emerge from the reviewing process unscathed. But let it also be noted that the reivewers are not infallible in their judgments. They hold somewhat different opinions about the most important qualities of a test and about what a specific test ought to measure. They do

---

[3]Robert L. Ebel, "Must All Tests Be Valid?" *American Psychologist*, vol. 16 (1961), 640–47.

[4]Oscar K. Buros, *The Sixth Mental Measurements Yearbook* (Highland Park, N.J.: The Gryphon Press, 1965).

not always show full awareness of the difficulties faced by commercially limited test publishers in meeting the highest standards of test quality. But despite these occasional shortcomings, the *Mental Measurements Yearbook* has contributed greatly to the production of better tests, and to more sophisticated evaluation and use of these tests. It is an indispensible guide to the prospective users of published tests.

In an effort to counterbalance the personal biases and idiosyncrasies of particular reviewers, and to be fair to test authors and publishers, the editor of the *Yearbook* attempts to include at least two reviews of each test. The prospective user should read and consider all of them. He will find them helpful, but he should not expect them to make the decision for him. That choice, often made tentatively pending actual experience with the test, should be based on a consideration of all of the characteristics of the test and of the user's purposes.

Another major influence toward the improvement of published tests was the development by a joint committee of three professional associations of a set of recommneded standards for such tests. These were first published in 1954, in two separate pamphlets of technical recommendations. A revised, combined version of the recommendations was published in 1966 under the title *Standards for Educational and Psychological Tests and Manuals*.[5]

The standards, designated as either essential, very desirable, or desirable, are grouped under six headings:

A. Dissemination of information
B. Interpretation
C. Validity
D. Reliability
E. Administration and scoring
F. Scales and norms

Sample standards illustrate their general nature.

A2. The test and its manual should be revised at appropriate intervals.
B3. The test manual should indicate the qualifications required to administer the test and to interpret it properly.
F5. Norms should be reported in the test manual in terms of standard scores or percentile ranks which reflect the distribution of scores in an appropriate reference group or groups.

Extensive debate preceded and has followed the publication of these standards. They are likely to be revised in the future. But the test publisher who follows them, except where he has adequate reason to believe they are wrong or do not apply, will produce a very good test.

[5](Washington, D.C.: American Psychological Association), p. 40.

SOURCES OF INFORMATION ABOUT PUBLISHED TESTS

A person who hopes to use a published test faces at least three problems:

1. Finding the names and sources of tests that might serve his purposes.
2. Becoming familiar with the test and associated materials.
3. Deciding which, if any, of the available tests will best serve his purposes.

For help in solving the first problem, the prospective user may turn to an introductory textbook in educational measurements, to an index of published tests, to the catalogs of test publishers, or to current periodicals that carry articles on or reviews of new tests.

Some textbooks designed for use in introductory courses in educational measurements present fairly detailed descriptions of some published tests and test batteries. The books by Mehrens and Lehmann,[6] by Noll,[7] and by Thorndike and Hagen[8] are excellent sources of descriptive information about a variety of published tests. The teacher who is looking for initial guidance in test selection will find these books, and others like them, very helpful.

There are several reasons why little if any descriptive information about specific tests will be presented in this book.

1. Space does not permit description of all the tests that ought to be included if any are.
2. Descriptive information tends to go out of date, swiftly in some cases, as new tests are introduced or substantial modifications are made in existing tests.
3. Few of the tests that might be mentioned are likely to be of great interest to a substantial proportion of a class that is taking a first course in measurement. It is hard to justify the requirement that *all* students in the class must learn the essential features of more than a very few, very widely used tests.
4. Finally, although descriptive information about particular tests is useful to have in a reference book, it is not very attractive or rewarding material for study or teaching. Simple presentation of the facts is about the only way of teaching them, and simple memorization is about the only way for students to learn them. These facts do not contribute to much of a structure of knowledge. Beyond knowing the meanings of the words used to present the facts, there is little to understand about them.

---

[6]William A. Mehrens and Irvin J. Lehmann, *Standardized Tests in Education* (New York: Holt, Rinehart and Winston, Inc., 1969).

[7]Victor H. Noll, *Introduction to Educational Measurement*, 2d ed. (Boston: Houghton Mifflin Company, 1965).

[8]Robert L. Thorndike and Elizabeth Hagen, *Measurement and Evaluation in Psychology and Education*, 3d ed. (New York: John Wiley Sons, Inc., 1969).

If descriptive information about particular tests were an essential part of the cognitive equipment of most classroom teachers, the fact that such knowledge is not easy or pleasant to acquire would be no valid argument against teaching or learning it. But this appears to be one case where storage of the needed information in reference works is preferable to storage of it in human minds. Thus, one useful source of information about published tests is some *other* textbook in educational measurement.

Another useful source, more comprehensive though less fully descriptive than a measurement textbook, is Buros' *Tests in Print*.[9] The *Mental Measurements Yearbooks*[10] also provide useful indices, though they are neither as comprehensive nor as convenient as *Tests in Print*. More limited indices can sometimes be found as journal articles or as separate publications in good education libraries.

Tests in Print, published in 1961, is a comprehensive bibliography of tests currently available in English-speaking countries. Each entry includes, where relevant, the following information:

1. The test title
2. The subjects for whom the test is appropriate
3. Publication dates
4. Number and nature of scores reported
5. Authors and publisher
6. Parts and subtests
7. Special comments
8. Cross-references to other entries in *Tests in Print* and to the
9. *Mental Measurements Yearbooks*

Updated editions of *Tests in Print* may appear in future years.

Another source of information on published tests is the Office of Special Tests at the Educational Testing Service, Princeton, New Jersey. Most of the tests mentioned on the lists published periodically by this office are experimental and not likely to be widely used. Nevertheless, the prospective user might find just what he is searching for among them.

The catalogs of test publishers provide another useful guide to published tests. Names and addresses of some of the major test publishers are listed in Exhibit 17.2. A more complete list is given in *Tests in Print*. A typical entry in one of the test catalogs is shown in Exhibit 17.3. As a source of information about tests, these catalogs can be very useful.

The best guide to articles in periodicals dealing with published tests is the *Education Index*. Some of these articles, particularly the test reviews, will deal at some length with specific tests. Other articles on some aspect of the trait being measured may mention published tests that have been, or might be, used. Those who read educational and psychological periodicals regularly will gradually become acquainted with a wide range of

[9]See fn., Ex. 17.1.
[10]See fn. 4.

EXHIBIT 17.2

Some Major Test Publishers

CTB/McGraw-Hill, Del Monte Research Park, Monterey, California 93940

Cooperative Tests and Services, Educational Testing Service, Princeton, New Jersey 08540

Harcourt Brace Jovanovich, Inc., 757 Third Avenue, New York, New York 10017

Houghton Mifflin Company, 110 Tremont Street, Boston, Massachusetts 02107

Personnel Press, Inc., 20 Nassau Street, Princeton, New Jersey 08540

The Psychological Corporation, 304 East 45th Street, New York, New York 10017

Scholastic Testing Service, Inc., 480 Meyer Road, Bensenville, Illinois 60106

Science Research Associates, Inc., 259 East Erie Street, Chicago, Illinois 60611

EXHIBIT 17.3

Typical Test Catalog Entry

SPITZER STUDY SKILLS TEST   GRADES 9–13
Herbert F. Spitzer

A five-part measure of important work-study skills: Using the Dictionary; Using the Index; Knowledge of Sources of Information; Understanding Graphs, Maps, and Tables; and Organization of Facts in Note Taking. Results of each subtest are sufficiently reliable to be useful for diagnostic purposes. Time: 2 hours 30 minutes (3 sittings). Scoring: Hand score IBM Answer Sheet with IBM Machine Key. Machine Score IBM Answer Sheet either locally or through Harcourt Brace Jovanovich's IBM Scoring Service. Norms: Percentiles.

SPITZER STUDY SKILLS TEST	FORMS	NET PRICE
Test booklet	AM, BM	$6.00 pkg/35
IBM answer sheet	AM, BM	1.75 pkg/35
IBM scoring—basic service (opt. See page 86.)		.40 per student
Specimen set		.40 each

Test package contains directions and IBM machine key. IBM answer sheet package contains class record.

published tests, But the search for a specific test via the *Eduaction Index* and the periodicals it covers is likely to be long and quite possibly unsuccessful.

GETTING ACQUAINTED WITH SPECIFIC TESTS

The second problem of the prospective test user is to become familiar with the test and associated materials once he has identified the ones that interest him. If the test is one that is widely used, he may find helpful discussions of it in textbooks of educational measurement or in articles in professional journals. The descriptive entries and critical reviews in the *Mental Measurements Yearbooks* will also be helpful if the test has been listed there. But the best way to become acquainted with a test is to purchase the specimen set that most test publishers offer; to take the test, score the answers, and interpret the score; and to read the manual and associated materials offered by the test publisher. Only when the prospective user has this first-hand acquaintance with a test and its accessories can he claim to be familiar with it.

Direct exposure to the test itself may go far toward solving the test user's third problem, that of deciding which if any of the available tests will best serve his purposes. He may also be aided by reading critical reviews of the test, if any are available, in current periodicals or in the *Mental Measurements Yearbooks*.

Obviously the careful selection of a published test is no simple, easy task. Items of relevant information are sometimes hard to find or completely unavailable. But in most cases, a poor choice is not due primarily to deficiencies of the test publisher. It is more often due to lack of care or lack of competence on the part of the test user.

A PROGRAM FOR USING PUBLISHED TESTS

Any school with a good educational program ought to encourage its teachers to supplement their own classroom tests with a few carefully selected and fully utilized published tests. It can do this by making limited funds available to each teacher for the purchase of any published test she would like to use in her classes.

Two strings should be attached to this offer. One, that an interpretive report of the results be prepared for pupils to take home to their parents. Each pupil's score on the test should be recorded on the copy of the report he takes home. The second is that an evaluative summary of the class results be prepared and submitted to the school administration.

These procedures are likely to provide strong stimulation to the faculty for in-service education in the selection of published tests and in the interpretation of test results. If the school staff includes one or more members who are experienced and knowledgeable in test selection and score interpretation, the program could result in substantial improvements in teacher competence in educational evaluation. Teacher competence is always individual. To cultivate that competence there are no good substitutes for individual opportunity and individual responsibility.

The procedures here suggested will not give the school a coordinated testing program. Unfortunately, in school testing, coordination is sometimes achieved at the cost of test relevance, of staff interest and support, and of fully used test results. Local option in the use of published tests has some very attractive features. It can be guaranteed to make at least some of the staff well acquainted with some of the available published tests, their characteristics, uses, and limitations. It may give them an independent assessment of the effectiveness of their efforts and cause them to reconsider their objectives and procedures. Self-imposed assessments are likely to be more tolerable and influential than externally imposed assessments.

One word of caution. Never should scores on a published test be regarded as sufficient evidence of a teacher's success or lack of it. Such a test always should be regarded as supplementary evidence, to be weighed lightly or heavily as circumstances seem to warrant, along with other evidences of pupil achievement and other evidences of teacher effectiveness.

SUMMARY

The major ideas developed in this chapter can be summarized in these statements.

1. Over 2,100 published tests of over 75 human achievements, abilities, or other characteristics are identified in Buros' *Tests in Print*.
2. It is economically feasible for publishers to develop and distribute tests for only the most widely recognized test needs.
3. Not all published tests measure what their titles indicate. Not all of them are of high quality.
4. The quality and usefulness of published tests depend not only on the characteristics that make classroom tests good but also on these additional elements: directions for convenient administration; provision for easy scoring; scores that are easy to interpret; appropriate dependable norms; equivalent forms; and reasonable cost.
5. There are good and usually sufficient reasons why statistical evidence for the validity of published tests is often scanty and sometimes totally absent.
6. Critical test reviews and professionally authorized test standards have done much to improve the quality of published tests.
7. Test publishers' catalogs and comprehensive lists of published tests such as those found in *Tests in Print* or the *Mental Measurements Yearbooks* are useful guides to published tests.
8. The best way to become acquainted with a specific published test is to pur-

chase and study carefully the materials in the specimen set most publishers offer.

9. School administrators can make good use of published tests by making limited funds available for the purchase of such tests by individual classroom teachers, in exchange for assurance that the results will be reported and interpreted to students, parents, and the school administration.

10. Scores on a published test should never be regarded as a sufficient basis for judging a teacher's effectiveness.

By weighing we know what things are light and what heavy. By measuring we know what things are long and what short. The relations of all things may be thus determined, and it is of the greatest importance to measure the motions of the mind. I beg your majesty to measure it.

SENECA (335 B.C.)

18

STANDARDIZED ACHIEVEMENT TESTS AND TEST BATTERIES

WHAT IS A STANDARDIZED ACHIEVEMENT TEST?

The term *standardized test* originally meant, and still means when used precisely, a test that:

1. has been carefully, expertly constructed, usually with tryout, analysis, and revision;
2. has explicit instructions for uniform (standard) administration; and
3. has tables of norms (standards) for score interpretation derived from administration of the test to a defined sample of students.

Used loosely, the term can refer to almost any published test or inventory, whether standardized in the manner just described or not. In this section, *standardized test* will be used in its more restricted sense, and attention

465

will be limited to the characteristics, values, and limitations of standardized tests of achievement. Consideration will be given to standard test scores and norms in the next chapter.

Most standardized achievement tests are composed of objective test items. It would be almost impossibly difficult to standardize the scoring of anything but an objective test. As a matter of fact, objective test items were invented to meet the needs of the wide-scale survey testing that led to the development of standardized tests. Only afterward did classroom teachers begin to use objective items in their own test construction.

SOME DIFFERENCES BETWEEN STANDARDIZED AND CLASSROOM TESTS

Standardized tests differ from classroom tests in a number of important ways. In the first place, they come to the user ready-made. He does not need to spend hours deciding what to test and how to test it, writing the items, reviewing and editing them, and finally having them printed for classroom use. If the standardized test is a good one, these tasks have been done by a group of test constructors that includes expert teachers and expert test specialists. In all probability, data from research studies relevant to the test have been used by the test construction group to help with the decisions they have had to make. The test construction team has probably worked long and hard and done its conscientious best to produce a good test.

All of this costs money, which the users of the test in the long run must supply. This leads to a second important difference between classroom tests and standardized tests. The standardized tests must be purchased. Prices vary, of course, but the teacher who plans to use a good group intelligence test for a class of 32 fifth grade pupils could expect the school to get a bill something like this:

35 reusable test booklets	$4.50
35 machine scorable answer sheets	1.75
1 machine scoring key	.35
1 manual	.60
	$7.20

A high school teacher of biology who wants to give a standardized test to her class of 20 students to supplement her own measures of achievement should get authorization for an expenditure something like this:

35 test booklets	$7.00
35 answer sheets	2.20
1 scoring key	.30
	$9.50

Thus the per-pupil cost of giving a single standardized test may range from about 20 cents to about 50 cents. If every teacher in a school of 1,000 pupils were to give one standard test a year in every subject, the total bill could come to several thousand dollars. This is not a large amount in relation to other educational costs. If good use is made of the test results, the expenditure is easy to justify.

A third important difference between standardized and teacher-made tests is in the content covered. A good teacher-made test includes a representative sample of the tasks that the students were taught to handle in that particular class. A standardized test, on the other hand, must limit its tasks to those likely to be taught in *most* classes studying a specific subject.

The authors of most standardized tests of achievement do make conscientious efforts to determine what is being commonly taught in most classes teaching a specific subject, since the volume of use of their test depends on its general acceptability. In some subjects of study, where course content is reasonably uniform from school to school and reasonably stable from year to year, the task of finding a substantial proportion of common elements in the total of what is being taught isn't impossibly difficult. But in areas where course content is not uniformly agreed upon, and in periods when enthusiasm for curricular reform sweeps the schools, the problems of the authors of a standardized achievement test may become almost insoluble.

It must not be assumed that in this matter of content coverage the advantage is all with the teacher-made test. Not all teachers building a classroom test do a careful, competent job of sampling what they actually have taught. What they have taught may be vastly different from what they should have taught. Often a great deal of expert judgment and careful consideration go into determining what to test in a standardized test of achievement. The teacher who rejects a standardized test on the ground that it doesn't cover what was taught in her course may find it hard to explain why her perceptions of what ought to be taught, or the perceptions of the author of the text she used, differed so much from those of the authors of the test.

Perhaps the fact that text authors are faced with the necessity of making their books unique, whereas test authors must try to include only what is common, is worth pointing out. Only by being different can a textbook be better, but simply being different does not make it better. The same principle applies to classroom teaching. The emphasis that standardized tests of achievement place on standard course content may be a valuable counterbalance to the forces that make for excessive diversity in textbooks and in teaching.

TWO PROBLEMS OF STANDARDIZED ACHIEVEMENT TESTING

Standard achievement tests are designed to measure achievement, but even among measurement specialists (perhaps *especially* among measurement specialists) there are doubts about the metric quality (that is, the logical and mathematical properties) of the measures obtained. For many years those who are concerned with measurement in education and psychology have looked enviously at the measurements of the physical scientists: at the definiteness of the dimensions they measure, at the precision and uniformity of the scales they use.

In the early days of standardized testing some educators hoped that they might achieve the same precision in measuring "mind" that the physical scientists had achieved in measuring matter. These hopes have never been realized. No standard units of mental development corresponding in definiteness and precision to the meter, the gram, or the second have been discovered or developed. Nor are there any instruments comparable to the meter stick, the analytic balance, or the chronometer to measure them.

Most measurement specialists now agree that there probably never will be such units or such instruments, for the things to be measured seem not to have any simple, stable dimensions. The devices we have been able to develop to measure these things lack the precision and durable usefulness of physical measuring instruments. Tests can affect strongly the thing being measured. They also wear out rapidly.

To know in advance the course over which a race is to be run helps the runner very little to increase his speed. But to know in advance what tasks will be set to test a mental ability can help the student greatly to do those tasks. A given set of tasks can constitute a representative sample of a student's abilities in a given field only if the student does not know in advance what the tasks will be. Mental tests cannot be used repeatedly without the possibility of serious loss in validity. So the dream of standard measures of educational development is likely to remain a dream.

However, if we will settle for more limited objectives in mental measurement and more limited success in attaining them, we will find many worthwhile educational uses for mental tests, whether standardized or teacher-made. Between the impossible dream of perfectly precise and permanently valid measures of educational development on the one hand, and the unjustified denial of the possibility of any useful mental measurements on the other, there are wide realms of opportunity. Some of these have already been explored and developed. Others remain as challenges for future scholars and teachers.

FACTORS LIMITING THE VARIETY OF AVAILABLE ACHIEVEMENT TESTS

The economic necessity, or advantage, of limiting the content of a particular test to the topics most frequently taught has restricted the fields for which standardized tests are available to those that enroll large numbers of students. This effect has been particularly apparent in recent years. More and more the offerings of test publishers have tended to concentrate on tests of general fields of knowledge rather than on specific course content. There are numerous tests of intelligence, numerous batteries of tests of general educational development, numerous tests of reading and of arithmetic. But the more specialized the subject and the more advanced the level, the more limited the potential market and thus, the fewer the offerings.

Some of those who develop and publish tests argue that this trend is educationally desirable. They contend that it is the general educational development of a student that is important, not his specific knowledge of the subject matter of specific courses. No doubt they are honestly persuaded that this is so, despite the obvious fact that the belief serves well to support large volume sales of general tests. But they must be mistaken.

In most walks of life where knowledge is used, general knowledge is not adequate. What the doctor or the lawyer or the editor or the artisan needs is specific knowledge. The English teacher may claim that her students studying *King Lear* or *Silas Marner* or *The Catcher in the Rye* are learning to understand and interpret and appreciate literature in general. But what one learns mostly in studying *King Lear* is that particular play. One learns, if he has a good teacher, what Shakespeare perceived and expressed about particular aspects of human frailty and nobility evoked by a specific situation. The quotations one remembers are specific quotations. The general ability we speak of probably consists entirely of an organized and integrated body of particulars.

Another factor that has caused a reduction in the variety of tests offered by publishers is persistent criticism from test specialists of the inadequacies of some of the "standardized" tests that were published in such abundance, and so hurriedly, during the early days of the testing movement. Critics pointed to inadequate research to determine appropriate content, inadequate item tryout and editorial review, inadequate norms, inadequate validity studies, and meager manuals. They succeeded in improving the general level of test quality, but at the cost of restricting those tests more and more to fields where large-volume sales could be anticipated.

In these circumstances it is legitimate to wonder if the critics have really served education well. Is there not a place, is there not a need, for tests that cover smaller units of instruction; tests that can be supported with smaller volume sales because they are less ambitiously conceived and less elaborately developed; tests that may even lack alternate forms, or norms, or validity studies? Perhaps some test publisher could perform an educational service by selecting the best of the many good tests that are produced around the country by expert teachers who are also skillful in test construction; by editing, publishing, cataloging, and offering such tests for sale. Published tests of achievement need not be limited to those that have been painstakingly standardized. They ought not to be limited to subjects where volume of sales is certain to be large.

ACHIEVEMENT TEST BATTERIES

Standardized tests of educational achievement are often developed, published, and administered in coordinated sets known as test batteries. The number of tests, or subtests, in a battery may vary from 4 or less to 10 or more. Here are some examples:

STANFORD ACHIEVEMENT TESTS (FIVE LEVELS: GRADES 1.6–2.5, 2.6–3.9, 4.0–5.5, 5.6–6.9, 7.0–9.6)

Reading	*Arithmetic*
Word reading	Computation
Paragraph meaning	Concepts
Vocabulary	Applications
Spelling	
Word study skills	*Social Studies*
Language	Concepts
	Study skills
	Science

IowA TESTS OF EDUCATIONAL DEVELOPMENT (GRADES 9–12)

1. Understanding of Basic Social Concepts
2. Background in the Natural Sciences
3. Correctness and Appropriateness of Expression
4. Ability to do Quantitative Thinking
5. Ability to Interpret in the Social Studies
6. Ability to Interpret in the Natural Sciences
7. Ability to Interpret Literary Materials
8. General Vocabulary
9. Uses of Sources of Information

SEQUENTIAL TESTS OF EDUCATIONAL PROGRESS (FOUR LEVELS: GRADES 4–6, 7–9, 10–12, 13–14)

Reading	Listening	Writing	Social Studies
Essay	Mathematics	Science	

The number of items per test may vary from 35 or fewer to 100 or more; the time per test 10 minutes to more than an hour. The administration of a battery like the Iowa Tests of Educational Development requires three or four half-day sessions.

A test battery can provide comprehensive coverage of most of the important aspects of achievement at the elementary school level, many at the secondary level, and some at the college level. The more uniform the educational programs of the students, the more suitable is a uniform test battery for all of them. Such a battery can be planned to avoid duplication in the content covered by the several tests and to minimize the number of serious omissions.

Use of a battery of tests that was developed as an integrated whole thus offers substantial advantages. The only significant disadvantage is the lack of flexibility in the battery. The battery may include some tests that interest a user very little and may omit some he would like very much. But this is part of the price that must be paid for the advantage of convenience in use, comprehensiveness of coverage, and comparability of scores. Test developers quite naturally seek to minimize these disadvantages. Usually they are quite successful in doing so. If they were not, test batteries would be much less popular than they have proved to be.

The coordination of achievement tests within a battery has another important advantage: it makes possible the provision of comparable scores and norms. This is important if a student's achievement in one area is to be compared with his achievement in another. If uncoordinated tests are used, a student might seem to do better on Test A than on Test

B simply because students of lower achievement made up the norm group
of Test A.

PROFILES OF TEST SCORES

Only if scores on the several tests used are comparable is a profile
of the student's scores on the several tests meaningful. An example of
one pupil's test score profile is shown in Exhibit 18.1. The horizontal

EXHIBIT 18.1

Example of Pupil Profile Chart

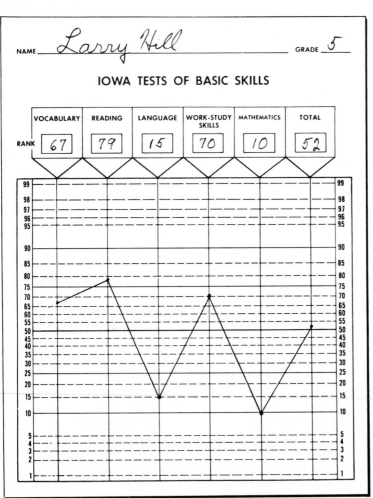

lines on the chart represent various percentile ranks. They are spaced as they would be if scores on the vertical scale were normally distributed. There is a vertical line on the chart for each test in the battery. The percentile ranks shown across the top of the chart are marked as dots on each vertical scale, and connected by lines to form the profile. Larry Hill is about average, overall. (His percentile rank for the total test is 52.) His best achievements are in reading, vocabulary, and work-study skills. His poorest are in language and mathematics.

It is important to remember, in using profiles, that small differences could result from errors of measurement. A slightly higher score on one test than another does not necessarily indicate higher achievement in that area. On the other hand, if a student's score on Test A is 52, and on Test B is 53, the slightly more probable explanatory hypothesis is that his achievement in B is actually higher than in A. Slightly less probable is the hypothesis that he is actually better at A than at B. Very much less probable is the hypothesis that he is equally good in both areas. Exact equality of achievement in two different areas is highly unlikely.

These observations are not intended to minimize the importance of errors of measurement. Nor are they intended to suggest that much confidence can be placed in any one of the hypotheses just mentioned. But they are intended to challenge the beliefs, sometimes expressed, that small score differences are totally devoid of significance or that they signify identity of achievement. Just as too much significance can be attached to these differences, so also too little significance, or the wrong significance, can be attached to them.

PERCENTILE BANDS

Some test publishers stress the fact that test scores are subject to error by refusing to report an exact percentile equivalent for each raw test score. Instead they report a range of values within which the true percentile equivalent probably lies. This range of percentiles is often referred to as a percentile band. For example, the manual may indicate that the equivalent percentile rank for a test score of 37 is some value between 28 and 57, pointing out that the exact equivalent is unknown since it depends on the unknown size and sign (positive or negative) of the error of measurement in the score.

The width of the percentile band depends on two factors, the reliability of the test and the degree of certainty that it includes the true value. Unreliable tests or high degrees of certainty lead to broad percentile bands. The degree of certainty desired is a matter of more or less arbitrary decision. There is no objective criterion that can be appealed to in determining it. And, unfortunately, the broader these percentile bands the less useful information the test provides.

One use of the percentile bands for the scores of a student on the tests of a battery is to indicate whether or not a difference between the scores is significant. If the percentile bands for two of the scores overlap, the manual suggests, little confidence should be placed in it as indicating a real difference. But if they do not overlap the difference may be regarded as significant of a true difference in achievement.

These suggestions guard against the danger of attaching too much importance to score differences that might be due to errors of measurement. But they invite two other misinterpretations. One is that differences below a somewhat arbitrary critical value have no significance at all. The other is that as the differences increase toward the critical value they change suddenly and categorically from insignificant to significant. The fact is, however, that insignificance does not end and significance begin at any particular size of score value. The larger the difference in scores, the more confidently one can believe in a corresponding difference in achievement. These facts are illustrated in Fig. 18.1, in which a statistically defensible relation between size of a difference and confidence in it is contrasted with that implied by the use of percentile bands in the way just described.

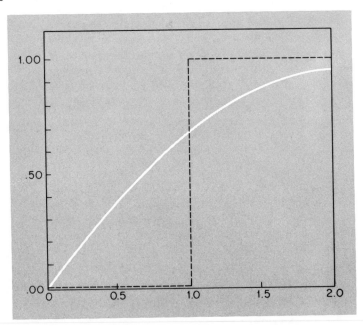

Horizontal Scale: Score difference divided by its standard error
Vertical Scale: Confidence the score difference is real
Solid Curve: Relation indicated by sampling theory
Dotted Lines: Relation implied by percentile bands

FIGURE 18.1
Confidence in a Score Difference

These two misinterpretations limit and distort the essential meaning of the test scores. In reducing the possibility of overly exact interpretation, they reduce the amount of information to be interpreted. And they complicate the process of score interpretation by requiring the test user to deal with two percentiles, neither of which is a good indication of the probable meaning of the score, instead of with one percentile representing the most probable meaning. For these reasons the value of percentile bands in improving score interpretation seems open to question.[1]

SUBTEST SCORES

Just as the tests that constitute a test battery provide separate measures of different aspects of achievement, it is possible to subdivide a single complex test into separately scored parts to obtain measures of different aspects of the complex. The desire to obtain as much information as possible from a test sometimes leads the test developer to offer a large number of part scores, each of which is based on only a few test items. There are two limitations to this process. One is that as the number of part scores is increased, the reliability of each diminishes. On many tests a part score based on as few as 10 or 15 items may report more error of sampling than true achievement. The other is that multiplying the number of scores a test yields complicates the process of using it without producing a corresponding gain in its value. Often all the test user really wants, and all he has time to use effectively, is a single overall measure of achievement in an area. On a standard test of achievement, therefore, the provision of a number of part scores should be viewed more with skepticism than with acclaim.

USES OF STANDARDIZED ACHIEVEMENT TEST SCORES

The primary and essential use of standardized achievement test scores is to provide a special kind of information on the extent of pupil learning. It is special because it is based on a concensus of expert teachers with respect to what ought to be learned in the study of a specific subject, a concensus external to and independent of the local teacher. It is special because it provides a basis for comparing local achievements with external norms of achievement in comparable classes. It is useful information

[1]P. Kenneth Morse, "Reporting Test Results: Percentile Bands vs. Percentile Ranks," *Journal of Educational Measurement*, vol. 1 (1964), 139–42.

because it helps to inform students, teachers, school administrators, and the public at large of the effectiveness of their educational efforts.

Schools have often been criticized for setting up testing programs, giving and scoring the tests, and then doing nothing with the test scores except to file them in the principal's office. If the school faculty and the individual teachers do not study the test results, identifying levels and ranges or achievement in the school as a whole and in specific classes, identifying students of high and low achievement; if the scores are not reported and interpreted to students, parents, and the public, these criticisms are justifiable. But if they mean that no coherent program of action triggered specifically by the test results and designed to "do something" about them emerged from the testing program, then the criticisms probably are not justified.

What a good school faculty does about scores from the standardized tests it gives is something like what a good citizen does with the information he gleans from a newspaper. Having finished the evening paper he does not lay it aside and ask himself, "Now what am I going to do about all this, about the weather, the accidents, the crimes, the legislative decisions, the clothing sales, the stock market reports, the baseball games won and lost, and all the rest?" He may, in response to one or two items, plan specific actions. But most of what is memorable he simply stores as a part of his knowledge. In hundreds of unplanned ways it will affect the opinions he expresses later, the votes he casts, the other decisions he makes. Information can be very useful ultimately even when it triggers no immediate response.

Educators who properly deplore the unwisdom of judging teacher competence solely on the basis of pupil test scores sometimes fail to see the equal unwisdom of taking action on school or pupil problems solely on the basis of those same test scores. Seldom do standardized test scores by themselves provide sufficient guidance for wise and effective educational actions. It follows that these test scores should be regarded primarily as sources of useful information, not as stimuli and guides to immediate action.

The ultimate, and occasionally immediate, actions that are taken on the basis of standardized achievement test scores fall into two general classes, instructional and evaluative. If the tests are given at the start of or during a specific course they can serve as guides to

1. placement in differentiated instructional "tracks,"
2. individualized instruction,
3. remedial instruction, or

as learning exercises or problems. The fall testing programs that have become popular in recent decades are intended to serve primarily these purposes.

If the tests are given at the end of a course or unit of instruction their function is primarily evaluative: of the pupils' success, of the teachers' effectiveness, of the curriculum's adequacy. To argue that terminal evaluations come too late to do any good is to ignore the fact that pupils are likely to continue to study in other courses, that teachers are likely to continue teaching in other classes, and that the curriculum or some revision of it will continue to be used in the future. Past successes and failures are useful guides to future improvements. In life there is no such thing as an absolutely final examination.

A school faculty or teacher that sees the need and has the opportunity should not hesitate to develop an action program partly on the basis of scores provided by standardized tests of achievement. But neither should feel that the testing was a waste of time unless such an action program is developed. The main immediate purpose to be served by standardized test scores is the provision of information, information that can contribute to the wisdom of a host of specific actions stimulated by other educational needs and developments.[2,3]

DIAGNOSTIC TESTING

Like some other concepts in education, diagnostic testing is more cherished as an ideal than effectively demonstrated in practice. Taking their cue from medicine, and noting that some pupils seem to be ailing educationally, the advocates of diagnostic testing propose to identify the causes of the educational ailment and to correct it. In the early days of objective testing, diagnostic tests in a number of school subjects were developed and published. Now, outside the fields of elementary reading and arithmetic, few standardized diagnostic tests are available. Even in these two fields, the diagnostic tests are not in themselves clear indicators of the sources of a student's difficulties in learning. They are simply tools that the skilled diagnostician can use to help him identify the problems.

One of the reasons for the lack of success in educational diagnosis in most fields other than the two just mentioned is that the medical model is inappropriate. Learning difficulties are not attributable in most cases to specific or easily correctable disorders. Instead, they usually result from accumulations of ignorance and of distaste for learning. Neither of these causes is hard to recognize; neither is easy to cure. Diagnosis is not the real problem, and diagnostic testing can do little to solve that problem.

[2]G. D. Moore and Leonard Feldt, "Positive Approach to the Use of Test Results," *National Elementary Principal*, vol. 42 (1963), 65–70.

[3]William A. Mehrens, "The Consequences of Misusing Test Results," *National Elementary Principal*, vol. 47 (1967), 62–64.

Another reason for this lack of success in educational diagnosis is that effective diagnosis and remediation take a great deal more time than most teachers have, or most pupils would be willing to devote. The diagnosis of reading difficulties is a well-developed skill, and remedial treatments can be very effective. Because reading is so basic to other learning, the time required for diagnosis and remediation is often spent ungrudgingly. But where the subject of study is more advanced and more specialized, the best solution to learning difficulties in one area, say algebra, physics, economics, or German, is to leave off study in that area and cultivate learning in other areas that present fewer problems.

Any achievement tests can provide "diagnostic" information of value to the individual pupil if he is told which items he missed. Then, if he chooses to do so he can, with the teacher's help, correct the mistakes or misconceptions that led him astray. Highly specific "diagnosis" and "remediation" of this sort can be effective and ought to be encouraged. Good diagnosis and remediation also take place informally in the give-and-take of recitation and discussion. This too ought to be encouraged. But more general, more formal, and elaborate efforts at diagnosis through testing seldom have been effective. Nor do they give promise of effectiveness in the foreseeable future.

SUMMARY

The following statements summarize the principal ideas developed in this chapter:

1. A standardized test has been expertly and carefully constructed, must be administered under standard (uniform) conditions, and is provided with tables of norms for score interpretation.
2. As compared with classroom tests, standardized tests are easier to get, more expensive to use, and restricted to more commonly taught content.
3. It has proved to be impossible for educators to achieve the same precision in measuring mind that physical scientists achieve in measuring matter.
4. Economic considerations tend to restrict standardized achievement tests to subjects almost all students study, or to areas of general education rather than to specific subjects.
5. Achievement test batteries provide for comprehensive coverage of achievements and for comparable scores in different areas of achievement.
6. Profiles of test scores indicate both the pupil's general level of achievement and his specific strengths and weaknesses.
7. Percentile bands call attention to the lack of precision in educational measurements at the cost of complicating those measurements and distorting their interpretation somewhat.
8. Subtest scores may be too unreliable to use effectively.

9. The primary, essential use of standardized achievement test scores is to provide information to all concerned with the educational process.
10. Standardized test scores are useful in facilitating instruction and in evaluating its results.
11. Except in the fields of elementary reading and arithmetic, diagnostic testing has proved to be of little educational value.

19

STANDARD SCORES, NORMS, AND THE PASSING SCORE

One of the distinguishing marks of a standardized test is the provision of norms to aid in score interpretation. For standard achievement tests these norms are usually in the form of a table of equivalents between raw scores (number right, sometimes corrected for guessing) and some type of derived score, such as

Grade equivalent scores
Age equivalent scores
Standard scores
Percentile ranks
Stanines

Effective use of standardized tests requires an understanding of these types of scores, and the ability to interpret them.[1] The first part of this chapter is intended to foster this ability.

[1] Robert L. Ebel, "How to Explain Standardized Test Scores to Your Parents," *School Management*, vol. 5 (1961), 61–64.

GRADE AND AGE NORMS

Grade and age norms are most appropriate for elementary school subjects like reading and arithmetic that are studied continuously at increasing levels of complexity and skill over a long series of grades. To obtain the table of equivalents the test must be given to a substantial number of pupils in each of the grades in which it is intended to be used. Then the median raw score of pupils in each grade, or of each age, is determined. The numerical designation of the grade, or the age in years, is considered to be the grade equivalent or the age equivalent of that particular raw score. Both grade and age equivalents are usually indicated to tenths of a unit, each tenth corresponding roughly to one month of schooling in a school year of approximately 10 months.

One usually obtains the actual equivalents reported in the table graphically by plotting the median test scores against grade or age scores, drawing a smooth curve through the points, and reading the score equivalents for each grade or age value from the curve. Suppose, for example that a reading test is given to one large and representative sample of pupils in grades 3 through 8 at the beginning of December, and another large sample about five months later at the end of April. The median scores for each grade might look something like those shown in Table 19.1.

TABLE 19.1.   MEDIAN READING TEST SCORES IN GRADES 3–8

Grade	Median Raw Score December	April
3	33	42
4	45	57
5	59	64
6	72	74
7	77	81
8	82	85

These data are shown plotted in Figure 19.1. Note that the median score for the third grade in the December testing is plotted as Grade 3.3 (third grade, plus three months). Similarly, the other December test medians are plotted as 4.3 (for grade 4), 5.3, 6.3, 7.3, and 8.3. The April medians are plotted as 3.8, 4.8, and so on. A smooth curve has been drawn to approach the points as closely as possible. Table 19.2 presents the grade equivalents of some of the raw test scores. These were obtained from Fig. 19.1 by reading straight across from the test score value to the curve and then straight down to the corresponding grade level.

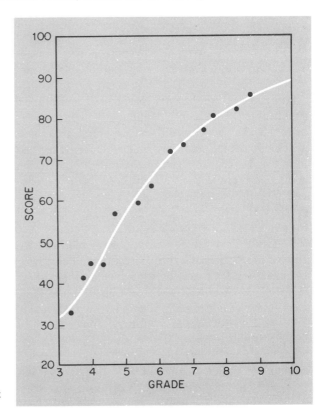

FIGURE 19.1
Plot of Median Raw Scores Against
Grade Levels

TABLE 19.2.   GRADE EQUIVALENTS OF READING TEST SCORES

Score	Grade	Score	Grade
85	8.8	55	4.8
80	7.6	50	4.5
75	6.8	45	4.1
70	6.2	40	3.8
65	5.6	35	3.4
60	5.2	30	2.8

Age equivalents are obtained similarly, though since the age data
are less uniform than the grade data, more points are usually plotted for
age equivalents. Often only four age levels per year are recognized, indicated by the numbers, for example, 11.0, 11.3 (three months past eleventh
birthday), 11.6, and 11.9.

Although grade and age norms are easy to interpret, they are also
subject to misinterpretations. Both grade and age equivalent scores involve
the assumptions that the subject tested is studied consistently, year after
year, and that a student's rate of increase in competence is reasonably

constant from year to year. They also assume that the test in question samples adequately what is being taught at all of the grade or age levels for which scores are reported. These assumptions are quite often violated. When they are, the grade or age scores can be quite misleading.

If a bright fifth grade boy gets a grade equivalent score of 7.4 on an arithmetic test, his parents (perhaps even his teacher!) may feel that he should skip from the fifth to the seventh grade arithmetic class. This would be a mistake. His score does not mean that he knows as much about arithmetic overall as the typical seventh grader. How could he, since he hasn't had a chance to learn the new things normally taught in the sixth and seventh grades? All his grade equivalent score of 7.4 means is that he understands whatever arithmetic the test covers about as well as a seventh grader does. No doubt he is good for his grade, but whether he is ready for a more advanced grade is quite a different question.

Grade and age equivalents have many of the same characteristics, and tell much the same story. In many schools grade grouping is essentially age grouping. In some, however, where there are frequent cases of grade skipping, or of failure and retention in grade, the age variation within a grade may be substantial. The older pupils in such a grade tend to make lower test scores and the younger pupils to make higher scores. Some test publishers report different norms for each age level within a grade, but the accurate establishment of such norms requires that enormous numbers of students be tested.

Further, the more highly differentiated these equivalents are, the less meaningful they become as standards of attainment. Overage students in the fourth grade may typically read less well than their classmates who have not been retarded, but this does not make their poor reading satisfactory, even for them. Girls in high school may do less well than boys in the study of algebra, but this does not mean that a poorer performance from them is just as satisfactory as a better performance from the boys.

NORMS AND STANDARDS

Norms, which report how students actually do perform, should not be confused with *standards*, which reflect estimates of how well they should perform. The standard of correctness in addition in arithmetic is 100 percent. The norm of pupil achievement on any given test may be only 70 percent. Nevertheless, evaluations of human achievements in most areas are relative, based on comparisons of an individual with his peers.

Norms inevitably function as a kind of standard. Few students are regarded as failures in an area of study if their performance is above the norm. Few are regarded as successes if their performance is below it. It is in this context that highly differentiated norms lose much of their significance. If the differentiation were carried far enough, the only reason why an individual student would not score at the norm appropriate for him would be that his score includes some error of measurement.

STANDARD SCORES AND PERCENTILES

A third kind of norm is provided by the various types of standard scores. Raw scores are usually transformed into standard scores on the basis of the raw score means and standard deviations. If X represents a student's raw score on a given test, M_x the mean score on that test in the norm or reference group, and σ_x the standard deviation of the scores in that group, then the student's standard z score would be found from the formula:

$$z = \frac{X - M_x}{\sigma_x}.$$

His standard T scores (linear transformation) would be

$$T = 10z + 50.$$

His standard score on the College Board or Graduate Record scale would be

$$\text{CEEB score} = 10T.$$

His standard score on the scale used with the Iowa Tests of Educational Development would be

$$\text{ITED score} = 5z + 15.$$

His stanine standard score (linear transformation) would be

$$\text{Stanine} = 2z + 5 \quad \text{(rounded to the nearest whole number)}.$$

The characteristics of these scales are summarized in Table 19.3, and in Figure 19.2.

To say that in some cases the transformation of raw scores to standard scores is linear means that if the pairs of corresponding values, raw score and standard score, were plotted on a graph they would all fall on a single straight line. This also means that the shape of the distribution of standard scores is identical with the shape of the raw score distribution, and that the asymmetry and irregularities of the raw score distribution are faithfully reproduced in the distribution of standard scores.

Perhaps they should be. On the other hand these irregularities may be due more to peculiarities of the test itself than to any essential characteristics of the thing being measured. If one wishes to assume that what is

TABLE 19.3. SUMMARY OF CHARACTERISTICS OF STANDARD SCORES

Characteristic	z	T	Type of Score CEEB	ITED	Stanine
Mean	0.0	50	500	15	5
Standard deviation	1.0	10	100	5	2
Maximum	+3.0	80	800	30	9
Minimum	−3.0	20	200	0	1
Negative values	Yes	No	No	No	No
Decimals	Yes	No	No	No	No
Transformation	Linear	Linear*	Linear	Linear*	Linear*

*In other, better, forms of *T*-scores, ITED scores, and stanines, the transformation is not linear. Instead, the form of the distribution of scores is adjusted to make it approximately normal.

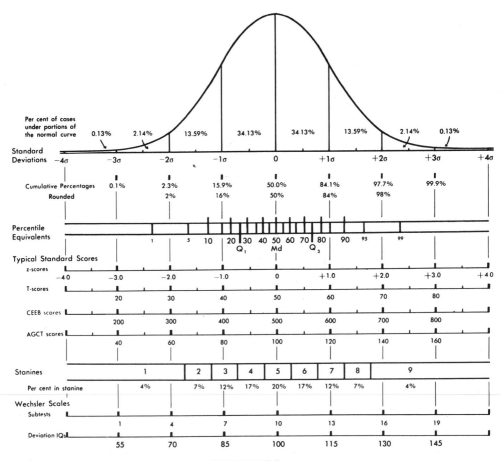

FIGURE 19.2

Chart Illustrating the Relations of Various Derived Scores to the Normal Distribution and to Each Other (*Courtesy of the Psychological Corporation*)

being measured is distributed normally, in a smooth, symmetrical fashion, it is possible to transform the raw scores nonlinearly so that the distribution of standard scores is normal. Such a normalizing transformation, sometimes called an area transformation, involves three steps.

1. The distribution of raw scores is converted into percentile ranks. (A method for doing this was described in Chapter 11.)
2. From a table of percentile ranks for normally distributed z scores read the normalized z score corresponding to each raw score percentile. (Such a table, derived directly from a table of areas under the normal curve, is presented here as Table 19.4.)

TABLE 19.4.   Percentile Ranks of Normalized z-Scores

z-Score	Percentile Rank	z-Score	Percentile Rank
3.0	99.9	−0.1	46.0
2.9	99.8	−0.2	42.1
2.8	99.7	−0.3	38.2
2.7	99.6	−0.4	34.5
2.6	99.5	−0.5	30.9
2.5	99.4	−0.6	27.4
2.4	99.2	−0.7	24.2
2.3	98.9	−0.8	21.2
2.2	98.6	−0.9	18.4
2.1	98.2	−1.0	15.9
2.0	97.7	−1.1	13.6
1.9	97.1	−1.2	11.5
1.8	96.4	−1.3	9.7
1.7	95.5	−1.4	8.2
1.6	94.5	−1.5	6.7
1.5	93.3	−1.6	5.5
1.4	91.9	−1.7	4.5
1.3	90.3	−1.8	3.6
1.2	88.5	−1.9	2.9
1.1	86.4	−2.0	2.3
1.0	84.1	−2.1	1.8
0.9	81.6	−2.2	1.4
0.8	78.8	−2.3	1.1
0.7	75.8	−2.4	0.8
0.6	72.6	−2.5	0.6
0.5	69.1	−2.6	0.5
0.4	65.5	−2.7	0.4
0.3	61.8	−2.8	0.3
0.2	57.9	−2.9	0.2
0.1	54.0	−3.0	0.1
0.0	50.0		

3. Convert the z scores into the desired T scores or stanines, using one of the formulas just given.

An illustration of this process, using the data of Table 11.5, is presented here in Table 19.5. It is impossible to see anything that looks like a normal distribution with so few test scores, but these data do illustrate the way in which normalized standard scores are derived.

TABLE 19.5.   CONVERSION OF EIGHT RAW SCORES INTO T-SCORES AND STANINES

Raw Scores	Exact Percentile	Normalized z-score	Normalized T-score	Normalized Stanine
43	93.75	1.5	65	8
42, 42, 42	68.75	0.5	55	6
41	43.75	−0.2	48	5
40, 40	25.00	−0.7	43	4
38	6.25	−1.5	35	2

The normative meaning of these standard scores is not so obvious or so easily explained as that of the grade and age scores, or of the percentile ranks. To understand it requires some knowledge of score distributions and of the descriptive statistics related to them—the mean and the standard deviation. They are more often used to provide a common, clearly defined scale for reporting and comparing the results from different tests. But they do have substantial normative meaning that can be useful if one knows about it and looks for it.

The calculation and interpretation of the other major type of normative score, the percentile rank, was discussed in Chapter 11. Percentiles offer the best all-round means of presenting normative information. They are precise and easy to interpret. More and more test authors and publishers are turning to the use of percentiles in their test manuals.

THE BASIS FOR TEST NORMS

Test norms to be accurate must be based on the test scores of large and representative samples of examinees, who have been tested under standard conditions, and who take the test as seriously, but no more so, than other students to be tested later for whom the norms are needed. That complex sentence outlines a very complex and difficult process.

Norms obviously must be obtained from pupils in schools that are willing to take time out from their other responsibilities to help with the norming administration. That very willingness may make them somewhat atypical of the population of schools and pupils generally. To get enough cooperation to provide a reasonably large norm sample is hard enough. To make it a representative sample is even harder. First one must decide what population it is supposed to represent. Then one must decide what the ideal sample to represent that population would be. Then one must try to actually test the students in such a sample.

In the early days of standard testing, publishers sometimes prided themselves on the large numbers of pupils on which their test norms were based. Often these large numbers had been obtained by testing all the pupils in a few very large school systems. But since there are great differences between school systems in the abilities of the pupils enrolled and in the quality of education provided, scores from only a few different schools cannot provide dependable norms. There are good reasons, as Flanagan has pointed out, for considering the school, not the pupil, as the unit to be sampled in obtaining test norms.[2] At least, one must consider *both* the number of schools and the number of pupils represented in the test norms to judge their adequacy.

The administration of tests to obtain normative data can take significant amounts of time away from the school's other important activities. The occasional reluctance of schools to cooperate is easy to understand, but it would be quite wrong for them to believe that test administration has no direct educational value for the students who participate in it. They learn while thinking about answers to the questions. If scores are reported they may learn from these too. A school that "doesn't have time" to cooperate in the tryout or norming of a standardized test must have a phenomenal program, and must be making amazingly good use of pupil and teacher time doing things that are more important.

But some schools do find the time requirement a deterrent. To reduce it, some test developers have broken down a test into smaller units so that items as well as pupils are sampled. Lord[3] and others[4] have described procedures for doing this that seem to work quite well in situations where the more usual techniques of tryout and norming would take too much school time.

A serious error that some test users have made is to use norms for individual pupil scores in interpreting school average scores. Although the mean of the school averages must be the same as the mean for the individ-

[2]John C. Flanagan, "Units, Scores and Norms," in *Educational Measurement*, ed. E. F. Lindquist (Washington, D.C.: American Council on Education, 1951), pp. 741–42.

[3]Frederic M. Lord, "Estimating Norms by Item Sampling," *Educational and Psychological Measurement*, vol. 22 (1962), 259–67.

[4]Thomas R. Owens and Daniel L. Stufflebeam, "An Experimental Comparison of Item Sampling and Examinee Sampling for Estimating Test Norms," *Journal of Educational Measurement*, vol. 6 (1969), 75–83.

ual pupil scores, the school averages are likely to be far less variable than the pupil scores. The *average* score in a truly excellent school may be lower than the scores made by one-third of the pupils from all schools, and the average score in very poor school may be better than the scores of one-third of all pupils. Thus when school averages are evaluated in terms of norms for pupil scores, degrees of excellence or of deficiency are likely to be badly understimated. The only proper basis for evaluation of school averages is a separate table of norms for school averages.

In order for norms to provide valid standards for evaluating achievement, the test must be given under the same conditions whenever it is used as it was when the norming scores were obtained. The directions, time limits, and pupil motivation should be the same. Any other circumstances that would affect the test performance, except the abilities of the particular students tested, should be the same.

This is no small order. No wonder it is sometimes done badly. No wonder test reviewers frequently complain about inadequate or inaccurate norms. No wonder some test specialists, comparing the great difficulty of getting good norms with their limited relevance and durability, have begun to wonder if the prize is worth the struggle.

There is also a subtle and indirect but also persuasive influence on test authors and publishers to develop norms that will make the test user's pupils, and the school's educational program, look good. It is highly unlikely that deliberately falsified norms have ever been published. But in the process of developing the norms, scores of decisions must be made, and these may affect the severity or leniency of the standards implied by the norms. Decisions that, taken individually, seem reasonable may have the cumulative effect of lowering norm standards substantially.[5] As a consequence test users sometimes find, when they shift from one test battery to another, that their pupils seem miraculously to have gained (or lost) a year or more of educational development.

The better test publishers have worked hard to overcome some of these problems and limitations of test norms, not only in their own tests but also in the whole enterprise of standardized testing. Standard populations of puplis have been proposed. A common "anchor test" to use as a basis for adjusting norms from different populations has been proposed. But none of these remedies has seemed feasible enough or potentially useful enough to be widely used.

The moral of all this for the test user is that he should incline more to be critical of test norms than to accept them unquestioningly. He should

[5]Jason Millman and John Lindolf, "The Comparability of Fifth-grade Norms of the California, Iowa and Metropolitan Achievement Tests," *Journal of Educational Measurement*, vol. 1 (1964), 135–37.

be aware of their possible shortcomings, and wary of putting too much trust in them. He should always ask what population was sampled and how it was sampled to get the norms reported.

ALTERNATIVES TO NATIONAL NORMS

Because accurate national norms are difficult to get and of limited relevance in many local situations, some test specialists have suggested that they should be abandoned in favor of purely local norms. These are adequate for pupil evaluations, but they provide no basis for judging whether the school's performance is better or worse than that of other schools. There is, however, a third alternative. Schools in similar situations, with similar interests and similar problems, can band together to form a kind of "common market" for educational testing. If they use the same tests under the same conditions they can pool the scores obtained, both pupil scores and school averages, and thus gain the benefits of external standards of achievement.

One notable and successful demonstration of this kind of cooperation in educational testing is provided by the Educational Records Bureau. This association of schools was conceived and guided during its formative years by Dr. Ben Wood. Its operations were managed with high professional competence for many years by Dr. Arthur Traxler. During the 1969–1970 school year over 900 independent schools and public schools were associated with it.

In addition to providing an economical source of supply for a carefully selected list of standardized tests, with directions for uniform administration, and with a central, economical scoring and reporting service, the Bureau provides its members with extensive and detailed norms for the tests. It reports the results of numerous research studies and holds an annual conference on testing and educational problems for its member schools. The Bureau has long been a constructive influence in American education.

Not every assocaition of schools for the purposes of educational cooperation needs to be as large and as elaborate as the Educational Records Bureau. However, the Bureau does provide a model that deserves to be copied more widely. It solves the most difficult problems of getting accurate, relevant test norms and simplifies the problems of designing, operating, and using a school testing program. Moreover, it provides for the in-service education of teachers and school administrators in effective educational measurement.

DETERMINATION OF THE PASSING SCORE

There is a widespread popular belief that any person who takes a test either passes or fails it. For tests used to measure amount of achievement, this is not true. However, it is substantially true of a minority of tests, those used to certify competence to practice, such as those used for licensure in the trades and professions.

A second popular belief is that when a test is used to pass or fail someone, the distinction between the two outcomes is clear-cut and unequivocal. This is almost never true. Determination of a minimum acceptable performance always involves some rather arbitrary and not wholly satisfactory decisions.

There are several approaches to the problem of setting a passing score. One is to decide on the minimum essentials of competence—what every practitioner must know, or be able to do, in order to practice effectively and safely. Tasks designed to test whether the applicant possesses this knowledge and these abilities are developed to constitute the test.

Theoretically, the passing score on such a test should be a perfect score. In practice, of course, to insist on a perfect score as the minimum passing score would be almost to guarantee that no one would pass. Minimum essentials are not obvious enough to all, the item writer's ability to test them unequivocally is not perfect enough itself, and the examinee's performance is not flawless enough to make a perfect score a reasonable minimum score. There needs to be some margin for errors on all counts.

A second approach is to broaden the scope of the ability to be tested somewhat, replacing the "minimum essentials" concept with the concept of "important fundamentals." Test construction is handled in the same manner, but the passing score is set somewhat below 100 percent correctness. Conventionally, passing scores on such tests have been 75 percent, 70 percent or even 65 percent correct.

This approach is more satisfactory than the first, but it has two weaknesses. The first is that the "conventional" passing score is an arbitrary percentage with no clearly rational justification. This weakness can be overcome to some degree by using this line of reasoning:

1. On a well-constructed objective test no examinee, however weak, should actually get a score less than the expected chance score on that test, but one or two should get close to the expected chance score.
2. On a well-constructed objective test the very best examinees should get scores at or near the maximum possible score.
3. Hence, the ideal mean score on such a test falls at a point midway between the maximum possible score and the expected chance score.
4. The passing score might then be defined as a point midway between the ideal mean score and the expected chance score.

TABLE 19.6. PASSING SCORES ON TWO HYPOTHETICAL TESTS

	True-false	Four-alternative
Number of items	100.0	100.00
Expected chance score	50.0	25.00
Ideal mean score	75.0	62.50
Minimum passing score	62.5	43.75

How this reasoning applies to two hypothetical tests is shown in Table 19.6.

If the test does not meet the criteria of goodness expressed in 1. or 2. above, being too easy or too difficult to give a mean score near the ideal mean and insufficiently discriminating to give a low score near the expected chance score, a better estimate of the passing score might be obtained by these modifications of the foregoing prodecures.

1. Average the lowest score and the expected chance score.
2. Average the actual mean score and the ideal mean score.
3. Define the passing score as a point midway between the two averages.

If the divergence between ideal and actual values is extreme, it might be advisable to forget the ideal values and define the passing score as the point midway between the mean score and the lowest score.

The second weakness of the definition of the passing score as some percentage of the total score is that it still leaves substantial elements of chance in determination of the passing score. The items may be more difficult, or less difficult or less discriminating, than the test constructor intended. Whether an examinee passes or fails a specific test may be determined by the questions in the test rather than by his level of professional competence.

The second weakness of this approach can be overcome to some degree by the derivation of the passing percentage from a subjective analysis of the relevance and difficulty of each item in the test. Table 19.7 illustrates four categories of relevance and three categories of difficulty, and

TABLE 19.7. RELEVANCE, DIFFICULTY, AND EXPECTED SUCCESS
           ON TEST ITEMS

Relevance Categories	Difficulty Levels		
	Easy	Medium	Hard
Essential	100%	—	—
Important	90	70%	—
Acceptable	80	60	40%
Questionable	70	50	30

gives the expected percentages of passing for items in each category. These expected percentages are what would be expected of a minimally qualified (barely passing) applicant.

Suppose, for example, that the number of items in a 100-item test falling in each category when the ratings of five judges are pooled were as shown in the second column of Table 19.8. Multiplying each of these numbers by the expected proportion of correct answers gives the products shown in the fourth column of Table 19.8. The sum of these products divided by 500 gives an estimate of the appropriate passing score.

TABLE 19.8. PASSING SCORE ESTIMATED FROM ITEM CHARACTERISTICS

Item Category	Number of Items*	Expected Success	Number × Success
Essential	94	100	9400
Important			
Easy	106	90	9540
Medium	153	70	10710
Acceptable			
Easy	24	80	1920
Medium	49	60	2940
Hard	52	40	2080
Questionable			
Easy	4	70	280
Medium	11	50	50
Hard	7	30	210
	500		37130

$$\frac{37130}{500} = 74.26$$

or 74% = passing score

*Actually the number of placements of items in the category by all five of the judges.

A third approach assumes that competence is essentially a relative term, and that the task of the certification test is simply to select the most competent and to reject those who are less competent. The test is still based on important fundamentals, but the passing score is not defined as some proportion of correct answers. Instead, it is defined as the score above which 50 percent, or 66 percent, or 90 percent of all scores fall. This means that the poorest one-half, or one-third, or one-tenth of the applicants fail regardless of the absolute value of their scores.

The obvious drawback of this approach is that it allows the passing score to vary according to the general level of competence of the examinees at a specific testing. If that general level is high, some fairly well qualified applicants may fail. If is it low, some poorly qualified applicants may pass.

Whether the passing score should be defined as a percent of the total score or as a percent of applicants to be passed probably should depend on the expected stability of the examinations in level of difficulty compared to the expected stability of the group of examinees in levels of ability. If one is more confident of the stability of examination difficulty than of examinee group ability, he may choose the percent of total score approach. But if his confidence leans in the other direction, he probably will choose the percentage of applicants to be passed.

A fourth approach combines the second and third, retaining some of the advantages of both. In it the passing score might be defined as 75 percent correct responses, provided at least 60 percent of the examinees but not more than 80 percent of them exceed this score. If less than 60 percent of the examinees exceed the 75 percent score, the passing score is the point midway between the 75 percent score and the score 60 percent of the examinees do exceed. If more than 80 percent of them exceed this score, the passing score is the point midway between the 75 percent score and the score 80 percent of the examinees exceed. The figures used in this example, 75 percent of the items, and 60 percent and 80 percent of the examinees, are simply illustrative. Depending on circumstances, an examining authority might want to raise or lower any of them. The object in setting these values is to keep the amount of content knowledge, and the proportion of passes and failures, within what seem to be reasonable bounds while making reasonable allowance for the unavoidable errors of measurement. This fourth alternative has not been widely used, but would seem to have considerable merit as a rational solution to a difficult problem.

A fifth approach uses the performance of certified practitioners as a basis for setting the passing score. It requires the certification test to be given to a large and representative sample of professionals who have been approved to practice and who are actually practicing. A decision is made by the certifying authority that any applicant who scores above the lowest quarter, lowest fifth, or lowest tenth of those actually practicing the profession deserves to be certified to practice it also. If the supply of applicants is good, and if the profession is seeking to upgrade itself rapidly, it may set the passing score fairly high on the scale of actual practitioner performances.

One problem with this fifth approach, of course, is getting the scores of a sufficient sample of practitioners, and of getting them to take the test conscientiously. A solution to this problem might be to break the test into representative sets of 15 to 25 items, asking each respondent to answer only those in one set. From their performances on these sets synthetic score distributions of the entire test could be constructed. This procedure, by limiting the exposure of the test to any one person, would help to safeguard test security. Two other steps might also be desirable:

1. Getting practitioner responses to the items in several forms of the test at the

same time. The fewer items any one person sees of the items in a single form of the test, the less its security is threatened.
2. Reminding practitioners who respond to the items of the importance to the profession and to themselves of safeguarding item security.

From the preceeding paragraphs it is clear that a variety of approaches can be used to solve the problem of defining the passing score. Unfortunately, different approaches are likely to give different results. Anyone who expects to discover the "real" passing score by any of these approaches, or any other approach, is doomed to disappointment, for a "real" passing score does not exist to be discovered. All any examining authority that must set passing scores can hope for, and all any of their examinees can ask, is that the basis for defining the passing score be defined clearly, and that the definition be as rational as possible.

SUMMARY

The main ideas developed in this chapter can be summarized in the following 12 statements.

1. Grade and age norms are most appropriate for elementary school subjects that are studied continuously over a long series of grades.
2. A grade equivalent score in arithmetic of 7.4 for a fifth grade boy does not mean that he is ready for seventh grade arithmetic.
3. Norms report what is, standards what ought to be, but national norms inevitably function as a kind of local standard.
4. The basic standard score is the z-score, in which a given raw score is expressed as a plus or minus difference from the mean in standard deviation units.
5. Normalized standard scores can be obtained by converting raw scores to percentile ranks and then entering a table which gives z-score equivalents of the percentile ranks.
6. To be accurate test norms must be based on large and representative samples of examinees, tested under standard conditions.
7. The adequacy of test norms depends on both the number of pupils and the number of schools represented in them.
8. Pupil norms are not appropriate for the interpretation of school averages.
9. Similar schools that cooperate in administering the same tests can secure highly relevant and useful norms.
10. The passing score may be defined as some fraction of the total test score, as some fraction of applicants to be passed, or as a score higher than that made by some fraction of certified practitioners.
11. The passing score may be defined on the basis of the pooled judgments of experts on the relevance and difficulty of each item in the test.
12. Passing scores cannot be discovered. They must be defined, but the definition should be as clear and as rational as possible.

It is probably unwise to spend much time in attempts to separate off sharply certain qualities of man, as his intelligence, from such emotional and vocational qualities as his interest in mental activity, carefulness, determination to respond effectively, persistence in his efforts to do so; or from his amount of knowledge; or from his moral or esthetic tastes.

E. L. THORNDIKE

20

INTELLIGENCE AND APTITUDE TESTS

A very important group of published tests is composed of those designed to measure intelligence. From the early years of this century up to the present many teachers, perhaps a majority of them, have regarded intelligence testing as an essential part of a good school testing program. Many of them believe that each person has a definite amount of intelligence, measured by his I.Q. (intelligence quotient), which was given him at birth and remains his as long as he lives. They feel that it is important for a teacher to know as precisely as possible what each student's I. Q. is, so that he can be educated up to his "capacity," without asking him to do more than he is able to do.

THE NATURE OF INTELLIGENCE

Despite widespread acceptance of the idea that intelligence exists, no one seems to have a very clear idea of what it is. Presumably it has a biological basis in neuroanatomy or in brain physiology. A few types of gross mental deficiency have been identified with severe metabolic defects.[1] Shultz, in an interesting popular article, has summarized evidence on the relation of mental deficiencies to prenatal "insults" (i.e. lack of oxygen, viral infection, injurious drugs, etc.)[2] But thus far no biological basis for differences in intelligence among normal human beings has been discovered.

In popular speech intelligence is often characterized as brightness or sharpness. These words suggest responsiveness, perceptiveness, and ability to cut through appearances and confusions to reach understanding. Lack of intelligence is characterized as dullness, which suggests a lack of responsiveness, perceptiveness, or understanding. But these metaphors help very little in understanding the nature of intelligence.

When psychologists are asked what intelligence is they give an amazing variety of answers, none of which is very specific.[3] One calls it ability to learn, that is, to do the work of the school. The lack of this ability is what Alfred Binet was interested in detecting in his early tests.[4] Another characterizes it as ability to reason, to solve problems, and use the "higher mental processes." Still another emphasizes original thinking and the ability to adapt to novel situations.

These different conceptions of the nature of intelligence have contributed to the development of a wide diversity of tasks for testing it. An outline of some of the better known types is presented in Exhibit 20.1. Illustrations of these types of tasks can be found in textbooks such as those by Anastasi[5] or by Thorndike and Hagen.[6] Most actual intelligence tests are composed of a selection of tasks like these.

---

[1]H. Eldon Sutton, "Human Genetics: A Survey of New Developments," *The Science Teacher*, vol. 34 (1967), 51–55.

[2]Gladys Denny Shultz, "The Uninsulted Child," *Ladies Home Journal*, vol. 73 (1956), 60–63.

[3]"Intelligence and Its Measurement: A Symposium," *Journal of Educational Psychology*, vol. 12 (1921), 123–47, 195–216.

[4]Alfred Binet, "Nouvelles recherches sur la mesure du niveau intellectual chez les enfants d'ecole," *Anneé Psychologique*, vol. 17 (1911), 145–201.

[5]Anne Anastasi, *Psychological Testing*, 3d ed. (New York: Crowell-Collier and Macmillan, 1968).

[6]Robert L. Thorndike and Elizabeth Hagen, *Measurement and Evaluation in Psychology and Education*, 3d ed. (New York: John Wiley Sons, Inc., 1969).

EXHIBIT 20.1

Tasks Used to Test Intelligence

VERBAL	OBJECT OR FIGURE
Synonyms	Object naming
Analogies	Object assembly
Commands	Picture vocabulary
Sentence completion	Picture completion
Sentence interpretation	Figure analogy
	Matrix progression
QUANTITATIVE	Maze tracing
Digit span	Figure drawing
Number series	
Arithmetic computation	ABSTRACT PROCESS
Arithmetic reasoning	Similarity (and difference)
Relative magnitudes	Classification
Water jar problems	Sequence
	Coding
INFORMATION	
General	
Common sense	
Absurdities	

EXHIBIT 20.2

Kinds of Tasks Used to Test Intelligence

I. VERBAL

1. *Synonyms (or antonyms)*
   Identify the pair of words in each set that are either synonyms or antonyms
   a. accident   b. bad   c. evil   d. worry
   a. accept   b. make   c. object   d. order

2. *Verbal analogies*
   Snow: Flake: (a) cloud: fleecy   (b) hail: storm   (c) icicle: eaves
   (d) rain: drop

3. *Commands*
   The task is to obey simple commands
   "Give me the pencil."
   "Put the book on the shelf."

4. *Sentence completion*
   While most teachers agree that educational tests are useful, one occasionally hears the suggestion that education could go on perfectly well, perhaps

much better than in the past, if tests and testing were _____
(a) abolished   (c) criticized   (e) praised
(b) continued   (d) investigated

5. *Sentence interpretation*
Given sentence: The date must be advanced one day when one crosses the International Date Line in a westerly direction.
Interpretive question: If a ship approaches the International Date Line from the East on Tuesday, what day is it on board the ship after the line has been crossed?

II. QUANTITATIVE

6. *Digit span*
The examiner says a series of numbers and asks the subjects to repeat them, forward or backward. The maximum number the student can repeat is his digit span.

7. Number series
1   3   5   7   9   ?
1   2   3   5   8   ?

8. *Arithmetic computation*
Add 23 to 66.
Divide 96 by 16.

9. *Arithmetic reasoning*
How many 5¢ candy bars can be bought with 30¢?
If concrete is to be made with 4 parts of sand to 1 part of cement, how many shovels of cement should be put with 16 shovels of sand?

10. *Relative magnitudes*
How much larger than 1/3 is 1/2?
A dollar is how many times as much as a dime?

11. *Water jar problems*
If you have a 7-quart jar and a 3-quart jar how can you get exactly 8 quarts of water?

III. INFORMATION

12. *General*
How many legs does a dog have?
What is the special name for a doctor who takes care of teeth?

13. *Common sense*
Why are street lights turned off in the morning?
Why do houses have windows?

14. *Absurdities*
What is foolish about these statements?
"The fish I tried to catch got away, but it made a delicious meal."
"If I get to the clubhouse first I'll put an X on the door. If you get there first, rub it out."

IV. OBJECT OR FIGURE

15. *Object naming*

    Examiner points to a cup, a book, a glove, etc., and asks the subject to name them.

16. *Object assembly*

    The task is to assemble pieces of a puzzle to form a common object in limited time.

17. *Picture vocabulary*

    Given several pictures in a set, the examinee is asked to indicate which best illustrates the meaning of a particular word.

18. *Picture completion*

    Tell me what part of this picture is missing.

19. *Figures analogies*

    A: B:: C:?

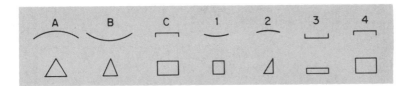

20. *Matrix progression*

    What figure belongs in the blank space?

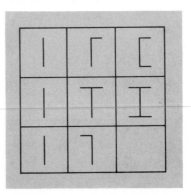

21. *Maze tracing*
    The task is to fine a clear path through
    a maze of lines

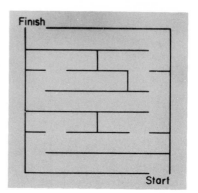

22. *Figure drawing*
    Draw a picture of a man.

V. ABSTRACT PROCESS

23. *Similarity (and difference)*
    Which of these is most like a calf?
    (a) a colt   (b) a cat   (c) a pony
    In what way is a tennis ball different from a baseball?

24. *Classification*
    The examinee is directed to sort a set of words, objects, symbols, etc., into
    a given set of categories.

25. *Sequence*
    Arrange the following words in the proper order
    afternoon   morning
    daybreak   noon
    evening   sunrise
    midnight   twilight

26. *Coding*
    Given a simple code, the task is to translate a set of symbols into the code.

Code	——	+	X	——	=
	1	2	3	4	5

Task	X	X	+	=	——	+

OPERATIONAL AND ANALYTIC DEFINITIONS OF INTELLIGENCE

One possible solution to the problem of defining intelligence is to use an operational definition. The test used to measure it defines what it is measuring. Intelligence is whatever the test measures. Different tests measure different kinds of intelligence. Obviously this approach, whatever its virtues in helping us to think more concretely about what we mean by intelligence, is not going to yield a single, generally acceptable definition.

Another possible solution is to use the methods of factor analysis on the responses of a wide variety of persons to a wide variety of tasks designed to measure intelligence. This approach has also been tried. It has shed much light on the extent to which proficiency on certain tasks tends to be related to, or independent of, proficiency on other tasks. But it has provided no compelling definition of intelligence. Each practitioner interprets its finding somewhat differently. One finds a common, general intellectual factor.[7] Another finds seven primary mental abilities.[8] Still another finds an elaborate multidimensional structure of intellect.[9] The tasks used to measure intelligence can be grouped as coarsely or subdivided as finely as one chooses. But none is excluded from the comprehensive definition, and the dimensions or elements of mental ability are no more discrete and distinguishable than the segments of a line.

EDUCATIONAL AND ENVIRONMENTAL TASKS

A few of the tasks used to test intelligence, such as giving synonyms, interpreting sentences, computing, and solving problems are objects of specific instruction in schools. Hence, almost identical tasks are likely to be found in general achievement test batteries. Ability to handle other tasks such as analogy problems, recognition of absurdities, and problems of classification and sequence, is usually learned incidentally at home, at play, in school, or elsewhere.

It is sometimes assumed that what a student succeeds in learning incidentally, on his own so to say, is a better indication of his intelligence than his success in learning what he has been taught. The assumption

[7]Charles E. Spearman, *The Abilities of Man* (New York: The Macmillan Company, 1927), 198 pp.

[8]L. L. Thurstone, "Primary Mental Abilities," *Psychometric Monographs*, no. 1 (1938).

[9]J. P. Guilford, "Intelligence: 1965 Model," *American Psychologist*, vol. 21 (1966), 20–25.

may be justified, but the evidence and logic needed to justify it are not obvious. Teaching does indeed assist learning, but it does not make learning automatic nor does it eliminate the need for effort and ability on the part of the students. Intelligence contributes to learning in school as well as out of it.

Obviously, if one wishes to compare the intelligence of children who have been to school with those who have not, he should not use tasks that the school tries to teach. As a general principle, if one seeks to infer basic ability to learn from measurements of success in learning, he should try to equalize opportunities to learn. He can do this by using as test items only problems that all children are likely to have equal opportunity to learn how to solve. But it is not at all obvious, indeed it is downright unlikely, as Coleman and Cureton point out, that school-attending children have more nearly equal opportunities for incidental learning than for school-directed learning.[10] Great as the differences may be among schools and teachers, they are probably not as great as the differences in environments and life styles among different families, different neighborhoods, and different regions of the country.

NONVERBAL AND CULTURE-FAIR TESTS

Some intelligence tests attempt to minimize, or to eliminate altogether, the influence of verbal ability on the test scores. The tasks are based on objects or drawings or figures, and require assembly, classification, arrangement, selection, manipulation, or some other response. Sometimes even the instructions involve no words, but are given in pantomime.

These tests are useful if students who speak different languages must be tested with the same test, or if a student with a severe language handicap must be tested. They appeal to those seeking measures of basic intelligence, uncontaminated by learning, particularly language learning. But there is no good reason to believe that these nonverbal tests get any closer to basic native intelligence than do the verbal tests. Ability to do well on them can also be learned. And since verbal facility is so important an element in school learning, and in most areas of human achievement, what the nonverbal tests succeed in measuring usually seems to have little practical usefulness.

---

[10]William Coleman and Edward E. Cureton, "Intelligence and Achievement: the 'Jangle Fallacy' Again," *Educational and Psychological Measurement*, vol. 14 (1954), 347–51.

Most intelligence tests not only require some degree of familiarity with a particular language, but also assume familiarity with a specific culture. This quality limits their usefulness in other cultures. It even casts some doubt on their purity as measures of basic, abstract intelligence. However, attempts to build culture-free tests have failed because testing requires communication and communication is impossible in the absence of culture: its concepts, symbols, and meanings.

Attempts to build culture-fair tests by eliminating items that discriminate between different cultures have been no more successful. If carried far enough, they result in eliminating all the items. There is no difference between individuals in their response to any test item that cannot be attributed to differences in culture, if culture is defined inclusively enough. Each of us lives in a somewhat different culture. Not only Eskimos and Africans but also Vermonters and Virginians, farmers and townspeople, boys and girls, even first-born and next born in the same family live in somewhat different "cultures." The differences are not equally great in all these instances, but they exist as differences in all cases, and they can be used to support the charge that any item that discriminates is unfair. It is logically impossible for a completely culture-fair test to discriminate among individuals, and there is no reason to use a test that does not discriminate.

TESTS OF ABSTRACT INTELLIGENCE

Those who conceive of intelligence as an abstract ability to think are likely to favor tasks that present novel problems, such as number series, water-jar problems, figure analogies, matrix progressions, or maze tracing. So long as the task is a problem requiring thought, so long as it is novel, its exact nature is relatively unimportant. Since the ability being tested is presumably a unitary, generally applicable ability, any novel problem will do. Nor is a diversity of problem tasks in the test deemed necessary. The assumption is that the examinee's success with any of them will depend not on the problem but only on the examinee's ability to reason.

But thinking is always based on content. What the examinee has or has not learned does make a difference in his ability to handle these tasks that supposedly involve only abstract reasoning. A little judicious coaching can help the student greatly to do well on them. How much their pre-coaching differences in performance may have been due to relevant incidental learning is an open question. The claim that these tasks measure abstract intelligence is thus open to question too.

INDIVIDUAL AND GROUP INTELLIGENCE TESTS

The earliest tests of intelligence were administered individually. Later, tests that could be administered simultaneously to all individuals in a group were developed. Both are still in use, because each has special advantages and limitations.

Some of the differences between individual and group intelligence tests are summarized in Exhibit 20.3. As a result of these characteristics, intelligence tests for young children, for those with reading disability, or for other special cases are usually adminstered individually. Group tests, because they are economical of time and money, are generally used for routine testing of older children. There is no important difference between the two types in reliability or validity.

EXHIBIT 20.3

Comparison of Individual and Group Intelligence Tests

ASPECT	INDIVIDUAL	GROUP
Task presentation	Oral	Written
Range of task types	Wider	Less wide
Dependence on reading	Minimal	Substantial
Mode of response	Oral-free	Multiple-choice
Flexibility in testing	High	Low
Age suitability	Younger	Older
Scoring	Semiobjective	Objective
Time required	Longer	Shorter
Cost	Higher	Lower
Reliability	High	High
Validity (where suitable)	Satisfactory	Satisfactory

TESTS OF SPECIAL APTITUDES

Somewhat related to tests of general intelligence, but often sounder conceptually and more useful practically, are tests of special aptitudes. They are sounder conceptually because what is to be measured is more restricted and more clearly defined. Fewer assumptions about the origin of the aptitude or its changelessness are made. They are more useful practically because their purposes are more specific and more readily attainable.

Some tests of special aptitude, such as academic aptitude, are quite comprehensive. Others, such as those of engine lathe aptitude, are rather specific. Often aptitude tests are grouped into batteries to provide for measurement of diverse aptitudes or to permit differential predictions of aptitudes for diverse activities. Texts by Cronbach,[11] Anastasi,[12] and Thorndike and Hagen[13] describe various aptitude tests and test batteries in some detail. In general, they are of high quality, although as Super's[14] classic reviews indicated, they are subject to further improvement.

Aptitude tests are sometimes criticized for seeking to predict success in training programs rather than to predict success on the job. A medical aptitude test, for example, is judged to be valid if it gives highest scores to those who do best in medical schools. But success in medical school does not always forecast success in the practice of medicine. One reason for this situation is, of course, that criteria of success in training programs are easier to define and to measure than criteria of on-the-job success. Another is that short-range predictions can be made with greater accuracy and assurance than can long-range predictions. Both of these reasons are valid. Long-range predictions are useful only to the degree that they are accurate. Predictions of success are useful only to the degree that success can be reasonably defined. If there is evidence of unreasonable disparity between competence in training and competence on the job, it may be the training program rather than the test that is in need of correction.

THE INTELLIGENCE QUOTIENT (I.Q.)

One of the concepts that has contributed most to the popularity, and to the misunderstanding, of intelligence tests is the intelligence quotient or I.Q. The German psychologist Stern suggested the use of intelligence quotients as meaningful interpretations of mental test scores.[15] Later, when he discovered that it was being represented as an index of permanent, general mental ability, he suggested that steps be taken to "kill the I.Q."

[11]Lee V. Cronbach, *Essentials of Psychological Testing* 3d. ed. (New York: Harper and Row, Publishers, 1970).
[12]*Psychological Testing.*
[13]*Measurement and Evaluation.*
[14]Donald E. Super, *The Use of Multifactor Tests in Guidance* (Washington, D.C.: American Personnel and Guidance Association, 1958).
[15]William Stern, *The Psychological Methods of Testing Intelligence,* trans. Guy M. Whipple (Baltimore: Warwick, 1914).

The apparent simplicity of the I.Q. concept is one reason for its popularity and for the misunderstandings associated with it. It is calculated from the formula:

$$I.Q. = 100 \times \frac{\text{Mental age}}{\text{Chronological age}}$$

Since the pioneer work of Alfred Binet, most mental test scores have been expressed as years and months of mental age. If a student taking an intelligence test answers correctly as many of the questions asked as does the average child who is 11 years and 3 months of age, then the student's mental age is reported as 11 years 3 months, or 135 months. But if the student's actual chronological age is only 10 years 6 months (126 months) his I.Q. is

$$100 \times \frac{135}{126} = 107$$

This is a ratio I.Q. It is easy to understand how it is calculated and what it means. But like many other simple generalizations, it fits the facts none too well.

To begin with, if it is a measure of some permanent quality of the mind, it ought to remain constant as the years pass. This means that mental age ought to increase as steadily as does chronological age, and at a constant rate of increase. The person of exceptional intellect who has an I.Q. of 150 based on a mental age of 15 at age 10 should have a mental age of 30 when he reaches 20 years, a mental age of 75 at 50 years, and a mental age of 120 at 80 years. Of course, nothing like this can be demonstrated. In fact it is virtually impossible to devise a test of general intelligence on which the average twenty-five year-old does much better than the average sixteen-year-old.

To explain this fact we may assume that general mental ability stops developing at about age 16. This is not unreasonable in relation to the general pattern of physical growth, although it should be noted that physical growth shows little of the constant rate of increase from year to year that the I.Q. assumes to be characteristic of mental growth. Nor does physical growth cease for many even at age 20, for they continue to put on weight well into middle age.

Another, different explanation for the apparent halt of mental development at about age 16 is that the educational experiences that most children share in schools, in homes, and at play—experiences that provide the background for answering intelligence test questions—stop occurring to all children in essentially the same way at about that age. Henceforth, fewer new experiences are encountered. Those that do occur are likely to differ more from person to person. The common experiences formerly provided in school, at home, and at play are replaced by differentiated experiences on the job or in different spheres of activity. Tests of *general* mental ability have no place for tasks based on *special* experiences. Finally, as Owens has reported, for those whose occupations or social positions involve them in verbal, quantitative, or other tasks like those represented on the tests, intelligence test scores continue to increase in adult life.[16,17]

Judged in the light of facts like these, the famous statement that Americans are, intellectually speaking, a nation of twelve-year-olds—a statement based on intelligence test results for World War I draftees—is seen to be more a reflection on the contents of the intelligence test than on the abilities of those tested. Walter Lippman discussed this and other apparent flaws in the concept of general intelligence in his debate with Lewis Terman in the pages of *The New Republic*.[18]

If the measurement of intelligence is limited to the years below 16, as it usually is in school practice, the logical difficulties with ratio I.Q.'s are less troublesome. But some remain. One would expect, on the assumption that an individual's intelligence is a constant characteristic, that the proportion of the population with I.Q.'s above, say, 116, or below, say, 84, ought to be the same for each age group. But it is difficult to build an intelligence test that shows this kind of stability.

To solve the problem, on the assumption that the fault lay in the test and not in the concept, many test developers have shifted from ratio I.Q.'s to deviation I.Q.'s. At each age a score one standard deviation above the mean score for the age group is taken to represent an I.Q. of 116[19] in that group. A score one standard deviation below is interpreted as an I.Q. of 84. All other I.Q.'s are similarly located with reference to the mean and standard deviation. Thus, deviation I.Q.'s are not really quotients at all. They are intelligence standard scores. Stern did not succeed in killing the I.Q., but time and experience have succeeded in discrediting the simple logic on which it was based.

There is a second reason for the popularity of the I.Q. and for some of the misunderstandings associated with it. I.Q. seems to be a common denominator for all measurements of mental ability. Regardless of the content of the test, whether verbal or nonverbal, whether based on school learning or on novel problems, if its scores come out as I.Q.'s, the impres-

[16]William A. Owens, Jr., "The Retest Consistency of Army Alpha after 30 Years," *Journal of Applied Psychology*, vol. 38 (1954), 154.

[17]William A. Owens, Jr., "Age and Mental Abilities: A Second Adult Followup," *Journal of Educational Psychology*, vol. 57 (1966), 311–25.

[18]Walter Lippman, "Intelligence Tests," *The New Republic*, vol. 32 (1922), and vol. 33 (1923).

[19]Some test makers use 115. Others have used other values near 116. But 116 is the value recommended in the booklet on test standards published by the American Psychological Association.

sion is created that it is measuring the same thing as every other intelligence test. The fact that different tests are based on quite different tasks is glossed over by the use of the same kind of unit to express the measurements obtained. Were it not for this apparent generality of mental ability, and for the apparent simplicity of its measurement, the concept of abstract intelligence probably would not have gained so strong a following in the educational establishment.

ACHIEVEMENT QUOTIENTS AND "UNDERACHIEVEMENT"

The success and popularity of I.Q. encouraged the development of other quotients in the early days of standardized testing. One of these was the Educational Quotient (E.Q.), defined as:

$$E.Q. = 100 \times \frac{\text{Educational age}}{\text{Chronological age}}$$

Another was the Achievement Quotient (A.Q.)

$$A.Q. = 100 \times \frac{\text{Educational age}}{\text{Mental age}}$$

But both of these depend on assumptions that are even more questionable than those involved in the I.Q. They are subject to even greater errors and ambiguities, and hence they have fared much less well. Indeed they are now both generally discredited, for the following reasons.

To determine a pupil's educational age, one must give him a test for which age equivalent scores are available. An age equivalent for a given number of right answers is the age level for which that number of right answers is the average score. To determine age equivalent scores for a test of educational achievement is troublesome and costly, and of questionable value. If all pupils studied the same topics in the same sequence over a range of grades, that is, if all of them followed the same curriculum, reporting levels of educational achievement as age levels would make some sense. But curricula are not the same, textbooks are not the same, tests are not the same. To use the average test performance of pupils following diverse curricula as a basis for measuring the achievement of a specific pupil who has been following a specific curriculum is not particularly reasonable.

There are a number of additional difficulties with the achievement quotient, as Conrad has pointed out.[20] Educational ages and mental ages

[20]Herbert S. Conrad, "Norms," *Encyclopedia of Educational Research*, rev. ed., Walter S. Monroe, ed. (New York: The Macmillan Company, 1950).

are abstractions that carry the implication that their values are independent of the particular tests used. This is not true. Further if the "ages" were determined by using different samples of the population, the quotients might be systematically biased upward or downward, or biased differently at different points along the scale. Finally, errors of measurement in each of the two ages tend to be compounded in the quotient calculated from them.

Because their untrustworthiness is widely recognized, and because the necessary age scores are difficult to obtain, achievement quotients have fallen into disfavor and disuse. But the notions of underachievement and overachievement, which involve the same questionable assumptions and the same operational difficulties, are still popular. Thorndike has discussed some of the limitations of these notions.[21] Education is more likely to gain than to lose if the concepts of over- and underachievement are consigned to the same oblivion that has overtaken achievement quotients.

THE INHERITANCE OF INTELLIGENCE

One particular aspect of the nature of intelligence has been the focus of controversy for more than a century. To what extent is it a native, inborn characteristic? To what extent is it acquired? It was Galton's interest in intelligence as an inheritable trait that opened up the modern era of scientific study of intelligence.[22] Since his time, hundreds of scholars have contributed research data and rational reflections in efforts to end the controversy.

There have been studies of descendants of the same parents that seemed to show mental ability or lack of it to run in families. There have been comparisons of the intelligence of identical twins, fraternal twins, and siblings that seemed to show a correlation between degree of genetic similarity and degree of similarity in intelligence. There have been studies of children reared in foster homes that seemed to show intelligence to increase in favorable environments and to decline in unfavorable ones. A few investigators have felt confident enough of their data, and of the logical soundness of their conceptual structures, to partition the observed variance in human intelligence into two components and to report what fraction of the total was due to heredity and what fraction to environment.

[21]Robert L. Thorndike, *The Concepts of Over- and Underachievement* (New York: Teacher's College Press, 1963).
[22]Francis Galton, *Inquiries into Human Faculty and Its Development* (London: Macmillan, 1883).

Jensen,[23] in a comprehensive review article that attracted considerable popular attention, concluded that there was evidence not only for the inheritance of intelligence but for substantial racial differences in intelligence. Some other scholars disagreed.[24,25,26]

The difficulties that have prevented a clear-cut, generally accepted answer to the question are mainly two:

1. The lack of any clearly identified biological structure or function that determines intelligence and that could be subject to the laws of heredity
2. The impossibility of isolating the influences of heredity and environment and of controlling and manipulating them sufficiently to obtain unequivocal results.

Few are inclined to doubt that a particular individual's intelligence has an inherited biological base, or that individuals differ in the quality of that base. Extreme cases of mental deficiency are pretty clearly inherited, just as in other instances they are pretty clearly acquired. But among normal individuals it is difficult to find evidence that differences in the biological base result in corresponding differences in developed intelligence.

In this respect mental intelligence may be analogous to physical health. Just as a person may be born with physical deformities or physiological deficiencies that impair health throughout life, so may he be born with anatomical or physiological deficiencies of the brain and nervous system that impair intelligence throughout life. But for the vast majority of mankind, both our physical health and our mental intelligence depend almost entirely on what happens to us, and above all on what we ourselves do with the capabilities we inherit.

We have something in common with computers of the same model that were designed to have identical capacities and, save for accidental flaws, do have identical capacities. What differentiates the work that computers do, or that we do, is what they, and we, have been programmed to do. One of our advantages over the computer is that we have a hand in writing the programs that guide our thoughts and actions.

On the basis of evidence now available there is no compelling reason to believe that much of a man's intelligence is inherited. If we do not need to believe it, we probably are better off not to believe it. It represents

[23]Arthur R. Jensen, "How Much Can We Boost I.Q. and Scholastic Achievement?" *Harvard Educational Review*, vol. 34 (1969), 1–123.

[24]Jerome S. Kagan, "Inadequate Evidence and Illogical Conclusions," *Harvard Educational Review*, vol. 34 (1969), 274–77.

[25]J. McV. Hunt, "Has Compensatory Education Failed? Has It Been Attempted?" *Harvard Educational Review*, vol. 34 (1969), 278–300.

[26]Lee J. Cronbach, "Heredity, Environment and Educational Policy," *Harvard Educational Review*, vol. 34 (1969), 338–47.

an unnecessary hypothesis of the kind that Newton deplored. And it would call into question the soundness of our commitment to political equality, and to equality of educational opportunity.

INTELLIGENCE OF YOUNG CHILDREN

If intelligence were a biological "given," the sooner after birth it could be measured the less the contaminating influence of environment, and the more accurate the measurement should be. Unfortunately, no one has discovered any satisfactory way of testing the ability of a person to learn before he has learned much. One can assume that the intelligence is there all right, but just inaccessible. Another assumption is that it doesn't exist in any real sense until it has been developed.

The intelligence of infants has been measured and studied extensively.[27] One salient finding is that early measurements correlate poorly with later measurements of the same individuals. Again, one can assume that the apparent instability is due to inadequate measurements, or that it is due to actual changes in the developing intelligence. Those who emphasize hereditary factors as determinants of intelligence will choose one explanation. Those who emphasize learning and experience will prefer the other. Whatever the explanation, the measurements are not good predictors of subsequent educational development.

INTELLIGENCE AND TEACHING

It is obvious that different persons show different degrees of ability to learn. Since the differences exist, why they exist might seem to be a matter of purely academic interest. For the teacher it is more important to know that they do exist than to try to answer the difficult question of how they came to exist. Yet a teacher's hypotheses about the source and nature of the differences can have important consequences in her teaching. If she believes that they are the consequences of inherited capacities that set limits to what a given person can learn, she may "waste" little time trying to teach those whose capacities are limited. If she believes that inherited capacity rather than acquired background knowledge is the main determinant of future learning, she may concentrate on trying to discover

[27]Nancy Bayley, "Mental Growth During the First Three Years," *Genetic Psychology Monographs*, vol. 14 (1933), 1–92.

hidden talent so that it may be developed. But if she believes that there are no effective biological limits to learning, she will not despair of helping anyone to learn more, and she will concentrate on developing ability rather than prospecting for it.

Teachers who see intelligence as an inherent characteristic that limits the learning of some pupils have tended to use I.Q. scores more to explain why some pupils do not learn than to help all pupils to learn more. They have tended to see intelligence as a characteristic in which races differ, as they differ in other inherited characteristics. Instead of using intelligence test scores to insure equality of educational opportunity, they have used them to deny it. This is why some school and school systems have dropped intelligence tests from their testing programs.[28]

If there were clear evidence that important biological differences in learning ability do exist among school children, that these differences account to a significant degree for differences in school achievement, and that intelligence tests can measure these biological differences, then we ought to accept that evidence and take it into account in our teaching practices. But the evidence is far from clear or conclusive. We do well not to imagine barriers to learning where none exist, nor to assume that brightness gives easy access to all knowledge.

USE OF INTELLIGENCE TESTS IN SCHOOLS

What does the foregoing discussion mean with respect to a school's use of intelligence tests?

1. It means that they should not try to determine each child's I.Q., which he may not really have, and which they cannot determine with any real accuracy or assurance in any case.
2. It means that they should not spend time and money on individually administered intelligence tests, even with very young pupils, except in unusual individual cases.
3. It means that they should regard intelligence tests as useful measures of a general ability in school learning, an ability that is based on prior learning.
4. It means that they should not identify underachievers or overachievers on the basis of intelligence test scores.
5. It means that they should prefer verbal to nonverbal intelligence tests, and tests that emphasize abilities developed in school, not as a result of out-of-school experiences.

---

[28]J. O. Loretan, "The Decline and Fall of Group Intelligence Testing," *Teachers College Record*, vol. 67 (1965), 10–17.

6. It means that they should not regard intelligence tests as essential to a good school testing program.
7. It means that they should avoid tests that try to measure abstract intelligence, abstract mental abilities, or "the higher mental powers."
8. It means that instead of choosing tests that purport to be "culture free" or "culture fair" they should choose tests whose content is relevant to the learning tasks of the school.
9. It means that they should not be surprised to get somewhat different I.Q.'s from somewhat different tests, or to find that the same student's I.Q. shifts upward or downward from time to time.
10. It means that they should abandon the I.Q. as a term and as a concept as quickly as possible, substituting percentiles or standard scores on specific tests of aptitude for learning.

My own view is that traits are only convenient names given to types or qualities of behavior which have elements in common. They are not psychological entities, but rather categories for the classification of habits.

MARK A. MAY

21

PERSONALITY, ATTITUDES, AND INTERESTS

PERSONALITY TESTS

Published tests of personality are relatively abundant. In the *Sixth Mental Measurements Yearbook*,[1] the number of entries in each of four major categories was:

Achievement	614
Personality	196
Intelligence	131
Other	278
	1,219

[1]Oscar N. Buros, *The Sixth Mental Measurements Yearbook* (Highland Park, N.J.: The Gryphon Press, 1965).

The personality tests range from rather comprehensive personality inventories and temperament surveys to rather specific tests designed to assess, for example, hypnotic susceptibility in children, or the dimensions of alcohol addiction in adults.

Despite the number and variety of personality tests, their usefulness in the process of education is open to question. In part this question arises from the uncertain technical quality of some of the published personality tests. But to an even greater extent it arises from doubts about what precisely is being measured.

WHAT IS PERSONALITY?

As used in ordinary speech, the term *personality* is very broad and inclusive. Traxler defined it as the "sum total of an individual's behavior in social situations." Some use the term even more broadly, including not only behavior but also intellect, achievement, stature, health, voice quality, beauty, and so on. Clearly we are not likely to get a single meaningful measure of how much a person has of such a complex mixture of characteristics. Clearly what we must measure are aspects of the total personality.

But even this does not solve the problem when we are concerned with the behavioral aspects of personality. The traits we give separate names to, such as friendliness, tolerance, integrity, loyalty, ambition, determination, optimism, and so on (the list can be almost infinite) overlap and interact so that it is difficult to define any of them clearly. Traits that cannot be defined clearly can never be measured precisely.

For ages men have sought to discover the underlying elements of behavior. The ancients thought they had it in their theory of the four humors—blood, phlegm, yellow bile and black bile—that contributed respectively warm friendliness, inertia, anger ,and melancholy to a person's temperament. Jung, Kretschmer, and others have tried to identify and distinguish a limited number of types of personality. In our day the factor analysts have sought for some simple structure of basic determiners of behavior, without apparent success.

It is not even clear that personality traits can be properly regarded as causes of behavior observed. Perhaps they are only names for the behavior, which itself is the consequence of previous experience interacting with a given present situation. Do some high school students refuse to study because of lack of motivation? Or is lack of motivation simply the term we use to describe their behavior, which is in fact the result of many previous experiences and current competing interests? We call generous a man who drops a $20 bill in the collection plate on Sunday. Does he do this *because* he is generous, or does the word generosity simply name a class of similar behaviors? If personality traits are not causes of behavior, perhaps educators should not waste too much time trying to measure them. For if trait names only describe behavior, the only point in measuring the trait in an individual would be to determine to what extent the particular trait name can be used appropriately in descriptions of his behavior.

MOTIVATION

One of the personality traits that teachers most often wish to measure is motivation. They see some of their students studying hard, and others avoiding study as much as possible. They explain the difference by saying that some students are well and others poorly motivated. But is motivation here a cause, or is it simply a description of the observed result? Is motivation a mysterious spiritual essence, or is it the result of a complex interaction of beliefs, values, and choices? Can it be measured apart from its manifestation in how hard the student actually works at learning?

The facts that motivation is more a consequence than a cause, and that it probably can never be "measured" effectively by any paper-and pencil-test, does not mean that teachers or students can ignore it. Hard work is essential to learning, and getting students to work hard is an essential part of teaching. This is not the place to discuss techniques of motivation even if the author had (which he probably does not) much that is new and useful to say on the subject. The techniques are varied, and their results are not wholly predictable. Often the essential motivational factors are out of the teacher's reach, even out of the school's. Sometimes, however, they are not. Some teachers are generally successful in motivating students. With some students they may be outstandingly successful. But it is a safe bet that their arsenal of secret weapons does not include a paper-and-pencil test of motivation. Motivation, like most other personality traits, is less a cause than a consequence.

PERSONALITY TESTS IN SCHOOL TRAINING PROGRAMS

If schools had systematic, rational programs for personality development, it would be essential to include personality tests in the school's total program of evaluation. But few schools have such programs, and the limited ones that these few schools have tried, designed to develop such personality traits as ambition, honesty, patriotism, and piety, have not been notably successful. Nor are there any clear guides as to the directions personality development should take. Surely the world would be a poorer place to live if all of us had the same "good" personality. Some of us have "difficult" personalities, difficult for our families and friends and even for us to live with. But if one were to eliminate from the list of the world's great men and women those who had serious personality defects of one kind or another, only a handful would remain.

This does not mean that the schools can ignore the serious personality problems some of their students face. For the student's sake, as well as for the order, effectiveness, and harmony of the school, these problems need to be solved as well as possible. But personality development probably cannot and probably should not replace cognitive development as the central mission of the school.

A further problem of personality measurement is that paper-and-pencil tests are not well suited to it. Much of personality has to do with typical behavior in actual situations. But the behavior exhibited on a paper-and-pencil test is a limited, artificial kind. Even if a student knows with reasonable accuracy how he would behave in the situation described (and often he does not know) he may find it advantageous to report something else. It is possible for an examinee to "fake good" on most personality tests if he chooses to do so. Sometimes the purpose of the test is disguised, but the more this is done the less confidence one can have that the responses are really related to the behavior that needs to be measured. Finally, no matter how disguised or presented, a paper-and-pencil test remains for the examinee essentially a cognitive task. The emotion that plays so large a part in responses that reflect personality is largely absent from the responses to a paper-and-pencil test.

A final problem with personality tests involves the matter of invasion of privacy.[2] Personality tests cause more trouble on this score by far than either aptitude or achievement tests. Those who design personality tests, seeking to probe the basic causes of behavior, often ask questions about intimate personal or family affairs, questions that may embarrass the respondent (Do you ever wet the bed?) or irk his parents (Do your parents quarrel?). Even if the tester could prove that knowing these facts enables him to help the student with his personal problems, the probing might be resisted. But in the almost universal absence of any such proof it is almost universally resented.

We have pointed out these difficulties with the use of personality tests in schools:

1. Personality traits are difficult to define because they probably do not exist as distinct entities.
2. The essentially cognitive nature of the tasks presented by paper-and-pencil tests, plus their susceptibility to faking, makes them poorly adapted to the measurement of personality traits.
3. Personality tests that seek to uncover basic causes of maladjustments are likely to probe sensitive areas of concern, and thus are likely to be resented.

[2]George K. Bennett, "Testing and Privacy," *Journal of Educational Measurement*, vol. 4 (1967), 7–10.

In view of these problems, and because most schools do not have, and perhaps should not have, systematic programs of personality development, personality tests probably have no place in their systematic testing programs. This does not, of course, rule out selective, clinical use of adjustment inventories or problem checklists to aid a counselor in his efforts to help a troubled student. But no one concerned in this process—counselor, student, teachers, or parents—should expect a personality test to reveal much of a person's basic structure of personality. Indeed the very notion of such a structure is probably something of an illusion. Nor should anyone expect a personality test to contribute very much to the solution of the problem.

PERSONALITY TESTS IN SELECTIVE ADMISSIONS

Those who are responsible for selecting students for admission to specific colleges, or to training for the professions, often seek to supplement the tests of cognitive ability they use with tests of personality. They recognize the crucial importance of personality to effective performance in training, and even more to subsequent success and happiness. They have spent hundreds of thousands of dollars to develop, try out, and evaluate diverse approaches to the measurement of aspects of personality. But as of this writing, no major selection testing program is making operational use of any personality test. Such tests have been used quite extensively by private agencies concerned with the selection of executives, but their practices in using personality tests have been criticized sharply, and with considerable justification.[3]

There are two reasons why personality tests are little used in responsible selection programs. One is the great difficulties we have mentioned of making good, useful personality tests. The other is real concern over the wisdom and the ethics of using them. It is not always, perhaps not even usually, the normal, happy, well-adjusted person who makes the greatest contribution to human welfare. History is full of the records of great men and women who suffered agony of spirit during their developing years. Geniuses are not all mad, but the line between madness and genius is often not at all clear. Denial of advanced education to a capable student who seems maladjusted or somewhat odd might be an extremely shortsighted policy. It might also be quite unfair to reject an applicant otherwise well qualified simply because he chooses to live his life somewhat differently from the way others do. The directors of selection testing programs are properly cautious about the use of personality tests.

[3] William H. Whyte, Jr., *The Organization Man* (New York: Simon and Schuster, Inc., 1956).

ATTITUDE AND INTEREST INVENTORIES

WHAT ARE ATTITUDES?

One aspect of an individual's personality is his attitudes. The concept of an attitude, like that of personality, is not easy to define precisely. It may be defined very generally as "the sum total of a man's inclinations and feelings, prejudice or bias, preconceived notions, ideas, fears, threats, and convictions about any specific topic."[4] Or it may be defined more narrowly as a tendency "to favor or reject particular groups of individuals, sets of ideas or social institutions."[5]

Attitudes result from our tendency to reach general conclusions on the basis of specific experiences. This ability to generalize is very useful. It is largely responsible for our intellectual development. Without it all that we learn would be specific and hence limited in use. It gives us laws of science, of ethics, and of government. It also gives us attitudes, biases, and misconceptions.

To have an attitude toward something is to be biased, favorably or unfavorably. Bias is commonly deplored. Its opposites—openmindedness, tolerance, fairness—are approved. But to stay openminded one must not make up his mind on the question, and that kind of indecision we are not likely to approve. Thus being biased (that is, having an attitude) toward something is not necessarily bad. Likewise being openminded is not always possible or desirable. We like others to be openminded to our ideas, but not to be easily persuaded when contrary ideas are presented.

Some attitudes involve mainly feelings. These are sometimes the results of conditioning. A child is conditioned to fear thunderstorms by the anxious behavior of a fearful mother. Or he may be conditioned to fear small dogs by the aggressive playfulness of a puppy. Or he may be conditioned to love reading by the pleasant experience of being read to at bedtime.

Other attitudes are primarily cognitive generalizations. A political leader's words and actions, or what we know about his friends and supporters may cause us to like and to trust him. If we do, we give him the benefit of the doubt. Or if a church states positions or takes actions that seem wrong to us, we may conclude that its whole influence is bad.

Cognitive attitudes are closely related to knowledge. The difference between them is chiefly in how universally they are accepted, or how easily

---

[4]L. L. Thurstone and E. J. Chave, *The Measurement of Attitude* (Chicago: University of Chicago Press, 1929), pp. 6–7.

[5]R. L. Thorndike and E. Hagen, *Measurement and Evaluation in Psychology and Education*, 3d ed. (New York: John Wiley & Sons, Inc., 1969), p. 382.

they can be shown to be true. What a person believes is made up of his knowledge and his attitudes. Those propositions that most informed persons regard as true make up his knowledge. Those on which significant differences of opinion exist constitute his attitudes. Attitudes are personal beliefs.

Several other terms that we commonly use in describing personality represent specific kinds of attitudes. Self-concepts are attitudes of a person toward himself. Interests are attitudes of desire for certain activities. Ideals are attitudes of desire for the attainment of certain goals. Values are attitudes of approval of specific things or accomplishments.

WHY DIFFERENT PEOPLE HAVE DIFFERENT ATTITUDES

There are several reasons why the beliefs that we call attitudes differ from person to person. One is that they involve broad generalizations, with much relevant and occasionally contradictory evidence. Another is that they deal less with things as they are than with things as they ought to be. Personal goals and values affect them. Consider these examples:

Earl Warren was an outstanding chief justice.
Communism is evil.
Pollution of our air and water must be stopped.
Our most urgent problem in the United States today is reestablishment of
  respect for law and order.

These propositions are all more or less debatable. They are too general and too loaded with value judgments to be *proved* true or false. But individuals and governments, after reflection and deliberation, will decide to act as if they were either true or false. Despite their somewhat limited justifiability, attitudes are powerful determiners of action.

Attitudes have a noteworthy self-sustaining and reinforcing property. Once a person develops an attitude toward something, once he arrives at an emotional feeling or a cognitive generalization about it, further experience is more likely to support than to weaken it. For the person henceforth tends to observe and to remember selectively. He will notice and believe incidents that support his attitude, that prove he is indeed correct in holding it. He will ignore or discredit incidents that seem to call the attitude into question. The vulnerability of a person's attitudes, the fact that they are not universally believed or easily shown to be true, makes one who holds them use every opportunity to strengthen and defend them.

A well-established attitude is very difficult to overthrow. Seldom can one person induce another to change one of his attitudes, however ill-founded it may seem to be. If a change comes, and attitudes do change, it is likely to be as result of a voluntary, internal decision. If evidence against an attitude accumulates, or if clinging to it entails penalties, the holder may gradually soften and ultimately reverse it.

HOW ARE ATTITUDES MEASURED?

Attitudes affect behavior and thus can be measured by observers making use of rating scales. However, the difficulties of finding qualified observers and of finding sufficient relevant incidents to observe usually make measurement based on direct observation unattractive. The easier and generally better way is to ask the individual himself to report what he believes or what he likes to do. Measurements of attitudes are usually based on the subjects's self-reports.

It is reasonable to presume that measurements based on self-reports could be falsified or faked. That is, the student could make himself to seem different from, or better than, his real self if it should serve his purposes to do so. Several studies confirm this expectation.[6] If one of the objectives in a course is to cultivate a certain attitude, some students will probably yield to the temptation to show more of the attitude than they actually possess. However, if the measurements are being made to aid the student in making sound decisions about his own future, the probability that the responses will be faked approaches zero. Efforts to minimize faking by disguising the purpose of the test have not proved effective, on the whole. Usually the disguise introduces more error due to indirect measurement than the amount of error due to faking it removes.

Instruments used to measure attitudes are usually referred to as attitude scales. Although many elaborate techniques of scale construction have been developed, including scalogram analysis (Guttman),[7] unfolding (Coombs),[8] and latent structure analysis (Lazarsfeld),[9] only two have come into wide use. These methods involve either scaled statements (Thurstone)[10] or scaled responses (Likert).[11]

[6]H. P. Longstaff, "Fakeability of the Strong Interest Blank and the Kuder Preference Record," *Journal of Applied Psychology*, vol. 32 (1948), 360–69.

[7]Louis Guttman, "The Basis for Scaleogram Analysis," in Samuel Stouffer and others, *Measurement and Prediction* (Princeton, N.J.: Princeton University Press, 1950), pp. 60–90.

[8]C. H. Coombs, *A Theory of Data* (New York: John Wiley & Sons, Inc., 1964), p. 585.

[9]Paul F. Lazarsfeld, "Latent Structure Analysis" in S. Kock, ed., *Psychology: A Study of a Science*, vol. 3 (New York: McGraw-Hill Book Company, 1959), pp. 476–542.

[10]L. L. Thurstone and E. J. Chave, *The Measurement of Attitude* (Chicago: University of Chicago Press, 1929).

[11]R. Likert, "A Technique for the Measurement of Attitude," *Archives of Psychology*, vol. 22, no. 140 (1932), pp. 1–55.

In the Thurstone technique a large set of statements describing varying attitudes toward something like an institution (for example, the church) or a development (for example, urbanization) is assembled or written. Judges are asked to sort these statements into groups that fall in equally spaced intervals along the attitude continuum from highly favorable to highly unfavorable. Statements that different judges place at widely different points on the continuum are discarded. From those that remain a smaller set representing the entire continuum as well as possible is selected. These statements constitute the attitude scale.

Each statement carries a scale value determined by the average of its placements by the several judges along the original continuum. The student whose attitude is to be measured is given the scaled statements in random order and asked to indicate which statements he can accept. His score is the average of the scale values of those statements.

Statements like the following might appear in a scale of attitudes toward permissiveness in child rearing.

	Scale Value
A child should be free to do as he pleases with his own playthings.	9.5
Decisions on matters of conduct should be made by parent and child jointly.	6.3
In modern times children are being allowed too much freedom.	3.5

The Likert technique also starts with a set of statements, though usually not so many are required. Further, instead of expressing a number of different degrees of favorableness or unfavorableness, each statement is intended to be clearly favorable or unfavorable. Neutral statements are avoided. The examinee responds to each item on a five-point scale of agreement:

	Numerical Scores	
	Favorable	Unfavorable
Strongly agree	5	1
Agree	4	2
Uncertain	3	3
Disagree	2	4
Strongly disagree	1	5

His score on the item depends, as indicated above, on the extent to which he agrees with statements favoring the attitude and disagrees with statements opposing it.

Here are three statements that might appear on a scale of political liberalism:

Unemployment insurance tends to encourage idleness.
Government serves the businessman better than it serves the laborer.
A family can live quite comfortably on welfare.

Items that discriminate best between those receiving highest and those receiving lowest scores on the total scale are retained for the final form of the scale.

The Likert technique is easier to use in developing an attitude scale than the Thurstone technique, and gives almost equally good results. It is currently the most widely used technique.

The number of attitudes that could be measured is almost infinite. Some of these are very general, like attitudes toward education or government. Others are quite specific, such as attitudes toward the Pope's encyclical on birth control. Shaw and Wright have collected and published a number of examples.[12]

HOW ARE INTERESTS MEASURED?

Interests are also measured by asking the subject directly what he likes or would like to do. Here again two somewhat different approaches have been used. The Strong Vocational Interest Blank[13] uses brief designations of such things as occupations, amusements, and activities, and asks the examinee to indicate whether he likes, dislikes, or is indifferent to them. The Kuder Preference Record presents the examinee with triads of activities and asks him to choose which he likes most and which he likes least of each triad.[14]

There are other significant differences between these two approaches to the measurement of interests. Scoring weights for alternative responses to items in the Strong were derived from the responses of men successfully engaged in various occupations. Scores are reported to indicate how well the interests of the examinee correspond to the interests of those in various occupations. In the Kuder Preference Record, the interests measured and the assignment of items to these interest scales was determined by an analysis of the responses of students to locate coherent clusters. Some of these clusters included activities that were mainly musical, and so on.

[12]Mervin E. Shaw and Jack M. Wright, *Scales for the Measurement of Attitudes* (New York: McGraw Hill Book Company, 1967).

[13]Edward K. Strong, Jr., *Vocational Interests of Men and Women* (Stanford, Calif.: Stanford University Press, 1943).

[14]G. F. Kuder, "The Stability of Preference Items," *The Journal of Social Psychology*, vol. 10 (1939), 41–50.

Thus, the scores reported indicate interests in types of activities rather than in particular occupations.

Both inventories have been widely used. The characteristics of both have been thoroughly investigated. The interests measured by both show considerable stability over time. Both considerable value as predictors of later occupational choice. But it is important to remember that they measure interests rather than abilities, and that although the two tend to be associated, the correlation is by no means perfect. A high interest score does not mean that a person will succeed in a particular occupation. What it does mean is that *if* he succeeds in it he will probably be happy in it.

SHOULD SCHOOLS SEEK TO DEVELOP ATTITUDES?

The cultivation of various presumably desirable attitudes is frequently mentioned as an educational objective for a course or a school. Less often does the teacher or the school have a systematic program for the attainment of such objectives. Almost never is a serious attempt made to measure the extent to which such objectives have been achieved.

Beyond question, schooling does lead to attitude changes. Many of these changes are results of the acquisition of new knowledge that calls old attitudes into question or suggests new ones. Many of them are the results of conditioning. For example, a well-liked teacher of history may give his students an enduringly favorable attitude toward the study of history. A poorly managed school may condition students to dislike the whole process of education.

But, regardless of how they are changed, if attitudes are, as we have suggested, simply beliefs that are not demonstrably true and that therefore may be false, it seems very doubtful that a teacher or a school should set out deliberately to inculcate them. It seems even more doubtful that an institution designed for the education of free men should use techniques of conditioning to inculcate the attitudes it approves. For attitudes accepted as a result of conditioning have not been freely chosen on their merits, as a free man's attitudes ought to be.

What this means is that a teacher or a school should not make the cultivation of a particular set of attitudes one of its explicitly stated and publicly announced primary objectives. Inevitably good teachers will have attitudes themselves that they believe to be both good and true. Inevitably these attitudes will affect the knowledge they choose to teach and perhaps even their manner of teaching. Inevitably these and other attitudes will get talked about in good class discussions. The teacher's attitudes will not remain hidden from the students. But under no circumstances should the students be held responsible, as a condition of satisfactory achievement, for accepting the teacher's attitudes. What they should be expected to do is to gain command of the knowledge that is relevant to these and alternative attitudes.

Such a procedure with respect to attitudes is not only the educationally ethical one, but also is likely to be the most effective pedagogically. A frontal attack on another person's attitudes is likely only to strengthen his commitment to them. But if attitudes are recognized as his to hold or to change, if he is challenged to examine them critically, and if his cognitive resources relevant to them are increased, he may find personal satisfaction in changing them himself. Attitude modification by indirection is probably the best strategy.

Neither this strategy nor any other will guarantee adoption by students of a single ideal set of attitudes, but this lack of certainty is more to be applauded than deplored. If the propositions that constitute our attitudes are uncertain knowledge, it is good to have different ones held and defended. Efforts to defend them, plus the test of time, are quite likely to lead ultimately to agreement on knowledge that is certain to replace the attitudes that are uncertain. And if we must live with some degree of error in our beliefs, as we inevitably must, it is best that such error not be universally accepted as truth.

Thus, the fact that attitudes are almost impossible to measure as educational achievements is no serious loss. We shouldn't include them among our explicit objectives, and we shouldn't try to teach them in any case. The fact that they are very difficult to measure as outcomes of instruction, however, has probably helped to keep the feet of idealistic teachers in paths of virtue.

SUMMARY

The principal ideas developed in this chapter can be summarized in the following eleven propositions.

1. The concept of personality is broad and the factors that influence its development are complex.
2. Personality trait names are more useful in describing behavior than in explaining it.
3. It is unlikely that paper-and-pencil tests of motivation will prove useful to the teacher.
4. The central mission of the school is cognitive development rather than personality development.
5. Personality tests are resented more often and more deeply as unwarranted invasions of privacy than are tests of cognitive achievements.
6. Personality tests have not been used effectively, and probably should not be used at all, in selective admission to educational programs.

7. Attitudes are generalizations whose validity is open to question.
8. A person's attitudes tend to be self-reinforcing.
9. The two principal techniques of attitude measurement are those developed by Thurstone and by Likert. Thurstone's technique uses scaled statements. Likert's technique uses scaled responses.
10. The two principle techniques of interest measurement are those developed by Strong and by Kuder. Strong's technique calls for expressions of liking, indifference, or dislike for particular activities. Kuder's technique calls for choice among alternative activities.
11. Schools probably should not set out to develop directly certain desired attitudes in their students.

We must never forget that to the degree that we are able
to measure medical competence, to just that same degree will
medical competence be available to our people.

NATHAN A. WOMACK, M. D.

22

TESTING PROGRAMS

A testing program is an arrangement for providing, administering, scoring, and reporting the results from a test or a group of related tests. Well-known examples are the Regent's examinations in New York State and the admissions tests of the College Entrance Examinations Board. A partial listing of testing programs designed to serve various purposes is presented in Table 22.1. These programs can be classified roughly into three broad categories:

1. those designed for the improvement of learning in the school
2. those designed for selective admission and scholarship awards
3. those designed for certification of competence

In this section some of the characteristics and problems of programs in each category will be discussed. No attempt will be made to describe any of the programs in detail. Numbers in parentheses in Exhibit 22.1 refer to addresses in Exhibit 22.2 where one can write for more information

EXHIBIT 22.1

Types of Testing Programs

PURPOSE	EXAMPLES
I Evaluation and Instruction	
To aid local schools in facilitation of learning and evaluation of results	Local Testing Programs (21) Iowa Testing Programs (14) Michigan School Testing Service (5) Educational Records Bureau (11)
To provide information on educational attainments and problems to government agencies and the public	National Assessment of Educational Progress (15) (10) New York Regents Examinations (19) California State Testing Program (9) Michigan Assessment of Education (4)
II Guidance and Selection	
To aid colleges in program evaluation	Graduate Record Examination (12) College Level Examination Program (10) Teacher Education Evaluation Program (12)
To encourage and reward advanced levels of secondary school education	Advanced Placement Program (12)
To aid colleges and secondary schools in guidance, selection, and admission	The College Board Programs (12) The American College Testing Program (1) The Secondary School Admission Testing Program (12)
To aid graduate and professional schools in guidance, selection, and admission	Graduate Record Examination (12) Miller Analogies Test (22) Admission Test for Medicine (22), Law (12), and Business (12)
To qualify students for selection or exemption from government service	Peace Corps Selection Test (18) Selective Service College Qualification Test (20) Foreign Service Examinations (3)
To aid in employee guidance, selection, and placement	General Aptitude Test Battery (24) Civil Service Examinations (7)
To select students for scholarship awards	National Merit Scholarship Testing Program (17)

III Certification of Competence

To certify professional competence	National Teacher Examinations (12) C.P.A. Accountant Examinations (2) National Board Medical Examinations (16) State Licensing Examinations (7) Chartered Life Underwriter Examination (12)
To certify competence in a foreign language	Graduate School Foreign Language Examinations (12)
To certify educational equivalence	New York College Proficiency Examination Program (19)
To certify technical competence	Examinations of the City and Guilds of London (6) State and City Licensing Examinations (7)

EXHIBIT 22.2

Names and Addresses of Program Sponsors

1. American College Testing Program
   P.O. Box 168
   Iowa City, Iowa 52240
2. American Institute of Certified Public Accountants
   666 Fifth Avenue
   New York, New York 10019
3. Board of Examiners for the Foreign Service
   U.S. Department of State
   Washington, D.C. 20520
4. Bureau of Research
   Michigan Department of Education
   106 S. Pine Street
   Lansing, Michigan
5. Bureau of School Services
   The University of Michigan
   401 S. Fourth Street
   Ann Arbor, Michigan 48103
6. City and Guilds of London Institute

   76 Portland Place
   London, W1N 4AA England
7. Civil Service Director
   (City or State Government)
8. College Proficiency Examination Program
   New York State Education Department
   Albany, New York 12224
9. Department of Education
   State of California
   721 Capitol Mall
   Sacramento, California 95814
10. Education Commission of the States
    822 Lincoln Tower
    1860 Lincoln Street
    Denver, Colorado 80203
11. Educational Records Bureau
    116 Maple Avenue
    Greenwich, Connecticut 06830

12. Educational Testing Service
    Princeton, New Jersey 18540
13. General Educational Development
    Testing Service
    American Council on Education
    1785 Massachusetts Avenue
    Washington, D.C. 20036
14. Iowa Testing Programs
    The State University of Iowa
    N101 East Hall
    Iowa City, Iowa 52240
15. National Assessment of Educational Progress
    300 Lincoln Tower
    1860 Lincoln Street
    Denver, Colorado 80203
16. National Board of Medical Examiners
    3930 Chestnut Street
    Philadelphia, Pennsylvania 19104
17. National Merit Scholarship Corporation

990 Grove Street
Evanston, Illinois 60201
18. Peace Corps
    Washington, D.C.
19. Regents Examination and Scholarship Center
    University of the State of New York
    The State Education Department
    Albany, New York 12224
20. Selective Service System National Headquarters
    1724 F Street
    Washington, D.C.
21. Superintendent of Schools
    (Local school system)
22. The Psychological Corporation
    304 East 45th Street
    New York, New York 10017
23. U.S. Civil Service Commision
    1900 E. Street
    Washington, D.C.

on some of these programs. A detailed discussion of the nature and functions of school testing programs has been published by the National Society for the Study of Education.[1]

SCHOOL TESTING PROGRAMS

Local schools and school systems frequently supplement teacher-made classroom achievement tests with school-wide testing, in order to:

1. provide information needed for instruction and guidance
2. evaluate local school achievement against external standards
3. stimulate and direct continuing efforts to improve curriculum and instruction in the local school

Sometimes these school testing programs are well planned and compet-

[1] Warren G. Findley, ed., *The Impact and Improvement of School Testing Programs.* 62nd Yearbook, Part II, National Society for the Study of Education (Chicago: University of Chicago Press, 1963), p. 304.

ently handled,[2,3] sometimes the results are put to good use, and sometimes the testing program is strongly supported by the faculty and the community. Unfortunately, these desirable conditions do not always exist. Sometimes a school's testing program is imposed by an administration that believes all good schools have such programs, without knowing very clearly what educational purposes they serve. In that situation the school's testing program is not likely to be very good, or very popular, or very well used.

The chief justification of a school testing program, of course, is the use made of the scores obtained.[4,5] To give the tests, obtain scores, and record each on the pupil's cumulative record card does not constitute sufficient use, ordinarily, to justify the testing. On the other hand, it is a mistake to develop such an elaborate program for "using" the test scores in teachers meetings, conferences with pupils and parents and various other kinds of action programs that the testing program begins to absorb more than its share of the school's time and budget.

REPORTING TEST SCORES

The most essential use to be made of test scores is simply to report them to all who need to know, along with a simple interpretation of what they mean.[6] They should be reported to the students, and usually to the parents as well. The teachers should receive them for initial review, and should keep them at hand for ready reference on future occasions. Summaries of the score distributions should be reported to the school authorities and to the community. If these things are done, many other important uses of the test scores will occur spontaneously. It is no more necessary to develop a comprehensive, formal program for using test scores than for using a dictionary or a typewriter. If they are at hand, and if their use is understood, they will be used whenever the occasion arises.

School officials have sometimes been negligent about reporting the results of their testing programs. Sometimes they have been unnecessarily

[2]Robert H. Bauernfeind, *Building a School Testing Program* (Boston: Houghton Mifflin Company, 1969).

[3]Arthur E. Traxler, "15 Criteria of a Testing Program," *The Clearing House*, vol. 25 (September 1950), 3–7.

[4]Arthur E. Traxler, "Use of Results of Large-scale Testing Programs in Instruction and Guidance," *Journal of Educational Research*, vol. 54 (October 1960), 59–62.

[5]G. D. Moore and L. Feldt, "Positive Approach to the Use of Test Results," *National Elementary Principal*, vol. 42 (1963), 65–70.

[6]Robert L. Ebel, "How to Explain Standardized Test Scores to Your Parents," *School Management*, vol. 5 (March 1961), 61–64.

cautious. Most test scores are not especially difficult to understand. When understood, they are almost never dangerous. A school should seldom, if ever, require all pupils to take a test whose results are not to be reported to them or their parents. Pupils and parents are partners with teachers and administrators in the educational process. The process works best if they are admitted to full partnerhsip. Recently the Commissioner of Education for the State of New York ruled that parents have a right to know the test scores of their children and other information in the school files of pupil records. The decision upset some educators who had grown accustomed to working with confidential files, but it seems fully justifiable on educational grounds. It is hard to imagine information that teachers need to know about a pupil that his parents should not also be allowed to know if they wish.

JUDGING TEACHER COMPETENCE

Should the results of standardized tests of student achievement given in a school program be used in evaluating the competence of teachers? The popular answer from teachers and most professional educators is a resounding No! Surely test results can never tell the whole story of a teacher's effectiveness. A superintendent who notes low achievement test scores for a class and who concludes on this evidence and this alone that the teacher is incompetent would be no wiser than a physician who notes a patient's complaint of pains in the lower abdomen and concludes on this evidence and this alone that the patient's appendix must be removed. Fortunately not many superintendents and not many physicians are foolish enough to jump to conclusions like these.

But would it not be equally foolish to deny, a priori and in all cases, that poor pupil achievement *might* be the result of poor teaching, just as pain in the lower abdomen might be caused by an infected appendix? If we agree that quality of teaching influences the quality of educational achievement, then we must also agree that good measures of that achievement have something to contribute to the complex process of evaluating teacher competence. If we do not agree that good learning requires good teaching, why try to hire good teachers or even to train them in the first place?

Now it is quite proper to call attention, as many educators have done, to the limitations of standardized tests as measures of pupil achievement, and to their additional limitations as bases for inferring teacher competence. Exhibit 22.3 presents some of the limitations of both kinds. But these limitations are by no means so serious, so inherent, and so un-

EXHIBIT 22.3

Limitations of Standard Test Scores

A. As measures of student achievement
   1. Lack of complete relevance to the objectives of a given course
   2. Lack of perfect score reliability owing to a limited number of items or poor item quality
   3. Susceptibility to coaching
   4. Tendency to lose validity with repeated use
   5. Possibility of improper administration or scoring
   6. Possibility of inappropriate or unreliable norms

B. As bases for inferring teacher competence
   1. Sensitivity to conditions other than teacher competence that affect learning
      a. Pupil ability levels
      b. School, family, and community support for learning
      c. Quality of educational curricula and instructional materials
   2. Insensitivity to the teacher's contributions that do not directly foster learnings
      a. Motivation
      b. Guidance
      c. School morale
      d. Direction of co-curricular activities
   3. Imperfection as measures of student achievement

avoidable as to destroy the value of standardized tests as part of the basis for judging pupil achievement or teacher competence. Those who object most strongly to the use of standard tests for these purposes would probably object with equal vigor to any other definite bases for measuring achievement or competence. It is more the fact that judgments are being made than the basis on which they are made that causes concern.

Yet despite the difficulty of the task and the uncertain quality of the result, judgments of teacher competence do have to be made. Almost every school and college has, and uses, procedures for differentiating the better from the poorer teachers. Teachers do differ in effectiveness. The pupils of good teachers learn more important things, and learn them better, than do the pupils of poor teachers. Hence, standard test scores do provide one kind of evidence of teacher effectiveness. They never tell the whole story, but they tell one important part of it. They should never be used exclusively or blindly, but neither should any other evidence of a teacher's competence or lack of it. The indications they can give should not be denied or disregarded.

DEVELOPING A SCHOOL TESTING PROGRAM

A school testing program, almost everyone now agrees, should not be imposed by administrative fiat on an unprepared and hence possibly unwilling school staff. But to democratize the approach by appointing a committee of teachers and administrators to plan the testing program is not always a satisfactory alternative. It may develop into a classic illustration of the stumbling efforts of the blind to lead the blind. The first requirement of a good school testing program is not that it be *democratically* planned, but that it be *competently* planned. Of course the teachers who must administer the testing program and use its results should be helped to understand what is to be done, and why. Their support for the program should be sought. However, support for the program will be easier to secure if it is competently planned than if it is incompetently planned.

A school planning to adopt or to modify its testing program has two options. One is to tailor a program to fit its own needs and purposes. This is an attractive alternative if the school has teachers, counselors, and administrators who know enough about tests and testing programs to plan a good one. The other is to participate in a cooperative interscholastic testing program such as the Iowa Testing Programs, the Michigan School Testing Service, or the Educational Records Bureau.

The main advantage of the local program is its specific adaptation to local conditions. Its main disadvantages are that it needs more expertness and time to plan and operate than the cooperative program requires, and the possible lack or inadequacy of relevant external standards of comparison. The external cooperative testing program may not ideally meet all of the local school's needs, but it is likely to bring expert planning, efficient and economical operation, relevant norms, and professionally competent resources for score interpretation and use. Unless a school feels sure of its competence and its resources for development of its own testing program, it should probably give careful consideration to the possibilities of participation in some cooperative program.

A good testing program is likely to cost some money—perhaps as much as several dollars per pupil per year. These costs cannot be disregarded. On the other hand, if seen in the perspective of other educational costs and of educational value received, they are by no means high. A school that absolutely cannot afford a good testing program can hardly afford to operate at all.

Whether a school elects to develop its own testing program or to participate in an established, cooperative program, and regardless of the number of its staff who have some competence in testing, it will usually benefit greatly from the appointment of a specialist to manage the testing program and the other testing activities of the school. Such a staff member can be given responsibility for efficient performance of a multitude of tasks associated with the program. He can also handle the administration of tests in other programs involving pupils of the school. If qualified to do so, he can serve as a consultant to teachers on their own evaluation problems. Unfortunately, the supply of talent in this area is less than abundant. Perhaps colleges of education have not done as much as they could and should to train easily identifiable specialists in school testing.

ADMISSION AND SCHOLARSHIP PROGRAMS

Testing programs for college admission and scholarship awards are usually designed and operated by agencies outside of the schools. They are of interest to pupils in the schools who wish to take them, and of concern to staff members of the schools who must arrange for their administration and sometimes for the interpretation of their scores. But they are not under the effective control of the schools, and are not integral parts of their educational programs.

With the increasing popularity of higher education, which has forced some colleges to become increasingly selective in admissions, and with increasing use of scholarships to help capable students of limited means to get a college education, participation in these programs has increased rapidly in recent years. The number of such programs has also increased. These developments have led to complaints from school administrators[7] and to responses from test specialists.[8,9,10] Some of the objections raised to external testing programs, and answers to the objections, are summarized here.

Objection: The different programs of this type serve similar purposes, use similar tests, and yield similar scores for the same student. The repeated testing involves needless duplication, needless testing time, and needless expense to all concerned.

[7] Joint Committee on Testing, *Testing, Testing, Testing*, Washington, D.C.: American Association of School Administrators, Council of Chief State School Officers, National Association of Secondary-School Principals (1962), p. 32.

[8] Frank B. Womer, "Pros and Cons of External Testing Programs," *The North Central Association Quarterly*, vol. 36 (Fall 1961), 201–10.

[9] Robert L. Ebel, "External Testing: Response to Challenge," *Teachers College Record*, vol. 64 (December 1962), 190–98.

[10] Paul L. Dressel, "Role of External Testing Programs in Education," *Educational Record*, vol. 45 (1964), pp. 161–66.

Answer: Multiple testing gives the student multiple opportunities and options. Though similar, the tests are not identical and give somewhat different indications of abilities. Taking each test is likely to be a useful learning experience for the student.

Objection: The tests, which emphasize particular kinds of verbal and numerical skills, do not give adequate opportunities to students with other kinds of special talents. They narrow the gate of admission to college too much.

Answer: The scope of verbal and numerical skills is broad. Together these skills encompass much that is fundamental to achievement in most areas of learning. Colleges are free to admit students with relatively low scores on admission tests if they give other indications of promise.

Objection: Truly creative intellects are penalized by multiple-choice tests because they often choose and can justify one of the "wrong" answers on the basis of brilliant insights that the test makers overlooked.

Answer: There is no empirical evidence to support this objection, partly because there is no obviously valid means of measuring the "true creative ability" of an intellect. On the other hand, there is ample evidence, which Chauncey and Hilton[11] have summarized, that aptitude tests *are* valid for the highly able.

Objection: Emphasis on aptitude test scores for college admission and scholarship awards encourages intensive coaching to do well on the tests, at the expense of more fundamental and lasting learning.

Answer: Experimental studies of coaching indicate that it yields small returns for the effort expended.[12] Good aptitude tests cover such a wide range of verbal and numerical understandings as to be practically uncoachable. What gains do result from the coaching are likely to be educationally helpful also.

Because of the legitimate interest of high school graduates in admission to college and in scholarship awards, a school cannot justify refusal to cooperate in these programs, even though the demands on staff cooperation and school facilities may seem heavy at times. With good guidance, students will avoid registration for tests that are unlikely to help them. The indirect influence of these testing programs on school morale, through the recognition and rewards they offer for effective learning, can more than repay the efforts the school expends in cooperation. Finally, if the school

[11]Henry Chauncey and Thomas L. Hilton, "Are Aptitude Tests Valid for the Highly Able?" *Science*, vol. 140, No. 8 (1965), 1297–1304.

[12]John W. French and Robert E. Dear, "Effects of Coaching on an Aptitude Test", *Educational and Psychological Measurement*, vol. 14 (1959), 319–30.

has a staff specialist who is assigned responsibility for managing the school's involvement in the program, the job is likely to be done well without unreasonable demands on other staff members.

CERTIFICATION OF COMPETENCE

The numerous testing programs that are operated to aid in the certification of professional or technical competence concern the schools very little. It is interesting to speculate on reasons why the teaching profession makes less use of written tests in the certification of competence to practice than almost any other profession, except perhaps the ministry. Let it be granted without argument that no written test can assess *all* aspects of skill or competence in the practice of a profession. The best it can do is to indicate whether a person knows enough about the work he hopes to do to be intellectually qualified. It cannot reveal how skillfully, or with what wisdom, he will use the knowledge that is his to command. But the aspects of competence that written tests can assess are important, and written tests can do an efficient valid job of assessing them. Some of the arguments that teachers use against written tests of professional competence are self-serving, defensive evasions. Neither the profession nor the public should tolerate them indefinitely.

Those who are responsible for the development of tests to be used in certifying competence should themselves be highly competent test developers. In some cases they are; in many they are not. Usually, and quite understandably, they are first and foremost experts in the profession or trade in which competence is to be examined and certified. They may work under the supervision of a specialist in testing, and they may gradually acquire through experience some sophistication in methods of testing. But lacking special training for the job they are asked to do, they may sometimes show less than the desired competence in doing it. Across the country and around the world there are many untrained or poorly trained test constructors doing their very limited best to handle some very important responsibilities. Universities that offer training in educational measurement ought to do much more than they have done in the past to provide good pre-service or in-service training for these workers.

Tests used to certify competence ought to be highly valid tests. To many this suggests that the tests ought to be validated against "appropriate" criterion measures. Unfortunately, as pointed out in Chapter 16, the problem of getting valid criterion measures is no easier to solve than the problem of getting valid test scores. Whether the test is validated directly, or indirectly via some criterion, there is no escape from the exercise of expert judgment in determining what ought to be measured and how it ought to be measured. The frequent absence of this kind of expert judgment in test development is a more serious weakness of many tests of professional competence than is the lack of adequate validation of the developed test.

In recent years concern has been expressed that certification tests and other ability tests may be biased against minority group members.[13] Sometimes evidence that applicants from these groups tend to make lower scores on the certification tests than do other applicants is cited to justify this concern. But to the extent that the certification test is a relevant test, such score differences simply indicate that the minority group applicants tend to be less well qualified than the other applicants. Society may decide that to help right old wrongs a preferential bonus should be added to the test scores of minority group applicants. War veterans have often been shown that kind of preference on civil service selection tests. And surely those who develop or use tests for certification of competence should try to get tests of the highest possible validity. But they should view with skepticism the claim that written tests are less valid for minority group members than for others.[14,15] In most situations valid written tests are less subject to racial, religious, or personal bias than any other aid to selection or certification.

SUMMARY

The principal ideas developed in this chapter can be summarized in the following nine propositions.

1. Testing programs are designed to facilitate learning in the school, selective admission and placement, award of scholarships, and certification of competence.
2. The chief justification of a local school testing program is the use the school makes of the test scores obtained.
3. If scores obtained from a testing program are reported and interpreted to teachers, pupils, and parents, no other formal or elaborate program for using them is necessary.
4. Standard test scores provide information that can contribute to evaluations of teacher competence, but such scores should never be used as the sole basis for making such evaluations.

[13]APA Task Force, "Job Testing and the Disadvantaged," *American Psychologist* vol. 24 (1969), 637–50.

[14]Julian C. Stanley and Andrew C. Porter, "Correlation of Scholastic Aptitude Test Score with College Grades for Negroes versus Whites," *Journal of Educational Measurement*, IV (1967), 199–218.

[15]T. Anne Cleary and Thomas L. Hilton, "An Investigation of Item Bias," *Educational and Psychological Measurement*, vol. 28 (1968), 61–75.

5. It is more essential that a school testing program be *competently* planned than that it be *democratically* planned.
6. In general, locally designed testing programs are likely to be somewhat more relevant to local needs, but somewhat less expertly designed than external testing programs.
7. External testing programs designed to serve admission and scholarship purposes have been criticized as needlessly duplicating each other, emphasizing only verbal and quantitative skills, penalizing creative thinkers, and making test-passing instead of learning the focus of a teacher's efforts. There is only a little validity in any of these charges.
8. The essential functions served by tests of technical or professional competence would be better served if those who develop such tests were better trained and paid more attention to the problems of test validity.
9. Valid tests are less likely than any alternative means of selection or certification to be biased against minority group members.

APPENDICES

Vague and insignificant forms of speech, and abuse of language,
have so long passed for mysteries of science; and hard or
misapplied words with little or no meaning have, by prescription,
such a right to be taken as deep learning and height of
speculation, that it will not be easy to persuade either those who
speak or those who hear them, that they are but the covers of
ignorance and hindrance of true knowledge.

JOHN LOCKE

GLOSSARY
OF TERMS USED IN
EDUCATIONAL MEASUREMENT

This glossary of 170 terms used in educational measurement is
intended primarily to aid the reader who encounters an unfamiliar term.
It can also be used profitably as the subject of direct, intensive study.
In educational measurement as in other special fields, study of the meaning
of technical terms helps to increase understanding of the concepts they
represent. It is thus an important aspect of achievement.

The explanations in this glossary have been made somewhat more
detailed than usual in the hope of increasing their contributions to understanding. An effort has been made, too, to make them conform to general
usage by specialists in educational measurement. However, since usage
varies and since many of these terms have not been given precise, authoritatively sanctioned definitions, no claim can be made that these are the
only correct descriptions of the meanings of each term listed. Other useful
glossaries of measurement terms by Gerberich, Lyman, Lennon, and

by the CaliforniaTest Bureau are available.[1] The terms included in this glossary are indexed separately here for the convenience of the reader.

1. achievement quotient
2. achievement test
3. affective outcome
4. age norm
5. age scale
6. ambiguity
7. analogies test
8. aptitude test
9. attenuation
10. attitudes
11. average

12. basic skills
13. battery of tests
14. behavioral goals
15. best-answer item
16. bimodal distribution
17. bluffing

18. cheating
19. classification exercise
20. cognitive outcomes
21. comparable scores
22. completion test
23. composite score
24. conditioning
25. content validity
26. control group
27. correlation coefficient
28. creativity
29. credit by examination
30. criterion
31. critical incident
32. critical thinking
33. cross-validation
34. culture-free test
35. cumulative frequency
36. cumulative record

37. decile
38. derived score

39. deviation
40. diagnostic test
41. differential aptitude battery
42. difficulty index
43. discrimination index
44. dispersion
45. distracter
46. distribution of scores

47. empirical key
48. equivalent forms
49. error of measurement
50. error variance
51. essay examination
52. evaluation
53. examination
54. expectancy table
55. external examination

56. face validity
57. factor analysis
58. forced-choice technique
59. frequency distribution

60. grade norm
61. graphic rating scale
62. guessing correcting

63. halo effect
64. heterogeneity
65. homogeniety
66. honor system

67. intelligence
68. internal consistency
69. internal criterion
70. interpretive test
71. inventory
72. I.Q.
73. item analysis
74. item stem
75. item-test correlation

---

[1] J. Raymond Gerberich, *Specimen Objective Test Items* (New York: David McKay Co., Inc., 1956), pp. 392–412; Howard B. Lyman, *Test Scores and What They Mean* (Englewood Cliffs, N.J.: Prentice-Hall, Inc., 1963), pp. 194–205; Roger T. Lennon, "A Glossary of 100 Measurement Terms," *Test Service Notebook, No. 13* (New York: Harcourt, Brace Jovanovich, Inc.); *A Glossary of Measurement Terms* (Los Angeles, Calif.: California Test Bureau), pp. 1–16.

76. knowledge
77. Kuder-Richardson formulas
78. mark
79. matching exercise
80. mastery test
81. mean
82. measurement
83. median
84. mental abilities
85. mental age
86. mental processes
87. mode
88. motivation
89. multiple-choice item

90. nonverbal test
91. norm
92. normal distribution
93. normalized standard scores

94. objective test
95. objectivity
96. open-book test
97. operational definition

98. passing score
99. percentile band
100. percentile rank
101. performance test
102. personality
103. power test
104. practice effect
105. probability
106. probable error
107. profile
108. projective test

109. quality scale
110. quantification
111. quartile
112. questionnaire

113. random numbers
114. random sample
115. range of scores
116. rate score
117. raw score
118. rectangular distribution
119. regression
120. relevance
121. reliability coefficient
122. representative sample
123. response count

124. response set
125. rote learning

126. sampling error
127. scale
128. scaling
129. scatter diagram
130. score
131. scoring formula
132. scoring key
133. sigma
134. significant difference
135. situational test
136. skewed distribution
137. Spearman-Brown formula
138. specific determiner
139. speed test
140. speededness
141. split halves reliability coefficient
142. standard deviation
143. standard error of measurement
144. standard score
145. standardized test
146. stanine score
147. statistic
148. statistical validity
149. subjective evaluation
150. subtest

151. table of specifications
152. take-home test
153. taxonomy
154. test
155. test anxiety
156. test exercise
157. testing program
158. test item
159. test-retest reliability
160. testwiseness
161. trait
162. true-false item
163. true score
164. *T*-score

165. underachievement
166. understanding

167. validity
168. variance

169. weighted scoring

170. *z*-score

1. An **Achievement Quotient** is calculated by dividing a student's achievement age by his mental age. Hence it is essentially a ratio of scores on two kinds of tests, achievement and aptitude. Presumably it shows how his actual achievement compares with his potential achievement. However, most test specialists now agree that achievement quotients present a greatly oversimplified and often misleading basis for judging achievement. Achievement quotients are sometimes referred to as "accomplishment quotients."

2. An **Achievement Test** is one designed to measure a student's grasp of some body of knowledge or his proficiency in certain skills. Such tests are often used to measure achievement in arithmetic, chemistry, English composition, typing, medical diagnosis, and other subjects of study. Most tests made by teachers for classroom use are achievement tests.

3. **Affective** outcomes of education involve feelings more than understandings. A person's likes and dislikes, his pleasures and annoyances, his satisfactions and discontents, his confidence and diffidence, his pride and humility, his ideals and values are some of the affective outcomes that education may develop in him.

4. An **Age Norm** is the average score on an aptitude or achievement test for pupils of a specific age group. Age norms are usually reported in tables showing the average scores of students in a series of different age groups.

5. An **Age Scale** is a test in which the items are arranged in groups on the basis of the earliest age at which a group of typical, normal pupils can answer those items correctly. Binet's intelligence test scale is an age scale.

6. **Ambiguity** is characteristic of statements that are obscure or indistinct in meaning, subject to two or more quite different interpretations.

7. An **Analogies Test** requires the examinee to supply the missing term necessary to yield two pairs of terms having the same relationship within each pair. It is a test designed to measure ability to perceive similarities and differences, as well as relationships, among words, figures, or ideas.

8. An **Aptitude Test** is one given to determine the potential of an individual for development along a special line or the extent to which he is likely to profit from instruction along that line. Tests of academic aptitude, scientific aptitude, music aptitude, clerical aptitude, and other special aptitudes are available.

9. **Attenuation** is the reduction of a coefficient of correlation from its theoretical true value due to errors of measurement in the variables being correlated. Errors of measurement could by chance make a coefficient of correlation higher than it ought to be, but the more common effect of such errors is to lower the coefficient obtained. Formulas are available for estimating the "true correlation" when the reliabilities of correlated measures are known.

10. **Attitudes** are predispositions to favor or oppose, to believe or to doubt some person, group, institution, process, or proposal. Thus they are akin to biases. They tend to be firmly held and vigorously defended even though (or perhaps because) they can not be proved conclusively to be correct. They usually involve generalizations that go beyond the available data. Discussions of divergent attitudes are likely to arouse emotions.

11. An **Average** is a number, not always an actual score, which represents the most typical or representative value in a group of scores. "Average" is a generic term designating any measure of a central tendency, such as the mean, median, or mode. In ordinary speech, the term "average" often means the same thing as the term "arithmetic mean."

12. **Basic Skills** are tool skills such as those involved in reading, language, and arithmetic. Their development is regarded as essential to the further study of content subjects, and they tend to be emphasized in the elementary grades.

13. The **Battery of Tests** is a set of several tests intended to be administered in succession to the same subjects. The tests in a battery are usually designed to yield comparable scores and are provided with norms on the same or comparable groups of subjects.

14. **Behavioral Goals** of education are those that describe specific acts that the student will perform either (a) in the process of being educated, (b) to show that he has been educated, or (c) to live effectively as a result of being educated. Behavioral goals can have the virtues of definiteness and specificity, but only at the cost of minute detail. They focus attention on overt behavior itself rather than on the knowledge and understanding that can guide behavior. They are well suited to programs of training. Some educators doubt that the essential goals of education can be expressed in behavioral terms.

15. The **Best Answer Item** is a multiple-choice item in which the incorrect responses are not totally wrong. The examinee's task is to select the best response, even though it may not be a perfectly correct response. In a best answer item the difference between the correct answer and the incorrect alternatives is a difference in degree of correctness.

16. In a **Bimodal Distribution** the measures tend to concentrate or pile up at two distinct points or regions along the score scale. The frequency distribution curve for a bimodal distribution has two pronounced humps or peaks, though these may not be of the same height.

17. **Bluffing** by a student on an examination is his attempt to create the impression that he knows more than he actually does know. It may involve use of an impressive vocabulary, sentences that are fluent but empty of meaning, or deliberate misinterpretation of a hard question to make it easier to answer. Bluffing is practiced mainly on essay and oral examinations.

18. **Cheating** by a student on an examination involves copying of a fellow student's answers, use of forbidden notes or references, or employment of a substitute to take the examination in his place. The intent is to obtain a higher score than the student could obtain fairly. Cheating may be practiced on either essay or objective examinations.

19. In a **Classification Exercise** the examinee's task is to assign each item or specimen given to the appropriate category or class. Or this task may be to decide whether a particular item does or does not belong in a specific class. The items to be classified may consist of names, descriptive phrases, pictures, statements, and so forth. The categories or classes the examinee is to use may be defined for him, or he may be required to infer the appropriate definition from the examples of items belonging in the class.

20. **Cognitive Outcomes** of education involve knowledge and understanding of the subjects of study. Whatever a student learns to know, or to understand, or to do mentally, is a cognitive outcome of education.

21. **Comparable Scores** are expressed on the same scale, and have the same mean and the same variability. If scores on several tests are truly comparable for a group of subjects, the distributions of their scores on each test would be identical, though the scores of any one student on the several tests might differ.

22. A **Completion Test** requires a subject to supply the missing part of a sentence, a series, or a graphic pattern. The most typical form of a completion exercise is that based on a complex sentence or a unified paragraph.

23. A **Composite Score** is a single value used to express the result of combining scores on several different tests. It may be some average of the scores of the individual tests or a summation of their weighted scores. Often the average or sum is converted to the appropriate value on some different standard score scale.

24. **Conditioning** is the process of changing the behavior of an organism by manipulation of stimuli (classical conditioning) or of responses (operant conditioning). Pavlov's salivating dogs illustrate classical conditioning. Skinner's bar-pressing rats or pecking pigeons illustrate operant conditioning. Much human learning, particularly in the pre-school years, involves conditioning.

25. The **Content Validity** of an educational achievement test is determined by the extent to which the items in the test adequately sample the areas of subject matter and the abilities that a course of instruction has aimed to teach.

26. A **Control Group** in an educational experiment is not subject to the experimental treatment but is otherwise as nearly as possible like the experimental group or groups. Tests given before the experimental treatment are used to establish the similarity of the control and experimental groups. Tests given to all groups after the experimental treatment are used to indicate the influence of that treatment on the experimental groups.

27. A **Correlation Coefficient** is a pure number, limited by the values plus 1 and minus 1, that expresses the degree of relationship between two sets of test scores or other measurements of each of the individuals in a group. The letter r is ordinarily used to represent the correlation coefficient. The most widely used coefficient of correlation is obtained from the Pearson product-moment formula, though a number of other formulas are also used.

28. **Creativity** is the name given to a presumed faculty, with which some are supposed to be more richly endowed than others, that enables them to excel in originating ideas (Aristotle), theories (Newton), poems (Keats), plays (Shakespeare), stories (Maupassant), symphonies (Beethoven), sculpture (Phidias), painting (Raphael,) and so on. The solid evidence that some common creative faculty caused this wide diversity of creative achievements is hard to find. Nor is it easy to demonstrate the presence of this faculty in a person before his creative achievement has been recognized. Hence, the concept of creativity is sometimes suspected of serving mainly as a pseudo-explanation of that achievement.

29. **Credit by Examination** involves the use of approved examinations for the granting of academic credit. Credit by examination may be used to shorten the time required for a capable student to earn an academic degree. It also provides a means for recognizing and rewarding an individual's achievement resulting from informal learning experiences or independent study.

30. A **Criterion** is a standard of judging. In test development it usually refers to a characteristic or a combination of characteristics used as a basis for judging the validity of a test or some other measurement procedure. The criterion for the validity of scores from an aptitude test is ordinarily some measure of academic achievement, perhaps obtained from a good achievement test.

31. A **Critical Incident** is the description of some occurrence involving a person that is taken to indicate unusual competence or lack of competence on his part. The term "critical incident" has been popularized by the work of John Flanagan and his associates. It has been used by them as a basis for defining job requirements and for developing proficiency tests.

32. **Critical Thinking** is careful, exact, discriminating thinking. Care in thinking is essential to critical thinking, but care cannot compensate for lack of knowledge and understanding of the subject about which the thinking is to be done. Care in thinking fosters understanding; understanding fosters care in thinking. Thus, critical thinking is only to a very limited extent a separate mental ability that can be developed apart from the relevant knowledge.

33. **Cross-validation** is a process of testing the quality of a test item, a test, or a test battery using data independent of that used originally to select or revise the items for the test. If the test is not cross-validated, that is, if the same data are used to test its quality as were used to develop it, the validity coefficients obtained are likely to be spuriously high.

34. A **Culture-free Test,** usually an intelligence test, is presumably insensitive to the effects of an individual's cultural background or environment on his score. Hence it is intended to provide valid measures of the individual genetic equipment for learning. It is now generally agreed that no culture-free test is possible, and that even a culture-fair test, on which examinees from different cultural backgrounds may expect to do equally well, may be almost impossible to achieve.

35. A **Cumulative Frequency** is a number obtained from a frequency distribution of scores that shows for any given score interval the number of the scores in the distribution that lie below and in that interval. Cumulative frequencies are useful in the computation of percentile ranks.

36. A **Cumulative Record** is a form, often printed on a large card or folder, on which to record the personal data, course grades, test scores, and other educationally useful information about a particular school pupil.

37. A **Decile** is any one of nine points that divide the score scale into 10 intervals, each of which includes one-tenth of the total frequency. Normally the score differences between successive deciles are unequal.

38. A **Derived** score is obtained by converting a score from one system of measurement into another. Raw scores on a test, consisting of the number of correct responses, with or without correction for guessing, are frequently converted into such derived scores as percentile ranks, z-scores, or T-scores. Some derived scores are quantitatively proportional to the original scores; some are not.

39. The **Deviation** of a test score is the difference between that score and some point of reference such as the mean, the median, or an arbitrary reference point. An average of the measures of deviation of the scores in the distribution provides a measure of the variability of those scores.

40. A **Diagnostic Test** is designed to reveal specific weaknesses or failures to learn in some subject of study such as reading or arithmetic. In a diagnostic test the main interest is in scores on individual items or on small groups of highly similar items.

41. A **Differential Aptitude Battery** is a group of diverse tests, yielding comparable scores and intended to show an individual's relative chances of success in each of a variety of activities. Differential aptitude batteries are sometimes developed on the basis of factor analysis studies.

42. The **Difficulty Index** of a test item is based on the proportion of examinees in a group who do not answer the test item correctly. The most common index of difficulty is the percent of incorrect response, though difficulty indices on other scales are sometimes encountered. When percent of incorrect response is used as the difficulty index, the higher the numerical value of the index, the greater the difficulty of the item.

43. A **Discrimination Index** is a measure of the extent to which students who are judged to be good in terms of some standard succeed on the item and those who are judged to be poor on the same standard fail it. A commonly used index of discrimination is simply the difference in a proportion of correct response between the group of those scoring in the top 27 percent on the total test and the group scoring in the bottom 27 percent on the same test. Other indices of discrimination are based on the coefficient of correlation between success on the item and total score on the test.

44. **Dispersion** refers to the scatter, variability, or spread of a distribution of scores around some central value such as the mean or median. The terms "dispersion" and "variability" are practically synonymous. Dispersion may be measured by the average deviation, the standard deviation, the variance, or the range.

45. The **Distracter** is any of the incorrect answer options in multiple-choice test items. A good distracter is chosen by many of the poorer students but few of the good students.

46. A **Distribution of Scores** is a tabulation or enumeration of the frequency of occurrence of each score in a given set of scores. A distribution of scores may be indicated graphically by a frequency polygon or by a histogram.

47. An **Empirical Key** to the correct answers of a test is based not on the judgments of the test constructor, but on the differences between the answers actually given by individuals belonging to different criterion groups, such as good or poor students, friendly or hostile students, and so on. In an empirical key the responses are often weighted so as to maximize the difference between the chosen criterion groups.

48. The items in **Equivalent Forms** of a test are the same in type, cover the same content, have the same distribution of difficulty values, and yield scores having the same mean, variability, and reliability. The existence of equivalent forms is particularly useful when the same characteristic of a student must be measured more than once. Test theorists have developed precise specifications for the statistical equivalence of alternate forms of a test.

49. An **Error of Measurement** is the difference between an obtained score and the corresponding true score. Any actual test score may be regarded as the sum of a true score and an error of measurement that may be either positive or negative. The median value of the numerical size of the errors of measurement in a particular set of test scores is called the probable error.

50. The **Error Variance** in a set of test scores is the mean of the squared errors of measurement for each score in the set. The reliability of a set of test scores is sometimes defined as the "proportion of the total score variance that is not error variance."

51. An **Essay Examination** consists of questions or instructions which require the examinee to compose a more or less extensive original written response. Essay test questions frequently begin with words like "discuss," "explain," or "describe." The examinee is allowed relative freedom in composing his response. This requires that its quality must be judged subjectively by one skilled and informed in the subject.

52. An **Evaluation** is a judgment of merit, sometimes based solely on measurements such as those provided by test scores but more frequently involving the synthesis of various measurements, critical incidents, subjective impressions, and other kinds of evidence.

53. An **Examination** is any process for testing the ability or achievement of students in any area. Often this process is based primarily on a particular instrument, such as a paper-and-pencil test. In ordinary speech, the terms "examination" and "test" are frequently used as synonyms. If a distinction between the two is to be made, "examination" should be regarded as more comprehensive and complex than "test."

54. In an **Expectancy Table** the rows ordinarily correspond to score intervals on some predictor of achievement and the columns correspond to score intervals on some measure of actual achievement. The figures in each cell of such a double-entry table indicate the relative frequency with which an individual having a given score on the predictor will receive a given score on the criterion of achievement. Expectancy tables serve somewhat the same function as validity coefficients for tests but provide more detailed information.

55. An **External Examination** is one chosen or prepared by someone other than the classroom teacher for administration to the students in that classroom. The tests used in statewide or nationwide testing programs, and sometimes those used in local testing programs, are external examinations.

56. A test possesses **Face Validity** if the questions in it appear to measure the knowledge or ability the test is intended to measure. Psychologists tend to discount face validity on the ground that appearances may be deceiving. However, if the observer is perceptive and experienced, his judgment that a test possesses face validity may carry considerable weight as an indication that it is valid.

57. **Factor Analysis** involves the use of a variety of mathematically sophisticated techniques to identify a small number of hypothetical characteristics that will count for the correlations between scores on a much larger number of tests for the individuals in a particular group.

58. The **Forced-choice Technique** makes use of multiple-choice items in which the examinee is required to select one of several choices, regardless of how much he may like all of them or how little he may like any of them. The forced-choice technique is used mainly with items intended to measure personality characteristics. In an ideal form of forced-choice item, the alternatives are equally acceptable and equally often chosen by members of a typical group. However, the choice of one alternative over another is more frequently made by persons having a specific personality characteristic than by those having its opposite.

59. A **Frequency Distribution** consists of a sequence of score intervals opposite each of which is recorded the number of scores in the total group falling in that interval. The terms "frequency distribution" and "distribution of scores" are nearly synonymous.

60. A **Grade Norm** is the mean or median achievement of pupils in a given school grade on a given standardized test. Grade norm tables usually present these mean scores for several adjacent grades. The practice of fractionating intervals between grades into tenths and of reporting estimated mean scores for each tenth of an interval is quite common.

61. A **Graphic Rating Scale** is a line whose ends represent contrasting extremes of a trait. The rater places a check mark at a point along the line corresponding to his judgment of how much or how little of the trait the particular individual possesses. Sometimes the line is divided into segments, each of which is accompanied by a brief verbal description of how much of the trait it represents.

62. A **Guessing Correction** is a factor that is added to or subtracted from the number of items correctly answered. The purpose of this correction is to make the score a student could expect to get by guessing blindly on certain questions no higher than the score of a student who omits those items in preference to guessing blindly on them. If the correction is effected by subtraction, the factor subtracted is the number of wrong responses divided by one less than the number of options per item. If the correction is effected by addition, the factor added is the number of items omitted divided by the number of options per item. A guessing correction, however, does not correct for a student's luck, or lack of it, in blind guessing.

63. **Halo Effect** describes a bias in ratings arising from the tendency of a rater to be influenced in his rating of specific traits by his general impression of the person being rated.

64. **Heterogeneity,** when applied to the individuals in a group or the items in a test, refers to the degree to which they are different or unlike. The individuals or items in a highly heterogeneous group are very unlike.

65. **Homogeneity,** as applied to the individuals in a group or the items in a test, refers to similarity. The items in a highly homogeneous test or the individuals in a highly

homogeneous group are all very much alike. A highly homogeneous group of students or set of test items is low in heterogeneity.

66. The **Honor System,** as applied to the administration of tests, requires students to be individually responsible for their own honesty and avoidance of cheating. To emphasize this responsibility, instructors and proctors are ordinarily absent from a room in which an examination is being given under the honor system. Some honor systems make students responsible for reporting any cheating on the part of their classmates.

67. **Intelligence** is the capacity to apprehend facts and propositions and their relations, and to reason about them. This capacity in rudimentary form must develop biologically with the embryo, but its psychological development, which probably accounts for the greater part of it in the mature mind, depends mainly on learning experiences. Genetic endowment controls the biological development of intellectual capacity, but for most persons intelligence is limited not by genetic endowment, but by learning experiences.

68. A test possesses high **Internal Consistency** if it is composed of items that all measure much the same thing and that are therefore highly intercorrelated. A measure of internal consistency provides one measure of test reliability.

69. An **Internal Criterion** is applied in judging the discriminating power of a test item when the score on the total test containing that item is used as a basis for choosing students for the high and low achievement groups. Although indices of discrimination based on the use of an internal criterion are always inflated somewhat, the degree of inflation is not large in moderately long tests. Further, good external criteria are seldom available.

70. In an **Interpretative Test,** the questions are based on background material supplied in the test itself. The background material may consist of excerpts of prose, poetry, statistical tables, pictures, or diagrams.

71. An **Inventory** consists of a number of questions, tasks, or other stimuli, designed more to provide a comprehensive description of some aspect of an individual's characteristics than to provide a quantitative measurement of one of those aspects. Inventories are more commonly used in the description of interest, attitudes, or personality traits than in the measurement of intellectual achievements.

72. **I.Q.** stands for "intelligence quotient," originally a ratio of the individual's mental age to his chronological age. (On modern intelligence tests it may be a standard score whose mean is 100 and standard deviation 16 in the appropriate reference population.) The I.Q. is the most commonly used index of brightness or rate of mental development.

73. **Item Analysis** involves the counting of responses to objective test items to determine the difficulty and discriminating power of the item. The difficulty of an item is usually expressed as the percent of the group of examinees who failed to answer the item correctly. Its discriminating power may be expressed as a difference between the proportions of good and poor students who answered the item correctly. Applied to multiple-choice items, the counting of responses from students of high and low overall achievements reveals the effectiveness of each distracter.

74. The **Item Stem** of a multiple-choice test item is the introductory question or incomplete statement. The examinee chooses an answer to or a completion of the item stem from among the options provided in the remainder of the item. A complete multiple-choice item consists of the item stem and the answer options.

75. An **Item-test Correlation** is the coefficient of correlation between scores on the item and scores on the test as a whole. If the item test correlation is calculated directly, the formulas for the biserial coefficient or the phi coefficient are ordinarily used. More

commonly, however, item-test correlations are read from specially prepared tables designed to give estimates of the Pearson product-moment coefficient of correlation.

76. **Knowledge** is a personal mental development, a structure of concepts and relations built by reflective thought out of information received. Any experience of participation, observation, reading or thinking *can* become part of a person's knowledge. It *will* become part of his knowledge if he thinks about it, makes sense of it, understands it. Only if it becomes part of his knowledge is he likely to be able to recall it and use it. Each person develops knowledge for himself. A teacher can give information, but not knowledge. Understanding is part of knowing. In the total absence of understanding there is no structure of knowledge, for to understand is to see relations, and out of these relations the structure of knowledge is built.

77. The **Kunder-Richardson Formulas** provide estimates of the reliability of a single test from a single administration. The information ordinarily required is the number of items in the test, the standard deviation of the test scores, and the difficulty of each item in the test, or the average difficulty of all items as reflected in the mean test score. Because of their convenience and their statistical soundness, the Kuder-Richardson formulas are now widely used in the estimation of test reliability.

78. A **Mark** is a rating of achievement assigned on the basis of some scale such as the five-letter A-B-C-D-F scale, the percentage scale, the stanine scale, or some other. Marks are widely used in reporting pupil achievements in various subjects to parents and in recording them on cumulative school records.

79. A **Matching Exercise** consists of two lists of statements, terms, or symbols. The examinee's task is to match an item in one list with the one most closely associated with it in the other.

80. A **Mastery Test** is not intended to indicate how much a student has achieved relative to other students, but only whether or not he has achieved enough to satisfy the minimum requirements of the teacher or the examining agency. The items of the mastery test are typically easier than those in the test intended to discriminate among different levels of achievement.

81. The **Mean** is a measure of the central tendency or of the average numerical value of a set of scores. It is calculated by adding all of the scores and dividing the sum by the number of scores.

82. **Measurement** is a process of assigning numbers to the individual members of a set of objects or persons for the purpose of indicating differences among them in the degree to which they possess the characteristic being measured. If any characteristic of persons or things can be defined clearly enough so observed differences between them with respect to this characteristic can be consistently verified, the characteristic is measurable. A more refined type of measurement involves comparison of some characteristic of a thing with a preestablished standard scale for measuring that characteristic.

83. The **Median** is the point in a score distribution that divides it into two parts containing equal numbers of scores. If the number of scores in the distribution is odd, the median is the middle score. If the number is even, the median is a point midway between the two scores nearest the middle. The median is identical with the fifth decile or the fiftieth percentile.

84. **Mental Abilities** is a term used to refer either to specific problem-solving routines, such as the ability to find the square root of a number, the ability to balance a chemical equation, or the ability to diagram a sentence; or to more general types of purposeful thinking, such as recognition, recall, comprehension, interpretation, application, analysis, synthesis, or evaluation. It is clear that specific problem-solving routines do exist and can be taught. The general mental abilities are useful categories for types of thinking, but probably do not exist, and cannot be taught, as general mental functions.

85. A person's **Mental Age** is his score on a test of mental ability expressed in terms of the chronological age in months of persons whose average test score is the same as his. Thus, if a child's mental test score is equal to that of the average eight-year-old on the same test, he has a mental age of eight years (96 months) regardless of his actual chronological age.

86. **Mental Processes** are hypothetical activities of the mind, presumably involving electrochemical changes in the brain. No good definitions and no generally accepted catalog of these processes exist. The relation between brain chemistry and conscious thought has not been clearly established. It is not definitely known that different "kinds of thinking" involve different mental processes (that is, different mental abilities). There is no clear, firm basis for classing some mental processes as "higher" and others as "lower." Thus, the concept of mental processes has proved to be of less use to the scientific psychologist than to the popular essayist.

87. The **Mode** is the most frequently occurring value in a frequency distribution. If the frequency distribution is displayed graphically, the mode is the score corresponding to the highest point on the curve.

88. **Motivation** is a term used to explain the presence or absence of apparent effort to attain a particular goal. Teachers use it to explain why some students study harder than other students. Motivation is useful as a categorical term for the complex of old habits, persistent goals, new incentives, and other influences that cause a given person to act in a given way in a given set of circumstances. But if motivation is regarded as some simple latent internal force or energy that good teachers are good at arousing to action, then both its reality and usefulness are questionable. Motivation is more complex than simple.

89. A **Multiple-choice Item** has two parts: the stem, consisting of a direct question or an incomplete statement, and two or more options, consisting of answers to the question or completions of the statement. The examinee's task is to choose the correct, or the best, answer option in terms of the question posed by the item stem.

90. A **Nonverbal Test,** usually an intelligence test, aims to minimize the importance of language skills as a factor determining the test score. In the purest form of nonverbal test there is no use of words, written or spoken, either by the examiner giving the test or by the subjects responding to it. More commonly, a nonverbal test is one in which no written directions are employed and to which the subject responds without using language. Such tests are commonly used in testing small children, illiterates, and others with language deficiencies.

91. A **Norm,** as the term is used in relation to test scores, is the average or typical test score (or other measure) for members of a specific group. Norms are often presented in tables giving the typical score values for a series of different homogeneous groups, such as students in a given grade or students of a given age.

92. A **Normal Distribution** is an ideal frequency distribution defined by a mathematical formula. It is represented by a symmetrical, bell-shaped curve characterized by scores concentrated near the middle and tapering toward each extreme. Tables have been prepared to show the height of the ordinate at various points along the base line (score scale) and for showing areas under the curve in various intervals along the base line. The heights of the ordinates indicate the relative frequencies of each score in the distribution. The areas under the curve over various score intervals indicate what proportion of the total number of scores fall in that interval.

93. **Normalized Standard Scores,** like other standard scores, have a predetermined mean and standard deviation. In addition they are derived in a way that makes the distribution of standard scores approximately normal, regardless of the shape of the distribution of raw scores on which they were based.

94. An **Objective Test** is one that can be provided with a simple predetermined list of correct answers, so that subjective opinion or judgment in the scoring procedure is eliminated. The scoring of true-false, multiple-choice, or matching exercises is completely objective. The scoring of short-answer or completion items is partly objective.

95. **Objectivity** is characteristic of statements that can be verified by an independent observer or judge. A person's descriptive statements about the world external to him are usually objective in this sense. His statements about his own feelings or values usually are not. Scores on objective tests tend to be more objective than scores on typical essay tests.

96. During an **Open-book Test,** the examinee may consult his textbook, reference books, or, sometimes, notes he has brought with him. The purpose of the open-book test is to emphasize command of knowledge, as distinguished from recall of factual information. Examinations of this type seem to be most popular in mathematics, engineering, and the sciences.

97. **Operational Definitions** of quantitative concepts (variables) describe how the amount of the variable can be determined. There are operational definitions of distance, illumination, atomic weight, vitamin potency, and gross national product. An operational definition of intelligence would be a description of the processes for constructing, administering, and scoring an intelligence test.

98. The **Passing Score** on a test is the lowest score that satisfies a particular requirement. It serves to separate examinees into two groups, those who will be given credit for a course, or license to practice a trade or profession, and those who will not. Determination of a passing score usually involves the making of a number of somewhat arbitrary decisions. For most tests used in education, there is no need to determine passing scores.

99. A **Percentile Band** is a range of percentiles within which a particular student's true percentile rank on the test is likely to fall. The use of percentile bands serves to emphasize the uncertainty associated with any test score, but it does this at the cost of precise information on the individual's most probable percentile rank.

100. The **Percentile Rank** of a particular score in a given distribution of scores is a number indicating the percentage of scores in the whole distribution that fall below the point at which the given score lies. Percentile ranks are sometimes also called "centile ranks," reflecting the fact that there are 100 units on the scale of such scores. Distribution of percentile (or centile) ranks is approximately rectangular, whereas most raw score distributions from which the percentile ranks are derived are roughly normal.

101. In a **Performance Test** the subjects ordinarily respond by overt action, that is by motor or manual behavior. In a performance test the subject is required to demonstrate his skill by manipulating objects or instruments.

102. **Personality** refers to the complex of characteristics that gives a particular person identity, distinguishing him from other persons. A person's appearance, habits, attitudes, interests, values, and knowledge all contribute to his personality. How his personality is perceived by others depends mainly on his behavior in social situations. Many trait names are used to describe personality, but it is wrong to think of these traits as causes of the behavior.

103. A **Power Test** is one on which the examinee's score depends on how much he is able to do, not how rapidly he is able to do it. Hence, in a power test there is either no time limit at all or a very generous time limit. The tasks in a power test are sometimes arranged in order of increasing difficulty, with the expectation that the examinee will stop when he reaches tasks of a level of difficulty beyond his capabilities.

104. **Practice Effect** is a term used to explain part of a change, usually an increase in the score of an individual when he takes the same test or essentially the same test,

more than once. The magnitude of these practice effects depends on the nature of the test, the interval between testings, and motivation of the student being tested.

105. The **Probability** of an occurrence is a decimal fraction expressing the ratio of actual occurrences to opportunities for occurrence. The analysis and computation of probabilities make up a special branch of mathematics.

106. The **Probable Error** of a set of test scores is the median error of measurement, in absolute value. Half the errors of measurement are larger and the other half smaller than the probable error of measurement. The probable error is usually calculated from the standard error and is equal to 0.6745 times the standard error of measurement. The probable error is a good measure of the estimated accuracy of a test score but not of its reliability, since a longer and more reliable test may have a larger probable error of measurement than a shorter, less reliable test.

107. A **Profile** is a graphic representation of the relative magnitude of a student's scores on several tests. In order for such a profile to be meaningful, the scores on all of the tests must be comparable scores, based on the same standard scale. Peaks on the profile represent those areas of ability or achievement in which the individual exceeds his own average. Valleys in the profile indicate those areas where he is weak relative to his achievement in other areas. The general level of the profile on the chart indicates the general level of his ability or achievement relative to those from which the test norms were obtained.

108. A **Projective Test** is intended to stimulate free expression by the examinee, guided and restricted as little as possible by directions from the examiner. The problems in a projective test are often intentionally ambiguous. The examinee's responses are analyzed for the purpose of revealing his interests, motivations, perceptions, problems, values, and modes of adjustment. The stimulus material for projective tests may consist of such things as ink blots, pictures, incomplete sentences, and so on. The examinee may be asked to describe what he sees in the stimulus material or to indicate what sense he can make out of it. Projective tests are used largely in the study of personality. The task presented by a projective test item is frequently said to be unstructured because of the examinee's relative freedom of response.

109. A **Quality Scale** consists of a series of typical specimens of such things as handwriting, composition, or drawings of a particular subject, arranged in an order of merit, usually with a numerical value assigned to each. Such a scale is then used as a standard of comparison for rating the quality of work of other examinees. The Thorndike Handwriting Scale is a familiar example of a quality scale.

110. The **Quantification** of a human characteristic, of a property of matter, or of anything else requires the specification of operations or the creation of an instrument by means of which appropriate numbers can be attached to various amounts of the characteristic or property. A thermometer is used to quantify temperature. A complex set of operations is used to quantify the red blood cell count of a person. A written test is often used to quantify achievement in a particular course of study. The process of quantification provides an operational definition of the thing being quantified. No measurement of anything is possible until some process for quantifying the attribute to be measured has been worked out.

111. A **Quartile** is one of three points along the score scale of a frequency distribution that divide the distribution into four parts of equal frequency. The first quartile corresponds to the twenty-fifth percentile, the second to the median, or fiftieth percentile, and the third to the seventy-fifth percentile.

112. A **Questionnaire** is a list of planned written questions relating to a particular topic, usually intended to gather descriptive information from a number of selected respondents. An important difference between a questionnaire and a test is that in a

questionnaire the responses are ordinarily summarized question by question, whereas in a test they are summarized respondent by respondent.

113. In a table of **Random Numbers** there is no observable system or order in the sequence of the digits. That is, one cannot predict with better than chance success which digit will occur at a given point in the table or which digit is likely to follow some other digit.

114. A **Random Sample** is a sample selected in such a way as to guarantee equal probability of selection to all possible samples of this size that could be formed from the members of the universe involved. It is also true that each element in the universe has equal probability of being included in a random sample. The problem of selecting a truly random sample from any population is not simple.

115. A **Range of Scores** is the smallest interval on the score scale that will include all the measures in the distribution. It is sometimes defined, more simply but somewhat inaccurately, as the difference between the highest and the lowest scores in the distribution. The range of scores provides a simple measure of the variability of the scores of the distribution.

116. A **Rate Score** is the measure of an individual's speed of performance of tasks of a specific type, stated either in terms of the number of units of work done in a given time or the number of units of time required to complete a given amount of work.

117. A **Raw Score** is the number first obtained in scoring the test, before any transformation to a standard score or other derived score. For objectively scorable tests, the raw score usually consists of the number of right answers, the number right minus some fraction of the number wrong, the time required for performance, the number of errors, or some other directly defined measure. On an essay test the raw score is often the scorer's estimate of the quality of the response, relative to some quantitative standard of perfection.

118. A **Rectangular Distribution** is a frequency distribution in which successive equal intervals along the score scale include the same frequency or number of scores. A distribution of percentile ranks is rectangular, not bell-shaped, as in the case of a normal distribution.

119. **Regression** in statistics refers to the tendency for predicted scores to lie closer to the mean than the predictor scores when the two are correlated and expressed on the same standard score scale. If the two measures were perfectly correlated, there would be no regression. Since height and weight are correlated positively, but not perfectly, the tallest individual in a group is likely to be heavier than the average individual but is unlikely to be the heaviest individual. The heights of fathers and sons are correlated, but not perfectly correlated. The fact that the sons of tall fathers tend to be taller than the average of their generation reflects this correlation. But the fact that the sons of tall fathers tend to be not as tall relative to the whole population as their fathers is an illustration of regression. Regression accounts for some of the findings that high-aptitude students seem to be underachievers and low-aptitude students overachievers.

120. The **Relevance** of a task in a test is the extent to which it contributes to the purposes of the test by virtue of the abilities it calls into play. For example, a question that asks students to give the dates of birth and death of several English poets may have low relevance in a test of poetic appreciation. On the other hand, a question asking a student to calculate the standard deviation of a set of scores might have high relevance in a test of ability to use statistical techniques. Relevance is one of the major aspects of quality in tests of educational achievement.

121. The **Reliability Coefficient** is the estimate of the coefficient of correlation between the scores for students in a particular group on two equivalent forms of the

same test. If equivalent forms of the same test are not available, one can estimate the reliability of a single form by splitting it into equivalent halves and using the correlation between scores on equivalent full-length tests. The reliability of a test may also be estimated on the basis of the variance of the test scores and of the item scores. Reliability is sometimes defined also as the proportion of total score variance that is not error variance, that is, attributable to errors of measurement.

122. The **Representative Sample** is one chosen in such a way as to make it more likely than a random sample to exhibit the same characteristics as the population. Representative samples are often stratified samples, with predetermined numbers of cases chosen randomly from different geographical areas, different age groups, or other subgroups that are thought to differ systematically with respect to the characteristic being measured.

123. A **Response Count** for an objective test item indicates the frequency with which one or more of the answer options were chosen by examinees in a particular group. Response counts are the bases for estimating the difficulty and discriminating power of the test items. They may be obtained by counting hands or, in some cases, by special counting or tabulating equipment.

124. A **Response Set** is a predisposition on the part of an examinee to differ systematically from other examinees in his handling of uncertain responses to a test item. For example, willingness to guess may be a response set. If two examinees have the same limited amount of information about the answer to a question, one of them may be willing to guess, the other may not. Some examinees may be systematically less reluctant to mark true-false statements false than other examinees. Response sets may or may not affect the reliability and validity of the measurements yielded by a test.

125. **Rote Learning** is memorization of a sequence of words or other symbols by repeated utterance or observation. Material learned by rote may or may not be meaningless to the person who has learned it, but the process of learning does not rely on meaningfulness as an aid to learning.

126. A **Sampling Error** is the difference between the value of some statistic, such as the mean or the standard deviation calculated from a sample, and that which would have been obtained if it had been calculated on the basis of the entire population. If, for example, the score of one fourth grade pupil in arithmetic were used as an indication of the level of achievement of the entire fourth grade, the difference between his score and the average score on the same test for all pupils in the grade would be a sampling error. Samples are seldom perfectly representative of populations. If they were, there would be no sampling error.

127. A **Scale** is a sequence of numbers whose use is defined and limited so they will have special significance in indicating various degrees of some trait or characteristic. For example, the scores obtainable from any test constitute a scale. Scales are sometimes represented graphically by intervals and subdivisions of intervals along a line.

128. **Scaling**, in the general sense of the term, involves the attachment of numbers to different statements, test items, stimuli, handwriting specimens, written compositions, and so forth, to indicate how much of some quality each of them possesses. Thus, it means almost exactly the same thing as *quantification*. In a more restricted sense it refers to a collection of special techniques for the construction of scales for measuring such things as quality of handwriting or attitude toward religion, scales on which the units are as nearly equal as possible, and sometimes on which a true zero point can be located. Psychometric scaling has been a fertile field for theoretical developments. Its useful applications in educational measurement have been less numerous.

129. A **Scatter Diagram** is a device for displaying the relationship between scores on two tests for the individuals in a group. Scores on one test are represented on the

vertical dimension, those on the other along the horizontal dimension. A dot, tally mark, or other symbol is entered on the diagram at such a position with reference to the horizontal and vertical scales as to reflect the pair of scores for a particular individual. If the scores on the two variables are highly correlated, the tally marks on the scatter diagram tend to fall close to a straight line. A scatter diagram is sometimes used as the starting point in the calculation of a coefficient of correlation. Because each tally mark represents scores on two variables, a scatter diagram is sometimes referred to as a "double-entry table."

130. A **Score** is a number assigned to an examinee to provide a quantitative description of his performance on a particular test. The original raw score is often converted into a standard score or some other derived score to facilitate comparison or interpretation.

131. A **Scoring Formula** indicates how the raw score on the test is to be obtained from the number of correct, incorrect, or omitted responses. The simplest scoring formula is "Score equals number right." If scores corrected for guessing are desired, the number of wrong responses divided by one less than the number of answer options per item is frequently subtracted from the number of correct responses. Alternatively, the number of omitted items divided by the number of answer options per item can be added to the number of right responses.

132. A **Scoring Key** indicates the correct answer to each item. The term "scoring key" is also applied to devices, such as stencils punched in positions corresponding to the correct answers or cut strips of paper with answers written on them, that facilitate the scoring of objective tests.

133. **Sigma** is a character in the Greek alphabet corresponding to the Roman letter "s" which, in lower-case form (σ), is used as the symbol for the standard deviation of a distribution. In upper-case form (Σ) it indicates the arithmetic operation of addition or summation. (When a distinction between the standard deviation of a sample and that of a population is important, the Roman letter "s" is used to indicate the standard deviation of the sample.)

134. A **Significant Difference,** statistically speaking, is a large enough difference between two comparable statistics computed from separate samples so that the probability that the difference may be attributed to chance is less than some defined limit. If the difference as large as the observed difference could not be expected to occur by chance more than five times in 100, the difference is sometimes said to be significant at the 5 percent level of confidence. The significance of a difference depends not only on the magnitude of the difference, but also upon the precision of the two measures used to obtain the difference. Hence, a difference too small to be of any significance can often be made statistically significant by the use of sufficiently large samples. Conversely, the use of very small samples can make measures so imprecise that a difference may be statistically insignificant even when it is large enough to be of considerable practical significance.

135. A **Situational Test** is based upon descriptions, verbal or pictorial or both, of specific situations, real or imagined. The examinee's task is to respond to some problem in, or question about, the situation. The response may be either an essay or an answer to an objective question. Situational test items have the virtue of concrete practicality. They have the weaknesses of inefficiency (few items per page or per hour of testing time) and of uncertain answers because of the difficulty of describing actual situations completely and unambiguously.

136. A **Skewed Distribution** is an asymmetrical distribution in which most of the scores are closer to one end of the distribution than they are to the other. Skewed distributions ordinarily have only one mode, but the tails or extremities are unequal in

length. If the longer tail of the distribution extends toward the lower end of the score scale, the distribution is said to be negatively skewed. If the longer tail extends to the higher end of the score scale, the distribution is said to be positively skewed.

137. The **Spearman-Brown Formula** is used to predict the reliability of a lengthened test, assuming that the material added to the test is highly similar to that already present in it. The Spearman-Brown formula may be written

$$r_n = \frac{nr_s}{1 + (n - 1)r_s}$$

when r_n is the reliability coefficient of the lengthened test, r_s the reliability coefficient of the original short test, and n the number of times that the original length has been increased. The Spearman-Brown formula has wide uses, but perhaps the most common use is in stepping up the correlation between scores on halves of a test to obtain an estimate of the reliability of the total test.

138. A **Specific Determiner** is some characteristic in the statement of a true-false test item that supplies an unintended clue to the correct answer. For example, statements including the words "every," "always," "entirely," "absolutely," and "never" are more likely to be false than true. Similarly the statements containing the words "sometimes," "usually," "often," and "ordinarily" are more likely to be true than false.

139. In a **Speed Test** the rapidity with which a task is completed is an important factor determining the score on the test. Some speed tests consist of tasks of uniform and relatively low difficulty so the student's score is determined almost entirely by how fast he works, not by the difficulty of the tasks he accomplishes. Any test with a time limit short enough to prevent many examinees from finishing is at least partially a speed test.

140. **Speededness** of a test is the extent to which an examinee's score on it depends on his quickness in working through it. It is sometimes measured by the proportion of examinees who *do not* reach and answer the last item in the test. For a good classroom test of achievement that proportion should be 10 percent or less.

141. A **Split-halves Reliability Coefficient** is obtained by using half the items on the test, sometimes the odd-numbered items, to yield one score for an examinee and the other half of the items to yield another, independent score. The correlation between the scores on these two half-tests, corrected with the aid of the Spearman-Brown formula, provides an estimate of the reliability of the total test.

142. The **Standard Deviation** is a measure of variability, dispersion, or spread of a set of scores around their mean value. Mathematically, the standard deviation is the square root of the mean of the squared deviations of the scores from the mean of the distribution of scores. The more closely the scores in a distribution cluster about the mean, the smaller the standard deviation. In a normal distribution, 68.26 per cent of all of the scores lie within one standard deviation of the mean.

143. The **Standard Error of Measurement** is an estimate of the standard deviation of the errors of measurement associated with the test scores in a given set. The standard error of measurement is estimated by multiplying the standard deviation of the scores by the square root of one minus the reliability coefficient. Approximately two-thirds of the errors of measurement in a given set of test scores will be less than the standard error of measurement. The largest error of measurement in a set of one hundred scores is likely to be less than three times the standard error of measurement.

144. A **Standard Score** is one derived from a raw score so that it can be expressed on a uniform standard scale without seriously altering its relationship to other scores in the distribution. A simple type of standard score is the z-score, which expresses each raw score as a positive or negative deviation from the mean of all raw scores on a scale

in which the unit is one standard deviation. In another type of standard-score scale, the transformation is arranged to yield a normal distribution of standard scores. The use of standard scores simplifies comparisons and interpretations of scores.

145. A **Standardized Test** is one that has been constructed in accord with detailed specifications, one for which the items have been selected after tryout for appropriateness in difficulty and discriminating power, one which is accompanied by a manual giving definite directions for uniform administration and scoring, and one which is provided with relevant and dependable norms for score interpretation. Standardized tests are ordinarily constructed by test specialists, with the advice of competent teachers, and are offered for sale by test publishers. Unfortunately not all tests offered as standardized tests have been prepared as carefully as the foregoing description suggests.

146. A **Stanine Score** (from standard nine) is a single-digit standard score on a nine-unit scale. The distribution of stanine scores in the population from which they were derived has a mean of 5 and standard deviation of 2. Stanine scores are normalized standard scores so that, in the population from which they were derived, the proportions of each stanine score are approximately these:

Stanine score	1	2	3	4	5	6	7	8	9
Percent of scores	4	7	12	17	20	17	12	7	4

147. A **Statistic** is a number used to describe or characterize some aspect of a sample. For example, the number of cases in the sample, the mean value of the measures in the sample, the standard deviation of those measures, and the correlation between two sets of measures for the members of the sample are statistics. Corresponding to every statistic in the sample there is a parameter in the population.

148. The **Statistical Validity** of scores from a test, or any other measures, is ordinarily indicated by the coefficient of correlation between those scores and appropriate criterion measures. For example, the statistical validity (predictive validity) of an aptitude test is expressed by the coefficient of correlation between the scores of students on the aptitude test and their subsequent scores on some good measure of achievement.

149. In the **Subjective Evaluation** of a student's answers to essay test questions, or of his performance in other situations, the score assigned is determined by the personal opinion and judgment of the scorer. It is not determined by a prescribed scoring key or by the specifications in detail of the requirements for answers that will receive various scores.

150. A **Subtest** is a part of a test, composed of similar items having a distinct purpose, for which a separate score may be provided. The reliability of scores on short subtests is generally low.

151. A **Table of Specifications** includes a test outline that specifies what proportion of the item shall deal with each content area and with each type of ability. It may also include other specifications, such as the number of items in the test, the time to be allowed for its administration, and descriptions of kinds of items that will or will not be included in the test. The content outline for a test is often presented in the form of a two-dimensional grid with content areas represented along one dimension and pupil abilities or educational outcomes along the other. The number or proportion of items to be devoted to each content area and to each educational outcome is specified in the table.

152. A **Take-home** test is one a student completes outside of class, using whatever help he can get from notes, references, or expert consultants. When used as a follow-up to the same test taken in class, a take-home test can be a valuable learning experience.

153. A **Taxonomy** is an orderly classification, usually of plants and animals, arranged according to their presumed natural relationships. Taxonomies of educational objectives have been prepared, but since verbal statements are less definite in meaning

than plant or animal structures are in form, and since natural relations among the statements are more difficult to discern, these educational taxonomies are less objective and less precise than their biological models.

154. A **Test** is a general term used to designate any kind of device or procedure for measuring ability, achievement, interest, and other traits. A test is also defined as any systematic procedure for comparing the behavior of two or more persons. In ordinary speech, the terms "examination," "quiz," and "test" are often used interchangeably. However, the term "quiz" oridinarily refers to something short and informal, the term "test" to a longer, more carefully prepared series of questions, and the term "examination" to a very comprehensive process.

155. **Test Anxiety** is the apprehensive uneasiness that precedes and accompanies the taking of an important test. In extreme cases the anxiety may upset the examinee so much that he fails to do justice to his ability on the test. In most cases, however, the anxiety facilitates maximum performance. Most examinees are subject to moderate degrees of test anxiety when facing or taking an important test.

156. A **Test Exercise** is a structural unit of a test for which a single set of directions is provided. A test exercise, unlike a test item, ordinarily requires more than one response.

157. A **Testing Program** is a plan of procedure for selecting, administering, and scoring a set of tests, and for reporting, interpreting and using the scores from those tests. Testing programs are designed by, and for use in, local school systems, for statewide use, or for nationwide use. If competently planned and executed, a testing program can make substantial contributions to the effectiveness of the educational efforts of a school system, a state, or a nation.

158. A **Test Item** is the smallest independent unit of a test. Each statement to be judged true or false, each question to which an answer is to be selected, each incomplete statement to which a completion is to be selected, each blank in a sentence or paragraph to be filled in, is a separate test item.

159. **Test-retest Reliability** is calculated by correlating scores for the same students on two administrations of the same test. The size of a test-retest reliability coefficient indicates not only the precision of measurement of the test, but also the stability of the trait being measured. Test-retest reliability coefficients do not indicate how adequately or representatively the items in the test sample the whole field to be covered by the test. Hence, retest reliability coefficients are usually higher than equivalent forms reliability coefficients. In general, the greater the interval of time between test and retest, the lower the retest reliability coefficient will be. Because of practice effects and the difficulty in maintaining motivation when examinees are asked to take the same test the second time, retest reliability coefficients are calculated less frequently than other types.

160. **Testwiseness** is knowledge that enables the examinee to make the highest scores on a test that can be made honestly. It includes knowledge of how to respond properly, to use time wisely, and to make full use of partial knowledge. It also includes knowledge of clues to the correct response that clumsy or careless item writers may leave in their test items. If a test is well constructed, testwiseness will help the examinee do as well as, but no better than, he ought to do. Examinee testwiseness does more to increase than to diminish the validity of scores from a good test.

161. A **Trait** is any attribute of persons that is possessed in differing amounts by different members of a group or class. It is a physical characteristic or a relatively stable mode of behavior. Such things as height, intelligence, quality of handwriting, or understanding of chemical principles are traits.

162. A **true-false Item** consists of a statement that the examinee is asked to judge to be true or false. A true-false item might be regarded as a form of the multiple-choice item in which only two answer options are provided and in which the answer options are the same for all items.

163. A **True Score** is an idealized error-free score for a specific person on a specific test. It may also be defined as the mean of an infinite number of independent measurements of the same trait, using equivalent forms of the test. The second definition assumes that as the number of independent measurements of the same trait in the same person is increased, the average value of the errors associated with those measurements approaches zero. The actual score a person does receive on a particular test can hence be regarded as the sum of his true score and a positive or negative error of measurement associated with that particular measurement.

164. A **T-score** is a normalized standard score on a scale such that the distribution of *T*-scores in the population from which they are derived has a mean of 50 and a standard deviation of 10. The original *T*-scores, devised by McCall and named in honor of Thorndike and Terman, were limited to scores that would be made on a standard test by an unselected group of twelve-year-old children.

165. **Underachievement** is the term used to describe the educational situation of a pupil whose aptitude test scores are substantially higher than his achievement test scores. Often such apparent discrepancies are due to a difference between the kind of achievement the aptitude test measures, and the kind that the achievement test measures (for both measure learned achievements). Sometimes the discrepancies are due to different bases used in norming the aptitude and achievement tests. Sometimes they are simply due to errors of measurement. Any marked discrepancy between the scores a student makes on different tests ought to be investigated and, if possible, explained. But teachers should guard against overly simple explanations. It is usually true that the underachieving student could do better "if he would only try," but so also could all of his "normally achieving" or "overachieving" classmates. Aptitude test scores may not provide valid indications of how good a pupil's achievements ought to be.

166. **Understanding** the information one receives involves relating it to what one already knows so that it becomes part of a coherent structure of knowledge. The more integrated, coherent knowledge a person has of a subject the better he understands it. Understanding of a concept or an idea is no more and no less than seeing its relations to other concepts and ideas. To develop a structure of knowledge, one must understand.

167. The **Validity** of a test is often defined as the degree to which it measures what it purports to measure, or as the extent to which a test does the job for which it is intended. Reliability is a necessary but not a sufficient condition for validity. The validity of an achievement test depends not only on the reliability of the scores it yields, but also on the extent to which the content of the test represents a balanced and appropriate set of tasks sampling the outcomes of the course or instructional program. For some types of tests for which good independent criterion measures are available, statistical coefficients of validity can be obtained. These are coefficients of correlation between scores on the test and the criterion measures.

168. The **Variance** is a measure of the dispersion of scores about their mean. The variance is the mean of the squared deviations of the scores from their mean. Hence, it is equal to the square of the standard deviation.

169. In **Weighted Scoring** the number of points awarded for a correct response is not the same for all items in the test. In some cases, weighted scoring involves the award of different numbers of points for the choice of different responses to the same item.

170. A **z-score** is a standard score. In a complete distribution of z-scores, the mean is zero and the standard deviation 1. Raw scores are converted into z-scores by subtracting the mean from the raw score and dividing the difference by the standard deviation. Thus, z-scores are equally likely to be positive or negative. They ordinarily range from about -3 to about $+3$. To avoid the loss of too much precision in converting raw scores to z-scores, the z-scores are ordinarily expressed to tenths or hundredths of the standard deviation unit. If a z-score is multiplied by 10 and added to 50, the result is another kind of standard score, sometimes designated as a "T-score."

Reading furnishes the mind only with the materials of knowledge;
it is thinking that makes what is read ours. We are of the
ruminating kind, and it is not enough to cram ourselves with
a great load of collections; unless we chew them over again, they
will not give us strength and nourishment.

JOHN LOCKE

B

PROJECTS AND PROBLEMS

These projects and problems, some of which are rather extensive, are intended mainly to provide occasions for applying or practicing the principles discussed in the preceeding chapters. Some of the first three may be used near the beginning of the course. The next four are general assignments that might be used any time during the course. The remaining 20 are related rather closely to specific chapters. Some are designed to provide a basis for class discussions. Others should be turned in for evaluation by the instructor.

I. Introductory Projects
1. Biographical sketch
2. A survey of experience and opinion
3. A survey of educational values

II. General Projects
4. Class notes
5. Sources of information

6. Article reports
7. Data on a measurement problem

III. Chapter-related Problems

8. Test plan (Chapter 5)
9. Grading essay test answers (Chapter 6)
10. Items to measure learning (Chapter 7)
11. Conversion of multiple-choice to true-false items (Chapter 7)
12. Discrimination items (Chapter 8)
13. Reading test items (Chapter 8)
14. Purchase of a scoring machine (Chapter 9)
15. Correction for guessing (Chapter 9)
16. Procedures for an oral examination (Chapter 10)
17. Score distribution statistics (Chapter 11)
18. Computation of percentiles (Chapter 11)
19. Computation of correlation coefficients (Chapter 11)
20. Letter mark and stanine assignment (Chapter 12)
21. Test evaluation (Chapter 13)
22. Item analysis data (Chapter 14)
23. Reliability coefficients (Chapter 15)
24. Reliability of essay test scores (Chapter 15)
25. Summary notes on a published test (Chapter 17)
26. Interpretation of standard test scores (Chapter 19)

BIOGRAPHICAL SKETCH

Write a brief (2-5 page) account of your background and of the experiences that have been most influential in shaping you into the person you now are. Be as candid as you can without revealing anything you would prefer to keep to yourself. Write as well as you can. Keep a copy of what you turn in, for it will not be returned to you. You are quite likely to find it interesting and useful to refer to in future years. If possible, attach a small photograph of yourself to the biography.

This sketch will serve three purposes: 1) to help your instructor get to know you better, 2) to indicate how well you can write on a subject you know better than anyone else, and 3) to help your instructor to remember you if he is asked to write a letter of recommendation at some future date.

If the paper is not typed, write it neatly. Do not use a cover page, or put it in a theme cover. It will be read and evaluated subjectively. No attempt will be made to grade it precisely.

A SURVEY OF EXPERIENCE AND OPINION

Answer each of the following 50 questions as carefully and as honestly as you can. A summary of the results in your class will be reported to you. If time permits, they will be used as a basis for class discussion. Mark your answers on a machine-scorable answer sheet, or otherwise, as your instructor directs.

1. In your high school experience, about what percent of the tests you took were objective tests (that is, multiple-choice, true-false, short answer, matching, and to forth) as opposed to essay or problem tests?
   1) Less than 25%   4) From 75% to 90%
   2) From 25% to 50%   5) More than 90%
   3) From 50% to 75%

2. In your college experience, about what percent of the tests you have taken have been objective tests?
   1) Less than 25%   4) From 75% to 90%
   2) From 25% to 50%   5) More than 90%
   3) From 50% to 75%

3. How often have you, personally, cheated on examinations you have taken?
   1) Never   4) Seven or more times
   2) Once or twice   5) I'd rather not say
   3) Three to six times

4. How often have you helped someone else to cheat on an examination?
   1) Never   4) Seven or more times
   2) Once or twice   5) I'd rather not say
   3) Three to six times

5. A student caught cheating on an examination should be
   1) Failed in the course
   2) Failed on that examination
   3) Receive a grade one unit lower than his score would justify on that examination
   4) Be required to take another examination
   5) Be counseled but not punished

6. How many courses that you wanted to take, and felt that you could have taken with benefit and satisfaction, have you avoided for fear of getting a low grade?
   1) None   4) Three
   2) One   5) Four or more
   3) Two

7. When, if ever, did you start to worry about the marks you might get in your school work?
   1) Almost as soon as I started to school
   2) In the early elementary grades
   3) In the upper elementary grades
   4) In high school
   5) In college

8. How severely have you been scolded or punished by your parents for low marks in school?
   1) I never got marks low enough to give cause for scolding or punishment.
   2) I was never blamed by my parents for the low marks I got.
   3) I was scolded for low marks but never punished.
   4) I was punished for low marks by the loss of privilege.
   5) I have been punished by a spanking or a whipping for low marks.

9. If you were to rank low marks as a cause of anxiety and unhappiness in your life among these other four common causes—illness, unpopularity with schoolmates, conflicts in the home, self-criticism over conduct or morals—where would low marks rank?
   1) At the top (the greatest cause of anxiety and unhappiness)
   2) Next to the top
   3) In the middle
   4) Next to the bottom
   5) At the bottom (the least cause of anxiety and unhappiness)

10. Which of these types of test do you personally prefer to take?
    1) An essay test or problems test
    2) A short answer or completion test
    3) A true-false test
    4) A multiple-choice test
    5) A combination test including several item types

11. Which of these types of test do you personally prefer to take?
    1) A supervised in-class test
    2) An unsupervised (honor system) in-class test
    3) An open book in-class test
    4) A take-home test
    5) An oral examination

12. Which of the following grading systems comes closest to the one you would regard as preferable for high school and college courses?
    1) Pass-fail in all courses
    2) The common A–B–C–D–F system
    3) A–B–C–D–F grades with + or − refinements
    4) A nine-point numerical scale (stanines)
    5) A system of percent grades, with 100 percent perfect and 70 percent passing

13. Ideally what proportion of a student's grade should depend on his examination scores?
    1) All of it   4) Less than half of it
    2) Most of it   5) None of it
    3) About half of it

14. Who should determine the goals of education in a particular course?
    1) Mainly the teacher
    2) Mainly the individual student
    3) Teacher and student jointly and equally
    4) The class as a group
    5) Each student for himself

15. Who is primarily and ultimately responsible for the success of the process of education?
    1) The student   4) The school
    2) The teacher   5) The society
    3) The parents

16. Which statement below comes closest to expressing your view of the essence of educational achievement?
    1) Learning how to learn
    2) Gaining command of useful verbal knowledge
    3) Cultivating the higher mental processes of reason, judgment, imagination and creativity
    4) Developing a favorable self-concept
    5) Learning to work effectively with others
17. What do you regard as the best justification for testing by a classroom teacher?
    1) To motivate study
    2) To diagnose difficulties in learning
    3) To provide a basis for more accurate grades
    4) To conform to traditional but largely ineffectual practices
    5) To provide students additional opportunities to learn

For questions 18 to 50 use the following set of responses:

   1) Agree
   2) Disagree
   3) Neither

Note: If you agree *in general,* or if you *tend to agree,* use response 1. Do not require perfect, total agreement. Use response 3 only if you have no opinion, or if your tendency to agree is about equal to your tendency to disagree.

18. Students tend to learn more in classes that emphasize student participation in discussion than in classes where the teacher does most of the talking.
19. Intelligence is more a developed than an inherited ability.
20. The elimination of failure from the educational experience is a desirable and an attainable educational goal.
21. Individual instruction tends to be more effective than group instruction.
22. The typical teacher's responsibilities for motivating student learning are greater than his responsibilities for directing the process of learning.
23. The relation between success in school and success on the job is very low.
24. The goal of teaching and of learning should be mastery even when attaining mastery takes some pupils much longer than others.
25. Schools have in the past paid too much attention to the pupil's intellectual development and too little to his social and emotional development.
26. Progress in education has been slowed by the reluctance of teachers to try out new ideas.
27. Discipline problems in a class are usually the fault of the teacher.
28. Present emphasis on tests and grades in American education is excessive.
29. Giving an hour test as often as once a month would be likely to do more to impede than to promote effective learning in most high school subjects.
30. In order to properly evaluate a student's educational achievement, it is necessary to know his I.Q.
31. A nationwide test of secondary school achievement would provide useful information to supplement the diploma of high school graduation.

32. College students should be permitted to gain credit toward graduation by passing examinations in certain courses, without enrolling or attending classes in them.

33. Pupils' standardized test scores provide information that is useful in judging the competence of the pupils' teacher.

34. In some college courses a term paper provides a better basis than any examination could provide of determining how much a pupil has learned.

35. The use of extrinsic rewards (grades, honors, credits, degrees, and so forth) to motivate learning is educationally undesirable.

36. Student achievement should be measured and expressed in terms of the amount of knowledge gained and the nature of abilities developed, not in terms of relative standing among the student's classmates.

37. The achievement of every important educational objective can be measured.

38. Educational objectives should be defined in terms of desired behavior.

39. The possibility of correct response by guessing is a serious weakness of objective tests.

40. A teacher should be able to determine the passing score on any of her tests before the test is given.

41. In essay testing effective use can be made of questions that have no right answer, but which show how a student thinks and what evidence he has available to use.

42. The widespread use of objective tests has encouraged a great deal of superficial rote learning.

43. Some students suffer so badly from test anxiety that they seldom do justice to themselves on a test.

44. The main cause of cheating on examinations is overemphasis on grades.

45. Hard questions should count more than easy questions in determining a student's score on an examination.

46. The questions in a good test range widely in difficulty.

47. One can make a test that is low in reliability more reliable simply by making it longer.

48. The statistical validity of most educational tests can be, and should be, determined.

49. Most students would do a better job of getting an education if the "system" did not force them to work for high grades.

50. Each instructor should be free to determine for himself what the overall distribution of grades in his course should be.

A SURVEY OF EDUCATIONAL VALUES

Your opinion is sought on two questions relative to each of the statements in the list below:

1. *Is it in fact true* that the typical elementary school teacher in the United States today is more concerned with what is mentioned first in the statement than with what is mentioned second?

2. *Should* a good elementary school teacher be more concerned with the first than with the second?

In each case your answer can be either *yes, no* or *I don't know.* If you use a machine scorable answer sheet, mark the first response position if you mean yes, the second if you mean no, and the third to indicate that you don't know or can't say.

The statements each contrast two alternative aims or methods of teaching. While both may be desirable, they are also competing alternatives in most cases. The teacher cannot give more emphasis to one without giving less to the other.

The first time you react to the 20 statements below do so in relation to the first of the two questions above, that is, ask yourself whether typical elementary school teachers today *actually do* emphasize the first more than the second. Enter this first set of responses in positions 1 through 20 on the answer sheet.

The second time through, react to the 20 statements in terms of the second question above, that is, ask yourself whether elementary school teachers *really should* emphasize the first more than the second. Enter this second set of responses in positions 21 through 40 on the answer sheet.

Here are the 20 statements, preceded by common general preamble(s) which they all complete.

Does (should) the typical elementary school teacher pay more attention to:

1. The intellectual development of her pupils than their adjustment to life?
2. Her pupil's thoughts than their feelings?
3. The thoughts of her pupils than their actions?
4. Her pupils as learners than as persons?
5. The future welfare of her pupils than their present enjoyment of living?
6. The needs of society for loyal, cooperative members than the needs of individuals for freedom and independence?
7. Encouraging conformity than individuality?
8. Using competition rather than cooperation as a motivator?
9. Encouraging convergent rather than divergent thinking?
10. Teaching subjects effectively than understanding pupils thoroughly?
11. The product rather than the process of learning?
12. Helping pupils learn what others have discovered than helping them discover things for themselves?
13. Instructing pupils who want to learn than motivating those who don't?
14. Directing the learning process rather than participating in it?
15. Initiating learning activities than responding to pupil questions and suggestions?
16. Her class as a group of similar children than as a collection of different individuals?
17. The common needs of all children than the unique needs of particular children?
18. Using tests to evaluate learning rather than to produce it?
19. Encouraging pupils to evaluate their achievements relative to that of other pupils rather than relative to their own past achievements?
20. Making accurate evaluations of pupil achievement herself than helping pupils make their own self-evaluations?

CLASS NOTES

Each student will be assigned responsibility for turning in a set of notes that report the important ideas developed in one class period. The notes should be recorded as a set of 5-15 separate complete sentences. The sentences should express important ideas developed by the instructor or by students relating to the subject of the course. Do *not* report what the instructor or the class did during the period. Instead, report some concept or relationship they should have learned. Identify your paper completely. A good example to follow is shown below. Plan to turn in your set of notes at the next class meeting after the one in which they were taken. They will be evaluated roughly for significance, comprehensiveness, and precision of statement. However, they will not be returned to you.

EDUCATION 465

Class Notes for June 23, 1971

1. A point of view toward educational testing involves a point of view toward learning, knowledge, intelligence, measurement, and objectivity.
2. The essential job of the school is to help students learn from the store of man's accumulated knowledge.
3. Learning has been defined as the modification of behavior in desired directions. It might be better to regard it as giving human beings the resources to determine their own directions.
4. The primary responsibility for learning rests with the learner.
5. Knowledge is anything one has experienced, either personally or vicariously.
6. Getting command of useful verbal knowledge is the main purpose of education.
7. The two major tasks of the teacher are to determine what knowledge is likely to be most useful and to manage the learning process so as to help the student gain command of it.
8. Intelligence has a biological base, but it is largely an acquired characteristic.
9. Present tests of intelligence measure acquired intelligence.

W. HAROLD BAKKER

SOURCES OF INFORMATION

With the help of one of the sources or guides listed here, find an answer to the questions that have been assigned from the following list. Write an answer to the question using a brief quotation from the source or, if that is not feasible, a brief statement of your own. Then cite the original reference to your answer (not an index or abstract) using as models for reference citation similar references in the text.

BOOKS AND PAMPHLETS

Buros, Oscar K., ed., *The Sixth Mental Measurements Yearbook*. Highland Park, N.J.: The Gryphon Press, 1965. This volume, like those preceding it in the series, provides critical reviews of hundreds of recently published standardized tests. Descriptive information concerning the tests is also furnished. There are complete indexes by title, type of test, and name of author or reviewer, as well as lists of test publishers. Reviews of recently published books in measurement are also included.

Buros, Oscar K., ed., *Tests in Print*. Highland Park, N.J., The Gryphon Press, 1961. Includes information on the nature and sources of published tests, but not critical reviews. It includes also the original Technical Recommendations for Psychological Tests and Diagnostic Techniques, and the original Technical Recommendations for Achievement Tests. Several indexes are provided.

Lindquist, E. F., *Educational Measurement*. Washington, D.C.: American Council on Education, 1951. 819 pp. A comprehensive book on testing containing chapters by 20 of the leading specialists in the field. It represents the most authoritative manual on testing currently available. Some of the chapters will be too technical for the beginning student. It is, however, an extremely valuable reference to one seriously concerned with test construction and use.

Standards for Educational and Psychological Tests and Manuals. Washington, D.C.: American Psychological Association, 1966. An inexpensive 40-page pamphlet that includes a set of recommendations to guide test publishers, and by implication test users, in the development of satisfactory standardized tests and related materials. It provides a concise summary of recommendations on some of the critical problems in testing.

PERIODICALS

Psychological Abstracts. Washington, D.C.: The American Psychological Association. This bimonthly publication lists classified references on most subjects of interest to psychologists, including educational measurement. Most references are followed by brief summaries or excerpts. An annual index, by authors and subjects, is provided.

"Educational and Psychological Testing," *Review of Educational Research*, vol. 34, no. 1 (February 1968). Washington, D.C.: American Educational Research Association. Occasionally before February, 1941, and regularly every three years thereafter until February 1968, an issue of this summary and bibliography of research studies in education has been devoted to educational and psychological testing. Useful analyses and research evidence on most testing problems can be located with the help of these periodic reviews. A recent issue listed over 800 periodical articles on testing and commented on many of them.

The Education Index. New York: The H. W. Wilson Company, 1929–present. 13 volumes. This collection of references to current periodical articles on education, classified by subject and author, is issued monthly and cumulated periodically. Most of the articles related to classroom testing will be found under the subject heading Tests and Scales, although some others will be found under the headings

Educational Measurements, Evaluation, Examinations, and Objective Tests. The Education Index is available in many college libraries and large general libraries.

QUESTIONS TO LOOK UP

1. What four basic test types are identified by Lindquist?
2. What is Professor Van Roekel's parting shot in his 1965 review of the Diagnostic Reading Tests?
3. What is the journal reference for S. Lemeshow's Problem Check List for teachers, published in 1968?
4. What scores were provided in 1960 by the common examinations of the National Teacher Examinations?
5. What significant conclusions concerning the relation between reading readiness scores and success in reading were reported by Jack Bagford in 1968?
6. What suggestion did James L. Angel make for the benefit of the Regents Examinations in New York State in his 1968 review of research on tests?
7. What three kinds of validity are discussed in the Standards for Educational and Psychological Tests and Manuals?

ARTICLE REPORTS

Read and report on five recent journal articles on testing. Choose articles that interest you and that you can understand. Locate the articles by consulting the Education Index. Write a report on each article, following the form and style of the example on this page. Limit your report to a single page. Use $8\frac{1}{2}$ by 11 paper. The references you submit will not be returned to you.

Sample Article Report

AUTHOR: Betts, Gilbert L.

POSITION: Editor, Educational Test Bureau, Minneapolis, Minnesota.

TITLE OF ARTICLE: "Suggestions for a Better Interpretation and Use of Standardized Achievement Tests."

REFERENCE: *Education*, vol. 71 (December 1950), 217–21.

THESIS: In order to get a meaningful measurement, achievement should be graded in relation to ability to achieve.

DEVELOPMENT: The intelligence test should be used as a measure of ability to achieve and the achievement test score should be used as a measure of achievement. The two scores should then be compared for purposes of judging achievement. The use of grade norms leads to mediocrity because the more capable students are not motivated. If they are rated against them-selves, they will receive more equal motivation. Improved use of tests begins with selection. Each test should be selected to cover the area that the tester desires to cover and to measure what he is desires to measure.

CONCLUSION: Achievement and intelligence should be compared by percentile ranks to see if the student is working up to his ability. All students should learn at their own rates but each should receive proper motivation in regard to his abilities.

EVALUATION: The author presents a very good argument in that good students are not properly motivated when achievement is judged solely on the basis of grade norms as is many times done. One trouble with his suggested remedy is that when the poor students are motivated on the basis of their own intelligence scores, which correlate very highly with achievement scores, there will probably be a tendency for them to become somewhat more satisfied with their performances as they are.

GLEN A. STEPHENSON
May 27, 1964
Ed. 465

DATA ON A MEASUREMENT PROBLEM

Using a reference located through the *Education Index*, *Psychological Abstracts*, the *Review of Educational Research*, or simply by leafing through issues of *Educational and Psychological Measurement*, the *Journal of Educational Measurement*, or other periodicals, find an article that presents solid data on a measurement problem that interests you. Data of this kind are almost certain to be numerical: numbers, proportions, averages, ratios, differences, standard deviations, correlation coefficients, significance levels, and so forth.

Write a brief summary of the study reported in the article, following the form illustrated below.

Guessing on Objective Tests

Problem:
How much guessing do students do on objective tests?

Procedure:
College students taking true-false tests in a course on educational testing were asked to check on their test copies any questions to which their answers were no better than blind guesses. The answers they gave to these questions were then marked on a separate "Guesses" answer sheet. The inducement

to report these guesses, and to report them accurately, was the promise that the student would be given credit for as many right answers as the laws of chance would predict, even if his actual guesses were not that good.

Data:

	Mid-term	Final	Mid-term	Final
1. Test	Mid-term	Final	Mid-term	Final
2. Date	7–7–67	7–25–67	10–23–67	12–4–67
3. Number of items	98	89	108	116
4. Number of students	158	158	121	121
5. Responses	15,484	14,062	13,068	14,036
6. Percent Correct	76	72	76	71
7. Guesses	486	905	620	1,108
8. Percent of Responses	3.1	6.4	4.7	7.9
9. Guesses Correct	271	494	336	575
10. Percent Correct	56	55	54	52
11. Test Reliability	0.79	0.89	0.79	0.81

Conclusion:

Students like these taking tests like these do relatively little blind guessing.

Reference:

Ebel, Robert L. "Blind Guessing on Objective Achievement Tests," *Journal of Educational Measurement* vol. 5 (Winter 1968), 321–25.

Here are some measurement problems for which you might want to collect data.

I. Functions
   A. Measurement of motivation
   B. Measurement of vocabulary
   C. Measurement of writing ability
   D. Prediction of success in college
   E. Credit by examination
   F. External examinations
   G. Wide-scale testing programs

II. Construction
   A. Types of objective test items
   B. Free response vs. choice-type tests
   C. Number of multiple-choice options
   D. Effects of position of correct response among multiple-choice options
   E. Specific determiners

   F. Negative suggestions effects of true-false test items

III. Administration
   A. Methods of presenting test items
   B. Open-book examinations
   C. Confidence weighting of objective test responses
   D. Testwiseness
   E. Effects of practice
   F. Effects of special coaching
   G. Response sets and objective test responses
   H. Test anxiety
   I. Persistence on objective tests
   J. Correctness of first impressions on objective test answers
   K. Test time limits
   L. Rate of work scores
   M. Correction for guessing

N. Accuracy of objective test scoring

IV. Evaluation
    A. Determination of the difficulty of objective test items

B. Item difficulty distributions
C. Indices of item discrimination
D. Reliability of essay test grades
E. Validity of the Spearman-Brown formula
F. Methods of scaling test scores

TEST PLAN
(Chapter 5)

Identify one of your needs for an important test, such as an hour-long final test, or an important series of shorter tests in elementary reading or arithmetic. Detail your plans for developing that test or series in a substantial paper (1000-1500 words). Organize the paper around the following headings.

1. *Identity of the Test.* Give the proposed test title, so as to indicate the subject, grade level, and type of test (for example, achievement, aptitude, diagnosis)
2. *Purpose of the Test.* Here state the purpose of the test and defend its educational value. Do not seem to attempt the impossible or even the unlikely of attainment, but show some commitment to excellence in education.
3. *Type and Number of Test Questions.* Identify the type or types of questions (for example, essay, short answer, true-false, multiple-choice) to be used, and the number of each. Defend your choices on the basis of item characteristics in relation to the purposes of the test and the time available.
4. *Abilities to be Measured.* What will be your criteria of relevance for the test items? What item content will you approve (understanding, problem solving, explanation, application, and so forth) or disapprove (rote memory, verbal recall, general intelligence, testwiseness). Defend your decisions. Provide one or two illustrations of each of the various kinds of items you plan to use.
5. *Content to be Covered.* Present a content outline and justify it.

This assignment will be graded for completeness and quality. Your instructor will not second-guess your decisions unless they are clearly wrong. He is more interested in the value of this activity as a learning exercise—in the questions it causes you to ask and answer—than in its limited values as a measure of your competence. However, since it involves a substantial amount of work, do not let sloppy appearance detract from its apparent worth.

GRADING ESSAY TEST ANSWERS
(Chapter 6)

This activity is based on the essay test question, the model answer to that question, and five student answers to the question. Your task is to assign a numerical grade to each student answer, using the scale of grades defined below.

9. Much better than the model
8. Some better than the model
7. As good as the model
6. Not quite as good as the model
5. A little more than half as good as the model
4. Half as good as the model
3. Not quite half as good as the model
2. Only a little that is correct or relevant
1. Totally incorrect or irrelevant

Make an initial grade decision paying attention only to the completeness and correctness of the statements made, and the absence of irrelevant statements. Then lower the initial grade by a point if ideas are poorly expressed or if there are serious errors in sentence structure, spelling, or punctuation. Write a brief statement explaining the grades you give to each answer. Do not confer with any other student in this class in deciding on these grades. Do not change your grade if you discover that others disagree with you.

A committee will collate the grades and report the distribution of grades assigned to each question. Results may be discussed in class. Later, data from this assignment may used to demonstrate how the reliability of these grades can be calculated.

A. *The Question:*

Identify and comment on the misconceptions (there are at least five) that surround the problem of guessing on objective tests.

B. *Model Answer:*

A number of misconceptions surround the problem of guessing on objective tests. One is that students are likely to do extensive blind guessing on objective tests. The fact is that well-motivated students taking an examination that is appropriate for them do relatively little blind guessing. Another is that a student who guesses may, if he is lucky, make a high score on an objective test by blind guessing alone. The fact is that the odds against a high score on a reasonably long objective test are astronomical.

A third misconception is that if an objective test score is corrected for guessing the effect of luck in guessing is removed or neutralized. The fact is that a correction for guessing hurts the lucky guesser far less than it hurts the unlucky guesser. Another misconception is that the student should avoid guessing if his score is to be corrected for guessing. Actually he has the best chance of making a high score by offering an answer to every question even when the correction is to be applied. Usually his answer will be better than a blind guess. Even if it is not, the penalty is not likely to hurt more than an omission would.

Finally there is the common misconception that guessing involves an element of cheating, with the student trying to get credit for answers he is not sure of. But since the purpose of the test is to measure amount of knowledge, a student ought to use all of it he possesses to give the best answers he can, even if he is quite uncertain of the correctness of some of them.

C. *Student Answers:*

1. There are many misconceptions that surround the problem of guessing on objective tests. It is some of these misconceptions that will be discussed in this paper.

   One common misconception that surrounds guessing on objective tests is that guessing is not helpful to maintaining a higher grade. We can see that this is truly a misconception because any answer is better than none and the guessed answer could be a right answer.

   Another misconception in this same idea is the view that correction for guessing makes a difference in the score. This is not true because the score is usually the same.

   Another is the psychological advantage.

2. First the chances of doing well on a test by blindly guessing alone are very slim, contrary to popular belief. Secondly, very few guesses are really blind guesses. Uncertainty may exist but some basis exists for the choice. Third, it is not undesirable to encourage students to make educated guesses. Life is full of uncertainties we must learn to cope with. We must often make decisions before all the needed information is available. Fourth, tests corrected for guessing yield results almost identical to those not corrected. Why waste valuable time, unless it be for public relation purposes? Fifth, objective tests are no more subject to "guessing" than are essay tests to "bluffing." Sixth, the better students receive the higher grades regardless of whether the test is corrected for guessing or not.

3. Test-wiseness is one problem surrounding guessing on objective tests. Students who know "how" to take a test can do well even when they aren't familiar with the material being tested if the questions contain specific determiners which give away the answer.

   Rote learning also promotes guessing on exams when application of knowledge is required.

4. One misconception surrounding the problem of guessing on objective tests is that students really do guess blindly. If a student has any information at all about the subject matter, he is not really guessing blindly; he only does that if he marks answers without any regard to the question.

   A second misconception is that guessing (with some information for background) is harmful. A student will often have to make decisions in life on things of which he is not certain. He will often have to use whatever resources he has available to make choices. This is not a harmful thing.

   A third misconception is that one can get a high score by guessing blindly. The longer the test, the smaller the probability that the student will get a high score by true blind guessing.

   A fourth misconception is that a guessing correction really corrects for guessing. When the formula $R = [W/(k - 1)]$ is used, subtractions are being made for all the questions a student missed, even if he was positive the answer was right; in other words, even though the answer was not a guess.

   A fifth misconception is that guessing is a large problem in objective tests, making luck more important than knowledge. A student with even a moderate command of the material has a better chance on the questions he must guess on because he is not guessing blindly.

Guessing does not seem to have much of an effect on the reliability of objective test scores.

5. The first misconception surrounding the problem of guessing on objective tests deals with a false assumption. Critics suggest that a correction for guessing assumes that incorrectly answered questions are guessed at blindly by the examinee; this not only is incorrect but it also has no relevance in the use of correction for guessing.

The second misconception deals with the correction for guessing. It is assumed (and sometimes so because of false representation) that guessing on a test—or at least its effects—are eliminated by this correction. Again—not true. Corrected and uncorrected tests correlate highly.

The third misconception assumes that if corrected and uncorrected tests correlate highly then correction for guessing does no good. Perhaps that is so with the correction per se but it has been shown that by telling a class a test will be corrected for guessing (but not necessarily doing this correction) the reliability of the test scores increased. In this sense some good has been done.

The fourth misconception deals with testwiseness. It is assumed that two people knowing absolutely nothing about a subject should both perform at about a chance level. However, a testwise student can pick out specific determiners and irrelevant clues and quite possibly function above the chance level.

The fifth (but not necessarily the last) misconception is that students should never just guess—because it is immoral, or lying, or misrepresentation, etc. Not true! A student might make a good guess based on his basic understanding of the material and justly score better. Actually, not guessing would probably give a less accurate measure of his ability.

ITEMS TO MEASURE LEARNING
(Chapter 7)

This assignment is based on 20 true-false test items that were intended to test for elements of knowledge that most college students are unlikely to have. Decide how you would answer each question and record the answers on a special answer sheet. Then your instructor will read, or show you the 10 paragraphs on which the questions were based. After you have heard or seen the background information you will be asked to respond again to the 20 questions. This time your answers may be recorded in spaces 21 to 40 on the special answer sheet.

A committee from the class, or a test scoring machine, will determine the proportion of correct answers given to each question each time it was taken (that is, before and after "instruction"). The difference between "proportion correct after" and "proportion correct before" will indicate how effective the instruction was in giving information and how effective the item was in measuring it. These differences will be reported to you and will form the basis for a discussion of good and poor true-false test items.

THE 20 TRUE-FALSE TEST ITEMS

1. Napoleon won most of his military campaigns.
2. Napoleon's downfall was his loss of the battle for Spain.
3. Six of the several known species of penguins are found on the Galapagos Islands near the equator.
4. Adult penguins have no natural enemies on the ice.
5. Sugar is often added to wine during fermentation to make it sweeter.
6. Most wines require fairly long aging periods before they reach the peak of their flavor.
7. Scientists have found that male sperm are stronger and live longer than female sperm; and this accounts for the sex ratio of males to females— 140 to 160 to 100.
8. Human population studies indicate that the general weakness of the male sperm accounts for the relationship of more birth defects, miscarriages, and death among males than females.
9. Infection was the major cause of death for soldiers in the Civil War.
10. Pneumonia was the most common illness suffered by soldiers in the Civil War.
11. After learning something, more of it is forgotten in the next few hours than in the next several days.
12. Lessons learned early in the morning are remembered better than those learned just before going to sleep.
13. In cases of severe shock, the victim's feet should be elevated.
14. Small amounts of an alcoholic beverage can be given to a shock victim if he is conscious.
15. When purchasing a home, realtors must be aware of its individual "sex appeal" to the buyer.
16. A man considers the price and location as the most important elements when purchasing a home.
17. Due to the many new techniques that have been developed by psychologists, mental illness is not considered to be one of our biggest problems today.
18. Some forms of mental illness can be inherited.
19. A recent survey indicates that many parents give stock to their children.
20. 6.5 percent of the stockholders in the United States are children.

CONVERSION OF MULTIPLE-CHOICE TO TRUE-FALSE ITEMS
(Chapter 7)

This exercise is based on part of a reading interpretation test consisting of four paragraphs of background information and nine multiple-choice questions intended to test comprehension of the background information. Your task is to convert each of the multiple-choice items into a true-false item that tests the same general idea. The items you write may be reviewed and evaluated by some of your classmates before they are turned in.

FINDERS KEEPERS

Have you ever heard the saying, "Finders keepers, losers weepers"? Do you believe it? If you do, you may get an unpleasant surprise some day. According to the law, the finder is *not* the keeper, and he may turn out to be the weeper himself.

In almost every state the law says that a person must make a "reasonable and immediate" effort to locate the owner of a lost article. In New York a finder can be sent to prison for as much as 10 years if he keeps a really valuable piece of property. Although the other states are not so strict, almost all of them have fines for keeping things, such as money or jewelry, that are found.

The person who finds an article may not be allowed to keep it, even if he cannot trace the owner. In Illinois, for example, the state takes any unclaimed finds. In Michigan, half the value of the find goes to the state. By an unusual Iowa law, the finder can keep 10 percent of the value of anything he comes across, even if the true owner is located. This law is hardly ever enforced, however, unless the find is worth a lot of money. In the other states, if the owner is located, he may give as big or little a reward as he likes.

The first and best rule for finders is to put an ad in the paper. The second rule is to take the money or valuables to the police and get a receipt for them. If the owner is not found, the police will see that you get your legal share. One last rule is also important: Make sure the article is really lost before you find it.

1. What is the purpose of the first paragraph?
   1) To show how little people know about "lost and found" laws.
   2) To scare the reader into returning things that he finds.
   *3) To give the reader an idea of what the article is about.
   4) To make the reader want to study law books.

2. In what way could a "finder" be a "weeper"?
   1) He might not get any reward for returning the article.
   *2) He might be fined or sent to jail for not trying to find the owner.
   3) The state might take the find away from him.
   4) The true owner might turn up and take back the find.

3. Which two paragraphs explain the legal side of finding things?
   1) 1 and 2
   *2) 2 and 3
   3) 2 and 4
   4) 3 and 4

4. What is the *main* idea of paragraph 2?
   *1) The law requires the finder to try to return the find.
   2) New York has very strict "lost and found" laws.
   3) People usually keep the things that they find.
   4) There is no way to enforce the "lost and found" laws.

5. Why are the words "reasonable and immediate" put in quotation marks in paragraph 2?
   1) The words are used in an unusual way.
   *2) The words are taken directly from the law.

3) The words are a direct quotation of what someone has said.

4) The words are not understood by everyone.

6. What is the purpose of paragraph 4?

*1) To give examples of "reasonable and immediate" efforts that can be made to locate the owner of a lost article.

2) To tell what one should do if he loses something valuable.

3) To explain how one can tell whether an article is really lost.

4) To emphasize the fact that the police can be helpful in locating owners of lost articles.

7. Suppose one found a watch in the lobby of a movie theater. Which of these, by itself, would *not* be a "reasonable and immediate" attempt to return the property?

1) Putting an ad in the "lost and found" column of a local newspaper.

2) Taking the watch to the police station.

3) Asking people near the spot if they had lost anything.

*4) Giving the watch to the manager of the theater.

8. What does the last sentence of the article mean?

1) Keep the article a few days before trying to return it.

*2) "Finding" can sometimes be very close to stealing.

3) An article that is hidden is not really lost.

4) Always obey the law when you find things.

9. Which of these would make the best title for this article?

*1) "Finders Keepers?"

2) "Rules for Finders"

3) "Losing Things"

4) "Do You Know the Laws?"

DISCRIMINATION ITEMS
(Chapter 8)

Write or copy a short paragraph of from three to seven sentences expressing ideas you think few, if any, of the other members of this class already know. Then, on another sheet, write three different, independent items, two true-false and one four-alternative multiple-choice, designed to test the knowledge of these ideas. None of the items should refer directly to the paragraph.

Your items and the paragraph on which they are based will be tried out by your classmates in one of the class meetings. The class will be divided into tryout groups of 6 to 10 members. The items written by members of the groups will be circulated within the group to obtain the pre-information responses. Each person, excepting the author of the item, will record his responses independently, guarding against being influenced by the responses others may have given. Then the items will be circulated again along with the paragraphs to obtain the post-information responses.

When all this has been done and the responses have been returned to the author of the items, he must do these four things:

1. Enter the key (correct response) for each item.
2. Calculate an index of discrimination for each item using this arithmetic:
   a. Number of post-information correct responses, minus
   b. Number of pre-information correct responses, divided by
   c. Number of total responses, pre or post (that is, one less than the number of members of the group).
3. Add the three indices of discrimination, taking account of signs (that is, subtracting the negative indices).
4. Fasten paragraph, items, responses, and calculations together and turn them in. Be sure your name is on each sheet.

Your instructor may supply you with special forms on one side of which you may write the items. The other side will provide spaces for recording the responses and calculating the discrimination indices.

READING TEST ITEMS
(Chapter 8)

Write five four-alternative multiple-choice test items on the passage below. The purpose of the items should be to test comprehension of the passage. Use the items on Finders Keepers, pp. 586-87, as models to follow. Your items should be appropriate for use in the upper elementary grades.

THE TRICK*

My practice was to work hard on a trick, privately, and when it was perfect, let my father see it. I would have the colt out in our vacant lot doing the trick as he came home to supper. One evening, as he approached the house, I was standing, whip in hand, while the colt, quite free, was stepping carefully over the bodies of a lot of girls, all my sisters and all their girl friends. My father did not express the admiration I expected; he was frightened and furious. "Stop that," he called, and the came running around into the lot, took the whip, and lashed me with it. I tried to explain; the girls tried to help me explain.

I had seen in the circus a horse that stepped thus over a row of prostrate clowns. It looked dangerous for the clowns, but the trainer had told me how to do it. You begin with logs, laid out a certain distance apart; the horse walks over them under your lead, and whenever he touches one you rebuke him. By and by he will learn to step with such care that he never trips. Then you sub-

*From *The Autobiography of Lincoln Steffens*, copyright 1931 by Harcourt Brace Jovanovich, Inc.; renewed, 1959 by Peter Steffens. Reprinted by permission of the publishers.

stitute clowns. I had no clowns, but I did get logs, and with the girls helping, we taught the colt to step over the obstacles even at a trot. Walking, she touched nothing. All ready thus with the logs, I had my sisters lie down in the grass, and again and again the colt stepped over them. None was ever touched.

My father would not listen to any of this; he just walloped me and when he was tired or satisfied and I was in tears, I blubbered a short excuse: "They were only girls." And he whipped me some more.

CORRECTION FOR GUESSING
(Chapter 9)

Anticipating an important objective test, a student asks whether or not the scores will be corrected for guessing. Write down the answer you would give him and your justification for it (200-500 words).

PURCHASE OF A SCORING MACHINE
(Chapter 9)

The principal of your school mentions that a salesman is trying to interest him in the purchase of a machine costing $3,000 for scoring classroom tests. Knowing of your interest in testing, he asks whether it would be a good idea, and if so, what capabilities the machine should have. Write the answer you would give him (200-500 words).

PROCEDURES FOR AN ORAL EXAMINATION
(Chapter 10)

Suppose that you have been appointed as one member of a committee of teachers to interview five applicants for a teaching vacancy in your school. The chairman has called a meeting of the committee to discuss and agree on the procedures to be followed. He knows that you recently took a course in which oral examination procedures were discussed. He asks you to prepare a list of 5 to 15 suggestions for making the committee's oral examinations as good as possible. Write down the suggestions you would present to the committee for their consideration. Do not copy verbatim any of the suggestions made in the chapter on oral examinations in this book. Prepare your suggestions in view of the specific problem facing your committee.

SCORE DISTRIBUTION STATISTICS
(Chapter 11)

This exercise is based on the two lists of spelling test scores presented in Table 11.1. In the example below the frequency distribution, median, mean, variance, and standard deviation of the List A scores have been produced or calculated. Your task is to prepare a similar display based on the List B scores. Use the same class intervals, and make the calculated values as accurate as those shown here. Show some concern for the neatness of your work. You need not show details of your calculations.

				List A
I.	Frequency Distribution			
	94–96	6		96
	91–93	5		91, 91, 93
	88–90	4		88
	85–87	3		87
	82–84	2		82, 84, 84
	79–81	1		80, 79
	76–78	0		76, 77, 76
	73–75	−1		75, 74, 73
	70–72	−2		71, 72
	67–69	−3		69, 67
	64–66	−4		65, 66, 65
	61–63	−5		61
II.	Median			76
III.	Mean			
	Σx			1942
	Mean (ungrouped data)			77.68
	Σfd			6
	Mean (grouped data)			77.72
IV.	Variance			
	Σfd^2			252
	Variance (deviation scores)			10.0224
	Variance (raw scores)			90.2016
V.	Standard Deviation			9.50

COMPUTATION OF PERCENTILES
(Chapter 11)

Prepare a chart like that shown in Figure 11.2 for computing the percentiles of the List B spelling test scores. Use the same method as was used with the List A scores. Prepare to turn in the chart.

COMPUTATION OF CORRELATION COEFFICIENTS
(Chapter 11)

Compute the product-moment coefficient of correlation (Formula 11.8) and the rank-difference coefficient (Formula 11.9) using the second 10 pairs of scores (Gary-Patricia) in Table 11.1. The task will be much simpler if you convert the scores into deviations, using the equivalents shown in Table 11.3. Thus the scores for Aaron, 65 and 67, would become −4 and −3 respectively. Those for Barbara would become −1 and −2, and so on. Show your work in displays like those of Tables 11.11 and 11.12.

LETTER MARK AND STANINE ASSIGNMENT
(Chapter 12)

The problem in this exercise is to assign letter marks and stanines to the achievement scores given below for a class at the indicated level of ability. Use the methods described on pages 342-48 of chapter 12. Show your work in the form used in the lower half of tables 12.3 and 12.5. You need not include the data for the problem, as given below, on the paper you prepare to turn in.

1. Class ability level measures
   a) Mean G.P.A. on previous year's courses: 2.44
   b) Mean percentile on aptitude test: 63
2. Achievement scores (number of students = 25)

190	176	157	151	137
181	173	157	147	133
180	164	155	147	133
180	162	152	144	132
177	157	151	138	130

TEST EVALUATION
(Chapter 13)

Choose an important (semester or term) test you have given or taken during the past year and obtain a copy of the test and answer key. If all of the tests available, or of interest to you, are brief (about 10 to 20 questions), base this assignment on a set of 3 to 5 such tests. Write a brief descriptive summary of the test (or tests). You may wish to mention something on these points:

 1. Test title
 2. Test author
 3. Course of subject
 4. Department or school
 5. Grade level
 6. Date of test
 7. Number of examinees
 8. Number of items of each type
 9. Time limits
10. Purpose of test

Write evaluative comments on the following characteristics, after reading discussions of them in this chapter.

1. Relevance
2. Balance
3. Efficiency
4. Objectivity
5. Specificity
6. Fairness
7. Speededness

Prepare a test analysis report like that shown in Exhibit 13.1 of the text. Include also a content analysis like that of Exhibit 13.3, a relevance report like that of 13.4, and a score distribution statistics display like that shown in the exercise of Chapter 9. List the indices of difficulty and discrimination for each item, and show calculation of the reliability coefficient for the scores.

If you do not have access to student answers to the test, use the response data for the item analysis problem on pages 593-94 as the basis for the test analysis. Do not be concerned by the fact that these response data have nothing at all to do with your test. The two parts of the analysis can be handled quite separately.

In a final section, make an overall summary evaluation of the test and offer suggestions for improving it. Attach a copy of the test and the answer key. In the case of an essay test, supply an ideal answer to each question. *Arrange the parts of the assignment in this order, and staple them together.*

 1. Test descriptive information
 2. Evaluative comments or elements of test quality
 3. Test analysis summary
 4. Content analysis
 5. Relevance report
 6. Score distribution statistics
 7. Indices of difficulty and discrimination
 8. Reliability calculation
 9. Summary evaluation
10. Test copy
11. Key to correct answers

Do not use a special theme or notebook cover. The paper you turn in will be graded on the basis of completeness and quality but may not be returned. You may want to make an extra copy for your own future reference.

ITEM ANALYSIS DATA
(Chapter 14)

Using the responses indicated below of 26 students (identified by letter and recorded in columns) to 25 multiple-choice test items (identified by number and recorded in rows), calculate an index of difficulty and an index of discrimination for each of the 25 items. Record these in a table to be turned in, using these headings:

ITEM ANALYSIS DATA

Item Number	Corrective Alternative	Number of Correct Responses Upper	Lower	Index Discrimination	Difficulty
1	2	6	3	0.43	36%
etc.					

RESPONSES OF 26 STUDENTS TO 25 MULTIPLE-CHOICE TEST ITEMS

		Student				
Item	Key	ABCDE	FGHIJ	KLMNO	PQRST	UVWXYZ
1	2	42222	24222	42211	42242	222122
2	2	22222	14224	00034	44222	211442
3	2	22131	21212	21211	13223	211313
4	2	32222	22443	11441	41422	411322
5	4	44442	44421	40121	24444	344442
6	3	42233	33332	33332	33321	333344
7	1	13123	11323	00301	23124	121101
8	3	33333	33433	31113	13313	313333
9	2	12232	22212	12242	31242	120342
10	2	22422	11212	11211	11223	142221
11	3	42222	22342	14024	24232	322211
12	3	33333	34243	44424	33343	443343
13	1	11111	11441	14042	44314	144414
14	1	11111	11311	41111	11111	111121
15	1	11311	13334	43333	43333	312111

Continued on page 594

Continued from page 593

		Student				
Item	Key	ABCDE	FGHIJ	KLMNO	PQRST	UVWXYZ
16	3	33333	33333	33333	23333	333333
17	2	22422	22244	23044	43444	443322
18	4	42334	43423	21404	21143	414441
19	2	21222	22222	42022	32221	221232
20	4	44444	44421	14221	23444	442444
21	2	22442	24214	42444	42421	424241
22	4	43444	34444	44443	33444	331444
23	1	11114	13333	30013	34403	313111
24	4	44444	44344	34343	43443	444444
25	1	11111	12123	11214	11121	411214

RELIABILITY COEFFICIENTS
(Chapter 15)

Using the data given below calculate a split-halves, a Kuder-Richardson 20, and a Kuder-Richardson 21 reliability coefficient. Show your work in displays like those of Exhibits 15.1 and 15.2.

Note: The easiest and most accurate way to get the quantity Σpq needed for K. R. 20 is to multiply the number of right answers to an item by the number of wrong answers. Add these products for all 10 items and divide by 225. In this problem

$$p = \frac{R}{15} \quad q = \frac{W}{15} \quad \text{so} \quad pq = \frac{R \times W}{225}$$

		Student															
Item	Key	A	B	C	D	E	F	G	H	I	J	K	L	M	N	O
1	2	4	2	2	2	2	2	4	2	2	2	4	2	2	1	1
2	2	2	2	2	2	2	1	4	2	2	4	0	0	0	3	4
3	2	2	2	1	3	1	2	1	2	1	2	2	1	2	1	1
4	2	3	2	2	2	2	2	2	4	4	3	1	1	4	4	1
5	4	4	4	4	4	2	4	4	4	2	1	4	0	1	2	1
6	3	4	2	2	3	3	3	3	3	3	2	3	3	3	3	3
7	1	1	3	1	2	3	1	1	3	2	3	0	0	3	0	1
8	3	3	3	3	3	3	3	3	4	3	3	3	1	1	1	3
9	2	1	2	2	3	2	2	2	2	1	2	1	2	2	4	2
10	2	2	2	4	2	2	1	1	2	1	2	1	1	2	1	1

RELIABILITY OF ESSAY TEST SCORES
(Chapter 15)

Eight students receive the scores shown below on the five questions of an essay test. Using the procedures described on pages 419-20, estimate the reliability of the eight scores. Show your work in a table like that of Exhibit 15.3.

Question	Student A	B	C	D	E	F	G	H	Sum
1	6	4	6	4	3	6	6	8	43
2	6	0	7	4	2	7	3	4	33
3	7	5	5	2	0	2	7	5	33
4	2	4	6	4	4	5	3	5	33
5	7	2	4	7	4	2	7	3	36
Total	28	15	28	21	13	22	26	25	178

SUMMARY NOTES ON A PUBLISHED TEST
(Chapter 17)

Choose from your instructor's files a published test that seems likely to be useful to you in your work. Prepare a concise summary of the principal features of the test, following the outline given below.

A. Identifying information
   1. Name of the test
   2. Publisher (and address)
   3. Date of publication
   4. Authors (and their positions)
B. Descriptive information
   1. Types and numbers of items
   2. Fields of knowledge sampled
   3. Means for recording and scoring answers
   4. Scores provided
   5. Time required
   6. Cost per pupil tested
C. Interpretive information
   1. Type and adequacy of norms
   2. Score reliability and measurement errors
   3. Data on item difficulty
   4. Evidence for test validity

D. Evaluative information
   1. Readability and attractiveness of test and answer sheets
   2. Readability and completeness of directions for administering, scoring and interpreting
   3. Favorable and critical comments from other reviewers (Buros or periodicals)
   4. Summary of your own evaluation

INTERPRETATION OF STANDARD TEST SCORES
(Chapter 19)

The table below gives the scores of Roland Elkins, a fifth grade pupil in your school, on a series of tests of basic skills. The tests were taken at midyear. Complete the table by determining stanine equivalents for the local percentiles. Mrs. Elkins has made an appointment to talk with you about the test scores, which she has not seen. Write out the main ideas that you would try to explain to her. You probably should touch on these:

1. What raw scores, grade equivalents, percentiles and stanines mean. (These tests were not corrected for guessing. The standard error of measurement of the grade equivalent scores is about 0.4.)
2. Why local percentiles differ from publishers' percentiles, and what the differences indicate in this case.
3. What the scores indicate about the achievements of Roland, in general and more specifically.

BASIC SKILLS TEST SCORES FOR ROLAND ELKINS

Test	Raw Score	Grade Equivalent	Publisher's Percentile	Local Percentile	Local Stanine
Vocabulary	21	5.3	46	46	
Reading	37	5.3	46	37	
Language	78	5.7	55	49	
Study skills	57	5.3	48	42	
Arithmetic	27	4.2	16	9	
Composite	—	5.2	45	37	

C
BIBLIOGRAPHY

The numbers in parentheses, following each entry, indicate pages where references appear in this text.

A Glossary of Measurement Terms. Los Angeles: California Test Bureau, 1960. (548)

Aiken, L. R., Jr. "Another Look at Weighting Test Items." *Journal of Educational Measurement* 3 (1966): 183–85. (258)

American Educational Research Association. *Technical Recommendations for Achievement Tests.* Washington, D. C., 1955. (436)

American Psychological Association. *Technical Recommendations for Psychological Tests and Diagnostic Techniques.* Washington, D.C., 1954. (437)

————. *Standards for Educational and Psychological Tests and Manuals.* Washington, D. C., 1966. (458)

American Psychological Association Task Force. "Job Testing and the Disadvantaged." *American Psychologist* 24 (1969): 637–50. (542)

Anastasi, A. *Psychological Testing.* 3d ed. New York: Crowell Collier and Macmillan, Inc., 1968. (437, 498)

————. "The Concept of Validity in the Interpretation of Test Scores." *Educational and Psychological Measurement* 10 (1950): 67–78. (442)

————. "The Invitational Conference on Testing Problems." In *Testing Problems in Perspective*. Washington, D. C.: American Council on Education, 1966. (19)

Angoff, W. H. "Scales With Non-meaningful Origins and Units of Measurement." *Educational and Psychological Measurement* 22 (1962): 27–34. (455)

Association of Certified Public Accountant Examiners. *Report of the CPA Examination Appraisal Commission*. New York: 1961. (150)

Ayres, L. P. *A Scale for Measuring the Quality of Handwriting of School Children*. Division of Education, Bulletin 113, New York: Russell Sage Foundation, 1912. (38)

Bagley, W. C. "An Essentialist's Platform for the Advancement of American Education." *Educational Administration and Supervision* 24 (1938): 241–56. (30)

————. "On the Correlation of Mental and Motor Ability in School Children." *American Journal of Psychology* 12 (1900): 193–205. (9)

Barnes, E. J., and Pressey, S. L. "The Reliability and Validity of Oral Examinations." *School and Society* 30 (1929): 719–22. (266)

Bauernfeind, R. H. *Building a School Testing Program*. Boston: Houghton Mifflin Company, 1969. (535)

Bayley, N. "Mental Growth During the First Three Years." *Genetic Psychology Monographs* 14 (1933): 1–92. (513)

Bennett, G. K. "Testing and Privacy." *Journal of Educational Measurement* 4 (1967): 7–10. (520)

Binet, A. "Nouvelles Recherches sur la Mesure du Niveau Intellectual chez les Enfants d'Ecole." *Anneé Psychologique* 17 (1911): 145–201. (498)

Binet, A., and Simon, T. *The Development of Intelligence in Children*. Translated by Elizabeth S. Kite. Baltimore: The Williams and Wilkins Co., 1916. (12)

Black, H. *They Shall Not Pass*. New York: William Morrow & Co., Inc., 1963. (29)

Blommers, P., and Lindquist, E. F. *Elementary Statistical Methods*. Boston: Houghton Mifflin Company, 1960. (283, 300)

Bloom, B. S. "Learning for Mastery." *UCLA, CSEIP Evaluation Comment*, 1, no. 2, Los Angeles: U.C.L.A., 1968. (85)

Bloom, B. S., and Krathwohl, D. R. *Taxonomy of Educational Objectives: Cognitive Domain*. New York: David McKay Co., Inc., 1956. (24, 60, 76, 109, 114)

Board of Examinations, University of Chicago. *Manual of Examination Methods*. University of Chicago Bookstore, 1937. (577)

"The Board of Examiners at the University of Chicago." *School and Society* 35 (1932): 116–17. (18)

Boas, G. "Superstitions in Education." *The Education Digest* 25 (1959): 1–4. (55)

Bolmeier, E. C. "Principles Pertaining to Marking and Reporting Pupil Progress." *School Review* 59 (1951): 15–24. (332)

Bormuth, J. R. *On the Theory of Achievement Test Items.* University of Chicago Press, 1970. (85, 204)

Brigham, C. C. *A Study of Error.* New York: College Entrance Examination Board, 1932. (15)

Brody, W., and Powell, N. J. "A New Approach to Oral Testing." *Educational and Psychological Measurement* 7 (1947): 289–95. (264)

Brooks, H. B. "What Can Be Done About Comparative Marks and Formal Report Cards?" *California Journal of Secondary Education* 10 (1935): 101–106. (313)

Burmester, M. A. and Olson, L. A. "Comparison of Item Statistics for Items in Multiple Choice and Alternate Response Form." *Science Education* 50 (1966): 467–70. (168)

Burnham, P. S., and Crawford, A. B. "The Vocational Interests and Personality Test Scores of a Pair of Dice." *Journal of Educational Psychology* 26 (1935): 508–12. (526)

Buros, O. K. *Tests in Print.* Highland Park, New Jersey: The Gryphon Press, 1961. (452)

———. *The Sixth Mental Measurements Yearbook.* Highland Park, New Jersey: The Gryphon Press, 1965. (20, 457, 517)

Calvert, E. T. "Supplemental Report on the 1973 Statewide Testing Program." *California Education* 2 (1965): 3–6. (26)

Carroll, J. "A Model for School Learning." *Teachers College Record* 64 (1963): 723–33. (85)

Carter, H. D. "How Reliable Are Good Oral Examinations?" *California Journal of Educational Research* 13 (1962): 147–53. (264, 266)

Carter, R. S. "How Invalid Are Marks Assigned by Teachers?" *Journal of Educational Psychology* 43 (1952): 218–28. (316)

Cashen, V. M., and Ramseyer, G. C. "The Use of Separate Answer Sheets by Primary Age Children." *Journal of Educational Measurement* 6 (1969): 155–58. (243)

Cattell, J. M. "Mental Tests and Measurements." *Mind* 15 (1890): 373–80. (9)

Chadwick, E. "Statistics of Educational Results." *Museum, A Quarterly Magazine of Education, Literature and Science* 3 (1864): 479–84. (8)

Chase, C. I. "The Impact of Some Obvious Variables on Essay Test Scores." *Journal of Educational Measurement* 5 (1968): 315–18. (132)

Chauncey, H. *Annual Report to the Board of Trustees.* Princeton, New Jersey: Educational Testing Service, 1949. (22)

Chauncey, H., and Dobbin, J. E. *Testing: Its Place in Education Today.* New York: Harper and Row, Publishers, 1963. (29)

Chauncey, H., and Hilton, T. L. "Are Aptitude Tests Valid for the Highly Able?" *Science* 148 (1965): 1297–1304. (540)

Cleary, A. T., and Hilton, T. L. "An Investigation of Item Bias." *Educational and Psychological Measurement* 28 (1968): 61–75. (542)

Coffman, W. E. "On the Validity of Essay Tests of Achievement." *Journal of Educational Measurement* 3 (1966): 151–56. (100)

Cohen, M. R., and Nagel, E. *An Introduction to Logic and Scientific Method.* New York: Harcourt Brace Jovanovich, 1934. (70)

Coleman, W., and Cureton, E. E. "Intelligence and Achievement: The 'Jangle Fallacy' Again." *Educational and Psychological Measurement* 14 (1954): 347–51. (504)

College Proficiency Examination Program. Albany, New York: The State Education Department, 1969. (7)

Conant, J. B. "Preliminary Report of the Committee on Testing to the President of Carnegie Foundation for the Advancement of Teaching." *School and Society* 64 (1946): 274–76. (22)

Conrad, H. S. "Norms." *Encyclopedia of Educational Research.* rev. ed. Edited by Walter S. Monroe. New York: The Macmillan Company, 1950. (510)

Cook, D. L. "An Investigation of Three Aspects of Free-Response and Choice-type Tests at the College Level." *Dissertation Abstracts* 15 (1955): 1351. (105, 125, 372)

———. "A Replication of Lord's Study of Skewness and Kurtosis of Observed Test-score Distributions." *Educational and Psychological Measurement* 19 (1959): 81–87. (285)

Cook, W. W. "Tests: Achievement." *Encyclopedia of Educational Research.* rev. ed. Edited by Walter S. Monroe. New York: The Macmillan Company, 1950. (440)

Coombs, C. H. *A Theory of Data.* New York: John Wiley & Sons, Inc., 1964. (524)

Counts, G. S. *Dare the School Build a New Social Order?* New York: The John Day Company, Inc., 1932. (33)

Cronbach, L. J. *Essentials of Psychological Testing.* 3d ed. New York: Harper and Row, Publishers, 1970. (507)

———. "Heredity, Environment and Educational Policy." *Harvard Educational Review* 39 (1969): 338–47. (512)

———. "Response Sets and Test Validity." *Educational and Psychological Measurements* 6 (1946): 475–92. (180)

Cronbach, L. J., and Warrington, W. G. "Efficiency of Multiple-choice Tests as a Function of Spread of Item Difficulties." *Psychometrika* 17 (1952): 127–47. (399)

Cureton, E. E. "Validity." In *Educational Measurement.* Edited by E. F. Lindquist. Washington, D. C.: American Council on Education, 1951. (440)

Curtis, F. D. "Types of Thought Questions in Textbooks of Science." *Science Education* 27 (1943): 60–67. (146)

Curtis, H. A., and Kropp, R. P. "A Comparison of Scores Obtained by Administering a Test Normally and Visually." *Journal of Experimental Education* 29 (1961): 249–60. (230)

———. *Experimental Analyses of the Effects of Various Modes of Item Presentation on the Scores and Factorial Content of Tests Administered by Visual and Audio-visual Means.* Tallahassee, Florida: Department of Educational Research and Testing, Florida State University, 1962. (230)

Curtis, S. J. *History of Education in Great Britain.* London: University Tutorial Press Ltd., 1967. (6, 7)

Davis, F. B. "Item Analysis in Relation to Educational and Psychological Testing." *Psychological Bulletin* 49 (1952): 97–121. (384)

DeZouche, D. "The Wound is Mortal: Marks, Honors, Unsound Activities." *Clearing House* 19 (1945): 339–44. (313)

Dickenson, H. F. "Identical Errors and Deception." *Journal of Educational Research* 38 (1945): 534–42. (239)

Diederich, P. B. "Pitfalls in the Measurement of Gains in Achievement." *School Review* 64 (1956): 59–63. (329)

————. *Short-cut Statistics for Teacher-made Tests.* Evaluation and Advisory Service Series No. 5, Princeton, N. J.: Educational Testing Service, 1960. (304, 388)

Dizney, H. "Characteristics of Classroom Test Items Identified by Students as 'Unfair.'" *Journal of Educational Measurement* 2 (1965): 119–21. (379)

Dressel, P. L. *Comprehensive Examinations in a Program of General Education.* East Lansing: Michigan State College Press, 1949. (109, 365)

————. "Role of External Testing Programs in Education." *Educational Record* 45 (1964): 161–66. (539)

DuBois, P. H. *A History of Psychological Testing.* Boston: Allyn and Bacon, Inc., 1970. (5)

————. "A Test Dominated Society: China 1115 B.C.–1905 A.D." *Proceedings of the 1964 Invitational Conference on Testing Problems.* Princeton, New Jersey: Educational Testing Service, 1965. (5)

Dyer, H. S. "Is Testing a Menace to Education?" *New York State Education* 49 (1961): 16–19. (29)

————. "What Point of View Should Teachers Have Concerning the Role of Measurement in Education?" *The Fifteenth Yearbook of the National Council on Measurements Used in Education.* East Lansing: Michigan State University, 1958. (92)

Ebel, R. L. "Estimation of the Reliability of Ratings." *Psychometrika* 16 (1951): 407–24. (411)

————. "The Reliability of an Index of Item Discrimination." *Educational and Psychological Measurement* 11 (1951): 403–409. (387)

————. "Writing the Test Item." In *Educational Measurement.* Edited by E. F. Lindquist. Washington, D. C.: American Council on Education, 1951. (102)

————. "Maximizing Test Validity in Fixed Time Limits." *Educational and Psychological Measurement* 13 (1953): 347–57. (108)

————. "Improving Evaluation of Educational Outcomes at the College Level." *Proceedings, 1953 Invitational Conference on Testing Problems.* Princeton, N. J.: Educational Testing Service, 1954. (245)

————. "Procedures for the Analysis of Classroom Tests." *Educational and Psychological Measurement* 14 (1954): 352–64. (360)

————. "Obtaining and Reporting Evidence on Content Validity." *Educational and Psychological Measurement* 16 (1956): 269–82. (442)

————. "The Problem of Evaluation in the Social Studies." *Social Education* 24 (1960): 6–10. (59)

————. "How to Explain Standardized Test Scores to Your Parents." *School Management* 5 (March, 1961): 61–64. (481, 535)

————. "Must All Tests Be Valid?" *American Psychologist* 16 (1961): 640–47. (457)

————. "Content Standard Test Scores." *Educational and Psychological Measurement* 22 (1962): 15–25. (86)

————. "External Testing: Response to Challenge." *Teachers College Record* 64 (1962): 190–98. (539)

————. "The Relation of Testing Programs to Educational Goals." *The Impact and Improvement of School Testing Program*. 62d Yearbook, Part II. National Society for the Study of Education. Edited by W. G. Findley. University of Chicago Press, 1963. (60)

————. "Confidence Weighting and Test Reliability." *Journal of Educational Measurement* 2 (1965): 49–57. (162)

————. "The Relation of Item Discrimination to Test Reliability." *Journal of Educational Measurement* 4 (1967): 125–28. (399)

————. "Blind Guessing on Objective Achievement Tests." *Journal of Educational Measurement* 5 (1968): 321–25. (161, 254)

————. "The Value of Internal Consistency in Classroom Examinations." *Journal of Educational Measurement* 5 (1968): 71–73. (408)

————. "The Relation of Scale Fineness to Grade Accuracy." *Journal of Educational Measurement* 6 (1969): 217–21. (334)

————. "Behavioral Objectives: A Close Look." *Phi Delta Kappan* 52 (1970): 171–73. (62)

————. "Knowledge vs. Ability in Achievement Testing." *Proceedings of the 1969 Invitational Conference on Testing Problems*. Princeton, N. J.: Educational Testing Service, 1970. (75)

Educational Policies Commission. *The Central Purpose of American Education*. Washington, D. C., 1961. (30)

Engelhart, M. D. "A Comparison of Several Item Discrimination Indices." *Journal of Educational Measurement* 2 (1965): 69–76. (388)

————. "Unique Types of Achievement Test Exercises." *Psychometrika* 7 (1942): 103–16. (102)

Eurich, A. C. "Four Types of Examinations Compared and Evaluated." *Journal of Educational Psychology* 26 (1931): 268–78. (105)

Feister, W. J., and Whitney, D. R. "An Interview With Dr. E. F. Lindquist." *Epsilon Bulletin* 42 (1968). (16)

Ferguson, G. A. *Statistical Analysis in Psychology and Education*. New York: McGraw-Hill Book Company, 1959. (283)

Ferguson, L. W., and Crooks, W. R. "Some Characteristics of the Quality Point Ratio." *Journal of General Psychology* 27 (1942): 111–18. (330)

Findley, W. G. "Rationale for the Evaluation of Item Discrimination Statistics." *Educational and Psychological Measurement* 16 (1956): 175–80. (390)

Findley, W. G., ed. *The Impact and Improvement of School Testing Programs*. 62d Yearbook, Part II. National Society for the Study of Education. University of Chicago Press, 1963. (60, 534)

Flanagan, J. C. "The Critical Requirements Approach to Educational Objectives." *School and Society* 71 (1950): 321–24. (60)

————. "Units, Score and Norms." In *Educational Measurement*. Edited by E. F. Lindquist. Washington, D. C.: American Council on Education, 1951. (489)

————. "The Effectiveness of Short Methods for Calculating Correlation Coefficients." *Psychological Bulletin* 49 (1952): 342–48. (388)

————. *Calculating Correlation Coefficients.* Pittsburgh, Pa.: American Institute for Research, 1962. (388)

————. "The Use of Educational Evaluation." In *Educational Evaluation: New Roles, New Means.* 68th Yearbook, Part II. National Society for the Study of Education. University of Chicago Press, 1969. (25)

Fremer, J., and Anastasio, E. "Computer-assisted Item Writing—I (Spelling Items)." *Journal of Educational Measurement* 6 (1969): 69–74. (204)

French, J. W., and Dear, R. E. "Effects of Coaching on an Aptitude Test." *Educational and Psychological Measurement* 19 (1959): 319–30. (540)

French, W. *Behavioral Goals of General Education in High School.* New York: Russell Sage Foundation, 1957. (62)

Fuess, C. M. *The College Board: Its First Fifty Years.* New York: College Entrance Examination Board, 1950. (10)

Galton, F. *Inquiries into Human Faculty and Its Development.* London: Macmillan & Co., Ltd., 1883. (511)

Gardner, E. F. "Normative Standard Scores." *Educational and Psychological Measurement* 22 (1962): 7–14. (455)

Gardner, J. W. *Excellence.* New York: Harper and Row, Publishers, 1961. (51, 308)

Gerberich, R. *Specimen Objective Test Items.* New York: David McKay Co., Inc., 1956. (102, 548)

Gerlach, V. S. "Preparing Transparent Keys for Inspecting Answer Sheets." *Journal of Educational Measurement* 3 (1966): 62. (243)

Glaser, R. "Instructional Technology and the Measurement of Learning Outcomes." *American Psychologist* 18 (1963): 519–21. (85)

Glaser, R., and Cox, R. C. "Criterion Referenced Testing for the Measurement of Educational Outcomes." *Instructional Process and Media Innovation.* Edited by R. A. Weisgerber. Chicago: Rand McNally and Co., 1968. (8)

Glasser W. *Schools Without Failure.* New York: Harper and Row, Publishers, 1969. (47)

Goheen, H. W., and Karruck, S. *Selected References on Test Construction, Mental Test Theory and Statistics.* Washington, D. C.: U. S. Government Printing Office, 1950. (577)

"The Graduate Record Examination." *School and Society* 54 (1941): 241–42. (19)

Graham, G. "Denmark's Oral Examinations." *Education* 83 (1963): 306–309. (263)

Gray, W. S., ed. *Tests and Measurements in Higher Education.* University of Chicago Press, 1936. (577)

Grieder, C. "Is It Possible to Word Educational Goals?" *Nation's Schools* 68 (1961). (60)

Guilford, J. P. "Three Faces of Intellect." *American Psychologist* 14 (1959): 469–79. (9)

————. "Intelligence: 1965 Model." *American Psychologist* 21 (1966): 20–25. (503)

Guilford, J. P.; Lovell, C.; and Williams, R. M. "Completely Weighted Versus Unweighted Scoring in an Achievement Examination." *Educational and Psychological Measurement* 2 (1942): 15–21. (259)

Gulliksen, H. "The Relation of Item Difficulty and Inter-item Correlation to Test Variance and Reliability. *Psychometrika* 10 (1945): 79–91. (118)

———. "Intrinsic Validity." *The American Psychologist* 5 (1950): 511. (437, 442)

Guttman, L. "The Basis for Scaleogram Analysis." In *Measurement and Prediction*. Samuel Stouffer et al. Princeton University Press, 1950. (524)

Hadley, T. S. "A School Mark—Fact or Fancy?" *Educational Administration and Supervision* 40 (1954): 305–12. (309–16)

Harris, C. W. *Problems in Measuring Change*. Madison: The University of Wisconsin Press, 1963. (329)

Hartnett, J. R. "Oral Examinations." *Improving College and University Teaching*, 13 (1965): 208–209. (263, 264)

Hartog, Sir P., and Rhodes, E. C. "A Viva Voce (Interview) Examination." In *The Marks of Examiners*. London: Macmillan and Co., Ltd., 1936. (266)

Hastings, J. T. "Tensions and School Achievement Examinations." *Journal of Experimental Education* 12 (1944): 143–64. (239)

Heckman, R. W.; Tiffin, J.; and Snow, E. "Effects of Controlling Item Exposure in Achievement Testing." *Educational and Psychological Measurement* 27 (1967) 113–25. (230)

Heston, J. C. *How to Take a Test*. Chicago: Science Research Associates, 1953. (234)

Hilgard, E. R., and Marquis, D. G. *Conditioning and Learning*. New York: Appleton-Century-Crofts, 1940. (34)

Hills, J. R., and Gladney, M. B. "Factors Influencing College Grading Standards." *Journal of Educational Measurement* 5 (1968): 31–39. (316)

———. "Predicting Grades from Below Chance Test Scores." *Journal of Educational Measurement* 5 (1968): 45–53. (161)

Hively, W.; Patterson, H. L.; and Page, S. "A 'Universe Defined' System of Arithmetic Achievement Tests." *Journal of Educational Measurement* 5 (1968): 275–90. (85)

Hoel, P. G. *Introduction to Mathematical Statistics*. New York: John Wiley & Sons, Inc., 1947. (284)

Hoffman, B. *The Tyranny of Testing*. New York: Crowell Collier and Macmillan, Inc., 1962. (133, 188)

Holzinger, K. J. *Statistical Methods for Students in Education*. Boston: Ginn and Company, 1928. (287)

Howard, F. T. "Complexity of Mental Processes in Science Testing." *Education No. 879*. New York: Teachers College, Columbia University, 1943. (158)

Huddleson, E. M. "Test Development on the Basis of Content Validity." *Educational and Psychological Measurement*, 16 (1956): 283–93. (446)

Hunt, J. M. "Has Compensatory Education Failed? Has It Been Attempted?" *Harvard Educational Review* 39 (1969): 278–300. (512)

Husén, R. "International Impact of Evaluation." In *Educational Evaluation: New Roles, New Means*. 68th Yearbook, Part II. National Society for the Study of Education. University of Chicago Press, 1969. (25)

"Intelligence and Its Measurement: A Symposium." *Journal of Educational Psychology* 12 (1921): 123–47, 195–216. (498)

Jensen, A. R. "How Much Can We Boost I.Q. and Scholastic Achievement?" *Harvard Educational Review* 39 (1969): 1–123. (512)

Jenkins, W. L. "A Short-cut Method for σ and r." *Educational and Psychological Measurement* 6 (1946): 533–36. (281)

Joint Committee of the American Association of School Administrators. *Testing, Testing, Testing.* Washington, D. C., 1962. (49, 539)

Judd, C. H. *Education as Cultivation of the Higher Mental Processes.* New York: The Macmillan Company, 1936. (74)

Kagan, J. S. "Inadequate Evidence and Illogical Conclusions." *Harvard Educational Review* 39 (1969): 274–77. (512)

Kalish, R. A. "An Experimental Evaluation of the Open-book Examination." *Journal of Educational Psychology* 49 (1958): 200–204. (120)

Kandel, I. L. *Examinations and Their Substitutes in the United States.* Bulletin 28. Carnegie Foundation for Advancement of Teaching. New York, 1936. (48)

Kearney, N. C. *Elementary School Objectives.* New York: Russell Sage Foundation, 1953. (62)

Kelley, E. C. "The Fully Functioning Self." *Perceiving, Behaving, Becoming.* 1962 Yearbook, Association for Supervision and Curriculum Development. Washington, D. C., 1962. (33)

Kelley, T. L. *Statistical Method.* New York: The Macmillan Company, 1924. (304)

———. "The Selection of Upper and Lower Groups for the Validation of Test Items." *Journal of Educational Psychology* 30 (1939): 17–24. (386)

Klein, S. P., and Hart, F. M. "Chance and Systematic Factors Affecting Essay Grades." *Journal of Educational Measurement* 5 (1968): 197–206. (133)

Kolesnik, W. B. *Mental Discipline in Modern Education.* Madison: The University of Wisconsin Press, 1958. (74)

Krathwohl, D. R. et al. *Taxonomy of Educational Objectives: Affective Domain.* New York: David McKay Company, Inc., 1964. (24)

Kuder, G. F. "The Stability of Preference Items. *The Journal of Social Psychology* 10 (1939): 41–50. (526)

Kuder, G. F., and Richardons, M. W. "The Theory of the Estimation of Test Reliability." *Psychometrika* 2 (1937): 151–60. (414)

Kuo, P. W. "The Chinese System of Public Education." *Education No. 64.* New York: Teachers College, Columbia University, 1915. (5)

Lange, A.; Lehmann, I. J.; and Mehrens, W. A. "Using Item Analysis to Improve Tests." *Journal of Educational Measurement* 4 (1967): 125–28. (401)

Lathrop, R. L. "A Quick but Accurate Approximation to the Standard Deviation of a Distribution." *Journal of Experimental Education,* 29 (1961): 319–21. (281)

Lazarsfeld, P. F. "Latent Structure Analysis." *Psychology: A Study of a Science,* vol. 3. Edited by S. Koch. New York: McGraw-Hill, 1959. (524)

Learned, W. S., and Wood, B. D. *The Student and His Knowledge.* New York: Carnegie Foundation for the Advancement of Teaching, 1938. (15)

Lennon, R. T. "A Glossary of 100 Measurement Terms." *Test Service Notebook.* no. 13. New York: Harcourt Brace Jovanovich. (548)

————. "Assumptions Underlying the Use of Content Validity." *Educational and Psychological Measurement* 16 (1956): 294–304. (446)

Levine, H. G., and McGuire, C. H. "The Validity and Reliability of Oral Examinations in Assessing Cognitive Skills in Medicine." *Journal of Educational Measurement* 7 (1970): 63–74. (263)

Ligon, E. M. "Education for Moral Character." *Philosophies of Education.* Edited by Philip H. Phenix. New York: John Wiley & Sons, Inc., 1961. (33)

Likert, R. "A Technique for the Measurement of Attitude." *Archives of Psychology* 22, no. 140 (1932). (524)

Linden, K. W., and Linden, J. D. *Modern Mental Measurement: A Historical Perspective.* Boston: Houghton Mifflin Company, 1968. (5)

Lindquist, E. F. "Factors Determining the Reliability of Test Norms." *Journal of Educational Psychology* 21 (1930): 512–20. (489)

————. "Some Criteria of an Effective High School Testing Program." *Measurement and Evaluation in the Improvement of Education.* Report of the Fifteenth Educational Conference 1950. Washington, D. C.: American Council on Education, 1950. (534)

————. "Impact of Machines and Devices on Developments in Testing and Related Fields." *Proceedings, 1953 Invitational Conference on Testing Problems.* Princeton, New Jersey: Educational Testing Service, 1954. (23)

————. "The Impact of Machines on Educational Measurement." In *Educational Evaluation: New Roles, New Means.* 68th Yearbook, Part II. National Society for the Study of Education. University of Chicago Press, 1969. (23)

————. *The Iowa Tests of Educational Development: Interpretation and Use of the Test Results by the Classroom Teacher.* Iowa City: College of Education, State University of Iowa, 1943. (21)

Lippman, W. "Intelligence Tests." *New Republic*, vol. 32 (1922): 213, 246, 275, 297, 328; vol. 33 (1923): 9, 145, 201. (14, 509)

Longstaff, H. P. "Fakability of the Strong Interest Blank and the Kuder Preference Record." *Journal of Applied Psychology* 32 (1948): 360–69. (524)

Lord, F. M. "The Relation of the Reliability of Multiple-choice Tests to the Distribution of Item Difficulties." *Psychometrika* 18 (1952): 181–94. (399)

————. "On the Statistical Treatment of Football Numbers." *American Psychologist* 8 (1953): 750–51. (292)

————. "A Summary of Observed Test-score Distributions With Respect to Skewness and Kurtosis." *Educational and Psychological Measurement* 15 (1955) 383–89. (285)

————. "The Measurement of Growth." *Educational and Psychological Measurement* 16 (1956): 421–37. (329)

————. "Do Tests of the Same Length Have the Same Standard Error of Measurement?" *Educational and Psychological Measurement* 17 (1957): 501–21. (424)

————. "Tests of the Same Length Do Have the Same Standard Error of Measurement." *Educational and Psychological Measurement* 19 (1959): 233–39. (424)

————. "Estimating Norms by Item Sampling." *Educational and Psychological Measurement* 22 (1962): 259–67. (489)

Loree, M. R. *A Study of a Technique for Improving Tests.* Unpublished doctoral dissertation. University of Chicago, 1948. (204)

Loretan, J. O. "The Decline and Fall of Group Intelligence Testing." *Teachers College Record* 68 (1965): 10–17. (514)

Lowell, A. L. "The Art of Examination. "*The Atlantic Monthly* 137 (1926): 58–66. (97)

Lyman, H. B. *Test Scores and What They Mean.* Englewood Cliffs, New Jersey: Prentice-Hall, Inc., 1963. (548)

Madsen, I. N. "To Mark or Not to Mark." *Elementary School Journal* 31 (1931): 747–755. (313)

Mager, R. F. *Preparing Instructional Objectives.* Palo Alto, California: Fearon, 1962. (62)

Mann, H. "Report of the Annual Examining Committees of the Boston Grammar and Writing Schools." *Common School Journal* 7 (1845): 326–36. (7)

Manuel, H. *Taking a Test.* New York: Harcourt Brace Jovanovich, 1956. (234)

Marshall, J. C., and Powers, J. M. "Writing Neatness, Composition Errors, and Essay Grades." *Journal of Educational Measurement* 6 (1969): 97–101. (132)

McCall, W. A. "A New Kind of School Examination." *Journal of Educational Research* 1 (1920): 33–46. (14)

————. *Measurement.* New York: The Macmillan Company, 1939. (39)

Mehrens, W. A. "The Consequences of Misusing Test Results." *National Elementary Principal* 47 (1967): 63–64. (477)

Mehrens, W. A., and Lehmann, I. J. *Standardized Tests in Education.* New York: Holt, Rinehart and Winston, Inc., 1969. (459)

Merwin, J. C., and Womer, F. B. "Evaluation in Assessing the Progress of Education to Provide Bases of Public Understanding and Public Policy." In *Educational Evaluation: New Roles, New Means.* 68th Yearbook, Part II. National Society for the Study of Education. University of Chicago Press, 1969. (26)

Meyer, G. "An Experimental Study of the Old and New Types of Examination: II Methods of Study." *Journal of Educational Psychology* 26 (1935): 30–40. (139)

————. "The Choice of Questions on Essay Examinations." *Journal of Educational Psychology* 30 (1939): 161–71. (148)

Michael, J. J. "The Reliability of a Multiple Choice Examination Under Various Test Taking Instructions." *Journal of Educational Measurement* 5 (1968): 307–14. (162)

Miller, C. D. et al. "Scoring, Analyzing and Reporting Classroom Tests Using an Optical Reader and 1401 Computer." *Educational and Psychological Measurement* 27 (1967): 159–64. (246)

Millman, J.; Bishop, C. H.; and Ebel, R. L. "An Analysis of Testwiseness." *Educational and Psychological Measurement* 25 (1965): 707–26. (239)

Millman, J., and Lindolf, J. "The Comparability of Fifth-Grade Norms of the California, Iowa and Metropolitan Achievement Tests." *Journal of Educational Measurement* 1 (1964): 135–37. (490)

Millman, J., and Pauk, W. *How To Take Tests.* New York: McGraw-Hill Book Company, 1969. (234)

Monroe, W. S., and Carter, R. E. *The Use of Different Types of Thought Questions in Secondary Schools and Their Relative Difficulty for Students.* Urbana: University of Illinois Bulletin, vol. 20, no. 34 (1923). (146)

Moonan, W. J. "A Table of Normal Distribution Frequencies for Selected Numbers of Class Intervals and Sample Sizes." *Journal of Experimental Education* 27 (1959): 231–35. (283)

Moore, G. D., and Feldt, L. "Positive Approach to the Use of Test Results." *National Elementary Principal* 42 (1963): 65–70. (477, 535)

Morrissett, I. "An Experiment With Oral Examinations." *Journal of Higher Education* 29 (1958): 185–90. (263)

Morse, K. P. "Reporting Test Results: Percentile Bands vs. Percentile Ranks." *Journal of Educational Measurement* 1 (1964): 139–42. (475)

Mosier, C. I. "A Critical Examination of the Concepts of Face Validity." *Educational and Psychological Measurement* 7 (1947): 192. (437)

National Council on Measurement in Education. *Multiple-Choice Items for a Test of Teacher Competence in Educational Measurement.* East Lansing: Michigan State University, 1962. (375)

National Education Association, Commission on Reorganizing Secondary Education. *Cardinal Principles of Secondary Education.* Washington, D.C.: U. S. Office of Education Bulletin No. 35, 1918. (58)

National Education Association, Educational Policies Commission. *The Central Purpose of American Education.* Washington, D. C.: National Education Association, 1961. (63)

National Society for the Study of Education. *Measurement of Understanding.* 45th Yearbook, Part I. University of Chicago Press, 1946. (109)

Noll, V. H. *Introduction to Educational Measurement.* Boston: Houghton Mifflin Company, 1965. (5, 459)

Odell, C. W. *Scales for Rating Pupils' Answers to Nine Types of Thought Questions in English Literature.* Urbana, Illinois: Bureau of Educational Research, 1927. (139)

———. "Marks and Marking Systems." *Encyclopedia of Educational Research.* Edited by Walter S. Monroe. New York: The Macmillan Company, 1950. (308, 309, 315, 317, 329)

Office of Education. *Life Adjustment Education for Every Youth.* Washington, D. C.: U. S. Office of Education, 1951. (33)

Ohlson, D. "School Marks Versus Intelligence Rating." *Educational Administration and Supervision* 13 (1927): 90–102. (330)

Olsen, M. *Summary of Main Findings on the Validity of the 1955 College Board General Composition Tests.* Princeton, New Jersey: Educational Testing Service, 1956. (138)

O'Malley, J. M., and Stafford, C. "Scoring and Analyzing Teacher-made Tests With an IBM 1620." *Educational and Psychological Measurement* 26 (1966): 715–17. (246)

Ordway, S. H. *Oral Tests in Public Personnel Selection.* Chicago: Civil Service Assembly, 1943. (264)

Osburn, H. G. "Item Sampling for Achievement Testing." *Educational and Psychological Measurement* 28 (1968): 95–104. (85)

Owens, R. E.; Hanna, G.; and Coppedge, F. "Comparison of Multiple Choice Tests Using Different Types of Distractor Selection Techniques." *Journal of Educational Measurement* 7 (1970): 87–90. (204)

Owens, T. R., and Stufflebeam, D. L. "An Experimental Comparison of Item Sampling and Examinee Sampling for Estimating Test Norms." *Journal of Educational Measurement* 6 (1969): 75–83. (489)

Owens, W. A., Jr. "The Retest Consistency of Army Alpha after 30 Years." *Journal of Applied Psychology* 38 (1954): 154. (509)

———. "Age and Mental Abilities: A Second Adult Follow-up." *Journal of Educational Psychology* 57 (1966): 311–25. (509)

Page, E. B. "Grading Essays by Computer." *Phi Delta Kappan* 47 (1966): 238–43. (151)

Palmer, O. "Seven Classic Ways of Grading Dishonestly." *The English Journal* 51 (1962): 464–67. (309, 317)

Paterson, D. G. "Do New and Old Type Examinations Measure Different Mental Functions?" *School and Society* 24 (1926): 246–48. (13, 125)

Petch, J. A. "Examinations." *Encyclopedia Brittanica* 8 (1960): 938. (6)

Peters, C. C., and Van Voorhis, W. R. *Statistical Procedures and Their Mathematical Bases.* New York: McGraw-Hill Book Company, 1940. (304, 334)

Phillips, A. J. "Further Evidence Regarding Weighted Versus Unweighted Scoring of Examinations." *Educational and Psychological Measurement* 3 (1943): 151–55. (259)

Popham, W. J., and Husek, T. R. "Implications of Criterion-referenced Measurement." *Journal of Educational Measurement* 6 (1969): 1–9. (85)

Posey, C. "Luck and Examination Grades." *Journal of Engineering Education* 23 (1932): 292–96. (127, 128)

Rice, J. M. "The Futility of the Spelling Grind: I." *Forum* 23 (1897): 163–72. (10)

———. *Scientific Management in Education.* New York: Hinds, Noble, and Eldredge, 1914. (10)

Richardson, M. W. "The Relation Between the Difficulty and the Differential Validity of a Test. *Psychometrika* 1 (1936): 33–49. (117, 399)

Richardson, M. W., and Stalnaker, J. M. "Comments on Achievement Examinations." *Journal of Educational Research* 28 (1935): 425–32. (43, 77, 100)

Riggs, C. C. *The Oral Interview as a Predictive Device in the Selection of Michigan State Troopers.* Master's thesis, East Lansing: Michigan State University, 1961. (264, 266)

Rippey, R. M. "A Comparison of Five Different Scoring Functions for Confidence Tests." *Journal of Educational Measurement* 7 (1970): 165–70. (162)

Rockefeller Brothers Fund. *The Pursuit of Excellence.* Garden City, New York: Doubleday & Company, Inc., 1958. (308)

Ross, C. C. *Measurement in Today's Schools.* 2d ed. Englewood Cliffs, New Jersey: Prentice-Hall, Inc., 1947. (164)

———. *Measurement in Today's Schools.* 3d ed. Edited by J. C. Stanley. Englewood Cliffs, New Jersey: Prentice-Hall, Inc., 1954. (437)

Ruch, G. M. *The Objective or New-type Examination.* Chicago: Scott, Foresman and Company, 1929. (127, 164, 320, 322)

Rulon, P. J. "A Simplified Procedure for Determining the Reliability of a Test by Split-halves." *Harvard Educational Review* 9 (1939): 99–103. (411)

————. "On the Validity of Educational Tests." *Harvard Educational Review* 16 (1946): 290–96. (439)

Rummel, J. F. *The Modification of a Test to Reduce Errors in the Classification of Examinees.* Unpublished dissertation. College of Education, The State University of Iowa, 1950. (285)

————. "Procedures for Computation of Zero-order Coefficients Among Several Variables." *Journal of Experimental Education* 20 (1952): 313–18. (298)

Ryans, D. G. "The Professional Examination of Teaching Candidates: A Report of the First Annual Administration of the National Teacher Examinations." *School and Society* 52 (1940): 276. (21)

Ryans, D. G. "The Results of Internal Consistency and External Validation Procedures Applied in the Analysis of Test Items Measuring Professional Information." *Educational and Psychological Measurement* 11 (1951): 549–60. (392)

Sabers, D. L., and Feldt, L. S. "An Empirical Study of the Effect of the Correction for Chance Success on the Reliability and Validity of an Aptitude Test." *Journal of Educational Measurement* 5 (1968): 251–58. (253)

Sabers, D. L., and White, G. W. "The Effect of Differential Weighting of Individual Item Responses on the Predictive Validity and Reliability of an Aptitude Test." *Journal of Educational Measurement* 6 (1969): 93–96. (259)

Sarason, I. G. "Empirical Findings and Theoretical Problems in the Use of Anxiety Scales." *Psychological Bulletin* 57 (1960): 403–15. (237)

Sax, G., and Collet, L. S. "An Epirical Comparison of the Effects of Recall and Multiple Choice Tests on Student Achievement." *Journal of Educational Measurement* 5 (1968): 169–73. (125)

————. "The Effects of Differing Instructions and Guessing Formulas on Reliability and Validity. "*Educational and Psychological Measurement* 28 (1968): 1127–2236. (253)

Sax, G., and Cromack, T. R. "The Effects of Various Forms of Item Arrangements on Test Performance." *Journal of Educational Measurement* 3 (1966): 309–11. (119)

Saxe, R. W. "Oral Examinations Evaluate Character, General Fitness. *Chicago Schools Journal* 44 (1962): 123–27. (264)

Seashore, C. E. "Some Psychological Statistics." *University of Iowa Studies in Psychology* 2 (1899): 1–84. (9)

Sgan, M. R. "First Year of Pass-fail at Brandeis University: A Report." *Journal of Higher Education* 40 (1969): 135–44. (333)

Shaw, M. E., and Wright, J. M. *Scales for the Measurement of Attitudes.* New York: McGraw-Hill Book Company, 1967. (526)

Shuford, E. H.; Albert, A.; and Massengill, H. E. "Admissible Probability Measurement Procedures." *Psychometrika* 31 (1966): 125–45. (162)

Shultz, G. D. "The Uninsulted Child." *Ladies Home Journal* 73 (1956): 60–63. (498)

Silberman, C. E. *Crisis in the Classroom.* New York: Random House, Inc., 1970. (36)

Simon, G. B. "Comments on 'Implications of Criterion Referenced Measurement.'" *Journal of Educational Measurement* 6 (1969): 259–60. (85)

Sims, V. M. "The Essay Examination Is a Projective Technique." *Educational and Psychological Measurement* 8 (1948): 15–31. (132)

Slakter, M. J. "The Effect of Guessing Strategy on Objective Test Scores." *Journal of Educational Measurement* 5 (1968): 217–21. (257)

———. "The Penalty for Not Guessing." *Journal of Educational Measurement* 5 (1968): 141–44. (257)

Smith, A. Z., and Dobbin, J. E. "Marks and Marking Systems." *Encyclopedia of Educational Research*. 3d ed. Edited by Chester W. Harris. New York: The Macmillan Company, 1960. (332)

Smith, B. O. *Logical Aspects of Educational Measurement*. New York: Columbia University Press, 1938. (39)

Smith, K. "An Investigation of the Use of 'Double Choice' Items in Testing Achievement." *Journal of Educational Research* 51 (1958): 387–89. (205)

Smith, R. V., and Freeman, H. V. "Report on Aptitude Testing in Dentistry at University of Iowa." *Proceedings, 12th Annual Meeting*. American Association of Dental Schools, 1936. (151)

Spearman, C. E. "The Theory of Two Factors." *Psychological Review* 21 (1914): 101–15. (13)

———. *The Abilities of Man*. New York: The Macmillan Company, 1927. (503)

Spencer, H. *Education: Intellectual, Moral and Physical*. New York: A. L. Burt; London: G. Manwaring, 1861. (56, 58)

Stallings, W. M., et al. "Pass-fail Grading Option." *School and Society* 96 (1968): 179–80. (333)

Stalnaker, J. M. "Essay Examinations Reliably Read." *School and Society* 46 (1937): 671–72. (100)

———. "The Essay Type of Examination." *Educational Measurement*. Edited by E. F. Lindquist. Washington, D. C.: American Council on Education, 1941. (148)

———. "A National Scholarship Program; Methods, Problems, Results." *Applications of Psychology*. Edited by L. L. Thurstone. New York: Harper and Brothers, 1952. (23)

———. "Evaluation and the Award of Scholarships." In *Educational Evaluation: New Roles, New Means*. 68th Yearbook, Part II. National Society for the Study of Education. University of Chicago Press, 1969. (23)

Stalnaker, J. M., and Stalnaker, R. C. "Open Book Examinations: Results." *Journal of Higher Education* 6 (1935): 214–16. (120)

Stalnaker, J. M., and Richardson, M. W. "Scholarship Examinations." *The Journal of Higher Education* 5 (1934): 305–13. (23)

Stanley, J. C. *Measurement in Today's Schools*. 4th ed. Englewood Cliffs, New Jersey: Prentice-Hall, Inc., 1964. (5)

Stanley, J. C., and Porter, A. C. "Correlation of Scholastic Aptitude Test Score with College Grades for Negroes Versus Whites." *Journal of Educational Measurement* 4 (1967): 199–218. (542)

Starch, D. *Educational Measurements*. New York: The Macmillan Company, 1916. (8)

Starch, D., and Elliott, E. C. "Reliability of the Grading of High School Work in English." *School Review* 20 (1912): 442–57. (12, 85)

———. "Reliability of Grading Work in History." *School Review* 21 (1913): 676–81. (138)

———. "Reliability of Grading Work in Mathematics." *School Review* 21 (1913): 254–59. (317)

State Education Department, Albany, New York. *Regents Examinations 1865–1965: 100 Years of Quality Control in Education.* Albany, New York, 1965. (8)

Stern, W. *The Psychological Methods of Testing Intelligence.* Translated by Guy M. Whipple. Baltimore: Warwick & York, 1914. (507)

Stoddard, G. D. *The Meaning of Intelligence.* New York: The Macmillan Company, 1943. (45)

Strong, E. K., Jr. "Vocational Interest Test." *Educational Record* 8 (1927): 107–21. (15)

———. *Vocational Interests of Men and Women.* California: Stanford University Press, 1943. (526)

Stroud, J. B. *Psychology in Education.* New York: David McKay Co., Inc., 1946. (42, 74, 315)

Super, D. E. *The Use of Multifactor Tests in Guidance.* Washington: American Personnel and Guidance Association, 1958. (507)

———. "The Multifactor Tests: Summing Up." *Personnel and Guidance Journal* 36 (1957): 17–20. (507)

Sutton, H. E. "Human Genetics: A Survey of New Developments. "*The Science Teacher* 34 (1967): 51–55. (498)

Swift, J. "On Poetry, a Rhapsody." *The Portable Swift.* New York: The Viking Press, Inc., 1948. (109)

Swineford, F. "Note on 'Tests of the Same Length Do Have the Same Standard Error of Measurement.'" *Educational and Psychological Measurement* 19 (1959): 241–42. (424)

Terman, L. "The Great Conspiracy." *New Republic* 33 (1922): 116–20. (14)

Terry, P. W. "How Students Review for Objective and Essay Tests." *Elementary School Journal* 33 (1933): 592–603. (139)

Terwilliger, J. S. "Individual Differences in Marking Practices of Secondary School Teachers." *Journal of Educational Measurement* 5 1968): 9–15. (315)

Test Development Division, E.T.S. *Multiple-Choice Questions: A Close Look.* Princeton, New Jersey: Educational Testing Service, 1963. (113)

Thorndike, E. L. *An Introduction to the Theory of Mental and Social Measurements.* New York: The Science Press, 1903. (11)

———. *Mental and Social Measurements.* 2d ed. New York: Teachers College, Columbia University, 1912. (308)

———. "The Nature, Purposes, and General Methods of Measurement of Educational Products." *The Measurement of Educational Products.* 17th Yearbook, Part II. National Society for the Study of Education, 1918. (11, 39, 110)

———. "In Defense of Facts." *Journal of Adult Education* 7 (1935): 381–88. (75)

Thorndike, R. L. *The Concepts of Over-and Under-achievement.* New York: Teacher's College Press, 1963. (511)

Thorndike, R. L., and Hagen, E. *Measurement and Evaluation in Psychology and Education.* 3d ed. New York: John Wiley and Sons, Inc., 1969. (438, 459, 498, 522)

Thurstone, L. L. *The Measurement of Values.* University of Chicago Press, 1959. (522)

———. "Multiple Factor Analysis." *Psychological Review* 38 (1931): 406–27. (20)

———. "Primary Mental Abilities." *Psychometric Monographs* no. 1, 1938. (9, 503)

———. "The Improvement of Examinations." *American Association of University Professors Bulletin* 34 (1948): 394–97. (89)

Thurstone, L. L., and Chave, E. J. *The Measurement of Attitude.* University of Chicago Press, 1929. (16, 522, 524)

Travers, R. M. W. *How to Make Achievement Tests.* New York: Odyssey Press, 1950. (365)

Travers, R. M. W., and Gronlund, N. E. "Meaning of Marks." *Journal of Higher Education* 21 (1950): 369–74. (315)

Traxler, A. E. "15 Criteria of a Testing Program." *The Clearing House* 25 (1950): 3–7. (535)

———. "The IBM Scoring Machine: An Evaluation." *1953 Invitational Conference on Testing Problems.* Princeton, New Jersey: Educational Testing Service, 1953. (18)

———. "Use of Results of Large-scale Testing Programs in Instruction and Guidance." *Journal of Educational Research* 54 (1960): 59–62. (535)

Trimble, O. C. "The Oral Examination: Its Validity and Reliability." *School and Society* 39 (1934): 550–52. (266)

———. *The Final Oral Examination, Purdue University Studies in Higher Education,* no. 25 (November, 1934). (263, 266)

Turnbull, W. W. "A Normalized Graphic Method of Item Analysis." *Journals of Educational Psychology* 37 (1956): 129–41. (384)

Tussing, L. "A Consideration of the Open-book Examination." *Educational and Psychological Measurement* 11 (1951): 597–602. (120)

Tyler, R. W. "A Generalized Technique for Constructing Achievement Tests." *Educational Research Bulletin* 10, Columbus: Ohio State University (1931): 199–208. (17, 62)

———. "The Objectives and Plans for a National Assessment of Educational Progress." *Journal of Educational Measurement* 3 (1966): 1–4. (26)

Vernon, P. E. *Educational Testing and Test Form Factors.* Research Bulletin 58–3. Princeton, N. J.: Educational Testing Service, 1958. (100)

Weidemann, C. C. "How to Construct the True-False Examination." *Education No. 225.* New York: Teachers College, Columbia University, 1926. (172)

Weiss, P. "Knowledge: A Growth Process." *Science* 131 (1960): 1716–19. (65)

Wesley, E. B., and Wronski, S. P. *Teaching Social Studies in High Schools.* 4th ed. Boston: D. C. Heath & Company, 1958. (146)

Wesman, A. G., and Bennett, G. K. "The Use of 'None-of-These' as an Option in Test Construction." *Journal of Educational Psychology* 37 (1946): 541–49. (218)

———. "Multiple Regression Versus Simple Addition of Scores in Prediction of College Grades. *Educational and Psychological Measurement* 19 (1959): 243–46. (258)

Whyte, W. H., Jr. *The Organization Man.* New York: Simon and Schuster, Inc., 1956. (521)

Wilhelms, F. T., ed. *Evaluation as Feedback and Guide.* 1967 Yearbook. Washington, D. C.: Association for Supervision and Curriculum Development, 1967. (30)

Wilks, S. S. "Weighting Systems for Linear Functions of Correlated Variables When There is No Dependent Variable." *Psychometrika* 3 (1938): 23–40. (258)

Wissler, C. "The Correlation of Mental and Physical Tests." *Psychological Review, Monograph Supplements* 8 (1901): 16. (9)

Womer, F. B. "Pros and Cons of External Testing Programs." *The North Central Association Quarterly* 36 (1961): 201–10. (539)

Wood, B. D. "Origin and Work of the Educational Records Bureau." *School and Society* 34 (1931): 835–37. (15)

———. "The Program of the Cooperative Test Service." *Tests and Measurements in Higher Education.* Edited by William S. Gray. Chicago: University of Chicago Press, 1936. (17)

Wood, B. D., and Beers, F. S. "Knowledge Versus Thinking?" *Teachers College Record* 37 (1936): 487–99. (75)

Woodworth, R. S. "Edward Lee Thorndike." *Biographical Memoirs* 27. National Academy of Sciences (1952): 209–37. (11)

Woody, T. *Educational Views of Benjamin Franklin.* New York: McGraw-Hill Book Company, 1931. (56)

Yerkes, R. M. "Psychological Examining in the United States Army." *Memoirs of the National Academy of Sciences* 15 (1921). (14)

INDEX

This index does not include the glossary terms, which are listed separately on pages 548–49. Names of authors cited are indexed with the references listed on pages 597–614.